OLD TESTAMENT

BIBLE STORIES

Jackson Day

OLD TESTAMENT BIBLE STORIES

Copyright © 2004 by Jackson Day. All rights reserved.
No part of this book may be reproduced, stored in a retrieval system or transmitted by any means, electronic, mechanical, photocopying, recording, or otherwise, without written permission from the author.

Bible Storytelling Project
P. O. Box 1248
Ashville, AL 35953

Http://biblestorytelling.org

Published 2007 by
Lightning Source
1248 Heil Quaker Blvd.
La Vergne, TN 37086

Printed in the United States of America

ISBN 978-0-9797324-0-9

CONTENTS

BIBLE STORY		TEXT	PAGE
	Preface		1
Chart	Summary of Old Testament Stories in Chronological Order		3
	Summary of Old Testament Stories in Chronological Order		3
Chart	Old Testament Prophecies about a Promised One		7
Chart	Panoramic View of Old Testament		8
Chart	Genesis		9
1	Creation	Gn 1:1 - 2:25	9
2	Beginning of Sin	Gn 3:1 - 4:16	14
3	Degeneration of Sinners	Gn 4:16 - 6:13	19
Chart	Time-Line of Methuselah		22
4	The Flood	Gn 6:11 - 9:29	23
5	Tower of Babel	Gn 10:1 - 11:32	27
6	Abraham: Faith Tested by Life's Circumstances	Gn 12 - 25	30
7	Jacob: Seeking Divine Blessings by Wheeling and Dealing	Gn 25:11 - 38:30	39
8	Joseph: Victory over Different Situations	Gn 37, 39 - 50	49
Chart	Exodus		58
Chart	Moses		58
9	Moses: Chosen, Protected and Sent	Ex 1 - 4	58
10	Liberating the Israelites from Slavery	Ex 4:27 - 12:50	64
11	Redeemed and Tested by God	Ex 12:43 - 18:27	71
12	The Legislator of the Ten Commandments	Ex 19 - 24	78
Chart	The Ten Commandments		82
13	Worship: God's Way or Man's Imitation	Ex 19 - 40; Lev 8 - 11	84
Chart	Offerings		92
Chart	Pure and Impure Food		93
Chart	Holy Days		93
Chart	Failures Recorded in Numbers		94
14	Complaining and Rebelling	Nu 11 - 33; Dt	95
Chart	Joshua		106
15	Joshua: Conquering the Promised Land	Jos 1 - 24	106
Chart	Judges		114
16	Judges: Cycles of Apostasies, Oppressions and Deliverances	Jdg 1 - 21	114
17	Ruth: Restructuring One's Life after a Forced Adaptation	Ru 1 - 4	127
Chart	Samuel		132
18	Samuel: Heard and Spoke the Word of God	1 Sam 1 - 8	132
Chart	The Kingdom of Israel		138
Chart	Saul		138
19	Saul: From God's Best to a Reject	1 Sam 9 - 15	138
20	Saul Descends while David Ascends	1 Sam 16 - 31	146
Chart	David		157

BIBLE STORY		TEXT	PAGE
21	King David	2 Sam 1-24; 1 Ki 1- 2; 1 Chr 28 - 29	157
Chart	Solomon		171
22	Solomon: A Wise Man Who Abandoned Wisdom	1 Ki 1 - 11; 2 Chr 1 - 9	171
Chart	Comparing the Two Kingdoms		181
23	The Kingdom is Divided	1 Ki 12 - 16; 2 Chr 10 - 16	182
24	Ahab, a King Who Fought the Lord; Elijah, a Prophet Who Fought for the Lord	1 Ki 16:29 - 22:40; 2 Ki 9:30 - 10:17	191
Chart	Jonah		202
25	Jonah: The Reluctant Prophet	Jnh 1 - 4	202
26	Prophets to Rebellious People	2 Ki 1 - 17	207
Chart	Nebuchadnezzar's Invasions of Jerusalem		218
27	Instability in the Partial Kingdom	2 Ki 18 - 25; 2 Chr 29 - 36	218
28	Babylonian Exile	2 Ki 24 - 25; Da 1 - 6; Jer 29	228
Chart	Chronological Order of the Reconstruction Historical Books		238
29	Restoration of Judah	Ezr; Ne	238

PREFACE

My childhood was spent on a farm twelve miles from the county seat town of LaFayette, Alabama. I was thirteen when I saw television for the first time. On many Sundays, my father's family went to my grandparents' house and sat on the front porch swapping stories. When I enrolled in Samford University in Birmingham, I became a barber to pay the bills. I worked for Jimmy Williams, a storytelling barber in Mountain Brook, a suburb of Birmingham. Customers often stayed in the barber shop hours after getting a haircut listening to Jimmy tell his stories. Others would drop by when they did not need a haircut just to hear a good story.

While storytelling was a part of my growing up, it was on the mission field that I realized its importance in teaching and preaching. In December 1970, my wife Doris and I were appointed as missionaries to Brazil with the International Mission Board. I was unable to train men with less than a primary education to preach using methods I had learned in seminary. One of my students was Jairo Lima, an uneducated brick layer, who learned to read after becoming a believer in Jesus. He loved to preach. When he told Bible stories and made applications, his listeners sat on the edges of their chairs with mouths wide open. In sharp contrast, when he tried to preach from one of Paul's letters, no one paid attention. Jairo helped me understand that the uneducated are usually great storytellers and can be effective church leaders when they preach or teach using Bible stories. Since 1974, I have trained church leaders to preach and teach using Bible stories. I also realized that when I myself told a Bible story as part of my sermons, those with limited education understood me.

In 1992, I discovered FIRM FOUNDATIONS, written by Trevor McIlwain. The author emphasizes telling Bible stories in chronological order to evangelize and plant churches. I made the decision to teach and preach the Bible stories in chronological order in a church we were planting in Lago Sul, Brasilia, Brazil. Lago Sul is an upper class community. The highly educated upper class loved the Bible stories. That was when I began to write the book that was published in Brazil as VELHO TESTAMENTO: NARRATIVAS BÍBLICAS, by SOCEP- Sociedade Cristã Evangélica de Publicações Ltda in 2000. I have adapted and rewritten into English the book which was first published in Portuguese.

Each Bible story included in this book contains:
✓ The structure of the story;
✓ The Bible Story, using the language I would use to tell it;
✓ Life-lessons discovered from the story;
✓ Questions helpful to generate discussion about the story.

THE STRUCTURE

Key-elements that help identify the structure of a Bible story are:
- **Context.** The context establishes the place and time in which the story occurred and identifies the characters who begin the story. The context also establishes the initial-situation of the story.
- **Key-person or persons.** These are the important characters in the story.
- **Key-location.** This is the principal location where the events took place.
- **Key-repetitions.** Events in a story are often tied together by words, themes, facts, or ideas that are repeated, either exactly or with minor variations. Repetitions are made in biblical stories in order to emphasize truths, to build to a climax, or to express strong emotions.
- **Key-attitudes.** Stories express attitudes and emotions. To be true to scripture, one must express the same attitudes as those expressed by the original storyteller.
- **Initial-problem.** The context establishes the initial-situation of the story. Bible stories begin with an event that is related to a problem or necessity that changes the initial situation.
- **Sequence of events.** The sequence of events is the outline of the story and lists the events in the order narrated. Attention is paid to dialogue, conflict, and contrast.
- **Final-situation of the story.** This observes the state of affairs at the end of the story.

THE STORY

Each Bible story is a contemporary paraphrase that was crafted by the author of this book. Friends with different educational backgrounds read the stories and marked the words and sentences that confused them. Then I made other modifications to make the stories more clearly understood.

LIFE-LESSONS

The life-lessons are truths that were discovered from the story.

The Bible teacher or preacher will find some of these life-lessons helpful in his preparation to teach or preach. He should also discover other life-lessons on his own.

QUESTIONS

Questions are listed that should help the listeners discover truths from the Bible Story. In my opinion, one of the best ways to teach Bible Stories is to tell the story, and without any explanation, start asking questions that help the students discover truths for themselves.

OTHER BIBLE STORYTELLING BOOKS

I prepared the book BIBLE STORYTELLING TOOLS, which gives guidelines on how to do Bible storytelling. I have used the book to train church leaders to evangelize, plant churches, teach, preach, and train others.

The book, NEW TESTAMENT BIBLE STORIES, is a continuation of this book, the OLD TESTAMENT BIBLE STORIES. It gives the New Testament events in chronological order and follows the same structure as this book.

CONCLUSION TO INTRODUCTION

The Bible has stories about Adam, Eve, Noah, Abraham, Moses, David etc.; however, the Bible is primarily the story of the GOD of Adam, Eve, Noah, Abraham, Moses, David etc. Each Bible story is similar to a pearl in a necklace. It has value and is capable of standing alone, but when strung together by a common thread, they become the necklace with ultimate value. The individual pearls would be: God and Adam and Eve, God and Noah, God and Abraham, God and Moses, God and David etc. The pearls strung together form the necklace of ultimate value: GOD'S STORY.

I hope this book will give you a panoramic view of the Old Testament. I pray you will find it useful in understanding, telling, teaching, and preaching Bible Stories.

EXPRESSIONS OF THANKS

I wish to express my thanks to those who had a part in making this book a reality.

I am thankful to the International Mission Board and the Southern Baptist Convention churches that made it possible for my wife and me to serve as missionaries to Brazil for 33 years.

I am thankful to the Brazilians who received our family and made us feel at home in their country. I am thankful for the Brazilian evangelical Christians who loved my family and allowed us to work beside them as co-workers. Many became as close to us as our blood relatives. I am thankful for the Brazilians who became my students. Working alongside my students helped me to become a Bible Storyteller.

SOCEP- Sociedade Cristã Evangélica de Publicações Ltda, is the publisher of my wife's and my books on Bible Storytelling in Portuguese. The owners and workers at SOCEP are within the circle of our closest friends. We thank God for them.

Berdie Hope was an English teacher before she and her husband Ben went to Brazil as IMB missionaries. They are now retired and live 26 miles from us. They are good friends. Berdie corrected my English and made suggestions to improve my writing.

While living in Brazil for 33 years, I struggled to think and write in Portuguese. Now, I have difficulty expressing myself in English. Several friends in the Ashville, Alabama, area agreed to read this book, mark what was confusing, and make suggestions. They are: Eddie Smith, Larry and Betty Robinson, Jack and Kay Collins, Charles and Patsy Fouts and Tony and Meredith Sparks. Diane Grill then corrected my final revision and made many suggestions to improve my writing.

The person who helped me the most with this book is the one who has been my helpmate since she agreed to marry me. I am thankful for all Doris Day has done to help me with this book.

SUMMARY OF OLD TESTAMENT STORIES IN CHRONOLOGICAL ORDER							
ADAM before 4000 B.C.	**NOAH** 2500 B.C.	**ABRAHAM** 2000 B.C.	**MOSES** 1500 B.C.	**DAVID** 1000 B.C.		**DANIEL** 586 B.C.	**EZRA** 516 B.C.
HISTORY OF THE ANCIENT WORLD		HISTORY OF ISRAEL					
Pre-Flood	Post-Flood	The People — The Patriarchs — The Israelites in Egypt	The Land — Leaving Egypt — Conquering the Land — Living in the Land	The Kingdom			
				United — Saul David Solomon	Divided 931 B.C. — ISRAEL: North *Jeroboam* JUDAH: South *Rehoboam*	Partial 722 B.C. — Only JUDAH	In Exile 586 B.C. — In BABYLON	Remnant 516 B.C. — RESTORATION OF JUDAH Ezra Esther Nehemiah

SUMMARY OF OLD TESTAMENT STORIES IN CHRONOLOGICAL ORDER

I. HISTORY OF THE ANCIENT WORLD

1. Creation

In the beginning, God created the heavens and the earth. To create, God spoke, and what he said came into being. God created man and woman in his image and gave them dominion over the animals and plants. He planted the Garden of Eden, and there he put the couple. In the garden, there was a tree whose fruit God commanded Adam and Eve not to eat. All of creation was, naturally, good in the beginning.

2. Fall

Satan used a snake to deceive Eve and to lead her to eat the forbidden fruit. She gave the fruit to Adam, who also ate it. At that time, evil and suffering entered the world. God promised Eve that one of her descendants would crush the snake's head. Adam and Eve were expelled from the Garden. Adam and Eve had two sons, Cain and Abel. Cain killed his brother Abel and left God's presence. God gave Adam and Eve other children. One son was called Seth. Some of Seth's descendants began to worship God. All of Cain's descendants polluted the world with sin until only one man, Noah, lived a life that pleased God. God decided to destroy the world.

3. Flood

God told Noah to build an ark. Noah, his family and some animals entered the ark. God destroyed the world with a flood but saved Noah, his family and the animals inside the ark. God set a rainbow in the clouds as a sign that he would never again destroy all life with a flood.

God told Noah and his sons to increase in numbers and fill the earth. However, in order not to scatter, they began building a tower in a place called Babel. God confused their language in such a way that they could not understand each other.

After God multiplied the languages, the nations scattered themselves over the face of the whole earth. Again they corrupted themselves and forgot God. They made idols of stone and wood. However, this time God did not punish them as before.

Old Testament Bible Stories © Jackson Day

II. ISRAEL

1. The People of Israel

The Patriarchs

God chose Abraham and commanded him to leave his country, his people and his father's household and go to the land that he would show him. Before Abraham even had children, God promised to give his descendants the land of Canaan, and that one of his descendants would bless all people groups on earth. God renewed his promise to Abraham's son, Isaac, and to his grandson, Jacob. Jacob sought to attain God's blessings through deceit. After being dominated by God, Jacob's name was changed to Israel. Jacob, or Israel, had twelve sons.

Israel's family was dysfunctional. Ten of his sons hated their brother Joseph and sold him as a slave. He was taken to Egypt.

God was with Joseph in Egypt, even when he was a slave and when he was falsely accused and imprisoned. God enabled Joseph to interpret the dreams of Pharaoh, the king of Egypt. Pharaoh made Joseph second in command over Egypt. Joseph saved the Egyptians and others in the surrounding countries during a time of widespread famine.

The Israelites in Egypt

During the famine, Israel's other sons discovered that their brother Joseph was second in command over Egypt. Joseph told his brothers that God used the evil they committed against him to save lives and to give them descendants. Pharaoh invited Joseph's father and his brothers, along with their children and grandchildren, to live in Egypt. After Israel died, his descendants continued living in Egypt. They did not return to Canaan, the land God promised Abraham, Isaac and Jacob. Joseph and all his generation died in Egypt.

Israel's descendants had many children. The descendants of each of Israel's sons became a tribe. The Pharaoh who was grateful to Joseph died. Approximately 400 years after Joseph, Egypt had a Pharaoh who became afraid of the Israelites and made plans to destroy them by enslaving, oppressing and treating them ruthlessly.

2. The Land of Canaan

The Israelites Leave Egypt for Canaan

God chose Moses to liberate the Israelites from Egyptian slavery. God sent nine plagues, but Pharaoh refused to let them go. After the ninth plague, God told Moses how the Israelites should prepare for the tenth plague. The head of each household should kill a year-old lamb and place its blood on the door-frame of his home. The Egyptians did not put blood on their door-frames. At midnight, the death angel killed the oldest son in every Egyptian home. Pharaoh commanded Moses to take the Israelites out of Egypt that very night.

God freed the Israelites from slavery in Egypt and began to guide them to the land of Canaan. During the day, he went ahead of them in a pillar of cloud, and by night, in a pillar of fire. When the Israelites arrived at the Red Sea, Pharaoh decided to recapture them. God separated the waters, and the Israelites passed through two walls of water on dry ground. They entered the desert, and God took care of their basic needs, providing them with water, food and protection from enemies.

God led the people up to Mount Sinai, where he gave the Ten Commandments to govern those he had liberated. They promised to obey all God's commands. However, when Moses returned to the mountain, they built a golden calf and worshiped it.

God guided the Israelites from Mount Sinai to the edge of the promised land. Moses sent twelve men to spy out the land. The spies returned explaining that the land was good, but the people were strong, some were giants, and the cities were fortresses. Ten spies claimed the inhabitants of the land were too strong for them. Joshua and Caleb said that with God they could conquer the land. The multitude lacked faith, rebelled against Moses and murmured against God. God punished them by requiring that the Israelites wander in the desert for 40 years until that generation died. Only two from that generation, Joshua and Caleb, would be allowed to enter the promised land.

God spoke face to face with Moses and he promised to send another one similar to Moses with whom he would also speak face to face.

Conquering the Land

The forty years passed, the disobedient generation died, and God led his people to the border of the promised land. Moses died, and Joshua replaced him as the leader of God's people. Joshua led the Israelites to conquer Canaan. Their first conquest was the city of Jericho. The Israelites invaded Canaan, conquered many of its inhabitants and began to live there. They served God while Joshua was alive and during the lifetime of the leaders who knew Joshua.

Living in the Land When it Was Governed by Judges

After the generation that knew Joshua died, the people forgot God. There was no king in Israel, and everyone did as he saw fit. As a consequence, every generation became worse than their father's generation. God handed them over to enemies who oppressed them. When they clamored to God for liberation, he sent a judge to liberate them and reestablish order. During the lifetime of that judge, the Israelites served God. After his death, they returned to idolatry, were oppressed, again cried out to God, and he sent another judge. Some of the well-known judges are Deborah, Barak, Gideon and

Samson. There were six cycles of rebellion, oppression, clamoring to God, and liberation.

The last judge was Samuel. He brought the Israelites back to God and led them to have victory over their enemies. After Samuel became old, he appointed his sons as judges over Israel. However, they were greedy and perverted justice by accepting bribes. The people wanted to have a king, just like the other nations. They no longer wanted God to govern them through the judges.

3. The Kingdom of Israel

3.1 The United Kingdom

King Saul

God chose Saul to be the king. All twelve tribes of Israel united in accepting Saul as their first king. When he first became king, Saul served the Lord and successfully waged war against Israel's enemies. Later, he forgot that the king, just as the people, must live under the authority and judgment of God. As king, he wanted to live above the law of God. After Saul's disobedience, God rejected him as king and chose David to occupy his place. Saul rejected God's choice and tried to kill David. After Saul's death, David became king.

King David

King David fought many battles with Israel's enemies and won them all. He was a man after God's own heart and, as a leader, gained the loyalty of his people. David wanted to build a temple. God refused to allow David to build the temple but promised that his son would build it and that one of his descendants would reign forever.

King David became so strong that it was not necessary for him to lead his army into battle. Once when his armies were at war, he remained in Jerusalem. He went to the roof of his home and saw a neighbor woman taking her bath. He committed adultery with her and then had her husband murdered. David confessed his sins and God again gave him the joy of salvation. However, a consequence of his sins was that he had no more victories, but faced problems in both his family and nation.

King Solomon

Before dying, David appointed his son Solomon as king. Solomon began his reign by loving God and seeking wisdom. In Jerusalem, he built the great Temple for the people to worship God. Afterwards, he married foreign women, even knowing that God had prohibited such marriages. God sent two prophets to warn Solomon, but he refused to listen to them. His wives led him to build temples so they could worship their gods. Then Solomon began to practice idolatry with his wives. Solomon's riches demanded high taxes and forced labor, which became a heavy burden for the people.

3.2 Divided Kingdom

When King Solomon died, his son Rehoboam reigned. The Israelites requested Rehoboam to lower taxes and reduce forced labor. Rehoboam responded that he would demand more than Solomon. Ten of the tribes rebelled against Rehoboam, causing a civil war and dividing the kingdom. Ten northern tribes split off from the kingdom whose king was a descendant of David. They chose Jeroboam as their king and formed a new kingdom, called Israel or the northern kingdom. Its capital was Samaria. Two tribes remained loyal to Rehoboam. His kingdom was called Judah or the Southern Kingdom. Its capital was Jerusalem. All the kings of Judah were descendants of David, while the kings of Israel were not.

Jeroboam, the first king of Israel, rebelled against God and made two golden calves, placing one in Bethel and the other in Dan in order to keep his citizens from going to Jerusalem to worship God in the Temple. All of Israel's kings followed Jeroboam's example; they were evil and idolaters. In Israel, idolatry and immorality went hand in hand.

The worst king of Israel was Ahab, who followed the counsel of his wicked wife, Jezebel. He worshiped the god Baal, practiced all kinds of violence and considered the prophet Elijah his enemy. God sent prophets to Israel. Elijah and Elisha are two of the most well-known prophets.

Judah was the other Kingdom. It was also called the Southern Kingdom. Its kings were all descendants of David. A few imitated King David and loved God, but most were evil and followed the example of Jeroboam, Israel's first king.

3.3 Partial Kingdom

All of Israel's kings led the people to practice idolatry and immorality. The Israelites sinned against God, worshiped other gods and followed the customs of the people that God had expelled from the land. God sent messengers called prophets; however, Israel rejected them. God punished Israel by allowing Assyria to conquer the nation. Many Israelites were taken captive to Assyria, and the Assyrians sent other conquered peoples to re-populate the land. There was intermarriage between the left-over Israelites and the immigrants. Their descendants were called the Samaritans. The Samaritans tried to worship the Lord God, and at the same time worship idols and other gods.

With the fall of Israel, there was left only the kingdom of Judah. The value of each king in

Judah was determined by comparing him to one of the two previously mentioned kings: King David, who remained faithful to God versus King Jeroboam of Israel, who rebelled against God. The primary kings that were faithful to God were Hezekiah and Josiah.

The kingdom of Judah experienced a spiral of moral decline. Kings, religious leaders and the people sinned progressively more, following the example of pagan people and worshiping their idols. The moral decay was interrupted by reforms of a few kings who were faithful to God. Because of this spiral of moral decline, God continued to warn them by means of his prophets, but they laughed at them, rejected their messages and mocked them. Many of the prophets spoke of a special person whom God was going to send.

3.4 Kingdom in Exile

Finally, God became so outraged with His people that he used Nebuchadnezzar, king of Babylon, to conquer and destroy Judah. Most of Judah's citizens were taken to Babylon. Only the poorest remained.

In Babylon, the citizens of Judah in exile finally learned the lessons taught by the prophets. They were to worship only the Lord God. They should refrain from inter-marriage with those who worshiped other gods and they were to observe the Sabbath.

Daniel and his friends were among the captives taken to Babylon as prisoners. They were firm in their faith in God and obeyed his laws, in spite of the persecutions and suffering they received.

The prophet Ezekiel lived in Babylon and preached God's messages directed to the people who were living there, he also sent messages to the residents of Jerusalem.

3.5 Remnant of the Kingdom

Seventy years after Judah was exiled in Babylon, the Persians conquered the Babylonians. The Persians allowed the Jews to return to their land. Most of the Jews preferred to remain in Babylon, but a remnant returned to Judah. Ezra and Nehemiah were leaders during the reconstruction. Ezra tells how the remnant rebuilt the Temple. Nehemiah supervised the rebuilding of Jerusalem's walls. The book of Esther tells the story of some Jews who did not return to Jerusalem.

As time went by, the people who returned to Jerusalem continued backsliding from God's standards. They disregarded the Sabbath, married foreign women and practiced pagan customs. Ezra, Nehemiah and the prophets put them back in line as they purified their nation from pagan influences and made sure that the services in the Temple were true to God. In the end, the remnant of Judah became a nation that rejected idolatry, rejected "mixed marriages" with those who served other gods, and observed the Sabbath. However, with the passing of time, they became rigid, concerned about legalism and incapable of love.

The Jews did not experience liberty after they returned to Judah. They were always dominated by foreign powers. Later, the Romans conquered the known world and ruled them for over 500 years. The Israelites anxiously awaited the coming of the Liberator that God promised Eve, Abraham, Moses, David and the prophets. After the remnant returned to Judah, God sent a few prophets and then he stopped sending special messages. Four hundred years passed without God sending a single prophet.

OLD TESTAMENT PROPHECIES ABOUT A PROMISED ONE

The chart below lists some of the prophecies about one who is the promised One.

TEXT	PROPHECY
Gn 3:15	A descendant of Eve will crush the head of the serpent.
Gn 12:3	Through Abraham, all peoples on the earth will be blessed.
Is 9:7;11:1-2	The promised One will be a descendant of David.
Is 7:14	A virgin will conceive and give birth to a son.
Mic 5:2	The Messiah will be born in Bethlehem.
Hos 11:1	He will flee to Egypt.
Dt 18:15	A great prophet is promised.
Zc 9:9	He will enter triumphantly into Jerusalem.
Ps 41:9	The traitor will be an intimate follower of his.
Zc 11:12	The Messiah will be betrayed for thirty silver coins.
Ps 27:12	False witnesses will speak against him.
Is 50:6	They will beat him and spit on him.
Is 53:3	He will be rejected by the Jews.
Ps 22:16	His hands and feet will be pierced.
Is 53:7	He will remain silent before his accusers.
Ps 22:18	They will cast lots for his garments.
Is 53:12	He will die with transgressors.
Ps 22:6-8	He will be scorned, despised and mocked.
Is 53:6,12	The sins of many will be laid on him.
Is 53:4-5	He will suffer for others.
Ps 69:4	He will be hated for no reason.
Ps 109:4	He will pray for his enemies.
Is 53:9	He will be buried with the rich.
Ps 16:10	He will not be abandoned in the grave, nor will his body see decay.
Ps 68:18	He will ascend on high.

PANORAMIC VIEW OF OLD TESTAMENT IN CHRONOLOGICAL ORDER

KEY PEOPLE							
ADAM before 4000 B.C.	NOAH 2500 B.C.	ABRAHAM 2000 B.C.	MOSES 1500 B.C.	DAVID 1000 B.C.		DANIEL 586 B.C.	EZRA 516 B.C.

HISTORY OF THE ANCIENT WORLD		HISTORY OF ISRAEL						
Pre-Flood	Post-Flood	**The People** The patriarchs The Israelites	**The Land** Returning to, conquering, and living in the land	**The Kingdom**				
				United	Divided 931 B.C.	Partial 722 B.C.	In Exile 586 B.C. A Remnant	Remnant 516 B.C.
Creation Adam and Eve Cain and Abel Lamech Seth Enoch Methu-selah	Noah Flood Babel	Abraham Lot Hagar and Ishmael Sodom Isaac Jacob/ Israel Joseph The Israelites in Egypt	Moses ▪Burning Bush ▪10 Plagues ▪Passover ▪Escape from Egypt ▪Crossing the Sea ▪Manna ▪Water from the Rock ▪10 Commandments ▪Golden Calf ▪Tabernacle ▪Report of Spies ▪Punishment of Rebellious Israelites ▪Moses' Sin ▪Bronze Snake ▪Balak and Balaam Joshua The Judges ▪Gideon ▪Samson Ruth Samuel	Saul David ▪Goliath ▪Jonathan ▪Bathsheba ▪Absalom Solomon ▪Wisdom ▪Temple ▪Wives	**ISRAEL:** North *Jeroboam* Ahab and Jezebel **JUDAH:** South *Rehoboam*	Only JUDAH Hezekiah Josiah	In BABYLON Daniel	Restoration of JUDAH Ezra Nehemiah Esther
					PROPHETS			
					Elijah Elisha Amos Hosea Jonah	Isaiah Jeremiah	Daniel Ezekiel	Haggai Zechariah Malachi

Old Testament Bible Stories © Jackson Day

GENESIS

	1	2	3	8:18	8:19	50
SUMMARY	Construction		Destruction		Reconstruction	
	The Beginning: The Creation		Sin and its Consequences		A New Beginning	
KEY-PERSON	Adam		Noah		Abraham	
KEY-SUBJECTS	Creation (1-2)		▪Fall of Man (3) ▪The Degeneration of Mankind (4-5) ▪The Flood (6:1-8:18)		▪Noah, after the flood (8:19-9:28) ▪The Nations (10) ▪Tower of Babel (11) ▪Abram/Abraham (12-25) ▪Isaac (25-26) ▪Jacob/Israel (27-35) ▪Joseph (37-50)	
	EVENTS: Predominantly global events				PEOPLE: Predominantly patriarchs, individuals	
THEME	Mankind was created		Mankind was preserved		Mankind was blessed	
SIGN	The Sabbath: God finished his creation work and separated work from rest		The cherubim and the sword: Separation because of sin		▪Rainbow: separation for a new beginning ▪Circumcision: separation from sin for God	
	1	2	3	11	12	50

CREATION
Genesis 1:1 - 2:25

STRUCTURE

Context:
No historical context precedes the creation event because it deals with the beginning of all things.

Key-person: God

Key-location: Heaven and earth

Key-repetitions:
▪God's action. God: created (1:1, 21,27); saw (1:4, 25, 31); made (1:7, 16, 25); called (1:10); set/put (1:17); blessed (1:22, 28); gave (1:29-31).
▪God commanded: let (1:3, 6, 9, 11, 14, 20, 24, 26); be (1:28); do not (1:15).
▪God said, and it was so (1:3, 6, 9, 11, 14, 20, 24).
▪There was evening, and there was morning (1:3, 6, 11, 19, 23, 31).
▪Separation: light from darkness (1:4); water above from water below (1:6-7); seas from dry land (1:9); work from rest (2:2); newlyweds from their parents (2:24).
▪God saw that it was good (1:4, 10, 12, 18, 21, 25, 31).
▪More of its own kind (1:11,12, 21, 25).
▪The creation of man (1:26-27; 2:7).
▪The responsibility of man over the creation: to rule (1:26, 28); to work and care for (2:15); to name the animals (2:19).

Key-attitudes:
▪A positive attitude: everything created was good.
▪God loves: he created a paradise for mankind.
▪Risk: God established boundaries and there was a risk that man would violate them.
▪The loneliness of man before the creation of woman.
▪The joy of man when he met Eve.

Initial-problem:
The earth was formless, empty of life and dark.

Sequence of events:
Creation
▪In the beginning, God created (1:1).
▪The earth was formless, empty and dark (1:1).
▪1st day: God created light and separated light from darkness (1:3-5).
▪2nd day: God created the sky to separate water above from water below (1:6-8).
▪3rd day: God gathered water into one place and separated dry land from the seas. God created plants

and trees (1:9-13).
- 4th day: God made the sun, moon and stars.
- 5th day: God created creatures of the sea and birds of the air. He blessed them and told them to multiply (1:20-23).
- 6th day: God created livestock, reptiles, and wild animals (1:24-25). He made man in his image (1:26-27), blessed him, commanded him to multiply and to rule over other living beings. God gave man plants to eat (1:28-30). God saw that all he had made was very good (1:31).
- 7th day: God rested and declared the seventh day holy (2:1-2).

Garden of Eden
- A summary of the creation: when God first created, there were no plants, no rain and no man; streams sprung from the ground; God formed man from dust and breathed into his nose (2:4-7).
- God planted a garden (2:8-9).
- A river that separated into four headwaters watered the garden (10-14).
- God permitted the man to eat everything in the garden except fruit from the Tree of the Knowledge of Good and Evil (2:15-17).

Creating the Home
- It was not good for man to be alone (2:18).
- Man named the animals (2:19-20).
- God made a woman for Adam (1:17; 2:18-23).
- A man should leave his parents, unite with his wife and the two should become one flesh (2:24).
- Adam and Eve were naked, but felt no shame (2:25).

Final-situation:
Everything God created was good. Adam and Eve lived in the Garden of Eden, were naked, but felt no shame.

BIBLE STORY

Creation

In the beginning God created the heavens and the earth. The earth was formless and empty. Darkness was over the surface of the deep, and God's Spirit was moving over the waters (1:1-2).

God said: "Let there be light," and there was light. God saw that the light was good, and he separated light from darkness. God called the light "day," and the darkness he called "night." And there was evening, and there was morning: the first day (1:3-5).

God said: "Let there be a space between the waters to separate water from water." And it was so. God made the space and some of the water was under the space and some of the water was high above it. God called the space "sky." And there was evening, and there was morning: the second day (1:4-8).

God said: "Let the water under the sky be gathered to one place so the dry ground will appear." And it was so. God called the dry ground "land," and the gathered waters he called "seas." And God saw that it was good.

Then God said: "Let the land produce vegetation: seed-bearing plants and trees on the land that bear fruit with seed in it. Every seed will produce more of its own kind of plant." And it was so. The land produced vegetation: plants that made seed that produced more of its own kind, and trees that made fruit with seed that produced more of its own kind. And God saw that it was good. And there was evening, and there was morning: the third day (1:9-13).

God said: "Let there be lights in the sky to separate day from night. Let these lights serve as signs to mark seasons and days and years. Let them be lights in the sky to give light on the earth." And it was so.

God made two great lights: the brighter light, the sun, to govern the day and the lesser light, the moon, to govern the night. God also made the stars. God put the lights in the sky to shine on the earth, to govern the day and the night, and to separate light from darkness. And God saw that it was good. And there was evening, and there was morning: the fourth day (1:14-19).

God said: "Let the water be filled with living creatures, and let birds fly in the sky above the earth." So God created the great creatures of the sea, every kind of fish, and every living thing that moves in the sea. Each one reproduces more of its own kind. God created birds that fly and they reproduce according to the kind from which they came. And God saw that it was good. God blessed them and said: "Be fruitful and grow in number and fill the water in the seas, and let the birds grow in number on the earth." And there was evening, and there was morning: the fifth day (1:20-23).

God said: "Let the land produce every kind of animal. Let each reproduce according to the kind from which it came. Let there be livestock, reptiles, and wild animals, each reproducing according to the kind from which it came." And it was so. God made the wild animals, livestock, and all the reptiles, each one reproducing according to the kind from which it came. And God saw that it was good (1:24-25).

Then God said: "Let us make man in our image and likeness, and let them rule over the fish of the sea and the birds of the air, over the livestock, over all the earth, and over all the reptiles." So God created man in his own image. He created them male and female. God blessed them and told them: "Have many children and increase in number; fill the earth and be its master. Rule over the fish of the sea and the birds of the air and over every reptile" (1:26-28).

God told the male and female: "I give you every seed-bearing plant on the earth and every tree that has fruit with seed in it. They will be food for you. I give all the green plants to all the animals to eat. Green plants will be food for every wild animal, every bird of the air and every reptile that crawls." And it was so.

God saw all that he had made, and it was very good. And there was evening, and there was morning: the sixth day (1:29-31).

The sky, the earth and all that filled them were successfully made down to the last detail (2:1).

By the seventh day God had finished his work; so on the seventh day, he rested from all his work. God blessed the seventh day and made it a holy day, because on that day he rested from all the creation work (2:2-3).

By faith we understand that the universe was formed at God's command (Hb 11:3).

Garden of Eden
This is another summary of the creation story of the sky and the earth. When the Lord God made the earth and the sky, there were no plants on the land, no rain, nor was there any man. However, the earth was watered by underground springs that sprang up at different places. A mist often rose from the earth and watered all the ground. The Lord God took dust from the ground and formed man. The Lord breathed the breath of life into the man's nose, and man became a living person (2:4-7).

Then the Lord God planted a garden in the east, in a place called Eden; and there he put the man he had formed. And the Lord God made all kinds of trees grow from the ground; trees beautiful to look at and good to eat. In the middle of the garden were the Tree of Life and the Tree of the Knowledge of Good and Evil. A river flowed through Eden and watered the garden. From that point it was divided into four headwaters (2:8-14).

The Lord God put the man in the Garden of Eden to work it and take care of it. The Lord God gave the man this warning: "You are free to eat from any tree in the garden; but you must not eat from the Tree of the Knowledge of Good and Evil. If you ever eat fruit from that tree, you will die" (2:15-17).

Creating the Home
The Lord God said: "It is not good for the man to be alone. I will make him a companion, a helper who is right for him." Now the Lord God had formed out of the ground all the beasts of the field and all the birds of the air. He brought them to the man so the man could name them. Whatever the man called each living creature, that became its name. So the man gave names to all the livestock, the birds of the air and all the wild beasts of the field.

But Adam found no suitable companion for himself. Then the Lord God caused the man to fall into a deep sleep. While the man was asleep, the Lord took one of the man's ribs and closed up the place with flesh. The Lord used the rib to make a woman. Then the Lord brought the woman to the man. The man exclaimed: "This is it! Her bones come from my bone and her flesh from my flesh! She shall be called 'woman,' for she was taken out of man" (2:18-23).

For this reason a man will leave his father and mother and be united to his wife, and the two people will become one flesh. The man and his wife were naked, but they felt no shame (2:24-25).

LIFE-LESSONS DISCOVERED IN THE STORY

1. The term GOD is the subject of the first sentence of the Bible (Gn 1:1). GOD is the subject of the entire Bible. He should be the primary subject of each person's life.

2. Only God existed in the beginning. Before God spoke, nothing existed (Gn 1:1-2). Creation is the time when God initiated the absolute beginning of history.

3. Jesus participated in creation. The New Testament teaches that before the world was created, Jesus Christ already existed, was with God and participated in the creation of the earth and sky. It was by means of Jesus that God created everything in the sky and on earth (Jn 1:1-3 and Cl 1:15-16).

4. The creation story reveals many facts about God's character and abilities in seed form. As the Bible Story continues, these seed-facts will grow larger and become more visible. The creation story reveals that:

4.1 God is omnipotent. He has all power to accomplish whatever he desires. To create is to make something out of nothing. Only God can make something out of nothing. The Creator who made everything out of nothing has the power to do anything he chooses.

4.2 God is omniscient. He has all knowledge. Nobody taught God how to make the sky, the earth, plant life and animal life. He had wisdom and knowledge to create everything, without anyone teaching him.

4.3 God is omnipresent. He is present everywhere. He doesn't need to rise up in order to reach high places. He doesn't need to walk or fly in order to arrive at some distant place. God is everywhere.

4.4 God is holy. He is perfect and good. That is the reason that he made everything good. In the beginning, nothing of the animal world would hurt man. Thorns, briars, weeds and poisonous fruits didn't grow then as they do now (Gn 1:31).

4.5 God is love. He made a perfect creation for mankind, because he is a loving and kind God.

4.6 God is active. God: created (1:1, 21, 27); saw (1:4, 25, 31); made (1:7, 16, 25); said (1:3, 6, 9, 11, 14, 20, 24, 26, 29); called (1:5, 8, 10); put (1:17); blessed (1:22, 28; 2:3).

4.7 The Trinity existed before the creation. The plural: "let us make man in our image", used in Gn 1:26, was God the Father, God the Son and God the Holy Spirit talking amongst themselves.

4.8 God does things in an orderly manner. The creation follows a growing order of dignity, until man is created in the image of God and has the responsibility of caring for the creation. God made the sun to rise and set each day. He made the moon and the stars to follow the same pathway year after year.

4.9 God's Word is powerful. With his spoken words, he created. He began with nothing, spoke and things were created (1:3, 6, 9, 11, 14, 20, 24).

5. It is by means of faith that we understand that God is the creator. The Bible teaches that everything was created by God, and it is by faith that we understand that it is the God of the Bible who accomplished the work of the creation (Hb 11:3).

6. Man's true value is determined by the worth God gives him. God values man above the rest of creation. The creation comes into existence following a growing order of dignity, until man is created in the image of God with the responsibility to be the administrator of all of God's creation.

7. Man was made in the image of God (1:26). He was created similar to God. The part of man that can not be seen has a mind, emotions and a will that is in the image of God. Man's body was created to house the part that was created in God's image. Of all the creation, only man was made in the image of God.

8. God is the best matchmaker. Adam fell asleep while God prepared a woman for him. God brought Eve to Adam (2:21-22). A well established home is also built by God (Ps 127:1). A person should not ignore God when seeking a marriage partner. He should allow God to direct the process of finding a marriage partner.

9. God is the creator of the family and gives guidelines on how to establish a healthy marriage (2:24):
    1st <u>Leave one's father and mother</u>. For the baby, child, and youth, the most important relationship one has is with his parents. The married person should stop giving preference to his parents and should consider his marriage partner the most important person in his life.
    2nd <u>Unite</u>. To unite means to glue or to cement. Jesus used this Genesis text to explain that a couple should remain married as long as both are living (Mt 19:4-6).
    3rd <u>Become one flesh</u>. God's plan is for a man and a woman to participate in the sex act after they have left their parents and have made a commitment to remain united as long as both are living. Everything that God created is very good (1:31); sex inside of marriage is good.

10. In the beginning, God made the family to be a priority for man (2:24). The most important relationship for a married person should be his own spouse. When marrying, he should leave his parents. The relationship with parents becomes less important than that with his new spouse.

11. Parents should release their hold on the child who marries and allow him to give priority to his mate. Since it is God's will for the married child to leave his father and mother, the parents should release their child, helping him to give priority to his new home (2:24).

12. Sex was created by God and it is good, when used according to God's plan (2:25 with 1:31). When God first made man, he told him to multiply and increase (1:28). A married couple enjoying sex has no reason to feel shame (2:25). The marriage bed is pure (Hb 13:4). It is only a sin to practice sex outside of God's plan.

13. Since the very beginning, it is part of God's plan for man to work. God told Adam to cultivate and care for the Garden of Eden (2:15).

14. God establishes limits determining what is right and wrong for man. From the time of creation, God established limits determining what is prohibited to man (2:16-17).

15. God's limits are for the protection of mankind. God prohibited Adam and Eve from eating from the Tree of Knowledge of Good and Evil in order to protect them from death (2:16-17).

16. Man is a steward and has the responsibility to administrate God's creation. At creation, all animal life was subject to man (1:28). God entrusted mankind with the privilege of working and caring for the land (2:15) and to subdue and rule over the animals (1:26, 28).

17. God concluded the activity of creation by resting. It is not the rest of inactivity; God nurtures what he created (2:1-3).

18. The Sabbath was a divine institution. God rested on that day (2:2-3). During Old Testament time, God's people rested from their work on the seventh day, to worship the Creator. The Sabbath rest was only imposed on Sinai, when it became the sign of the alliance between God and Israel (Ex 31:12-17). From the time of creation, God gave an example that man should imitate (Ex 20:11; 31:17). God's greatest work in the Old Testament was the creation, and it was celebrated on the seventh day. God's greatest work in the New Testament was Jesus' resurrection. During New Testament time, Jesus' disciples began meeting to worship God on the first day of the week, the day Jesus resurrected (Jn 20:19, 26; I Cor 16:2).

QUESTIONS

1. What most impresses you about the creation story?
2. What does the creation teach us about God's character and abilities?
3. What was the condition of the world before God began to prepare it as a place for people to live?
4. How was the creation of man different from the creation of other things?
5. What do these differences tell us about ourselves?
6. After God created man, what responsibilities did man receive from God?
7. What responsibility does mankind have for the world that God created?
8. What limits did God establish for man?
9. What does the creation teach us about God's plan for the family?
10. Why did God rest on the Sabbath day?
11. If God can create the universe out of nothing, in what ways can God make a difference in your life?
12. What is your relationship to the God who created the universe out of nothing?

BEGINNING OF SIN
Genesis 3:1 - 4:16

STRUCTURE

Context:
In the beginning, only God existed. Until he spoke, nothing else existed. Everything God made was good. There was nothing in the world that would hurt or harm man. Thorns, weeds, poisonous fruits and violent animals didn't exist.

God made man different from the rest of his creation. Man was made in the image of God, received responsibilities to take care of the creation and was to rule over the animals. God made the Garden of Eden for Adam and Eve. He gave them freedom to enjoy fruit from all the trees in the garden except from the Tree of Knowledge of Good and Evil. Adam and Eve were naked, but felt no shame.

Key-person: Adam and Eve

Key-location: Garden of Eden

Key-repetitions:
- Eat the fruit (3:1, 2, 3, 5, 6, 11, 12, 13, 17, 22).
- Accusations: God accused Adam (3:11); Adam accused God and Eve (3:12); Eve accused the snake (3:13); God accused Cain (4:9-13); Cain accused God (4:13).
- Punishment: the snake's (3:14-15); the woman's (3:16); the man's (3:17-19); Cain's (4:11-12); and for whoever kills Cain (4:15).
- Pain: for the woman (3:16); for the man (3:17-19); for Cain (4:13).
- Conflict: between snake and woman (3:15); the snake's descendants and the woman's (3:15); Cain and Abel (4:8-9); God and Cain (4:10-16).
- God asked questions to those who did wrong: Adam (3:9, 11); Eve (3:13); Cain (4:6, 9, 10).

Key-attitudes:
- The snake's deception.
- Eve's lack of confidence in God's Words.
- Adam and Eve's shame after eating the forbidden fruit.
- God's sadness when he declared punishments.
- God's pleasure with Abel and his displeasure with Cain.
- Cain's anger.
- Cain's resentment because of his punishment.

Initial-problem:
The snake asked the woman: "Did God really say: 'You must not eat from any tree in the garden'?"

Sequence of events:

Adam and Eve Disobey God
- The snake asked Eve if all fruits in the Garden were forbidden (3:1).
- Eve answered that there was one fruit they could not eat nor touch; if they did so, they would die (3:2).
- The snake said they would not die, but they would have knowledge (3:4).
- Eve saw that the fruit was good, ate, gave to Adam and he ate (3:5-6).

Results of Disobedience
- Adam and Eve saw that they were naked and made clothes from fig leaves (3:7).
- Adam and Eve hid from God (3:8).
- God called Adam, who claimed to have hidden because he was naked (3:9-10).
- God asked Adam if he had eaten the forbidden fruit. Adam accused God and the woman. Eve accused the snake (3:12-13).
- God announced punishment for: the snake, (3:14-15), the woman (3:16) and the man (3:17-19).
- God promised that a descendant of Eve would crush the snake's head and that the snake would wound his heel (3:15).
- God made leather garments for Adam and Eve (3:21).
- Adam and Eve were banished from the garden (3:22-24).

Cain and Abel
- Adam and Eve had two sons: Cain and Abel (4:1-2).
- Cain offered some fruits to God and Abel offered the first-born of his flock to God. God rejected Cain's offering, but accepted Abel's (4:3-5).
- Cain was angry. God warned Cain about his anger (4:6-7).
- Cain killed Abel (4:8). Cain belonged to the evil one (1 Jn 3:12).
- God confronted Cain and pronounced his punishment (4:8-12).
- Cain protested and God replied (4:13-14).
- Cain went out from the Lord's presence (4:16).

Final-situation:
Adam and Eve were banished from the Garden of Eden. Their son Cain killed his brother and went out from the Lord's presence.

BIBLE STORY

Adam and Eve Disobey God

Now the snake was the cleverest of all the wild animals the Lord God had made. The snake spoke to the woman: "Did God really say: 'You must not eat fruit from any tree in the garden'?"

The woman answered the snake: "No, that is not right. We may eat fruit from the trees in the garden. God did say: 'You must not eat fruit from the tree that is in the middle of the garden, you must not even touch it, or you will die.'"

The snake replied to the woman: "You will not die. For God knows that when you eat of it, your eyes will be opened to see what's really going on. You will be just like God, knowing good and evil."

The woman saw that the tree was beautiful, its fruit was good for food, and she realized what she would get out of it: she'd know everything. So she took some of its fruit and ate it. She also gave some of the fruit to her husband, and he ate it. Then both of them had their eyes opened, and they saw themselves naked! They sewed fig leaves together to make something to cover themselves around the hips (3:1-7).

Results of Disobedience

That evening, the man and his wife heard the sound of the Lord God strolling in the garden in the cool part of the day. They hid from the Lord God among the trees of the garden.

But the Lord God called to the man: "Where are you?"

The man answered: "I heard you in the garden. I was afraid because I was naked; so I hid."

God asked: "Who told you that you were naked? Did you eat fruit from the tree that I commanded you not to eat from?"

The man replied: "The woman you put here with me: she gave me fruit from the tree, so I ate it."

The Lord God asked the woman: "What have you done?"

The woman replied: "The snake deceived me, and I ate the fruit."

The Lord God said to the snake: "Because you did this, you're cursed, cursed beyond all livestock and all wild animals! You are cursed to crawl on your belly and eat dust all your life. You and the woman will be enemies to each other. Your descendants and her descendants will be enemies. The woman's descendant will injure your head, and you will injure his heel."

The Lord God told the woman: "I will cause you to have much trouble when you are pregnant. You will have great pain when you give birth to babies. Yet, you will desire your husband's affections, and he will rule over you."

The Lord God said to the man: "You listened to your wife; you ate fruit from the tree which I commanded you not to eat from. Therefore, the ground is cursed because of you. You will work very hard to get food from the ground. Getting food from the ground will be painful. You will be working in pain all the days of your life. The ground will produce thorns and thistles for you, and you will eat the plants of the field. You will sweat in the fields to get your food until you return to the ground. You started out as dirt. When you die, you will end up as dirt" (3:8-19).

Adam named his wife Eve, because she would become the mother of everyone who ever lived (3:20).

The Lord God made leather clothing for Adam and his wife and dressed them. The Lord God said: "The man has now become like one of us. He knows good from evil. He must not be allowed to reach out his hand, take fruit from the Tree-of-Life and eat it. If he does, he will live forever." So the Lord God expelled the man from the Garden of Eden. He sent the man out to work the ground, the same dirt out of which he had been made. The Lord threw them out of the garden and stationed an angel-cherubim on the east side of the Garden of Eden. He also put a sword of fire that revolved around in every direction to prevent people from getting to the Tree-of-Life (3:21-24).

Cain and Abel

Adam slept with his wife Eve. She became pregnant and gave birth to Cain. She said: "With the help of the Lord, I have given birth to a man." Later she gave birth to his brother Abel. Now Abel became a herdsman and kept flocks, while Cain became a farmer and worked the soil (4:1-2).

Time passed. Cain brought some produce from his farm as an offering to the Lord. But Abel brought choice cuts of meat from the firstborn of his flock. The Lord accepted Abel and his offering, but rejected Cain and his offering (Gn 4:3-4). It was by faith that Abel offered God a better sacrifice than Cain did. By faith he was commended as a righteous man, when God spoke well of his offerings (Hb 11:4).

Cain became very angry; his face was dark with rage. The Lord asked Cain: "Why are you angry? Why is your face so dark with rage? If you do what is right, I will accept you. But if you do not do what is right, sin is crouching at your door waiting to pounce; it is out to get you, but you must tame it" (Gn 4:5-7).

One day Cain said to his brother Abel: "Let's go out into the field." While they were in the field, Cain attacked his brother Abel and killed him (4:8). Cain belonged to the evil one and murdered his brother because his own actions were evil and his brother's were righteous (1 Jn 3:12).

The Lord asked Cain: "Where is your brother Abel?"

Cain replied: "I don't know. Is it my job to take care of my brother?"

The Lord asked: "What have you done? Listen! Your brother's blood cries out to me from the ground. From now on you will receive nothing but curses from the ground; which opened its mouth to receive your brother's blood, murdered by your hand. When you work the ground, it will no longer yield good crops for you. You will be a restless tramp upon the earth, a wanderer from place to place."

Cain complained to the Lord: "My punishment is too much. I can't take it! Today you are driving me from the land, and I can never again face you. I will be a homeless fugitive and a tramp wandering on the earth. Whoever finds me will kill me."

The Lord answered Cain: "Not so; if anyone kills Cain, he will suffer vengeance seven times greater than your punishment." Then the Lord put a mark on Cain. It was a warning to anyone who met him not to kill him (4:8-15).

Cain went out from God's presence and lived in No-Man's-Land, east of Eden (4:16).

LIFE-LESSONS DISCOVERED IN THE STORY

1. God has absolute authority, which gives him power to determine what is right and wrong for mankind. God established limits and told Adam what he should do and what he should not do (1:28; 2:16-17).

2. God didn't create man for him to live by his own thoughts or ideas. Man was created to be guided by the words of God.

3. People have freedom of choice; they may sin or they may resist temptation. God established limits (2:16-17); however, man was not made as a machine which has no choice.

4. Temptation comes from outside of a person (3:1). The snake served as a mask for a being that was hostile to God and enemy to man when he tempted and deceived Eve. The Bible recognizes the snake as being the opponent, Satan, the devil (Jb 1:6; 2 Cor 11:3; Rv 12:9; 20:2). Satan used the snake as a disguise to deceive Eve.

5. The tempter is intelligent, and he is a liar. The snake spoke the opposite of what God spoke to Adam (3:4-5). In doing so, he accused God of being a liar. However, Satan is the liar (Jn 8:44).

6. God always speaks the truth. Jesus declared himself to be "the truth" (Jn 14:16) Satan is a liar and the father of liars (Jn 8:44). The person who rejects God's truth will accept Satan's lie.

7. The person who modifies God's Words is not prepared to resist Satan. God said they could not eat of the fruit of the Tree of Knowledge of Good and Evil (2:16-17). Eve increased God's demands, saying that they were neither to eat nor touch the tree (3:3). Eve was not prepared to resist Satan, because she modified the Word of God.

8. Sin does not deliver the malicious blessings it promises. Satan promised the blessing of knowledge, but he didn't mention sin's undesirable consequences (3:4-5).

9. Sin: so easy the act, so painful the consequences. It was easy for Eve to take the forbidden fruit, eat it and give it to Adam (3:6). However, the results of sin were painfully hard (3:16-19).

10. The sinner suffers the consequences of sin:

    10.1 Sin brings death (Gn 2:17; Rom 6:23).

    10.2 Sin produces fear and shame. After sinning, Adam and Eve felt fear and shame, and hid from God (3:7-8).

    10.3 Sin separates people from God. After sinning, Adam and Eve hid from God (3:8). They were expelled from the garden where they had walked with God (3:23). Cain went out from the Lord's presence (4:16). The worst punishment for sin is loss of fellowship with God.

    10.4 Sin separates one person from another. After eating the forbidden fruit, Adam accuses Eve (3:12). Years later, Cain killed his brother, Abel (4:8).

    10.5 The sinner seeks to deny responsibility for his own sin. Adam placed blame on both God and Eve (3:12). Eve placed blame on the snake (3:13). Cain tried to excuse himself, asking if he were responsible for his brother (4:9).

    10.6 Sin creates problems in the home. Adam accused Eve after he ate the forbidden fruit (3:12). Cain was angry with his brother and murdered him (4:8). Most family problems are the results of sin committed by family members.

    10.7 Sin affects the guilty in their essential activities: the woman as a mother and wife (3:16), the man as a worker (3:17-19).

11. God desires fellowship with the people he created. It was his practice to meet with Adam and Eve, to walk with them, and to talk with them. He found them hiding because of sin, and he called out: "Where are you?" (3:9).

Old Testament Bible Stories © Jackson Day

12. Nobody can hide from God. Adam and Eve were unable to hide from God among the trees (3:8-9).

13. People, by their own effort, cannot become acceptable to God. God didn't accept Adam and Eve with the clothes they made using leaves. God made clothes from the skins of animals for them (3:21).

14. The sinner is responsible for his actions. Adam shifted the blame both to God and to Eve for his action (3:12), but God blamed Adam for listening to his wife and eating the forbidden fruit (3:17).

15. God's action on behalf of the sinner is man's only hope for liberation from sin's consequences. God promised that one of Eve's descendants would crush the snake's head, while the snake would wound his heel (3:15).

16. Man is a sinner and is unable to save himself from the consequences of sin; he needs a Savior. After the first sin, God made plans to save the sinner; he promised: "A descendant of the woman will crush the snake's head" (3:15). This is the first prophecy regarding Jesus.

17. God demands death as a payment for sin. God killed an animal, removed the skin, made leather garments, and clothed Adam and Eve (3:21).

18. After Adam and Eve sinned, Satan started to govern the world. God had given man the responsibilities to govern it. When Adam and Eve ate the forbidden fruit, they gave Satan the right to govern. Jesus calls Satan: "The prince of this world" (Jn 12:31). Paul calls Satan "The ruler of the kingdom of the air" (Eph 2:2) and "The power of this dark world" (Eph 6:12).

19. When Adam and Eve sinned, the human race suffered a fall. The part of a person that was made in the image of God was contaminated by Satan. One of the results of sin is that Satan now contaminates the mind, emotions, and will of each human being.

20. The worshiper who does not offer his best to God opens the door for sin to assault him. God expects those who worship him to offer him their best. Cain offered God "some" of his produce while Abel's offering was the very best he had. Sin, like a crouching tiger, is ever ready to attack (4:3-7).

21. God seeks to recover the sinner who is headed in the wrong direction. Cain made wrong choices, but God spoke to him, alerting him that his anger resulted in sin crouching at his door (4:6-7).

22. A religion that doesn't obey God, leads one to commit evil. Cain had a religion, and he brought offerings to God. Cain's religion led him to:
    ■Practice evil;
    ■Be angry with God;
    ■Kill his brother;
    ■Lie to God;
    ■Despise the invitation to repent and receive forgiveness;
    ■Become a wandering tramp;
    ■Leave God's presence;
    ■Experience God's punishment (4:8-16).

23. An angry person is in danger of refusing to hear God's Word. Cain was angered and refused to hear God's warning (4:5-8).

24. Sin wants to dominate the person who is a victim of temptation. However, the tempted person should dominate sin. God warned Cain: "...sin is crouching at your door; it desires to have you, but you must tame it" (4:6-7). This is figurative language, that refers to a wild animal being tamed or domesticated. Sin, desirous of attacking its victim, should be dominated. Romans 7:18-23 reveals man's fight against temptation.

25. Each person is responsible to control his own anger. After God asked Cain why he was angry, God told him that sin was crouching at his door waiting to attack him, but he needed to master it (4:3-7).

26. Uncontrolled anger hurts others. Cain allowed his anger to control him and he killed his brother, Abel (4:8).

27. The person who doesn't listen to God will listen to Satan. Satan is not mentioned, in the Genesis text; however, he was involved. Cain "...belonged to the evil one and murdered his brother" (1 Jn 3:12). Jesus taught that Satan is a liar and a murderer from the beginning (Jn 8:44).

28. To harm another person is to sin against God. God, the Creator, will punish anyone who deliberately harms another person. Cain's cruelty to Abel was a sin against God (4:8-10).

29. The person who despises God's invitation to repent and receive forgiveness is in the process of leaving God's presence. Cain didn't listen to God's warning (4:6-7), and he rejected God's confronting him about his sin (4:10-14). As a result, he left God's presence (4:16).

30. To lament suffering that is the consequence of sin is different from repentance. Cain protested against his punishment for his sin, but he did not confess to his crime, nor did he admit the justice of his punishment (4:13-14).

QUESTIONS

1. Before their sin, how did Adam and Eve have fellowship with God?
2. What gives God the right to determine what is right or wrong?
3. How was Eve tempted? How did the tempter deceive her?
4. After their sin, how did Adam and Eve react when they heard God in the garden? How do people today try to hide from God?
5. How did Adam and Eve cover their nakedness? Did God accept them with their clothes made from fig leaves?
6. Who did Adam and Eve blame after they ate the forbidden fruit?
7. What are some of the consequences of disobeying God?
8. How does Satan continue to tempt and deceive people?
9. Why did Cain become so angry that he killed Abel?
10. Cain was a religious man who brought sacrifices to God, yet he refused to listen to God. Why are some religious people responsible for such hideous evil?

DEGENERATION OF SINNERS
Genesis 4:16 - 6:13

STRUCTURE

Context:
Adam and Eve disobeyed God and were banished from the Garden of Eden. The part of them made in the image of God, that enabled them to think, feel, make decisions and walk in perfect fellowship with their Creator, had been contaminated by Satan's influence. Adam and Eve's children were born outside the garden. Their son Cain killed his brother Abel, then he left the presence of God.

Key-person: Cain, Lamech, Seth, Enoch, Noah

Key-location: Outside of the Garden of Eden

Key-repetitions:
- The accomplishments of Cain's descendants: Cain built a city (4:17); Lamech married two women, killed two men and sang a song celebrating his actions (4:19-24); Jabel was the first of the cattlemen and those living in tents (4:20). Jubal was the first musician, the inventor of the harp and flute (4:21); Tubal-Cain forged all kinds of tools out of bronze and iron (4:22).
- Of Adam's descendants through Seth, it is mentioned how many years the first son of each generation lived: Adam 930 (5:3-5); Seth 912 (5:6-8); Enosh 905 (5:9-11); Kenan 910 (5:12-14); Mahalalel 905 (5:15-17); Jared 962 (5:18-20); Enoch 360 (5:21-24); Methuselah 969 (5:25-27); Lamech 776 (5:28-31).
- Evil in the world: Cain killed Abel and left God's presence (4:8-16); Lamech married two wives and killed two men (4:19-24); the sons of God married whomever they chose (6:2); mankind was wicked and everyone's thoughts were always evil (6:5); the earth was corrupt (6:11, 12) the earth was full of violence (6:11, 13).
- The ones who were faithful to God: those who called on the Lord during the time of Seth and Enosh (4:26), Enoch (5:24); Noah (6:8).

Key-attitudes:
- The pride of Cain's descendants because of their accomplishments.
- The privilege of a long life experienced by Seth's descendants; the family line of those who called on the name of the Lord.
- God's pleasure with Enoch and Noah.
- God's frustration with the human race, with the exception of Enoch and Noah.
- God's patience in waiting 120 years before punishing the people.

Initial-problem:
Cain went out from the presence of the Lord.

Sequence of events:

Cain and His Descendants
- Cain went out from the presence of the Lord (4:16).
- Cain had a son named Enoch. Cain built a city (4:17-18).
- Lamech married two women. His sons brought progress in the form of: Jabel, raising cattle; Jubal, music; and Tubal-Cain, manufacturing tools (4:19-22).
- Lamech killed two men and sang a song celebrating his action (4:23-24).

Seth and His Descendants
- Adam and Eve had another son Seth. His descendants called on the name of the Lord (4:25-26).
- Enoch walked with the Lord and God took him (5:21-24).
- Methuselah, the father of Lamech and the grandfather of Noah, lived 969 years (5:21, 27).

God Plans to Destroy Mankind
- The sons of God married whoever they chose (6:1-2).
- God gave mankind 120 years (6:3).
- The Nephilims were the heroes of old (6:4).
- The Lord saw man's wickedness and that everyone's thoughts were evil. The Lord planned to destroy the world because of corruption and violence (6:5-13).
- Noah pleased God (6:8-9).

Final-situation:
Because of corruption and violence in the world, God planned to destroy it, with the exception of Noah.

BIBLE STORY

Cain and His Descendants

Cain went away from the Lord's presence and lived in No-Man's-Land, east of Eden (4:16).

Cain's wife gave birth to their son Enoch. Cain built a city and named it after his son Enoch. Five generations later, a descendant of Cain was named Lamech (4:17-18).

Lamech married two women, Adah and Zillah. Adah gave birth to Jabal; he was the first person to live in tents and raise cattle. His brother Jubal was the first musician, the inventor of the harp and the flute. Lamech's other wife, Zillah, gave birth to Tubal-Cain, who made all kinds of tools out of bronze and iron (4:19-22).

Lamech said to his wives: "Adah and Zillah, listen to me; wives of Lamech, hear me out. I killed a man for wounding me, I killed a youth for hitting me. Anyone who kills Cain will be punished seven times, anyone killing me to get revenge will be punished seventy-seven times" (4:23-24).

Seth and His Descendants

When Adam was 130 years old, Eve gave birth to another son and named him Seth. Eve said: "God has granted me another child to take the place of Abel, since Cain killed him." Seth had a son, and he named him Enosh. At that time men began to call on the name of the Lord God in prayer. Adam was 930 years old when he died (4:25 - 5:5).

Several generations later, one of Seth's descendants was named Enoch. Enoch became the father of Methuselah. Enoch lived 365 years. Enoch prophesied: "The Lord is coming to judge everyone, and to convict all the ungodly of all the ungodly acts and of all the harsh words ungodly sinners have spoken against him" (Jd 14-16). Enoch walked with God; then one day he was gone; God took him away (Gn 5:21-24).

Enoch's son, Methuselah, was 187 years old when his son Lamech was born. Methuselah lived 969 years, and then he died (5:26-27).

Lamech was 182 years old when his son Noah was born (5:28-29).

Lamech lived 777 years (5:30-31). After Noah was 500 years old, he became the father of Shem, Ham and Japheth.

People increased in number on the earth. Many daughters were born. The sons of God saw that the daughters of men were beautiful. They looked them over and chose the wives they wanted for themselves. Then the Lord said: "My Spirit will not contend with humans forever, because they are mortal. They can only expect to live a hundred and twenty years" (6:1-3).

The Nephilims were giants who came from the sexual union between the sons of God and the daughters of men. They were heroes, the mighty warriors of ancient stories (6:4).

God Plans to Destroy Mankind

The Lord saw that the human beings on earth were very wicked. Everyone's thoughts were only about evil all the time. The Lord was sorry that he had made human beings; his heart was filled with pain. The Lord said: "I will get rid of the human beings that I created. I will destroy every person, every animal, every creature that moves along the ground, and every bird of the air, because I am sorry that I made them" (6:5-7).

But Noah was different. Noah pleased God. Noah was a righteous man; he was a man of integrity in his community. He walked with God. Noah had three sons: Shem, Ham and Japheth. God saw how corrupt and how violent the earth had become. Everyone on earth was corrupt. Everyone on earth did only evil.

So God told Noah: "I am going to put an end to the human race, for people have filled the earth with violence. I am going to destroy all people from the earth. So make yourself an ark of cypress wood; make rooms in it and coat it with tar pitch inside and out" (6:8-13).

LIFE-LESSONS DISCOVERED IN THE STORY

1. Moral, social and spiritual degeneration exist when a civilization progresses without obeying God. Cain's descendants built a city, raised cattle, made musical instruments and tools, but they didn't remember God. Their civilization experienced both progress and moral degeneration (4:16-22).

2. The urban man who excludes God from his thoughts will be condemned by God because of his sins. However, he may appear to benefit from the comforts and pleasures of urban life. Cain, who left the presence of God, became the builder of the first city (4:17). The descendants of Cain experienced progress (4:19-22), but divine judgment is the result of moral decay (6:5-7). Other cities in Genesis also experienced urban progress, yet disobeyed God and were condemned by him. They are: Babel (11:1-9) and Sodom (13:13; 18:20; 19:1-25).

3. Those who experience material progress are still subject to divine judgment. Lamech practiced polygamy. Lamech's sons founded the civilized skills of animal husbandry, making musical instruments and blacksmith craftsmanship (4:19-22). God decided to destroy the ancient world because of its wickedness (6:5-7).

4. The sinner who is proud of his sin is in deep spiritual depravity. Lamech took for himself two wives. He rejoiced because he killed two men and made a song celebrating his action (4:23-24). When people approve of sin and treat it as if it were good, they stoop to the lowest level of degeneration (Is 5:20; Rom 1:32).

5. A marriage without God's approval results in evil. Lamech took for himself two wives (4:19). Men chose for themselves wives, motivated by physical attraction, without seeking God's orientation. This was one of the main reasons that led God to plan to destroy the earth (6:2-3).

6. The person who is proud of his sins does not accept punishment; he desires to inflict great suffering on anyone who would punish him. Lamech stated that if anyone revenged Cain for murdering his brother Abel, then seven people in the revenger's family were to be killed.

Therefore, if Lamech is killed in revenge for murdering two people, vengeance should not stop until seventy-seven were killed. He implies that his family should revenge his death by wholesale slaughter (4:23-24).

7. People are divided into two different groups: those that walk with God and those that are moving away from God. Some of those who walked with God are: Abel (4:4), descendants of Seth (4:26), Enoch (5:22) and Noah (6:8). Some of those who moved away from God are: Cain (4:16), his descendants, Lamech (4:19-24) and those who married being motivated by physical attraction (6:2).

8. Righteousness is possible in the midst of evil. Enoch and Noah were exceptions who lived in a corrupt society (5:24; 6:9) Their relationship was with God and not with their culture.

9. Living a long life and living a quality life is not the same thing. Enoch walked with God for 365 years (5:24) while Methuselah lived 969 years, and he died in the flood (5:27).

10. Salvation does not depend upon one's family; it is individual. Enoch, who walked with God, was Methuselah's father (5:21-24). Methuselah was the grandfather of Noah (5:25-29). Methuselah heard his grandson Noah preach for 120 years (6:3). However, Methuselah died in the flood.

11. God is omniscient and knows everything. God is aware of both man's actions and man's thoughts. He knew Cain was in danger of allowing his anger to dominate him, and he knew when Cain killed his brother (4:5-9). The Lord saw man's wickedness and knew that his thoughts were inclined towards evil (6:5-7).

12. God punishes those who practice evil. God planned to punish those who practiced cruelty (6:5-8).

13. In the midst of moral and spiritual decay, the hope of the world is the few who hear God's message and have faith in him. The hope for the ancient world was the few descendants of Seth who were faithful to God.

14. Hope exists in the middle of degeneration, because God continues to communicate with people. God spoke to Cain (4:6-7; 9-15), he communicated with Enoch (5:22-24), he spoke to Noah (6:13-21) and Noah transmitted God's message to the people (2 Pt 2:5).

15. When those with a godly heritage treat courtship and marriage the same way as those who do not know God, they are giving God reasons to punish their people group. The sons of God saw that the daughters of men were beautiful, and they married any of them they chose. Then the Lord decided that there would be a 120 years until the flood (6:1-3).

16. The thoughts that a person entertains in his mind will be expressed by his actions. The result of everyone having only evil thoughts all day long (6:5) was that the earth became wicked, corrupted and full of violence (6:11).

17. Divine justice requires God to punish people who practice widespread evil. The human race deteriorated to the point where, with the exception of Noah, there was universal evil. Everyone had only evil thoughts all day long (6:5). The flood would be the result of God's judgment on human evil (6:11-13).

18. When God is judging and punishing, his grace is still active. God made plans both to destroy the corrupt and to save Noah (6:14-18).

QUESTIONS

1. What are some of the things that Lamech did wrong?
2. What were Lamech's attitudes about his wrong actions?
3. Why was the situation of Lamech worse than that of Cain?
4. What progress did Lamech's descendants contribute to the ancient world?
5. How were Cain's descendants different from Seth's?
6. Who were some of Seth's descendants who walked with God?
7. How were Enoch and Noah different from other people?
8. Why did Noah find favor with God?
9. How was God able to see people's actions and to know that their thoughts were evil?
10. Why did God plan to punish the world?
11. What gives God the right to punish?
12. Do you consider yourself as one who is walking with God or as one who is walking away from God?

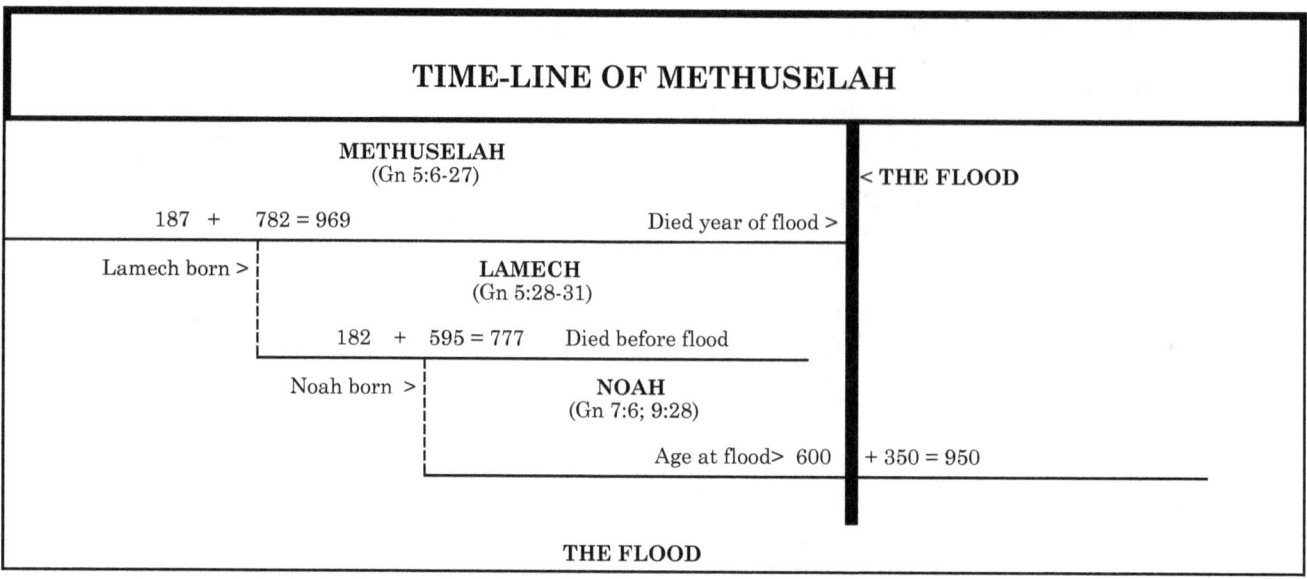

THE FLOOD
Genesis 6:11 - 9:29

STRUCTURE

Context:
Adam and Eve sinned against God and were banished from the Garden of Eden. Their children, Cain and Abel, were born outside the garden. Cain killed his brother Abel. Then he went out from the presence of God. Cain's descendants experienced both progress and moral decay. Adam and Eve had another son, Seth. Some of Seth's descendants walked with God. After many generations, moral decay, corruption and violence increased until all the people were evil, except for Noah. God regretted having made man and informed Noah of his plan to destroy the world.

Key-person: Noah

Key-location: The ancient world and the ark

Key-repetitions:
- Destroy (6:3, 7, 13, 17; 7:21; 8:21-22; 9:11, 15).
- Ark (6:13-16; 7:1, 9, 23; 8:1, 4, 6-10, 16-19; 9:10).
- Take into the ark: Noah's family (6:18; 7:1, 7, 13); animals, birds (6:19-20; 7:2-3, 8, 14-16); food (6:21).
- Animals (6:7, 19-21; 7:8, 14-15, 21, 23; 8:1, 17-20; 9:2-3, 10, 11, 12, 15).
- God commands (6:14, 19; 7:1, 2; 8:15, 17; 9:1, 4, 7).
- Covenant (6:18; 9:9, 11, 12, 13, 15, 16, 17).
- Waters: rose (7:17, 18, 19, 20); receded (8:1, 3, 5, 7, 8, 11, 13).
- Time mentioned: God gave the people 120 years (6:3); age of Noah (7:6; 9:28-29); 7 days after Noah entered the ark (7:10); flood lasted 40 days (7:17); the inundation lasted 150 days (7:24; 8:1-3); on the 17th day of the 7th month, the ark stopped on a mountain (8:4); at the end of 40 days, Noah sent out a raven and a dove (8:6-8); the dove returned and Noah waited 7 more days and again sent it out (8:10); Noah waited 7 more days and sent out the dove the third time (8:12); after 29 days, the flood waters had dried up (8:13); after another 57 days, the earth was dry (8:14-18); Noah lived 350 years after the flood. He was 950 years old when he died (9:28-29).

Key-attitudes:
- God's displeasure with the human race.
- Noah's faith.
- God's concern to save a remnant of both people and animals.
- Noah's gratitude when he left the ark.
- The disgrace of the drunken and naked Noah.
- Ham's disrespect for his father.
- Shem and Japheth's respect for their father.
- Noah's anger at his son, Ham, and his grandson, Canaan.

Initial-problem:
With the exception of Noah and his family, all the people on the earth were wicked.

Sequence of events:

The Flood
- The wickedness of the world (6:1-6).
- God decided to destroy the world (6:7). There would be 120 years until the destruction (6:3).
- Noah found favor in God's eyes (6:8).
- God advised Noah of his plan to destroy the world and commanded him to build an ark: 450 feet long, 75 feet wide and 45 feet high and to finish it to within 18 inches of the top. Make three decks. Put in a door. God established a covenant with Noah. Noah obeyed God (6:13-22).
- Noah announced God's Word while he built the ark (2 Pt 2:5).
- Noah, his wife, sons and daughters-in-law entered the ark with a male and female of every kind of animal (7:1-16) and 7 pairs of animals considered clean (7:2-3).
- God closed the door to the ark (7:16).
- The flood lasted 40 days and covered everything. 150 days after the flood began, the ark rested on the Ararat Mountain Range (7:17-24; 8:1-3).
- After 73 days, other mountain peaks became visible (8:4-5).
- After 40 days, Noah sent out a raven and a dove. The dove returned to the ark (8:6-8).
- After 7 more days, Noah sent out the dove. It returned with an olive leaf in its beak (8:10-11).
- After 7 more days, he sent the dove out, but it did not return (8:12).
- After 29 days, the flood water had dried up, and Noah removed the ark's covering (8:13).
- After another 57 days, the earth was dry, and God commanded Noah, his family and the animals to leave the ark (8:14-18). They were in the ark a total of 370 days.

After the Flood
- Noah built an altar and offered sacrifices to God (8:20).
- God commanded Noah and his sons to increase in number and fill the earth (9:1,7).
- God made a covenant with Noah and promised never again to destroy all life with a flood (8:21-22; 9:11).
- As a sign of his promise, God gave the rainbow (9:12-17).

Noah Became Drunk
- Noah planted a vineyard, drank wine, became drunk and lay naked inside his tent. Ham told his brothers about Noah's condition and they covered their father (9:20-25).

- Noah cursed Ham's son, Canaan (9:25-27).
- Noah lived 350 years after the flood. He died when he was 950 years old (9:28-29).

Final-situation:
Noah became drunk and lay naked inside his tent. His son Ham disrespected him, and Noah cursed Ham's son Cannan.

BIBLE STORY

The Flood

The earth was corrupt and full of violence. The Lord said: "My Spirit will not contend with humans forever, because they are mortal. They can only expect to live a hundred and twenty years" (6:1-3).

Noah was a good man. God said to Noah: "I have decided to destroy all people on earth because they have filled the earth with violence. Build yourself an ark of cypress wood. Make rooms in it and coat it with tar pitch inside and out. Make the ark 450 feet long, 75 feet wide and 45 feet high. Make a roof for it and finish the ark to within 18 inches of the roof in order to have a skylight all the way around the ark. Make three decks, a lower, a middle and an upper deck. Put a door in the side of the ark.

I will bring flood-waters on the earth that will destroy everything alive under the sky. Everything on earth will be destroyed.

But I will establish my covenant with you: you will board the ark; you, your sons, your wife, and your sons' wives with you. You are to bring into the ark two of each living creature, male and female, to keep them alive with you. There will be two of every kind of bird, two of every kind of animal and two of every kind of crawling creature that will come to you to be kept alive. Gather every kind of food that you will need to eat and store it away as food for you and for them." Noah did everything God commanded him to do (6:11-22).

Noah announced God's message while he built the ark (2 Pt 2:5).

The day came when the Lord told Noah: "Board the ark, you and your whole family, because out of everyone in this generation, you are the righteous one. Take on board with you seven pairs, each male with its female, of every kind of clean animal that I have chosen for eating and for sacrifice. And take seven pairs of every kind of bird, and a pair, each male with its female, of every kind of unclean animal. This will allow every kind of life to reproduce again after the flood ends. Seven days from now I will send rain on the earth. It will rain for forty days and forty nights, and I will eliminate from the earth every living creature I have made" (7:1-4).

Noah did everything the Lord commanded him to do. Noah was six hundred years old when the flood waters came. Noah, his wife, his sons Shem, Ham and Japheth and their wives boarded the ark to escape the flood. Male and female pairs of clean and unclean animals, of birds and of all crawling creatures came to Noah. They boarded the ark in pairs, male and female. Then the Lord shut the door behind Noah. After being in the ark seven days, the flood waters came. The rain came in mighty torrents from the sky, and the underground springs erupted for forty days and forty nights (7:5-16).

For forty days the flood waters kept coming. The waters rose, and the ark floated. The waters rose until the highest mountain peaks were covered. The high water mark was twenty feet above the mountains. Every living thing that lived on the earth died: birds, livestock, wild animals, crawling creatures and humans: all dead. Everything that lived on dry land and breathed with its nose died. Only Noah and those with him in the ark were left.

The flood waters covered the earth for a hundred and fifty days (7:17-24).

But God remembered Noah, all the wild animals and the livestock that were with him in the ark. God sent a wind over the earth, the underground springs stopped flowing, and the flood waters began to go down. A hundred and fifty days after the flood began, the ark came to rest on the Ararat Mountain Range. Seventy-three days later, other mountain peaks became visible (8:1-5).

Forty days later, Noah opened the window in the ark and released a raven. The raven flew back and forth waiting for the earth to dry. Then Noah sent out a dove; it could not find a dry place to perch and returned to the ark. Seven days later, Noah again sent the dove out from the ark. The dove returned to him in the evening with a freshly-plucked olive leaf in its beak! Then Noah knew that the flood-water had almost receded from the earth. A week later he sent the dove out a third time. This time it did not come back (8:6-12).

Twenty-nine days after that, Noah removed the roof from the ark and saw that the water was gone. After another 57 days went by, the earth was completely dry. Then God said to Noah: "Leave the ark; you, your wife, your sons and their wives. Bring out all the living creatures that are with you; the birds, the animals, and all the crawling creatures; so they can breed, reproduce and increase in number." So Noah, his family and all the animals departed from the ark (8:13-19). They had been in the ark for a total of 337 days.

After the Flood

Then Noah built an altar to the Lord. He selected clean animals and clean birds from every species and sacrificed them as burnt offerings on the altar. The Lord smelled the pleasing aroma and said to himself: "I will never again curse the ground because of humans, even though their thoughts are evil from childhood. I will never again destroy all living creatures as I did this time. As long as earth continues, planting and harvest, cold and hot, summer and winter, day and night will never cease" (8:20-22).

Then God blessed Noah and his sons. He said to them: "Have many children, grow in number and fill the earth. All wild animals and birds and fish will be afraid of you, for I have placed them in your power. You are responsible for them. Everything that lives and moves will be food for you. Earlier, I gave you green plants, now I give you everything for food. But you must not eat meat that still has blood in it, because blood gives life. I will demand an accounting from every animal. I will demand the life of any animal that kills a person. I will demand the life of any one who takes another person's life; for to kill a human being is to kill one made like God.

Noah, I want you and your family to have many children. Grow in number; multiply, scatter and populate the whole earth" (9:1-7).

Then God said to Noah and to his sons: "I now establish my covenant with you, your descendants and with every living creature, a covenant for all generations to come. Flood-waters will never again destroy all life; flood-waters will never again destroy the earth. I have placed my rainbow in the clouds as a sign of the covenant between me and the earth. Whenever the rainbow appears in the clouds, I will remember my everlasting covenant with you and all living creatures, that never again will flood-waters destroy all life" (9:8-17).

Noah's sons who came out of the ark were Shem, Ham and Japheth. Ham was the father of Canaan. All the people who were scattered over the earth came from these three sons (9:18-19).

Noah Became Drunk

Noah became a farmer and planted a vineyard. He made some wine from his grapes, drank it, got drunk and passed out naked inside his tent. Ham, the father of Canaan, saw that his father was naked inside the tent and went outside and told his two brothers. But Shem and Japheth took a garment and held it between them from their shoulders. Then they walked backward into the tent and let the garment fall across their father to cover his nakedness. Their faces were turned the other way so that they could not see their father's naked body. When Noah awoke from his drunken stupor and found out what Ham, his youngest son had done to him, he cursed Ham's son Canaan. Noah said: "May there be a curse on Canaan! May Canaan be the lowest slave to his brothers. May the Lord, the God of Shem be blessed! May Canaan be the slave of Shem. May God give more land to Japheth; may Japheth live in the tents of Shem, and may Canaan be his slave" (9:20-27).

After the flood, Noah lived another 350 years. He was 950 years old when he died (9:28-29).

LIFE-LESSONS DISCOVERED IN THE STORY

1. God's patience is limited. A time will come when God will remove the opportunity that people now have for salvation. God promised he would give to the people 120 years. This was time for them to repent and turn from their sins (6:3). The time passed, the punishment came. Opportunity for salvation disappeared when God closed the ark's door.

2. The world's important people won't escape God's punishment. The Nephilims were the heroes of their time, and they were punished (6:4). Great and powerful men may escape punishment in earthly justice; however, they won't escape punishment in the coming divine justice.

3. God is omniscient and knows everything. He knew what the people did and thought (6:5).

4. A person may have a right relationship with God, even if he is surrounded by wicked people. Noah lived in a society where wickedness was rampant. Yet Noah was a righteous man who walked with God (6:9).

5. God condemns and destroys sinners. The flood proves that God will punish the sinners (2 Pt 2:4-10).

6. Salvation is obtained only by the means established by God. There was only one entrance door to the ark (6:16). There was only one ark in which people could escape God's punishment in the flood.

7. People are separated into two groups: people with faith who obey God are separated from those who do not believe and obey (2 Pt 2:5). Noah was separated from those outside the ark who didn't have faith in God (Gn 7:11-16; 2 Pt 2:4-5). (See Mt 24:37-41.)

8. People need to prepare for God's coming judgment. Those with faith in Jesus will be saved from judgment that will punish those without faith in God. The flood was a judgment of God that prefigures the last times (Lk 17:26-27; Mt 24:37-42). The salvation granted to Noah represents the salvation that comes as a result of Jesus Christ's resurrection (1 Pt 3:20-22).

9. God wants people to receive his Word. He spoke to Noah (6:13-21; 7:1-4; 8;15-17; 9:1-7, 8-17). Noah announced God's message while he built the ark (2 Pt 2:5).

10. Those who know that God promises to punish sinners need to announce God's message and alert others. Noah announced God's message while he built the ark (2 Pt 2:5).

11. It is better to face unpleasant circumstances with God's protection than to face destruction without his protection. With all the animals inside the ark, no one could withstand the stink from the manure if it were not for the danger of the flood-waters outside.

12. There are times when a church with problems stinks; however, it is better to be inside a stinking church with problems than to be in the world that will be destroyed by God. The ark is often used to illustrate the church. With the manure from all the animals in the ark, no one could have withstood the stink if it were not for the flood outside.

13. God is faithful to fulfill his promises. He kept his promise to punish the ancient world with the flood, and he has kept his promise to never again destroy the world with flood-waters.

14. God desires a covenant relationship with all people. He established a covenant with Noah and his descendants (6:18; 9:9, 11, 12, 13, 15, 16, 17).

15. Faith in God is manifested by obedience. The book of Hebrew teaches that it was by faith that Noah heard God's warnings and prepared an ark for the salvation of his household (Gn 7:5-16; Hb 11:7). Although salvation is by faith and not by works (Eph 2:8-10), faith is accompanied by action (Jm 2:17).

16. God prohibits murder of humans. God established capital punishment as the penalty because of the unique value of humans; they are made in the image of God (9:5-6).

17. God's servants face temptations and risk assuming a lifestyle normal for those who live without considering God. After Noah was saved from the flood, he drank wine, became drunk and lay naked inside his tent (9:20-21).

18. God's servant needs to remain alert in order to avoid falling into sin and creating a scandal. After being saved from the flood, Noah got drunk and conducted himself indecently (9:20-21). Jesus teaches the need to watch and pray in order to resist temptation (Mt 26:41).

19. Alcoholic drink can result in disastrous consequences. The Bible shows the destructive results of alcoholic drink. Noah lost his composure and exposed himself (Gn 9:20-22); Lot lost conscience and committed incest (Gn 19:32-35); Amnom died victim of alcoholic influence; while drunk, he could not resist when attacked (2 Sm 13:28-29); King Belshazzar lost his sobriety, his kingdom and his life (Dan 5:1-30).

20. Mistakes committed during the normal course of the life can result in disastrous consequences. Noah became drunk and acted indecently. Noah's son, Ham, disrespected his father. As a result, Ham's son, Canaan was cursed (9:20-27).

21. Parents' sins may give occasion for their children to commit sins. Noah being drunk and naked, gave occasion for his son to disrespect him (9:20-24).

22. One who disrespects his parents risks harming his own children. Ham disrespected his father. Noah in turn, cursed Ham's son, Canaan (9:25-27). The curse fell on the offender's son (10:6). Ham disrespected his father, and his descendants were cursed.

QUESTIONS

1. During Noah's lifetime, how did God know what men were thinking and doing?
2. Why did God decide to destroy the ancient world with a flood?
3. What did Noah do when God informed him of his plans for the flood?
4. What does the ark teach us about God's judgment and his punishment of sinners?
5. How does Noah's life illustrate the connection between faith in God and obedience to God?
6. During the flood, how many means of salvation did God provide?
7. When Noah left the ark, what was the first thing he did?
8. What was the covenant God made between Noah and his descendants?
9. What is the visible sign of God's promise that he would never again destroy the world with a flood?
10. What was Noah's failure after the flood?
11. What do Noah's actions teach us about the danger of parents' sinning in the presence of their children?
12. The next time God exercises universal judgment, will you be with the group he punishes, or with the group he saves?

TOWER OF BABEL
Genesis 10:1 - 11:32

STRUCTURE

Context:
The waters receded after the flood, and the land dried. Noah's family and all the animals left the ark. Noah built an altar and offered sacrifices to God. God accepted Noah's offering (8:20-22). God commanded Noah's descendants to multiply and scatter through the whole earth (9:7). God gave the rainbow as a sign that he would never again destroy the world with a flood (9:12-17). After the flood, all of the people on earth were descendants of Noah.

Key-person: The settlers of Shinar

Key-location: A plain in Shinar

Key-repetitions:
- Descendants of Noah's sons are mentioned by giving the firstborn son's name of each generation, along with names of sons born to him (10:1-32).
- Language/speech (11:1, 6,7,9).
- Tower (11:4, 5).
- City (11:4, 5, 8).
- Build/make (11:3, 4, 5, 8).
- Scatter over the earth (9:7; 11:4, 8, 9).
- Descendants of Shem: the name of the first son born for ten generations is mentioned with the fact that the father had other sons and daughters and his age at death (11:10-25).

Key-attitudes:
- The pride and arrogance of those who built the tower of Babel.
- The superiority of God over mankind.

Initial-problem: All the people spoke the same language, and men on the plain of Shinar decided to build a city in order not to scatter.

Sequence of events:

Beginning of Nations
- The descendants of Noah sons, Shem, Ham and Japheth increased; they became clans and the clans became nations. The nations spread out (10:1-32).

Tower of Babel
- All of the people spoke one language (11:1).
- Men on the plain of Shinar made bricks and used tar for mortar (11:1-3).
- The men decided to build a city with a tower in order to make a name for themselves and in order not to be scattered (11:4).
- God came down to see the men's activities (11:5).
- God confused the language, so they would not understand what others were saying (11:7).
- That is how God scattered the people over the whole earth (11:8).

Descendants from Shem to Abram
- Ten generations from Shem to Abram (11:10-32).

Final-situation:
God confused the language spoken by everyone, and the people dispersed. Abram, one of the descendants of Shem, settled in Haran.

BIBLE STORY

Beginning of Nations
Noah had three sons: Shem, Ham and Japheth. The descendants of each son increased in number until they became clans. The clans increased in number until they established nations. The nations spread out over the earth after the flood (10:1-32).

Tower of Babel
At this time everyone on the earth spoke the same language. Everyone used the same words. As people moved eastward, they came upon a plain in Shinar (Babylonia) and settled there. They said to each other: "Come, let's make bricks and bake them thoroughly." They used hard-burned brick instead of stone, and tar for mortar (11:1-3).

Then they said to each other: "Come, let us build for ourselves a city, with a tower that reaches to the heavens. Let's make ourselves famous, then we will not be scattered over all the earth" (11:4-5).

But the Lord came down to see the city and the tower that the people were building. The Lord said: "One people, one language; these people are united. This is only the beginning of what they will do. Anything they plan to do will be possible for them. Come, let us go down and confuse their language so they will not understand each other." That is how God stopped their building the city and scattered them all over the earth. The place was called Babel, which means "confusion", because there the Lord turned their language into "babble." From there the Lord scattered them all over the whole earth (11:6-10).

Descendants from Shem to Abram
Shem was one of the sons of Noah. An account of the descendants of Shem, for ten generations, is given. The name of the first son of each generation is given along with how many years he lived until the generation of Terah (11:11-25).

Terah had three sons: Abram, Nahor and Haran. Haran had a son named Lot and a daughter named

Milcah. Haran died in Ur of the Chaldeans, the land of his birth. He was survived by his son, his daughter, his two brothers and his father (11:26-28).

Abram and Nahor both married. Abram married his half-sister Sarai (20:12) and Nahor married their orphaned niece Milcah. Abram's wife Sarai was barren; she had no children (11:29-30).

Terah took his son Abram, his grandson Lot, and his daughter-in-law Sarai, and together they set out from Ur of the Chaldeans to go to the land of Canaan. But when they reached the city of Haran, they settled there. Terah lived 205 years, and he died in Haran (11:31-32).

LIFE-LESSONS DISCOVERED IN THE STORY

1. God, the creator, expects man to obey his commands. God's command was: "Fill the earth" (Gn 1:28) and "multiply, scatter and populate the whole earth" (9:7).

2. Man is sinful. He refuses to obey clear commands from God. God's command was to scatter and populate the whole earth (9:7). Those who settled on the plain in Shinar decided to build a tower that would reach to the heavens in order not to scatter over the whole earth (11:4-5).

3. Those who disobey God's commands will be judged and punished by him. The builders of the tower refused to obey God by scattering. God intervened, gave different languages to the people, and forced them to scatter (11:6-7).

4. A people group that unites in their sin will be judged and punished by God. The people in Shinar united to build the tower, refusing to obey God by scattering. God intervened, gave different languages to the people, and forced them to scatter (11:6-7).

5. When people try to reach God through their own efforts, they always fail. Man-made religion seeks to reach up to God. This is in contrast with the Christian faith, where God comes down to man (11:5, 7). The only way to reach God is to receive God who is reaching for man. The builders of the tower were unsuccessful in their attempt to reach heaven.

6. People, by their own efforts, are unable to protect themselves from God's judgment. God gave Noah the rainbow as a sign that never again would he destroy the world with a flood (Gn 9:11-17). However, the inhabitants of Shinar began to build a tower that would reach high in the sky, beyond the danger of another flood (11:4). They were unable to make a tower that would put them beyond the reach of God's judgment. God came down to punish them (11:7).

7. When people seek unity and harmony without obeying God, the result will be confusion (11:7-8). Unity and harmony without God are impossible.

8. Those who have admirable objectives, yet do not obey God, experience confusion. Those who started building the tower desired unity (11:4-5); however, they disobeyed God's command to scatter (9:7) and the result was the confusion of languages (11:7-8).

9. Working hard is a virtue; however, working hard will not make a person acceptable to God, or worthy of heaven. Those in Shinar worked hard to make bricks by hand and to construct buildings (11:3-4), yet their efforts were rejected by God (11:5-9).

10. Working hard while living independently from God leads to futility. The hard working builders did not accomplish their purpose of reaching the heavens because God confused their language and scattered them (11:5-9).

11. The Tower of Babel explains the problem of diversity of languages. It also explains the lack of harmony which results from communication problems.

12. Man cannot win when he struggles against God's orders. God's command was to scatter; the people decided to stay in one location. God took control of the situation and dispersed the people.

13. God is supreme and sovereign. God's plan was for the people to scatter and populate the whole earth (9:7). The people decided not to scatter (11:4). However, God's intervention with the confusion of the languages forced the dispersion of the human race.

14. God is omniscient. He knew what the builders of the tower were thinking, what they were doing, and what they were capable of doing (11:5-6).

15. Communication problems are the result of sin problems. Misunderstanding that comes from different languages is the result of people disobeying God when they decided to build a tower (11:4).

16. God began to correct the confusion of Babel on the day of Pentecost. Jews from every nation were present in Jerusalem on that day, yet each one heard the apostles speaking in his own language (Ac 2:7-11).

17. Correction of the confusion that resulted from Babel, is still incomplete (Ac 6:1; 10:28, 34-35; Gl 2:11-13). The church still experiences confusion

as a result of different languages, cultures and races.

18. The correction of the confusion that is the result of Babel will be completed in heaven. A great multitude from every nation and language will speak the same words (Rv 7:9).

19. The Bible gives methods to combat confusion in the church in Mt 5:23-24; 18:15-17 and Rom 12:18. If you offend somebody, seek reconciliation (Mt 5:23-24). If somebody sins against you, seek reconciliation (Mt 18:15-17). In all that depends on you, live in peace with others (Rom 12:18).

20. Each church should be a community where the confusion of Babel is corrected. In the church there is no Greek nor Jew (Gl 3:28). The leadership of the church at Antioch was composed of a mixture of races and nationalities (Ac 13:1-2).

QUESTIONS

1. How did the post-flood generation react to God's command to scatter and populate the whole earth (9:7)?
2. Why did Noah's descendants begin to build the Tower of Babel?
3. What does the story about the Tower of Babel teach us about God?
4. What does the story about the Tower of Babel teach us about people?
5. When people were trying to reach up into heaven, God came down to the city. What does that teach us about God and people?
6. What were some of the admirable objectives that the citizens of Babel had?
7. Why is it that people with admirable objectives, who are disobeying God's commands, experience confusion?
8. Why do so many languages exist?
9. What can you do to help correct the confusion that is the result of many languages?
10. How does disobeying God result in confusion today?

ABRAHAM: FAITH TESTED BY LIFE'S CIRCUMSTANCES
Genesis 12 - 25

STRUCTURE

Content:
After the flood, God commanded Noah's descendants to multiply and scatter throughout the whole earth (9:7). Men on the plain of Shinar decided to build a city with a tower in order not to scatter (11:4). God confused the language spoken by everyone and the people dispersed. Abram, one of the descendants of Shem, settled in Haran.

Key-person: Abram/Abraham

Key-location: Canaan

Key-repetitions:
- Covenant (15:18; 17:2, 4, 7, 9, 10, 11, 13, 14, 19, 21).
- God promises Abraham: to bless him and to make him a blessing (12:1-4); to give him numerous descendants (15:4-5; 17:7-8, 16-21; 18:9-15; 22:17-18); if there were 10 righteous, to save Sodom (18:32); to bless him richly (22:15-18).
- Altar/call on the name of the Lord (12:7-8; 13:4, 18; 22:9-14).
- Abraham claimed Sarah as his sister (12:10-20; 20:1-18).
- Son/offspring/descendants: Abram didn't have children (11:30; 15:2); God promised descendants (15:4-5; 17:7-8, 16-21; 18:9-15; 22:17-18); Ishmael (16:1-16; 21:8-21; 25:9); Isaac (21:1-7, 8; 22:1-14; 24:1-8, 52-67; 25:9).
- In the context of mentioning the name of Lot, God appeared to Abraham: God told Abram to leave his father's household. Lot went with him (12:1-4); after the conflict that resulted in Lot separating from Abram, God promised to give Abram's descendants all the land he could see (13:1-18); Sodom was conquered; Lot was taken prisoner and Abram freed him (14:1-16). Then God promised Abram a son and established a covenant with him (15:1-21); When God destroyed the city of Sodom, he remembered Abraham and removed Lot from the catastrophe (19:15-29).

Key-attitudes:
- Abraham's faith; also, faith that wavered when tested by the circumstances of life.
- Abraham's willingness to yield to Lot.
- Abraham's anguish because he did not have a son.
- Abraham's weakness to resist Sarah's suggestions.
- A negative attitude toward Lot.
- A positive attitude toward Abraham.
- Sarah's disgust of Hagar and Ishmael.
- Abraham's willingness to sacrifice Isaac to God.

Initial-problem:
God called Abram to leave his country and his people.

Sequence of events:

God Calls Abram
- God called Abram to leave his family and his country. He promised to bless Abram and make him a blessing (12:1-3).
- Abram was 75 years old. Lot went with him (12:4-5).
- Abram arrived in Canaan. God promised to give the land to his offspring. Abram built an altar (12:6-9).

Abram in Egypt
- There was a famine, Abram went to Egypt and claimed Sarai was his sister (12:10-13).
- Pharaoh sent Abram out of Egypt (12:14-20).

Abram and Lot Separate
- Abram returned to Canaan. At Bethel, he called on the Lord (13:1-5).
- There was a conflict between Lot's and Abram's herdsmen. Abram let Lot choose where he would go. Lot chose the fertile plain of Jordan and left Abram the dry hilly land (13:6-11).
- Lot went near Sodom (13:12-13).
- The Lord promised Abram's offspring all the land he could see. Abram built an altar (13:14-18).
- Sodom was conquered, along with Lot. Abram, with 318 men, rescued Lot and the citizens of Sodom (14:1-16).
- Abram refused gifts from the king of Sodom but was blessed by Melchizedek, king of Salem (14:17-24).

God's Covenant with Abram
- The Lord promised Abram a son, and that his descendants would be as the stars. Abram believed. The Lord considered him as righteous (15:1-6).
- The Lord told Abram his descendants would be enslaved 400 years. He made a covenant to give Canaan to Abram's descendants (15:7-21).
- Abram had a son named Ishmael with Sarai's servant Hagar (16:1-16).
- Abram was 99 years old when God changed his name to Abraham and Sarai's to Sarah. God promised to give Canaan to Abraham's descendants. Circumcision was a sign of the covenant. God promised Abraham and Sarah a son (17:1-22).
- Abraham, Ishmael and all the men in his household were circumcised (17:23-27).
- God again appeared to Abraham and said Sarah would have a son. Sarah laughed. The Lord asked: "Is anything too hard for the Lord?" (18:1-15).

Destruction of Sodom
- The Lord told Abraham he planned to visit Sodom. Abraham pleaded with God to spare Sodom if there

were 50 righteous men there. Abraham lowered the number gradually to 10 (18:16-33).
■ The Lord did not find ten righteous men in Sodom. His angels found men determined to have sex with other men. They told Lot to flee with his family. Lot's wife looked back, and became a pillar of salt (19:1-27).
■ God remembered Abraham, and brought Lot out of the catastrophe (19:28-29).
■ Lot went to live in a cave. His two daughters got him drunk and slept with him. Each had a son with him (19:30-38).

Abraham and His Son Isaac

■ Sarah and Abraham had a son named Isaac (21:1-7).
■ When Isaac was weaned, Ishmael mocked him. Sarah told Abraham to get rid of Hagar and Ishmael (21:8-13).
■ Abraham sent Hagar and Ishmael off. When they were out of water, God opened her eyes and she saw a well. Ishmael lived in the desert and became an archer (21:14-20).
■ God tested Abraham, asking him to sacrifice Isaac. Abraham and Isaac went to the place of sacrifice together (22:1-8).
■ When Abraham took the knife to slay Isaac, an angel stopped him (22:9-12).
■ A ram was caught in a thicket by its horns. Abraham sacrificed it and named the place: "The Lord Will Provide" (22:13-14).
■ The angel promised Abraham numerous descendants and that through his offspring all nations would be blessed (22:15-19).
■ Abraham heard that his brother Nahor had 8 sons (22:20-24).
■ Sarah was 127 years old when she died. Abraham buried her in a cave (23:1-20).

A Wife for Isaac

■ Abraham ordered his chief servant to get a wife for Isaac. The servant went to the town of Nahor and prayed that the girl who offered water for his camels would be the right wife for Isaac. Rebekah gave water to his camels. Rebekah returned with the servant and became Isaac's wife (24:1-67).
■ Abraham died when he was 175 years old (25:1-10).

Final-situation:

The angel of the Lord promised Abraham that he would make his descendants as numerous as the stars in the sky and as the sand on the seashore and that through his offspring all nations on earth would be blessed. Abraham's son Isaac took Rebekah to be his wife. Abraham died.

BIBLE STORY

God Calls Abram

One day the Lord said to Abram: "Leave your country, your family and your father's home and go to the land I will show you" (12:1).

The Lord made the following promises to Abram:
1st "I will make you into a great nation;
2nd I will bless you;
3rd I will make you famous;
4th You will be a blessing to others;
5th I will bless those who bless you;
6th I will curse those who curse you;
7th All peoples on earth will be blessed through you" (12:2-3).

Abram was seventy-five years old when he left Haran. Lot went with him. Abram took his wife Sarai, his nephew Lot and everything he owned. They set out for the land of Canaan (12:4-5).

After arriving in Canaan, the Lord appeared to Abram and said: "I will give this land to your descendants." So Abram built an altar to the Lord. He moved on to Bethel, built another altar and called on the name of the Lord (12:6-9).

Abram in Egypt

There was a severe famine in Canaan, and Abram went down to Egypt. Just before they entered Egypt, he said to his wife Sarai: "You are very beautiful. When the Egyptians see you, they will kill me but will let you live. Therefore, tell them you are my sister, so that my life will be spared" (12:10-13).

The Egyptians praised Sarai's beauty to Pharaoh, and he took her into the king's palace. Pharaoh was kind to Abram because he thought Abram was Sarai's brother. He gave Abram sheep, cattle, donkeys, servants and camels. But the Lord sent terrible diseases on Pharaoh and his household because of Abram's wife Sarai. Pharaoh summoned Abram and accused him sharply: "What have you done to me? Why didn't you tell me Sarai was your wife? Why did you tell me she was your sister? Here is your wife. Take her and get out!" Then Pharaoh commanded his men to make Abram leave Egypt. Abram left Egypt with everything he owned (12:14-20).

Abram and Lot Separate

Abram, his wife and Lot left Egypt and returned to Canaan. Abram was very rich, loaded with livestock, silver and gold. They returned to Bethel; there Abram called on the name of the Lord (13:1-5).

Lot also had many sheep, cattle and servants. The land could not support both Abram's and Lot's herds. Fights broke out between Abram's herdsmen and Lot's herdsmen. Abram said to Lot: "Let's not have fighting between you and me, or between your herdsmen and mine, for we are family. Let's part company. If you go to the left, I'll go to the right; if you go to the right, I'll go to the left."

Lot saw that there was much water in the fertile plain of the Jordan, so he chose for himself the Jordan valley and left for Abram the dry, hilly land. The two men parted company (13:6-11).

Abram lived in the land of Canaan, while Lot lived among the cities of the plain and pitched his tents near the wicked city of Sodom (13:12-13).

After Lot left, the Lord said to Abram: "Lift up your eyes and look north, south, east and west. All the land that you see I will give to you and your descendants forever. I will make your descendants as many as the dust of the earth; if anyone could count the dust, then he could count your descendants." Abram moved his tents to Hebron and built an altar to the Lord (13:14-18).

Four kings joined together to war against the king of Sodom and his allies. The four kings conquered Sodom. They took everything the people of Sodom owned. They took Lot, Abram's nephew who was living in Sodom. They took everything he owned. One of Lot's servant's escaped and fled to Abram. When Abram heard that Lot had been taken captive, he called out 318 trained men born in his camp and went in pursuit. During the night Abram divided his men and made a surprise attack against Sodom's conquerors. Abram recovered everything the enemy had stolen. He brought back his nephew Lot, together with other conquered citizens of Sodom (14:1-16).

Two kings, Melchizedek, king of Salem, and the king of Sodom came out to meet Abram.

Melchizedek king of Salem brought out bread and wine. He was a priest of God, and he blessed Abram, saying: "Blessed be Abram by God, Creator of heaven and earth. And blessed be God Most High, who delivered your enemies into your hand." Then Abram gave him a tenth of all the recovered plunder.

The king of Sodom said: "Give me the people and keep the goods for yourself."

But Abram replied: "I will not keep anything that is yours, not even a thread or a shoestring. That way, you will never be able to say: 'I made Abram rich.' I will accept nothing but what my men have eaten and the share that belongs to the men who went with me" (14:17-24).

God's Covenant with Abram

Afterwards, the Lord spoke to Abram in a vision: "Do not be afraid, Abram. I am your shield; your reward will be great."

But Abram replied: "O Sovereign Lord, what good are your blessings when I have no son. A servant in my household will be my heir."

The Lord replied: "This man will not be your heir, but a son coming from your own body will be your heir."

God led Abram outside and said: "Look up at the heavens and count the stars. Can you do it? Your descendants will be like that, too many to count."

Abram believed the Lord, then God considered him righteous on account of his faith (15:1-6).

The Lord also told Abram: "Your descendants will be strangers in a country not their own. The people there will make them slaves and do cruel things to them for four hundred years. Then I will punish the nation that enslaves them. Then your descendants will leave that land, taking great wealth with them." On that day the Lord made a covenant with Abram and said: "To your descendants I give this land" (15:7-21).

Sarai and Abram had no children. Sarai took her maid, an Egyptian girl named Hagar, and told Abram to sleep with her. Sarai told Abram: "The Lord has not allowed me to have children. Sleep with my maid. Maybe I can build a family through her." Abram agreed. He slept with Hagar, and she became pregnant. When she knew she was pregnant, she became proud and arrogant toward her mistress, Sarai.

Sarai told Abram: "It is all your fault. I put my servant in your arms, and now that she knows she is pregnant, she despises me."

Abram replied: "Your servant is your business. Do with her whatever you think best." Then Sarai beat Hagar; so she ran away.

An angel of the Lord found Hagar near a spring in the desert and told her: "Go back to your mistress and put up with her abuse. I will increase your descendants until they will be too numerous to count. You shall name your son Ishmael. He will be a wild donkey of a man and will live in hostility toward all his brothers."

So Hagar bore Abram a son named Ishmael. Abram was eighty-six years old when Hagar bore him Ishmael (16:1-16).

When Abram was ninety-nine years old, the Lord appeared to him and said: "I am God Almighty; obey me and do what is right. I will confirm my covenant between us and will give you a huge family."

Abram fell flat on his face, and God said to him: "This is my covenant with you: You will be the father of many nations. No longer will you be called Abram; your name will be Abraham. I will make nations of you, and kings will come from you. I will make my covenant an everlasting covenant between me and you and your descendants from now on: I will be your God and the God of your descendants. I will give the whole land of Canaan as an everlasting possession to you and your descendants; and I will be their God. As for you, you must honor my covenant, you and your descendants. Circumcise every male, and it will be the sign of the covenant between me and you. For the generations to come every male in your household who is eight days old must be circumcised."

God also said to Abraham: "As for Sarai your wife, you are no longer to call her Sarai; her name will be Sarah. I will bless her and will give you a son by her. I will bless her so that she will be the mother of nations; kings will come from her."

Abraham laughed, thinking: "Can a man have a son when he is a hundred years old? Can Sarah bear a child at the age of ninety?" And Abraham said to God: "Please let Ishmael be the son you promised."

God replied: "No. Your wife Sarah will bear you a son, and you will call him Isaac. I will establish my covenant with him as an everlasting covenant for his descendants after him. And as for Ishmael, I will bless him also; but I will establish my covenant with Isaac, whom Sarah will bear to you by this time next year." God left when he finished speaking with Abraham (17:1-22).

Abraham took every male in his household and circumcised them. Abraham was ninety-nine years old when he was circumcised, and his son Ishmael was thirteen. Abraham, Ishmael and every male in Abraham's household were circumcised on the same day (17:23-27).

On another occasion, God appeared to Abraham while he was sitting at the entrance to his tent in the heat of the day. Abraham looked up and saw three men standing nearby. He hurried from his tent to meet them and bowed low to the ground. He said: "If I have found favor in your eyes, don't go any further. Rest here in the shade of this tree while I get water to wash your feet and bread for you, so you can regain your strength."

They answered: "Very well, do as you say."

Abraham ordered Sarah to prepare bread and a servant to butcher a calf. Abraham brought them some bread, milk and roast beef. He set these before them. While they ate, he stood near them under a tree.

They asked him: "Where is your wife Sarah?"

Abraham answered: "There, in the tent."

The Lord said: "I will return to you next year at this time, and Sarah your wife will have a son." Now Sarah was listening at the tent door, just behind the Lord. Abraham and Sarah were already old. Sarah laughed to herself thinking: "My husband and I are too old to have a baby!"

Then the Lord said to Abraham: "Why did Sarah laugh and say: 'I am too old to have a baby.' Is anything too hard for the Lord? I will return to you about this time next year and Sarah will have a son!"

Sarah was afraid, so she lied and said: "I did not laugh."

The Lord replied: "Yes, you did laugh" (18:1-15).

Destruction of Sodom

Abraham walked with the men when they got up to leave. They looked down toward Sodom. Then the Lord said: "Shall I hide from Abraham what I am about to do? Abraham will surely become a great and powerful nation. All nations on earth will be blessed through him."

Then the Lord told Abraham: "The cries of the victims in Sodom and Gomorrah are deafening; the people there are evil. I will go down and see if they are as bad as I have heard."

The two men went on toward Sodom, but Abraham stood in the Lord's path, blocking his way. Abraham asked: "Will you kill the good people along with the wicked? What if there are fifty good people in the city? Will you destroy it and not spare the place for the sake of the fifty good people in it? Far be it for you to kill the good with the wicked."

The Lord said: "If I find fifty good people in the city of Sodom, I will spare the entire city for their sake."

Abraham spoke up again: "Now that I have been brave to speak to the Lord, what if the fifty fall short by five: Will you destroy the whole city because of the missing five?"

The Lord answered: "If I find forty-five there, I will not destroy it."

Abraham once again spoke: "What if only forty are found there?"

The Lord answered: "For the sake of forty, I will not do it."

Then Abraham said: "What if only thirty can be found there?"

The Lord answered: "I will not do it if I find thirty there."

Abraham said: "What if only twenty can be found there?"

The Lord replied: "For the sake of twenty, I will not destroy it."

Abraham said: "May the Lord not be angry, but let me speak just once more. What if only ten can be found there?"

The Lord answered: "For the sake of ten, I will not destroy it."

The Lord finished speaking with Abraham and left; and Abraham returned home (18:16-33).

The Lord did not find ten good men in Sodom. Instead, he found men determined to have sex with other men.

The two angels, who had the appearance of men, arrived at Sodom in the evening. Lot was sitting in the gateway of the city. He got up to meet them and bowed down. He said: "My lords, please come to my house to spend the night. You can wash your feet, sleep and then go on your way in the morning."

The angels answered: "No, we will spend the night in the square."

But Lot insisted so strongly that they did go with him and entered his house. He prepared a meal for them. Before they had gone to bed, all the men from the city of Sodom; both young and old, surrounded the house. They called to Lot: "Where are the men who came to you tonight? Bring them out to us so that we can have sex with them."

Lot went outside and closed the door behind him. He said: "No, my friends. Don't do this wicked thing. Look, I have two daughters who are virgins. I will give them out to you, and you can do what you like with them. But don't do anything to these men, they are my guests and I must protect them."

They replied: "Get lost! You came here as a stranger and now you want to play the judge!" They moved forward to break down the door.

The angels pulled Lot back into the house, shut the door and temporarily blinded the men of Sodom so that they couldn't find the door. The angels said to Lot: "Do you have any other family in the city, sons, daughters, in-laws, or anyone else? Get them out of here. The stench of the place has reached to heaven, and God has sent us to destroy it."

So Lot went out and spoke to his daughters' fiances. He said: "Evacuate this place; the Lord is about to destroy the city!" But his future sons-in-law thought he was joking.

At the coming of dawn, the angels urged Lot, saying: "Hurry! Take your wife and your two daughters, or you will be destroyed when the city is punished."

Lot hesitated. The angels took their hands and led them safely out of the city. As soon as they had brought them out, one of them said: "Flee for your lives! Don't look back. Flee to the mountains or you will be destroyed!"

But Lot said to them: "No, my lords, please! You have shown great kindness to me in sparing my life. But I can't flee to the mountains; the disaster will catch me, and I'll die. Look, here is a town near enough to run to, and it is small. Let me flee to it. Then my life will be spared."

The angel replied: "Very well. We agree. But flee quickly, because I cannot do anything until you reach it."

By the time Lot reached Zoar, the sun had risen over the land. Then the Lord rained down burning sulfur from heaven upon Sodom and Gomorrah. Thus he eliminated all life on the Jordan Valley: people, plants and animals alike.

But Lot's wife looked back, and she became a pillar of salt (19:1-27).

Early the next morning Abraham returned to the place where he had stood with the Lord. He looked down toward Sodom and he saw dense smoke rising from the land, like smoke from a furnace. When God destroyed the cities of the plain, he remembered Abraham, and he brought Lot out of the catastrophe that destroyed the cities (19:28-29).

Lot was afraid to stay in Zoar so he and his two daughters left Zoar and settled in the mountains. They lived in a cave. One day the older daughter said to the younger: "Our father is old. No man is around here to sleep with us. Let's get our father to drink wine, and then we will sleep with him, so that our clan will not come to an end."

That night they got their father drunk, and the older daughter went and lay with him. He was not aware of when she lay down or when she got up. The next day the older daughter said to the younger: "Last night I slept with my father. Let's get him drunk again tonight, and you go in and lie with him so we can preserve our family line through our father."

So they got their father drunk again, and the younger daughter lay with him. Again, he was not aware of when she lay down or when she got up.

So both of Lot's daughters became pregnant by their father with baby boys. The older daughter named her son Moab. The younger daughter named her son Ben-Ammi (19:30-38).

Abraham went to the city of Gerar. He told everyone that Sarah was his sister. King Abimelech brought her to his palace. Before he had a chance to sleep with Sarah, God warned the king in a dream that she was married. The king strongly criticized Abraham (20:1-18).

Abraham and His Son Isaac

The Lord fulfilled his promise: Sarah became pregnant and gave Abraham a son at the time God had promised. Abraham named him Isaac. When Isaac was eight days old, Abraham circumcised him. Abraham was a hundred years old when Isaac was born.

Sarah said: "God has brought me laughter. I have given Abraham a son in his old age" (21:1-7).

On the day Isaac was weaned, Abraham gave a great feast. Sarah saw Ishmael, the son or Hagar, teasing Isaac. Sarah said to Abraham: "Get rid of that slave woman and her son, for that slave woman's son will never share in the inheritance with my son Isaac."

The matter upset Abraham because Ishmael was also his son. God told Abraham: "Do not be so distressed about the boy and your maid. Listen to whatever Sarah tells you. The descendants I promised you will be from Isaac. I will make Ishmael into a nation also, because he is your son too" (21:8-13).

Early the next morning, Abraham took some food and a canteen of water, gave them to Hagar, and sent her off with Ishmael. She went on her way and wandered in the desert of Beersheba.

When the water was gone, Hagar put the boy under a bush. Then she went away a short distance and sat down, about a bowshot away, for she thought: "I cannot watch the boy die." And as she sat there, she began to sob.

God heard the boy crying, and the angel of God called to Hagar from heaven: "What is wrong, Hagar? God has heard the boy crying. Help the boy up and take him by the hand, for I will make him into a great nation." Then God opened her eyes and she saw a well of water. So she went and filled the canteen with water and gave the boy a drink. God was with the boy as he grew up. He lived in the desert and became an archer (21:14-20).

Many years later God tested Abraham. The Lord said: "Abraham, take your only son Isaac, whom you love, and go to the region of Moriah. Sacrifice him there as a burnt offering on one of the mountains I will point out to you."

Early the next morning Abraham got up, saddled his donkey and set out for the place designated by God. He took with him Isaac, two servants, fire and enough wood for the burnt offering. On the third day, Abraham looked up and saw the place in the distance. He said to his servants: "Stay here with the donkey while I and the boy go over there. We will worship, and then we will come back to you."

Abraham took the wood for the burnt offering and placed it on his son Isaac, and he himself carried the fire and the knife. The two of them went on together. Isaac asked Abraham: "Father, the fire and wood are here, but where is the lamb for the burnt offering?"

Abraham answered: "My son, God himself will provide the lamb for the burnt offering." The two of them went on together (22:1-8).

When they reached the place, Abraham built an altar and arranged the wood on it. Then he tied up his son Isaac and laid him on the altar. Abraham took his knife and was about to kill his son. But the angel of the Lord called out to him: "Abraham! Abraham! Do not lay a hand on the boy. Now I know that you fear God, because you have not kept from me your son, your only son" (22:9-14).

Abraham looked up and there in a thicket he saw a ram caught by its horns. He went over and took the ram and sacrificed it as a burnt offering instead of his son. Abraham called that place: "The Lord Will Provide."

The angel of the Lord called to Abraham from heaven a second time: "Because you have done this and have not withheld your son, your only son, I will surely bless you and make your descendants as numerous as the stars in the sky and as the sand on the seashore. Through your descendant, all nations on earth will be blessed, because you have obeyed me."

Then Abraham returned to his servants, and they set off together for Beersheba. Abraham stayed in Beersheba (22:15-19).

Some time later Abraham was told: "Milcah is also a mother; she has borne eight sons to your brother Nahor" (22:20-24).

Sarah was a hundred and twenty-seven years old when she died. Abraham bought a cave to serve as the family cemetery and there he buried his wife Sarah (23:1-20).

A Wife for Isaac

Abraham was well advanced in years when he ordered his chief servant to return to the country he came from in order to find a wife for his son Isaac. Abraham said: "The Lord God, who brought me out of my father's household and my native land, will send his angel before you so that you can get a wife for my son from there."

The servant took ten camels and all kinds of valuable things. He made his way to the town of Nahor. He arrived in town at evening, the time women go out to draw water. He prayed: "O Lord God of my master Abraham, give me success today. May it be that when I say to a girl: 'Please let down your jar so I may have a drink,' and she says: 'Drink, and I'll water your camels too;' let her be the one you have chosen for your servant Isaac. By this I will know that you have shown kindness to my master."

Before he had finished praying, Rebekah came out with her jar on her shoulder. Her grandfather was Nahor, Abraham's brother. The girl was very beautiful, and a virgin. She filled her jar with water. The servant hurried to her and said: "Please give me a little water from your jar."

Rebekah replied: "Drink, my lord," and gave him a drink. Then she said: "I'll draw water for your camels too." She emptied her jar into the trough, ran back to the well, and drew enough water for all his camels.

Abraham's servant took a gold nose ring and two gold bracelets, and gave them to Rebekah. He asked: "Whose daughter are you?"

She answered: "I am the daughter of Bethuel, the son that Milcah bore to Nahor. We have plenty of straw and fodder, as well as room for you to spend the night."

Then the man bowed down and worshiped the Lord. The girl ran and told her mother's household about these things. Rebekah's brother was named Laban. He saw the nose ring and the bracelets on his sister's arms, and ran out to the well. Laban told Abraham's servant: "Come in the house, you who are blessed by the Lord."

The servant went to the house. Laban gave him food. But the servant said: "I will not eat until I have told you why I have come. I am Abraham's servant. The Lord has blessed my master abundantly, and he has become wealthy. My master's wife Sarah has borne him a son in her old age, and he has given him everything he owns. And my master sent me to his father's family to get a wife for his son." The servant told them about his prayer and how Rebekah gave drink to his camels.

Laban and Bethuel answered: "This is from the Lord. Here is Rebekah; take her and go, and let her become the wife of your master's son, as the Lord has directed."

Abraham's servant bowed down to the ground before the Lord. Then he brought out gold and silver jewelry and articles of clothing and gave them to Rebekah. He also gave costly gifts to her brother Laban and to her mother.

The next day, Rebekah's family blessed her and sent her away with Abraham's servant.

Isaac brought Rebekah into his mother's tent and he married her. Isaac loved Rebekah and was comforted after his mother's death (24:1-67).

Abraham took another wife and she bore him other sons. But while he was still living, he gave gifts to those sons and sent them away from his son Isaac. Abraham left everything he owned to Isaac.

Abraham lived a hundred and seventy-five years. When he died, his sons Isaac and Ishmael buried him in the cave Abraham had bought. There Abraham was buried with his wife Sarah (25:1-10).

LIFE-LESSONS DISCOVERED IN THE STORY

1. God's promise to Abram: "All the peoples on earth will be blessed through you" (12:3) is a reference to the future coming of Jesus Christ. Through Jesus, all people can have a personal relationship with God and be blessed. This is the second reference made to one who is coming in the future. The first was in Gn 3:15.

2. The Lord has the right to give orders to people. He had the right to order Abram to leave his country, his people and his father's household (12:1).

3. God communicates with people. He spoke directly to Abram and told him what he should do (12:1-4). God continues to speak. Today he mainly speaks through his Bible, through prayer and to people who gather together to study the Bible.

4. Man's destiny depends upon his faith in God; and faith is proven by action. Abram broke away from his country and family bonds, left with his sterile wife (11:30), for an unknown location (12:1), because God called him and promised him a posterity (12:1-4). Abram's faith was tested by God's delay in keeping his promise. Abram's faith was reinforced when God renewed his promise (15:5-6) and it was tested when God demanded the sacrifice of Isaac (22). The existence and the future of the elect people depended upon Abram's faith in action (Hb 11:8-9).

5. The person who has faith in God will be tested by circumstances of life. One passes the test when he shows his faith by doing the will of God. One fails the test of faith when he does not obey God. Abraham is an example of one whose faith was tested by the circumstances of life.

6. God calls his servant to accept a difficult task and promises to bless him and make him a blessing. Whoever wants to be a blessing and to be blessed must accept difficult tasks. God called Abram to leave his country, his people and his father's household and go to the land he would show him. God also promised to bless him and make him a blessing (12:1-4).

7. The one who partially obeys God will suffer the consequences of his disobedience. Abram's obedience was partial when leaving his father's household, in that he took Lot with him (12:4).ABram always brought problems for Abram: there was conflict between Lot's herdsmen and Abram's (13:1-14); Abram had to rescue Lot after Sodom was conquered (14:1-16); Abraham was concerned when he knew God was about to destroy Sodom, where Lot lived (18:23-33).

8. A crisis tests the trust one has in God. A time of famine tested Abram's faith. Without consulting God, he went on his own initiative to Egypt (12:10). In Egypt he was afraid and lied, saying Sarai was his sister (12:11-13).

9. When a Christian stops trusting God and depends upon his own resources, others may be harmed. In a time of famine, Abram went to Egypt and lied saying that Sarai was his sister. The Lord inflicted diseases on Pharaoh. Pharaoh expelled Abram from Egypt (12:10-20).

10. God's disobedient servants give non-believers reasons to feel hostility toward them. After Abram lied, saying that Sarai was his sister, Pharaoh expelled Abram from Egypt (12:15-20).

11. A servant of God may be rich. Abram was very rich (13:2). The rich can serve God, when he acquires his wealth by lawful means, when he recognizes that everything belongs to God, and when he seeks divine orientation on how to use his wealth.

12. The principles that guide a person, when he faces a crossroad that requires a life changing decision, will influence his future. Lot could no longer stay with Abram. Abram chose to peacefully resolve the conflict. Lot chose prosperity and comfort when he chose the fertile plain of Jordan and left Abram the dry hilly land (13:6-11). Lot went near Sodom (13:12-13). He suffered when tragedy struck Sodom (14:11-12; 19:1-29).

13. The New Testament considers Melchizedek (14:18-21) as being a type of Christ (Hb 7). Melchizedek was similar to Christ in:
    1) He was both king and priest, like Jesus;
    2) No mention is made of his ancestors, nor of his descendants, just as Jesus is the Eternal Son of God;
    3) He was greater than Abraham. Abram gave a tenth to Melchizedek, who being the greater, blessed Abram.

14. A person who believes that God will do what he promises is considered righteous by God. Abram believed the Lord, and he credited it to him as righteousness (15:6). Abram trusted God to do what appeared to be impossible, to enable him in his old age to have a son (15:5-6).

15. The basis for salvation is faith that God keeps his promises. Abram believed God, and it was credited to him as righteousness (15:6). People of the Old Testament looked forward to the coming of Christ, and they were saved by his propitiatory death. Today God credits righteousness to those who believe Jesus the Lord was raised from the dead (Rm 4:18-25).

Old Testament Bible Stories © Jackson Day

16. Faith and works walk hand in hand. Abram believed God and it was credited to him as righteousness (15:6). Paul used this text to prove that justification depends upon faith and not the works of the Law (Rm 4:3; Gl 3:6). However, Abraham's faith determined his action. James invoked the same text to condemn faith without works as being dead (Jm 2:23).

17. God's servants should practice hospitality. Abraham's hospitality (18:1-15) became the basis for the injunction given in the New Testament: "... some people have entertained angels without knowing it" (Hb 13:2).

18. God is omniscient. He knew everything the people of Sodom were doing (18:20). He also knows what people do today.

19. God is a righteous judge. He has patience with sinners; however, when he decides to punish, nobody can stop him. Sodom is an example of that (19:23-29). God exercised grace and granted Abraham's request to spare the city if there were only ten righteous people. However, when God decided to act, judgment came.

20. The person who has a relationship with God can be a powerful intercessor. Abraham's prayers in favor of Sodom would have saved the city if there had been ten righteous people in the city (18:23-32).

21. A good beginning is not a guarantee of a good ending. Lot had the privilege of beginning with Abraham and had the same advantages. Lot became a wealthy man. However, the desire for an easy life with financial advantages brought him to a sad ending (13:10-13).

22. The person who knows God, but prefers an easy life and the comfort of a sinful environment, will pay a high price. Lot preferred the easy life close to the wicked city of Sodom (13:10-13). He suffered when his future sons-in-law didn't believe in his word (19:14), when he lost his wife (19:26) and everything that he possessed in Sodom.

23. The Christian who imitates Lot, having faith in God but making decisions based upon what brings financial advantages, will suffer some of the same consequences of the wicked who are being punished by God. When Lot separated from Abram, he chose the fertile valley of Jordan with the wicked city of Sodom (13:10-13). Lot's relatives didn't believe him when he warned them of Sodom's destruction (19:14). Lot lost his wife, and he lost all his possessions in Sodom (19:26). He lost everything when God judged the sinners he associated with in Sodom.

24. The Christian who is similar to Lot, who compromises godly principles for financial advantages, will lose credibility when he desires to communicate the Word of God. When Lot separated from Abram, he chose the fertile valley of Jordan with the wicked city of Sodom (13:10-13). Lot's future sons-in-law didn't believe him when he informed them of Sodom's destruction (19:14).

25. The practice of having sexual relations with the same sex, which is often called sodomy because of the city of Sodom, is abominable to God (Lev 18:22; 20:13; Rm 1:27, 31-32). The men of Sodom wanted to sexually abuse the angels who, in the form of men, visited Sodom (19:4-9).

26. It is God's mercy that saves the sinner from divine punishment. Lot and his daughters were saved from the destruction of Sodom because of God's mercy (19:14). Eternal salvation is also the result of God's mercy (Eph 2:8-9).

27. A person under the influence of alcohol may do things he would avoid if he were sober. Lot lost consciousness and committed incest (Gn 19:32-35). The Bible shows the danger of alcoholic drink: Noah got drunk and exposed himself (9:20-21); Amnom died victim of his drunkenness. While drunk, he could not offer resistance when attacked (2 Sm 13:28-29); Belsazzar lost his sobriety, his respect for the sacred, his kingdom and his life (Dan 5:1-30).

28. Man's efforts to be religious are incompatible with the action of the Holy Spirit. The New Testament compares Ishmael, the son of Hagar, as born "according to the flesh," as man's efforts to be religious (Gl 4:22-23). Isaac, the son of Sarah was born as the result of God's promise (Gl 4:23). Human effort is always incompatible with the action of the Spirit (Gl 4:29-30).

29. God is omnipotent. He had the power to give a son to Abraham and Sarah, even though both of them were advanced with age (18:14; 21:1-2).

30. God can delay the execution of his promises; however, he always fulfills them. God took many long years from the time he promised Abraham a son, until Isaac was born (21:1-2).

31. The spiritual leader needs to be faithful to his own family. Twice, when Abraham was afraid somebody would kill him in order to have his wife, he put Sarah into a dangerous situation (12:10-20; 20:2-3). When Hagar was pregnant with Abram's son and Sarai was jealous, Abram was fast in washing his hands of the results of his actions (16:1-6). When Sarah demanded that Hagar and Ishmael be sent away; Abraham was too weak to demand justice in his own home. He, a rich man, committed an injustice when he sent them away with only water and bread (21:9-21).

32. Hagar's behavior is an example of a rejected person's suffering. Hagar was sent away by Abraham. She was angry, depressed and helpless. She wandered without direction (21:16). She received help from two sources:
    1st She clamored to God, who opened her eyes. Rejection generates anger, that generates depression, and the rejected only has eyes for his problems and doesn't see any solution. When Hagar looked to God, he opened her eyes to see the well that was nearby.
    2nd Assuming her responsibility to her son helped Hagar's recovery. Life isn't finished when somebody is rejected, neither do responsibilities go away. Being rejected by a man didn't remove God's willingness to help Hagar survive and continue her life.
33. God gives his servants tests in order to strengthen their faith. God put Abraham to the test in order to strengthen his faith, not in order to get him to do evil (22:1). See James 1:12-15. The test, instead of destroying Abraham, brought him to the summit of his relationship with God.
34. God provided the perfect sacrifice to substitute for sinful man. God provided a ram in the place of Isaac (22:13). God made sure the ram was caught by its horns in a bush. If it had been caught by any other part of its body, he would have injured himself, trying to escape. God only accepts a perfect and healthy animal as a sacrifice. The sheep died in the place of Isaac. Abraham called the place where God provided the sheep to substitute Isaac: "The Lord will provide." The lamb that substituted Isaac is an illustration of Christ, who was offered in substitution for all who have faith in him (Hb 10:5-10).
35. The search for a marriage partner should begin with seeking God in prayer. When Abraham's servant was sent to find a wife for Isaac, he prayed, seeking orientation from God (24:12-14).
36. Answered prayer is a reason to worship God. After God answered Abraham's servant's prayer by leading him to Rebekah, he fell on his face and worshiped the Lord (24:26-27, 52).
37. Those who serve God sometimes fail; just as Abraham did; they fail both God and their fellow man. However, God continues giving his servants another opportunity. God is faithful, even when his servants are not.

QUESTIONS

1. What does Abraham's life teach us about God?
2. What are some examples of Abraham doing right?
3. What are some examples of Abraham doing wrong?
4. What does Abraham's life teach us about God's relationship with his servant who fails?
5. What does Abraham's life teach us about the need to have patience to wait for God to fulfill his promises?
6. What is the most important lesson you learned from Abraham's life?
7. What can you learn from Lot?
8. What does the destruction of Sodom teach us about God's judgment?
9. What were some of the trials Abraham faced?
10. What does Abraham's life teach us about faith?
11. In your current spiritual state, who do you most identify with:
    ■A citizen of the wicked city of Sodom?
    ■A worldly Christian like Lot: you believe in God; however, your lifestyle is similar to those who don't confess belief in God?
    ■A person of faith like Abraham: you are imperfect, sometimes you fail; however, you are still progressing in your walk with God?

JACOB: SEEKING DIVINE BLESSINGS BY WHEELING AND DEALING
Genesis 25:11 - 38:30

STRUCTURE

Context:
The Lord promised Abraham that his descendants would be as numerous as the stars in the sky and as the sand on the seashore, that through his offspring all nations would be blessed, and that his promises would be fulfilled through Isaac's descendants. Isaac took Rebekah to be his wife. Abraham died when he was 175 years old.

Key-person: Jacob

Key-location: Canaan and Haran

Key-repetitions:
- Jacob took advantage of others: traded stew in exchange for Esau's birthright (25:29-34); deceived Isaac in order to receive the blessing promised to Esau (27:1-29); arranged for weak animals to remain with Laban and the strong ones to become his (30:25-43).
- Conflict between: Isaac and Rebekah over the favorite son; Jacob and Esau over the rights of the firstborn; Jacob and Laban; Rachel and Leah; Laban's sons and Jacob; Jacob's son and Shechem; Joseph and his brothers.
- God speaks to: Jacob (28:13-15; 31:3; 32:25-30; 35:1, 10-12; 46:2-4); Laban (31:23).
- Altar/Pillar: altar (26:25; 33:20; 35:1-7); pillar (28:18, 22; 31:13,45, 51-52; 35:14, 20).

Key-attitudes:
- Isaac's preference for Esau and Rebekah's preference for Jacob.
- Selfishness and greed of Jacob.
- Conflict.
- Cowardice of Jacob.
- Jacob's fear: when he fled from Esau, when he fled from Laban; when Esau was coming to meet him; when his sons killed the men from Shechem.
- Esau's anger at Jacob.
- Laban and his son's contempt for Jacob.
- Jacob's love for Rachel and his dislike for Leah.
- The fury of Jacob's sons when their sister was raped.

Initial-problem:
Rebekah was barren. Isaac prayed, and Rebekah became pregnant with twins who butted heads while still inside her.

Sequence of events:

Isaac, Rebekah and Their Twin Sons
- Rebekah was barren. Isaac prayed and Rebekah became pregnant with twins (25:19-23).
- Esau was born first. Jacob followed, his hand grasping Esau's heel (25:24-26).
- Esau became a hunter; Jacob stayed among the tents. Isaac loved Esau; Rebekah loved Jacob (25:27-28).
- Jacob traded stew for Esau's birthright (25:29-34).
- During a famine, Isaac claimed that Rebekah was his sister (26:1-11).
- Isaac became wealthy; the Philistines envied him. King Abimelech sent him away (26:12-22).
- At Beersheba, God promised to bless Isaac and increase his descendants. Isaac built an altar (26:23-25).
- Abimelech made a treaty with Isaac to do him no harm (26:26-33).
- Esau's two Hittite wives brought grief to Isaac and Rebekah (26:34-35).
- Isaac told Esau to hunt wild game and prepare food. Then he would bless him (27:1-4).
- Rebekah was eavesdropping. She helped Jacob deceive his father (27:5-17).
- Jacob deceived his father and received the blessing Isaac intended to give to Esau (27:18-29).
- Esau realized Jacob had deceived his father and he begged for a blessing. Esau planned to kill Jacob (27:30-41).

Jacob Flees from Esau
- Rebekah told Jacob to flee to her brother Laban. Isaac blessed Jacob and sent him on his way (27:42 - 28:5).
- Esau married one of Ishmael's daughters (28:6-9).
- At night, Jacob dreamed of a stairway reaching to heaven. The Lord gave promises to Jacob. Jacob set up a memorial pillar, called that place Bethel and made promises to God (28:10-22).

Jacob with Laban. He Marries and Has Children
- Laban had two daughters, Leah and Rachel. Jacob agreed to work 7 years for Laban in exchange for marrying Rachel. But, Laban gave him Leah and gave her a maid named Zilpah. A week later, Laban gave Rachel to Jacob in exchange for 7 more year's work. Laban gave Bilhah to Rachel as a maid. Jacob loved Rachel more than Leah (29:1-31).
- Leah gave birth to sons: Reuben, Simeon, Levi and Judah. Then she stopped having children (29:32-35).
- Rachel was jealous of Leah and gave Jacob her maid Bilhah. Bilhah gave birth to Dan and Naphtali (30:1-8).
- Leah gave Jacob her maid Zilpah. Zilpah gave birth to Gad and Asher (30:9-13).
- Rachel bartered with Leah. In exchange for mandrake plants, Leah slept with Jacob. Leah became pregnant with Issachar. She gave birth to

Zebulun and later to Dinah (30:14-21).
- Rachel then had a son, Joseph (30:22-24).
- After Joseph was born, Jacob wanted to return home. He agreed to work for Laban in exchange for his receiving: speckled or spotted sheep, dark-colored lambs and spotted or speckled goats. Jacob took fresh-cut branches and made white stripes on them. He placed them in front of the stronger females who were in heat, and they gave birth to animals that became Jacob's (30:25-43).

Jacob Fleeing from Laban
- Laban's sons accused Jacob of gaining wealth at their father's expense. The Lord told Jacob to return to his father's land. His wives agreed to go with him (31:1-16).
- Rachel stole her father's household gods. Jacob concealed his plans from Laban and fled with all he had to Gilead (31:17-21).
- Laban pursued Jacob. God warned Laban to be careful not to say anything to Jacob (31:22-24).
- Laban accused Jacob, who defended himself (31:25-32).
- Laban searched Jacob's baggage for his idol-gods, and did not find them (21:33-35).
- Jacob angrily accused Laban of unfairness. He claimed if God had not been with him, Laban would have sent him away empty-handed (31:36-42).
- Laban and Jacob built a monument. Each agreed not to pass it in order to harm the other (31:43-53).
- Jacob offered a sacrifice meal. The next morning Laban returned home (31:54-55).
- Jacob sent messengers to his brother Esau. The messengers reported Esau was coming with 400 men. Jacob was afraid. He divided his people and animals into two camps. Then Jacob prayed (32:3-13).
- Jacob hoped to pacify Esau with gifts (32:14-21).
- Jacob's family crossed a creek, but Jacob stayed behind. "A man" (God) wrestled with him. The man touched the socket of Jacob's hip. Jacob's name was changed to Israel. Jacob called the place Peniel (32:22-31).

Jacob Returns to Canaan
- Esau with 400 men arrived. Jacob bowed down to him. Esau embraced Jacob, and they wept. Esau resisted taking gifts, but Jacob insisted. Esau returned to Seir (33:1-16).
- Jacob went to Shechem in Canaan and set up an altar (34:17-20).
- Dinah was raped by Shechem. Then he wanted to marry her. Jacob's sons deceived Shechem and killed all the men in the city. Jacob condemned Simeon and Levi (34:1-31).
- God told Jacob to return to Bethel. Jacob told his household to get rid of foreign gods. Jacob built an altar in Bethel (35:1-8).
- God appeared to Jacob, blessed him, changed his name to Israel, told him to increase in number and promised that nations and kings would come from him. He said he would give the land promised to Abraham and Isaac to Jacob and his descendants. Jacob set up a stone pillar (35:9-15).
- They moved on from Bethel. Rachel died giving birth to her son Benjamin (35:9-20).
- Reuben slept with Israel's concubine Bilhah (35:21-22).
- Jacob had twelve sons:
    - The sons of Leah: Reuben, Simeon, Levi, Judah, Issachar and Zebulun;
    - The sons of Rachel: Joseph and Benjamin; the sons of Rachel's maid Bilhah: Dan and Naphtali;
    - The sons of Leah's maid Zilpah: Gad and Asher (35:21-26).
- Isaac was 180 when he died. Esau and Jacob buried him (35:27-29).

Final-situation:
After spending 20 years with his Uncle Laban, Jacob returned to Canaan with: two wives, two concubines and twelve sons. God confirmed that Jacob's name was changed to Israel and promised that the land he gave to Abraham and Isaac he would give to Jacob and would pass it on to his descendants.

BIBLE STORY

Isaac, Rebekah and Their Twin Sons
Isaac was forty years old when he married Rebekah, daughter of Bethuel and sister of Laban. Rebekah could not have children and Isaac prayed for her. The Lord answered his prayer, and Rebekah became pregnant with twins. The babies kicked hard inside her, so she asked: "Why is this happening to me?" The Lord told her: "Two nations are in your womb, and two peoples butting heads while still in your body; one people will be stronger than the other, and the older will serve the younger" (25:19-23).

When her time came to give birth to the twins, the first baby was born red, and his whole body was like a hairy robe, so they named him Esau (Hairy). His brother followed, his hand grasping Esau's heel. He was named Jacob (Heel). Isaac was sixty years old when Rebekah gave birth to them. The boys grew. Esau became a skillful hunter, an outdoors man. Jacob was a quiet man, staying among the tents. Isaac, who loved wild game, loved Esau, but Rebekah loved Jacob (25:19-28).

Once when Jacob was cooking stew, Esau came in from hunting, starved. Esau said to Jacob: "Quick, let me have some of that red stew! I'm starved!"

Jacob replied: "Make me a trade: my stew for your birthright."

Esau said: "I'm about to die; what good is the birthright if I'm dead?"

Jacob said: "Swear to me first." So Esau swore an oath, selling his rights as the firstborn to Jacob.

Jacob gave Esau some bread and stew. Esau ate, drank, got up and left. So Esau showed how little he cared about his rights as the firstborn son (25:29-34).

There was a famine as bad as the one during the time of Abraham. Isaac went down to Abimelech, king of the Philistines in Gerar. The Lord appeared to Isaac and said: "Do not go down to Egypt; live in this land and I will be with you and will bless you. I will give you and your descendants all these lands and I will confirm the oath I swore to your father Abraham. I will make your descendants as numerous as the stars in the sky. Through your descendants all nations on earth will be blessed, because Abraham obeyed me" (26:1-5).

So Isaac stayed in Gerar. When the men of that place asked him about his wife, he said: "She is my sister," because he thought: "The men of this place might kill me to get Rebekah, because she is beautiful."

One day, King Abimelech saw Isaac fondling Rebekah. Abimelech summoned Isaac and said: "She is your wife! Why did you say, 'She is my sister'?"

Isaac answered him: "Because I thought someone who wanted her might kill me."

Abimelech said: "One of the men might have slept with your wife, and you would have made him guilty of a great sin" (26:6-11).

The Lord blessed Isaac when he planted crops, and he took in a huge harvest. He became wealthy. He had so many flocks, herds and servants that the Philistines envied him. They sought revenge by throwing dirt into all the wells Abraham's servants had dug. Then Abimelech said to Isaac: "Move away from us; you have become too powerful for us." So Isaac moved away and encamped in the Valley of Gerar (26:12-22).

From there Isaac went up to Beersheba. The Lord appeared to him and said: "I am the God of your father Abraham. Do not be afraid, for I am with you; I will bless you and will increase the number of your descendants because of my servant Abraham." Isaac built an altar there and called on the name of the Lord (26:23-25).

Meanwhile, King Abimelech came to him from Gerar with his personal adviser and commander of his forces. They made a treaty with Isaac to do him no harm. Then they left him in peace (26:26-33).

When Esau was forty years old, he married two native Hittite women who were a source of grief to Isaac and Rebekah (26:34-35).

When Isaac was old and nearly blind, he called for Esau his older son and said: "My son."

Esau answered: "Here I am."

Isaac said: "I am now an old man and don't know when I might die. Now get your quiver of arrows and bow. Go to the open country to hunt some wild game and prepare the kind of tasty food I love. Bring it to me to eat, then I will bless you before I die" (27:1-4).

Rebekah was eavesdropping as Isaac spoke to Esau. When Esau left to hunt game, Rebekah said to her son Jacob: "I overheard your father say to your brother Esau, 'Bring me some game and prepare me some tasty food to eat, so that I may bless you before I die.' Now, my son, listen carefully and do what I tell you: Go out to our flock and get two of the best young goats. I will prepare them into a meal for your father, just the way he likes it. Then take it to your father to eat, and he will bless you before he dies."

Jacob replied: "But Mother, Esau is a hairy man, and I have smooth skin. If my father touches me, he will think I am tricking him. I'll bring down a curse on myself instead of a blessing."

His mother answered: "My son, let the curse fall on me. Just go and get them for me."

Jacob got the goats and brought them to his mother. She prepared some tasty food. Rebekah took Esau's best clothes and put them on Jacob. She also covered his hands and the smooth part of his neck with goatskins. Then she gave Jacob the food she had prepared (27:5-17).

Jacob went to his father and said: "My father."

Isaac said: "Yes, which son are you?"

Jacob answered: "I am Esau your firstborn. I have done what you told me. Please sit up and eat some meat of the animal I hunted for you. Then bless me."

Isaac asked his son: "How did you find it so quickly, my son?"

Jacob replied: "The Lord your God gave me success."

Then Isaac said to Jacob: "Come near so I can touch you, to know if you really are my son Esau or not."

Jacob moved close to his father. Isaac touched him and said: "The voice is the voice of Jacob, but the hands are the hands of Esau. Are you really my son Esau?"

Jacob replied: "I am."

Isaac said: "My son, bring me some of your game. I will eat it and bless you." Jacob brought it to him and he ate. He also brought him some wine. Then Isaac said: "Come close my son, and kiss me."

Jacob kissed his father and Isaac caught the smell of his clothes. Finally, he blessed him and said: "The smell of my son is like the smell of a field that the Lord has blessed. May God give you of heaven's dew and of earth's richness, an abundance of grain and new wine. May nations serve you and peoples bow down to you. May you be master over your brothers, and may the sons of your mother bow down to you. May those who curse you be cursed and those who bless you be blessed" (27:18-29).

Jacob received the blessing and left his father's presence. Then Esau returned from hunting. He also prepared a meal and brought it to his father and said: "My father, sit up and eat some of my game, so that you may bless me."

Isaac asked him: "Who are you?"

His son answered: "I am your son, your firstborn, Esau."

Isaac trembled violently and said: "Who was it, then, that hunted game and brought it to me? I ate it just before you came and I blessed him. It is too late to take back my blessing!"

Esau sobbed violently; he bitterly cried out to his father: "Bless me also, my father!"

But Isaac said: "Your brother came deceitfully and took your blessing."

Esau said: "Not for nothing was he named Jacob, the Heel. Twice he has tricked me: First he took my birthright; now he's taken my blessing! Haven't you saved a blessing for me?"

Isaac answered: "I made him master over you and made all his relatives his servants, and I have sustained him with grain and new wine. So what can I possibly do for you, my son?"

Esau said to his father: "Do you have only one blessing, my father? Bless me too, my father!" Then Esau sobbed inconsolably.

His father Isaac answered him: "Your dwelling will be away from the earth's richness, away from heaven's dew. You will live by the sword and you will serve your brother. But when you can't take it any more, you will throw his yoke from off your neck."

Esau hated Jacob. He brooded: "The days for mourning my father's death are near; then I will kill my brother Jacob" (27:30-41).

Jacob Flees from Esau

Esau's threats were reported to Rebekah. She sent for Jacob and told him: "Your brother Esau is plotting vengeance against you. He is going to kill you. Now, my son, do what I say: Flee at once to my brother Laban in Haran. Stay with him until your brother's fury subsides. When your brother is no longer angry with you, I'll send word for you to come back. I don't want to lose both of my sons on the same day."

Rebekah told Isaac: "I'm sick to death of these Hittite women Esau married. If Jacob also marries a native Hittite woman, my life will not be worth living."

So Isaac called for Jacob, blessed him and commanded: "Do not marry a Canaanite woman. Go to the house of your mother's father Bethuel. Marry one of Laban's daughters. May God Almighty bless you and make you fruitful and increase your numbers. May he give you and your descendants the blessing given to Abraham, so that you may take possession of the land where you now live as an alien." Isaac sent Jacob on his way to Rebekah's brother Laban (27:42 - 28:5).

Esau learned that Isaac had commanded Jacob: "Do not marry a Canaanite woman." Esau realized how displeasing the Canaanite women were to his father; so he married one of Ishmael's daughters, in addition to the two wives he already had (28:6-9).

Jacob set out for Haran. When the sun went down, he stopped for the night. He put a stone under his head and lay down to sleep. He had a dream where he saw a stairway resting on the earth, with its top reaching to heaven, and the angels of God were ascending and descending on it. Above it stood the Lord who said: "I am the Lord, the God of your father Abraham and the God of Isaac. I will give you and your descendants the land on which you are lying. Your descendants will be like the dust of the earth, and you will spread out to the west and to the east, to the north and to the south. All peoples on earth will be blessed through you and your offspring. I am with you and will watch over you wherever you go, and I will bring you back to this land. I will not leave you until I have done what I have promised you."

When Jacob awoke from his sleep, he thought: "Surely the Lord is in this place, but I didn't know it. This place frightens me! This is God's house; this is the Gate of Heaven!"

Jacob took the stone he had used for his pillow and set it up as a memorial pillar and poured oil over it. He called that place Bethel (God's house). Jacob vowed: "I want God to be with me, watch over me on this journey and give me food to eat and clothes to wear. Then I will return safely to my father's house. If the Lord does these things, he will be my God and this stone that I have set up as a pillar will be God's house. And I will give God one-tenth of all he gives me (28:10-22).

Jacob with Laban. He Marries and Has Children

Jacob continued on his journey and came to the land of the eastern peoples. He saw a well with three flocks of sheep lying near it. Jacob asked the shepherds: "My brothers, where are you from?" "We're from Haran," they replied.

He asked them: "Do you know Laban, Nahor's grandson?"

The shepherds answered: "Yes, we know him."

Jacob asked them: "Is he well?"

The shepherds answered: "Yes, he is, and here comes Laban's daughter Rachel with the sheep."

When Jacob saw Rachel, he went over and watered his uncle's sheep. Then Jacob kissed Rachel and began to weep. He told Rachel that he was a nephew of her father and a son of Rebekah. She ran and told her father. Laban hurried to meet Jacob. He embraced him, kissed him, brought him to his home and said: "You are my own flesh and blood."

Jacob stayed with him for a whole month and Laban told him: "You are a relative of mine, but it is not right for you to work for me without pay. What should I pay you?"

Laban had two daughters; Leah was the older and she had weak eyes. Rachel was the younger and she was beautiful. Jacob loved Rachel and said: "I'll work for you seven years in return for you letting me marry your younger daughter Rachel."

Laban said: "It's better that I give her to you than to some other man. Stay here with me."

Jacob served seven years to get Rachel, but they seemed like only a few days to him because he loved her. Then Jacob said to Laban: "Give me my wife. My time is completed, and I want to consummate my marriage."

Laban invited everyone around and threw a

feast. When evening came, he took his daughter Leah and brought her to the marriage bed, and Jacob slept with her. Laban gave his servant girl Zilpah to Leah as her maid.

Morning came; Leah was in the marriage bed! Jacob accused Laban: "What have you done to me? I worked for you so I could marry Rachel! Why did you deceive me?"

Laban replied: "In our country we do not allow the younger daughter to marry before the older daughter. Finish your honeymoon week, then I will give you the younger one also, in return for another seven years of work."

Jacob completed the honeymoon week with Leah, and then Laban gave him Rachel to be his wife. Laban gave his servant girl Bilhah to Rachel as her maid. Jacob also slept with Rachel. He loved Rachel more than Leah. Jacob worked for Laban another seven years (29:1-31).

The Lord saw that Jacob loved Rachel more than Leah. The Lord enabled Leah to have children, but Rachel was barren. Leah became pregnant, gave birth to a son and named him Reuben, for she said: "The Lord has seen my troubles. Surely now my husband will love me." She conceived again, gave birth to a second son and said: "The Lord heard that I am not loved, so he gave me this son." She named him Simeon. She conceived again, gave birth to a third son and said: "Now my husband will become attached to me; I have born him three sons." She named him Levi. She conceived again, gave birth to a fourth son and said: "This time I will praise the Lord." She named him Judah. Then she stopped having children (29:32-35).

Rachel, realized she was not giving Jacob any children. She was jealous of her sister and told Jacob: "Give me children, or I'll die!"

Jacob became angry with her and answered: "Can I do what only God can do? He has kept you from having children!"

Rachel said: "Here is Bilhah, my slave girl. Sleep with her so that she can give birth to a child for me. I can build a family through her."

Jacob slept with Bilhah, who became pregnant and gave birth to a son. Rachel said: "God listened to my plea and gave me a son." She named him Dan. Rachel's servant Bilhah conceived again, gave birth to a second son. Then Rachel said: "I struggled hard with my sister, and I have won." She named him Naphtali (30:1-8).

Leah stopped having children, so she gave her slave girl Zilpah to Jacob as a wife. Leah's servant Zilpah bore Jacob a son. Leah said: "I am lucky!" So she named him Gad. Leah's servant Zilpah bore Jacob a second son. Leah said: "Now women will call me happy," and she named him Asher (30:9-13).

During wheat harvest, Reuben went into the fields, found some mandrake plants, and brought them to his mother Leah. Rachel said to Leah: "Please give me some of your son's mandrakes."

Leah replied: "You already took away my husband. Will you take my son's mandrakes too?"

Rachel said: "Give me your son's mandrakes and in return you can sleep with Jacob tonight."

When Jacob came in from the fields that evening, Leah met him and said: "You must sleep with me, I have bartered my son's mandrakes for a night with you." That night Leah became pregnant and bore Jacob a fifth son. Leah said: "God has rewarded me." She named him Issachar. Leah conceived again and bore Jacob a sixth son. She said: "Now my husband will treat me with honor, because I have given him six sons." She named him Zebulun. Later she gave birth to a daughter and named her Dinah (30:14-21).

Then God answered Rachel's prayer and enabled her to have children. She gave birth to a son and said: "God took away my disgrace." She named him Joseph, and said: "May the Lord give me another son" (30:22-24).

After Joseph was born, Jacob said to Laban: "Let me go to my own home and country. Give me my wives and children. I have earned them by working for you. You know how much work I've done for you."

But Laban replied: "If I have found favor in your eyes, please stay. I have learned by divination that the Lord has blessed me because of you. Name your wages, and I will pay them."

Jacob said to him: "You know how I have worked for you and how your livestock has increased under my care. The little you had before I came has increased greatly, and the Lord has blessed you wherever I have been. But when may I do something for my own family?"

Laban asked: "What shall I pay you?"

Jacob replied: "I will go on tending your flocks and watching over them. Go through all your flocks today and remove from them every speckled or spotted sheep, every black lamb and every spotted or speckled goat. They will be my wages."

Laban answered: "Agreed! We will do what you asked."

That day Jacob removed all the streaked or spotted goats and sheep and all the black sheep. He placed them in his sons' care. Jacob continued to care for the rest of Laban's flocks. Jacob took fresh-cut branches from poplar, almond and chestnut trees and made white stripes on them by peeling the bark and exposing the white inner wood of the branches. Whenever the stronger females were in heat, Jacob placed the branches in troughs in front of the animals so they would mate near the branches. If the animals were weak, he would not place them there. The weak animals went to Laban, and the strong ones to Jacob. In this way Jacob grew very rich. He had large flocks, male and female servants, camels and donkeys (30:25-43).

Jacob Fleeing from Laban

Jacob heard that Laban's sons were saying: "Jacob has taken everything our father owned. Jacob became rich at our father's expense." Jacob noticed that Laban's attitude toward him had changed.

The Lord told Jacob: "Return to your father's

land and to your relatives. I will be with you."

Jacob sent word to Rachel and Leah to come out to the fields where he kept his flocks. He said: "I notice your father's attitude has changed toward me. But the God of my father has been with me. You know how hard I've worked for your father. But he cheated me by changing my wages ten times. But God has not allowed him to harm me. If he said: 'The speckled ones will be your wages,' then all the flocks gave birth to speckled young; if he said: 'The streaked ones will be your wages,' then all the flocks bore streaked young. God has taken away your father's livestock and has given them to me. The angel of God said to me in a dream: 'I am the God who appeared to you at Bethel. There you anointed a pillar and you made a promise to me. Leave this land at once and go back to your native land.'"

Rachel and Leah replied: "Our father has no inheritance to give us. He treats us like strangers. He sold us to you, then he used up what was paid for us. God took this wealth from our father. Now it belongs to us and our children. So do whatever God told you to do" (31:1-16).

Jacob left with his children, his wives, his livestock and all the goods he had accumulated to return to his father Isaac in the land of Canaan.

Laban was off shearing sheep. Rachel stole her father's household idols. Laban worshiped those idols as his gods. Jacob hid his plans for running away from Laban; he fled with all he had and headed for the hill country of Gilead (31:17-21).

Three days after Jacob left, Laban learned that Jacob had fled. Laban took his relatives with him and pursued Jacob for seven days before he caught up with him in the hill country of Gilead. At night, God told Laban in a dream: "Do not say anything to Jacob, either good or bad" (31:22-24).

Laban overtook Jacob and said to him: "What have you done? You've deceived me. You've carried off my daughters like captives in war. Why did you run off secretly and deceive me? You didn't even let me kiss my grandchildren and my daughters good-bye. I have the power to harm you; but last night the God of your father said to me, 'Be careful not to say anything to Jacob, either good or bad.' You left because you longed to return to your father's house. But why did you steal my gods?"

Jacob answered Laban: "I was afraid, because I thought you would take your daughters away from me by force. If you find anyone with your gods, he will be killed." Jacob didn't know that Rachel had stolen the gods (31:25-32).

Laban went into Jacob's tent, into Leah's tent and into the tent of the two maids, but he found nothing. Then he entered Rachel's tent. Rachel had hidden the household gods inside her camel's saddle and was sitting on them. Laban searched through everything in the tent but found nothing. Rachel told her father: "Don't be angry with me. I cannot stand up in your presence; I'm having my period." Laban searched but couldn't find the household gods.

Jacob was angry and lit into Laban: "What is my crime? What sin did I commit that you hunted me down? You ransacked my goods and found nothing that belongs to you. I worked for you for twenty years. Your sheep and goats did not miscarry, nor did I eat rams from your flocks. I did not bring you animals torn by wild beasts; I bore the loss myself. And you made me pay for whatever was stolen. The heat consumed me in the daytime and the cold at night. I worked like a slave for you for twenty years. I worked fourteen years for your two daughters and six years for your flocks. You changed my wages ten times. If the God of my father, the God of Abraham and the God of Isaac, had not been with me, you would have sent me away empty-handed. But God saw my hardship, and last night he rebuked you" (31:25-42).

Laban defended himself: "The women are my daughters, the children are my children, and the flocks are my flocks. Yet what can I do today about these daughters of mine, or about the children they have borne? Come now, let's settle things between us; let's make a covenant. God will be the witness between us."

So they took stones and piled them in a heap as a monument. Laban said: "This monument of stones will be a witness between you and me today. May the Lord keep watch over us while we are separated from each other. God will know if you mistreat my daughters or if you marry other women besides my daughters. This pile of rocks and this stone pillar is a reminder: I will not go past them to your side to harm you nor will you go past them to my side to harm me" (31:43-53).

Jacob offered a sacrifice and invited his relatives to a meal. They ate and then spent the night. Early the next morning Laban kissed his grandchildren and his daughters, blessed them and then he left to return home (31:54-55).

Jacob sent messengers to Esau who was in the country of Edom. He told them to tell Esau: "Your servant Jacob says: 'I have been with Laban and remained there till now. I have cattle, donkeys, sheep, goats and servants. I am sending this message to my master, and ask you to accept us.'"

The messengers returned and reported to Jacob: "We went to your brother Esau, and now he is coming to meet you. Four hundred men are with him."

Jacob was terrified. He divided his flocks, herds, camels and people into two camps. He thought: "If Esau attacks one group, the group that is left may escape."

Jacob prayed: "God of my father Abraham, God of my father Isaac! Lord, you told me: 'Return to your country and your relatives, and I will make you prosper.' I am unworthy of all the kindness and goodness you have shown me. I had only my staff when I crossed this Jordan, but now I own enough to have two camps. Save me from my angry brother Esau. I am afraid he will kill us all: me, the mothers and their children. But you said, 'I will surely make you prosper and will make your descendants as numerous as the sand of the sea'" (32:3-13).

Jacob spent the night there, and he selected a gift for his brother Esau: two hundred female goats and twenty male goats, two hundred ewes and twenty rams, thirty female camels with their young, forty cows and ten bulls, and twenty female donkeys and ten male donkeys. He put them in the care of his servants, each herd by itself. He said to his servants: "Go ahead of me, and keep some space between the herds."

He instructed the leader of each herd: "My brother Esau will meet you and ask: 'Whose servant are you. Where are you going? Whose animals are these?' You are to answer: 'They belong to your servant Jacob. He sent them to you, my master Esau, and he is coming behind us.'" Jacob thought: "I will pacify him with these gifts I am sending on ahead; later, when I see him face to face, perhaps he will welcome me" (32:14-21).

So Jacob's gifts went on ahead of him, but he himself spent the night in the camp. That night Jacob took his two wives, his two maids and his eleven sons and crossed the ford of the Jabbok River. After he had sent them across, he sent over all his possessions.

Jacob stayed behind alone, and a man wrestled with him till daybreak. When the man saw that he could not overpower him, he struck Jacob's hip and put it out of joint. Then the man said: "Let me go, for it is daybreak."

But Jacob replied: "I will not let you go unless you bless me."

The man asked him: "What is your name?"

He answered: "Jacob."

Then the man said: "Your name will no longer be Jacob, but Israel, because you have wrestled with God and with men and have won." Then he blessed Jacob there.

Jacob called the place Peniel, saying: "I saw God face to face. But, my life was spared."

The sun rose as he left Peniel, and he was limping because of his hip. To this day the Israelites do not eat the tendon attached to the hip socket, because Jacob's hip socket was touched near the tendon (32:22-31).

Jacob Returns to Canaan

Jacob looked up and saw Esau, coming with his four hundred men. He divided the children among Leah, Rachel and the two maids. He put the maids and their children in front, Leah and her children next, and Rachel and Joseph in the rear. Jacob himself went out front. He bowed down to the ground seven times as he walked toward his brother.

But Esau ran to meet Jacob and embraced him; he threw his arms around his neck and kissed him. They both wept. Then Esau looked up and saw the women and children and asked: "Who are these with you?"

Jacob answered: "They are the children God has graciously given your servant."

Then the women and their children approached and bowed down.

Esau asked: "What do you mean by all these herds I met?"

Jacob answered: "They were to please you, my master."

Esau replied: "I already have plenty, my brother. Keep what you have for yourself."

Jacob replied: "No, please! If you can find it in your heart to welcome me, accept this gift from me. For to see your face is like seeing the face of God smiling on me. Please accept the present that was brought to you." And because Jacob insisted, Esau accepted it.

Then Esau said: "Let us be on our way; I'll travel with you."

Jacob replied: "The children are weak. And the flocks and herds are nursing, making for slow going. If they are driven hard just one day, all the animals will die. My master, go on ahead of me, your servant. I will let the animals and the children set the speed for us to travel. I will come to my master in Edon."

Esau started back to Edon (33:1-16).

Jacob, however, went in another direction. When he pitched his tent at the city of Shechem in Canaan, he set up an altar (34:17-20).

One day, Dinah, the daughter of Leah and Jacob, went to visit some women in that land. When Shechem son of Hamor, the ruler of that area, saw her, he raped her. Then he fell in love with Dinah and spoke kindly to her.

Shechem said to his father Hamor: "Get me this girl so I can marry her."

Jacob heard that Shechem had raped his daughter Dinah. But, his sons were in the fields with his livestock; so he kept quiet about it until they came home.

Then Shechem and his father, Hamor, went out to talk with Jacob. Now Jacob's sons had come in from the fields as soon as they heard what had happened. They were outraged, explosive with anger.

But Hamor said to Jacob and his sons: "My son Shechem is in love with your daughter. Please let him marry her. Intermarry with us. You can settle among us; the land is open to you. Live in it, trade in it, and acquire property in it."

Shechem spoke up for himself: "Please accept my offer. I will give you whatever you ask. Make the price for the bride as great as you like, and I'll pay whatever you ask me. Just let me marry Dinah."

Because their sister Dinah had been raped, Jacob's sons replied deceitfully: "We can't do such a thing; we can't give our sister to a man who is uncircumcised. We will give our consent to you on one condition: you become like us by circumcising all your males. But if you will not agree to be circumcised, we'll take our sister and go."

Hamor and his son Shechem went to the gate of their city to speak to their fellow townsmen. They said: "These men are friendly toward us. Let them live in our land and trade here. We can marry their daughters and they can marry ours. But the men will consent to live with us as one people only on one condition: that our males be circumcised, just as they themselves are. Won't their livestock, their property and all their other animals become ours? Let's do what they say, and they will settle among us."

All the men agreed with Hamor and his son Shechem; every male in the city was circumcised. Three days later, the men who were circumcised were in great pain. Two of Jacob's sons, Simeon and Levi, Dinah's brothers, took their swords and attacked the unsuspecting city, killing every male. They killed Hamor and his son Shechem, took Dinah from Shechem's house and left. When the rest of Jacob's sons came upon the dead bodies, they looted the city where their sister had been raped.

Jacob said to Simeon and Levi: "You have made my name stink among the people here in Canaan. We are few in number; if they join forces against us, my household will be destroyed."

But they replied: "We will not allow our sister to be treated like a prostitute" (34:1-31).

God spoke to Jacob: "Go back to Bethel and settle there. Build an altar to the God who appeared to you when you were fleeing from your brother Esau."

So Jacob told his household and to all who were with him: "Get rid of your foreign gods, take a bath and change your clothes. Then let us go up to Bethel. There I will build an altar to God, who answered me in the day of my distress and who has been with me wherever I have gone."

So they gave Jacob all their foreign gods and their lucky-charm earrings. Jacob buried them under the oak at Shechem. Then they set out. The terror of God fell upon the towns all around them so that no one pursued them. Jacob and all the people with him came to Bethel. There he built an altar, and he called the place El Bethel, because it was there that God revealed himself to him when he was fleeing from his brother (35:1-8).

God appeared to Jacob again, blessed him and said: "Your name is Jacob, but that is your name no longer. Your name will be Israel. I am God Almighty. Have children and increase in number. You will be the ancestor of many nations and kings. The land I gave to Abraham and Isaac I also give to you, and I will pass it on to your descendants." Then God left him.

Jacob set up a stone pillar at the spot where God spoke to him. He poured a drink offering on and also poured oil on it (35:9-15).

After they moved on from Bethel, Rachel died giving birth to her son, Benjamin. Rachel was buried on the way to Bethlehem. Over her tomb Jacob set up a pillar (35:9-20).

On one occasion, Reuben went in and slept with his father's concubine Bilhah. Israel learned about Reuben's action (35:21-22).

Jacob had twelve sons:
- The sons of Leah: Reuben the firstborn, Simeon, Levi, Judah, Issachar and Zebulun.
- The sons of Rachel: Joseph and Benjamin.
- The sons of Rachel's maid Bilhah: Dan and Naphtali.
- The sons of Leah's maid Zilpah: Gad and Asher (35:21-26).

Finally, Jacob made it home to his father Isaac near Hebron, where Abraham and Isaac had stayed. Isaac was a hundred and eighty years old when he died. His sons Esau and Jacob buried him (35:27-29).

LIFE-LESSONS DISCOVERED IN THE STORY

1. God fulfills his promises, even though he may not be in a hurry to do so. God told Abraham that he would fulfill his covenant promise through Isaac's descendants (Gn 12:1-3 and 17:19). Isaac had to wait twenty years before children were born to him. He was forty years old when he married (25:20) and he was 60 when Esau and Jacob were born (25:26).

2. God hears his servant's prayers. Isaac prayed in favor of Rebekah, who was barren, and she became pregnant with twins (25:21-22).

3. When a parent favors one child more than another, conflict is generated in the home. Isaac loved Esau, the hunter, while Rebekah loved Jacob, the son who cooked (25:27-28). There was serious conflict in their home.

4. The one who despises privileges will lose them. Esau didn't attribute value to the covenant between God and Abraham, nor to the privileges of being the firstborn son. He traded his firstborn rights for bread and stew (25:29-34).

5. The person who is most attractive to his fellow man, may not be the person God chooses to use. Esau the hunter was more attractive than Jacob the cook. However, Esau was godless because he sought immediate gratification, and didn't value spiritual privileges (Hb 12:16).

6. God can choose an unattractive person and use divine discipline to turn him into someone useful. In the first phase of his life, Jacob was a wheeler dealer who used deceit to obtain advantages over others. He used deceit to obtain things God had promised as a result of the covenant established with Abraham. Through divine discipline, God changed Jacob's name to Israel, and he changed Jacob's character.

7. There are times when a person can't correct the results of wrong actions, even if he repents and

regrets his action. After Esau traded his birthright for a single meal, he was rejected when he wanted to inherit a blessing, though he sought the blessing with tears (Hb 12:17).

8. Decisions made by someone who values temporary pleasures more than eternal rewards often bring permanent damages. When Esau was hungry, he valued immediate gratification more than the future long-term benefits of being the firstborn. He lost both material and spiritual privileges that could have been his as the firstborn (25:29-34).

9. Children are usually predisposed to imitate their parent's mistakes. During a time of famine, Isaac lied, saying that his wife was his sister (26:7). Twice, his father Abraham had done the same thing (12:13; 20:2, 13). Isaac was predisposed to imitate his father's mistakes rather than trust the Lord for protection (26:2-3, 6-7).

10. When a married partner gives priority to a child rather than his spouse, communication problems are generated. Isaac loved Esau, while Rebekah loved Jacob. Rebekah learned about Isaac's plans to bless Esau by eavesdropping instead of being informed by her husband (27:5). She also helped her favorite son deceive his father (27:5-17).

11. The wife and mother who gives priority to her children instead of her husband will suffer solitude. When Rebekah deceived her husband in order to help Jacob, her husband Isaac was betrayed, she lost relationship with Esau, and she was left alone when Jacob fled from Esau (27:30 - 28:5).

12. It is not God's will for a person to do evil expecting it to bring about positive results. It was not God's will for Rebekah and Jacob to deceive Isaac and betray Esau in order to receive the paternal blessing, expecting that the results would be positive (27:1-35).

13. The person who cunningly takes advantage of others will have enemies. Twice Jacob took advantage of Esau: when he traded Esau stew for his birthright and when he deceived his father to receive Esau's blessing. After those events, Esau hated Jacob (27:36-41).

14. People don't deserve blessings and privileges that they receive from God. Jacob's heart was not directed toward God; however, God's heart was directed toward Jacob. Jacob the deceiver didn't deserve God's blessing that was first given to Abraham, then passed onto Isaac and then transmitted to him (28:1-4; 32:9-12).

15. God chooses whomever he desires to accomplish specific tasks. Just as Isaac was chosen instead of Ishmael, Jacob was chosen instead of Esau. Through Jacob and through his descendants all nations would be blessed. This is another promise related to a future Messiah (28:12-16).

16. God is omnipresent. He is at every place, even when people aren't aware of his presence. Jacob wasn't aware that God was present with him (28:17).

17. Sin finds the sinner. The deceiver will be deceived. The thief will be robbed. Just as Jacob took advantage of Esau (25:29-34; 27:17-29), Laban also took advantage of Jacob by giving him Leah as a wife instead of Rachel (29:21-27).

18. God uses his servant to be a blessing for others. Laban was blessed because of Jacob's being with him (30:27).

19. God's patience doesn't become exhausted because of his servant's flaws. God took many years with Jacob, disciplining him, driving him, and even using Jacob's mistakes and sins.

20. God's servant is protected by divine care and not by human cunningness. God protected Jacob from Laban's avenging him. It was not Jacob's cunningness, but God's care that saved his life (31:24, 29).

21. True prayer comes from a person who knows the greatness of God, his own weakness and misconduct, and that he is totally dependent upon God for the solution of his needs. In his prayer, Jacob (32:9-12) recognized divine initiative in manifesting grace to his father and to himself (32:9). He recognized his own failure and recognized God as the source of everything good and perfect (32:10). He recognized his need for God to protect him (32:11). He recognized that he could trust God to do what he had promised (32:12).

22. The person who is aware of both the extent of his needs and his own impotence is in a condition to experience the power of God. Jacob knew Esau was coming with four hundred men. Jacob was afraid of Esau's violent anger; Jacob was aware of his own impotence to do battle with Esau, and Jacob knew he needed protection. Only then did he voluntarily surrender to God with mind, body and spirit (32:22-29).

23. A person is transformed when he has an experience with God. Jacob's name was changed to Israel, and he was transformed into a different person (32:28). He stopped being the wheeler dealer who cunningly took advantage of others; he became a person dependant on divine guidance. He stopped being the cowardly frightened man; he became one who was able to face the future with confidence in the grace and power of God. He stopped being the man who took from his brother with his cunning ways; he

became one who sought peace with his brother by giving him presents (33:8-11).

24. One of the characteristics of an evil man is that he does not fulfill his commitments. Simeon and Levi betrayed the commitment they had made with Shechem. Their actions placed their entire family in danger of being eliminated and greatly upset Jacob (34:1-31). Paul states that one of the characteristics of wickedness is deceit (noncompliance of commitments) (Rm 1:31).

25. The youth from a Christian home who despises his spiritual inheritance and participates in the social life of those without God, will suffer. Worldliness not only impedes spiritual blessing, it carries real danger. Dinah was a descendant of Abraham, Isaac and Israel; through them she possessed a spiritual inheritance. But she went out to spend time with the women of the land and to participate in their social life (34:1). The women of the land were pagans who didn't know God. Participating in their social life, she placed herself in danger where it was easy for Shechem to abuse and rape her (34:1-2, 13, 27).

QUESTIONS

1. What kind of family did Isaac, Rebekah, and their twin boys have?
2. What are some of the ways that parents today contribute to problems in their own home?
3. How did Jacob obtain Esau's birthright?
4. How did Jacob obtain his father's blessing?
5. What happened to Jacob the night he was fleeing from Esau and he used a rock for a pillow?
6. How did Laban deceive Jacob on his wedding night?
7. How did Jacob obtain his four wives?
8. What was the source of disharmony in Jacob's family?
9. How did Jacob obtain the wealth of his father-in-law?
10. What kind of experience did Jacob have the night before his reunion with Esau?
11. Describe the reunion of Jacob and Esau.
12. What happened when Dinah went to visit some of the women of the land?
13. What can you learn from Jacob's life that is helpful to you?

Old Testament Bible Stories © Jackson Day

JOSEPH: VICTORY OVER DIFFERENT SITUATIONS
Genesis 37, 39-50

STRUCTURE

Context:
God promised Abraham to give his descendants the land of Canaan. He renewed his promise to Abraham's son Isaac. Isaac had twin sons, Esau and Jacob. Jacob deceived his father in order to obtain the blessing promised to his brother Esau. To escape Esau's vengeance, Jacob fled to Laban, his mother's brother. After spending 20 years with Laban, Jacob returned to Canaan with two wives, two concubines, eleven sons and one daughter. God changed Jacob's name to Israel and said that the land promised to Abraham and Isaac would be passed on to Jacob's descendants.

Key-person: Joseph

Key-location: Canaan and Egypt

Key-repetitions:
- Clothes (cloak, coat, clothes): Jacob made a coat for Joseph (37:3-4); Joseph's brothers stripped him of his coat (37:23); Reuben tore his clothes (37:29); the brothers dipped Joseph's coat in blood and took it back to their father (37:31-33); Potiphar's wife caught Joseph by his cloak, he left it with her and she used it to falsely accuse him (39:11-18); Joseph changed clothes before going to Pharaoh (41:14); Pharaoh dressed Joseph in robes of fine linen (41:42).
- Joseph in a position of authority: in his dreams (39:5-11); at Potiphar's home (39:1-6); in prison (39:20-23); as governor of Egypt (41:37-44); Joseph's brothers bowed down to him (42:6).
- Joseph defeated and then raised up: from slave to administrator (39:1-6); from prisoner to responsible for other prisoners (39:22-23); left prison to become governor (41:14-44).
- Dreams/visions: Joseph (37:5-11); chief cupbearer and chief baker (40:1-23); Pharaoh (41:1-7); Israel (46:1-4).
- Joseph suffering injustice: his father loved him more than his other sons (37:3-4); his brothers sold him into slavery (37:12-36); Potiphar's wife falsely accused him (39:11-19); Potiphar put him in prison (39:20-21); the cupbearer forgot Joseph (40:1-23; 41:9).

Key-attitudes:
- Jacob's preference for Joseph.
- Young Joseph's arrogance.
- The brothers' hatred for Joseph.
- Hope in the midst of despair is expressed each time Joseph was defeated and then recovered.
- Potiphar's wife's obsession to have sex with Joseph.
- Potiphar's anger when he heard his wife's accusations.
- Pharaoh was troubled by his dreams.
- Joseph's courage when he told Pharaoh that it is God who gives interpretations to dreams, and when he gave counsel to Pharaoh.
- The despair of Israel's family because of the famine.
- Joseph's cautiousness when he saw his brothers in Egypt.
- Israel's fear of losing another son.
- The brothers' fear when they realized who Joseph was.
- The desire of Jacob to be buried in Canaan.

Initial-problem:
When Joseph was 17 years old, he gave his father a bad report on his brothers (37:2).

Sequence of events:
Joseph and His Brothers
- Seventeen year old Joseph gave his father a bad report on his half-brothers (37:1-2).
- Jacob loved Joseph and made a coat for him. His brothers hated him (37:3-4).
- Joseph dreamed that his brothers bowed to him (37:5-11).
- Jacob sent Joseph to check on his brothers (37:12-17).
- Joseph's brothers plotted to kill him; then sold him to the Ishmaelites (37:18-29).
- The brothers dipped Joseph's coat in blood and took it to Jacob (37:30-35).

Joseph, Suffering in Egypt
- The Ishmaelites took Joseph to Egypt and sold him to Potiphar (37:36; 39:1).
- The Lord was with Joseph. Potiphar made Joseph his personal aid (39:2-6).
- Potiphar's wife invited Joseph to go to bed with her. He refused. She falsely accused him. Potiphar threw Joseph into prison (39:7-20).
- The Lord was with Joseph, and the prison warden put him in charge of the other prisoners (39:21-23).
- In prison, Joseph interpreted dreams for Pharaoh's chief cupbearer and his chief baker (40:1-23).

Joseph in a High Position in Egypt
- Pharaoh had one dream about cows that came out of the Nile and another about heads of grain (41:1-7).
- No one could interpret Pharaoh's dream. The chief cupbearer remembered Joseph (41:8-14).
- Pharaoh sent for Joseph. Joseph stated that it is God who gives interpretations. Pharaoh told Joseph his dreams. Joseph interpreted the dream: God was going to send seven years of abundance then seven

Old Testament Bible Stories © Jackson Day

years of famine. Joseph suggested that Pharaoh appoint someone to prepare for the famine (41:15-36).
- Pharaoh appointed Joseph to govern Egypt and gave him a wife (41:37-45).
- Joseph stockpiled food produced during the seven years of abundance (41:46-49).
- Joseph had two sons: Manasseh and Ephraim (41:50-52).
- The seven years of famine began. Joseph sold grain (41:53-57).
- In Canaan, Israel sent 10 of his sons to buy food in Egypt (42:1-5).
- In Egypt, Joseph's brothers didn't recognize him and bowed down to him. Joseph accused them of being spies. He kept Simeon in Egypt. He sent the others home with grain and silver in their sacks, and orders to return only if they brought their younger brother (42:6-28).
- The 10 brothers returned to Canaan and told their father everything. Israel said his younger son would not return with them (42:29-38).
- Israel wanted his sons to return to Egypt to buy food. The sons only returned when Israel agreed to send Benjamin (43:1-14).
- In Egypt, Joseph had his brothers eat with him (43:15-25).
- Joseph cried when he saw Benjamin. The brothers were seated in the order of their ages (43:26-34).
- Joseph had his cup put in Benjamin's sack, then sent his steward to search for it (44:1-15).
- Joseph said Benjamin would be his slave. Judah begged to take his place (44:16-34).
- Joseph lost control, cried, sent his attendants away and revealed himself to his brothers. He told them that God sent him ahead of them. He told them to get their father, their household, their flocks and return to Egypt (45:1-15).
- Pharaoh heard that Joseph's brothers had come (45:21-24).

Israel's Family in Egypt

- Israel at first was stunned, then wanted to go to Egypt and see Joseph (45:25-28).
- At Beersheba, God spoke to Israel (Jacob) in a vision (46:1-4).
- Seventy of Israel's descendants ended up in Egypt (46:5-29).
- Joseph went to his father and told him to settle in Goshen (46:30-34).
- Joseph presented five of his brothers to Pharaoh (47:1-6).
- Joseph brought his father to Pharaoh. Joseph settled his family in the district of Rameses and provided them with food (47:7-12).
- Joseph collected all the money in Egypt and in Canaan in payment for grain. Then he sold food in exchange for livestock. Then he sold food in exchange for land (47:13-22).
- Joseph provided the people with seed and established a land law: a fifth of the produce belongs to Pharaoh (47:23-26).
- Israel lived 17 years in Egypt. Israel requested for Joseph not to burry him in Egypt (47:27-31).
- Joseph took his two sons Manasseh and Ephraim to Israel. Israel blessed them, placing his right hand on the younger son's head (48:8-22).
- Israel pronounced blessing and prophecies for each son and their descendants. He gave instructions to be buried with his ancestors, then he died (49:1-33).
- Israel was embalmed and his body returned to Canaan for burial (50:1-14).
- After the funeral, Joseph's brothers requested he forgive them. Joseph replied: "Am I in the place of God? You intended evil for me, but God intended good for me and to accomplish what is now being done, the saving of many lives" (50:15-21).
- Joseph requested that his bones be carried to Canaan when the Israelites returned there. He was 110 when he died (50:22-26).

Final-situation: Joseph, his brothers, and their families continued living in Egypt after Israel's death. Before dying, Joseph requested that his brothers carry his bones with them when they return to the land promised to Abraham.

BIBLE STORY

Joseph and His Brothers

Jacob lived in the land of Canaan where his father had lived. His son Joseph was seventeen when he tended flocks with his half-brothers, the sons of his father's wives Bilhah and Zilpah. Joseph reported to his father the bad things they were doing (37:1-2).

Joseph was born when his father Israel was old. Israel loved Joseph more than any of his other sons. He made a brightly-colored long-sleeved coat for Joseph. His brothers noticed their father's partiality; they hated Joseph and could not speak a kind word to him (37:3-4).

Joseph had a dream. He told it to his brothers, and they hated him even more. He announced: "Listen to this dream I had. We were binding sheaves of grain out in the field. Suddenly my sheaf rose and stood up; your sheaves gathered around mine and bowed down to it."

His brothers asked him: "Do you think you will rule over us? Will you actually boss us?" They hated him more because of his cocky attitude when he talked about his dream.

Joseph told his brothers about another dream: "I had another dream. I saw the sun, moon and eleven stars bow down to me!"

His father rebuked him: "What is this dream you had? Will your mother, your brothers and I actually bow down to you?" His brothers were jealous of him, but his father brooded over the matter (37:5-11).

Joseph's brothers went away from home to

pasture their father's flocks. A few days later, Israel told Joseph: "Go and see how your brothers and the flocks are doing, and bring word back to me" (37:12-17).

Joseph tracked his brothers down. When they saw him in the distance, they plotted to kill him. They said to each other: "Here comes that dreamer! Let's kill him and throw his body into a well and say that a wild animal killed him. We'll see what comes of his dreams."

Reuben intervened to rescue Joseph. He said: "Let's not kill him. Shed no blood. Throw him alive into this well, but don't hurt him."

When Joseph reached his brothers, they stripped him of his fancy coat and threw him into a dry well.

Then they sat down to eat. Looking up, they saw a caravan of Ishmaelites. Judah said: "Brothers, what will we gain if we kill our brother and conceal the evidence. Let's sell him to the Ishmaelites; after all, he is our brother, our own flesh and blood."

The other brothers agreed. They pulled Joseph up out of the well and sold him for twenty pieces of silver to the Ishmaelites, who took him to Egypt (37:18:29).

Reuben was not with his brothers when the traders came by. When Reuben returned to the well and saw that Joseph was not there, he ripped his clothes in despair. He went back to his brothers and said: "The boy isn't there! What am I going to do?"

They took Joseph's coat, slaughtered a goat and dipped the coat in the blood. They took the fancy coat back to their father and said: "We found this. Examine it, do you think this is your son's coat?"

Israel recognized it and said: "It is my son's coat! A wild animal has torn Joseph to pieces." Israel refused to be comforted and said: "In mourning I will go down to the grave" (37:30-35).

Joseph, Suffering in Egypt

Meanwhile, the Ishmaelites took Joseph to Egypt and sold him to Potiphar, one of Pharaoh's officials. He was captain of the palace guard (37:36; 39:1).

The Lord was with Joseph, and things went well with him. Potiphar saw that the Lord was with Joseph and that the Lord gave him success in everything he did. Potiphar made Joseph his personal servant. He entrusted everything he owned to Joseph's care. The Lord blessed the home of the Egyptian because of Joseph. With Joseph in charge, Potiphar did not concern himself with anything except to decide which food he wanted to eat (39:2-6).

Joseph was well-built and handsome. Potiphar's wife became infatuated with Joseph and said: "Come to bed with me!"

Joseph refused and replied: "Look, my master has put me in charge of everything he owns. He does not concern himself with anything in the house. The only thing he hasn't turned over to me is you; you are his wife! How then could I do such a wicked thing and sin against God?" The woman pestered Joseph every day, but he refused to go to bed with her or even to spend time with her.

One day when Joseph went into the house to do his work, none of the household servants were inside. His master's wife grabbed him by his coat saying: "Come to bed with me!" But Joseph left his coat in her hand and ran out of the house. She realized that he left his coat and ran outside, so she screamed for her house servants and crying hysterically told them: "This Hebrew came to insult us! He tried to rape me, but I screamed. My scream scared him and he ran away, but he left his coat beside me."

She kept his coat until her husband came home. Then she told him her story: "That Hebrew slave you bought us tried to use me as his plaything. But as soon as I screamed for help, he fled, leaving his coat."

Potiphar was furious; he took Joseph and threw him into the prison where the king's prisoners were confined (39:7-20).

The Lord was with Joseph in prison. He caused the prison warden to like him. The warden put Joseph in charge of all the prisoners and let him manage the whole prison operation. The Lord was with Joseph and gave him success in everything he did (39:21-23).

Some time later, Pharaoh was angry with his chief cupbearer and his chief baker, and put them in the same prison where Joseph was confined. The captain of the guard assigned them to Joseph. After they had been in custody for some time, both the cupbearer and the baker had a dream the same night, and each dream had its own meaning.

Joseph came to them the next morning, noticed that they were dejected and asked them: "Why are you sad today?"

They answered: "We both had dreams, but no one can interpret them."

Joseph replied: "Interpreting dreams is God's business. Tell me your dreams."

The chief cupbearer told Joseph his dream: "In my dream I saw a vine with three branches in front of me. It budded, it blossomed, and its clusters ripened into grapes. I was holding Pharaoh's cup, so I took the grapes, squeezed them into Pharaoh's cup and gave it to him."

Joseph said: "This is what the dream means: the three branches are three days. Within three days Pharaoh will restore you to your position, and you will give Pharaoh his cup, just as you did before. When you are free, remember me. Tell Pharaoh about me and get me out of this prison! I was kidnaped from the land of the Hebrews; I have done nothing to deserve being put in prison."

The chief baker saw that Joseph had given a favorable interpretation, and he spoke up: "I also had a dream: There were three bread baskets on my head. In the top basket were all kinds of baked goods for Pharaoh, but the birds were eating them out of the basket on my head."

Joseph replied: "This is what it means: the three baskets are three days. Within three days Pharaoh will cut off your head and hang you on a tree and the birds will pick your bones clean."

The third day was Pharaoh's birthday, and he threw a feast for all his officials. He had the chief cupbearer and the chief baker brought to the party. He restored the chief cupbearer to his position, so that he once again put the cup into Pharaoh's hand, but he hanged the chief baker. Everything happened just as Joseph had said it would.

The chief cupbearer forgot about Joseph (40:1-23).

Joseph in a High Position in Egypt

Two years later, Pharaoh had a dream: He was standing by the Nile River and seven cows, sleek and fat, came out of the river and grazed on the marsh grass. After them, seven other cows, all skin and bones, came up out of the Nile. The skinny cows ate up the seven sleek, fat cows. Then Pharaoh woke up.

He fell asleep again and had a second dream: Seven heads of grain, healthy and good, grew on one stalk. After them, seven other heads of grain sprouted: thin and burned by the hot east wind. The thin heads of grain swallowed up the seven healthy, full heads. Pharaoh woke up and realized it was all a dream (41:1-7).

The next morning, Pharaoh told the magicians and wise men of Egypt his dreams, but no one could interpret them.

Then the chief cupbearer spoke up: "Today I remember my sins. Pharaoh was once angry with his servants, and he imprisoned me and the chief baker. Each of us had a dream the same night. Now a young Hebrew was there with us. We told him our dreams, and he interpreted them for us. And things turned out exactly as he interpreted them to us" (41:8-14).

Pharaoh at once sent for Joseph. Joseph shaved, cut his hair, changed his clothes, and went to Pharaoh.

Pharaoh told Joseph: "I dreamed a dream, and no one can interpret it. But I have heard that when you hear a dream, you can interpret it."

Joseph replied: "Not I, but God will give Pharaoh the interpretation of his dreams."

Pharaoh told his dream: "I was standing on the bank of the Nile, when seven cows, fat and sleek came out of the river and grazed on the marsh grass. After them, seven other cows, all skin and bones, came up. I had never seen such ugly cows in all of Egypt. The skinny, ugly cows ate up the fat cows. But after they had done so; they looked just as skinny and ugly as before. In another dream: I also saw seven heads of grain, full and good, growing on one stalk. After them, seven other heads sprouted; withered, thin and burned by the hot east wind. The thin heads of grain swallowed up the seven good heads. I told this to the magicians, but none could interpret it for me."

Joseph told Pharaoh: "The two dreams of Pharaoh are one and the same. God has revealed to Pharaoh what he is about to do. The seven good cows are seven years, and the seven good heads of grain are seven years. The seven sick, ugly cows that came up afterward are seven years, and so are the seven worthless heads of grain burned by the east wind: They are seven years of famine. God has shown Pharaoh what he is about to do. Seven years of great abundance are coming throughout the land of Egypt, but seven years of famine will follow them. Pharaoh needs to look for a wise man and put him in charge of Egypt. Then Pharaoh needs to appoint managers to take a fifth of the harvest during the seven good years. This food should be held in reserve, to be used during the seven years of famine. That way, Egypt will not be ruined by the famine" (41:15-36).

The plan seemed good to Pharaoh and to all his officials. Pharaoh asked them: "Can we find a better man than Joseph? God's spirit is truly in him!"

Pharaoh said to Joseph: "You are the man! God revealed all this to you; therefore, I put you in charge of my palace, and all my people will submit to your orders. Only as king will I be greater than you." Then Pharaoh took his signet ring from his finger and put it on Joseph's finger. He outfitted him with coats of fine linen and put a gold chain around his neck. He had him ride in a chariot as his second-in-command. Pharaoh gave Joseph an Egyptian name, Zaphenath-Paneah, and gave him Asenath, a priest's daughter, to be his wife (41:37-45).

Joseph was thirty years old when he went to work for Pharaoh. As soon as Joseph left Pharaoh's presence, he traveled throughout Egypt. He stockpiled food in the cities that was produced in the seven years of bumper crops. Joseph stockpiled huge quantities of grain, as much as the sand of the sea (41:46-49).

Before the years of famine came, two sons were born to Joseph. The firstborn he named Manasseh and said: "God made me forget all my trouble and all my father's family." The second son he named Ephraim and said: "God made me prosper in the land of my suffering" (41:50-52).

Egypt's seven years of bumper crops came to an end; seven years of famine began. The famine was severe everywhere. Egypt was the only country with food. Joseph opened the storehouses and sold grain to the Egyptians. All the people in that part of the world came to Egypt to buy grain from Joseph (41:53-57).

Canaan also experienced famine. Israel told his sons: "Grain can be found in Egypt. Go down there and buy some for us, so that we may live and not die."

Joseph's ten half-brothers went down to Egypt to buy grain. Israel was afraid that harm might come to Benjamin, Joseph's brother, so he did not send him (42:1-5).

Joseph was the one who sold grain to all the people. Joseph's brothers arrived and they bowed face-down to him. Joseph recognized them immediately, but treated them as strangers and spoke roughly to them. He asked: "Where do you come from?"

They replied: "From Canaan, to buy food."

Joseph's brothers did not recognize him. Joseph remembered his dreams and said to them: "You are spies! You have come to look for our weak spots."

They answered: "No, my lord, we come as your servants just to buy food. We are all sons of one man. We are honest men, not spies."

Joseph said: "No! You have come to see where our land is unprotected."

They replied: "There were twelve of us brothers, sons of the same father in the land of Canaan. The youngest is with our father, and one is no more."

Joseph said to them: "You are spies! And this is how you will be tested: You will not leave this place unless your youngest brother comes here. Send one of your number to get your brother; the rest of you will be kept in prison." And he put them all in custody for three days.

On the third day, Joseph said to them: "One of your brothers will stay here in prison. The rest of you will take grain back for your starving households. But you must bring your youngest brother to me."

They said to one another: "Now, we are being punished for what we did to our brother. We saw how terrified he was when he begged for his life. We would not listen; now we're the ones in trouble."

Reuben broke in: "I told you not to hurt the boy. But you wouldn't listen! Now we must pay for his murder."

Joseph had used an interpreter so they did not realize that he understood them. He left them and cried. When he was able to speak again, he took Simeon and had him tied up while they watched. Joseph gave orders: "Fill their bags with grain, put each man's money back in his sack, and give them provisions for their journey." After this was done for them, they loaded their grain on their donkeys and left (42:6-26).

They stopped for the night and one of the brothers opened his sack to get feed for his donkey. He saw his silver in the mouth of his sack and exclaimed: "My silver has been returned; it is in my sack!" They trembled and said: "What has God done to us?" (42:27-28).

They returned to Canaan and told their father everything that had happened. They said: "The man who rules the land spoke harshly to us and accused us of spying on the land. He told us: `This is how I will know whether you are honest men: Leave one of your brothers with me. Take food for your starving families and go. But bring your youngest brother to me. Then I will know that you are not spies but honest men. Then I will give your brother back to you.'"

As they were emptying their sacks, in each man's sack was his purse of silver! They were frightened. Israel (Jacob) said to them: "You are robbing me of my children. Joseph is gone, Simeon is gone, and now you want to take Benjamin!"

Reuben replied: "You may put both of my sons to death if I do not bring Benjamin back to you. Trust me, I will bring him back."

Israel said: "Benjamin will not go with you; his brother is dead and he is all I have left. If harm comes to him on the journey, you will bring my gray head down to the grave in sorrow" (42:29-38).

When they had eaten all the food they had brought from Egypt, Jacob said: "Go back and buy us more food."

Judah replied: "The man warned us: `You will not see my face again unless your brother is with you.' If you will not send him, we will not go down."

Israel (Jacob) asked: "Why did you bring this trouble on me by telling the man you had another brother?"

They replied: "The man questioned us, asking pointed questions about our family. We only answered his questions. How did we know he would say: `Bring your brother here'?"

Judah pushed his father: "Send the boy along with me and we will go at once, otherwise we will all die of starvation. I myself will guarantee his safety. If I do not bring him back to you, I'll take all the blame. If we had not delayed, we could have gone and returned twice."

Then Israel gave in: "If it must be, do this: Put some of the best products from the land in your bags and take them to the man as a gift. Take double the amount of silver with you; you must return the money that was put back into your sacks. Take your brother and go back to the man at once. And may God Almighty grant you mercy so the man will let your other brother and Benjamin come back with you. As for me, if I lose everything, I lose everything" (43:1-14).

The brothers hurried to Egypt and presented themselves to Joseph. Joseph told his steward: "Take these men to my house and prepare dinner; they are to eat with me at noon."

The brothers were frightened when they were taken to Joseph's house. They thought: "We were brought here because he thinks we ran off with the money on our first trip. He is going to turn us into slaves."

They spoke to Joseph's steward: "Please, we came down here the first time to buy food. But when we stopped for the night, we opened our sacks and each of us found his silver. We don't know who put our silver in our sacks."

The steward answered: "It's all right. Your God must have put it there. Then he brought Simeon out to them. The steward took the men into Joseph's house, gave them water to wash their feet and provided fodder for their donkeys. They prepared their gifts for Joseph's arrival at noon (43:15-25).

When Joseph came home, they presented to him

their gifts and bowed down before him. He asked them: "How is your aged father you told me about? Is he still living?"

They replied: "Our father is still alive and well." They again bowed before him.

Joseph recognized his brother Benjamin, his own mother's son. Deeply moved, he went into his bedroom and cried. After he washed his face, he came out and, controlling himself, said: "Serve the food." Joseph was served at his private table, the brothers by themselves, and the Egyptians who ate with him by themselves. Egyptians would not eat with Hebrews. The men were seated in the order of their ages, from the oldest to the youngest; and they looked at each other in amazement. The brothers feasted with Joseph (43:26-34).

Joseph ordered his house steward: "Fill the men's sacks with all the food they can carry, and put each man's silver in the mouth of his sack. Then put my silver cup in the youngest one's sack."

At dawn the men were sent on their way with their donkeys. They were barely out of the city when Joseph said to his steward: "Run after those men at once, and when you catch them, say: `Why have you repaid good with evil? This is the cup my master drinks from and uses for explaining dreams. You did a wicked thing!"

The steward caught up with them, and repeated Joseph's words. But they replied: "What are you talking about? We would never do anything like that! Why would we steal silver or gold from your master? If that cup is found on any of us, he'll die, and the rest of us will become your slaves."

The steward replied: "Only the one who stole the cup will become my slave; the rest of you will go free."

Each of them quickly lowered his sack to the ground and opened it. The steward searched their sacks. The cup was found in Benjamin's sack. At this, they ripped their clothes in despair, loaded their donkeys again and returned to the city (44:1-15).

Joseph was still in the house when his brothers came in. They threw themselves face-down on the ground before him. Joseph said to them: "What is this you have done? Don't you know that a man like me would discover this?"

Judah replied: "What can we say to my master? How can we prove our innocence? God is punishing us for our sin. We stand ready to be your slaves; both we and he in whose sack the cup was found."

But Joseph said: "Only the man who stole the cup will become my slave. The rest of you, go back to your father in peace."

Judah said: "Please, sir, let your servant speak. Don't think I'm presumptuous; you're the same as Pharaoh as far as I'm concerned. My lord asked us: `Do you have a father or a brother?' And we answered, `We have an aged father, with a young son born to him in his old age. His brother is dead, and he is the only one left alive from that mother. His father loves him.' If the boy is not with us when I go back, my father will die of sorrow. I guaranteed the boy's safety to my father. I told him: `If I do not bring him back to you, you can blame me all my life!' Please sir, let me remain here as your slave in place of the boy. Let the boy return with his brothers. Don't let me go back to watch my father die in misery!" (44:16-34).

Joseph could not control himself any longer. He cried out to his attendants: "Leave! Everyone leave my presence!" His sobbing was so violent that the Egyptians heard him. Joseph said to his brothers: "I am Joseph! Is my father still living?" His brothers couldn't say a word; they were terrified! Then Joseph said to his brothers: "I am your brother Joseph, the one you sold as a slave to go to Egypt! God sent me ahead of you to preserve your lives. For two years there has been famine in the land. For five more years there will be no plowing and no harvest. God sent me ahead to save your lives. God made me a counselor to Pharaoh and ruler of all Egypt. Hurry back to my father. Tell him: `Your son Joseph says: God made me ruler of all Egypt. Come to me; don't delay. You shall live in the region of Goshen and be near me; you, your children and grandchildren, your flocks and herds, and all you have. I will provide for you, because there will still be five more years of famine. Bring my father down here quickly.'"

Then Joseph hugged his brother Benjamin and wept, and Benjamin embraced him, weeping. Then Joseph kissed all his brothers and cried as he hugged them. Only then were his brothers able to talk to him (45:1-15).

The story reached Pharaoh's palace that Joseph's brothers had come. Pharaoh and his officials were pleased. Joseph gave his brothers carts and provisions for their journey. He sent his brothers away, and told them: "Don't quarrel on the way!" (45:21-24).

Israel's Family in Egypt

They arrived in Canaan and told their father: "Joseph is still alive! He is ruler of all Egypt!" Israel was stunned. They told him everything Joseph said. After seeing the carts Joseph had sent to carry him back, Israel said: "I'm convinced! My son Joseph is still alive. I will go and see him before I die" (45:25-28).

Israel set out with everything he owned. When he reached Beersheba, he offered sacrifices to the God of his father Isaac.

And God spoke to Israel in a vision that night: "Jacob! Jacob!"

Jacob replied: "Here I am."

The Lord replied: "I am God, the God of your father. Don't be afraid to go down to Egypt. I will make your descendants a great nation there. I will go down to Egypt with you, and I will also bring you back again. And Joseph's own hand will close your eyes" (46:1-4).

Israel's sons took with them all their livestock and all their possessions. The members of Jacob's family, who ended up in Egypt, numbered seventy (46:5-29).

Joseph went to Goshen to meet his father Israel. As soon as Joseph saw him, he threw his arms around his father and wept for a long time.

Israel said to Joseph: "Now I am ready to die; I have seen for myself that you are alive."

Joseph said to his father's family: "I will go and speak to Pharaoh. You will be allowed to settle in the region of Goshen. Egyptians look down on anyone who is a shepherd" (46:30-34).

Joseph took five of his brothers and presented them before Pharaoh.

Pharaoh asked the brothers: "What is your occupation?"

They replied: "Your servants are shepherds. "We have come to live here awhile, because the famine is severe in Canaan, and your servants' flocks have no pasture."

Pharaoh told Joseph: "Settle your father and your brothers in the best part of the land. Let them live in Goshen. And if you know of any among them with special ability, put them in charge of my own livestock" (47:1-6).

Next, Joseph brought his father Jacob in and presented him to Pharaoh. Jacob blessed Pharaoh. Pharaoh asked Jacob: "How old are you?"

Jacob replied: "My life has been a journey wandering from place to place. I have lived only a hundred and thirty years. My years have been few and difficult. My ancestors lived much longer than I." Then Jacob blessed Pharaoh and left.

Joseph settled his family in the best part of Egypt and provided them with food (47:7-12).

The famine was severe, and Joseph collected all the money that was in Egypt and in Canaan in exchange for grain. When the money was gone, Joseph sold them food in exchange for their livestock. Then all the Egyptians sold their land in exchange for food (47:13-22).

Joseph told the people: "I bought you and your land for Pharaoh. I will give you seed so you can plant the ground. At harvest time, you must give a fifth of it to Pharaoh. The other four-fifths you may keep as seed for the fields and as food."

So Joseph established a land law in Egypt: a fifth of the produce belongs to Pharaoh. Only the priests were able to keep their land (47:23-26).

The Israelites settled in Egypt in the region of Goshen and they acquired property. They had many children and increased in number. Jacob lived in Egypt seventeen years. He lived to be a hundred and forty-seven years old. When the time came for Israel to die, he called for his son Joseph and requested: "Do not bury me in Egypt, but when I rest with my fathers, carry me out of Egypt and bury me where they are buried."

Joseph replied: "I will do what you ask" (47:27-31).

Some time later Joseph learned that his father was very sick. So he took his two sons Manasseh and Ephraim along with him to see his father.

Israel said to Joseph: "God Almighty appeared to me at Luz in the land of Canaan, and there he blessed me and told me, 'I will give you many children. I will make you a community of peoples, and I will give this land as an everlasting inheritance to your descendants.' Your two sons born to you in Egypt before I came to you here will be counted as mine; Ephraim and Manasseh will be mine, just as Reuben and Simeon are mine" (48:1-7).

Israel noticed Joseph's sons and said: "Bring them to me so I may bless them."

Because of old age, Israel could hardly see. Israel kissed and embraced Joseph's sons.

Then Joseph removed them from Israel's knees and bowed down with his face to the ground. Joseph took both of them to Israel, Ephraim facing Israel's left hand and Manasseh facing Israel's right hand. But Israel reached out his right hand and put it on Ephraim's head, though he was the younger, and crossing his arms, he put his left hand on Manasseh's head, even though Manasseh was the firstborn.

Then he blessed Joseph and said: "My ancestors Abraham and Isaac walked with God. He has been my shepherd all my life to this day. He was the Angel who delivered me from all harm. I pray that he will bless these boys. May they be called by my name and the names of my fathers Abraham and Isaac, and may their children increase in number on the earth."

When Joseph saw his father placing his right hand on Ephraim's head, he was displeased; so he took hold of his father's hand to move it from Ephraim's head to Manasseh's head. Joseph said to him: "No, my father, this one is the firstborn; put your right hand on his head."

But his father refused and said: "I know, my son, I know what I'm doing. He too will become great. Nevertheless, his younger brother will be greater than he, and his descendants will become a group of nations." He put Ephraim ahead of Manasseh (48:8-20).

Then Israel said to Joseph: "I am about to die, but God will be with you and take you back to the land of your fathers" (48:21-22).

Then Jacob called for his sons and said: "Gather around so I can tell you what will happen to you in days to come. Then he pronounced blessing and prophecies for each son and their descendants. The descendants of each son became a tribe of Israel. There are twelve tribes of Israel (49:1-28).

Then he gave them these instructions: "Bury me with my fathers in the cave which Abraham bought as a burial place. There Abraham and his wife Sarah were buried, there Isaac and his wife Rebekah were buried, and there I buried Leah."

When Jacob finished instructing his sons, he drew his feet up into the bed, breathed his last breath and died (49:29-33).

Joseph threw himself upon his father, wept over him and kissed him. Joseph directed the physicians to embalm his father. The physicians took forty days to embalmed him, and the Egyptians mourned for him seventy days.

Joseph went to Canaan to bury his father. Pharaoh's high-ranking officers joined Joseph's family for the trip. Only the children were left in Goshen. It was a huge funeral procession. Jacob's sons carried him to the land of Canaan and buried him in the cave Abraham had bought as a burial place. After burying his father, Joseph returned to Egypt, together with his brothers and all the others who had gone with him (50:1-14).

After the funeral, Joseph's brothers talked among themselves: "What if Joseph pays us back for what we did to him?" They sent word to Joseph, saying: "Your father left this command before he died: 'Tell Joseph to forgive his brothers the great evil they did to him.' Joseph, we beg you to forgive our wrong. We are servants of your father's God." When their message arrived, Joseph wept.

His brothers came to him in person, threw themselves down before him and said: "We are your slaves."

Joseph replied: "Don't be afraid of me. Am I God? You intended evil for me, but God intended good for me and to accomplish what is now being done, the saving of many lives. Don't be afraid. I will provide for you and your children" (50:15-21).

Joseph stayed in Egypt, along with all his father's family. Before his death, Joseph said to his brothers: "I am about to die. God will certainly come to your aid and take you out of this land and back to the land he promised Abraham, Isaac and Jacob. Make sure you carry my bones when you leave this place."

Joseph died when he was a hundred and ten years old. Doctors embalmed him and placed his body in a coffin in Egypt (50:22-26).

LIFE-LESSONS DISCOVERED IN THE STORY

1. An individual can bring problems upon himself by provoking others. Joseph provoked his brothers when he reported his brothers' wrongdoing (37:2) and by the way he described his dreams (37:5-11).

2. God is omniscient and knows our future. He knew what would happen to Joseph and to Israel's family. Joseph didn't know how his dreams would be accomplished; however, God made it clear that he would be the leader of his family.

3. God enables his servants to have victory over the circumstances of life. God doesn't allow his servants to face situations without giving them conditions to face them. Joseph's life illustrates this truth.

4. A person who is despised and rejected by his own family can be a servant of God. Joseph was despised by his brothers (37:2-11).

5. God can even transform evil intentions of one's own family members and use them for good. God used the evil intentions of Joseph's brothers for good (50:20).

6. One who faithfully serves God may experience difficulties; however, God is in control. Joseph faced many difficulties: he was despised in his own home (37:1-11); sold as a slave (37:12-28); tempted (39:6-13); falsely accused (39:14-19); and imprisoned because of false accusations (39:19-20).

7. God can use people's evil intentions for the good of his servant and his kingdom. God used the evil intentions of Joseph's brothers to take him to Egypt where he would be responsible for saving many lives (50:20). (See Rm 8:28.)

8. Life is full of injustices. Joseph suffered many injustices. Jesus promised: "In the world you will have trouble" (Jn 16:33).

9. God's faithful servant will suffer temptations. Joseph suffered strong sexual temptations (39:6-12).

10. Victory is gained by God's servant who is tempted to sin, yet resists. Joseph was victorious because he ran from the woman who tempted him (39:12).

11. The person who tempts others to do wrong often resents those who resist temptation and may seek revenge. Potiphar's wife sought revenge when Joseph resisted her seduction (39:14-19).

12. The person who chooses to do the right thing and speaks the truth may suffer retaliation from the wicked. Joseph was hated by his brothers when he reported their evil action (37:2-4); and when he fled from sexual temptation, he was falsely accused (39:6-20).

13. God is present with his servants when they suffer injustice because of their righteousness. God was with Joseph when his brothers sold him into slavery (39:2) and when he was imprisoned (39:23). God is an ever-present help in trouble (Ps 46:1).

14. The youth who resists strong temptations increases his potential to serve God as an adult. Joseph resisted immorality (39: 8-12) and God made him governor of Egypt (41:37-40). Daniel resolved not to defile himself (Dan 1:8) and became a man in a high position (Dan 2:48).

15. It is important to consider one's relationship with God as a positive reason for resisting temptation instead of only considering an action as prohibited. Joseph's motivation for resisting temptation was: "How could I do such a wicked thing and sin against God?" (39:9).

16. It is better to suffer because of making the right choice than to deserve punishment for one's sins. Joseph suffered because he resisted the woman's immoral advances (39:13-20). (See 1 Pt 3:14-17.) Joseph's brothers knew they deserved to be punished (Gn 42:21-22).

17. One should walk with God in both the mountains and the valleys of his life. God was with Joseph in slavery (39:2) and in prison (39:23). Joseph recognized God's action in his life when he rose to power (41:16, 52; 45:4-5; 50:20). (See Ph 4:12.)

18. The one who remains faithful to God during the crisis experiences of life, will experience victory. Joseph had been hated by his brothers and falsely accused by Potiphar's wife; however, God was with Joseph and brought good from the evil intentions of others (39:2, 23; 40:8; 41:16; 45:7-8; 50:19-20).

19. Forgiveness should be given to the person who admits his wrongdoing. Joseph's brothers were aware of their evil actions toward him (42:21; 50:17). Joseph forgave his brothers (50:20-21).

20. An evil person may change his character and actions. However, one who has suffered injustice at the hands of an evil person needs to see proof that the offender has changed before trusting him. Joseph revealed himself to his brothers only after carefully testing them to see if their character had changed (42:1 - 44:34).

21. The person who forgives those who mistreated him demonstrates the way God graciously forgives undeserving sinful people. Joseph forgave his brothers for selling him into slavery, and he offered to care for them and their families (50:15-21).

22. God can bring good out of bad situations. God brought good from the evil actions of Joseph's brothers (50:20). God brought good from the bad situations in Joseph's life: Joseph was raised in a dysfunctional family; his brothers sold him into slavery; Potiphar's wife falsely accused him; he was imprisoned under false accusations; the cupbearer neglected to remember him; and he went through seven years of famine.

QUESTIONS

1. How did Jacob's (Israel's) actions contribute to conflict among his children?
2. What did Joseph do to provoke his brothers?
3. Why did Joseph's brothers sell him into slavery?
4. How did Joseph resist sexual temptation?
5. What injustices did Joseph experience?
6. Where was God when Joseph suffered one injustice after another: when he was sold into slavery, falsely accused and imprisoned?
7. How did Joseph become governor in Egypt?
8. How was God able to do whatever he desired in Egypt, a nation that did not know him nor worship him?
9. How did Joseph reveal himself to his brothers?
10. How did Joseph testify about God after he became governor of Egypt?
11. How was God able to transform the evil intentions of Joseph's brothers into good?
12. Which of Joseph's problems have you experienced (family problems; injustice; temptation; false accusations, etc.)?
13. When you suffered difficult situations,
   ■What helped you obtain victory?
   ■What hindered you and contributed to your defeat?

EXODUS									
1	5	12	15	19	25	32	35	40
Israel in Egypt		Journey to Sinai		Israel at Sinai				
Oppression in Egypt		Redeemed from Egypt		Consecrated at Sinai Instructed at Sinai				Worship in the Tabernacle
▪Oppression of Israel ▪Moses in Egypt and in Midian	Pharaoh and the plagues of Egypt	▪Leaving Egypt ▪Redeemed by the blood of the lamb and by God's power over the sea ▪Led by a pillar of cloud and a pillar of fire	Provisions in the desert: ▪ Water ▪ Food ▪ Protection from enemies	The Law		The Tabernacle		
Conflict with the oppressor		Redemption	Trained and tested in the desert	Accepting the Law		Disobedience and condemnation	▪Tabernacle ▪Priest ▪Sacrifices	
1	5	12	15	19	25	32	35	40

MOSES		
Prince of Egypt Ex 2:1-15	**Shepherd of sheep** Ex 2:16 - 4:31	**Shepherd of Israel** Ex 5 - Deut 34
In Egypt	In the wilderness of Midian	Wandering in the wilderness
40 years of luxury	40 years of humility	40 years of service
Self-confidence	Insecurity	Confidence in God

MOSES: CHOSEN, PROTECTED AND SENT
Exodus 1 - 4

STRUCTURE

Context:
God promised to give Abraham's descendants the land of Canaan. He renewed his promise to Abraham's son Isaac and to his grandson Jacob. God changed Jacob's named to Israel and said that the land promised to Abraham and Isaac would be passed on to Jacob's descendants. Jacob (Israel) had 12 sons. His favorite son, Joseph, was sold into slavery by his brothers. God enabled Joseph to become governor of Egypt. During a time of drought, Joseph's brothers went to Egypt seeking food. Joseph revealed himself to his brothers, invited them to move to Egypt and provided for their needs.

The drought ended. However, Joseph, his brothers, and their families continued living in Egypt. Before dying, Joseph requested that his brothers carry his bones with them when they returned to the land promised to Abraham.

Key-person: Moses

Key-location: Egypt, Midian, and Mount Horeb

Key-repetitions:
▪The Israelites kept on reproducing and constantly grew in number (1:7, 9, 10, 12, 20).
▪The Israelites suffered in Egypt (1:7, 11-12, 13-14, 15-18, 22; 2:11, 23-24; 3:7-9).
▪The Lord was aware of the Israelites' suffering (2:22; 3:7-9, 16-17).
▪The Lord is the God of Abraham, Isaac and Jacob (3:6, 15, 16; 4:5).
▪Moses objected to returning to Egypt and God answered his objections (3:11-12, 13-18, 4:1-9, 10-12, 13-17).

Key-attitudes:
▪Pharaoh's fear of the Israelites.
▪Agony and suffering of the Israelites.
▪Self-confidence felt by Prince Moses.
▪The Israelites' rejection of Prince Moses when he attempted to help them.
▪Moses' insecurity when the Lord commanded he return to Egypt.

- God's anger at Moses when he kept refusing to return to Egypt.

Initial-problem:
A king came to power in Egypt who did not know about Joseph; he feared the Israelites and elaborated plans to destroy them.

Sequence of events:
Oppressions in Egypt
- The descendants of Israel became numerous (1:1-7).
- A king who did not know about Joseph came to power in Egypt (1:8).
- The king was afraid of the Israelites and made plans to destroy them (Ex 1:6-10):
  - 1st Through slavery (1:11-14).
  - 2nd By ordering the Hebrew midwives to kill each Hebrew baby boy (1:15-21).
  - 3rd By ordering that each Hebrew baby boy be thrown into the Nile (1:22).

Moses in Egypt
- A Levite woman hid her baby son for three months. She then placed him in a basket and set it afloat along the banks of the Nile. The baby's sister remained nearby (2:1-4).
- Pharaoh's daughter found the basket and paid the baby's mother to nurse him. After the child was weaned, Pharaoh's daughter adopted him and named him Moses (2:1-10).
- When Moses was 40 years old, he visited the Israelites (Hb 11:23) and killed an Egyptian. The next day he tried to separate two fighting Hebrews. One asked if he was also going to kill him (Ex 2:11-14).

Moses Flees to Midian
- Pharaoh tried to kill Moses, but Moses fled to Midian. There he defended the daughters of Jethro. Moses went to live with Jethro and married his daughter, Zipporah. They had a son (2:16-22).
- Egypt's king died. God saw what was going on with the Israelites (2:23-25).

God Speaks to Moses from a Burning Bush
- Moses was shepherding the flock at Mt. Horeb. An angel appeared to him from within a burning bush that did not burn up. Moses went to see the strange sight (3:1-3).
- The Lord called to Moses from within the bush and told him: to remove his sandals; that he was the God of Abraham, of Isaac and of Jacob; that he had come to rescue the Israelites from the Egyptians and would bring them into a good land; that he was sending Moses to bring the Israelites out of Egypt (3:1-10).
- Moses brought up objections as to why he could not bring the Israelites out of Egypt, and God answered his every objection (3:13 - 4:31).
  - 1st Moses objected: "Who am I, that I should go? God answered: "I will be with you' (3:11-12).
  - 2nd Moses objected: "Suppose they ask me: `What is his name?" God answered: "I AM WHO I AM" (3:12-22).
  - 3rd Moses objected: "What if they don't believe me or listen to me?" The Lord gave Moses three miraculous signs.
    - *1st Sign*: A staff changed to a snake and then back into a staff (4:1-5).
    - *2nd Sign*: A hand turned into leprous and then was healed (4:6-7).
    - *3rd Sign*: Water turned into blood (4:8-8).
  - 4th Moses objected that he had difficulty speaking. The Lord answered: "Who gave man his mouth?" (4:10-12).
  - 5th Moses asked God to send someone else. The Lord became angry with Moses and told him his brother Aaron would speak for him (4:13-17).

Moses Starts Back to Egypt
- Moses obtained permission from Jethro to return to Egypt (4:18).
- Moses with his wife and sons started back to Egypt. God told Moses that Pharaoh would refuse to allow Israel to go; therefore, God would kill Pharaoh's firstborn (4:19-23).
- The Lord told Aaron to meet Moses in the desert. Moses told Aaron everything the Lord had sent him to speak and to do (4:24-28).

Final-situation:
The Lord commanded Moses to return to Egypt. Moses with his wife and sons started back to Egypt (4:19-23). The Lord also sent Aaron to meet Moses (4:24-28).

BIBLE STORY

Oppressions in Egypt
Jacob with seventy of his descendants went to Egypt. Joseph was already in Egypt (1:1-5).

The generation that included Joseph and his brothers all died. But the descendants of Israel kept on reproducing and became exceedingly numerous. The land was filled with them. A king who did not know about Joseph came to power. He told his people: "The Israelites have become too numerous for us. We must deal shrewdly with them or they will become even more numerous. If war breaks out, they will join our enemies, fight against us and leave the country." He elaborated plans to destroy the Israelites (Ex 1:6-10):

1st <u>The king planned to destroy the Israelites through slavery</u>.
The Egyptians put slave masters over the Israelites to oppress them with forced labor. They built cities for Pharaoh. The harder the Egyptians worked the Israelites, the more children they had.

The Egyptians feared the Israelites and made their lives miserable with hard labor; making brick and mortar and with work in the fields (1:11-14).

2nd <u>The king planned for the Hebrew midwives to kill Hebrew baby boys</u>.

Pharaoh spoke to the two Hebrew midwives, whose names were Shiphrah and Puah: "When you help the Hebrew women in childbirth, observe the sex of the baby. If it is a boy, kill him; but if it is a girl, let her live." The midwives feared God and refused to obey the king's orders. They let the boys live. Pharaoh called the midwives and asked them: "Why didn't you obey my orders? Why have you let the boys live?"

The midwives answered: "Hebrew women are not like Egyptian women; they are vigorous and give birth before the midwives arrive." God was pleased with the midwives. The Israelites continued to increase in number. And because the midwives feared God, he gave them families of their own (1:15-21).

3rd <u>The king planned for all baby Hebrew boys to be thrown into the Nile River</u>.

Then Pharaoh issued an order to all his people: "Every Hebrew boy that is born, you must throw into the Nile, but let every girl live" (1:22).

Moses in Egypt

A man and a woman from the tribe of Levi married. She gave birth to a son. She saw that he was a fine child and hid him for three months. When she could no longer hide him, she took a basket made of papyrus, waterproofed it with tar and pitch, and placed the baby in it. She set it afloat in the reeds along the bank of the Nile where there was less danger of crocodiles and where the current would not take it away. Miriam, the baby's sister, stood at a distance to see what would happen.

Pharaoh's daughter went down to the Nile to bathe. Her her attendants strolled along the river bank. She saw the basket among the reeds and sent her slave girl to get it. She opened it, saw the crying baby and felt sorry for him. She said: "This is one of the Hebrew babies."

Miriam, the baby's sister, asked Pharaoh's daughter: "Do you want me to get a nursing Hebrew mother to nurse the baby for you?"

Pharaoh's daughter answered: "Yes, go."

The girl fetched the baby's mother. Pharaoh's daughter told her: "Take this baby and nurse him for me. I will pay you." The woman took the baby and nursed him. After the child was weaned, the mother took him to Pharaoh's daughter who adopted him as her son. She named him Moses (Pulled-Out), saying: "I pulled him out of the water" (2:1-10).

Time passed. Moses became a man. When Moses was forty years old, he visited his fellow Israelites (Hb 11:23).

Moses went to where his own people were and watched them at their hard labor. He saw an Egyptian beating a Hebrew, one of his relatives. Glancing this way and that and seeing no one, he killed the Egyptian and buried him in the sand.

The next day he went out again and saw two Hebrew men fighting. He asked the one who started it: "Why are you hitting your fellow Hebrew?"

The man answered: "Who made you ruler and judge over us? Are you going to kill me the way you killed the Egyptian?" Moses panicked and thought: "People know about what I did" (Ex 2:11-14).

Moses Flees to Midian

Pharaoh heard about it and tried to kill Moses, but Moses fled to the land of Midian. He sat down by a well.

Jethro, a priest of Midian, had seven daughters. They came to the well to water their father's sheep. Some shepherds drove the girls away, but Moses came to their rescue and watered their sheep.

When the girls returned to their father, Jethro, who was also called Reuel, said: "That didn't take long. Why have you returned so early today?"

They answered: "An Egyptian rescued us from the shepherds. He even drew water for us and watered the sheep."

Jethro asked: "And where is he? Why did you leave him behind? Invite him to have something to eat with us."

Moses agreed to stay with Jethro. Jethro gave his daughter Zipporah to Moses in marriage. Zipporah gave birth to a son, and Moses named him Gershom, saying: "I have become an alien in a foreign country" (2:16-22).

Many years after Moses went to Midian, the king of Egypt died. The Israelites groaned under their slavery and cried out. Their cries were heard by God. He remembered his covenant with Abraham, with Isaac and with Jacob. God saw what was happening and was concerned about the Israelites (2:23-25).

God Speaks to Moses from a Burning Bush

Moses shepherded his father-in-law's flock for forty years. On one occasion, he led the flock to the far side of the desert to Horeb, the Mountain of God. The angel of the Lord appeared to him in flames of fire blazing from within a bush. Moses saw that the bush was blazing away, but it did not burn up. Moses thought: "Wow! What a strange sight; I'll go see why this bush doesn't burn up."

The Lord saw him stop to look and called out from within the bush: "Moses! Moses!"

Moses answered: "Yes? I'm here."

God replied: "Do not come any closer. Remove your sandals. You are standing on holy ground!" *(In Egypt, slaves went barefoot.)* The Lord continued: "I am the God of your father, the God of Abraham, the God of Isaac and the God of Jacob."

Moses hid his face, afraid to look at God.

The Lord said: "I have seen the misery of my people in Egypt. I have heard them crying out for deliverance from their slave masters. I know about their suffering. Now I have come down to rescue them from the grip of the Egyptians and to bring them up out of that land into a good and spacious land, a land flowing with milk and honey. The Israelites' cry for help has reached me. I've seen the way the Egyptians are oppressing them. It's time for you to go back. I am sending you to Pharaoh to bring my people, the Israelites, out of Egypt" (3:1-10).

Moses raised objections as to why he couldn't bring the Israelites out of Egypt, and God answers his every objection (3:13 - 4:31).

1st Objection and God's answer:
Moses objected: "Why me? Who am I, that I should go to Pharaoh and lead the Israelites out of Egypt?"

God answered: "I will be with you. This will be proof that it is I who have sent you: When you have brought the people out of Egypt, you will worship God on this mountain" (3:11-12).

2nd Objection and God's answer:
Moses objected: "Suppose I go to the Israelites and say to them, 'The God of your fathers has sent me to you,' and they ask me: 'What is his name?' What shall I tell them?"

God answered: "I AM WHO I AM. Tell the Israelites: 'I AM sent me to you.'"

God continued speaking: "Go, assemble the leaders of Israel and tell them: 'The Lord, the God of your fathers; the God of Abraham, Isaac and Jacob, appeared to me and said: I have seen what has been done to you in Egypt. I have determined to bring you up out of your misery in Egypt into the land of the Canaanites; a land flowing with milk and honey.' Israel's leaders will listen to you. Then you and the leaders will go to the king of Egypt and say to him: 'The Lord, the God of the Hebrews, has met with us. Let us take a three-day journey into the desert to offer sacrifices to the Lord our God.' The king of Egypt will not let you go unless forced to. So I will intervene and hit Egypt where it hurts with all the wonders that I will perform among them. After that, he will let you go. And I will make the Egyptians favorably disposed toward this people. When you leave you will not leave empty-handed. Every woman is to ask her neighbor for articles of silver and gold, for jewelry and clothing, which you will put on your sons and daughters. And so you will clean the Egyptians out" (3:12-22).

3rd Objection and God's answer
Moses objected: "What if they don't believe me or listen to me and say: 'The Lord did not appear to you'?"

The Lord answered by giving Moses three miraculous signs that would help the Israelites believe him.

1st Miraculous sign
The Lord said: "What is that in your hand?"
Moses replied: "A staff."
The Lord commanded: "Throw it on the ground."
Moses threw it on the ground. It became a snake. Moses jumped back, and fast! Then the Lord said to him: "Reach out and grab it by the tail." So Moses reached out and grabbed the snake and it turned back into a staff.

The Lord said: "This is so that they may believe that the Lord, the God of their fathers; the God of Abraham, the God of Isaac and the God of Jacob, has appeared to you."

2nd Miraculous sign
Then the Lord commanded: "Put your hand inside your shirt. So Moses put his hand into his shirt, and when he took it out, it had turned leprous, like snow.

God said: "Now put it back into your shirt." Moses put his hand back into his shirt, and when he took it out, it was healthy like the rest of his flesh.

3rd Miraculous sign
Then the Lord said: "If the first miraculous sign doesn't convince them, the second one should. If they don't believe you after those two signs, take some water from the Nile and pour it on dry ground. The water will become blood when it hits the ground" (4:1-9).

4th Objection and God's answer
Moses objected: "O Lord, I have never been an eloquent speaker, neither in the past nor since you have spoken to me. I stutter and stammer."

The Lord answered: "Who gave man his mouth? Who makes some deaf or mute? Who gives some sight or makes some blind? Is it not I, the Lord? Now go; I will help you speak and will teach you what to say" (4:10-12).

5th Objection and God's answer
Moses objected: "O Lord, please send someone else to do it."

The Lord became angry with Moses and said: "What about your brother, Aaron the Levite? He is good with words. He is already on his way to meet you. You shall speak to him and tell him what to say. I will help both of you speak and will teach you step by step. He will speak to the people for you, and it will be as if he were your mouth, and you will decide what comes out of it. Now take this staff in your hand so you can perform miraculous signs with it!" (4:13-17).

Moses Starts Back to Egypt
Moses returned to Jethro his father-in-law and said: "Let me go back to my own people in Egypt to see if they are still alive."

Jethro said: "Go, and peace be with you" (4:18).

The Lord had told Moses in Midian: "Go. Return to Egypt. The men who wanted to kill you are dead." So Moses took his wife and sons, put them on a donkey and started back to Egypt. And he took the staff of God in his hand.

The Lord said to Moses: "When you return to Egypt, see that you perform before Pharaoh all the wonders I have given you the power to do. But I will harden his heart so that he will refuse to let the people go. Then tell Pharaoh: 'This is what the Lord says: Israel is my firstborn son. I told you: Free my firstborn son so he may worship me. But you refused to let him go; so I will kill your firstborn son'" (4:19-23).

The Lord said to Aaron: "Go into the desert to meet Moses." So he met Moses at the Mountain of God and kissed him. Then Moses told Aaron everything the Lord had sent him to speak, and also about all the miraculous signs he had commanded him to do (4:24-28).

LIFE-LESSONS DISCOVERED IN THE STORY

1. A political leader's perverse plans cannot prevent God from accomplishing his divine plans. Pharaoh could not destroy the Israelites, the people of God (Ex 1:8-22).

2. The value God gives to human life should lead Christians to take a stand against abortion. The midwives feared God and refused to kill the Hebrew baby boys (Ex 1:15-17).

3. When facing a conflict between God's orders and civil authority, one should obey God rather than a person. God doesn't expect a Christian to obey a civil authority who demands that citizens disobey God. The midwives disobeyed the king's orders and refused to kill the Israelite baby boys (Ex 1:17-21). (See Ac 5:29.)

4. God is active, even when people see no visible evidence of his activity. The Israelites, suffering under Egyptian slave masters, felt abandoned by God and were unaware that he was preparing Moses to free them.

5. God coordinates events in order to protect and to guide his servants. Divine providence was evident when God coordinated circumstances to protect Moses' life and place him in the king's palace. There he received an education that prepared him to be a leader who could lead the Israelites to the promised land (Ex 2:1-10).

6. Sin finds the sinner. A person cannot hide his sins. Moses thought no one saw him kill and bury the Egyptian. But others knew of his actions (Ex 2:11-20).

7. A person, depending upon his own abilities and using human methods, cannot do God's work. Moses tried to help God free the Hebrews from slavery by killing the Egyptians one by one. He was depending upon his force and skills (Ex 2:11-20). (See Zechariah 4:6.)

8. There are crisis situations when God's presence and intervention is the only thing that prevents his people from being totally destroyed. The Israelites were similar to the burning bush that was in danger of being totally destroyed. Just as the presence of God within the burning bush prevented its being consumed, his presence with Israel prevented Pharaoh from destroying them (Ex 3:1-3).

9. Any place where a person is aware that God is present and communicating becomes: "Holy Ground." Horeb, also called Sinai, was the place where God revealed himself to Moses (3:2) and where, later on, he gave the Law to his people (3:12; chapters 19-20). The things God said and did on the mountain were what made it "Holy Ground."

10. A person who knows that God is speaking should become a voluntary slave ready to obey God's orders. When Moses stood before the burning bush, God ordered: "Remove your sandals. You are standing on Holy Ground!" In Egypt, slaves went barefoot. God wanted Moses to become his slave (3:5).

11. People understand who God is by both his salvation actions and his spoken revelation. God would reveal himself to Israel by his acts of redeeming them from slavery. He also revealed himself by his spoken word to Moses and to others through Bible history. For the rest of Bible history, God is known as the one who brought Israel out of Egypt, out of the land of slavery (Ex 20:2).

12. God is eternal. He has always existed, and he will always exist. God told Moses to inform the Israelites that "I Am" had given him orders. That means that he never had a beginning, will never have an ending and he is independent of all people and of all things (Ex 3:14).

13. The course of SALVATION HISTORY may be summarized in terms of: God promises, God acts. Throughout SALVATION HISTORY: God promises; he remembers his promise; he chooses somebody to be the liberator; and God acts in a saving way, using the liberator. Moses was the liberator that saved Israel from slavery in Egypt. The New Testament reveals that Jesus is the Liberator who frees the sinner from slavery to sin.

14. God knows each person by name and he communicates with people as individuals. He called Moses by name and declared himself to be the God of Abraham, of Isaac, and of Jacob (3:4-6).

15. The Lord desires to be the God of each individual person. The God who revealed himself to people in the past is revealing himself to individuals in the present. The Lord declared that he was the God of those who lived before Moses; of

Old Testament Bible Stories © Jackson Day

Abraham, of Isaac, and of Jacob (3:4-6). At the time, God was speaking to Moses because he desired to be the God of Moses. The New Testament reveals that belief in Jesus is the only way a person can know the Lord God as his personal God.

16. The Lord God has the right to choose anyone he desires to do whatever task he chooses for them to do. Moses didn't want to be chosen by God; however, God was entitled to choose him (3:10-4:16).

17. When God chooses a person for a task, his presence enables the chosen one to do the job. God told Moses he was sending him to Pharaoh to bring the Israelites out of Egypt. Moses objected: "Why me? Who am I, that I should go...?" God answered that he would be with Moses (Ex 3:10-12).

18. Low self-esteem is a virtue when it leads a person to trust in God. However, if low self-esteem results in a person's believing that God could not use him, then it is a sin that results in spiritual-paralysis. Moses had such a low self-esteem that his mind was closed to doing God's will (Ex 3:11 - 4:17).

19. God is angry at the person who refuses to obey clearly-understood divine orders. The Lord became angry when Moses kept rejecting the divine invitation to return to Egypt (4:14).

20. The one who put limitations on his serving God may suffer the results of those limitations. Moses objected that because he stuttered, he could not relay God's Words to the people (Ex 4:10-12). God determined that Aaron would be Moses' spokesman (Ex 4:14-16). Later on, that arrangement complicated Moses's life when Aaron made a golden calf for the Israelites to worship (Ex 32:1-6, 22-25) and when he rebelled against Moses (Nu 12:1-16).

21. When a person has experiences with God, he should become a witness, telling others about God's Words and actions. The Lord ordered Moses to inform the leaders of Israel about God's Words (Ex 3:16-17).

QUESTIONS

1. Why did Pharaoh become afraid of the Israelites?
2. How did Pharaoh try to destroy the Israelites?
3. When Pharaoh was making plans to destroy the Israelites, where was God and what was he doing?
4. How did God coordinate events that both protected baby Moses and prepared him to become a leader?
5. How has God coordinated events in your life, to either protect or prepare you?
6. What happened when Moses was full of self-confidence and tried to free the Israelites with his own strength?
7. Where did Moses go when he fled Egypt?
8. How did God reveal himself from within the burning bush?
9. Why was the ground around the burning bush "Holy Ground"?
10. What is the meaning of the name God gave himself: "I AM"?
11. Why was Moses so insecure that he rejected God's invitation to return to Egypt and liberate the Israelite slaves?
12. What were some of the excuses Moses gave for refusing God's invitation, and how did God answer those excuses?
13. What are some of the excuses you use for refusing to obey God?
14. What were some of the miraculous signs that God gave Moses to convince the Israelites that God was sending him?
15. Moses showed self-confidence when he killed the Egyptian. Forty years later he showed low self-esteem when God instructed him to return to Egypt.
    ■Do you have a greater problem with self-confidence or low self-esteem?
    ■Which is more damaging to God's work: self-confidence or low self-esteem?

LIBERATING THE ISRAELITES FROM SLAVERY
Exodus 4:27-12:50

STRUCTURE

Context:
God promised to give Abraham's descendants the land of Canaan. Joseph, a descendant of Abraham, became governor of Egypt and saved the country during a prolonged drought. During the drought, Joseph invited his family to move to Egypt. Joseph, his brothers and their families continued living in Egypt after the drought ended, and they had everything they needed. Years later, Egypt had a king who knew nothing about Joseph, was afraid of the Israelites, and made plans to do away with them.

About 350 years went by with the Israelites in Egypt before Moses was born. Moses lived as a prince in the king's palace for forty years. He tried to help the Israelites by killing an Egyptian. Then he had to flee to the desert, where he became a shepherd for forty years. When God instructed Moses to return to Egypt to liberate the Israelites from slavery, Moses objected. After God answered his objections, Moses returned to Egypt.

Key-person: Moses

Key-location: Egypt

Key-repetitions:
- Moses used the excuse that he stuttered (4:10; 6:13, 30).
- Moses prayed; God responded (5:22-6:1; 8:12-13, 29-34; 9:33; 10:18-19).
- Plagues (10 in number).
- Beginning with the second plague, after every plague: Pharaoh sent for Moses and Aaron; asked for the Lord to free Egypt from the plague; promised to let the Israelites go; Moses prayed; God removed the plague; Pharaoh saw relief from the plague; his heart hardened and he wouldn't let the Israelites leave.
- Competition between Moses and the Egyptian magicians (7:9-12, 20-22; 8:5-7, 16-19; 9:11).
- The Lord told Pharaoh to let the Israelites go (5:17:16; 8:1; 9:1, 13; 10:3).
- The Lord spoke to Moses (6:1, 10, 13; 7:1, 9, 14; 8:1, 16, 20; 9:8; 10:1, 12, 21).
- God made a distinction between Israel and Egypt. The Israelites did not suffer the plagues that punished Egypt (8:22; 9:4-7, 25-26; 10:22-23; 11:6-7; 12:12-13).
- The Israelites asked their neighbors for clothes and jewels (3:22; 11:2-3; 12:35-36).

Key-attitudes:
- Israel's leaders were grateful when Moses first told them God was concerned about them.
- Pharaoh felt rage when his absolute authority as king was challenged.
- The Israelites were angry at Moses when Pharaoh increased their work load.
- Moses felt disillusioned when Pharaoh increased the Israelites' suffering.
- Pharaoh stubbornly persisted in struggling against God.
- There was conflict between Moses, Pharaoh and the magicians.
- God manifested a determination to free his people.
- The Egyptians were afflicted after the death of their firstborn.
- After the tenth plague, the Egyptians were anxious for the Israelites to leave.

Initial-problem:
Moses and Aaron gathered Israel's leaders and told them everything the Lord had told Moses. The Israelites were thankful the Lord had heard their cries. Then, Moses and Aaron went to Pharaoh and told him that the Lord said: "Let my people go."

Sequence of events:

Moses and Aaron with the Israelite Leaders
- When Moses and Aaron met with Israel's leaders, they believed that the Lord had seen their misery. They worshiped him (4:29-31).
- Moses and Aaron told Pharaoh to let God's people go. Pharaoh answered that he did not know the Lord and would not let Israel go! He accused Moses of stopping the people from working (5:1-5).
- Pharaoh ordered the slave-masters not to supply the Israelites with straw, but to maintain the daily quota. The Israelite foremen appealed to Pharaoh for relief (5:5-18).
- The Israelites blamed Moses and Aaron for their suffering. Moses prayed (5:19-22).
- The Lord answered Moses, but the Israelites would not listen to him (6:1-9).

Moses and Aaron with Pharaoh
- The Lord commanded Moses and Aaron to tell Pharaoh everything God told them. Moses objected that he stuttered (6:10-30).
- The Lord stated that Pharaoh wouldn't listen to Moses, but he would bring the Israelites out of Egypt. Moses and Aaron did just as the Lord commanded them (7:1-7).
- Aaron threw his staff in front of Pharaoh and it turned into a snake. The Egyptian magicians did the same thing but Aaron's staff swallowed their staffs (7:8-13).

Plagues One Through Nine
- **1st Plague: Water to Blood.** Aaron struck the Nile River with his staff, and all the water was changed into blood. Egyptian magicians did the same thing (7:14-24).
- **2nd Plague: Frogs.** Frogs covered the land. The magicians also produced frogs. Pharaoh requested

Moses to pray for the Lord to rid them of the frogs. Moses told Pharaoh to set the time for him to pray. Pharaoh replied: Tomorrow. The Lord did what Moses asked, but Pharaoh hardened his heart, just as the Lord had said (7:25-8:15).

- **3rd Plague: Gnats**. Aaron struck the ground with his staff and dust throughout Egypt became gnats. The magicians could not produce gnats. Pharaoh's heart was hardened (8:16-19).
- **4th Plague: Flies**. Flies infested Egypt, but not where the Israelites lived. Pharaoh told Moses they could sacrifice in Egypt. Moses replied they must journey into the desert, because their sacrifices would offend the Egyptians. Pharaoh agreed, Moses prayed, the flies left, but Pharaoh hardened his heart (8:20-32).
- **5th Plague: Death of the Egyptians' Livestock**. The Egyptian's livestock died; the Israelites' animals lived. Pharaoh wouldn't let the people go (9:1-7).
- **6th Plague: Boils**. Moses tossed soot into the air and it caused boils on men and animals. The magicians were covered with the boils. The Lord hardened Pharaoh's heart (9:5-12).
- **7th Plague: Hail**. The Lord sent hail that smashed everything growing and stripped every tree. Goshen was free from the hailstorm. Pharaoh summoned Moses, asked him to pray and said the Israelites could go. Moses prayed, the hail storm stopped and Pharaoh hardened his heart (9:13-35).
- **8th Plague: Locust**. The Lord sent locust that ate everything left after the hail. Pharaoh summoned Moses. Moses prayed; the locust left. The Lord hardened Pharaoh's heart (10:1-20).
- **9th Plague: Total Darkness**. Total darkness covered Egypt for three days. Pharaoh summoned Moses and said the Israelites could go, but without their livestock. Moses replied that they used their livestock in worshiping. The Lord hardened Pharaoh's heart. Pharaoh said that Moses would die if he saw him again. Moses replied that Pharaoh wouldn't see him again (10:20-29).
- Moses told Pharaoh that about midnight every firstborn son in Egypt would die. There would be wailing throughout Egypt but silence among the Israelites. Moses, hot with anger, left Pharaoh (11:1-9).

Tenth Plague: Israelites' First Passover; Death for the Egyptians

- The Lord told Moses that on the tenth of the month, each family was to choose a healthy one year old male animal and keep it penned until the fourteenth. Then they would slaughter it, put some blood on their doorframes and roast the animal. On that night the Lord would strike down every firstborn in Egypt, but he would pass over the houses with blood (12:1-13).
- God instructed that the generations to come would honor that day as a celebration to the Lord (12:14-21).
- **10th Plague: Death of Firstborn**. Moses instructed Israel's leaders to select and slaughter the Passover lamb and to put blood on the doorframe. The Israelites obeyed. At midnight the Lord struck down every firstborn in Egypt (12:17-30).

Exodus from Egypt

- Pharaoh summoned Moses and Aaron and ordered the Israelites to leave. The Egyptians urged the people to leave. The Israelites asked the Egyptians for articles of silver and gold, and for clothing. The Egyptians gave the Israelites what they asked for (12:30-36).
- The Israelites started their journey. They had lived in Egypt for 430 years (12:31-42).
- The Lord gave Moses and Aaron rules for the Passover, for on that very day the Lord brought the Israelites out of Egypt (12:43-50).

Final-situation:

After 430 years in Egypt, the Israelites left, on their way to Canaan.

BIBLE STORY

Moses and Aaron with the Israelite Leaders

Moses and Aaron brought together the leaders of Israel. Aaron told them everything the Lord had told Moses. Moses demonstrated the three miraculous signs:

1st A staff changed to a snake and then back into a staff (4:1-5);
2nd A hand turned leprous and then healed (4:6-7);
3rd Water turned into blood (4:8-8). The leaders believed that the Lord was concerned about them and had seen their misery. They bowed down and worshiped (4:29-31).

After that, Moses and Aaron went to Pharaoh and told him: "The Lord, the God of Israel, says: `Let my people go, so that they may hold a festival to me in the desert.' "

Pharaoh said: "Who is the Lord, that I should obey him and let Israel go? I do not know this Lord and I will not let Israel go!"

Moses and Aaron said: "The God of the Hebrews has met with us. Let us take a three-day journey into the desert to offer sacrifices to the Lord our God lest he strike us with either plagues or with the sword."

Pharaoh replied: "Moses and Aaron, why are you taking the people away from their work? You are stopping this multitude of people from working" (5:1-5).

Pharaoh took immediate action. He ordered the slave masters: "Don't supply the Israelites with straw for making bricks; make them gather their own. But don't reduce the daily quota. They are lazy; that is why they are crying out: `Let us go and sacrifice to our God.' If they work harder, they will stop listening to lies."

The Israelites scattered all over Egypt to gather stubble to use for straw. The slave masters kept demanding: "Complete the work required for each day." The slave masters beat the Israelite foremen and asked them: "Why didn't you meet your quota of bricks yesterday and now again today?"

The Israelite foremen appealed to Pharaoh for relief: "Why have you treated your servants this way? Nobody gives us any straw, yet they tell us: `Make bricks!' Your servants are being beaten, but the fault is with your own people."

Pharaoh said: "You are lazy! That's why you whine wanting to sacrifice to your Lord. Get to work. You will not be given any straw, yet you must produce your daily quota of bricks" (5:5-18).

The Israelite foremen left Pharaoh, found Moses and Aaron and told them: "May the Lord punish you for what you've done! You've made us stink to Pharaoh and his officials! You've put a sword in their hand to kill us."

Moses prayed: "O Lord, why are you treating this people so badly? Is this why you sent me? Since I spoke to Pharaoh in your name, things got worse for this people!" (5:19-22).

The Lord answered Moses: "Now you will see what I will do to Pharaoh: Because of my strong hand he will drive them out of his country. Therefore, say to the Israelites: `I am the Lord, and I will bring you out from under the yoke of the Egyptians. I will free you from slavery. I will redeem you with mighty acts of judgment. I will take you as my own people, and I will be your God. Then you will know that I am the Lord your God, who brought you out from under the yoke of the Egyptians. And I will bring you to the land that I promised to give Abraham, Isaac and Jacob. I will give it to you as your own country. I am the Lord.'"

Moses told this to the Israelites, but they didn't listen to him; they were beaten down in spirit by harsh slave conditions (6:1-9).

Moses and Aaron with Pharaoh

The Lord told Moses: "Tell Pharaoh king of Egypt, to let the Israelites go from his country."

But Moses answered: "If the Israelites won't even listen to me, why would Pharaoh listen? Besides, I stutter!" (6:10-13).

The Lord commanded Moses and Aaron to bring the Israelites out of Egypt clan by clan and to tell Pharaoh everything God told them.

But Moses objected: "Since I stutter, why would Pharaoh listen to me?" (6:26-30).

The Lord told Moses: "I have made you as a god to Pharaoh; your brother Aaron will be your prophet. You are to speak everything I command you, and your brother Aaron will tell it to Pharaoh. Then he will let the Israelites go from his country. But I will harden Pharaoh's heart. Though I multiply miraculous signs and wonders, Pharaoh will not listen to you. With mighty acts of judgment I will bring out my people the Israelites. Then the Egyptians will know that I am the Lord."

Moses and Aaron did just as the Lord commanded them. Moses was eighty and Aaron eighty-three when they spoke to Pharaoh (7:1-7).

The Lord said to Moses and Aaron: "When Pharaoh says to you, `Perform a miracle,' say to Aaron: `Take your staff and throw it down in front of Pharaoh.' Your staff will turn into a snake."

Moses and Aaron went to Pharaoh. Aaron threw his staff down in front of Pharaoh and it became a snake. The Egyptian magicians did the same thing. Each one threw down his staff, and they all turned into snakes. But Aaron's staff swallowed their staffs. Yet Pharaoh's heart became hard and he would not listen to them, just as the Lord had said (7:8-13).

Plagues One Through Nine
■ **1st Plague: Water to Blood**

The Lord told Moses: "Pharaoh's heart is stubborn. In the morning, go to Pharaoh when he goes to the Nile River. Say to him: `The Lord, the God of the Hebrews, has sent me with this message: Let my people go, so that they may worship me in the desert. But you have not listened. This is how you will know that I am the Lord: With the staff that is in my hand I will strike the Nile River, and it will be changed into blood. The fish in the Nile will die, and the river will stink; the Egyptians won't be able to drink its water.'"

Aaron raised his staff and struck the Nile River. All the water was changed into blood. The fish in the Nile died, and the river smelled so bad that the Egyptians could not drink its water. Blood was everywhere in Egypt.

The Egyptian magicians did the same things using their magical skills. Pharaoh's heart became hard. All the Egyptians dug along the Nile to get drinking water, because they could not drink the Nile water (7:14-24).

■ **2nd Plague: Frogs**

Seven days passed after the Lord struck the Nile. The Lord told Moses to tell Pharaoh: "Let my people go, so that they may worship me. If you refuse, I will plague your whole country with frogs. They'll come into your palace, into your bedroom, onto your bed, into your officials' houses, among your people, into your ovens and into your pots and pans."

Aaron stretched out his hand over the waters of Egypt, and the frogs came up and covered the land. The magicians did the same things by their secret arts; they also produced frogs.

Pharaoh summoned Moses and Aaron and requested: "Pray to the Lord to rid us of these frogs and I will let your people go to offer sacrifices to the Lord."

Moses answered: "Certainly. Set the time for me to pray. Then you'll be rid of the frogs, except for those in the Nile."

Pharaoh replied: "Tomorrow."

Moses replied: "Tomorrow it is. Then you will know there is no one like the Lord our God. The frogs will leave you. The only frogs left will be those in the Nile."

Moses and Aaron left Pharaoh. Moses cried out

to the Lord. The Lord did what Moses asked. The frogs died in the houses, in the courtyards and in the fields. They were piled into heaps, and the land reeked of them. When Pharaoh saw the relief from the frogs, he hardened his heart and would not listen, just as the Lord had said (7:25-8:15).

■3rd Plague: Gnats

The Lord told Moses to instruct Aaron to strike dust on the ground with his staff. Aaron obeyed, stretched out the staff and struck dust on the ground. Then all the dust throughout Egypt became gnats. The magicians tried to produce gnats by their secret arts, but could not.

The magicians told Pharaoh: "This is the finger of God." But Pharaoh's heart was hardened, and he would not listen, just as the Lord had said (8:16-19).

■4th Plague: Flies

The Lord told Moses: "Get up early in the morning and confront Pharaoh as he goes to the water. Tell him: 'The Lord says: Let my people go, so they may worship me. If you do not let them go, I will send swarms of flies on you, your officials, your people. But I will deal differently with the land of Goshen, where my people live; no swarms of flies will be there. That will show you that I am the Lord in this land. I will make a distinction between my people and your people. This miraculous sign will occur tomorrow.'"

The next day dense swarms of flies poured into Pharaoh's palace. The land of Egypt was ruined by flies.

Pharaoh summoned Moses and Aaron and said: "Go, sacrifice to your God, but do it here in this country."

Moses answered: "The sacrifices we offer the Lord our God would offend the Egyptians and they would stone us. We must take a three-day journey into the desert to offer sacrifices to the Lord our God, as he commands us."

Pharaoh said: "I will let you go to offer sacrifices to the Lord your God in the desert, but you must not go very far. Now pray for me."

Moses answered: "I will pray to the Lord, and tomorrow the flies will leave. Only be sure that Pharaoh does not deceive us again by not letting the people go to offer sacrifices to the Lord."

Moses left Pharaoh. He prayed, and the Lord did what Moses asked: The flies left Pharaoh, his officials and his people; not a fly remained. But Pharaoh hardened his heart and would not let the people go (8:20-32).

■5th Plague: Death of the Egyptians' Livestock

The Lord told Moses to go tell Pharaoh: "The Lord, the God of the Hebrews, says: Let my people go, so they may worship me. If you refuse, the Lord will bring a terrible plague on your livestock in the field: horses, donkeys, camels, cattle, sheep and goats; striking them with a severe plague. The Lord will make a distinction between the livestock of Israel and that of Egypt, so that no animal belonging to the Israelites will die." The next day all the Egyptians' livestock died, but not one animal belonging to the Israelites died. Pharaoh sent men to investigate and found that not even one of the Israelites' animals had died. Yet his heart was unyielding and he would not let the people go (9:1-7).

■6th Plague: Boils

The Lord told Moses and Aaron: "Take fistfuls of soot from a furnace and have Moses toss it into the air in the presence of Pharaoh. It will become fine dust all over Egypt, and festering boils will erupt on men and animals throughout the land."

They took soot from a furnace, stood before Pharaoh and Moses tossed it into the air. It caused festering boils on men and animals. The magicians could not even stand before Moses because they were covered with the boils. The Lord hardened Pharaoh's heart, and he would not listen to Moses and Aaron, just as the Lord had said to Moses (9:5-12).

■7th Plague: Hail

The Lord told Moses to confront Pharaoh early in the morning and tell him: "The Lord, the Hebrews' God, says: Let my people go, so they can worship me, or I will send the full force of my plagues against you and your people, so you may know that there is no one like me in all the earth. I have raised you up for this very purpose, that I might show you my power and that my name might be proclaimed in all the earth. At this time tomorrow I will send the worst hailstorm ever experienced by Egypt. Give an order now to bring your livestock and everything you have in the field to a place of shelter. The hail will fall on every man and animal that is still in the open field, and they will die."

Pharaoh's officials who feared the Word of the Lord quickly brought their slaves and livestock inside. But those who didn't take the Lord's word seriously left their slaves and livestock outside.

The Lord said to Moses: "Stretch your hand toward the sky. Signal the hail to fall all over Egypt." Moses stretched out his staff. The Lord sent lightning, thunder, and hail. It was the worst storm in Egypt's history. The hail struck everything in the fields, both men and animals; it smashed everything growing in the fields and stripped every tree. The flax and barley were destroyed, since the barley had headed and the flax was in bloom. The wheat was not destroyed, because it ripened later. Only the land of Goshen, where the Israelites lived was free from the hailstorm.

Pharaoh summoned Moses and Aaron and said: "This time I've sinned. The Lord is right, and I and my people are wrong. Pray to the Lord, for we've had enough thunder and hail. I'll let you go."

Moses replied: "As soon as I'm out of the city, I'll stretch out my hands to the Lord in prayer. The thunder will stop and the hail will end so you'll know that the land is the Lord's land. But I know that you and your officials still do not fear the Lord God."

Moses left the city and spread out his hands. The thunder and hail stopped; the storm cleared. When Pharaoh saw that the storm was gone, he kept on sinning: his heart turned rock-hard. He refused to let the Israelites go, just as the Lord had said through Moses (9:13-35).

■8th Plague: Locust

Moses and Aaron went to Pharaoh and told him: "The Lord, the God of the Hebrews, says: `How long will you refuse to humble yourself before me? Let my people go, so they can worship me. If you refuse, tomorrow I'll bring locusts into your country that will cover every inch of the ground. They will devour everything left from the hailstorm and will clear-cut every tree. They'll invade every house in Egypt. None of your ancestors have seen anything like it." Then Moses left Pharaoh.

Pharaoh's officials told him: "How long are you going to let this man harass us? Let the people go and worship the Lord their God. Don't you see that Egypt is ruined?"

Moses and Aaron were brought back to Pharaoh. He told them: "Go, worship the Lord your God. But just who is going?"

Moses answered: "We'll be taking young and old, sons and daughters, flocks and herds, because we are to celebrate a festival to the Lord."

Pharaoh replied: "You have evil intentions! No! Just the men can go. Go ahead, worship the Lord, since that's what you want!" Then Moses and Aaron were thrown out of Pharaoh's presence.

The Lord told Moses: "Stretch out your hand and signal the locusts to swarm over Egypt and devour every blade of grass in the fields, everything left by the hail."

Moses stretched out his staff. The Lord sent an east wind that blew all that day and night. By morning the east wind brought in the locusts. They invaded the land and covered every square inch of Egypt; all the ground was black. They ate everything not destroyed by the hail. Nothing green remained on tree or plant in all the land.

Pharaoh quickly summoned Moses and Aaron and said: "I have sinned against the Lord your God and against you. Overlook my sin once more and pray to the Lord your God to take this deadly plague away from me."

Moses left Pharaoh and prayed. The Lord reversed the wind into a strong west wind which took every single locust and dumped them into the Red Sea. The Lord hardened Pharaoh's heart, and he wouldn't let the Israelites go (10:1-20).

■9th Plague: Total Darkness

The Lord told Moses: "Stretch your hand and signal for darkness to spread over Egypt. Moses stretched out his hand; total darkness covered Egypt for three days. No one could see anyone else or even leave his place for three days. However, there was light where the Israelites lived.

Pharaoh summoned Moses and said: "Go, worship the Lord but leave your flocks and herds behind. Even your women and children may go with you."

Moses replied: "Our livestock must go with us; not a hoof is to be left behind. We use some of them in worshiping the Lord our God."

The Lord hardened Pharaoh's heart, and he wouldn't let them go. Pharaoh said to Moses: "Get out of my sight! I don't want to see you again! The day you see my face you will die."

Moses replied: "Have it your way. You won't see my face again" (10:20-29).

Moses told Pharaoh the Lord's message: "About midnight I will pass throughout Egypt. Every firstborn son in Egypt will die, from the firstborn son of Pharaoh, who sits on the throne, to the firstborn son of the slave girl and all the firstborn of the cattle as well. Widespread wailing will erupt throughout Egypt; wailing worse than ever before and worse than it will ever be again. But there will be silence among the Israelites, not even a dog will bark. Then you will know that the Lord makes a clear distinction between Egypt and Israel." Moses, hot with anger, left Pharaoh.

Moses and Aaron performed all these wonders before Pharaoh, but the Lord hardened Pharaoh's heart, and he would not let the Israelites go out of his country (11:1-9).

Tenth Plague: Israelites' First Passover; Death for Egyptians

The Lord told Moses and Aaron: "This month is to be the first month of your year. Tell the Israelites that on the tenth day of this month each man is to take a lamb for his family, one lamb for each household. If any household is too small for a whole lamb, they must share one with their nearest neighbor. Choose a healthy-one-year-old male animal, either a sheep or goat. Keep it penned until the fourteenth day of the month, then slaughter it at twilight. Take some of the blood and put it on the sides and tops of the doorframes of the houses where they eat. At night they are to eat the meat roasted over the fire. Roast it; head, legs and inner parts. If any is left till morning, you must burn it. You are to eat it with your cloak tucked into your belt, your sandals on your feet and your staff in your hand. Eat in haste; it is the Lord's Passover. On that same night I will go through Egypt and strike down every firstborn; both men and animals. I will bring judgment on all the gods of Egypt. I am the Lord! The blood will serve as a sign on your houses. When I see the blood, I will pass over you. No destructive plague will touch you when I strike Egypt (12:1-13).

"The generations to come after you will honor this day as a celebration to the Lord. For seven days you are to eat bread made without yeast. On the first day hold a sacred assembly, and another one on the seventh day. Do no work at all on these days, except to prepare food for everyone to eat. Celebrate the Feast of Unleavened Bread, because it was on this very day that I brought your clans out of Egypt. Celebrate this day as a lasting ordinance for the generations to come" (12:14-21).

■10th Plague: Death of Firstborn

Moses instructed Israel's leaders: "Select the animals for your families and slaughter the Passover lamb. Take a bunch of hyssop, dip it into the bowl of blood and put some blood on the top and on both sides of the doorframe. No one is to leave his house until morning. When the Lord goes through the land to strike down the Egyptians, he will see the blood on the doorframe and will pass over that doorway. He will not permit the destroyer to enter your houses. Obey these instructions as a lasting ordinance for you and your descendants. When your children ask you: 'What does this ceremony mean?' Tell them: 'It is the Passover sacrifice to the Lord, who passed over the houses of the Israelites in Egypt and spared our homes when he struck down the Egyptians.'" The people bowed down and worshiped. The Israelites did exactly what the Lord commanded Moses and Aaron.

At midnight the Lord struck down every firstborn in Egypt, from the firstborn of Pharaoh, who sat on the throne, right down to the firstborn of the prisoner locked up in the dungeon, and the firstborn of all the livestock. Pharaoh, his officials and all the Egyptians got up during the night. There was loud wailing in Egypt. There was not a house without someone dead! (12:17-30).

Exodus from Egypt

During the night Pharaoh summoned Moses and Aaron and said: "Get out of here, you and your Israelites! Go, worship the Lord as you have requested. Take your flocks and herds, as you've insisted, but go! And also bless me."

The Egyptians couldn't wait to get rid of them, they urged the people to hurry and leave. The Israelites did as Moses instructed and asked the Egyptians for articles of silver and gold, and for clothing. The Lord made the Egyptians readily give the Israelites what they asked for; so they picked the Egyptians clean (12:30-36).

The Israelites started their journey with about six hundred thousand men on foot, besides women and children. (There were about two million and five hundred thousand people.) They took with them large herds of livestock. The Israelites lived in Egypt for 430 years. At the end of the 430 years, to the day, the Lord's people left Egypt (12:31-41).

LIFE-LESSONS DISCOVERED IN THE STORY

1. God desires to communicate with those who govern. He communicated with Moses and with Pharaoh, king of Egypt.

2. The leader who refuses to listen to God's Word will mistreat his people. Many leaders have followed Pharaoh's example: they refuse to listen to God's Word, and they reject actions that would benefit their people if they, as leaders, would reduce their power or wealth.

3. The person who rejects God's truth often considers God's spokesman as an enemy. Moses was God's spokesman, but Pharaoh considered him an agitator who deserved punishment (5:5; 10:28).

4. Those whose visions are limited to current circumstances refuse to hear God's voice, because they believe they will be harmed. Moses and Aaron spoke to Pharaoh, who increased the Israelites' workload. Then the Israelites wouldn't listen to Moses when he gave them God's Word (6:9).

5. Wicked leaders can't prevent God from acting in benefit of his people. Pharaoh could not prevent God from liberating Abraham's descendants. God sent ten plagues which forced Pharaoh to free the Israelites.

6. God, being all powerful, can dominate human cruelty and can even use evil intentions for good. God used Pharaoh's rebellion to show Egyptians that the Lord is the only living, true and powerful God, and that the Egyptians' gods were unable to protect them from the God of Israel.

7. Satan and his servants have limited power; however, God is all powerful. There was a competition between Moses and the Egyptian magicians (7:11, 22; 8:7, 18). With their arts, the Egyptian magicians were able to reproduce the first two plagues (7:20-22; 8:6-7). But they were unable to compete with God.

8. Those whose source of spiritual power is not from God, increase people's problems instead of solving them. With their arts, the Egyptian magicians were able to reproduce the first two plagues (7:20-22; 8:6-7). They did not have the power to revert the process of the plagues.

9. Events that punish God's enemies may at the same time benefit those who trust the Lord. The plagues had a double nature: punishment and salvation. The plagues manifested God's punishment against Egypt, while also manifesting divine action to liberate the Israelites. Christians should interpret each event as part of God's good purpose for their life (Rom 8:28). Since no event can destroy a believer's faith, each event contributes to increasing faith that overcomes the world (1 Jn 5:4).

10. Punishment that comes from God may also represent divine mercy. Until the seventh curse, Pharaoh had been treated with mercy. His life had been prolonged so that the name and power

of the Lord would be exalted (9:14-16). Each plague represented an opportunity for the king to repent.

11. Every time a person resists God, he becomes more stubborn. However, no one can struggle against God and win. The king struggled against God and thought that the Lord could not make him give in. Even after all the terrible plagues, Pharaoh was stubborn and refused to free the Israelites (11:10).

12. God punishes those who resist him, but he saves those who trust him and accept his plan for salvation. God punished the Egyptians, but he freed Israelites who accepted his plan and put blood on their doorposts (12:26-29).

13. God makes distinction between those he is saving and those who are destined for punishment. God made a distinction between the Israelites and the Egyptians (9:6-7; 11:7). God made a distinction between Noah's family inside the ark and those outside (Gn 6:21-23). Believers in Jesus will be protected from the punishment that will afflict those who reject Jesus.

14. The punishment for sin is death. Death was part of God's judgment against Egypt; just as death is part of the universal judgment against sin (Gn 2:17). The Israelites were also sinful and deserved to die for their sins. When they killed the lambs and spilled their blood, they agreed that the punishment for sin is death. Punishment for sin is not just physical death, but it is eternal separation from God in the Lake of Fire.

15. The New Testament introduces Jesus as being the Lamb of God who liberates people from their sins (Jn 1:29; 1 Cor 5:7; 1 Pet 1:19; Rev 7:9; 21:22). The Lord Jesus was born without sin and lived a life without sin. As the Lamb of God, Jesus died to save the sinner from a death he deserves.

16. God only liberates those who accept his salvation plan. During the Exodus, only those inside houses with blood on the doorpost escaped death (Ex 12:1-36). The Lord rejected the garments Adam and Eve made for themselves (Gn 3:21). He refused Cain's offering (Gn 4:5, 7). Noah built the ark exactly as God instructed. During the flood, there was only one ark and it only had one door (Gn 6:16). The New Testament reveals that Jesus is the only way to God (Jn 14:6).

QUESTIONS

1. What was the reactions of the leaders of Israel when Moses first told them that the Lord was concerned about them?
2. What was Pharaoh's reaction when Moses and Aaron told him that the Lord God wanted him to let God's people go?
3. When those who govern imitate Pharaoh and reject the Word of the Lord, what happens to ordinary citizens?
4. Why was Pharaoh unable to prevent Abraham's descendants from leaving Egypt?
5. How did Moses use prayers during the time when he was in conflict with Pharaoh?
6. Describe the competition that took place between Moses and Aaron, and the Egyptian magicians.
7. What were some of the plagues that God sent to the Egyptians?
8. What distinction did God make between the Egyptians and the Israelites?
9. How did the plagues manifest two sides of God's character: the side that punishes and the side that saves?
10. What happens to the person who imitates Pharaoh and struggles against God?
11. What was the last plague that God sent against the Egyptians?
12. How did the Israelites prepare for the tenth plague?
13. What was the reaction of Pharaoh and the Egyptians after the deaths of the firstborn?
14. What does this Bible story teach us about God?
15. If the angel of death were to visit your home, which group would you be assigned to: those being punished by God or those being saved by God?

REDEEMED AND TESTED BY GOD
Exodus 12:43 - 18:27

STRUCTURE

Context:
There were 70 family members with Israel when he moved from Canaan to Egypt. They multiplied until there was about two million and five hundred thousand descendants of Israel in Egypt. They became slaves to the Egyptians. The Lord used Moses to confront Pharaoh and demand that the Israelites be allowed to leave Egypt. The Lord sent ten plagues against the Egyptians before Pharaoh allowed the Israelites to leave. After 430 years in Egypt, the Israelites left, on their way to Canaan.

Key-persons: Moses, the Israelites, Jethro

Key-locations: Red Sea, Marah, Desert of Sin and Rephidim

Key-repetitions:
- Each time the Israelites faced a problem: the people complained, Moses prayed and then God acted. This happened when: the Israelites saw Egyptians chasing them (14:1-30); at Marah where the water was bitter (15:22-25); at the Desert of Sin when they remembered food in Egypt (16:1-35); and at Rephidim where there was no water (17:1-7).
- The Israelites feared they would die in the desert (14:10-12; 16:3; 17:3).
- Ordinances that remember God's actions: Passover (13:1-10); consecrate to God every firstborn male (13:11-16).
- God's provisions in the desert: the cloud and the fire (13:20-22); water (15:13-25; 17:1-6); food (16:13-19); protection from the Egyptians (14:10-28) and from the Amalekites (17:8-13).
- The glory of the Lord: manifested in the destruction of the Egyptians (14:4, 12); manna (16:7); the cloud (16:10). The Lord will gain glory (14:4, 17,18).
- The Lord tested the Israelites (15:25; 16:4-8).

Key-attitudes:
- God desired for the Israelites to remember his delivering them from Egypt.
- Ecstasy was felt by the Israelites leaving Egypt.
- Joy was felt by the Israelites when they saw the drowned Egyptian soldiers.
- The Israelites feared dying in the desert.
- The Israelites complained each time they faced a crisis.
- Moses felt frustrated when the Israelites complained, but he also felt confidence in God.
- Moses felt anger toward the Israelites when they disobeyed God.
- Jethro felt concern for the overworked Moses.

Initial-problem:
When Pharaoh let the people go, God didn't lead them by the shortest route, through the Philistine country. He led them to make camp in front of the Red Sea.

Sequence of events:

Rules for Remembering Passover
- The Lord established a yearly Passover celebration and gave rules for observing it (12:43-50).
- Moses told the people how they were to celebrate the Passover in future years: observe it during the first month; eat bread made without yeast; on the seventh day celebrate a festival; and on that day tell your son the reason for the celebration (13:1-10).
- Moses told the people that after the Lord brings them into Canaan, they were to set aside for him every firstborn male (13:1-2, 11-16).

Leaving Egypt
- God led the people by the desert road toward the Red Sea. Moses took Joseph's bones with him (13:17-19).
- The Lord went ahead of them in a pillar of cloud by day and in a pillar of fire by night (13:20-22).
- The Israelites reversed their directions. Pharaoh gave chase (14:1-9).
- When the Israelites saw the Egyptians, they cried out in terror. Moses told them to watch the Lord deliver them. The Lord told Moses to raise his staff and split the water. He promised to gain glory through Pharaoh (14:10-18).
- The angel of God shifted from being in front of Israel's army and got behind them. The pillar of cloud also shifted to the rear and came between the Egyptians and the Israelites. Moses stretched out his hand over the sea, the sea-waters split and the Israelites walked through the sea. The Egyptians pursued them and the sea covered the entire Egyptian army. The Israelites put their trust in the Lord and in Moses (14:19-31).
- Moses and the Israelites sang, celebrating God's actions in Israel's favor (15:1-18).
- Miriam led the women in singing (15:19-21).

God's Provisions in the Desert
- At Marah: the water was bitter, the Israelites complained, Moses prayed, the Lord showed him a stick to throw into the water, and the water turned sweet (15:22-26).
- At the Desert of Sin they complained about the food (15:27 - 16:3).
- The Lord told Moses he would rain down bread from heaven. Moses instructed the people as to how they were to gather the bread (16:4-8).
- The glory of the Lord was visible in the cloud. God told Moses the Israelites would eat meat. That evening quail flew into camp and the next morning

manna was on the ground. Moses instructed them as to how they were to gather the manna. Some disobeyed Moses. Manna was not to be gathered on the Sabbath (16:9-36).

■ At Rephidim: there was no water, the people complained, Moses prayed, God told him to strike a rock, and water gushed out (17:1-7).

■ At Rephidim, Amalekites attacked the Israelites. Joshua fought them while Aaron and Hur helped hold up Moses' hands (17:8-16).

Moses Chooses Helpers

■ Jethro took Moses' wife and sons to him. Moses told him everything the Lord had done. Jethro presented sacrifices to God (18:1-12).

■ The next day Moses judged the people. Jethro accused Moses of working too hard and advised him: represent the people before God; teach them; and select capable men, who fear God, have integrity, are incorruptible, and appoint them to serve as judges for simple cases (18:13-23).

■ Moses did as Jethro suggested. Jethro returned to his own country (18:13-26).

Final-situation:

Moses chose some capable men to help him lead the Israelites.

BIBLE STORY

Rules for Remembering the Passover

As the Israelites were leaving Egypt, the Lord established a yearly celebration for future generations to remember the Passover. The night of the first Passover, all the Israelites obeyed the instructions the Lord had commanded Moses and Aaron. And on that very day the Lord brought the Israelites out of Egypt (12:43-50).

Moses told the people how to celebrate the Passover in future years: "Remember this day because the Lord brought you out of Egypt, out of slavery, with a mighty hand. When the Lord brings you into the land he swore to give your forefathers, you are to observe this ceremony during the first month of the year. For seven days eat bread made without yeast and on the seventh day celebrate a festival to the Lord. On that day tell your son: `I do this because of what the Lord did for me when I came out of Egypt.' This observance will be for you like a sign on your hand and a reminder on your forehead that the law of the Lord is to be on your lips. For the Lord brought you out of Egypt with his mighty hand. You must keep this ordinance at the appointed time year after year" (13:1-10).

Moses also told the people: "After the Lord brings you into the land of the Canaanites, you are to set aside to him every firstborn male, whether man or animal. All the firstborn males of your livestock belong to the Lord. In days to come, when your son asks you: `What does this mean?' say to him: `With a mighty hand the Lord brought us out of Egypt, out of the land of slavery. When Pharaoh stubbornly refused to let us go, the Lord killed every firstborn in Egypt, both man and animal. That is why I sacrifice to the Lord the first male offspring of every womb and redeem every firstborn son.' The observance functions like a sign on your hand and a symbol on your forehead that the Lord brought us out of Egypt with his powerful hand" (13:1-2, 11-16).

Leaving Egypt

When Pharaoh let the people go, God didn't lead them by the shortest route, through the Philistine country. For God said: "If they face war, they will change their minds and return to Egypt." So God led the people around by the desert road toward the Red Sea. The Israelites went up out of Egypt in military formation.

Moses took the bones of Joseph with him because Joseph had made the sons of Israel swear an oath when he said: "God will surely come to your aid, and then you must carry my bones from here with you" (13:17-19).

As they left Egypt, by day the Lord went ahead of them in a pillar of cloud to guide them and by night in a pillar of fire to give them light. Thus they could travel by day or night. The pillar of cloud by day and the pillar of fire by night never left their place in front of the people (13:20-22). The cloud and the fire were God's provisions that permitted the Israelites to live and travel in the desert. Desert days are extremely hot, and its nights are cold. The clouds kept the days from becoming hot, and the fire kept the nights from becoming cold. The glory of the Lord appeared in the cloud (16:10).

The Lord instructed Moses to tell the Israelites to turn around and start back the way they had come and make camp. God's reason was: "Pharaoh will think: `The Israelites are wandering around. They're lost; they're confused. They are hemmed in by the desert.' I will harden Pharaoh's heart, and he will chase after them. But I will put my glory on display through Pharaoh and his army. The Egyptians will know that I am the Lord." So the Israelites reversed their directions.

Pharaoh and his officials changed their minds about the Israelites and said: "What have we done? We let the Israelites go; we lost their slave labor!" He had his chariot harnessed and took his army with him. The Lord hardened the heart of Pharaoh king of Egypt, so that he chased the Israelites, who were marching out boldly. The Egyptians, all Pharaoh's horses and chariots, horsemen and troops, pursued the Israelites and overtook them as they camped by the sea near Pi Hahiroth (14:1-9).

The Israelites saw the Egyptians marching after them and cried out in terror to the Lord. They told Moses: "Was it because there were no graves in

Egypt that you brought us to the desert to die? What have you done to us by taking us out of Egypt? Didn't we tell you in Egypt, `Leave us alone; let us serve the Egyptians'? It was better for us to serve the Egyptians than to die in the desert!"

Moses replied: "Don't be afraid. Stand firm and watch the Lord deliver you today. Look at the Egyptians; you will never see them again! The Lord will fight for you; you need only to be still."

The Lord told Moses: "Why cry out to me? Order the Israelites to move. Raise your staff and stretch out your hand over the sea. Split the water! The Israelites will walk through the sea on dry ground. I will harden the hearts of the Egyptians so that they will go in after them. I will gain glory through Pharaoh and his entire army; his chariots and his horsemen. The Egyptians will know that I am the Lord when I gain glory through Pharaoh, his chariots and his horsemen" (14:10-18).

The angel of God, who had been in front of Israel's army, shifted and got behind them. Also, the pillar of cloud that had been in front shifted to the rear and came between the camp of Egypt and the camp of Israel. Throughout the night the cloud brought darkness to one side and light to the other side. Neither camp went near the other during the night.

Then Moses stretched out his hand over the sea, and the Lord used a terrific East wind to drive the sea back and turned it into dry land. The sea-waters split. The Israelites walked through the sea on dry ground, with a wall of water on their right and on their left.

The Egyptians pursued them. All Pharaoh's horses and chariots and horsemen raced after them into the sea. The Lord threw the Egyptian army into panic by making the wheels of their chariots come off so that they were stuck. The Egyptians said: "Run away from the Israelites! The Lord is fighting on their side against Egypt."

The Lord told Moses: "Stretch out your hand over the sea, and the waters will flow back over the Egyptians." Moses stretched out his hand over the sea, and the sea returned to its place. The water flowed back and covered the entire army of Pharaoh that had chased the Israelites into the sea. Not one of them survived.

But the Israelites walked through the sea on dry ground, the waters forming a wall to their right and to their left. That day the Lord delivered Israel from the hands of the Egyptians. Israel saw the Egyptians lying dead on the shore. The Israelites saw the great power the Lord displayed against the Egyptians. They feared the Lord and put their trust in him and in Moses his servant (14:19-31).

Then Moses and the Israelites sang a song celebrating the actions of God in Israel's favor. They sang a victory song of thanksgiving. God the Redeemer, God the Warrior, God the Almighty was worshiped. They sang:

I'm singing to the Lord,
what a victory!
The horse and its rider
he pitched into the sea.

God is my strength,
God is my song,
God is my salvation.
This is the kind of God I have.

Pharaoh's chariots and his army
he has hurled into the sea.
The best of Pharaoh's officers
are drowned in the Red Sea.

Who compares with you among gods, O Lord?
Who compares with you in holy majesty?
in awesome glory?
Wonder-working God?

In your unfailing love you will lead
the people you have redeemed.
In your strength you will guide them
to your holy dwelling.

You will bring them in and plant them
on the mountain of your inheritance--
the place, O Lord, you made for your dwelling,
your sanctuary, O Lord, that you established
with your hands.

The Lord will reign
for ever, for eternity! (15:1-18)

Miriam the prophetess was Moses and Aaron's sister. She took a tambourine, and all the women followed her, with tambourines and dancing. Miriam led them in singing:
Sing to the Lord,
what a victory!
The horse and its rider
he hurled into the sea. (15:1-21)

God's Provisions in the Desert
Moses led Israel from the Red Sea and they went into the Desert of Shur. The Middle Eastern deserts were usually not characterized by sand dunes; rather the wilderness lands through which the Israelites traveled were rocky, dry wastelands. They traveled for three days in the desert without finding water. When they came to Marah, the water was bitter and they couldn't drink it. The people complained to Moses, saying: "What are we to drink?"

Moses cried out in prayer to the Lord. The Lord showed him a stick of wood. Moses threw it into the water, and the water turned sweet. That's the place where the Lord made rules and decrees for them, and there he tested them. He said: "If you listen, obey the voice of the Lord your God and do what is right in his eyes, if you obey his commands and keep all his laws, I will not strike you with any of the diseases I inflicted on the Egyptians, for I am the Lord, your healer" (15:22-26).

They came to Elim, where there were twelve springs and seventy palm trees. They camped near the water. On the second month and fifteenth day after they had left Egypt, they set out from Elim and came to the Desert of Sin. In the desert the whole community complained against Moses and Aaron bickering: "Why didn't the Lord let us die in comfort in Egypt? There we sat around pots of meat and ate all the food we wanted, but you have brought us out into this desert to starve this entire company to death" (15:27 - 16:3).

The Lord told Moses: "I will rain down bread from heaven for you. The people are to go out and gather each day's ration. I'm going to test them and see whether they will follow my instructions. On the sixth day they are to gather twice as much as they gather on the other days."

Moses and Aaron told the Israelites: "This evening you will know that it was the Lord who brought you out of Egypt; in the morning you will see the glory of the Lord. He's heard your complaints against him. You will know that it was the Lord when he gives you meat to eat this evening and bread in the morning. He has heard your complaints against him. You aren't complaining against us, but against the Lord" (16:4-8).

The Israelite community looked toward the desert, and there was the glory of the Lord visible in the cloud. The Lord told Moses: "I have heard the complaints of the Israelites. Tell them: `At twilight you will eat meat, and in the morning you will eat your fill of bread. Then you will know that I am the Lord your God.'"

That evening quail flew in and covered the camp, and in the morning there was a layer of dew around the camp. When the dew was gone, thin flakes as fine as frost appeared on the desert ground. When the Israelites saw it, they asked each other: "What is it?" They didn't know what it was.

Moses told them: "It is the bread the Lord has given you to eat. These are the Lord's instructions: `Each one is to gather as much as he needs. Gather about two quarts for each person in your tent.'"

The Israelites went to work; some gathered more, some less. Each one gathered as much as he needed.

Moses told them: "No one is to store any of it until morning."

However, some did not obey Moses; they kept part of it until morning, but it was full of maggots and smelled bad. Moses lost his temper with them.

Each morning everyone gathered as much as he needed, and when the sun grew hot, it melted away. On the sixth day, they gathered twice as much, about four quarts per person. They saved it until the Sabbath morning, as Moses commanded, and it did not stink or get maggots in it. Moses said: "Today is a Sabbath to the Lord and you will not find any of it on the ground today. Six days you are to gather it, but on the seventh day, the Sabbath, there will not be any."

However, some of the people went out on the seventh day to gather manna, but found none. The Lord told Moses: "How long will you disobey my commands and not follow my instructions? Remember, the Lord has given you the Sabbath; on the sixth day he gives you bread for two days. Everyone is to stay in his tent on the seventh day; no one is to go out." So the people rested on the seventh day.

The Israelites called the bread manna (What is it?). It was white like coriander seed and tasted like wafers with honey. They ate manna forty years, until they reached the border of Canaan (16:9-36).

Directed by God, the whole Israelite community set out from the Desert of Sin, traveling from place to place. They camped at Rephidim, but there was not a drop of water for the people to drink. They confronted Moses: "Give us water to drink!"

Moses replied: "Why do you quarrel with me? Why are you testing the Lord?"

The people were thirsty and they quarreled with Moses: "Why did you bring us out of Egypt and drag us here with our children and animals to die of thirst?" They tested the Lord when they questioned: "Is the Lord here with us, or not?"

Moses cried out in prayer to the Lord: "What can I to do with these people? They are ready to stone me."

The Lord answered Moses: "Walk out ahead of the people and take in your hand the staff with which you struck the Nile. I will be present with you on the rock at Horeb. Strike the rock, and water will gush out of it for the people to drink." Moses obeyed (17:1-7).

The Amalekites attacked the Israelites at Rephidim, the desert place where water was gushing out from the rock. Moses said to Joshua: "Choose some of our men and go fight the Amalekites. Tomorrow I will stand on top of the hill holding God's staff."

Joshua fought the Amalekites. Moses, Aaron and Hur went to the top of the hill. As long as Moses held up his hands, the Israelites won, but whenever he lowered his hands, the Amalekites won. Moses' hands grew tired, and they took a stone and put it under him, and he sat on it. Aaron and Hur held his hands up, one on each side, so that his hands remained steady till sunset. So Joshua defeated the Amalekite army in battle.

The Lord told Moses: "Write this on a scroll as a reminder, because I will completely blot out the memory of Amalek from off the Earth."

Moses built an altar and called it: "The Lord is my Banner" (17:8-16).

Moses Chooses Helpers

Jethro, priest of Midian and Moses' father-in-law, heard the report of all that God had done for Moses and how the Lord had brought Israel out of Egypt.

Moses had sent his wife Zipporah and their two sons back to Jethro's home. Jethro sent word to

Moses: "I, your father-in-law, am coming to you with your wife and two sons."

Moses went out to welcome his father-in-law. He bowed to him and kissed him. They greeted each other and then went into the tent. Moses told his father-in-law about everything the Lord had done to Pharaoh and the Egyptians in helping Israel. He told about the hardships they had experienced on the journey, and how the Lord had delivered them.

Jethro was delighted to hear about all the good that the Lord had done for Israel in delivering them from Egyptian oppression. He said: "Praise the Lord, who delivered you from the hand of the Egyptians and of Pharaoh. Now I know that the Lord is greater than all other gods, because he did this to those who had treated Israel cruelly." Then Jethro presented a burnt offering and other sacrifices to God (18:1-12).

The next day Moses took his seat to judge the people. Many stood around him from morning till evening. Jethro saw all that Moses was doing and said: "Why are you doing all this by yourself? Why are you the only judge, while all these people stand around you from morning till evening?"

Moses answered: "The people come to me to seek God's will. Whenever they have a dispute, it is brought to me, and I decide between the parties and teach them God's laws and instructions."

Jethro replied: "What you are doing is wrong. You'll burn out and the people right along with you. The work is too heavy for you to handle alone. I will give you some advice so that God will be in this with you. Represent the people before God. Teach them rules and laws. But select capable men from all the people; men who fear God, men of integrity, men who are incorruptible; and appoint them as officials over groups organized by thousand, by hundred, by fifty, and by ten. Have them serve as judges; the simple cases they decide, the difficult cases they bring to you. Your load will be lighter, because they will share it with you. If you do this, and God so commands, you will be able to stand the strain, and all these people will flourish."

Moses listened to his father-in-law and did everything he said. He chose competent men from all Israel and made them leaders over the people who were organized by the thousand, by the hundred, by fifty, and by ten. They took over the everyday work of judging the routine cases. The difficult cases they brought to Moses.

Then Moses said good-bye to his father-in-law who returned to his own country (18:13-26).

LIFE-LESSONS DISCOVERED IN THE STORY

1. God liberates only those who accept his plans. The Israelites were delivered from slavery because they accepted God's plan and painted their doorframe with blood. Today, people can be delivered from slavery to sin by accepting God's plan and believing in Jesus Christ who shed his blood on the cross.

2. The home should be the primary place where children are taught about God's redemptive acts in history. The father has the main responsibility of being the spiritual leader and teaching his children. During the Passover celebration, the fathers should tell their children they were celebrating the Passover because of everything the Lord did for the Israelites when they left Egypt (Ex 13:1-10).

3. People who are liberated by God are guided by him. Just as the pillar of cloud and the pillar of fire guided the Israelites (Ex 13:20-22), followers of Jesus are guided by the Bible and the Holy Spirit.

4. The "Glory of the Lord" means people can see visible evidence of God's presence. The pillar of cloud was a visible sign of God's presence with the Israelites in the desert. The glory of the Lord appeared in the cloud (Ex 16:10).

5. In the New Testament, John 1:14 calls Jesus the "Glory" of God. Just as the pillar of cloud and the pillar of fire were visible signs of God in the desert (Ex 16:10), in the New Testament, Jesus is the visible sign of God's presence.

6. The brilliance of God's presence illuminates the most arid desert of life, just as the pillar of fire illuminated the desert nights for the Israelites.

7. There are occasions when God takes his people through danger, but when he does, he gives them evidence of his power and presence. Pharaoh decided to recapture the Israelites; he was behind them, and the sea was in front of them. God split the sea and the Israelites walked across between two walls of water (Ex 14:21-22); however, God allowed the waters to return over Pharaoh's army (Ex 14:26-30). At Rephidim, when the Amalekites attacked the Israelites, God helped Joshua to defeat them (Ex 17:8-16).

8. God comes to the aid of his people because of his mercy and compassion, not because people deserve his help. When the Egyptian army appeared, the Israelites didn't deserve to be saved; they didn't have faith, and they criticized Moses (Ex 14:10-12).

9. Desperation may initiate a pulse of faith that gives a person courage to do the impossible. The Israelites' terror of Pharaoh's army, with the certainty that God was their only hope, gave them courage to walk across the sea between two walls of water (Ex 14:15-25).

10. Worship celebrates both God's actions in past historical events and in recent present events. The Lord established a yearly Passover celebration where they were to remember the historical Passover event (Ex 12:43-50). Also, immediately after the Egyptian soldiers drowned in the sea, the Israelites sang songs celebrating the actions of God in Israel's favor (Ex 15:1-21).

11. God the Redeemer deserves to be worshiped. Exodus 15:1-21 is mainly a song celebrating the actions of God in favor of Israel. God, the Redeemer, was worshiped.

12. God values women, giving them an important part of his redemptive history. His church should value women and consider them as co-servants in God's work. The prophetess Miriam led the women in singing and dancing (Ex 15:20-21). She is one of the great women of the Bible.

13. God leads those he redeems into crisis situations where solutions are beyond human ability. God delivered the Israelites, and then led them into the desert where they were unable to provide for their bare necessities: water, food and protection from enemies. Without divine provisions, they would have died in the desert.

14. Those who remember the "good old days" suffer from selected amnesia; they remember the good while forgetting the bad. While in the desert, the Israelites remembered comfort in Egypt and the pots of meat they ate there (Ex 16:3); however, they forgot the bitterness of slavery.

15. Sometimes God tests his people through abundance and prosperity. Character may be at greater risk in prosperity than in adversity. The Lord told Moses: "I will rain down bread from heaven for you. The people are to go out and gather each day's ration. I'm going to test them and see whether they will follow my instructions" (Ex 16:4).

16. God is capable of providing for the basic needs of those he liberates. God supplied the basic needs of the Israelites in the desert:
    water (Ex 15:22-25; 17:5-7);
    ■Food (Ex 16:11-18);
    ■Protection from enemies (Ex 17:8-16).

17. According to Jesus' interpretation: the manna God provided in the desert illustrates the fact that Jesus is spiritual food for his disciples (Ex 16:11-18; Jn 6:26-58).

18. Circumstances don't determine one's attitudes or reactions, but reveal what is inside of a person. The Israelites faced problems beyond their abilities to solve, and they lost faith, complained and criticized Moses. Moses was faced with the same circumstances, yet he had faith and prayed asking God for help. Circumstances were not responsible for the Israelites' complaining, but revealed that they had within themselves the disposition to complain. Faced with the same circumstances, Moses revealed his disposition to trust God, expecting him to solve the problem.

19. In time of trial, God's people must depend upon both prayer and action in order to experience divine liberation. When Moses lifted his hands, he used the typical gesture the Israelites use when praying (Ps 63:4). Both prayer and action are essential. While Moses was on the mountain praying, Joshua and his soldiers were in the valley fighting (Ex 17:8-16).

20. A leader without helpers will weaken and lose his ability to help his followers. When the arms of Moses became tired, Aaron and Hur placed a stone for Moses to sit down, and they held his hands up. They helped Moses hold his arms up, and this enabled Joshua to defeat the Amalekites (Ex 17:11-13). Jethro accused Moses of working too hard and advised him to select capable men and appoint them to serve as judges for simple cases (Ex 18:13-23).

21. The leader who centralizes everything around himself will harm those he leads. Moses had centralized everything around himself, and Jethro informed him that his actions were detrimental for the people. Moses was getting tired, and the people were tiring also (Ex 18:13-27).

22. The leader needs to accept appropriate advice from others. Moses received and accepted advice from Jethro (Ex 18:13-27).

23. If Satan can't get a spiritual leader to fall into sin, he can destroy his ministry by getting him overworked, causing his health to be destroyed. Moses faced that danger, when he was overworked, judging the people from morning until sunset (Ex 18:13-27).

24. In correcting another person's mistake, it is necessary to:
    ■Condemn behavior that is not acceptable;
    ■Give suggestions on how the person can correct himself;
    ■Accept and value the person who is making a mistake.
    Jethro attacked Moses' behavior and gave suggestions on how to solve the problem. He didn't attack Moses the person. Moses' behavior was unacceptable while Moses the person was appreciated (Ex 18:13-27).

25. The leader should work accompanied by others. Jethro advised Moses to choose capable assistants and to place them as officials over the people (Ex 18:19-26).

26. It is necessary for spiritual leaders to be morally

qualified. Jethro advised Moses to choose and appoint as officials: capable men, who feared God, had integrity, and were incorruptible (Ex 18:21).

27. The spiritual leader's main responsibilities are described in Exodus 18:19-21:
    ■Pray (Ex 18:19).
    ■Teach the word of God and train people to serve him (Ex 18:20). Moses taught the Israelites God's laws and trained capable men to be judges.
    ■Guide people to make specific applications, in specific situations (Ex 18:20).
    ■Give responsibilities to qualified people (Ex 18:24-26). Moses chose capable men and gave them the task of judging.

QUESTIONS

1. What ceremonies did the Lord give the Israelites to help them remember their Exodus from Egypt?
2. How did the Lord guide the Israelites and show them where to go?
3. What was the Israelites' reaction when they saw Pharaoh's armies following them?
4. How did God liberate the Israelites from the Egyptians at the Red Sea?
5. How did the Israelites celebrate their crossing of the Red Sea?
6. What were the main problems the Israelites faced in the desert?
7. What were some of the things the Israelites complained about when they were in the desert?
8. When the Israelites were in the desert, how did God provide for their basic needs of: water; food and protection from enemies?
9. Have you experienced God's providing for your basic needs?
10. When the Israelites faced crises, how did the people react and how did Moses react?
11. When you face crises, how do your reactions reveal your character? Do you need to change your reactions?
12. How are there similarities between the way God treated the Israelites who were liberated in Egypt and the way he treats those who become followers of Jesus?
13. What mistakes did Jethro observe Moses making?
14. How did Jethro help correct Moses' mistake?
15. How can you help your spiritual leader?

THE LEGISLATOR OF THE TEN COMMANDMENTS
Exodus 19 - 24

STRUCTURE

Context:
God promised to give Abraham's descendants the land of Canaan. Jacob was Abraham's grandson. His name was changed to Israel. Israel had 12 sons. During his lifetime, Israel, with 70 of his descendants, left Canaan to live in Egypt. The Israelites multiplied in number and became slaves to the Egyptians. God sent Moses to Pharaoh, king of Egypt, with the request: "Let my people go."

When Pharaoh stubbornly refused to let the Israelites go, the Lord killed every firstborn in Egypt, both man and animal. Then the Israelites left Egypt and traveled to the Red Sea. Pharaoh chased after them. God split the waters and the Israelites walked through the sea on dry ground, the waters forming a wall to their right and to their left. When Pharaoh's army chased them into the sea, the water flowed back and covered the entire army. Not one of them survived.

After crossing the Red Sea, the Israelites traveled in the desert where God provided for their basic needs: the pillar of cloud and pillar of fire guided them; he provided them with water, food and protection from their enemies.

Moses chose some capable men to help him lead the Israelites.

Key-person: Moses

Key-location: Mount Sinai

Key-repetitions:
- The Israelites were unanimous in responding: "We will do everything the Lord said" (19:7; 24:3).
- The Lord spoke to Moses (19:3, 9, 10, 20, 24; 20:1, 22; 24:1).
- Moses reported the Lord's words to the people (19:7, 25; 24:3).
- Eight of the Ten Commandments begin with a negative order: "You shall not" (20:3-17).
- God emphasized the historical fact that it was he who brought the Israelites out of Egypt (19:4; 20:2).
- God established boundaries at the foot of the mountain that the Israelites were not to cross (19:12, 21, 23, 24).
- The Israelites trembled with terror when they stood at the foot of the smoking mountain where there was thunder, lightning, a thick dark cloud, and a loud trumpet blast (19:16; 20:18).

Key-attitudes:
- God felt that the Israelites were indebted to him since he liberated them from slavery in Egypt.
- The Israelites trembled with terror when they faced the smoking mountain where there was thunder, lightning, a thick dark cloud, and a loud trumpet blast.
- The predominance of God is expressed in everything that happened.
- The Israelites expressed firmness when they proclaimed: "We will do everything the Lord said."

Initial-problem:
The Lord told Moses to tell the Israelites: "You saw what I did to Egypt, and how I carried you on eagles' wings and brought you to myself. If you obey me and keep my covenant, then out of all peoples you will be my special treasure."

Sequence of events:

At the Foot of Mount Sinai
- The Israelites camped in the Desert of Sinai facing the mountain (19:1-2).
- The Lord told Moses to tell the Israelites: they saw what he did to Egypt; they saw how he carried them; if they obeyed him they would be his special treasure (19:3-6).
- The people responded: "We will do everything the Lord said" (19:7-8).
- The Lord told Moses the people could listen to God speaking to him in a thick dark cloud (19:9).

Preparing for the Lord's Presence
- The Lord told Moses to prepare the people to meet the Holy God. They were to put boundaries around the mountain, and whoever crossed them would die. Moses prepared them for the holy meeting (19:9-15).
- On the appointed day: there was thunder and lightning; a dark cloud covered the mountain; smoke billowed up; a loud trumpet blast was heard; and the mountain trembled. Everyone in camp trembled with terror. Moses spoke and the voice of God answered him (19:16-19).
- God told Moses to again warn the people not to cross the boundaries. Then he told Moses to bring Aaron up the mountain. Moses told the people what God said (19:20-25).

The Ten Commandments
- God said: "I am the Lord your God, who brought you out of Egypt, out of the land of slavery (20:1-2).
  1) You shall have no other gods before me (20:3).
  2) You shall not make for yourself an idol. You shall not bow down to them or worship them (20:4-6).
  3) You shall not misuse the name of the Lord your God (20:7).
  4) Observe the Sabbath day by keeping it holy (20:8-11).
  5) Honor your father and your mother (20:12).
  6) You shall not murder (20:13).
  7) You shall not commit adultery (20:14).

8) You shall not steal (20:15).
9) You shall not give false testimony (20:16).
10) You shall not covet (20:17).

▪People heard thunder, saw lightning, heard a trumpet blast, saw the smoking mountain, and they trembled with fear. They asked Moses not to let God speak to them because they were afraid of dying. Moses replied that the fear of God would keep them from sinning (20:18-21).

▪After giving the Ten Commandments, the Lord gave Moses other laws and regulations for the Israelites to obey (20:21 - 24:3).

▪The Lord promised rewards if the Israelites obeyed his laws (Lev 26:3-13) and punishment if they disobeyed them (Lev 26:14-17).

▪Moses gave the Israelites God's laws and regulations. They answered: "Everything the Lord said, we will do" (Ex 24:3).

Final-situation:
Moses told the people everything the Lord had said, all the laws and regulations. The Israelites answered in unison: "Everything the Lord said, we will do."

BIBLE STORY

At the Foot of Mount Sinai
The Israelites set out from Rephidim. Three months to the day after they left Egypt, they came to the Desert of Sinai and camped in the desert facing the mountain (19:1-2).

As Moses went up to meet God, the Lord called down to him from the mountain: "Tell the people of Israel: 'You saw what I did to Egypt, and how I carried you on eagles' wings and brought you to myself. If you obey me and keep my covenant, then out of all peoples you will be my special treasure. The whole Earth is mine to choose from, but you will be special, a kingdom of priests and a holy nation.' This is what you are to tell the Israelites" (19:3-6).

Moses went back and called the leaders of the people together and told them the words the Lord commanded him to speak. The people were unanimous in responding: "We will do everything the Lord said." Moses took their answer back to the Lord.

The Lord told Moses: "I am going to come to you in a thick dark cloud. The people can listen to me speaking with you and trust you when I speak with you." Again Moses told the Lord what the people had said (19:7-9).

Preparing for the Lord's Presence
The Lord told Moses: "Go to the people and for the next two days get them ready to meet the Holy God. Have them wash their clothes and be ready by the third day. On the third day the Lord will come down on Mount Sinai and make his presence known to all the people. Put boundaries around the mountain and tell the people: 'Warning! Don't climb the mountain; don't even touch the foot of it. Whoever touches the mountain shall die. Also, no one is to touch the offender, he is to be stoned or shot with arrows. Whether man or animal, he shall be put to death.' A long blast from the ram's horn will signal it is safe to go up the mountain."

Moses went down the mountain and prepared the people for the holy meeting. They washed their clothes and he told the people: " Be ready in three days. Abstain from sexual relations" (19:9-15).

On the morning of the third day there was thunder and lightning, a thick dark cloud covered the mountain, and they heard a very loud trumpet blast. Everyone in camp trembled with terror. Moses led the people out of the camp to meet God. They stood at the foot of the mountain. Mount Sinai was covered with smoke because the Lord descended as fire. Smoke billowed up from it like smoke from a furnace. The mountain trembled in huge spasms. The trumpet blast grew louder and louder. Moses spoke, and the voice of God answered him (19:16-19).

The Lord called Moses up to the peak and Moses climbed up to the top of Mount Sinai. The Lord told him: "Go down and warn the people so they do not break through the boundaries to get a look at the Lord and many of them perish. Even the priests must prepare themselves for the holy meeting, or the Lord will break out against them."

Moses replied: "The people cannot come up Mount Sinai because you yourself warned us, 'Put boundaries around the mountain and set it apart as holy.'"

The Lord replied: "Go down and bring Aaron back up with you. But make sure the priests and the people don't force their way through to come up to the Lord."

So Moses went down to the people and told them (19:20-25).

The Ten Commandments
God spoke all these words: "I am the Lord your God, who brought you out of Egypt, out of the land of slavery (20:1-2).

1st "You shall have no other gods before me (20:3).

2nd "You shall not make for yourself an idol. Make no carved gods in the form of anything in heaven above or on earth beneath or in the waters below. You shall not bow down to them or worship them; because I, the Lord your God, am a jealous God. I punish children to the third and fourth generation for the sins of their fathers who hate me. But I show love to a thousand generations of those who love me and keep my commandments (20:4-6).

3rd "You shall not misuse the name of the Lord your

God. The Lord will not hold anyone guiltless who misuses his name (20:7).

4th "Observe the Sabbath day by keeping it holy. Work six days and do all your work, but the seventh day is a Sabbath to the Lord your God. Don't do any work on it, neither you, nor your son, nor your daughter, nor your servant nor your maid, nor your animals, nor the foreign guest visiting your town. In six days the Lord made Heaven, Earth, sea, and everything in them, but he rested on the seventh day. Therefore, the Lord blessed the Sabbath day; he set it apart as holy (20:8-11).

5th "Honor your father and your mother, so that you will live a long time in the land the Lord your God is giving you (20:12).

6th "You shall not murder (20:13).

7th "You shall not commit adultery (20:14).

8th "You shall not steal (20:15).

9th "You shall not give false testimony about your neighbor (20:16).

10th "You shall not covet your neighbor's house, nor his wife, nor his servant, nor his maid, nor his ox nor his donkey, nor anything that is your neighbor's" (20:17).

The people saw the thunder and lightning, heard the trumpet blast, saw the smoking mountain, and they trembled with fear. They pulled back and stayed at a distance. They told Moses: "You speak to us and we will listen, but don't have God speak to us or we'll die."

Moses replied: "Do not be afraid. God has come to test you; the fear of God within you will keep you from sinning."

The people kept their distance, while Moses approached the thick dark cloud where God was (20:18-21).

After giving the Ten Commandments, the Lord gave Moses other laws and regulations the Israelites were to obey (20:21 - 24:3).

The Lord promised rewards if the Israelites obeyed him: "If you obey my commands, I will send rain in the rainy seasons, the ground will yield its crops and the trees their fruit. You will thresh grain until grape harvest, and grape harvest will continue until planting time. You will eat all the food you want and live in safety. I will make your country a place of peace; you will sleep without fear. I will get rid of savage beasts; war will not pass through your country. You will chase your enemies and defeat them. I will make you prosper, make you increase in number, and I will keep my covenant with you. You will still be eating last year's harvest when you clean out your barns to make room for the new crops. I will make my residence among you; I won't avoid or shun you. I will stroll among you and be your God; you will be my people. I am the Lord your God, who rescued you from Egypt so that you would no longer be slaves to the Egyptians. I broke the bars of your yoke and enabled you to walk freely with heads held high (Lev 26:3-13).

The Lord promised punishment if the Israelites disobeyed his laws: "If you refuse to obey me, if you won't observe my commands, if you reject my decrees, if you hate my laws and if by disobedience you make a shamble of my covenant; I will do this to you: I will bring upon you sudden terror, wasting diseases, high fever, blindness and drain away your life. You will plant seed in vain, because your enemies will eat the crops. I will turn my back on you; your enemies will defeat you. People who hate you will govern you. You will flee even if no one is chasing you" (Lev 26:14-17).

Moses told the people everything the Lord had said, all the laws and regulations. The Israelites answered in unison: "Everything the Lord said, we will do" (Ex 24:3).

LIFE-LESSONS DISCOVERED IN THE STORY

1. The Legislator of the Ten Commandments is a Holy God, while man is a sinner. The boundaries prohibiting people and animals from climbing Mount Sinai emphasize that God is holy and sinful man cannot approach him (19:12).

2. God will judge and punish those who dare enter God's holy presence while they are contaminated by sin. Anyone who crossed the boundaries established by God would be put to death (19:12-13).

3. God establishes absolutes for his people. Anyone who crossed boundaries established by God would be put to death (19:12-13). The Ten Commandments establish absolutes; God determines that some things are right and some things are wrong (20:1-17).

4. The Legislator of the Ten Commandments is the All Powerful God. The Egyptians alleged that their gods' power made Egypt the most powerful nation of the world. Each of the ten plagues that God ordered against Egypt was a blow against one of their gods. God Almighty's power destroyed Pharaoh's power and proved that the

Lord God of Israel is stronger than the gods of Egypt (20:1-2).

5. The Legislator of the Ten Commandments is a God who liberates. The Israelites were redeemed by God after putting the lamb's blood on their doorpost and when God split the Red Sea for them. He liberated the Israelites from slavery in Egypt. When God began to give the Ten Commandments, he claimed: I am the Lord your God, who brought you out of Egypt, out of the land of slavery (20:1-2).

6. The Legislator of the Ten Commandments is a God who guides. God redeemed the Israelites from slavery in Egypt and began to guide them to Canaan. He guided them with a pillar of cloud by day and in a pillar of fire by night (13:20-22). God gave the Ten Commandments in order to guide those he had liberated so they would know how to live. The Ten Commandments lead us to live a life guided by God.

7. The Legislator of the Ten Commandments is a demanding God. He demands absolute control of all the areas of his followers' lives. But after everything that God Creator, God All Powerful, God Liberator has done for his people, he has the right to be demanding.

8. The Legislator of the Ten Commandments demands absolute control over all his followers lives. When God was preparing the people to receive the Ten Commandments, he said: If you obey me and keep my covenant, then out of all peoples you will be my special treasure. And the people responded: We will do everything the Lord said (19:3-8). God demanded that his people do everything that he orders.

9. The Legislator of the Ten Commandments demands control over all human relationships. God demands that one's relationship with him determines the relationship one has with other people. The first four commandments speak of people's relationship to God (20:3-11). The last six commandments speak of people's relationship with one another (20:12-17).

10. The Legislator of the Ten Commandments demands that people control tendencies they have that would offend God. It may be that a person does not commit the offenses that the Commandments prohibit, but each person has the tendency or the desire to disobey each commandment.
■Youths have the tendency of thinking that they know more than their parents.
■Human nature has the tendency of wanting to kill those who mistreat them.
■People have the tendency of thinking that sex outside of marriage would be exciting.
■People have the tendency of wanting to lie in order to take advantage of others.
■People have the tendency of desiring to take for themselves what belongs to others.

11. The Lord's people hold a staggering responsibility for their descendants. God promised to punish children to the third and fourth generation for the sins of their ancestors who hate him, but to show love to generations of those who love him and keep his commandments (20:4-6).

12. Jesus affirms that the Ten Commandments are valid for his disciples. He emphasized that he did not come to abolish the Law but to fulfill it (Mt 5:17-18).

13. Jesus increases the demands made in the Ten Commandments. In the Sermon on the Mountain, Jesus explained to his disciples how he was intensifying the demands made in the Ten Commandments. The Ten Commandments demand that a person's behavior be put under God's control. Jesus increases the requirement by demanding that a person's thoughts and desires be put under divine control. For instance:
■The Ten Commandments demand: "You shall not murder." Jesus demands that one doesn't feel hatred nor call his brother a fool (Mt 5:21-22).
■The Ten Commandments demand "You shall not commit adultery." Jesus demands that a man not look at a woman with the purpose of fantasizing about having sex with her (Mt 5:27-28).

14. The Ten Commandments are for people who have been liberated by God. After God liberated the Israelites from slavery, he gave them the Commandments. They were given to a people who were liberated from slavery and were enjoying freedom.

15. The Ten Commandments are rules that enable God's people to enjoy freedom. If people desire to enjoy freedom, they must obey the Ten Commandments. Freedom is lost where the Ten Commandments are violated. Freedom is lost when:
■Children do as they please and dishonor their parents;
■Life is cheap and people kill others whenever they desire;
■Matrimonial vows are violated, sex is practiced on the level of the barnyard, and men have less respect for a woman than a bull has for the cows;
■Property lines are not respected and the strong takes what they desire from the weak;
■Injustice prevails because lies are freely told in the court room;
■Gossipers destroy reputations with lies.

16. Fear of God's punishment will protect a person from sinning. The Israelites heard the thunder and saw lightning. They heard the trumpet

blast, saw the smoking mountain and they trembled with fear. Moses told them: "The fear of God within you will keep you from sinning" (20:18-21).

QUESTIONS

1. Why did God give the Ten Commandments to the Israelites?
2. Explain the paradox: the only truly free person is the one who is God's servant and obeys his laws.
3. What right did God have to demand that the Israelites obey his Ten Commandments?
4. Why did God set boundary limits around Mount Sinai?
5. Why were the Israelites afraid to go close to Mount Sinai?
6. Which of the commandments make demands on a person's relationship with God?
7. Which of the commandments place demands on a person's relationship with other people?
8. What was the Israelites' reaction when they first heard the commandments?
9. How do the Ten Commandments apply to us today?
10. In his Sermon on the Mountain, what did Jesus have to say about the Law?
11. Is there something you should change in your life as a result of this study?

THE TEN COMMANDMENTS
Exodus 20:1-17

COMMANDMENT	INTERPRETATION	INTENSIFIED BY JESUS	COMMENTARY
1. You shall have no other gods before me (20:3).	God does not divide his glory with anyone. He is the only true God (Dt 4:39; Is 45:5).	Love the Lord your God with all your heart and with all your soul and with all your strength (Mt 22:36-38); No one can serve two masters (Mt 6:24).	God is the only God who liberates people. One should not love, worship or give loyalty to anything or anyone more than he does to the Lord God.
2. You shall not make an idol nor worship them (20:4-6).	Visual objects used in worship become stumbling blocks to true worship. Examples: images of Jesus, of angels, of apostles, of saints, or of created things.	Jesus is the visual revelation of the invisible God (Col 1:15; Jn 14:9).	Worship of the true God cannot be limited by symbols made by humans. Images, rituals, and symbols that become essential for someone to worship become idols.
3. You shall not misuse the name of the Lord your God (20:7).	It is prohibited to swear by God's name for the purpose of taking advantage of someone else.	Jesus requires that our words be pure, transparent and honest. He prohibited swearing (Mt 5:33-37).	Hypocrisy is condemned. It is prohibited to use the appearance of religion as a means to do evil. A profession of faith in God should be accompanied by a life that proves the spoken words (Col 3:17).
4. Observe the Sabbath day by keeping it holy. Work six days (20:8-11).	The Sabbath Day is a remembrance that God rested after his creation work (Ex 20:11). It commemorates the rest offered to the Israelites after God freed them from slavery (Dt 5:14). Both worship and the interruption from work is required.	The Sabbath was made for man, instead of man being made to serve the Sabbath by keeping legalistic rules. Jesus has authority over the Sabbath (Mk 2:27-28). It is lawful to do good on the Sabbath (Mk 3:4). Jesus' disciples began to assemble on the first day of the week to remember his resurrection. (Jn 20:1, 26; Ac 20:7; 1 Cor 16:2; Rev 1;10).	One should do his work in six days and have one day for rest and worship.

Old Testament Bible Stories © Jackson Day

THE TEN COMMANDMENTS
Exodus 20:1-17

COMMAND-MENT	INTERPRETATION	INTENSIFIED BY JESUS	COMMENTARY
5. Honor your father and your mother (20:12).	Children should obey their parents, unless obeying parents requires them to disobey the Lord (Eph 6:1-3).	God's will for adult children has priority over the parents' desires for their children (Lk 9:59-60). The married child should leave his parents to unite with his spouse (Mt 19:5). Religion should not be used as an excuse for disobeying God and neglecting needy parents (Mt 15:4-6).	Those who build a society where parents and the elderly are honored can expect to be respected in their old age. When youth is adored and old aged is feared and despised, the culture is in decline.
6. You shall not murder (20:13).	Do not kill your enemy. Life is valuable, it is a gift from God. The Law distinguishes between intentional murder and accidental homicide (21:12-14). This command does not prohibit the death penalty (21:15-16), nor war. The Law holds responsible the person who by negligence allowed someone to be killed (Ex 21:29, 34; Dt 22:8).	Jesus prohibited anger and offensive words along with forbidding murder (Mt:5:21-22).	■Lamech's Law: (He killed those who wounded him). Treat your enemy worse than he treats you (Gn 4:23-24). ■Moses's Law: Treat your enemy equal to the way he treats you; life for life, an eye for an eye. ■Jesus' Law: Treat your enemy better than he treats you. Return good for evil (Mt 5:44).
7. You shall not commit adultery (20:14).	The person who has sex with another person's spouse is sinning against God and against his fellow man (Gn 39:9).	Monogamy was God's plan for the human race from the time of creation. Divorce, polygamy and even fornication were tolerated in Old Testament Law due to the hardness of the human heart (Mt 19:8). Christ prohibits thinking about such actions (Mt 5:28). (See 1 Cor 6:15; Mt 19:4-6.)	Sex is valuable and should be protected within the boundaries of marriage. Sex outside of marriage is prohibited. It is also prohibited to throw stones at the person who committed adultery (Jn 8:7).
8. You shall not steal (20:15).	The Old Testament emphasizes that the powerful should not use their power to take from the weak (Dt 27:19; Pv 22:22; Is 3:15; 5:8; Am 4:1). Ways to steal are mentioned in Ja 5:4; Dt 19:14; 25:14; 27:19; Lev 19:13.	Three attitudes presented in the Parable of the Good Samaritan (Lk 10:25-37): ■Thieves: what is yours is mine, and I will take it; ■Priest and Levite: what is mine is mine, and I will keep it; ■Samaritan: what is mine is yours, and I will share.	Steal no more; but work, doing something useful in order to have something to share with the needy (Eph 4:28).
9. You shall not give false testimony (20:16).	In Old Testament Law, most crimes involved capital punishment. A "false testimony" would be equivalent to murder.	The Devil is the father of every lie (Jn 8:44). On Judgment Day, each one will give an account of every careless word spoken (Mt 12:36-37). What was said in secret will be announced openly (Lk 12:3).	Always speaking the truth is the means to avoid telling lies. The commandment can be generalized to include prohibiting false criticism and gossip that harms another (Lev 19:16).
10. You shall not covet (20:17).	Desires that are prohibited stimulate envy and motivate people to do such evil such as: kidnaping, robbing, manipulating, or harming others in order to obtain what is lawfully another's.	From the heart comes evil thoughts of: murder, adultery, sexual immorality, theft, false testimony, slander (Mt 15:11, 16-20).	The desire to use improper means to obtain what belongs to another, demonstrates that one is dissatisfied with what he received from God and lacks faith in his love.

Jesus summarized all the commandments with the statement: "Love the Lord your God with all your heart and with all your soul and with all your mind.... and love your neighbor as yourself" (Mt 22:37-40).

WORSHIP: GOD'S WAY OR MAN'S IMITATION
Exodus 19-40; Leviticus 8 - 11

STRUCTURE

Context:
The Lord liberated the Israelites from slavery in Egypt. After leaving Egypt, they crossed the Red Sea. Pharaoh's soldiers attempted to follow the Israelites across the Red Sea and drowned. The Israelites traveled through a desert and God guided them with a pillar of cloud and a pillar of fire. He provided them with water, food and protection from their enemies.

At Mount Sinai, the Lord gave Moses Ten Commandments and other laws and regulations for the Israelites to obey. He promised rewards if they obeyed him and punishment if they disobeyed.

Moses gave the Israelites all of God's laws and regulations, and they answered in unison: "Everything the Lord said, we will do."

Key-persons: Moses and Aaron

Key-location: Mount Sinai

Key-repetitions:
- Bezalel; his artistic skills and his using those skills to make the Tabernacle and all its furnishings (Ex 31:2; 35:30; 36:1, 2; 37:1; 38:22).
- The Israelites revolted against God: when Aaron made the golden calf (Ex 32:1-5); when Nadab and Abilhu offered forbidden fire (Lev 10:1-3).
- Obeyed exactly as God commanded: in the celebration of the festivals (Ex 23:15; 34:18); in the construction of the Tabernacle (Ex 25:1-9; 31:11; 35:10; 36:1; 40:19, 21, 23, 25, 29, 32); when Moses went up Mount Sinai (34:4); the priests, their garments and their consecration (Ex 39:1; 5-7, 21, 31-32, 41-42; 40:16; Lev 8:1 - 9:21).
- Anger: God was angry (Ex 32:7-10; 33:33:3; Lev 10:1-3). Moses was angry (Ex 32:19-20).
- God appeared in a cloud (Ex 19:9; 24:16-19; 33:9; 34:5; 40:34-36).
- Tabernacle (Ex 25:1-9; 26:1-36; 27:1-21; 28:43; 29:4, 10-11, 30-44; 30:1-36; 31:1-11; 35:11-21; 36:1-37; 38:8-31; 39:32-40; 40:2-38).
- Consecrated: the Tabernacle (Lev 8:10-11, 15); the priest (Lev 8:1-2, 12-13, 22-28, 30).

Key-attitudes:
- Moses worshiped the Lord.
- The splendor and glory of the Lord appearing in the clouds.
- The Israelites' insecurity when Moses was absent.
- Aaron was unstable and vulnerable to the influence of others.
- God's anger at the Israelites who worshiped the golden calf and at Nadab and Abihu when they offered forbidden fire.
- The attention to detail in doing exactly as the Lord commanded.
- The irreverence of Nadab and Abihu when they offered unauthorized fire.

Initial-problem:
The Lord told Moses to come up to him on the mountain.

Sequence of events:

Moses on Mount Sinai
- The Lord told Moses to come up to him on the mountain. Moses set out with Joshua and left Aaron and Hur in charge. He stayed on the mountain forty days and nights (Ex 24:12-18).
- The Lord told Moses to ask the Israelites to bring him an offering for the tabernacle and its furnishings (Ex 25:1-9).
- God gave Moses detailed instructions on how to construct the tabernacle and all its furnishings (25:10 - 27:21).
- God chose Aaron and his sons to serve as priests (Ex 28:1-3).

The Golden Calf
- Moses delayed on the mountain and the Israelites asked Aaron to make gods for them. Aaron shaped an idol in the form of a calf. The people called it their god. Aaron announced a feast. The people sacrificed offerings, ate, drank and had a party (Ex 32:1-6).
- The Lord told Moses the Israelites had become corrupt. God threatened to destroy them (32:7-10).
- Moses pleaded with the Lord to spare them and the Lord decided not to destroy them (32:11-14).
- Moses descended the mountain with two tablets in his hands. Moses and Joshua heard the sound of singing from the camp (32:15-18).
- Moses saw the calf; his anger flared and he destroyed it (32:19-20).
- Moses asked Aaron how he could lead them into such sin. Aaron blamed the people (32:21-25).
- Moses said: "Whoever is for the Lord, come to me." The Levites rallied to him. Moses told them to kill their fellow Israelites. They killed about 3,000 (32:25-30).
- The next day Moses told the people they had committed a great sin. He went back to the Lord and prayed pleading with him to forgive them (32:21-35).
- The Lord threatened to no longer go with the people. Moses pleaded, and God decided to do what Moses asked (33:1-17).
- Moses chiseled out two stone tablets, and the Lord wrote his commandments on them (34:1-4).
- Moses was on the mountain with the Lord forty days and forty nights (34:27-28).
- When Moses came down from Mount Sinai his face glowed, and he covered it with a veil when he was with the people (34:29-36).

Tabernacle Constructed

- Moses told the Israelites to bring offerings for the tabernacle. All who were willing brought to the Lord freewill offerings (Ex 35:4-29).
- They brought more than enough, and Moses restrained them from bringing more (Ex 36:3-7).
- The Lord chose Bezalel, gave him his Spirit and artistic ability to make the tabernacle and all its furnishings. He gave Bezalel and Oholia the ability to teach others to do the work following the Lord's commands (35:30 - 36:3).

Courtyard of the Tabernacle

- Surrounding the main building of the tabernacle was a courtyard 150 feet long and 75 feet wide. The courtyard was surrounded by a fence (Ex 27:9-19; 38:1-8).
- At the front of the courtyard stood the altar of burnt-offering (Ex 27:9-18; 38:1-8).
- Bezalel made a washbasin that was placed between the altar and the tabernacle (Ex 30:17-21; 38:8).

The Tabernacle

- The tabernacle was a rectangular tent structure, 45 feet long and 15 feet wide. The tent was divided into two rooms: a holy place and a Holy of Holies (26:1-33).
- The Holy of Holies contained the ark of the covenant. The covering for the ark was called the mercy-seat. At either end of the mercy-seat, stood two gold angels. The ark contained only the two tablets of stone (Ex 25:10-22; 37:1-9).
- The Holy Place had three pieces of furniture: (1) the table of shewbread (Ex 25:23-30; 37:10-16; 40:22); (2) the golden candlestick (Ex 25:31-40; 37:17-24; 40:24); (3) the altar of incense (Ex 30:1-10; 37:25-29).
- The tabernacle had a wooden framework. On top of the frame was 3 coverings (Ex 26:1-37; 36:8-38).
- The tabernacle-tent was held in position by ropes secured to the ground by bronze tent-pins (Ex 27:19; 38:31).
- Everything was done just as the Lord commanded Moses (Ex 39:32, 42-43).
- Moses set up the tabernacle-tent and the glory of the Lord filled the tabernacle. Whenever the cloud lifted from above the tabernacle, the Israelites would follow it (Ex 40:34-38).

Consecration of Aaron and His Sons

- Moses washed Aaron and his sons and put on their priestly garments (Lev 8:1-9).
- Moses anointed the tabernacle and its furnishings with oil. He anointed Aaron and then his sons (Lev 8:10-13).
- Aaron and his sons helped Moses present the bull for the sin offering (Lev 8:14-17).
- Moses presented one ram for the whole-burnt-offering (Lev 8:18-21).
- Moses presented a second ram for the ordination-offering. Moses consecrated Aaron and his sons when he sprinkled oil and blood on them and their garments (Lev 8:22-30).
- Moses told them not to leave the tabernacle for the seven days that would complete their ordination. Aaron and his sons did everything the Lord commanded through Moses (Lev 8:31-36).
- On the eighth day Aaron killed: the calf as a sin offering for himself; animals for the whole-burnt-offering; the goat for the people's sin offering; the ox and ram as the people's fellowship offering. Aaron blessed the people. Fire came from the Lord and consumed the burnt offering. The people shouted for joy and fell face down (Lev 9:1-24).
- Nadab and Abihu offered unauthorized fire and were consumed by fire. Moses told Aaron and his other sons not to mourn (Lev 10:1-7).
- The Lord instructed Aaron that he and his sons were not to drink fermented drink whenever they went into the tabernacle. They were to teach the Israelites God's decrees (Lev 10:8-11).

Final-situation:

The tabernacle was constructed as God's dwelling place among the people and Aaron and his sons were consecrated priests.

BIBLE STORY

Moses on Mount Sinai

The Lord told Moses: "Come up the mountain to me. Wait here, and I will give you two stone tablets with the law and the commandments. I have written these to teach the people."

Moses set out with his aide Joshua. Moses told the older leaders: "Wait here for us until we come back to you. Aaron and Hur are with you, and anyone involved in a dispute can go to them."

Moses went up on the mountain, the cloud covered it, and the glory of the Lord settled on Mount Sinai. On the seventh day the Lord called to Moses from within the cloud. To the Israelites, the glory of the Lord looked like a consuming fire on top of the mountain. Moses entered the cloud as he climbed the mountain. He stayed on the mountain forty days and forty nights (Ex 24:12-18).

The Lord instructed Moses: "Tell the Israelites to bring me an offering. These are the offerings you should receive from them: gold, silver and bronze; blue, purple and scarlet yarn and fine linen; goat hair; ram skins dyed red and hides of sea cows; acacia wood; olive oil; spices and fragrant incense; onyx stones and other gems. Then have them make a tabernacle (tent) for me, and I will dwell among them. Make this tabernacle and all its furnishings exactly like the plans I will show you (Ex 25:1-9). Moses received detailed instructions on how to construct the tabernacle and for each of its furnishings that would be used for worship (Ex 25:10 - 27:21).

God instructed Moses that Aaron along with his sons would serve as priests. God instructed: "Make

Old Testament Bible Stories © Jackson Day

sacred clothes for your brother Aaron, to give him dignity and honor. Tell all the skilled men that they are to make clothes for Aaron, for his consecration, so he may serve me as priest" (Ex 28:1-3).

The Golden Calf

The people saw that Moses stayed a long time on the mountain. They rallied around Aaron and said: "Make us gods who will go before us. We don't know what happened to that Moses who brought us out of Egypt."

Aaron answered: "Take off the gold earrings and bring them to me." All the people took off their earrings and brought them to Aaron. He took the gold, melted it and used an engraving tool to make an idol in the shape of a calf.

The people shouted with enthusiasm: "These are your gods, O Israel, who brought you up out of Egypt."

Aaron built an altar before the calf and announced: "Tomorrow is a feast day to honor the Lord." Early the next day the people offered whole-burnt-offerings and fellowship-offerings. They sat down to eat and drink, and got up to have sex. It became a wild party! (Ex 32:1-6).

The Lord told Moses: "Go! Get down there! Your people, whom you brought up out of Egypt, have become corrupt. They quickly turned away from what I commanded them. They made themselves an idol cast in the shape of a calf. They bowed down to it, sacrificed to it and said, 'These are your gods, O Israel, who brought you up out of the land of Egypt. These people are a stubborn, hard-headed people! Now give my anger free reign to burst into flames and destroy them. Then I will make you into a great nation."

But Moses begged: "O Lord, don't let your anger destroy your people. You brought them out of Egypt with your great power and strength. Why let the Egyptians say: "He brought them out, to kill them in the mountains?' Stop your anger; relent, don't bring disaster on your people! Remember your servants Abraham, Isaac and Israel, to whom you gave your word, telling them: 'I will make your descendants as numerous as the stars in the sky. I will give your descendants all this land that I promised them, and it will be theirs forever.'"

Then the Lord reconsidered and decided not to destroy the people (32:7-14).

Moses went down the mountain with the two tablets of the Testimony in his hands. The tablets were the work of God; the engraving on the tablets was written by God.

Joshua heard the noise of the people shouting and said to Moses: "The sound of war is in the camp."

Moses replied: "It is not the sound of victory, it is not the sound of defeat; it is the singing of people throwing a party that I hear" (32:15-18).

Moses approached the camp. He saw the gold calf and the dancing; his anger flared. He threw down the tablets, breaking them to pieces at the foot of the mountain. Moses took the calf they had made, melted it down with fire, ground it to powder, scattered it on the water and forced the Israelites to drink it (32:19-20).

Moses asked Aaron: "What did these people do to you, that you led them into such great sin?"

Aaron answered: "Master, don't be angry. You know these people are always ready to do wrong. They said to me: 'Make us gods who will lead us. We don't know what happened to this Moses who brought us up out of Egypt.' So I told them: 'Take off your gold jewelry.' They gave me the gold. I threw it into the fire, and out came this calf!" (32:21-25).

Moses saw that the people were running wild. Aaron allowed them to get out of control. Their enemies would laugh at them. Moses stood at the entrance to the camp and said: "Whoever is for the Lord, come to me." All the Levites rallied to him.

Moses gave them a command from the Lord: "Each man strap on your sword and go through the camp from one end to the other killing your brother, your friend and your neighbor." The Levites obeyed. About three thousand Israelites were killed that day. Moses said: "You have been set apart to the Lord today at a great cost. You were willing to kill your own sons and brothers, and God has blessed you" (32:25-30).

The next day Moses told the people: "You have committed a great sin. But I will go up to the Lord; perhaps I can do something so your sins will be removed." Moses went back to the Lord and prayed: "Oh, what a great sin these people have committed! They have made themselves gods of gold. But now, please forgive their sin; but if not, then erase me out of the book in which you have written the names of your people."

The Lord replied: "I will only erase from my book those who sin against me. Now go, lead the people to where I told you. My angel will lead you. When the time comes for me to punish, I will punish them for their sin." The Lord sent a plague on the people because of what they did with the calf Aaron had made (32:21-35).

The Lord told Moses: "Tell the Israelites: 'You are one hard-headed people. I will send an angel to lead you, I will not go with you. If I were to go with you, I might destroy you'" (33:1-6).

Moses replied: "If your Presence does not go with us, do not send us up from here."

The Lord answered Moses: "I will do the very thing you have asked, because I am pleased with you and I know you by name" (33:12-17).

The Lord told Moses: "Chisel out two stone tablets like the originals, and I will engrave on them the same words that were on the first tablets, which you broke. So Moses chiseled out two stone tablets like the originals (34:1-4). Moses was on the mountain with the Lord forty days and forty nights without eating bread or drinking water. And Moses wrote the words of the Ten Commandments on the stone tablets (34:27-28).

Moses came down from Mount Sinai with the two tablets of the Testimony in his hands. He was unaware that his face glowed because he had spoken with the Lord. Aaron and the Israelites saw his radiant face and they were afraid to come near him. But Moses called to them, they came to him, and he spoke to them. Afterward all the Israelites came near him. He gave them all the commands the Lord had given him on Mount Sinai.

When Moses finished speaking to them, he put a veil over his face. But when he went before the Lord, he removed the veil. When Moses came out and told the Israelites what the Lord commanded, they saw that his face glowed. Then Moses would cover his face with the veil until the next time he went in to speak with the Lord (34:29-36).

Tabernacle Constructed

God had told Moses that the Israelites were to make a tabernacle for him (Ex 25:1-9). God gave Moses detailed instructions on how to construct the tabernacle and for each object that would be used in worship (25:10 - 27:21).

Offering for the Tabernacle

Moses told the Israelites: "The Lord has commanded you to take an offering. Everyone who is willing is to bring to the Lord an offering of gold, silver and bronze; blue, purple and scarlet yarn, fine linen; goat hair; ram skins and hides of sea cows; acacia wood; olive oil; spices; incense; onyx stones and other gems.

Everyone who was willing brought an offering to the Lord for the work on the tabernacle, for all its service, and for the sacred garments (Ex 35:4-29).

The people continued to bring freewill offerings morning after morning. They brought more than enough for doing the work the Lord commanded to be done. Then Moses gave an order: "No man or woman is to make anything else as an offering for the sanctuary." The people were restrained from bringing more, because there already was more than enough to do all the work (Ex 36:3-7).

Moses told the Israelites: "The Lord has chosen Bezalel of the tribe of Judah and has filled him with the Spirit of God. The Lord has given Bezalel skill, ability and knowledge in all kinds of crafts; to make artistic designs of gold, silver and bronze, to cut and set stones, to carve wood and to do all kinds of artistic craftsmanship. The Lord gave both Bezalel and Oholiab the ability to teach others. He gave them skill to do all kinds of work as craftsmen, designers, embroiderers, and weavers. Bezalel, Oholiab and every person to whom the Lord has given skill and ability are to do the work just as the Lord commanded" (Ex 35:30 - 36:3).

Courtyard of the Tabernacle

Bezalel made a fence of curtains to form a courtyard around the main building of the tabernacle. The curtains were 150 feet long in its North-South directions and 75 feet wide in its East-West directions. The fence-curtains were 7 ½ feet high, formed of pillars with silver-work, resting in brass sockets, placed 7 ½ feet apart, and hung with fine linen. There were 60 pillars, 20 each on the longer sides (North and South), and 10 each on the shorter (East and West). On the eastern side was the entrance. This was formed by a screen 30 feet wide. At the back of the courtyard in the western half the tabernacle itself was set up. At the front of the courtyard in the eastern half stood two items: the altar of burnt-offering and the washbasin (Ex 27:9-19; 38:9-20).

The Altar of Burnt-Offering

At the front of the courtyard, toward the east, stood the altar of burnt-offering.

Bezalel made the altar of burnt-offering from acacia wood. He made it 7 ½ feet square and 4 ½ feet high. He made a grate of bronze mesh. Each corner projected out like a horn. He made buckets for removing the ashes along with shovels, basins, forks and fire pans. He used bronze to make all the utensils for the altar. He placed four rings at each of the four corners of the bronze grating to hold the poles used for carrying the altar (Ex 27:9-18; 38:1-8).

The Washbasin

Bezalel made a large bronze washbasin that was placed between the altar of burnt-offering and the tabernacle. The priests were to wash their hands and feet in it (Ex 30:17-21; 38:8).

Tabernacle's Two Rooms

The tabernacle was a rectangular oblong tent structure, 45 feet long and 15 feet wide. The tent had two rooms divided by an intricate veil of blue, scarlet, and purple linen embroidered with cherubim. The two divisions of the tabernacle were: a Holy Place (30 feet long by 15 feet wide) and a Holy of Holies (15 feet square) (Ex 26:1-33).

The Holy of Holies and the Ark

The inner, western room was called the Holy of Holies. It was 15 feet square. It contained one piece of furniture, the ark of the covenant.

Bezalel made a chest of acacia wood that was overlaid within and without with pure gold. He made it 45 inches long, 27 inches wide and 27 inches deep. The ark had golden rings on each side so it could be transported with poles that were placed through the rings (Ex 25:10-16; 37:1-5).

The lid for the ark was of solid gold and was called the mercy-seat. The lid was 45 inches long and 27 inches wide. At either end of the mercy-seat stood two gold angels. They faced each other with their wings spread over the lid, hovering over the mercy-seat and looking down on it. This was the meeting-place of the Lord God and his people. The ark contained only the two tablets of stone (Ex 25:16-22; 37:6-9).

The Holy Place

The outer eastern room was called the Holy Place. It was 15 feet wide and 30 feet long. It was entered through the blue, scarlet, and purple linen curtains which served as a door. This door was always aligned toward the east.

The Furniture Inside the Holy Place

The table of shewbread was placed on the north side of the Holy Place in front of the curtain (Ex 40:22). Bazalel and Oholiab made the table of acacia wood, overlaid with gold, with a molding all around it of gold. There were gold rings at its corners that served as holders for the poles used to carry the table. The poles were made of acacia wood and covered with a veneer of gold. The table's dimensions were 36 inches long, 18 inches wide, and 27 inches high (Ex 25:23). On it were placed 12 cakes, renewed each week, in two piles (Lev 24:5-9), together with dishes, incense cups, flagons and bowls for drink offerings, all of pure gold (Ex 25:23-30; 37:10-16).

The seven-branched golden candlestick was placed on the south side of the Holy Place across from the table (Ex 40:24). Bazalel made the candlestick of pure gold, making its stem and branches, cups, calyxes and petals all of one piece. It consisted of a pedestal, a central stem with three curved branches on either side, all elegantly wrought with cups of almond blossoms, calyxes and flower petals. Upon the six branches and the central stem were seven lamps from which the light issued. Connected with the candlestick were snuffers and snuff-dishes for the wicks, all of gold. The candlestick was formed from a seventy-five-pound brick of pure gold (Ex 25:31-40; 37:17-24).

The altar of incense was placed on the western side of the Holy Place, next to the veil. The small altar was 18 inches square, and 36 inches high. Each corner stuck out like horns. Bazalel and Oholiab made the altar of acacia wood overlaid with gold. Upon this altar, the morning and evening sweet-smelling incense was burned. It had a golden rim, golden rings, and gold-covered staves (Ex 30:1-10; 37:25-29).

Tabernacle's Framework

The tabernacle had a wooden framework. The framework was composed of 48 boards of acacia wood. Twenty were used on the north side, 20 on the south side and 8 on the west side. Each board was 15 feet in height, and 2 feet 3 inches wide and were overlaid with gold. On top of the frame was 3 coverings; The inside covering consisted of 10 curtains of fine twined linen, woven with blue, purple, and scarlet, and with figures of cherubim. The curtains were joined together to form a single great curtain 60 ft. long, and 42 ft. wide (Ex 26:1-6). The middle covering was formed by 11 curtains of goat's hair that were coupled into one great curtain 66 feet long and 45 feet wide (Ex 26:7-13). The top covering was made of rams' skins dyed red, and of seal-skins or porpoise-skins (Ex 26:1-14; 36:8-19).

The door of the tent was on the east side and formed a screen, embroidered with colors, and pending from five pillars in bronze sockets. The hooks were of gold, and the pillars and their capitals overlaid with gold (Ex 26:1-37; 36:8-38).

The tabernacle was a tent in shape, with ridge-pole, and a sloping roof, raising the total height to 22 feet and 6 inches. Passing over the ridge pole, and descending at an angle, 21 feet on either side, the inner curtain would extend 7 feet and 6 inches beyond the walls of the tabernacle, making an awning of that width north and south, while the goats'-hair covering above it, three feet wider, would hang below it 18 inches on either side. The whole tent would be held in position by ropes secured by bronze tent pins to the ground (Ex 27:19; 38:31).

Everything was done just as the Lord commanded Moses. Moses inspected the work and saw that they had done all the work exactly as God had commanded. (Ex 39:32, 42-43).

Moses set up the courtyard around the tabernacle, and he put up the curtain at the entrance to the courtyard. When Moses finished the work, the cloud covered the tabernacle, and the glory of the Lord filled it. Moses could not enter the tabernacle because the cloud had settled upon it, and the glory of the Lord filled the tabernacle.

Whenever the cloud lifted from above the tabernacle, the Israelites would begin to travel; but as long as the cloud stayed put, they did not travel. The cloud of the Lord was over the tabernacle by day, and fire was in the cloud by night. The Israelites could see the cloud during all their travels (Ex 40:34-38).

Consecration of Aaron and His Sons

The Lord told Moses to bring Aaron, his sons, their garments, and the special oil used in anointing people and things to the service of the Lord. "Also bring the bull for sin offering, two rams and the basket of bread made without yeast. Then gather the entire congregation at the entrance to the tabernacle." Moses did as the Lord commanded (Lev 8:1-4).

Moses brought Aaron and his sons forward and washed them with water. He put the priestly garments on Aaron, just as the Lord commanded (Lev 8:5-9).

Moses consecrated the tabernacle: he took anointing oil and sprinkled the tabernacle and all its furnishings. He consecrated the altar: he sprinkled oil on the altar and all its utensils seven times. He consecrated Aaron: he poured anointing oil on Aaron's head. Then he brought Aaron's sons forward and put priestly garments on them, as the Lord commanded Moses (Lev 8:10-13).

Moses presented the bull for the sin offering. Aaron and his sons put their hands on its head. Moses purified the altar: he killed the bull, and with his finger he took some of its blood and put it on all the horns of the altar. He poured the rest of the blood at the base of the altar. Moses took all the fat from the inner organs of the bull and burned it on the altar. But the bull with its hide, its meat and its intestines, he cremated outside the camp, just as the Lord commanded Moses (Lev 8:14-17).

Moses then presented the ram for the whole-burnt-offering. Aaron and his sons put their hands on its head. Moses killed the ram and splashed it's blood against all sides of the altar. He burned the whole ram on the altar as the Lord commanded Moses (Lev 8:18-21).

Moses presented the second ram for the ordination-offering. Aaron and his sons put their hands on the ram's head. Moses killed it and smeared some of its blood on the lobe of Aaron's right ear, on the thumb of his right hand and on the big toe of his right foot. Moses brought Aaron's sons forward and smeared some blood on the lobes of their right ears, on the thumbs of their right hands and on the big toes of their right feet. Then he splashed blood against the altar on all sides.

Moses took a wafer and loaf of bread from the basket of bread made without yeast. He put these on the fat and right thigh of the ram. He put all these in the hands of Aaron and his sons and waved them before the Lord as a wave-offering. Then Moses took it all back from their hands and burned them on the altar on top of the whole-burnt-offering as an ordination-offering.

Moses consecrated Aaron, his sons and their garments. Moses took some anointing oil and some blood from the altar and sprinkled Aaron, his sons and their garments (Lev 8:22-30).

Moses told Aaron and his sons: "Cook the meat at the entrance to the tabernacle and eat it there with the bread from the basket of ordination offerings. Then burn up the rest of the meat and the bread. Do not go out through the entrance of the tabernacle for the seven days that will complete your ordination. What has been done today was commanded by the Lord to make atonement for you. You must stay at the tabernacle's entrance day and night for seven days. Do what the Lord requires, lest you die." So Aaron and his sons did everything the Lord commanded through Moses (Lev 8:31-36).

On the eighth day after their consecration; Moses summoned Aaron, his sons and the leaders of Israel. Moses told Aaron: "Come to the altar and sacrifice your sin offering and your burnt offering and make atonement for yourself and the people, as the Lord has commanded" (Lev 9:1-).

Aaron came to the altar and killed a bull calf as a sin offering for himself. Then he killed a ram for the whole-burnt-offering. His sons handed him the blood, and he splashed it against each side of the altar. They handed him the whole-burnt-offering piece by piece and he burned them on the altar (Lev 9:8-11).

He brought the whole-burnt-offering and offered it in the prescribed way. He also brought the grain offering, took a handful of it and burned it on the altar in addition to the morning's burnt offering (Lev 9:12-14).

Next, Aaron presented the offering that was for the people's sin offering. He took the goat, killed it and offered it for a sin offering just as he did with the first one (Lev 9:15-17).

He killed the ox and the ram as the fellowship offering for the people (Lev 9:18-21).

Then Aaron lifted his hands toward the people and blessed them. Aaron had finished offering the sin offering, the whole-burnt-offering and the fellowship offering. Then he stepped down from the altar.

Moses and Aaron then went into the tabernacle. When they came out, they blessed the people. The glory of the Lord appeared to all the people. Fire came out from the Lord. It burned up the burnt offering and the fat on the altar. When people saw this, they shouted for joy and fell face down (Lev 9:22-24).

Aaron's sons, Nadab and Abihu, offered unauthorized fire before the Lord. The only coals that could be used to keep the altar of incense perpetually burning were those taken from the altar of sacrifice. They took their pans for burning incense, put fire in them from a source other than the altar of sacrifice, and added incense. Fire blazed out from the Lord, burned them, and they died. Moses told Aaron: "This is what the Lord meant when he said: `To the one who comes near me, I will show myself holy; in the sight of all the people I will be honored.'"

Aaron remained silent.

Moses summoned two of Aaron's cousins and told them: "Carry your dead cousins outside the camp, away from the Holy Place." So they carried them, still in their priestly garments outside the camp, as Moses ordered.

Then Moses said to Aaron and his other two sons: "No mourning rituals for you. Do not let your hair become unkempt, do not tear your clothes, or you will also die and the Lord will be angry with all the people. But your relatives, all the house of Israel, in fact, may mourn for those the Lord destroyed by fire. Do not leave the entrance to the tabernacle lest you die, because the Lord's anointing oil is on you." So they obeyed Moses (Lev 10:1-8).

The Lord instructed Aaron: "You and your sons must not drink wine or other fermented drink whenever you go into the tabernacle, or you will die. This rule will continue from now on. Distinguish between the holy and the common, between the unclean and the clean. You must teach the Israelites all the laws the Lord gave to Moses (Lev 10:9-11).

LIFE-LESSONS DISCOVERED IN THE STORY

1. God expects the people he liberates to obey him. God liberated the Israelites from slavery, and he commanded them to obey him (Ex 19:3-8).

2. A person can only arrive in God's presence by accepting God's plan (Ex 25 - 31). God instructed Moses to guide the Israelites to built a tabernacle where he would inhabit with them, where they would bring their sacrifices and where they would worship him (Ex 25:1-8). Everything in the tabernacle should be built exactly as the Lord commanded Moses (Ex 25:9).

3. Worship that takes a person into God's presence must follow God's plan down to the smallest detail. The tabernacle had to be made exactly according to the model that God showed Moses (Ex 25:9). During the Old Testament, the sinner who came to God, according to God's plan, was forgiven and freed from judgment of his sins. The New Testament reveals that a person can only come to God through Jesus, who shed his blood on the cross (Jn 14:6; Ac 4:12).

4. The sinner is separated from God because of his sin. The Tabernacle had a thick curtain dividing the two rooms to remind the Israelites that they were separate from God due to their sin (Ex 26:31-33). (See Is 59:2.) The day Jesus was sacrificed for our sins, this veil was torn from top to bottom (Mt 27:51). After Jesus' death, entrance into complete fellowship with God is only possible through the person of Christ (Hb 10:19-22).

5. The spiritual leader who seeks to please his followers instead of pleasing God, becomes guilty of these things: he is unfaithful to God, those who are his responsibility get out of control, his followers are without God's orientation, and he makes it easy for them to sin. Aaron accepted the people's request and made the golden calf; he allowed them to get out of control and to commit a horrible sin (Ex 32:1-6, 21-25).

6. When God's people feel insecure, they are in danger of returning to practices they followed before they knew God. The Israelites learned the habit of idolatry in Egypt, and a few days without hearing Moses' voice was reason for them to sink back into idolatry (Ex 32:1-5).

7. The majority decision may be the wrong decision. The majority of the Israelites were wrong when they wanted a golden calf to worship (Ex 32:1-2).

8. People who are in the act of disobeying God try to figure God into their wicked actions. God commanded the Israelites not to make idols nor to bow down to them nor worship them (20:4-6). However, when Aaron made a golden calf idol, he announced: "Tomorrow is a feast day to honor the Lord" (32:5).

9. The sinner usually excuses himself for his wrongdoing by shifting the blame to someone else. After Aaron made the golden calf, he blamed the people (Ex 32:22-24). Beginning with Adam, the sinner seeks to make excuses and blame another for his sin (Gn 3:12).

10. Others may pressure a person to do wrong, but the responsibility for sin is individual. The Israelites pressured Aaron to make the golden calf. However, Aaron made it, and Moses wanted to know why he caused the people to do such a horrible sin (Ex 32:21).

11. The person who obeys God has the ability to intervene in prayer on the behalf of others. Because Moses prayed, the Lord decided not to bring the threatened disaster on the Israelites (Ex 32:7-14).

12. The person who loves God, becomes angry at the same things that make God angry. God was angry at the Israelites for making the golden calf (Ex 32:7-10). When Moses saw the calf; his anger flared and he destroyed it (Ex 32:19-20).

13. Others will be more aware that an individual glows with the presence of God than the person who is glowing. When Moses came down from Mount Sinai, he was unaware that his face glowed, yet others saw his glow (Ex 34:29-36).

14. Intimacy with God often intimidates others. Aaron and the Israelites were intimidated by Moses when his face was radiant (Ex 34:29-30).

15. God gives his people the opportunity of giving Freewill Offerings. The motivation for a freewill offering is the simple joy of giving. Moses told the Israelites: "The Lord has commanded you to take an offering. Everyone who is willing is to bring to the Lord an offering....Everyone who was willing brought an offering to the Lord for the work on the tabernacle" (Ex 35:4-29).

16. A person who is filled with and controlled by the Holy Spirit is capable of doing the Lord's work. God chose Bezalel to do the art work for the Tabernacle. The Lord gave him: the gift of the Holy Spirit, skill, ability, knowledge to do artistic work and the ability to teach others (35:30-35). The Holy Spirit inhabited, guided and controlled Bezalel; enabling him to do the art work on the tabernacle and its furnishings, exactly like God had commanded.

17. God works through people who submit both to divine authority and earthly authority. Bezaleel followed God's instructions and submitted

himself to work under Moses' authority (36:1-7).

18. The tabernacle is the symbol of God's dwelling with his people (Ex 25:8; 1 Kn 8:27). This idea reaches its completion in the incarnation of the Word ("The Word became flesh, and dwelt (Greek "tabernacled") among us" (Jn 1:14). (See 2 Cor 6:16.)

19. The Epistle to the Hebrews teaches that the tabernacle represents the earthly and heavenly spheres of Christ's activity. The tabernacle was but a shadow of the eternal substance, an indication of the true ideal (Hb 8:5; 10:1). Jesus serves in a tabernacle made by God, not by men (Hb 8:2). Jesus is the high priest of the perfect tabernacle (Hb 9:11). Christ did not enter into the Holy of Holies made by men. The man-made one is a copy of the real one. Jesus went into heaven itself where he appears before the face of God for us (Hb 9:24).

20. Each part of the tabernacle referred to the person of Jesus. The tabernacle had to be just like God ordered for each part to teach something about Jesus, his birth, his life, his death, his resurrection and his return to the Father in heaven. The ark of the covenant with its mercy-seat symbolizes that God makes people right with himself through their being made free from sin through Jesus Christ. (See Rm 3:24-25.) The twelve cakes of shew-bread symbolize the twelve tribes of Israel. The cakes' presentation is an act of gratitude for food that supports life, and, symbolically, a dedication of the life thus supported. The candlestick symbolizes the calling of Israel to be a people of light. (See Mt 5:14-16.) The rising incense symbolizes the act of prayer. (See Rv 5:8; 8:3.)

21. God establishes only one way by which people may enter into his presence. There was only one door to the tabernacle 26:36; 36:37).

22. The sacrificial system God required of the Israelites had two obvious functions: there must be payment for sin, and God establishes the payment plan.

23. Spiritual leaders have a special responsibility to obey God in every detail. God is not satisfied if they simply get close to obeying him. Aaron and his sons did everything the Lord commanded through Moses (Lev 8:1-36).

24. Spiritual leaders who disobey God will receive divine judgment and punishment. Nadab and Abihu offered unauthorized fire before the Lord. They abused their office as priests, and God destroyed them with a blast of fire (Lev 10:2).

25. Spiritual leaders who lead others to worship, must exemplify God's holiness through obedience. Aaron's sons, Nadab and Abihu, offered unauthorized fire before the Lord. God killed them with fire (Lev 10:1-2). More is required of the person who has been entrusted with much (Lk 12:48).

26. Alcoholic drink results in disastrous consequences for spiritual leaders. God killed two of Aaron's sons for offering unauthorized fire (Lev 10:2). He instructed Aaron that he and his other sons were not to drink wine or other fermented drink whenever they went into the tabernacle (Lev 10:9). This implies that the two were drunk when they offered unauthorized fire. The Bible shows destructive results of alcoholic drink. Noah lost his composure and exposed himself (Gn 9:20-22); Lot lost consciousness and committed incest (Gn 19:32-35); Amnom died victim of alcoholic influence; while drunk, he could not resist when attacked (2 Sm 13:28-29); King Belshazzar lost his sobriety, his kingdom and his life (Dan 5:1-30).

QUESTIONS

1. When Moses returned to the mountain and remained 40 days, what did the Israelites do?
2. What happens when a spiritual leader follows Aaron's example and does whatever his followers desire?
3. What was Moses' reaction when the Lord threatened to no longer go with the Israelites?
4. Why was Bezalel able to make the tabernacle and all its furnishings?
5. Why did the tabernacle and all its furnishings need to be made exactly as God commanded?
6. Does God still require that worship be done exactly as he commands and that spiritual leaders do exactly as he commands?
7. What happened the first time Moses set up the tabernacle?
8. How were Aaron and his sons consecrated?
9. Why were two of Aaron's sons, Nadab and Abihu, consumed by fire?
10. With whom do you most identify:
    ■ Moses – You are struggling to lead people to do everything God commands?
    ■ Aaron – God has given you responsibility to lead, yet you are a people pleaser?
    ■ Bezalel – You are best able to serve God by working with your hands?
    ■ One of the Israelites – You profess to love and obey the Lord, yet every time a problem appears, you give no evidence of knowing the Lord?

OFFERINGS

OFFERING	OCCASION OR MOTIVE	SIGNIFICANT
Voluntary Offerings		
Burnt Offering (Lev 1:1-17; 6:8-13) Could be a young bull, goat, lamb, pigeon or turtle dove; but it must be a perfect specimen. The entire animal was burned on the altar.	Was offered in the evening and morning, as well as on the Sabbath, at annual feast, and on other special days. To make atonement for sin and/or a demonstration of dedication.	Points toward Christ on the cross. Christ gave himself without defect to God (Hb 9:14; Ph 2:6-8).
Grain Offering (Lev 2:1-16; 6:14-23) Offered from the harvest of the land and was composed of fine flour combined with oil, frankincense and salt. Could not contain yeast. A portion of offering was burned on the altar; the remainder was given to the priest.	Gratitude for the beginning of harvest.	A promise to obey God.
Fellowship Offering (Lev 3:1-17; 7:11-34; 22:18-30) The instructions for this offering were similar to that of the burnt offering; however, only certain parts of the internal organs were burned. Priests received the breast and right thigh, and the giver received a quantity of meat for a celebration meal.	Fellowship: 1. Expression of thankfulness because of an unexpected blessing (7:12-15). 2. The result of a vow (7:16). 3. Freewill offering to express thankfulness (7:16).	▪The one making the offering is dedicated to God and is at peace with him. ▪The blood of Christ shed on the cross brings peace to people (Cl 1:20) and is celebrated when we participate in the Lord's Supper (1 Cor 10:16). ▪Jesus is our peace (Eph 2:14).
Required Offerings		
Sin Offering (Lev 4:1 - 5:13) Four classifications of sinners: 1. Priest (4:3); 2. The community (4:13); 3. Leader (4:22); 4. A member of the community (4:27).	Basically, this offering applies to a situation when a guilty person needs to be cleansed from his sin (5:1-4). Offering required for: ▪Priest or the community: a young bull. ▪Leader: male goat. ▪Individual: female goat. ▪Poor person: 2 doves or 2 pigeons.	▪Christ, who had no sin, became sin for us, so that in him we might become the righteousness of God (2 Cor 5:21). ▪God presented Jesus Christ as a sacrifice of atonement. He bore our sins on the cross (Is 53:6, 7; 1 Pt. 2:24; Rm. 3:25-26).
Guilt Offering (5:14 - 6:7; 7:1-10) ▪A sin that results in lost to another person requires restitution (5:16; 6:5). Beyond bringing an offering to God, it was necessary to make restitution, plus pay 20 % interest to the person who suffered loss (6:5).	Applies to a situation when a person disrespected something holy or whose sin brought losses to another person. The sacrifice was accompanied by some kind of repayment or restitution offered to the one who was offended.	▪One who is responsible for another's losses should make restitution, producing fruit worthy of repentance (Mt 3:8). ▪A person should seek reconciliation with the person who has something against him (Mt 5:24). ▪God was reconciling the world to himself in Christ (2 Cor 5:19). ▪God credits righteousness to the believer in Jesus Christ (1 Cor 1:30; Rm 4:3).

PURE AND IMPURE FOOD

ANIMALS	PURE	IMPURE
Mammals	Two qualifications: 1. Split hoof; 2. Chews the cud (Lev 11:3-7 & Deut 14:6-8).	Those that only chew the cud or only have a split hoof (11:4) and any that do not qualify as pure.
Birds	Those that were not mentioned as prohibited (Lev 11:13-19).	Those that attack animals and those that eat dead animals (Lev 11:13-19 & Deut 14:11-20).
Reptiles	None	All (Lev 11:29-30).
Animals that live in the water (fish)	Two qualifications: have fins and scales (Lev 11:9-12 & Deut 14:9-10).	Any that do not have both fins and scales.
Insects	Those in the locust, cricket and grasshopper families (Lev 11:20-23).	Those that have wings and walk on all four feet (Lev 11:20).

Basic reasons:
1. Hygiene: many of the forbidden animals were carriers of diseases;
2. Religious: some of the animals considered impure were associated with pagan religions.

HOLY DAYS
Leviticus 23-25

HOLY DAYS	TEXTS	MONTH/DAY of Jewish Calendar
Sabbath	Lev 23:3; Ex 20:8-11; Dt 5:12-15	7th day of each week
Passover: Remembers when the Death Angel passed over the Israelites' homes in Egypt.	Ex 12; Lev 23:5; Nm 28:16; Dt 16:1-2	Twilight of 1/14
Unleavened Bread	Lev 23:6-8; Ex 23:15; Nm 28:17-25; Dt 16:3-8	1/15-21
First-fruits: Harvest Feast	Lev 23:9-14; Ex 23:16; Nm 28:26-31	
Pentecost: Feast of Weeks	Lev 23:15-22; Ex 34:22; Dt 16:9-12	3/6
Feast of Trumpets	Lev 23:23-25; Nm 29:1-6	7/1
Day of Atonement: Present sin offering for priest and the nation	Lev 16:29-34; 23:26-32; Nm 29:7-11	7/10
Feast of Tabernacles: Remembers Israel's wandering in the wilderness.	Lev 23:33-44; Nm 29:12-40; Dt 16:13-15	7/15-21
Sabbath Year	Lev 25:1-7; Ex 23:10-11	Every 7th year
Year of Jubilee	Lev 25:8-55	Every 50th year

FAILURES RECORDED IN NUMBERS

TEXT	WHO	FAILURE	DISCIPLINE	EXPRESSION OF DIVINE MERCY	OBSERVATION
11:1-9, 18-30	The People	1st Complaining: ▪Complained about hardships and manna.	Fire from the Lord (11:1); ate until vomited (11:20); plague (11:33).	God sent them quail, but punished the complainers.	God satisfied their physical appetite, but spiritually they were starving. God shows love, but exercises justice.
11:10-17	Moses	2nd Complaining: ▪Moses felt that his burden was too heavy.		Seventy men who were leaders received God's Spirit. They were to help Moses carry the burden of the people.	Complaining people become a heavy burden for their leader. The leader's strength comes from God, not from the people's emotional instability.
12:1-16	Miriam and Aaron	3rd Complaining: ▪They talked against Moses because of his wife.	Miriam had leprosy for 7 days.	God defended his own honor and that of his servant.	▪Silence is often the best answer to false accusations. ▪A leader who rebels holds back progress.
13	10 spies	▪They gave a bad report that expressed unbelief in God (13:28-33).	Died in a plague (14:37).	The surviving Israelites would wander in the wilderness for 40 years. Then they would have another opportunity to conquer the land.	Ten spies saw the giants, forgot God and were afraid. Two saw the giants, remembered God and were courageous.
14	The people	4th Complaining: ▪They complained against Moses and Aaron and rebelled against God (14:1-10). ▪They had unbelieving hearts (Hb 3:7-19).	▪Wandering in the wilderness; ▪Dying in the wilderness (14:28-34).	God delayed granting his blessings, but did not abandon his plan to give them the promised land.	Lack of faith resulted in prolonged wandering.
16:1-4	Korah, Dathan and Abiram	5th Complaining: ▪Rebelled against Moses (16:1-3). ▪Jealous.	The ground split apart and swallowed them (16:31-33).		Those who rebel against God-established leaders, rebel against God himself.
16:41-50	The people	6th Complaining: ▪Grumbled against Moses and Aaron.	Plague and death of 14,700.	The intervention of Moses and Aaron prevented total destruction of the complaining people.	God is impatient with his people when they complain and grumble.
20:2-6	The people	7th Complaining: ▪Complained about the food and because there was no water.		God told Moses how to obtain water.	Complainers who lack faith and don't show respect, provoke their leaders.
20:2-13	Moses	He struck the rock twice when God's command was to speak to it.	Moses and Aaron could not enter the promised land.	Even though Moses disobeyed God, water came from the rock.	Even though the people provoked Moses to anger, he was responsible for his own sin.
21:5-9	The people	8th Complaining: ▪Grew impatient and complained against God and Moses.	Poisonous snakes killed many.	The Bronze Snake symbolizes Jesus (Jn 3:14-15).	▪A long-lasting problem tests people's patience. ▪A complaining people may test God's patience.
22 - 25	Balaam	▪Balaam was a mercenary who rushed to make a profit with his spiritual gifts (Jd 11). ▪Balaam told Balak how to corrupt Israel with idolatry and immorality (Num 31:16).	Balaam was killed while with God's enemies (31:8).	An angel blocked Balaam's pathway to hinder Balaam's evil intentions (22:21-35).	▪A mercenary spiritual leader facilitates the corruption of God's people. ▪God prevents a curse being placed on his people; however, they can be corrupted.
25	The people	Israelite men indulged in sexual immorality and idolatry (25:1-3).	▪Sinners killed by hanging. ▪24,000 died in plague (25:4-9).	The zeal of Phinehas caused God to withdraw the plague (25:6-9).	▪Wicked counsel results in tragedy. ▪Prostitution and idolatry are linked together.

Old Testament Bible Stories © Jackson Day

COMPLAINING AND REBELLING
Numbers 11 - 33; Deuteronomy

STRUCTURE

Context:

The Lord liberated the Israelites from slavery in Egypt. After leaving Egypt, they crossed the Red Sea. They traveled through a desert where God guided them and provided them with water and food, and protected them.

At Mount Sinai, the Lord gave Moses the Ten Commandments and other laws. God promised rewards if they obeyed him and punishment if they disobeyed. Moses gave the Israelites all of God's laws and regulations, and they answered in unison: "Everything the Lord said, we will do."

The Lord told Moses to come up to him on the mountain. Moses delayed on the mountain, and the Israelites asked Aaron to make them gods. Aaron shaped an idol in the form of a calf. The people called it their god. Moses came down from the mountain, saw the calf and destroyed it.

Moses went back up the mountain and prayed, pleading with God to forgive the Israelites.

The Israelites brought offerings to make the Tabernacle. The Lord chose Bezalel to make the Tabernacle and all its furnishings. The Tabernacle was constructed as God's dwelling place among the people. Aaron and his sons were consecrated priests.

Key-person: Moses

Key-location: The wilderness

Key-repetitions:
- People complained, then God usually disciplined: Israelites complained about hardship and manna. Fire and a plague came from God (11:1-9, 18-30); Moses felt his burden was too heavy (11:10-17); Miriam and Aaron complained against Moses because of his wife. Miriam had leprosy for 7 days (11:10-17); Ten spies complained about giants in the promised land. They died in a plague (13:28-33; 14:37); the Israelites believed the 10 spies and complained against Moses, Aaron and God. They wandered in the wilderness for 40 years (14:1-34); Korah, Dathan and Abiram complained against Moses. The ground split apart and swallowed them (16:1-33); Israelites complained because there was no water (20:2-6); Israelites grew impatient and complained against God and Moses. Snakes killed many (21:5-9).
- Revolted against God: God declared the Israelites would wander in the wilderness for 40 years. A group went up toward the hill to conquer the promised land (14:39-45); Korah, Dathan and Abiram got a group of 250 leaders to rebel against Moses (16:1-33); Moses struck the rock twice when God's command was to speak to it (20:2-13); Balaam disobeyed God when he went to Balak (22:21-35) and when he told the king how he could get the Israelites to sin (Nu 31:16); Israelites practiced sexual sins and idolatry (25:1-9).
- Face-down on the ground: Moses and Aaron fell face-down before the Lord (14:5; 16:4, 22, 45; 20:6); Balaam fell face-down before the Angel of the Lord (22:31).

Key-attitudes:
- The constant complaining on the part of the Israelites.
- The frustration Moses felt when criticized.
- The 10 spies' unbelief and their fear of the giants.
- Caleb and Joshua's belief in God and their courage to confront an angry multitude.
- God's anger because of the constant complaining and attacks on Moses and Aaron.
- The Israelites' impatience with the long journey filled with constant hardships.
- Balaam's ambition and greed for financial gain.
- The Israelite men desired to have sex with the Moabite women.
Phinehas was zealous in protecting God's honor.
- Moses feared the tribes of Reuben and Gad would discourage the Israelites when they desired to remain on the east side of the Jordan River.

Initial-problem:

The Israelites complained about their hardships.

Sequence of events:

Complaining and Revolting Against God
- The Israelites complained. The Lord burned the outer boundaries of the camp (11:1-3).
- Troublemakers craved other food and the Israelites complained about the manna (11:4-9).
- Moses complained that his burden was heavy. The Lord told Moses to select 70 leaders to help him carry the burden (11:10-17).
- The Lord promised meat. Moses questioned God and the Lord replied that Moses would see that God can do what he promises (11:16-23).
- Moses selected the 70 men. They prophesied (11:24-30).
- God sent quail in from the sea. He also struck those who craved other food with a plague (11:31-34).
- Miriam and Aaron criticized Moses because of his wife. The Lord gave Miriam leprosy for 7 days (12:1-16).

The Spies Report; The People Revolt
- Moses sent 12 men to spy out the promised land (13:1-3, 17-21, 25).
- The spies stated that the land was good, but the people were strong and the cities were fortified (13:16-29).
- Caleb said they could possess the land. But 10 spies gave a bad report about giants in the land (13:30-31).
- That night all the Israelites complained. They

Old Testament Bible Stories © Jackson Day

wanted to return to Egypt. Joshua and Caleb argued that the Lord was with them (14:1-10).
■The Lord threatened to destroy the Israelites. Moses said the Egyptians would accuse God of killing them because he was unable to take them to the promised land. Moses pleaded for forgiveness (14:10-19).
■The Lord said the Israelites would wander in the wilderness for 40 years until all who were over 20 years of age died. The 10 spies who gave a bad report died. Joshua and Caleb survived (14:20-38).

More Complaining and More Revolting
■A group set out toward the hill country and were defeated (14:39-45).
■Korah, Dathan, Abiram and On rebelled against Moses and gathered 250 others to confront Moses and Aaron(16:1-7).
■The earth opened up and swallowed everyone connected with Korah, and the Lord cremated the 250 men who had joined the rebellion (16:12-35).
■The Israelites accused Moses and Aaron of killing the Lord's people. The Lord sent a plague. Aaron made atonement for the people. The plague stopped, but 14,700 died (16:41-46).
■Moses put 12 staffs in the Tabernacle, one from each tribe. Aaron's staff sprouted and produced almonds (17:1-13).
■At the Desert of Zin, Miriam died and was buried (20:1).
■The people opposed Moses and Aaron because there was no water. The Lord told Moses to speak to a rock, but Moses hit it twice. Therefore, Moses and Aaron were unable to lead the Israelites into the promised land (20:2-13).
■Aaron died on top of the Mountain Hor (20:22-28).
■The Israelites grew impatient and criticized God and Moses. The Lord sent snakes. Many Israelites died. At the Lord's command, Moses made a bronze snake and put it up on a pole (21:4-9).

Balaam the Mercenary
■The people of Moab were terrified of the Israelites. Balak summoned Balaam to come and curse the Israelites. God told Balaam not to go. Balak sent other messengers. Balaam started back with them. Three times an angel blocked the way for Balaam's donkey. God gave the donkey speech. Balaam refused to curse the Israelites, because God was with them (22-24); however, he told Balak how to cause the Israelites to sin (31:16).
■The Israelite men began sinning sexually with Moabite women and worshiping the Baal of Peor.
■The Lord told Moses to hang those guilty of idolatry. An Israelite man brought a Midianite woman into his family tent. Phinehas drove a spear through both of their bodies. That stopped a plague that killed 24,000. Phinehas and his descendants would always be priests (25:1-15).
■The Lord told Moses to pay back the Midianites. Moses sent twelve thousand men into battle. They killed every Midianite man and the prophet Balaam (31:1-12).
■Moses was furious with the army officers who allowed the women to live. Only virgins were allowed to live (31:13-18).

The Tribes Who Chose to Stay on the East of Jordan
■The families of Reuben and Gad had herds and desired the conquered land east of the Jordan River. Moses accused them of discouraging the Israelites. The families of Reuben and Gad agreed that the men would cross the Jordan with the other Israelites and would not return to their homes until every Israelite had received his inheritance (32:1-16).

Moses' Last Instructions to the Israelites
■Moses told the Israelites that they were to cross the Jordan into Canaan, drive out all the inhabitants and destroy their idols. They were to distribute the land according to family groups. He warned that if they did not drive out the inhabitants of the land, then God would punish them (33:50-56).
■By the side of the Jordan River, Moses made the speeches that are found in the book of Deuteronomy:
  ●"Be careful to do exactly as the Lord your God has commanded you...." (Dt 5:28-33).
  ●"....Love the Lord your God with all your heart, with all your soul and with all your strength...." (Dt 6:4-9).
  ●".... when you eat and are satisfied, be careful that you do not forget the Lord, who brought you out of Egypt, out of the land of slavery" (Dt 6:10-12).
  ●"Today, the Lord your God commands you to follow his decrees and laws. Be careful to observe them with all your heart ...." (Dt 26:16-19).
  ●The Lord God says: "... I have placed in front of you... death and destruction. I command you today to love the Lord your God, to walk in his ways... then you will live and grow in number.... if ... you are not obedient... you will be destroyed.... I place before you life and death, blessings and curses. Now choose life!...." (Dt 30:15-20).

Final-situation:
Moses gave his last instructions to the Israelites, preparing them to enter the land the Lord promised them.

BIBLE STORY

Complaining and Revolting Against God

The Israelites complained about their hardships. God heard them, and his anger flared. Fire from the Lord blazed up and burned the outer boundaries of the camp. The people cried out to Moses; Moses prayed to the Lord and the fire died down (11:1-3).

The troublemakers craved other food. The Israelites complained whiningly: "If only we had meat to eat! We remember the fish we ate for free in Egypt; we also had cucumbers, melons, leeks, onions and garlic. Now nothing tastes good here. All we have is manna, manna, manna and more manna!"

The manna was like small white seed and looked like resin. The people gathered it, and then ground it in a handmill or crushed it between stones. They cooked it in a pot or made it into cakes. It tasted like bread baked with olive oil. When the dew settled on the camp each night, so did the manna (11:4-9).

Moses heard every family wailing in front of their tents. The Lord became angry, and Moses got upset. He asked the Lord: "Why have you brought me this trouble? What did I do to deserve this? Why did you make me responsible for this people? Am I their father? Why do you make me carry them in my arms, as a nurse carries an infant, to the land you promised their ancestors? Where can I get meat for all these people? They keep crying to me: 'We want meat to eat!' The burden is too heavy for me to do this by myself. If this is how you are going to treat me, then kill me right now; don't let me face my own downfall."

The Lord told Moses: "Gather seventy of Israel's leaders and take them to the Tabernacle. I will come meet with you there, and I will take some of the Spirit that is on you and place it on them. They will help you carry the burden so you won't have to carry it alone" (11:10-17).

The Lord instructed Moses to tell the people: "Make yourselves holy. Get ready for tomorrow, when you will eat meat. The Lord heard your crying: 'We want meat! We were better off in Egypt!' The Lord will give you meat, and you will eat it. You will eat it for a whole month, until it comes out of your nostrils and you hate it. This is because you rejected the Lord and cried out: 'Why did we ever leave Egypt?'"

Moses answered: "I am surrounded by six hundred thousand men, and you say, 'I will give them meat to eat for a whole month!' Where is it coming from?"

The Lord replied: "Do you think I am weak? You will now see if I can do what I promise."

Moses went out and told the people what the Lord said. He brought together seventy of their leaders and had them stand around the Tabernacle. The Lord came down in the cloud and took some of the Spirit that was on Moses and put it on the seventy leaders. The Spirit rested on them; they prophesied, but their prophesying was a one time event. Then Moses and the leaders of Israel returned to the camp (11:16-30).

God set in motion a wind that drove quail in from the sea. They piled up three feet deep in the camp and as far out as a day's walk in every direction. For two days the people gathered quail. No one gathered less than sixty bushels. They spread them out all around the camp. But while the meat was still in their mouth, before they could swallow it, God's anger blazed out, and he struck them with a terrible plague. There they buried the people who had craved other food (11:31-34).

Miriam and Aaron began to talk against Moses because of his Cushite wife. He had married a Cushite black woman. They asked: "Has the Lord spoken only through Moses? Hasn't he also spoken through us?" The Lord overheard their complaining.

Moses was a very humble man, more humble than anyone else living on the earth.

The Lord suddenly spoke to Moses, Aaron and Miriam: "Come out to the Tabernacle, all three of you." They came out. The Lord came down in a pillar of cloud and stood at the entrance to the Tabernacle. He summoned Aaron and Miriam. When both of them stepped forward, he said: "Listen to what I am telling you. When a prophet of the Lord is among you, I make myself known to him in visions, I speak to him in dreams. But I don't do it that way with my servant Moses; I trust him to lead my people. I speak face to face to him, clearly and not in riddles. He has seen the form of the Lord. You should be afraid to speak against my servant Moses!"

The Lord's anger blazed out against them. The cloud lifted and Miriam had turned leprous, her skin was like snow. Aaron saw that she had leprosy, and he said to Moses: "Please, my master, do not let her be like a stillborn infant coming from its mother's womb without half its flesh!"

Moses cried to the Lord: "O God, please heal her!"

The Lord replied: "If her father had spit in her face, she would have been in disgrace for seven days. Quarantine her outside the camp for seven days." Miriam was quarantined outside the camp for seven days, and the people did not march until she was readmitted.

After that, the people relocated and encamped in the Desert of Paran (12:1-16).

The Spies Report; The People Revolt

The Lord told Moses: "Send men to explore the land of Canaan, which I will give to the Israelites. Send one leader from each ancestral tribe."

Moses obeyed and sent twelve spies out. Moses told them: "Go up through the hill country. See what the land is like. Check out the people: are they strong or weak, few or many? What kind of land do they live in? Is it good or bad? What kind of towns do they live in? Are they unwalled or fortified? How is the soil? Is it fertile or poor? Are there trees on it or not? Do your best to bring back some of the fruit of the land." It was the season for the first ripe grapes.

While exploring the land, they cut off a branch bearing a single cluster of grapes. It took two men to carry it on a pole between them. They also picked some pomegranates and figs. After forty days of scouting out the land, they returned to the camp (13:1-3, 17-21, 25).

They presented themselves to Moses and Aaron and the whole Israelite community. They gave the story of their trip: "We went into the land to which you sent us. It does flow with milk and honey! Just look at this fruit. But the people who live there are strong. Their cities are fortified and huge (13:16-29).

Caleb interrupted, called for silence and said: "Let's go up and take possession of the land. We can certainly do it."

But ten of the spies argued: "We can't attack those people; they are stronger than we are." And they gave the Israelites a bad report about the land. They said: "The land would devour us! All the people we saw there are giants. Beside them, we felt like grasshoppers, and we looked like grasshoppers to them" (13:30-31).

That night all the Israelites complained against Moses and Aaron. The whole assembly grumbled: "Why didn't we die in Egypt? Or in this desert? Why did the Lord bring us to this land only to be killed by the sword? Our wives and children will become plunder. We would be better off returning to Egypt!" And they said to each other: "Let's choose a leader and go back to Egypt."

Moses and Aaron fell face-down in front of the whole Israelite assembly. Joshua and Caleb, members of the spy group, tore their clothes and said to the entire Israelite assembly: "The land we walked through and explored is exceedingly good. If the Lord is pleased with us, he will lead us into that land, and he will give us the land; a land flowing with milk and honey. Only do not rebel against the Lord. Don't be afraid of those people. We will swallow them up. Their protection is gone. The Lord is on our side. Do not be afraid of them!"

But the entire assembly talked about stoning those two (14:1-10).

The glory of the Lord appeared at the Tabernacle. The Lord spoke to Moses: "How long will these people treat me with contempt? How long will it be before they believe me, in spite of all the miraculous signs I have performed among them? I will strike them with a plague and destroy them, but I will make you into a nation greater and stronger than they ever were."

Moses replied to the Lord: "The Egyptians will hear about it! The Egyptians will tell everyone: `The Lord was not able to bring these people into the land he promised them; so he killed them in the desert.' Now show your strength. Do what you said when you declared earlier: `The Lord is slow to anger. The Lord has great love. The Lord forgives sin and rebellion. Yet he does not leave the guilty unpunished. When parents sin, he will also punish their children, grandchildren, great-grandchildren and great-great-grandchildren.' Show your great love, forgive the sin of these people, just as you have pardoned them from the time they left Egypt until now" (14:10-19).

The Lord replied: "I have forgiven them, as you asked. Nevertheless, I make this promise to those men who saw my glory and the miracles I performed in Egypt and in the desert, but who disobeyed me and tested me ten times: not one of them will ever see the land I promised to their forefathers. No one who has treated me with contempt will ever see it. But my servant Caleb has a different spirit and follows me completely; I will bring him into the land he walked through, and his descendants will inherit it. Turn back tomorrow and set out toward the desert along the route to the Red Sea."

The Lord commanded Moses and Aaron to tell the grumbling Israelites: "The Lord is going to treat you the way you said he would. Every one of you, twenty years old or more, every one of you whiners and grumblers; your corpses are going to litter the wilderness. Not one of you will enter the land and make your home there, except Caleb and Joshua. Your children that you said would be taken as plunder, I will bring them in to enjoy the land you rejected. But your corpses will rot in this desert. Your children will live as shepherds in the wilderness for forty years, suffering for your unfaithfulness, until the last of your corpses lies in the desert. For forty years, one year for each of the forty days you explored the land, you will suffer for your sins and know what it is like to have me against you. I, the Lord, have spoken."

The men who spied out the land and returned to give a bad report which caused the whole community to grumble were struck down and died of a plague. Of the twelve men who scouted the land, only Joshua and Caleb survived (14:20-38).

More Complaining and More Revolting
Moses reported the Lord's words to the Israelites. They mourned bitterly. Early the next morning they started out toward the high hill country. They said: "We have sinned; we will go up to the place the Lord promised."

But Moses told them: "Why are you disobeying the Lord's command? This will not succeed! Do not go up. The Lord is not with you. You will be killed by your enemies."

Nevertheless, in their presumption they went up toward the high hill country. Neither Moses nor the Ark of the Lord moved from the camp. The Amalekites and Canaanites who lived in the hill country came out of the hills, attacked them and beat them (14:39-45).

Korah, Dathan, Abiram and On rebelled against Moses. These four men gathered 250 other Israelite men who were prominent community leaders. They came as a group to confront Moses and Aaron and said to them: "You have gone too far! All the people are holy, every one of them, and the Lord is with them. Why then do you put yourselves above everyone else in the Lord's assembly?"

When Moses heard this, he fell face-down on the ground. Then he told Korah and his followers: "Tomorrow morning the Lord will show who belongs to him and who is holy. Get some pans for burning incense, and put fire and incense in them before the Lord. Then the Lord will decide who is holy. You Levites have gone too far!" (16:1-7).

Moses summoned Dathan and Abiram. But they said: "We will not come! You brought us up out of a land flowing with milk and honey to kill us in the desert. Now you also want to lord it over us. Fact is, you haven't produced. You haven't taken us to a land flowing with milk and honey. You haven't given us the promised inheritance of fields and vineyards. No, we will not come!"

Moses became very angry. He said to the Lord: "Don't accept their offering."

Moses said to Korah: "You and all your followers are to appear before the Lord tomorrow. Also Aaron will appear. Each man is to take his censer pan and put incense in it. You and Aaron are to present your censers also." So each man took his censer, put fire and incense in it, and stood with Moses and Aaron at the entrance to the Tabernacle. Korah gathered all his followers who were against Aaron and Moses at the entrance to the Tabernacle. Then the glory of the Lord appeared to the entire assembly. The Lord said to Moses and Aaron: "Separate yourselves from this assembly so I can put an end to them at once."

But Moses and Aaron fell face-down and cried out: "O God, God of everything living, will you be angry with the entire assembly when only one man sins?"

The Lord replied to Moses: "Tell the assembly to move away from the tents of Korah, Dathan and Abiram."

Moses warned the assembly: "Move back from the tents of these wicked men!" So they moved away from the tents of Korah, Dathan and Abiram.

Then Moses said: "This is how you will know that the Lord sent me to do all these things and that it was not my idea: If these men die a natural death like most men, you will know the Lord did not send me. But if the Lord does something totally new, and the earth opens up and swallows them, with everything that belongs to them, and they go down alive into the grave; then you will know that these men have insulted the Lord."

When Moses finished speaking, the ground split open. The earth opened up and swallowed everyone connected with Korah and everything they owned. At their cries, all the Israelites around them fled, shouting: "The earth is going to swallow us too!"

And the Lord sent fire that cremated the 250 men who were offering the incense (16:12-35).

The next day the Israelite community complained against Moses and Aaron: "You have killed the Lord's people."

Suddenly the cloud covered the Tabernacle, and the glory of the Lord appeared. The Lord said to Moses: "Get away from this assembly so I can destroy them this very minute." Moses and Aaron threw themselves face-down on the ground.

Moses told Aaron: "Take your censer-pan. Put fire from the altar and incense in it. Hurry to the assembly to make atonement for them. The Lord is angry with them, the plague has started!" Aaron did as Moses directed. He ran into the midst of the assembly. The plague had already started among the people. So Aaron offered the incense and made atonement for them. He stood between the living and the dead, and the plague stopped. But 14,700 people died from the plague. Then Aaron returned to Moses at the entrance to the Tabernacle, for the plague had stopped (16:41-46).

The Lord spoke to Moses: "Get twelve staffs from the Israelites. Get one from the leader of each of their ancestral tribes. Write each man's name on his staff. Put Aaron's name on the staff from the tribe of Levi. Place each staff in the Tabernacle in front of the Testimony. The staff of the man I choose will sprout. I'm going to stop this constant grumbling against you by the Israelites."

The Israelites gave Moses twelve staffs, one for the leader of each of their ancestral tribes, and Aaron's staff was among them. Moses placed the staffs before the Lord in the Tabernacle.

The next day Moses saw that Aaron's staff, which represented the house of Levi, had sprouted. In fact, it had also budded, blossomed and produced almonds. Moses brought out all the staffs for the Israelites to see. They looked at them, and each man took the staff with his name on it.

The Lord told Moses: "Put back Aaron's staff in front of the Testimony, to be kept as a sign to rebels. This will put an end to their grumbling against me, and save their lives." Moses carried out the Lord's instruction (17:1-13).

In the first month the whole Israelite community arrived at the Desert of Zin, and they stayed at Kadesh. There Miriam died and was buried (20:1).

There was no water, and the people gathered in opposition against Moses and Aaron. They criticized Moses: "We wish we had died when our brothers fell dead before the Lord! Why did you bring the Lord's community into this desert to die, people and cattle alike? Why did you bring us up out of Egypt to this terrible place? It has no grain no figs, no grapevines no pomegranates, and no water to drink!"

Moses and Aaron went to the entrance to the Tabernacle and threw themselves face-down. They saw the glory of the Lord. The Lord spoke to Moses: "Take the staff, and you and your brother Aaron gather the assembly together. Speak to that rock that is in front of them, and it will pour out water."

Moses and Aaron rounded up the assembly in front of the rock. Moses spoke: "Listen, you rebels! Must we bring you water out of this rock?" Then Moses raised his arm and struck the rock two times with his staff. Water gushed out. The community and their livestock drank.

The Lord spoke to Moses and Aaron: "You did not trust me, you did not honor me as holy in the sight of the Israelites; therefore, you will not bring this community into the land I will give them."

These were the waters of Meribah, where the Israelites quarreled with the Lord and where he showed himself holy among them (20:2-13).

The whole Israelite community came to Mount Hor. The Lord said to Moses and Aaron: "Aaron will not enter the land I give the Israelites, because you both rebelled against my command at the waters of Meribah. Take Aaron and his son Eleazar up Mount Hor. Remove Aaron's priest-clothes and put them on his son Eleazar, for Aaron will die there."

Moses did as the Lord commanded. Aaron died there on top of the mountain. Then Moses and Eleazar came down from the mountain. When the Israelites learned that Aaron had died, they went into thirty days of mourning (20:22-28).

They traveled from Mount Hor along the route to the Red Sea. The people grew impatient on the way; they became irritable and spoke out against God and Moses. They said: "Why did you bring us up out of Egypt to die in the desert? There is no bread! There is no water! We detest this miserable food!"

Then the Lord sent them poisonous snakes. They bit the people, and many Israelites died. The people came to Moses and said: "We sinned when we spoke against the Lord and you. Pray to the Lord; ask him to take the snakes away from us."

Moses prayed for the people.

The Lord told Moses: "Make a snake and put it up on a pole. If anyone who is bitten looks at it, he will live." So Moses made a bronze snake and put it up on a pole. Anyone who was bitten by a snake and looked at the bronze snake lived (21:4-9).

Balaam the Mercenary

The Israelites traveled to the plains of Moab and camped near the Jordan River across from Jericho. The people of Moab were terrified because there were so many Israelites. The Moabites said to their leaders: "This mob is going to take everything around us, like an ox that eats all the grass of the field."

Balak, the king of Moab, sent messengers to summon the prophet Balaam. Balak said: "A people has come out of Egypt; they are all over the place and have settled next to me. Come and curse them for me. They are too powerful for me. Maybe then I will defeat them and drive them out of the country. For I know that those you bless are blessed, and those you curse are cursed."

The messengers took money to pay Balaam. They told him what Balak said. Balaam was a mercenary who rushed to make a profit with his spiritual gifts (Jd 11).

Balaam told them: "Spend the night here, and I will tell you what the Lord tells me."

God came to Balaam and said: "Don't go with them. Don't curse those people, because they are blessed."

The next morning Balaam told Balak's messengers: "Go back home. The Lord refuses to let me go with you."

The Moabite messengers returned to Balak and told him: "Balaam refused to come with us."

Balak sent other nobles, more distinguished than the first with his message: "Don't refuse to come to me, because I will pay you well. Come and curse these people for me."

Balaam answered them: "Even if Balak gave me his palace filled with silver and gold, I couldn't defy the command of the Lord my God. Now stay with me tonight as the others did, and I will find out what the Lord will tell me this time."

That night God came to Balaam and said: "Since these men have come to summon you, go with them, but only do what I tell you."

Balaam got up the next morning, saddled his donkey and went with the noblemen from Moab. But God became angry because Balaam went. The angel of the Lord stood in the road to block his way. Balaam was riding his donkey. The donkey saw the angel blocking the road with a sword in his hand, and she turned off the road into a field. Balaam beat her to force her back onto the road.

Then the angel of the Lord blocked the way again, standing in a narrow path between two vineyards, with walls on both sides. The donkey saw the angel and pressed close to the wall, crushing Balaam's foot against it. So he beat her again.

For the third time, the angel blocked the way. He stood in a narrow passage where there was no room to turn, either to the right or to the left. The donkey saw the angel and lay down under Balaam. Balaam lost his temper and beat the donkey with his staff. Then the Lord gave speech to the donkey; she said to Balaam: "What have I done to you? Why have you beat me these three times?"

Balaam answered the donkey: "You have made a fool of me! If I had a sword, I would kill you right now."

The donkey replied: "Am I not your trusty donkey, which you have ridden, for years up until now? Have I ever done this to you before?

Balaam replied: "No."

Then the Lord let Balaam see the angel. He saw the angel blocking the road with a sword in his hand. Balaam threw himself on the ground, face-down.

The angel of the Lord asked him: "Why have you beaten your donkey these three times? I have come here to block your way because your path is a reckless one before me. The donkey saw me and turned away from me these three times. If she had not turned away, I would have killed you, but I would have spared her."

Balaam said to the angel: "I have sinned. I did not know you were blocking the road. Now if you don't like what I am doing, I will go back."

The angel told Balaam: "Go with the men, but speak only what I tell you." So Balaam went with Balak's noblemen.

Balak came out to meet Balaam and said to him:

"Didn't I send you an urgent summons? Why didn't you come to me? Did you think I not able to reward you?"

Balaam replied: "Well, I am here now, but I can only speak words that God puts in my mouth."

Balak sacrificed cattle and sheep, and gave some to Balaam and the nobles who were with him. The next morning Balak took Balaam up to a high place where he could see some of the Israelites (22:1-41).

Balaam said: "Build me seven altars here, and prepare seven bulls and seven rams for me." Balak obeyed Balaam, and the two of them offered a bull and a ram on each altar.

The Lord put a message in Balaam's mouth for Balak: "Balak brought me from the eastern mountains to curse Jacob and to damn Israel for him. How can I curse those whom God has not cursed? How can I damn those whom the Lord has not damned?"

Balak said to Balaam: "What have you done to me? I brought you here to curse my enemies; all you have done is bless them!"

Balaam answered: "I must only speak words that the Lord puts in my mouth!" Balaam continued to utter one blessing after another for the Israelites. He refused to curse those God blessed (23:1 - 24:25). He told Balak that the Israelites could not be cursed, because God was with them; however, Balaam told him how to corrupt them with idiolatry and immorality (31:16). Balaam taught Balak how to cause the Israelites to sin by eating food offered to idols and by taking part in sexual sin (Rev 2:14).

While Israel was camped at Shittim, the men began sinning sexually with Moabite women. The women invited them to their sacrifices to their gods, and they engaged in sex as a part of their worship. So Israel joined in worshiping the Baal of Peor. The Lord burned with anger against them.

The Lord spoke to Moses: "Take all the leaders of these people, kill them by hanging and leave them exposed in broad daylight in order to turn the Lord's fierce anger away from Israel."

So Moses told Israel's judges: "Each of you must execute the men under your jurisdiction who have become worshipers of Baal of Peor."

Just then, while everyone was weeping at the Tabernacle's entrance, an Israelite man brought a Midianite woman into his family tent in plain sight of everyone. Phinehas, a grandson of Aaron the priest, saw what he was doing. So he left the assembly, grabbed a spear, followed the Israelite into the tent, and drove the spear through both of their bodies. Then the terrible plague against the Israelites stopped. The plague had killed 24,000 people.

The Lord said to Moses: "Phinehas, the grandson of Aaron the priest, has turned my anger away from the Israelites. He was zealous for my honor among them; therefore, I did not kill them all. As a result, I am making a covenant with him. He and his descendants have an agreement with me, and they will always be priests. This is because he was zealous for the honor of his God and made atonement for the Israelites" (25:1-15).

The Lord said to Moses: "Pay back the Midianites for what they did to the Israelites. After that, you will die."

So Moses addressed the people: "Get some men ready to go to war. The Lord will use them to pay back the Midianites. Send into battle a thousand men from each tribe of Israel." So Moses sent twelve thousand armed men into battle.

They fought against Midian, as the Lord commanded Moses, and killed every man. Among their victims were the five kings of Midian and the prophet Balaam.

The Israelites captured the Midianite women and children and took all the Midianite herds, flocks and goods as plunder. They burned all the towns where the Midianites had settled. They took all the plunder to Moses and Eleazar the priest (31:1-12).

Moses was furious with the army officers who returned from the battle. Moses asked them: "Have you allowed all the women to live? They were the ones who followed Balaam's advice and seduced the people of Israel away from God, causing the plague that struck the Lord's people. Now kill all the boys. Kill every woman who has slept with a man. The younger women who are virgins, you can keep alive for yourselves (31:13-18).

The Tribes Who Chose to Stay on the East of Jordan

The families of Reuben and Gad had very large herds and flocks. They saw that the lands that had just been conquered were suitable for livestock. So they came to Moses and Eleazar the priest and to the leaders of the community and said: "The land the Lord subdued before the people of Israel is just right for livestock, and your servants have livestock. If we have found favor in your eyes, give us this country for our inheritance. Do not make us cross the Jordan."

Moses answered the families of Reuben and Gad: "Shall your countrymen go to war while you sit here? Why do you discourage the Israelites just when they are going over into the land the Lord has given them? This is what your ancestors did when I sent them to look over the land. After they viewed the land, they discouraged the Israelites from entering the land the Lord had given them. The Lord got angry that day, and he swore this oath: `Because they have not followed me wholeheartedly, none of the men who are twenty years old or older who came up out of Egypt will see the land I promised to Abraham, Isaac and Jacob. None except Caleb and Joshua, for they followed the Lord wholeheartedly.' The Lord's anger burned against Israel, and he made them wander in the wilderness for forty years, until the whole generation that had done evil in his sight was gone.

"And here you are, a mob of sinners, stepping up to replace your ancestors and making the Lord even more angry with Israel. If you turn away from following him, he will again leave all this people in the desert, and you will cause their destruction."

Then they came close to Moses and said: "We want to build pens here for our livestock and cities for our women and children. But we are ready to arm ourselves and go to the front lines leading the Israelites to their place. Meanwhile, our women and children will live in fortified cities for protection from the inhabitants of the land. We will not return to our homes until every Israelite has received his inheritance. We will not receive any inheritance on the other side of the Jordan, because our inheritance has come to us on the east side of the Jordan."

Then Moses said to them: "You must do these things. You must go across the Jordan to fight before the Lord until he has driven his enemies out of the land. After the Lord helps us conquer the land, you will have fulfilled your duty to the Lord and to Israel. And this land will be your possession before the Lord (32:1-16).

Moses' Last Instructions to the Israelites

The Israelites were on the plains of Moab by the Jordan River across from Jericho. The Lord told Moses to tell the Israelites: "When you cross the Jordan into Canaan, drive out all the inhabitants of the land before you. Destroy all their carved images and their cast idols, and demolish all their high places. Take possession of the land and settle in it, for I have given you the land to possess. Distribute the land by lot, according to your family groups. To a larger family group give a larger inheritance, and to a smaller group a smaller one. Whatever falls to them by lot will be theirs. Distribute it according to your ancestral tribes. But if you do not drive out the inhabitants of the land, those you allow to remain will become barbs in your eyes and thorns in your sides. They will bring you trouble in the land where you will live. And then I will punish you as I planned to punish them" (33:50-56).

By the side of the Jordan River, Moses made the speeches that are found in the book of Deuteronomy. Here are some of the things included in Moses' speeches:

"Be careful to do exactly as the Lord your God has commanded you; do not turn aside to the right or to the left. Walk in all the way that the Lord your God has commanded you. Then you will live and prosper and prolong your days in the land that you are about to possess" (Dt 5:28-33).

"Hear, O Israel: The Lord our God, the Lord is one. Love the Lord your God with all your heart, with all your soul and with all your strength. These commandments that I give you today are to be upon your hearts. Impress them on your children. Talk about them wherever you are: when you sit at home, when you walk along the road, when you lie down and when you get up. Tie them as reminders on your hands and bind them on your foreheads. Write them on the doorframes of your houses and on your gates" (Dt 6:4-9).

"The Lord your God will bring you into the land he promised to give your ancestors Abraham, Isaac and Jacob. You will enter a land with large, flourishing cities you did not build, houses filled with all kinds of good things you did not provide, wells you did not dig, and vineyards and olive groves you did not plant. Then when you eat and are satisfied, be careful that you do not forget the Lord, who brought you out of Egypt, out of the land of slavery" (Dt 6:10-12).

"Today, the Lord your God commands you to follow his decrees and laws. Be careful to observe them with all your heart and with all your soul. Today, you have declared that the Lord is your God and that you will walk in his ways, that you will keep his decrees, commands and laws, and that you will obey him. Today, the Lord has declared that you are his people, his treasured possession and that you are to keep all his commands. He has promised that he will give you praise, fame and honor. He will make you greater than all the other nations he made. You will be a people holy to the Lord your God" (Dt 26:16-19).

The Lord God says: "Look at what I've done for you today: I've placed in front of you life and prosperity, death and destruction. For I command you today to love the Lord your God, to walk in his ways, and to keep his commands, decrees and laws; then you will live and grow in number. And the Lord your God will bless you in the land you are entering to possess. But I warn you: if your heart turns away and you are not obedient, and if you are drawn away to bow down and worship other gods, I declare to you that you will be destroyed. You will not live long in the land you are crossing the Jordan to enter and possess.

Today, I call heaven and earth as witnesses against you. I place before you life and death, blessings and curses. Now choose life! Then, you and your children may live. Love the Lord your God, listen to his voice, and hold fast to him. For the Lord is your life, and he will give you many years in the land he swore to give to your fathers, Abraham, Isaac and Jacob (Dt 30:15-20).

LIFE-LESSONS DISCOVERED IN THE STORY

1. When a person faces problems, his character is revealed. As a result, two people can face the same problem in different ways. The ten spies saw the giants and forgot about God's power, while Caleb and Joshua saw God's power and didn't fear the giants (Nu 13:25-33; 14:5-9).

2. Caleb's answer to the ten spies who feared the giants (Nu 13:30-33; 14:7-8) teaches three facts about facing obstacles:

1) Obstacles are real. The men were of great stature (Nu 13:32).
2) Obstacles should be faced. "Let us arise" (Nu 14:30).
3) Obstacles can be overcome by people who believe and obey God. Caleb believed that God was with them and they could defeat the giants (Nu 14:8-9).

3. When God's people face a great challenge, they should not allow the negative factors to overcome their confidence that God helps his people and keeps his promises. The ten spies saw the giants, and they forgot about God (Nu 13:25-33). Joshua and Caleb saw the giants and trusted God (Nu 14:5-9).

4. Murmuring is a sign of distrust of God. The Israelites' murmuring was proof that they didn't believe that God could give them the promised land (Nu 14:1-4).

5. The person who lacks faith, treats God as though he were a liar; however, God is faithful and punishes those who refuse to believe him. Eve didn't believe God's promise that she would die if she ate fruit from the Tree of Knowledge of Good and Evil and she was deceived by the snake. The people didn't believe Noah's message and were left outside the ark. The Egyptians didn't believe that God was the Almighty, that he would defeat their country, kill their firstborn and kill their army by drowning in the sea. The Israelites didn't believe that God could give them the promised land and became wanderers in the desert for 40 years, when they could have been enjoying the promised land.

6. Those who forget God's actions of the past, rebel against him because they lack faith to trust God for victory over present situations. Each time the Israelites forgot God's past actions in their favor, they failed to trust him to give them victory over current situations and problems, and they erred. When Moses was on the mountain for forty days, they felt insecure without his presence and made the golden calf (Ex 32:1-35). When they heard the ten spies' report, they lacked faith to conquer Canaan, rebelled and rioted against God (Nu 13-14).

7. Whenever God's people lack faith when facing a problem, they become roamers who are marking time, when they could be experiencing victories. The Israelites didn't believe that God could give them the promised land. They wandered in the wilderness for 40 years, when they could have been enjoying the promised land (Nu 13-14).

8. God's people who were delivered by him in the past, but who believe God is unable to help them with their current problems, will accuse God of being responsible for their problems and will end up marking time instead of conquering their problems with God's power. The Israelites accused God of bringing them to the land to be killed (Nu 14:2-4).

9. The majority is often wrong. The majority of the Israelites were wrong when they wanted a golden calf to worship (Ex 32:1-2). The ten spies were wrong when they saw the giants and lacked faith in God. The minority of two, Joshua and Caleb, were right when they trusted God to give them victory over the giants (13:27-33; 14:6-7). The majority of ten was wrong when it complained against Moses, Aaron and God while the minority of three, Moses, Aaron and Joshua, was right (14:1-2). We need to be followers of Jesus who will be true to him, even if no one else joins us.

10. God's people who lack faith, may prevent those with faith from achieving God's purposes. The majority of the Israelites lacked faith and prevented Joshua and Caleb, who had faith, from entering the promised land for forty years (Nu 13:30; 14:6-7, 26-38).

11. The consequence of disobeying God may be that a person will experience his greatest fears. The greatest fear of the Israelites was that they would die in the wilderness (Nu 14:2-3). The result of not believing in God was that they wandered in the desert until they died (Nu 14:34).

12. "The wages of sin is death." The ten spies who didn't have faith in God suffered immediate death (Nu 14:35-37). (See Rm 6:23.)

13. Complaining is a sign of lack of faith in God and can test the patience of the Lord. The Israelites were camped in a location that lacked water. They complained and accused Moses and Aaron because they had no water. They didn't ask the Lord to give them water because they didn't trust him (Nu 20:3-5). Paul referred to this episode and gave the counsel: "Do not complain as some of them did" (1 Cor 10:10).

14. Even when others provoke somebody to sin, that person is responsible for his own sin. The people's constant complaining provoked Moses to sin. However, God condemned Moses for the sin of unbelief and for not honoring the Lord as holy before the people. The people provoked Moses to sin; however, God did not excuse Moses (Nu 20:12).

15. What appears to be one act of misconduct may make a person responsible for multiple sins. The incident when Moses hit the rock made him guilty of multiple sins (Nu 20:2-13):
1) Moses mismanaged his anger when he called the people "rebels" when God told him to bring forth water (20:10);
2) Moses suggested that he and Aaron had the

power to provide water (20:10);
   3) Moses hit the rock when God ordered him to speak to it (20:11);
   4) Moses did not believe the Lord (20:12);
   5) Moses did not honor the Lord as holy before the people (20:12).

16. The spiritual leader who sins, gives a false impression of the nature of God. The New Testament reveals that the rock that provided water is an illustration of Christ (1 Cor 10:4). When Moses hit the rock instead of speaking to it, it contaminated an illustration of the Lord Jesus (Nu 20:6-12). The first time Israel needed water, God commanded Moses to hit the rock (Ex 17:6) to illustrate the fact that Jesus would be hurt on the cross so that we could receive the water of eternal life. The second time Israel needed water, God ordered Moses to speak to the rock. This illustrates the fact that Jesus only had to die once for our sins. The sin of Moses gave a false impression of the nature of God and destroyed a divine illustration about Jesus.

17. The spiritual leader who sins is very visible. Look at the stars at night. There are thousands of stars; even so, the one that we most notice is the falling star. There are thousands of evangelical leaders; however, the ones that receive the most attention are those who are falling.

18. In one situation God may instruct his servant to act in a certain manner, and later, when a similar situation occurs, God may instruct his servant to act in a different manner. Twice the Israelites had no water. The first time God ordered Moses to hit the rock (Ex 17:1-7), the second time, God ordered Moses to speak to the rock (Nu 20:8). When, on the second occasion, Moses repeated the same action as the first, he committed a sin (Nu 20:12).

19. Years of fidelity to God don't compensate for a sin. Moses had been a faithful leader for forty years. The forty years of fidelity didn't compensate for the one time Moses disrespected an order of God. When Israel entered the promised land, Moses could not accompany them (Nu 20:12).

20. Complaining can test the Lord's patience. The Israelites' complaining tested God's patience (Nu 21:4-6; 1 Cor 10:9) and he sent poisonous snakes that bit and killed many of the Israelites.

21. God's punishment for sin should lead to repentance. The Israelites' complaining tested the Lord's patience (1 Cor 10:9). God punished them with poisonous snakes (Nu 21:6). Then the Israelites recognized their sin (Nu 21:7).

22. Salvation is available only to those who accept the plan established by God. When the poisonous snakes invaded the Israelites' camp, the Lord instructed Moses to make a snake and put it up on a pole. Then anyone who was bitten was to look at it and live. Moses made a bronze snake and put it up on a pole. Anyone who was bitten by a snake and looked at the bronze snake lived (21:4-9). There was only one way to be saved from the snake bite: trust God's promise and look at the bronze snake.

23. The bronze snake on the pole (Nu 21:8-9) illustrates important truths about Jesus. Jesus explained to Nicodemus that his death on the cross would be the same thing as when Moses lifted up the snake (Jn 3:14-15). A person is saved today when by faith, he looks at Jesus, who took the responsibility for our sin when he hung on the cross. The bronze snake illustrates the following truths about Jesus:
    ■ The snake illustrates that sin requires God's judgment;
    ■ It illustrates the cross. Jesus was raised up on the cross to draw to God all who look at him with faith;
    ■ Look and be healed from the snake bite illustrates the simplicity of salvation. Believe on Jesus and be saved.

24. The person who knows God, but makes decisions based upon what gives him the most financial profit, suffers from spiritual blindness. Balaam (Nu 22:1-35) was a mercenary who negotiated with his spiritual gifts (Jd 11). He knew that God did not want him to go to king Balak and curse Israel. However, he insisted with God until he received permission to go. But it was given in a way that reproved Balaam's weakness (Nu 22:20). On the way to king Balak, God placed an angel to block Balaam's way. Balaam didn't see the angel, but his donkey did. A donkey has more spiritual vision than a person who knows God but is blinded by greed. A donkey has more spiritual vision and wisdom than God's servant who desires to negotiate his spiritual gifts and sell them to the highest bidder. A donkey has more spiritual vision than the Christian who knows God, understands God's will, yet makes his decisions based upon what brings him the most profit.

25. Sometimes when God uses a miracle to speak, it is because the person is so stubborn, it takes a miracle to get his attention. God enabled the donkey to speak to Balaam (Nu 22:28-30). The New Testament explains that this miracle hindered the prophet's intention to curse Israel (2 Pe 2:15-16). God, using an unusual means to communicate, may be a sign that a person is so hard-headed that extra revelation is necessary to get his attention.

26. A mercenary spiritual leader facilitates the corruption of God's people. Balaam is an example (Nu 22-25). The doctrine of Balaam was

that the people could not be cursed against divine will. However, they could be corrupted (Nu 31:16). Balaam taught Balak how to cause the Israelites to sin by eating food offered to idols and by taking part in sexual sin (Rev 2:14).

27. God punishes the mercenary spiritual leader who negotiates to sell his services to the highest bidder. Balaam desired to die as a good man (Nu 23:10), but he was killed as an infidel, and an enemy of God (Nu 31:8).

28. Idolatry and immorality often walk hand in hand. The women who followed Balaam's advice led Israelite men to both worship the god Baal-Peor and take part in sexual sin (Nu 25:1-2; 31:8; Rev 2:14). (See 1 Cor 6:13-20.)

29. The world surrounding the church tries to attract Christians using ungodly activities. The people surrounding the Israelites got them to participate in sexual sins and idol worship (Nu 25:1-2; 31:8; Rev 2:14). The pagans who lived close to Israel were always attracting the Israelites to idolatry and immorality.

QUESTIONS

1. When the twelve spies searched out the promised land, what was the majority report of ten and the minority report of two?
2. How did the Israelites respond to the spies' report, and what was the result of their response?
3. What are some of the "giants" you face and how are you dealing with them?
4. What were some of the things that provoked Israel to complain?
5. What were some of the results of their complaining?
6. What does the incident when Aaron and Miriam criticized Moses because of his marriage to a black woman teach us about interracial marriages?
7. Moses had faithfully led the Israelites for 40 years. Why was he unable to lead them into the promised land?
8. What does the episode of the poisonous snakes teach us about God, punishment, and salvation?
9. What does the story about Balaam teach us about the person who knows God, yet only considers financial matters when making decisions?
10. The pagans who surrounded Israel enticed the Israelites to participate in sexual sins and idol worship. How do people who surround you entice you to disobey God?

JOSHUA				
1 — 5	6 — 12	13 — 21	22 — 24	
CONQUERING CANAAN		DIVIDING THE LAND	JOSHUA'S FAREWELL	
PREPARATION: Entering Canaan	**VICTORY:** Conquering Canaan	**INHERITANCE:** Dividing Canaan	**CONSECRATION:** Conditions for staying in the land	
Jordan River	Canaan	2 ½ Tribes: east of Jordan 9 ½ Tribes: west of Jordan		
1 month	7 years	8 years		
1 — 5	6 — 12	13 — 21	22 — 24	

JOSHUA: CONQUERING THE PROMISED LAND
Joshua 1 - 24

STRUCTURE

Context:
Forty years had passed since the incident when Moses sent 12 men to spy out the promised land. When the spies returned, ten gave a bad report about giants in the land. Two of the spies, Joshua and Caleb, argued that since the Lord was with them, they could conquer the land. The Israelites listened to the ten, complained and wanted to return to Egypt. God declared a punishment for their unbelief: Those who were over 20 years old and lacked faith would wander in the wilderness for 40 years, until they were all dead. Moses, Aaron, Caleb and Joshua were the only ones who believed God would give them the land. However, Moses and Aaron were not allowed to enter the land because Moses struck the rock to get water, when God had told him to speak to it. The forty years of wandering had passed, and the time had come for them to take possession of the land God had promised them.

Key-person: Joshua

Key-location: Canaan

Key-repetitions:
- Land. The following facts about the land are mentioned many times: promised by God; conquered; not conquered; divided.
- Fear (1:9; 2:9, 24; 5:1; 8:1; 9:24; 10:2; 10:8; 11:6; 14:8; 22:24).
- Obeyed: God or Moses' Law (1:7-8; 22:3, 5; 23:6; 24:24);Joshua obeyed the Lord's instructions (11:9, 12,15; 14:5); God was not obeyed (5:6); Joshua was obeyed (1:17-18; 22:2).
- Promises kept: Spies to Rahab (2:12-21; 6:17, 22-23); Israel to the Gibeonites (9:19-21); God and Moses to Caleb (14:10-12); God keeps his promises (23:14-16).
- The Israelites killed all of the residents: of Jericho (6:21-26); of Ai (8:24); the Amorites (10:9-26); of Makkedah (10:28-30); of Libnah (10:30); of Lachish (10:32-35); of Hebron (10:37); of Hazor (11:11);of Leshem (19:47).
- The person Joshua.
- Joshua was esteemed/famous (3:7; 4:14; 6:27).
- God gave the Israelites victory: He dried up the Jordan River (3:1-7). He gave victory over their enemies: the city of Jericho (6:16); Ai (8:18); the Amorites (10:10-13); the cities of Makkedah (10:30); Hebron (10:37); Hazor (11:11); Leshem (19:47). The Lord was fighting for Israel (10:42); The Lord drove out super-powerful nations before them; no one was able to stand up to them (23:8-11).
- Failures of the Israelites: Acan disobeyed God (7:1); Joshua blamed God when the men of Ai defeated the Israelites ((7:6-12); Joshua made an agreement with the Gibeonites without consulting God (9:3-15); the Israelites failed to conquer a large portion of the land (13:2).

Key-attitudes:
- The challenge Joshua faced in replacing Moses as leader.
- The conflict between the Israelites and the residents of the land.
- The people of the land were terrified of the Israelites.
- The respect the Israelites felt toward Joshua.
- The challenge the Israelites faced to conquer the land and to be faithful to God.
- The danger of disobeying God and of mixing with the people of the earth.
- The cunning deceit of the Gibeonites.

Initial-problem: The Lord told Joshua that Moses was dead and that the Israelites were to get ready to cross the Jordan River into the land he was about to give to them.

Sequence of events:

Entering Canaan

- Moses was 120 years old when he climbed Mount Nebo, saw Canaan, and died. The Israelites grieved for 30 days (Dt 34:1-8).
- Joshua was filled with wisdom (Dt 34:9).
- The Lord told Joshua that Moses was dead and ordered him to prepare to cross the Jordan. God promised to be with Joshua, and told him to be strong, be courageous and to obey his Law. God promised to give Joshua success (Jos 1:1-9).
- Joshua ordered the leaders to prepare the people to cross the Jordan (1:10-11).
- Joshua sent out two spies to Jericho. A prostitute named Rahab hid them. They promised to spare her and her family. The spies returned and reported to Joshua (2:1-24).
- The water from the Jordan River stopped flowing. All Israel walked across on dry ground (3:1-17).
- The Lord exalted Joshua (4:14).
- The kings west of the Jordan were terrified (5:1).
- The Israelite men were circumcised (5:2-8).
- The Israelites celebrated the Passover. After they ate food grown in that country, manna stopped coming (5:9-12).

Conquering Canaan

- For six days the Israelites marched around Jericho once each day in silence. On the seventh day, they circled the city seven times. The seventh time around, the trumpets sounded, the people shouted, and the wall collapsed. They offered the city to the Lord. They killed every living thing, except they spared Rahab and her family. They burned everything in the city, except they put the silver and gold and articles of bronze and iron into the Lord's treasury (6:1-27).
- Achan took some of the things that should have been offered to the Lord. The men from Ai defeated the Israelites. The Lord revealed Achan's sin. Achan and everything connected with him was stoned, then burned (7:1-26).
- God gave them victory over Ai (8:1-29).
- The Gibeonites tricked Joshua into making a peace treaty with them (9:1-26).
- Five kings combined their armies to attack Gibeon. Joshua attacked the five kings, and the Lord gave him victory. The sun stopped in the middle of the sky for a full day (10:1-26).
- The south (10:1-43) and the north (11:1-23) of Canaan were conquered.
- The Lord fought for Israel (10:42).
- The Israelites kept for themselves all the plunder, but they killed all the people. Then the land had rest from war (11:13-23).

Dividing Canaan; Refuge-Cities

- The land was divided among the twelve tribes (13:7 - 19:51). The tribe of Levi received no inheritance (13:32-33) but did receive designated cities (21:1-42). The land was divided just as the Lord had commanded Moses (14:5).
- Caleb requested the hill country that the Lord promised him, and Joshua gave him Hebron as his inheritance (14:6-15).
- After Joshua was an old man, there was still land to be conquered (13:1, 6; 18:3).
- Joshua designated refuge-cities (20:1-9).

The Eastern Tribes Return Home

- Joshua allowed the men to return home from the tribes of Reuben, Gad and the eastern half-tribe of Manasseh. He challenged them to remain faithful to God. They built an altar by the Jordan and the Israelites gathered at Shiloh to go to war against them. The two tribes and the half-tribe explain the reason for the altar (22:1-34).

Joshua's Farewell

- Joshua called the Israelites together and gave them a farewell speech (23:1 - 24:28).
- He challenged them to: obey the Law; not worship other gods; and not ally themselves with the survivors of the land. Just as everything good that the Lord promised came true, so the Lord would keep his threats if they disobeyed him (23:6-16).
- Joshua challenged the Israelites: Throw away false gods or choose a god they would rather serve, but he and his household would serve the Lord. The people answered that they would never forsake the Lord (24:14-18).
- Joshua died at 110 years old (24:29).
- Israel served the Lord while Joshua and their leaders who had experienced everything the Lord had done for Israel remained alive (24:31).

Final-situation:

Israel served the Lord during Joshua's lifetime and during the lifetime of their older leaders who had experienced everything the Lord had done for Israel (24:31).

BIBLE STORY

Entering Canaan

Moses climbed up Mount Nebo, which is across from Jericho, and the Lord showed him all the land of Canaan. The Lord told Moses: "This land I promised to Abraham, Isaac and Jacob when I said: `I will give it to your descendants.' I let you look at it, but you will not cross over into it."

Then Moses, the Lord's servant, died there. The Lord buried him, but no one knows where his grave is. Moses was a hundred and twenty years old when he died, yet he had perfect vision and he was still strong. The Israelites grieved for Moses for thirty days (Dt 34:1-8).

Now Joshua, son of Nun, was filled with wisdom because Moses had laid his hands on him (Dt 34:9).

After Moses died, the Lord spoke to Joshua: "Moses my servant is dead. Now, you and all the people, get ready to cross the Jordan River into the land I am about to give to you. I will give you every place where you set your foot, just as I promised Moses. For as long as you live, no one will be able to stand up against you. Just as I was with Moses, so I will be with you. I will never leave you nor forsake you. Be strong; be courageous! You will lead these people to inherit the land I promised to give to their ancestors. Be strong; be courageous. Be sure to obey all the law my servant Moses gave you. If you follow it exactly, you will be successful in everything you do. Do not let this Book of the Law depart from your mouth; study it day and night, obey everything written in it. Then you will succeed. I have commanded you: Be strong; be courageous; do not be afraid; do not get discouraged. The Lord your God is with you every step you take" (Jos 1:1-9).

Joshua ordered the leaders to go throughout the camp and command the people: "Pack your supplies. In three days you will cross the Jordan River to go in and take possession of the land the Lord your God is giving you for your own" (1:10-11).

Joshua secretly sent out two spies with orders: "Go. Look over the land. Check out Jericho." They went to Jericho and stayed in the house of a prostitute named Rahab.

Someone told Jericho's king: "Israelite men arrived tonight to spy out the land."

The king sent a message to Rahab: "Bring out the men who came to stay the night in your house, because they came to spy out the whole country."

But Rahab had taken the two men up to the flat roof on her house. She hid them under the stalks of flax that were spread out on the roof. She told the king's men: "Yes, two men came here, but I did not know where they came from. When it was time to close the city gate at nightfall, the men left. Go quickly. You may catch up with them." The king's men set out to hunt the spies, following the road that led to the place where people cross the Jordan River.

Rahab went up on the roof and told the spies: "I know the Lord has given your people this land. We are terrified of you. We heard how the Lord dried up the water of the Red Sea for you when you left Egypt. We heard how you completely destroyed the kings east of the Jordan. Our men are afraid to fight you. The Lord your God is God of the heaven above and of the earth below. Please swear to me by the Lord that you will show kindness to my family. I showed you mercy; now show my family mercy. Spare our lives. Swear that you will save us from death."

The spies promised: "Our lives for your lives! If you don't tell what we are doing, we will treat you right and show mercy to you when the Lord gives us the land."

Her house was built on the city wall, and she used a rope to lower the men through a window. She advised them: "Go to the hills so the pursuers will not find you. Hide there for three days and then go on your way."

The spies told her: "In order for us to keep this oath, you must do the following when we enter the land: tie this red rope out the window through which you lowered us down, and bring all your family into your house. If anyone goes outside your house into the street and is killed, it's his own fault; we will not be responsible. Anyone who is in the house with you, we take full responsibility; if anyone lays a hand on one of them, it's our fault. But if you tell what we are doing, our oath to you is cancelled."

She replied: "Agreed, it is as you say." She sent them away. Then she tied the scarlet cord in the window.

They headed into the hills and stayed there for three days. The king's men searched all along the road and returned without finding them. Then the two spies returned to Joshua and told him everything that had happened to them. They told Joshua: "The Lord has given the whole land into our hands; all the people are terrified of us" (2:1-24).

Early the next morning, Joshua and all the Israelites set out traveling to the Jordan River. They camped by the river before crossing over. Three days later, the officers went through the camp, giving orders: "When you see the priests carrying the Ark of the Covenant of the Lord your God, start moving and follow it. But stay about a thousand yards behind the ark; do not go near it."

Joshua told the people: "Make yourselves holy for the Lord; tomorrow the Lord will do amazing things among you."

Joshua told the priests: "Take up the Ark of the Covenant and step out ahead of the people." The priests lifted the ark and carried it ahead of the people.

The Lord told Joshua: "Today I will begin to make you great in the eyes of all Israel. They will know that I am with you just as I was with Moses."

Joshua addressed the Israelites: "Attention! Listen to the Word of the Lord. You will see proof that the living God is with you and that he will drive out the people of the land. The Ark of the Covenant of the Lord of all the earth will go ahead of you into the Jordan River. When the priests who carry the ark of the Lord enter the water, the river will stop flowing. Water flowing downstream will be cut off and pile up in a heap as if a dam were there."

The people broke camp to cross the Jordan. They were led by the priests with the Ark of the Covenant. The Jordan was at flood stage during harvest. But when the feet of the priests who carried the ark touched the Jordan water's edge, the water from upstream stopped flowing. It piled up in a heap a great distance away. The priests stood firm on dry ground in the middle of the Jordan, while all Israel walked across on dry ground (3:1-17).

That day the Lord exalted Joshua in the sight of all Israel; and they respected him just as they had respected Moses (4:14). The kings west of the Jordan and the Canaanite kings along the coast heard how the Lord had dried up the Jordan until the Israelites had crossed over; they were scared; they were afraid to face the Israelites (5:1).

The Lord commanded Joshua: "Make knives from flint stones and circumcise the Israelites a second time." All men of military age who came out of Egypt had been circumcised. But those died in the desert. However, their sons born in the desert since leaving Egypt had not been circumcised. After all the men had been circumcised, they remained where they were camped until they were healed.

While camped at Gilgal on the plains of Jericho, the Israelites celebrated the Passover. The day after the Passover, they ate food grown in that country. The manna stopped coming the day they ate food from that land. There was no longer any manna for the Israelites (5:2-12).

Conquering Canaan

Jericho was shut up tight because of the Israelites. No one went out; no one came in. The Lord told Joshua: "I have delivered Jericho into your hands, along with its king and its fighting men. For six days, march around the city with the army one time every day. Seven priests carrying trumpets of rams' horns will march in front of the ark. On the seventh day, march around the city seven times, with the priests blowing the trumpets. Then have them sound a long blast on the trumpets; when you hear that, all the people are to give a loud shout. Then the city wall will collapse, and the people will go up, straight into the city."

The Israelites obeyed the Lord's instructions. On the first day, an armed guard marched in front; next came the trumpet-blowing priests; they were followed by priests carrying the ark, and then came the rear guard. Those marching did not speak a word. The ark of the Lord circled the city once. Then the people returned to camp and spent the night there. On the second morning, the priests took up the ark of the Lord. Armed men went first. Next came the seven trumpet-blowing priests who were followed by priests carrying the ark. The rear guard came last. They marched around the city once and returned to the camp. They did this for six days.

On the seventh day, they got up at daybreak and marched around the city the same way, except on that day they circled the city seven times. The seventh time around, the priests sounded the long trumpet blast and Joshua commanded: "Shout! The Lord has given you this city! The city and all that is in it are to be destroyed as an offering to the Lord. Only Rahab the prostitute and all those in her house shall be spared, because she hid the spies we sent. But do not take anything that should be destroyed as an offering to God. If you do, then you yourselves will be destroyed; you will endanger the camp of Israel, and you will make trouble for everyone. All silver and gold, all articles of bronze and of iron are holy to the Lord and must go into his treasury."

The trumpets sounded, the people shouted, and the wall collapsed; every man charged straight in, and they took the city. They offered the city to the Lord and destroyed with the sword every living thing in it; men and women, young and old, cattle, sheep and donkeys.

Joshua ordered the two men who had spied out the land: "Enter the prostitute's house and rescue her and all who are connected to her, just as you promised her."

Joshua spared Rahab the prostitute, with her family and all who belonged to her. But they burned the whole city and everything in it, except they put the silver and gold and articles of bronze and iron into the Lord's treasury. Joshua then pronounced a solemn oath: "Cursed before the Lord is the man who sets out to rebuild this city of Jericho."

So the Lord was with Joshua, and he became famous throughout the land (6:1-27).

Achan, a man from the tribe of Judah, took some things that should have been offered to the Lord. The Lord's anger burned against Israel.

Joshua sent men from Jericho to spy out the region of Ai. After spying out Ai, they returned and reported to Joshua: "Don't send many warriors against Ai. Send two or three thousand men since only a few men are there." So about three thousand men went up; but the men of Ai defeated the Israelites and killed thirty-six Israelites. The hearts of the people melted and became like water.

Joshua ripped his clothes and fell face-down to the ground before the Lord's ark, remaining there till evening. Israel's leaders did the same, and they threw dirt on their heads. Joshua said: "Ah, Sovereign Lord, why did you bring this people across the Jordan to defeat us by the Amorites? O Lord, what can I say, now that Israel has been defeated by its enemies? The other people of the country will hear about this; they will gang up on us and wipe out our name from the earth. Then what will you do for your own great name?"

The Lord told Joshua: "Stand up! Why are you down on your face? Israel sinned; they took forbidden plunder and put them with their own possessions. The Israelites cannot stand against their enemies; they turn their backs and run because they have been made liable to destruction. I will not help you unless you destroy whatever among you is devoted to destruction."

The Lord revealed to Joshua that Achan, of the tribe of Judah, had taken some forbidden plunder from Jericho. Joshua confronted Achan: "Give glory to the Lord God of Israel. Tell me what you have done."

Achan replied: "I sinned against the Lord God of Israel. I saw in the plunder a beautiful robe from Babylonia, five pounds of silver and one and one-quarter pounds of gold; I wanted them, so I took them. They are buried inside my tent, with the silver under the robe."

Joshua, together with all Israel, took Achan and everything connected with him: the silver, the robe, the gold, his sons, daughters, cattle, donkeys and sheep, and his tent to the Valley of Achor. Then all Israel stoned him. After they had stoned the rest, they burned them. Then the Lord turned from his fierce anger (7:1-26).

The Israelites again attacked the city of Ai. God gave them victory, and the city of Ai was totally destroyed (8:1-29).

The people of Gibeon heard what Joshua had done to Jericho and to Ai. The Gibeonites decided to trick the Israelites. A delegation loaded their donkeys with worn-out sacks and old wineskins. The men put old patched sandals on their feet and wore old clothes. They took dry, moldy bread. They went to Joshua and said to him and the men of Israel: "We have come from a distant country; make a treaty with us."

Joshua asked: "Who are you and where do you come from?"

They answered: "Your servants have come from a distant country because of the fame of the Lord your God. We heard reports of all that he did in Egypt, and all that he did to the kings east of the Jordan. Our leaders and our people told us to meet with you and tell you: 'We are your servants; make a peace treaty with us.' Our bread was warm and fresh when we left home. But now see how dry and moldy it is. Our leather wineskins were new when we filled them with wine, but see how cracked they are. And our clothes and sandals are worn out by the long journey."

The men of Israel looked them over and accepted the evidence, but they did not ask the Lord what to do. Joshua made a peace-treaty with them to let them live, and the Israelite leaders promised to keep the agreement.

Three days after making the peace-treaty with the Gibeonites, the Israelites learned that they lived near them. But the Israelites did not attack the Gibeonites, because Israel's leaders had sworn an oath to them by the Lord, the God of Israel.

The whole assembly complained to the leaders, but all the leaders answered: "We gave them our oath by the Lord, the God of Israel. We will let them live, so that we will not be accused of breaking the oath we swore to them. Let them live; however, they will cut wood and carry water for our entire community." So the leaders kept their promise, and they did not kill them (9:1-26).

Jerusalem's king heard that Joshua took Ai and totally destroyed it and its king, just as he had done to Jericho and its king. He also learned that the people of Gibeon made a peace treaty with Israel. He was shocked because Gibeon was an important city and all its men were good fighters. Five kings, including the king of Jerusalem, combined their armies and set out to attack Gibeon.

The Gibeonites sent word to Joshua in the camp at Gilgal: "Do not abandon your servants. Come quickly and save us! Help us! All the kings from the hill country joined forces against us."

So Joshua marched up from Gilgal with his entire army. The Lord told Joshua: "Do not be afraid of them; I have given them into your hand. Not one of them will be able to stand up to you."

Joshua marched all night from Gilgal and took them by surprise. The Lord threw them into confusion, and Israel experienced a great victory at Gibeon. The enemy fled, Israel pursued and the Lord threw large hailstones down on them. God killed more with the hailstones than the Israelites killed with the sword.

On that day Joshua shouted to the Lord, and all Israel heard: "Sun, stop! Stand still over Gibeon. Moon, halt! Stand still over Aijalon Valley." The sun stopped in the middle of the sky and waited to go down for a full day. There has never been a day like it before or since, a day when the Lord took orders from a man! Truly, the Lord fought for Israel!

So Joshua and the Israelites destroyed them completely; he left no survivors (10:1-26).

The south (10:1-43) and the north (11:1-23) of Canaan were conquered. Joshua conquered the kings and their lands in one campaign, because the Lord, the God of Israel, fought for Israel (10:42). Joshua took all the cities and their kings and killed them with the sword. He totally destroyed them, as Moses had commanded. The Israelites kept for themselves all the plunder and livestock of these cities, but they killed all the people with the sword. Joshua did not leave incomplete anything that the Lord commanded Moses. Except for those living in Gibeon, not one city made a peace treaty with the Israelites. Joshua took the entire land, just as the Lord had directed Moses, and he parceled it out as an inheritance to Israel according to their tribal divisions. Then the land had rest from war (11:13-23).

Dividing Canaan; Refuge-Cities

The land was divided among the twelve tribes (13:7 - 19:51). Each tribe received its own parcel of land. However, the tribe of Levi received no inheritance. The Lord, the God of Israel, was their inheritance, as he promised them (13:32-33). The Levites did receive designated cities with surrounding pasture land within the regions designated to the different tribes (21:1-42). So the Israelites divided the land, just as the Lord had commanded Moses (14:5).

Caleb approached Judah and spoke: "You remember what the Lord said to Moses at Kadesh Barnea concerning you and me. I was forty years old when Moses the servant of the Lord sent me from Kadesh Barnea to spy out the land. And I brought him back an honest and accurate report. But my companions who went up with me discouraged the people and filled them with fear. However, I wholeheartedly followed the Lord my God. On that day Moses promised me: 'The land on which your feet have walked will become your land. Your children will own it forever, because you followed the Lord God.' The Lord kept his promise. He kept me alive for forty-five years since the time he said this to Moses. Now I am eighty-five years old! I am as strong today as I was the day Moses sent me out; I'm as ready to go out to battle now as I was then. Now give me this hill country that the Lord promised me. You yourself heard then that the Anakites were there and their cities were large and fortified. But with the Lord helping me, I will drive them out just as he said."

Joshua blessed Caleb and gave him Hebron as his inheritance. After this, there was peace in the land (14:6-15).

After Joshua was an old man, the Lord told him: "You are old, and there are still very large areas of land to be taken" (13:1). God also promised: " I myself will drive out the people of the land before the Israelites (13:6).

Joshua said to the Israelites: "How long will you put off taking possession of the land that the Lord, the God of your fathers, has given you?" (18:3).

The Lord told Joshua: "Tell the Israelites to designate refuge-cities, as I instructed you through Moses. Anyone who kills a person accidentally may flee to the refuge-city and find protection from the avenger of blood, the relative who has the duty to kill the murderer." So six of the Levites' cities were designated as refuge-cities. They were spaced throughout the country. Any Israelite or any alien living among them who accidentally killed someone could flee to those refuge-cities and not be killed by the avenger of blood prior to standing trial (20:1-9).

The Eastern Tribes Return Home
Then Joshua summoned the men from the tribes of Reuben, Gad and the eastern half-tribe of Manasseh. He told them: "You have obeyed all that Moses the servant of the Lord commanded; you have obeyed me in everything I commanded. You carried out the mission the Lord your God gave you. Now the Lord your God has given your brothers rest as he promised. Return to your homes in the land that Moses the servant of the Lord gave you on the east side of the Jordan. But be careful to keep the commandment and the law that the Lord's servant Moses gave you: Love the Lord your God, walk in all his ways, obey his commands, hold fast to him and serve him with all your heart and all your soul."

Then Joshua blessed them and sent them away, and they returned to their homes. When they came to Geliloth near the Jordan in the land of Canaan, they built a huge altar by the Jordan. When the Israelites heard that the three tribes built the altar, the whole assembly of Israel gathered at Shiloh to go to war against them.

The Israelites sent Phinehas the priest and ten tribal leaders, one from each of the tribes gathered at Shiloh to Reuben, Gad and the half-tribe of Manasseh. They confronted them: "How could you turn against the God of Israel and build your own altar in rebellion against him? If you rebel against the Lord today, tomorrow he will be angry with the whole community of Israel. If the land you possess is somehow contaminated, come over to the Lord's land, where the Lord's tabernacle stands, and share the land with us. But do not rebel against the Lord or against us by building your own altar apart from the altar of the Lord our God."

Then Reuben, Gad and the half-tribe of Manasseh replied: "The Lord is our God! The Lord knows why we did this! And let Israel know! If we built our own altar to turn away from the Lord and to offer burnt offerings and grain offerings, or to sacrifice fellowship offerings on it, may the Lord himself punish us. No! We did it for fear that some day your descendants might say to ours: `You are not connected with God. The Lord made the Jordan a boundary between us and you Reubenites and Gadites. You have no share in the Lord!' That is why we built an altar, but not for burnt offerings or sacrifices. We built this altar as a witness between us and you and our children coming after us, that we will worship the Lord at his tabernacle with our burnt offerings, sacrifices and fellowship offerings. Then in the future your descendants will not be able to say to ours: `You have no share in the Lord.' No! We would not rebel against the Lord. We would not turn away from him today by building an altar for burnt offerings, grain offerings and sacrifices, to rival the true altar of the Lord our God that stands in front of his tabernacle."

Phinehas and Israel's tribal leaders were satisfied when they heard the answer from Reuben, Gad and Manasseh. Phinehas the priest, told them: "Today we know that the Lord is with us; we know you are loyal to the Lord in this matter. We know that you will not cause God to punish us."

Phinehas and the tribal leaders returned to Canaan and reported to the Israelites. They were pleased with the report, praised God and talked no more about going to war against their brothers. The Reubenites and the Gadites named the altar: "A Witness Between Us that the Lord is God" (22:1-34).

Joshua's Farewell
God gave the Israelites peace with their surrounding enemies. When Joshua became an old man, he called the Israelites together and gave them a farewell speech. He reminded them of all that the Lord God had done for them and challenged them to take possession of the land not yet conquered (23:1 - 24:28).

In his speech, he told them: "Be strong; obey all that is written in the Book of the Law of Moses, without turning aside to the right or to the left. There are still people living among us who are not Israelites, and they worship their own gods. Do not become friends with them. Do not speak the names of their gods or swear by them. Do not worship or pray to their gods. Hold fast to the Lord your God. The Lord has driven out super-powerful nations before you; no one has been able to stand up to you. Be careful to love the Lord your God. If you turn away and ally yourselves with the survivors of these nations that remain among you; if you intermarry with them and associate with them, then the Lord your God will not get rid of these enemies for you. They will cause you pain like a whip on your back and thorns in your eyes. Then you will become the ones who will be driven out of this good land, which the Lord your God has given you. Just as everything good that the Lord promised has come true, so the Lord will bring to pass all the evil he has threatened. If you violate the covenant of the Lord your God and serve and worship other gods, the Lord's anger will blaze against you; you will quickly perish from the good land he has given you" (23:6-16).

In his farewell speech, Joshua said: "Now fear the Lord; faithfully serve him. Throw away the false gods your ancestors worshiped on the far side of the River and in Egypt. Serve the Lord. But if you decide that it's a bad thing to serve the Lord, then choose for yourselves a god you'd rather serve, and do it today. Choose one of the gods your ancestors served beyond the River, or the gods of the Amorites, in whose land you are living. But as for me and my household, we will serve the Lord."

The people answered: "No! We will never forsake the Lord to serve other gods! It was the Lord our God himself who brought us and our fathers up out of Egypt. We were slaves in that land, but the Lord did great things for us while we watched. He protected us on our entire journey and among all the nations we traveled through. And the Lord drove out before us all the nations who lived in the land. We too will serve the Lord, because he is our God!" (24:14-18).

Joshua, the servant of the Lord, died when he was a hundred and ten years old (24:29).

Israel served the Lord during the time Joshua was living. They continued to serve him during the lifetime of their older leaders who had experienced everything the Lord had done for Israel (24:31).

LIFE-LESSONS DISCOVERED IN THE STORY

1. When God takes away one spiritual leader, he will replace him with another. When Moses died, the Israelites lost their leader, but God replaced Moses with Joshua (1:2-5).

2. A new leader should lead his followers beyond where the former one took them. Moses led the people out of Egypt and through the wilderness. Joshua led them across the Jordan River and led them to conquer Canaan.

3. God is sovereign; he has the power to do whatever it takes to carry out his plans. He had the power to stop the Jordan River from flowing, and he enabled the Israelites to walk across the river-bed on dry ground (3:1-17).

4. God is faithful and keeps his promises. God gave the Israelites the land he had promised to Abraham and to his descendants (Gn 12:6-7; 13:14-15; 15:18-21). No promise of God failed (Jos 21:45).

5. The spiritual leader needs to give priority to God's written word. He needs to: study it; obey it to the smallest detail and lead his followers to obey it. The Lord promised Joshua that if he held fast to the Law, studied it and obeyed everything written in it, then he would succeed (1:3-9). Joshua obeyed the Lord's instructions (11:9, 12,15; 14:5), he taught the people to obey the Lord's Words (22:5; 23:6).

6. The spiritual leader needs to have courage and to take seriously God's Word in order to prosper and to have success. The Lord told Joshua to be courageous and to obey all the law Moses gave him. The Lord promised him that if he held fast to the Law, studied it and obeyed everything written in it, then he would succeed (1:3-9).

7. The sinner will be forgiven and become an instrument used by God when he meets the following pre-conditions: trust God, confess his confidence in God and take a stand to serve him. The prostitute Rahab had faith in God, confessed her faith to the Israelite spies and helped them. Her life was spared (2:9-11). Her faith resulted in God's considering her a righteous person, and it produced action that benefitted God's people. Her name is included in the list of the heroes of faith (Heb 11:31). She became an ancestor of King David and of Jesus Christ (Mt 1:5-16).

8. God is omniscient. He is aware of a person's secret actions. He knew when Achan disobeyed divine instruction by taking forbidden things and hiding them (7:1).

9. One person's sin can make trouble for others and even endanger everyone in his community. Achan is an example: his sin harmed the whole nation (7:1-12).

10. After God's people experience victory, the danger exists that they will forget the need to seek divine direction for every decision. Israel followed God's order and experienced victory over Jericho and Ai. However, they did not consult the Lord before making a peace-treaty with the Gibeonites (9:1-15).

11. It is easy for the servant of God to be deceived when he doesn't consult God before making important decisions. Israel was deceived, not because of the Gibeonites' trickery, but because they did not ask the Lord what to do (9:14-15).

12. Even after a leader makes a wrong decision, he may be able to lead his followers to experience great victories. Joshua is an example: He failed to consult God before making a peace-treaty with the Gibeonites (9:3-15), but he was still able to lead the people to conquer the land of Canaan.

13. Righteous people keep their promises, even those they regret making, and even when the promise becomes an impediment to reaching

their goals. The Israelites realized they had been tricked into making an undesirable peace-treaty with the Gibeonites; however, they kept their promise because they did not want to be accused of breaking their oath (9:20).

14. God designed a plan to provide for those who work full-time for him. The tribe of Levi did not receive land as an inheritance. The Lord, the God of Israel, was their inheritance (13:32-33). The priests were supported by a portion of the tabernacle offering, and the Levites were supported by tithes (Nu 3:1-10; 18:1-7).

15. Those who refuse to believe God's promises create barriers for those who have faith in God. When Moses first sent out the 12 spies, Caleb and Joshua believed that with God's help they could conquer the promised land. However, when their ten companions lacked faith, the Israelites were required to wander in the wilderness for 40 years (Nm 13-14). Caleb, a man of faith, waited forty-five years before he could defeat the giants who terrorized his ten companions (Jos 14:6-12).

16. The Lord gives prolonged strength to those who trust him. Caleb, an 85 year old man with faith in God, defeated the city of giants that terrified the ten unbelieving spies of 45 years earlier (14:6-15).

17. Often it is necessary for a person to struggle in order to obtain blessings promised by God. The Lord gave the Israelites the promised land of Canaan, and he gave them rest from war. However, it was necessary for Israel to fight battles in order to take possession of the land (21:43-44). One should be eager to make his calling and election sure (2 Pt 1:10).

18. Procrastination in obeying God may result in being unfaithful to God. Joshua asked why some of the tribes were putting off the job of possessing the land (18:3-6).

19. When someone is accused of wrongdoing, God's people should stand up for justice, protect those not yet proven guilty, and examine carefully all sides of the story. The refuge-cities were to assure that the accused had justice. The people were to be intolerant of the sin, yet impartial in judgment so that the accused could have a fair trial (20:1-9). (See Nu 35:6-8.)

20. When someone is accused of wrong doing, beware of reacting before discovering the facts. When the 2 and ½ eastern tribes built an altar at the Jordan River, the other tribes feared that those tribes were rebelling and starting their own religion. Phinehas led a delegation to learn the truth and avoided a civil war (22:11-34).

21. God keeps his promises, both to bless those who faithfully serve him and to punish those who disobey him. Joshua told the Israelites: "Just as everything good that the Lord promised has come true, the Lord will bring to pass all the evil he threatened if you violate the covenant of the Lord your God and serve and worship other gods... " (23:6-16).

22. True worship begins at home. If parents do not practice and teach God's Words at home, they are partly to blame when their children do not serve the Lord. Joshua promised that he and his house would serve the Lord (24:15).

QUESTIONS

1. What did God tell Joshua after Moses died?
2. How did the Israelites cross the Jordan River?
3. What does Rahab the prostitute teach us about God and his people?
4. How was the city of Jericho conquered?
5. How did Achan's sin bring disaster to all the Israelites?
6. How was Joshua deceived by the Gibeonites?
7. Explain the paradox: The Lord gave the Israelites the land of Canaan; however, they had to fight to take possession of the Promised Land.
8. What was the importance of Joshua's farewell speech and his statement: "As for me and my house, we will serve the Lord" (24:15)?
9. What does the confusion that resulted when the eastern 2 and ½ tribes built an altar by the Jordan River, teach us about resolving conflict?
10. What could a spiritual leader learn from Joshua's life?

JUDGES		
1 — 3:4	3:5 — 16	17 — 21
DETERIORATIONS	CYCLES OF APOSTASIES, OPPRESSIONS AND DELIVERANCES	CORRUPTIONS
Reason for the Cycles	The Cycles History of the Judges	Other Examples of Corruption
Living with the Canaanites	Trouble with the Canaanites	Living like the Canaanites
Failure to conquer the people of the land / Judged by God because of the failure	The history of six cycles of Apostasies, Oppressions, Supplications and Deliverances. Each cycle begins with the fact: "The Israelites did evil in the eyes of the Lord." There are 13 judges who liberated and led Israel.	Idolatry / Immorality / Civil War
2 — 3:5	3:5 — 16:31	17 — 18 — 19 — 20 — 21

JUDGES: CYCLES OF APOSTASIES, OPPRESSIONS AND DELIVERANCES
Judges 1 - 21

STRUCTURE

Context:
Under Joshua's leadership, Israel conquered Canaan, the land the Lord God had promised to Abraham and his descendants. Israel served the Lord during Joshua's lifetime and during the lifetime of their older leaders who had experienced everything the Lord had done for Israel (24:31).

Key-person: Deborah and Barak, Gideon, and Samson

Key-location: Canaan

Key-repetitions:

Repetition of Six Cycles of Apostasy, Oppression, Supplication and Deliverance						
	1st 3:7-11	2nd 3:12-30	3rd 4:1-5:31	4th 6:1-8:35	5th 10:6-12:7	6th 13:1-16:31
Apostasy	3:7	3:12	4:1	6:1	10:6	13:1
Oppression	3:8	3:12-14	4:2	6:2	10:7	13:1
Supplication	3:9	3:15	4:3	6:6-7	10:10, 15	Not mentioned
Deliverance	3:9	3:15	4:4-7	6:12-14; 7:19-25	11:29, 33	13:3, 5; 15:20
Judges	Othniel	Ehud	Deborah	Gideon	Jephthah	Samson

- Judges.
- There was no king in Israel (17:6; 18:1; 19:1; 21:25).
- God used people who were aware of their own weakness: Barak (4:8) and Gideon (6:15).
- God used people and or things considered weak: Deborah (4:4-16) and Jael (4:17-23) who were women; Gideon and his 300 men (7:6-8); the jawbone of a donkey used by Samson (15:15).

Key-attitudes:
- The repeated failures of the Israelites.
- God's constant mercy
- The despair and humiliation of the oppressed Israelites.
- The insecurity of Barak and Gideon
- Samson's lewdness, his weakness for women.
- Conflict: The Israelites' conflict with their enemies and conflict among themselves.

Initial-problem:
After Joshua's death, the Israelites disobeyed God by putting the Canaanites to forced labor and allowing them to stay in the land.

Sequence of events:

Israel's Apostasy

- The Israelites never expelled all the Canaanites from their land (1:1-28).
- The Lord's angel told them that they had disobeyed him and that the people of the land would be like thorns and their gods would be traps to them. The people wept (2:1-5).
- The people served the Lord as long as Joshua was alive and during the lifetime of the older leaders (2:7-9).
- Another generation grew up that served the god Baal and the goddess Ashtoreth. The Israelites experienced cycles of: The Lord raised up enemies who oppressed them; they cried for help; the Lord raised up a judge who delivered them; when the judge died, the people returned to their old ways and became worse than their fathers (2:6-19).
- The Lord's anger blazed against Israel. He no longer drove out the people of the land, but left them as a test to see if the Israelites would obey his commands. The Israelites intermarried with the people and served the gods of those people (2:20 - 3:5).

Deborah and Barak

- The Israelites did evil in the eyes of the Lord. Sisera, the commander of Jabin's army, had 900 iron chariots and oppressed the Israelites for 20 years. They cried to the Lord for help (4:1-3).
- Deborah, a prophetess and judge, sent a message to Barak: The Lord commands you to take 10,000 soldiers to Mount Tabor and he will give Sisera into your hands (4:4-7).
- Barak replied he would go if Deborah also went. She answered that he would not get the glory; the Lord would let a woman defeat Sisera (4:8-10).
- Heber the Kenite had pitched his tent by the great tree near Kedesh (4:11).
- Barak advanced, and the Lord confused Sisera and his army. Barak and his men defeated Sisera's army and killed every man (4:1-16).
- Sisera fled on foot to Jael's (Herber's wife) tent. She used a tent peg to kill Sisera (4:17-22).
- God defeated Jabin (4:23).
- Deborah and Barak sang a song praising God and honoring Jael (5:1-31).
- The land had peace for forty years (5:31).

Gideon

- The Israelites did evil, and the Lord put them under the domination of Midian for 7 years. The Israelites cried out to the Lord (6:1-5).
- The Lord sent a prophet who told them they were suffering because of their disobedience (6:6-10).
- The Lord's angel came to the winepress where Gideon was separating wheat from the chaff and told him: "The Lord is with you, mighty warrior" (6:11-12).
- Gideon asked why had the Lord abandoned them. The Lord answered that he was sending Gideon to save Israel. Gideon replied he was too weak (6:13-15).
- The Lord said he would be with Gideon (6:16).
- Gideon requested a sign. Gideon prepared an offering of a young goat, and much bread. Fire flared from the rock and consumed the offering (6:17-24).
- That night Gideon tore down Baal's altar, cut down the Asherah pole and built an altar to the Lord. The townspeople wanted to stone him; but Joash, Gideon's father, answered that if Baal were a god, he could defend himself (6:25-32).
- 130,000 Midianites and other eastern peoples camped in the Valley of Jezreel. (See 8:10). Then Gideon blew his trumpet and 32,000 men responded to his summons (6:33-35).
- Twice Gideon used a fleece of wool to request confirmation from God (6:36-40).
- The Lord told Gideon that he had too large an army and that all who were afraid should leave. 22,000 men left; leaving 10,000 (7:1-3).
- The Lord separated those who lapped the water with their tongues from those who kneeled down to drink. Three hundred were left. The rest returned to their tents but left their jars and trumpets (7:5-8).
- Gideon visited the enemy camp and heard a man describe his dream of a loaf of barley bread that struck the tent and overturned it (7:9-15).
- Gideon divided the 300 men into three companies. He gave each man a trumpet and an empty jar with a burning torch inside. They separated around the edge of the camp. Everyone blew his trumpet, smashed his jar, held his torch and shouted: "A sword for the Lord and for Gideon!" Gideon's men stayed in place, but inside the camp, the men began shouting, running away and fighting each other (7:16-22).
- Other Israelites came out to chase the Midianites. Gideon sent messengers for the men of Ephraim to cut off the fords of the Jordan River. They secured the fords. They captured and killed two of the Midianite leaders, Oreb and Zeeb (7:23-25).
- The Ephraimites criticized Gideon because he had not called them to fight Midian. Gideon answered that they were the ones to capture the commanders (8:1-3).
- Gideon and his 300 crossed the Jordan in pursuit of Zebah and Zalmunna, the kings of Midian. Zebah and Zalmunna were left with 15,000 men. One hundred and twenty thousand had been killed. In a surprise attack, Gideon captured the two kings and defeated the enemy army (8:4-17).
- Zebah and Zalmunna had killed Gideon's brothers. Gideon killed them (8:18-21).
- The Israelites asked Gideon to rule over them. He refused. He requested that each man give him an earring from their share of the plunder. The gold earrings came to 43 pounds. Gideon used the gold to make an idol. Israel prostituted itself by worshiping the idol, and it ensnared Gideon and his family to sin (8:22-27).
- During Gideon's lifetime, the land enjoyed peace for 40 years (8:28-32).
- After Gideon died, the Israelites prostituted themselves to the Baal gods, and they failed to honor Gideon's family (8:33-35).

Samson

- The Israelites did evil, and the Lord delivered them to the Philistines for 40 years (13:1).
- Manoah's wife was childless. The Lord's angel told her she would have a son who would be a Nazirite from birth. He would begin delivering Israel (13:2-5).
- The woman told her husband about the angel's visit. Manoah prayed, asking for the angel to return to teach them how to raise the boy. When he returned, Manoah sacrificed a goat with a grain offering, and the angel ascended in the altar fire (13:6-23).
- The baby boy was named Samson (13:24-25).
- Samson saw a Philistine woman at Timnah and demanded her for his wife (14:1-4).
- On his way to Timnah, Samson killed a lion. Later, he found bees and honey in the lion's carcass (14:5-9).
- At his wedding feast Samson made a bet for 30 changes of clothes with 30 men that they could not find the answer to a riddle. His wife nagged him until she got the answer. Then she told the men (14:10-18).
- Samson killed 30 men and gave their clothes to those who had solved the riddle. In anger he went to his father's house. Samson's wife was given to the best man at the wedding (14:19-20).
- Later, Samson returned to his wife and discovered she had been given to another man. Samson sought revenge by using 300 foxes to set fire in the Philistines' fields (15:1-5).
- The Philistines then burned Samson's wife and her father to death. Samson sought revenge by slaughtering many Philistines. Then he returned to Judah (15:6-8).
- The men of Judah tied Samson with rope and took him to the Philistines. Samson broke the ropes and used a donkey jawbone to kill 1,000 men. He was thirsty and cried out to the Lord. God split a rock basin and water gushed out (15:9-19).
- Samson judged Israel for 20 years (15:20).
- Samson went to Gaza to see a prostitute. At midnight he removed the city gates and carried them to the top of a hill (16:1-3).
- Samson fell in love with Delilah. The Philistine rulers offered her silver if she discovered the secret of his strength (16:4-5).
- Delilah nagged Samson for the secret of his strength and how he could be subdued. Samson played games with her, telling her that he would be subdued: if anyone tied him with seven bow strings that have not been dried (16:6-9); if anyone tied him securely with new ropes (16:10-12); if they used the loom and wove the seven braids of his hair into cloth and tightened it (16:13-16).
- Finally Samson told her his secret: his hair had never been cut. Delilah got Samson to sleep. A man shaved his head. The Lord abandoned him (16:17-19).
- The Philistines seized Samson, gouged out his eyes, put him in prison and made him grind grain (16:20-21).
- His hair began to grow again (16:22).
- The Philistine rulers gathered to celebrate and sacrifice to their god Dagon. They made Samson put on a show for them. There were 3,000 people on the temple roof watching (16:23-27).
- Samson asked God for strength to get revenge on the Philistines. He pushed against the two central pillars that supported the temple. It crashed and Samson killed more when he died than while he was alive (16:23-30).
- His family buried him. He was a judge for 20 years (16:31).
- In those days Israel had no king; everyone did what he thought was right (21:25).

Final-situation:

In those days Israel had no king, and everyone did what he thought was right. As a result, each generation became worse than the generation of their fathers.

BIBLE STORY

Israel's Apostasy

After Joshua's death the Israelites continued to have victory over the Canaanites (1:1-26). When Israel became stronger, they put the Cananites to forced labor, but they never required all the Canaanites to leave their land. The Canaanites continued living in the land with them (1:27-28).

The Lord's angel went up from Gilgal to Bokim and said: "I brought you up out of Egypt; I led you into the land that I promised to give to your ancestors. I said: 'I will never break my covenant with you. But in return, you must never make a covenant with the people of this land. You must destroy their altars.' Yet you have disobeyed me. Why have you done this? Therefore, I will not drive them out before you; they will be thorns in your sides and their gods will be a trap to you."

After the Lord's angel spoke these things, the Israelites wept aloud (2:1-5).

The people served the Lord as long as Joshua was alive. They continued serving him during the lifetime of the older leaders who outlived Joshua, and who had seen all the great things the Lord had done for Israel. Joshua died at the age of a 110 (2:7-9).

After that generation died and their children grew up. They did not know the Lord nor what he had done for Israel. Then the Israelites did evil in the eyes of the Lord and served Baal's idols. They deserted the Lord, the God of their fathers, who had led them out of Egypt. They followed and worshiped other gods, gods of the peoples around them. They provoked the Lord to anger as they served the god Baal and the goddess Ashtoreth. Baal was the god of the storm and rains; therefore, he was thought to control vegetation and agriculture. Ashtoreth was the mother goddess of love, war and fertility. The Lord was hot with anger against Israel, and he handed them over to raiders who plundered them. The Israelites were unable to resist their enemies because the Lord fought on the side of their enemies. The Lord was true to his word and defeated them. They were in great distress. Then the Lord raised up judges, who saved them out of the hands of these raiders. Yet the Israelites would not listen to their judges.

Their enemies brought great distress on the Israelites. Then the Israelites cried for help. And each time the Lord had mercy on them and raised up a judge. The judges were not judges in courts of law; they were leaders who rescued the people in times of emergency. The Lord was with the judge and delivered them from their enemies as long as the judge lived. But when the judge died, the people returned to their old ways and became worse than their fathers, running after other gods and serving and worshiping them. They prostituted themselves to other gods! They quickly turned from the way of obeying the Lord's commands. They stubbornly refused to give up their evil practices (2:6-19).

Therefore, the Lord's anger blazed against Israel. The Lord said: "Because this nation has violated my covenant that I made with their ancestors and has not listened to me, I will no longer drive out before them the nations Joshua left when he died. I will use those nations to test Israel and see whether they will keep the way of the Lord as their ancestors did." Those nations were left to test the Israelites to see whether they would obey the Lord's commands. Those nations were left to teach the descendants of the Israelites who had not fought in those wars how to fight.

The Israelites lived among the people of the land. The Israelites began to marry the daughters of those people and they allowed their daughters to marry the sons of those people. The Israelites served the gods of those people (2:20 - 3:5).

Deborah and Barak

The Israelites once again did evil in the eyes of the Lord. So the Lord sold them into the hands of Jabin, king of Canaan, who reigned from Hazor. Sisera was the commander of Jabin's army. Sisera had nine hundred iron chariots and oppressed the Israelites for twenty years. Chariots were the most feared and powerful weapons of the day. Some chariots had razor-sharp knives extending from the wheels, designed to mutilate foot soldiers. Therefore, the Israelites cried to the Lord for help (4:1-3).

Deborah, a prophetess, was judge over Israel at that time. The Israelites came to her to have their disputes decided. She sent a message to a man named Barak: "The Lord, the God of Israel, commands you: `Go, take with you ten thousand soldiers from Naphtali and Zebulun and lead the way to Mount Tabor. I will lure Sisera, the commander of Jabin's army, with his chariots and his troops to the Kishon River and I will give him into your hands.'"

Barak said to Deborah: "If you go with me, I will go; but if you don't go with me, I won't go."

Deborah said: "Of course I will go with you. But because of your attitude, the honor will not be yours, for the Lord will let a woman defeat Sisera." Ten thousand men followed Barak, and Deborah also went with him.

Now Heber the Kenite had parted company with the other Kenites who were descendants of Moses' brother-in-law. Heber's tent was by the great tree near Kedesh, and he was friendly with Jabin.

Someone told Sisera that Barak had gone up to Mount Tabor. Sisera gathered together his nine hundred iron chariots and all the soldiers with him.

Deborah told Barak: "Go! Today is the day the Lord has given Sisera into your hands. Has not the Lord already cleared the way for you?" So Barak went down Mount Tabor, followed by ten thousand men. At Barak's advance, the Lord confused Sisera and his army and chariots. The Lord sent rain (5:4) and the Kishon River overflowed and swept Sisera's men away. The chariots bogged down in the mud (5:21). Barak and his men used their swords to defeat Sisera's army. Sisera jumped from his chariot and fled on foot. But Barak pursued the chariots and army. Sisera's entire fighting force was killed; not a man was left.

Sisera; however, was running for his life and fled on foot to the tent of Jael. She was the wife of Heber, a member of the Kenite clan. Jabin king of Hazor and Heber the Kenite were friendly with one another.

Jael stepped out to meet Sisera and said: "Come into my tent. Don't be afraid." So he entered her tent, and she covered him with a blanket.

Sisera said: "I'm thirsty. Please give me some water." She opened a leather bag in which she kept milk and gave him a drink. Then she covered him up again.

Sisera told Jael: "Stand in the entrance to the tent. If someone comes by and asks you, `Is anyone here?' say `No one is here.'"

When Sisera was asleep from exhaustion, Jael picked up a tent peg and a hammer; she went quietly to him and drove the peg through the side of Sisera's head and into the ground, and he died.

Barak arrived in pursuit of Sisera. Jael went out to greet him and told him: "Come, I will show you the man you're looking for." Barak entered her tent where Sisera lay dead, with a tent peg through his head.

On that day God defeated Jabin, the Canaanite king, before the Israelites. And the Israelites grew stronger and stronger against Jabin until they destroyed him (4:1-23).

On that day Deborah and Barak sang a song praising God and honoring Jael (5:1-31).

Then the land had peace for forty years (5:31).

Gideon

Again the Israelites did evil in the eyes of the Lord. The Lord put them under the domination of

Midian for seven years. Midian was so oppressive that the Israelites prepared hideouts for themselves in mountain clefts, caves and strongholds. Whenever the Israelites planted their crops, the Midianites, Amalekites and other eastern peoples invaded the country. They camped on the land and destroyed the crops that the Israelites had planted. They left nothing for Israel to eat. They took all their sheep, cattle and donkeys. They came up with their livestock and their tents like swarms of locusts. It was impossible to count the men and their camels. Midian so impoverished the Israelites that they cried out to the Lord for help (6:1-5).

The Israelites cried to the Lord for help against Midian. The Lord sent them a prophet, who said: "This is what the Lord, the God of Israel, says: I delivered you from Egypt, I freed you from the land of slavery. I rescued you from Egypt's brutality and from every oppressor. I saved you from the people of Canaan. I drove them from before you and gave you their land. I said to you: `I am the Lord your God; do not worship the gods of the Amorites, in whose land you live.' But you did not listen to me" (6:6-10).

One day the Lord's angel came and sat down under the oak in Ophrah that belonged to Joash the Abiezrite. Joash was the father of Gideon. Gideon was separating some wheat from the chaff in a winepress. Threshing, the process of separating the grains of wheat from the useless outer shell called chaff, was normally done on the top of a hill, where the wind could blow away the lighter chaff when the beaten wheat was thrown into the air. If Gideon had done this, he would have been seen by the Midianite raiders. Therefore, he separated wheat from the chaff in a winepress, a pit that was hidden from view. He did this to keep the wheat from the Midianites. The Lord's angel appeared to Gideon and said: "The Lord is with you, mighty warrior."

Gideon replied: "But sir, if the Lord is with us, why has all this happened to us? Where are all his miracle wonders that our fathers told us about when they said: `Did not the Lord bring us up out of Egypt?' But now the Lord has abandoned us and turned us over to Midian."

The Lord answered: "Go with your strength and save Israel out of Midian's hand. Am I not sending you?"

Gideon asked: "But Lord, how can I save Israel? My clan is the weakest in the Manasseh tribe, and I am the runt in my family."

The Lord answered: "I will be with you, and you will strike down all the Midianites together."

Gideon replied: "If you are serious about this, give me a sign that it is really you talking to me. Please do not leave until I come back and bring my offering and set it before you."

The Lord said: "I will wait until you return."

Gideon went in, prepared a young goat, and used over twenty quarts of flour to make bread without yeast. He put the meat in a basket and its broth in a pot; he brought them out and offered them to the angel under the shade of the oak tree.

The Lord's angel said to him: "Take the meat and the unleavened bread, place them on this rock, and pour out the broth." Gideon did as he was told. The angel stretched out the tip of the stick he was holding and touched the meat and the unleavened bread. Fire flared from the rock, consuming the meat and the bread! And the angel of the Lord vanished. When Gideon realized that it was the angel of the Lord, he exclaimed: "Ah, Sovereign Lord! I have seen the angel of the Lord face to face!"

But the Lord said to him: "Peace! Do not panic. You will not die."

So Gideon built an altar to the Lord there and called it The Lord is Peace (6:11-24).

That same night the Lord told Gideon: "Take two bulls that belong to your father. Take the seven year old one as the second bull. Tear down your father's altar to Baal and cut down the Asherah fertility pole beside it. Then build a proper kind of altar to the Lord your God on the top of this hill. Using fire wood from the Asherah pole that you cut down, offer the second bull as a whole-burnt-offering."

So Gideon took ten of his servants and did exactly what the Lord told him. But because he was afraid of his family and the men of the town, he did it at night.

Early in the morning the men of the town got up and saw that the altar for Baal had been demolished, the Asherah pole beside it had been cut down, and a bull had been sacrificed on the newly built altar!

They asked each other: "Who did this?"

After many questions they found their answer: "Gideon son of Joash did it."

The men of the town demanded of Joash: "Bring out your son. He must die! He broke down Baal's altar and cut down the Asherah pole beside it."

But Joash replied to the hostile crowd: "Are you going to plead Baal's cause? Are you going to save him? Whoever fights for Baal shall be put to death by morning! If Baal really is a god, he can defend himself when someone breaks down his altar." So that day they nicknamed Gideon "Jerub-Baal." The name means: "Let Baal fight him." He got the nickname because he broke down Baal's altar (6:25-32).

Now all the Midianites, Amalekites and other eastern peoples joined forces and crossed over the Jordan and camped in the Valley of Jezreel. (There were more than one hundred and thirty-five thousand soldiers.) (See 8:10.) Then the Spirit of the Lord came upon Gideon, and he blew his ram's horn trumpet, summoning the Abiezrites to follow him. He sent messengers throughout Manasseh, calling them to arms, and also sent messengers into Asher, Zebulun and Naphtali. Thirty-two thousand Israelite men came (6:33-35).

Gideon said to God: "If you will use me to save Israel as you have promised, look, I will place a wool fleece on the threshing floor. If dew is only on the fleece and all the ground is dry, then I will know that you will use me to save Israel, as you said." And that is what happened. Gideon rose early the next day; he squeezed the fleece and wrung out the dew, a bowlful of water.

Then Gideon said to God: "Do not be angry with me. Let me make just one more request. Allow me one more test with the fleece. This time make the fleece dry and the ground covered with dew." That night God made it happen. The fleece was dry; the ground was wet with dew (6:36-40).

Early in the morning, Gideon and all his men camped at the spring of Harod. The Midianites were camped north of them in the valley near the hill of Moreh. The Lord told Gideon: "Your army is too large for me to deliver Midian into your hands. The Israelites will brag saying they won the battle with their own strength. Announce to the people: `Anyone who is afraid may turn back and leave Mount Gilead.'" So twenty-two thousand men left, while ten thousand remained (7:1-3).

But the Lord said to Gideon: "There are still too many men. Take them down to the water, and I will make a final cut. If I say: `This one shall go with you,' he shall go; but if I say:`This one shall not go with you,' he shall not go."

So Gideon took the men down to the water. There the Lord told him: "Separate those who lap the water with their tongues like a dog from those who kneel down to drink, with their face in the water." Three hundred men cupped their hands to bring water to their mouths. They lapped with their tongues from their cupped hands. All the rest got down on their knees to drink and put their face in the water.

The Lord said to Gideon: "I will use the three hundred men who lapped at the stream to save you and give the Midianites into your hands. Let all the other men go home." So Gideon sent the rest of the Israelites to their tents, but kept the three hundred. He took the jars and trumpets of those who went home (7:5-8).

Now the camp of Midian was in the valley below Gideon. That night the Lord told Gideon: "Get up, go down against the camp, because I am going to give it into your hands. But if you are afraid to attack, go down to the camp with your servant Purah and listen to what they are saying. When you hear what they are saying, you'll be bold." So Gideon and Purah his servant went down to the outposts of the camp. The Midianites, the Amalekites and all the other eastern peoples had settled in the valley, thick as locusts. Their camels could no more be counted than the sand on the seashore.

Gideon arrived just in time to hear a man telling a friend his dream. "I dreamed that a round loaf of barley bread came tumbling into the Midianite camp. It struck the tent so hard that the tent overturned and collapsed."

The man's friend responded: "This can be nothing other than the sword of Gideon, the Israelite. God has given the Midianites and the whole camp into his hands."

When Gideon heard the dream and its interpretation, he worshiped God. He returned to the camp of Israel and called out: "Get up! The Lord has given the Midianite camp into your hands" (7:9-15).

Gideon divided the three hundred men into three companies. He gave each man a trumpet and an empty jar. A burning torch was inside each jar.

Gideon told them: "Watch me. Do what I do. When I get to the edge of the camp, do exactly what I do. When I and all who are with me blow our trumpets, then from all around the camp blow yours and shout: `For the Lord and for Gideon.'"

Gideon and the hundred men with him reached the edge of the enemy camp at the beginning of the middle watch, just after they had changed the guard. All three groups of Gideon's men blew their trumpets and smashed the jars that were in their hands. They held the torches in their left hands and the trumpets in their right hands. Then they shouted: "A sword for the Lord and for Gideon!" Each of Gideon's men stayed in his place around the camp. But inside the camp, the men of Midian began shouting and running away.

When the three hundred trumpets sounded, the Lord caused the men throughout the camp to turn on one another with their swords. The enemy soldiers ran for their lives. Gideon sent messengers throughout the hill country of Ephraim, saying: "Come down against the Midianites and capture the fords of the Jordan ahead of them as far as Beth Barah. Do this before the Midianites can get to the river and cross it."

So all the men of Ephraim were called out and captured the fords of the Jordan as far as Beth Barah. They also captured two of the Midianite leaders, Oreb and Zeeb. They killed Oreb and Zeeb. They pursued the Midianites and brought the heads of Oreb and Zeeb to Gideon, who was by the Jordan (7:16-25).

The Ephraimites criticized Gideon: "Why have you treated us like this? Why didn't you call us when you went to fight Midian?"

Gideon answered them: "What have I done compared to you? God gave you Midian's commanders, Oreb and Zeeb. What have I done compared to you?" At this, their resentment against him subsided (8:1-3).

Gideon and his three hundred men arrived at the Jordan and crossed over. Now Zebah and Zalmunna were in Karkor with a force of about fifteen thousand men, all that were left of the armies of the eastern peoples; a hundred and twenty thousand swordsmen had been killed. Gideon went up by the route of the caravan trails east of Nobah and Jogbehah. He found and attacked the unsuspecting army. Zebah and Zalmunna, the two kings of Midian, fled, but he chased and captured the two kings. Gideon and his men defeated the enemy army.

Gideon then returned from the battle.

Gideon asked Zebah and Zalmunna: "You killed some men on Mount Tabor. What were those men like?"

The two kings answered: "Men like you, each one

with the bearing of a prince."

Gideon replied: "Those were my brothers, my mother's sons. As surely as the Lord lives, if you had spared their lives, I would spare yours." Then he spoke to Jether, his oldest son and said: "Kill them!" But Jether did not draw his sword, because he was only a boy and was afraid.

Zebah and Zalmunna said: "Come, do it yourself, it is a man's job." So Gideon stepped forward and killed them. Then he took the ornaments off their camels' necks (8:4-21).

The Israelites said to Gideon: "Rule over us, you, your son and your grandson, because you have saved us from Midian's tyranny."

Gideon replied: "I will not rule over you; my son will not rule over you. The Lord will rule over you. I do have one request. Would each of you give me an earring from your share of the plunder?" The Ishmaelites men wore gold earrings and Gideon's men had their pockets full of them.

They answered: "We'll be glad to give them." So they spread out a garment, and each man threw a ring from his plunder onto it. The gold earrings came to about forty-three pounds. That did not include the other gifts the people gave Gideon. They gave him the ornaments, the pendants, the purple garments worn by the kings of Midian and the chains that were on their camels' necks. Gideon used the gold to make an idol, which he placed in Ophrah, his hometown. All Israel prostituted themselves by worshiping the idol. It became a trap that caused Gideon and his family to sin (8:22-27).

Thus Midian's tyranny was broken by the Israelites. During Gideon's lifetime, the land enjoyed peace for forty years. Gideon died at a good old age and was buried in the tomb of his father Joash. That tomb is in Ophrah where the Abiezrites live (8:28-32).

No sooner had Gideon died than the Israelites again prostituted themselves to the Baal gods. They set up Baal-Berith as their god and did not remember the Lord their God, who had rescued them from all their enemies who resided all around them. They also failed to honor Gideon's family for all the good things he had done for them (8:33-35).

Samson

Again the Israelites did evil in the eyes of the Lord, so the Lord delivered them into the hands of the Philistines for forty years (13:1).

There was a man named Manoah from the city of Zorah. Manoah was from the tribe of Dan. His wife was unable to have children. The angel of the Lord appeared to Manoah's wife and told her: "You are barren and childless, but you will become pregnant and have a son. Do not drink wine nor any other fermented drink. Do not eat anything ritually unclean. You will conceive and give birth to a son. Never cut his hair. No razor may be used on his head, because the boy is to be a Nazirite. He will be given to God from the moment of his birth. He will begin the deliverance of Israel from Philistine oppression" (13:2-5).

The woman went to her husband and told him: "A man of God came to me. He looked like an angel of God, very awesome. I didn't ask him where he came from, and he didn't tell me his name. But he said to me: `You will become pregnant and give birth to a son. Now then, drink no wine nor any other fermented drink and do not eat anything ritually unclean, because the boy will be a Nazirite dedicated to God from birth until the day of his death.'"

Manoah prayed to God: "O Lord, I beg you, let the man of God come to us again to teach us how to raise this boy who is to be born."

God heard Manoah, and the Lord's angel came again to the woman while she was out in the field; but her husband Manoah was not with her. The woman hurried to tell her husband: "He's back! The man who appeared to me the other day!"

Manoah got up and followed his wife. When he came to the man, he asked: "Are you the one who spoke to my wife?"

The man replied: "I am."

Manoah asked him: "When your words come true, what do you have to tell us about the boy's life and work?"

The angel of the Lord answered: "Your wife must do all that I told her. Eat nothing that grows on a grapevine. She must not drink any wine nor other fermented drink. She must not eat anything ritually unclean. She must obey everything I commanded her."

Manoah said to the angel of the Lord: "We would like you to stay until we prepare a young goat for you."

The Lord's angel replied: "Even if I stay, I will not eat your food. But if you prepare a whole-burnt-offering, offer it to the Lord." Manoah did not realize he was talking to the angel of the Lord.

Then Manoah inquired of the Lord's angel: "What is your name, so that we may honor you when your word comes true?"

The angel replied: "Why do you ask my name? It's too wonderful for your understanding."

Manoah took a young goat, together with the grain offering, and sacrificed it on a rock to the Lord. The Lord did an amazing thing while Manoah and his wife watched: As the flame leaped up from the altar toward heaven, the angel of the Lord ascended in the altar fire. Manoah and his wife saw this and fell face-down to the ground. When the Lord's angel did not show himself again, Manoah realized that he was the angel of the Lord.

Manoah told his wife: "We are condemned to die! We have seen God!"

But his wife answered: "If the Lord had meant to kill us, he would not have accepted a whole-burnt-offering and grain offering from our hands, nor given us this birth announcement" (13:6-23).

The woman gave birth to a boy and named him Samson. The boy grew and the Lord blessed him.

The Spirit of the Lord began to work in Samson while he was at a camp in Dan (13:24-25).

Samson went down to Timnah and saw a young Philistine woman. When he returned, he said to his father and mother: "I saw a Philistine woman in Timnah; now get her for me as my wife."

His parents replied: "Surely you can find a woman from Israel to marry. Must you go to the uncircumcised Philistines to get a wife?"

But Samson said to his father: "Get her for me. She's the right one for me."

His parents did not know that God was behind this. The Lord was seeking an occasion to start a fight with the Philistines; for at that time they were ruling over Israel (14:1-4).

Samson went down to Timnah together with his father and mother. As they approached the vineyards of Timnah, suddenly a young lion came roaring toward Samson. The Spirit of the Lord came upon him with great power and he ripped the lion apart with his bare hands, as he might have torn a young goat. But he did not tell his parents what he had done. He went down and talked with the Philistine woman and he liked her.

Several days later, when he went back to marry her, he made a little detour to look at the lion's carcass. In it was a swarm of bees and some honey. Samson scooped up the honey with his hands and ate as he went along. When he rejoined his parents, he gave them some, and they too ate it. But he did not tell them that he had taken the honey from the lion's carcass (14:5-9).

Now his father went down to make arrangements with the woman. Samson prepared a feast there, as was customary for bridegrooms. The townspeople sent thirty men to be with Samson.

Samson told the thirty men: "Let me tell you a riddle. If you can give me the answer within the seven days of the feast, I will give you thirty linen garments and thirty changes of clothes. If you can't tell me the answer, you must give me thirty linen garments and thirty changes of clothes."

The thirty men replied: "Tell us your riddle; let's hear it."

Samson replied: "Out of the eater came something to eat; out of the strong came something sweet."

For three days they could not give the answer.

On the fourth day, they said to Samson's wife: "Sweet-talk your husband into explaining the riddle for us, or we will burn you and your father's household. Did you invite us here to bankrupt us?"

Then Samson's wife turned on the tears and threw herself on him, sobbing: "You hate me! You don't really love me. You've told my people a riddle, but you haven't told me the answer."

Samson replied: "I haven't even told my own parents, so why should I tell you?" She cried the rest of the seven days of the feast. On the seventh day, worn out by her nagging, he finally told her. She in turn explained the riddle to her people.

Before sunset on the seventh day the men of the town said to Samson: "What is sweeter than honey? What is stronger than a lion?"

Samson said to them: "If you had not plowed with my heifer, you would not have solved my riddle" (14:10-18).

Then the Spirit of the Lord came upon him and gave him power. He went down to Ashkelon, killed thirty of their men, stripped them of their belongings and gave their clothes to those who had solved the riddle. Burning with anger, he went home to his father's house. And Samson's wife was given to the best man at the wedding (14:19-20).

Later on, during wheat harvest, Samson took a young goat and went to visit his wife. He said: "I'm going to my wife's bedroom." But her father would not let him go in.

The father told Samson: "I concluded that you hated your wife, and I gave her to your best man. Isn't her younger sister more beautiful? Take her instead."

Samson said to him: "This time I have a good reason to get even with you Philistines; I will wreak havoc on them."

Samson went out and caught three hundred foxes. He took two foxes at a time and tied their tails together. Then he tied a torch to the tails of each pair of foxes. He set fire to the torches and let the terrified foxes loose in the Philistines' fields of ripe grain. Everything burned, both stacked and standing grain, together with the vineyards and olive groves (15:1-5).

The Philistines asked: "Who did this?"

They were told: "Samson, son-in-law of the Timnite who took his wife and gave her to his best man."

The Philistines went up and burned her and her father to death.

Samson then said: "Since you've acted like this, I won't stop until I get my revenge on you." He attacked them viciously and slaughtered many of them. Then he went down and stayed in a cave at Etam Rock (15:6-8).

The Philistines went up and camped in Judah. The men of Judah asked: "Why have you come to fight us?"

The Philistines answered: "We have come to capture Samson; we are going to do to him as he did to us."

Then three thousand men from Judah went down to the cave at Etam Rock and said to Samson: "Don't you realize that the Philistines are rulers over us? What have you done to us?"

Samson answered: "I merely did to them what they did to me."

The men from Judah said: "We've come to tie you up and hand you over to the Philistines."

Samson requested: "Promise that you won't kill me yourselves."

The men from Judah answered: "Agreed. We will only tie you up and hand you over to them. We will not kill you." So they bound him with two new ropes and led him up from the rock and took Samson to the

Philistines who came toward him shouting in triumph. The Spirit of the Lord came upon him and gave him power. The ropes on his arms became like charred flax, and the bindings dropped from his hands. Samson saw a fresh donkey jawbone. He grabbed it and killed a thousand men.

Then Samson said: "With a donkey's jawbone, I have made donkeys of them. With a donkey's jawbone, I have killed a thousand men."

When he finished speaking, he threw away the jawbone.

Samson was very thirsty, and he cried out to the Lord: "You have given your servant this great victory. Must I now die of thirst and fall into the hands of the uncircumcised?" Then God split open the rock basin, and water gushed out. When Samson drank, he felt his strength return (15:9-19).

Samson judged Israel for twenty years in the days of the Philistines (15:20).

One day Samson went to Gaza, where he saw a prostitute. He went in to spend the night with her. The news got around: "Samson is here!" So they surrounded the place and lay in wait for him all night at the city gate. They made no move during the night, saying: "At dawn we'll kill him."

Samson stayed in bed with the prostitute until midnight. Then he got up and seized the city gate along with the two door posts. He tore them loose, bar and all. He lifted them to his shoulders and carried them to the top of the hill that faces Hebron (16:1-3).

Some time later, he fell in love with a woman in the Valley of Sorek. Her name was Delilah. The Philistine rulers approached her and said: "Seduce him. Discover the secret of his great strength and how we can overpower him so we may tie him up and dominate him. Each one of us will give you twenty-eight pounds of silver" (16:4-5).

So Delilah said to Samson: "Tell me the secret of your great strength and how you can be tied up and subdued."

Samson answered her: "If anyone ties me with seven bow strings, the kind made from fresh animal tendons, that have not been dried, I'll become as weak as any other man."

Then the rulers of the Philistines brought her seven fresh bowstrings that had not been dried, and she tied him with them. With men hidden in another room, she called to him: "Samson, the Philistines are about to capture you!" But he snapped the bowstrings as easily as a piece of string snaps when it comes close to a flame. The secret of his strength was still a secret.

Then Delilah said to Samson: "You have made a fool of me; you lied to me. Be serious; tell me how you can be tied up."

He said: "If anyone ties me securely with new ropes that have never been used, I'll become as weak as any other man."

So Delilah took new ropes and tied Samson. Then, with men hidden in another room, she called to him: "Samson, the Philistines are about to capture you!" But he snapped the ropes off his arms as if they were threads. The secret of his strength was still a secret.

Delilah then said to Samson: "You are still playing games with me. You have been making a fool of me and lying to me. Tell me how you can be tied up."

He replied: "Use the loom for making cloth from thread. Weave the seven braids of my hair into the cloth. Tighten it with a pin. Then I'll become as weak as any other man." So while he was sleeping, Delilah took the seven braids of his head, wove them into the fabric and tightened it with the pin.

Again she called to him: "Samson, the Philistines are about to capture you!" He awoke from his sleep and pulled up the pin and the loom, with the fabric. The secret of his strength was still a secret.

Then Delilah said to him: "How can you say, `I love you,' when you won't even trust me? This is the third time you have made a fool of me and haven't told me the secret of your great strength." She nagged him day after day until he could not take any more.

So he told her everything. "I have never had my hair cut. No razor has ever been used on my head, because I have been set apart to God as a Nazirite since birth. If my head were shaved, my strength would leave me, and I would become as weak as any other man."

Delilah saw that he had told her everything so she sent word to the Philistine rulers: "Come back once more; this time he has told me everything." So the Philistine rulers returned with the silver they had promised her. Delilah got Samson to go to sleep with his head lying in her lap. Then she motioned to a man to shave off his seven braids of hair. Immediately he began to grow weak. His strength left him.

Then she called: "Samson, the Philistines are about to capture you!"

He awoke from his sleep and thought: "I'll get loose as I did before and shake myself free." He did not know that the Lord had abandoned him (16:6-19).

Then the Philistines seized him, gouged out his eyes and took him down to Gaza. They put bronze chains on him and put him in prison and made him grind grain (16:6-21).

But the hair on his shaved head began to grow again (16:22).

Now the Philistine rulers gathered to celebrate. They offered a great sacrifice to their god Dagon saying: "Our god has delivered Samson, our enemy, into our hands."

When the people saw Samson, they praised their god, saying: "Our god has delivered our enemy into our hands, the one who killed many of us."

While they were in high spirits, they shouted: "Bring out Samson to entertain us." So they sent for and brought Samson out of the prison, and he put on a show for them.

They had him standing between the pillars of the temple of Dagon. A servant held Samson's hand and acted as his guide. Samson made a request to the servant: "Put me where I can touch the pillars that support the temple. I want to lean against them." Now the temple was crowded with men and women; all the Philistine rulers were there. There were about three thousand men and women on the roof watching Samson perform. Then Samson prayed to God: "O Sovereign Lord, remember me. O God, please strengthen me just once more, and let me with one blow get revenge on the Philistines for my two eyes." Then Samson reached toward the two central pillars that held up the temple and pushed against them, his right hand on the one and his left hand on the other. Samson said: "Let me die with the Philistines!" Samson pushed with all his might, and the temple crashed on the rulers and all the people in it. Thus he killed many more when he died than he had killed while he was alive (16:23-30).

His brothers and all his relatives went down to get his body. They brought him back and buried him in the tomb of Manoah his father. Samson was a judge for the people of Israel for twenty years (16:31).

In those days Israel had no king; everyone did what he thought was right (21:25).

LIFE-LESSONS DISCOVERED IN THE STORY

1. God's people experience victory in their lives only when they are faithful to him. The book of Judges teaches that the people of Israel prospered and enjoyed victories over their enemies only when they were faithful to God.

2. God is active in history. The book of the Judges gives a theological vision of history. Israel abandoned God for Baal. God then abandoned Israel allowing oppressors to dominate them; Israel called on God for help; then God sent a liberator to deliver the Israelites. History repeated itself. God was the Theocratic King who raised up people who represented him as judges within the nation.

3. The infidelity of God's people always results in misfortune and defeat. The infidelity of the Israelites, when they worshiped other gods, always brought the misfortune of an oppressive enemy.

4. Disobeying an explicit order from God results in discipline and punishment. The Israelites disobeyed God when they refused to expel the former residents of the land (Dt 7:1-6; Jdg 1:27-28; 2:1-3). Israel wanted to maintain the Canaanites as slaves and cheap labor. The result was disastrous. The book of Judges tells stories about the results of their worshiping other gods; they were repeatedly dominated by enemies.

5. The person who believes it is to his advantage to disobey God's orders will suffer disaster. God gave explicit commands for the Israelites to get rid of all the people who had lived in Canaan. (See Dt 7:1-6.) Israel thought it was to her financial advantage to keep the Canaanites as slave labor (Jdg 1:27-28). Israel suffered because the Canaanites became enemies who oppressed them, and their gods became traps that ensnared them (2:1-3).

6. God's love is without limit and he is always ready to forgive the sinner who repents, believes in him and calls on him. The Israelites suffered the consequences of rebelling against God. Whenever they clamored to God, motivated by their pain and suffering, he sent a judge to rescue them. In spite of the fact that the Israelites constantly deviated from God's orientation, every time they clamored to God, he heard them and forgave (2:11-19; 6:6).

7. People who do not respond to God's love, may seek him when in pain. The Israelites did not remain faithful to God when they were blessed with the benefits of his love. However, whenever they suffered, they remembered God and clamored to him.

8. Sinful man is unable to save himself from the consequences of his sin. The Israelites were being punished for sin; whenever they repented and called on him, God sent judges. The judges were unable to save the Israelites with their own strength. God was the one who gave the judges wisdom, guidance and strength to free the Israelites.

9. People are sinners, and each generation faces its own dominant style of sin. The generation that left Egypt lacked faith that God would enable them to defeat the Canaanites. The sin that dominated the generation that wandered in the desert was murmuring and complaining. The sin that dominated the generation after Joshua, was refusing to obey God's explicit orders and expel the Canaanites from the land (2:2-3).

10. God considers the infidelity of his people as spiritual adultery. God used marriage to illustrate the covenant relationship between himself and Israel. God was the husband who protected and provided for his bride, while Israel was the beloved bride. When the Israelites worshiped other gods, God condemned them for participating in an adulterous relationship involving spiritual prostitution (Jdg 2:17). (See Jer 3:1-13.)

11. Inside spiritual decay results in outside oppression. The Israelites, who did not obey God's order to get rid of the people of the land,

experienced inside spiritual decay when they began to worship the gods of the land and to intermarry with the people of the land. For not obeying God, the Israelites were dominated by enemies (2:11-15).

12. The lifestyle of those who worship false gods entices those who serve the Lord. The generation of Israelites after Joshua abandoned the faith of their parents and worshiped the gods of their neighbors (2:11-15). The desire to be accepted by those who surround us can lead us into behavior that is unacceptable to God.

13. Women have an important place in the history of God's people. Deborah was a prophetess who judged Israel and settled disputes on God's behalf (4:4). She was a prophetess, like Miriam (Ex 15:20) and Huldah (2 Kin 22:14). God gave credit for the defeat of Sisera to a woman named Jael and not to a man (Jdg 4:9, 21).

14. Songs of praise focus attention on God, give his people an outlet for celebration and remind them of God's faithfulness and character. An important part of worship is praising God, both for what he did in past history and for what he is doing in the present. The song of Deborah is an example of singing praises to God for victory (5:1-32). Exodus 15 is also a song celebrating the actions of God in favor of Israel.

15. God likes to use things and people considered weak. In Judges, God used people considered weak. For instance: Deborah, a woman (4:4-16); Gideon and his 300 men (7:6-8); and Samson used a donkey's jaw bone (15:15). (See 1 Cor 1:26-29.)

16. God uses people who are aware of their own weaknesses. Barak (4:8) and Gideon (6:15) didn't consider themselves capable of leading an army to free the Israelites. Others who lacked faith in themselves are Moses (Ex 4:13) and Jeremiah (Jer 1:16). (See 2 Cor 3:4-6.)

17. It is easy for a person to overlook personal accountability and blame his problems on God. Gideon questioned God about the problems his nation faced and about God's apparent lack of help. He didn't acknowledge that the people brought calamity upon themselves when they decided to disobey and neglect God (6:13).

18. In times of calamity, the Lord's people often conclude that he has abandoned them. Gideon felt that the Lord had abandoned the Israelites and turned them over to Midian (6:13).

19. The person who begins to serve God may be criticized by God's people, the very people who should support him. Gideon obeyed God and tore down the altar of the pagan god Baal. Afterwards, his fellow Israelites wanted to kill him (6:25-30). God said that idolaters must be stoned to death (Dt 13:6-11) but the Israelites had become so immoral they wanted to stone Gideon.

20. Fear results in a person's seeking extra signs from God when he should be taking action to obey God's commands. Gideon didn't use the fleece of wool to discover God's will (6:37), because the angel had already told him what he should do (6:14, 16). The fleece of wool was used to strengthen his weak faith. Proverbs 3:5 and James 1:5-8 give advice on discovering God's will. Also, whenever a person receives a command from God, he should obey it instead of seeking more confirmation.

21. A small number of the weak who put their trust in God have advantage over the multitudes who are strong but do not have God on their side. Gideon the coward was hiding in a wine press from the Midianites. He belonged to the weakest clan in his tribe, and he was the runt in his family (6:11-14). God used Gideon and three hundred men to defeat thousands (7:16-25).

22. God wants to receive honor for his actions. The Lord reduced Gideon's army to three hundred men. God knew that a larger victorious army would brag saying they won the battle with their own strength. He wanted the people to know that the victory came from the Lord. The Lord of the army was one who deserved all the credit (7:2-8).

23. The Lord can lead his people to use a new strategy that has never been used before. When Moses was leader, Joshua fought the Amalekites in the valley while Moses observed from a mountain with Aaron and Hur holding up his hands (Ex 17:8-16). Joshua was the leader in the battle against Jericho. For six days the Israelites marched around Jericho once each day. On the seventh day, they circled the city seven times (Jos 6:1-27). But Gideon used a new strategy against the Midianites. He divided 300 men into three companies who went to the edge of the enemy camp. Each smashed a jar, held a torch in his left hand, held a trumpet in his right hand and shouted: "A sword for the Lord and for Gideon!" (Jdg 7:16-22).

24. The diplomatic person who doesn't care who gets the praise helps keep peace in God's kingdom. Israel's tribal family of the Ephraimites criticized Gideon because he did not invite them to fight Midian. Gideon replied that they deserved more praise for killing the two commanders than he did for killing all the soldiers. At this, their resentment against him subsided (8:1-3).

25. Not every essential chore brings recognition; many necessary tasks are considered dirty work

by some. Ephraim's leaders felt left out because Gideon had not called them to join the battle, but had left them in place to cut off the escaping Midianites (8:1-3).

26. It is often easier to be faithful to God during a crisis time than during prosperity. Gideon was faithful to God during the crisis of war, but after victory when he enjoyed prosperity, he was unfaithful. He made an idol and had children with a lot of different women (8:22-30).

27. Parents should look to God for guidance on how to raise their children. Manoah prayed for God to give him and his wife wisdom to raise their son (13:8). It should be recommended that every father pray Manoah's prayer.

28. Parents can and should dedicate their child to God. However, it is the child who must decide for himself if he will be faithful to God. Manoah and his wife consecrated their child Samson to God from the time he was conceived. As man, he constantly violated his Nazirite vows in order to satisfy carnal appetites. He used God-given capacities to satisfy selfish desires. He was strong as a giant and weak as a child. He fascinated the women and was deceived by them. He made trouble for the Philistines; however, he didn't free the Israelites from oppression. He took revenge on an oppressor that he had to live with, and his actions made him a person to be ridiculed (13-16).

29. Strength in one area of life does not make up for weakness in other areas. Samson's physical strength did not make up for his moral weakness.

30. The person who is dedicated to God, but seeks sex outside of the marriage, faces destruction. An example is Samson and Delilah (16:4-21).

31. A woman who uses sex to manipulate men is a curse to those who enjoy her body. The man who allows a woman to manipulate him in order to gain sexual privileges is giving the woman the ability to ruin him. Motivated by greed, Delilah used Samson's infatuation with her to manipulate him and caused his downfall (16:1-21).

32. The selfish person who is in spiritual decline may be used by God; however, that person will experience discipline and destruction. Samson is an example. God used Samson to bring temporary benefit to the Israelites. However, Samson didn't use God-given talents for the purpose of helping his people. He only used his force to avenge. His defeat was the result of: forgetting to appreciate God's presence; seeking to satisfy personal appetites with pagan girlfriends; practicing sins without feeling remorse nor confessing them; surrendering to an uncontrolled sexual appetite and constantly violating his Nazirite vows to God. God called Samson to judge Israel, and endowed him with spiritual power; however, Samson didn't accomplish any permanent benefit for Israel, and he died in captivity, humiliated by the Philistines.

33. God's servant who is determined to do what he wants to do, risks losing divine power without even being aware of it. When Samson lost his God-given power, he didn't even realize that God had abandoned him, and he went to face the Philistines and was defeated (16:18-21).

34. The person who chooses to disobey God will face undesirable consequences resulting from his choice. Samson chose to be with Delilah, and the consequences of his choice were: he lost his strength, he was captured, his eyes were put out and he was publicly humiliated (16:1-27).

35. The individual is often unaware of the manifestation or lack of manifestation of God's power in his life. When Samson lost his God-given power, he didn't even realize that God had abandoned him when he faced the Philistines and was defeated (Jdg16:18-21). When Moses came down from Mount Sinai, he was unaware that his face glowed, yet others saw the glow (Ex 34:29-36).

36. God in his Word establishes some absolutes about what is right and wrong. Whenever people reserve for themselves the right to decide what is right and wrong, they will choose evil and sin against God. During the time of the judges, there was no king in Israel, and everyone did what he thought was right. The result was that the people sinned against God and every generation became more evil than the generation before them (Jdg 2:6-13; 21:25).

QUESTIONS

1. After Joshua died, how did the Israelites displease the Lord?
2. What do the historical events recorded in the book of Judges teach us about God?
3. How did God punish the Israelites when they worshiped idols and other gods?
4. When the Israelites were oppressed for disobeying God, how did they again obtain God's help?
5. Why was Barak unable to receive honor for winning the battle over Sisera?
6. Why did God reduce the number of the men in Gideon's army to only three hundred?
7. How was God able to use people who recognized their weakness, during the time of the judges?
8. What can we learn from Samson about a person who is called by God, and spiritually empowered by God, but desires to satisfy selfish desires?
9. What does the book of Judges teach us about the results when each individual decides for himself what is right or wrong?
10. What did you learn from Deborah, Barak, Gideon and Samson that you should apply to your own life?

RUTH: RESTRUCTURING ONE'S LIFE AFTER A FORCED ADAPTATION
Ruth 1 - 4

STRUCTURE

Context:
The story of Ruth happened during the time when judges ruled in Israel. In those days Israel had no king; everyone did what he thought was right and each generation became worse than the one of his parents.

Key-persons: Naomi, Ruth and Boaz

Key-location: Moab and Bethlehem

Key-repetitions:
- Problems: hunger (1:1); death (1:3; 5); Naomi telling her daughters-in-law to return to their mother's home (1:11-14); embittered Naomi (1:13; 20); need of food (2:2); the danger of Ruth being abused (2:8; 22); Naomi needed to find a husband for Ruth (3:1); there was a kinsman-redeemer who was a closer relative to Ruth than Boaz (3:12-13).
- Boaz helped Ruth: he made it easy for her to gather grain (2:9, 15-16); he offered water and food (2:8, 14); he encouraged her (2:11-12); he offered her protection (2:9, 16, 22); he valued her as a person (2:11, 3:11).

Key-attitudes:
- The persistence of Ruth in facing obstacles.
- The bitterness of Naomi.
- The virtue of Ruth.
- The kindness of Boaz.
- Happiness for Naomi after facing many problems.

Initial-problem:
During the time when judges ruled in Israel, there was a famine in Judah. Elimelech, his wife Naomi and their two sons left Judah to go to the country of Moab.

Sequence of events:

Naomi and Ruth Return to Bethlehem
- When judges ruled, everyone did as he saw fit (Jdg 21:25).
- There was a famine in Judah. Elimelech, his wife Naomi and their two sons Mahlon and Kilion, left home for Moab (1:1-2).
- Elimelech died. The sons married Moabite women, Orpah and Ruth. After 10 years the two sons died (1:2-5).
- Naomi heard that there was food in Judah. She and her daughters-in-law set out for Judah. Naomi told her daughters-in-law to return to their mother's home. They resisted (1:6-10).
- Naomi insisted that her daughters-in-laws return home. Orpah kissed Naomi good-bye, but Ruth insisted she would not leave Naomi (1:10-18).
- Naomi told the Bethlehem women not to call her Naomi (happy) but to call her Mara (bitter) (1:19-21).

Ruth and Boaz
- Naomi and Ruth arrived in Bethlehem at the beginning of the barley harvest (1:22).
- Boaz, a prominent man, was a relative of Elimelech (2:1).
- Ruth went to Boaz's fields to gather grain (2:1-3).
- Boaz sought information about Ruth. He showed kindness to her. She expressed her gratitude (2:5-13).
- At lunch break, Boaz gave Ruth food and ordered his workmen to be kind to her (2:14-16).
- Ruth gathered about one-half bushel of barley. Ruth told Naomi she had worked in Boaz's field. Naomi praised the Lord and said Boaz was one of their kinsmen-redeemers. They agreed that Ruth should continue in Boaz's field (2:17-23).
- Naomi said it was time for her to get a husband for Ruth. She told Ruth to go to the threshing floor and lie down at Boaz's feet, and he would tell her what to do. Ruth followed Naomi's instruction. Boaz discovered Ruth lying at his feet. Ruth asked him to spread the corner of his cover over her because he was a kinsman-redeemer (3:1-9).
- Boaz praised Ruth. Then he said that there was a kinsman-redeemer who was a closer relative than he. Ruth slept near his feet until dawn when Boaz gave her six measures of barley. Ruth returned to Naomi (3:10-18).
- Boaz went to the town gate and met with the other kinsman-redeemer and asked him if he would be the kinsman-redeemer for Ruth. The man refused and Boaz said that he would buy Naomi's land and marry Ruth. The town elders blessed Boaz and his marriage (4:1-12).
- Boaz married Ruth and she gave birth to a son. The town women rejoiced with Naomi. Naomi cared for the baby (4:13-16).
- The baby was named Obed. Obed was Jesse's father, and Jesse was the father of David (4:17-22).

Final-situation:
Ruth, the daughter-in-law of Elimelech and Naomi, had a son named Obed. He would become the grandfather of David.

BIBLE STORY

Naomi and Ruth Return to Bethlehem

In the days when judges ruled, Israel had no king; everyone did as he saw fit (Jdg 21:25).

During the time when the judges led Israel, there was a famine in the land. Elimelech, his wife Naomi, and their two sons Mahlon and Kilion, were Ephrathites from Bethlehem, Judah. They left home to live in the country of Moab (1:1-2).

Elimelech died, and Naomi was left with her two sons. Her sons married Moabite women, one named Orpah and the other Ruth. After they lived in Moab for ten years, the sons Mahlon and Kilion also died. Naomi was left alone in Moab without her two sons or her husband (1:2-5).

Naomi heard that the Lord had come to the aid of his people by providing food for them. She got ready to return to her home in Judah. Naomi and her two daughters-in-law left the place where she had been living and set out on the road that would take them to Judah.

After a short time on the road, Naomi told her two daughters-in-law: "Go back to your mother's home. May the Lord show kindness to you, as you have shown to your deceased husbands and to me. May the Lord give each of you a new home and a new husband."

She kissed them. They cried out loud: "No, we will go with you to your people" (1:6-10).

But Naomi said: "Return home, my dear daughters. Why would you come with me? Do you think that I am going to have more sons, who could become your husbands? Return home, my daughters; I am too old to get another husband. Even if there was still hope for me; if I had a husband tonight and then gave birth to sons, would you remain unmarried until the babies grew up? No, dear daughters. It is more bitter for me than for you. The Lord is against me!"

The women cried again. Then Orpah kissed her mother-in-law good-bye; but Ruth clung to Naomi.

Naomi said: "Look, your sister-in-law is going back to her people and her gods. Go with her."

Ruth replied: "Don't force me to leave you or to turn back from you. Where you go I'll go, and where you stay I'll stay. Your people will be my people and your God my God. Where you die I'll die, and that is where I will be buried. I ask the Lord to punish me terribly if I do not keep this promise: nothing but death will separate you from me." Naomi realized that Ruth was determined to go with her, so she stopped arguing with her (1:10-18).

When the two women arrived in Bethlehem, the whole town was buzzing with talk. The women exclaimed: "Can this really be Naomi?"

Naomi told them: "Don't call me Naomi, which means happy. Call me Mara, which means bitter. The Almighty has made my life bitter. I left here full of life, but the Lord has brought me back empty. Why call me Naomi when the Lord has afflicted me; the Almighty has ruined me" (1:19-21).

Ruth and Boaz

Naomi returned from Moab accompanied by Ruth, her daughter-in-law, the foreigner from Moab. They arrived in Bethlehem at the beginning of the barley harvest (1:22).

There was a prominent rich man living in Bethlehem named Boaz. He was a relative of Naomi's deceased husband Elimelech.

One day Ruth, the Moabitess foreigner, said to Naomi: "Let me go to the fields. Maybe someone will be kind and let me gather the grain he leaves in the field."

Naomi replied: "Go ahead, dear daughter."

Ruth went out and started gleaning in the fields behind the harvesters. It just so happened that the field belonged to Boaz, who was a close relative of Elimelech, her father-in-law (2:1-3).

Boaz arrived from Bethlehem and greeted the harvesters: "The Lord be with you!"

The workers replied: "The Lord bless you!"

Boaz asked the foreman of his harvesters: "Whose young woman is that?"

The foreman replied: "She is the Moabitess, who came back from the country of Moab with Naomi. She asked permission: `Please let me follow the harvesters and gather the grain that they leave on the ground.' She went into the field and worked steadily from morning till now. She only took a short rest in the shelter."

Then Boaz spoke to Ruth: "My daughter, listen to me. Don't go to any other field to glean. Stay here in my field to gather grain. Stay here with my servant girls. Watch where the men are harvesting, and follow along after my servant girls. I warned the men not to harass you. When you are thirsty, go and get a drink from the water jars the servants have filled."

Ruth dropped to her knees and bowed her face to the ground. She exclaimed: "Why have you treated me so kindly; me, a foreigner?"

Boaz replied: "I've heard all about you, how you helped your mother-in-law after the death of your husband. You left your father and mother and your homeland and came to live with a people where you did not know anyone. May the Lord repay you for what you have done. You will be paid in full by the Lord, the God of Israel, under whose wings you have come to seek protection."

Ruth answered: "Oh, you are very kind to me, sir. You have given me comfort. You have given me hope, though I do not belong here. I am not even one of your servant girls" (2:5-13).

At the lunch break, Boaz said to Ruth: "Come here. Eat some bread. Here, dip it in the wine vinegar."

Ruth sat down with the harvesters. Boaz gave her some roasted grain. She ate until she was full and had some left over. Ruth rose and went back to glean. Then Boaz ordered his men: "Let her gather even around the bundles of grain. Don't embarrass her. Make it easy for her, pull out some stalks for her from the bundles and leave them for her to pick up. Don't rebuke her" (2:14-16).

So Ruth gathered grain in the field until evening. She separated the grain from the chaff. There was about one-half bushel of barley; it amounted to almost a full sack. She carried it back to town, and her mother-in-law saw how much she had gathered. Ruth also gave Naomi the left overs from lunch.

Naomi asked her: "Where did you gather all that grain today? Where did you work? God bless the man who took such good care of you!"

Ruth told her mother-in-law about the place where she had been working and said: "The name of the man I worked with today is Boaz."

Naomi told Ruth: "The Lord bless him! The Lord has not stopped showing his kindness to the living and the dead. That man is our close relative; he is one of our kinsmen-redeemers."

Then Ruth said: "Boaz told me to stay with his workers until they finish harvesting all his grain."

Naomi told Ruth her daughter-in-law: "That will be good for you, my dear daughter. Stay with his servant girls, because in someone else's field you might be raped."

Ruth continued working with Boaz's servant girls. She gathered grain until both the barley and wheat harvests were finished. Ruth continued living with Naomi, her mother-in-law (2:17-23).

One day Naomi, Ruth's mother-in-law, said to her: "My dear daughter, it is time for me to find a home for you where you will be well provided for. Is not Boaz, with whose servant girls you have been, a close relative of ours? Tonight he will be winnowing barley on the threshing floor. Wash and perfume yourself, and put on your best clothes. Then go down to the threshing floor, but don't let him see you until he has finished eating and drinking. When he slips off to sleep, watch where he lies down. Go uncover his feet and lie down. He will tell you what to do."

Ruth answered: "I will do whatever you say." She went down to the threshing floor and put her mother-in-law's plan into action.

Boaz had a good time, eating and drinking his fill. He felt great. He went off to get some sleep beside the pile of grain. Ruth approached quietly, lifted the cover from his feet and lay down. About midnight, something startled Boaz and he rolled over. He was startled! There was a woman lying at his feet.

Boaz asked: "Who are you?"

She answered: "I am your servant Ruth; spread the corner of your cover over me. You are my close relative; you are a kinsman-redeemer."

Boaz replied: "The Lord bless you, my daughter. What a splendid expression of love. You could have had the pick of any of the young men around. You have not run after the younger men, whether rich or poor. Now, my daughter, don't be afraid. I will do everything you ask. All my fellow townsmen know that you are a woman of amazing character. You are right, I am a close relative to you, but there is a kinsman-redeemer closer than I. Stay here for the night. In the morning, if he wants to exercise his rights and responsibilities as the closest kinsman-redeemer, he'll have his chance. But if he refuses to take care of you, I myself will marry you. Then I will buy Elimelech's land for you. Go back to sleep until morning."

Ruth slept near his feet until dawn, but rose while it was too dark to be recognized. Boaz told his servants: "Don't let it be known that a woman came to the threshing floor."

Boaz told Ruth: "Bring me the shawl you are wearing and spread it out." When she did so, he poured into it six measures of barley and put it on her. Then he went back to town.

When Ruth came to her mother-in-law, Naomi asked: "How did it go, my dear daughter?"

Ruth told Naomi everything Boaz had done for her and added: "He gave me these six measures of barley, saying: `Don't go back to your mother-in-law empty-handed.'"

Then Naomi said: "Wait, my daughter, until you find out what happens. Boaz will not rest until the matter is settled today" (3:1-18).

Meanwhile Boaz went straight to the town gate and sat there. The kinsman-redeemer who was a closer relative than Boaz came along. Boaz said: "Come over here, my friend. Take a seat." So he went over and sat down.

Boaz gathered ten of the town elders and said: "Sit here, we've got some business to take care of," and they sat down. Boaz said to the kinsman-redeemer: "Naomi, who has come back from Moab wants to sell the piece of land that belonged to our relative Elimelech. I thought you ought to know about it. Buy it back if you want it, and make it official in the presence of these seated here. If you will redeem it, do so. You are first in line to do this, and I'm next after you."

The kinsman-redeemer replied: "I will redeem it."

Then Boaz said: "When you buy the land from Naomi and from Ruth the Moabitess, you must marry Ruth, the dead man's wife. You will have the kinsman-redeemer responsibility to have children with her, and the land will stay in her dead husband's family."

At this, the kinsman-redeemer said: "Oh, I can't do that. It might endanger my own estate. I might lose what I can pass on to my own sons. You redeem it yourself."

Long ago in Israel, this is how they handled official business regarding matters of property and inheritance: one party took off his sandal and gave it to the other. This was their proof of legalizing a transaction in Israel.

So the kinsman-redeemer said to Boaz: "Buy it yourself." And he took off his sandal as proof that the deal was settled.

Boaz announced to the town elders and all the people: "Today you are witnesses that I have bought from Naomi all the property of Elimelech, Kilion and Mahlon. I have also acquired Ruth the Moabitess, Mahlon's widow, as my wife. I'll take her as my wife and keep the name of the deceased alive along with his inheritance. The name of the deceased will not disappear from among his family or from the town records. Today you are witnesses!"

Then the town elders and all those at the gate said: "We are witnesses. May the Lord make the woman who is coming into your home like Rachel and Leah, the two women who built up the house of Israel. May the Lord make you a pillar in Ephrathah and famous in Bethlehem! Through the children the Lord gives you by this young woman, may your family rival the family of Perez, the son Tamar bore to Judah" (4:1-12).

Boaz married Ruth, and she became his wife. The Lord enabled her to conceive, and she gave birth to a son. The town women told Naomi: "Praise be to the Lord, who gave you this grandson. May he become famous in Israel! He will make you young again and take care of you in your old age. Your daughter-in-law, who has given him birth, loves you and is better to you than seven sons."

Then Naomi took the child, laid him in her lap and cared for him (4:13-16).

The neighborhood women called him: "Naomi's baby boy." But his name was Obed. Obed was Jesse's father, and Jesse was the father of David (4:17-22).

LIFE-LESSONS DISCOVERED IN THE STORY

1. Tragedies are a reality of life. There was a famine in the days when judges ruled Israel (1:1). Elimeleach died and left Naomi a widow (1:3). Naomi's two sons died and she was left without a husband and without children (1:4-5).

2. A person can serve God, even when others do not. Ruth lived during the time of judges (Rt 1:1) when there was no king in Israel, and each one did what he thought was right (Jdg 17:6; 21:25). Ruth lived in a time of idolatry, prostitution, immorality and cruelty, yet she maintained her character, living above the culture of the times.

3. Tragedy brings forced adaptations. Because of famine, Elimelech's family went to live in the country of Moab (1:2). The death of Elimelech and his two sons left Naomi in a foreign country, without protection and without support (1:5). Naomi decided to return to her country, where she had family (1:6). Naomi's decision forced her daughters-in-law to give up their home with her. They were forced to make a decision: go back to their parents' house or go with Naomi to a foreign country (1:8).

4. Reaction to forced adaptation influences the outcome of restructuring one's life. Bitterness was Naomi's reaction (1:13, 20). Resuming life by considering what was best for herself was Orpah's reaction. She said goodbye to her mother-in-law and went back to her parents (1:14). Ruth restructured her life with commitments and determination. She committed herself to stay with Naomi (1:16) and to get food (2:2). She was persistent in harvesting grain (2:6). She was committed to protecting her reputation (3:11).

5. Fidelity and devotion are praiseworthy character traits. Ruth's fidelity and devotion were not determined by what was to her personal advantage, by customs of the time, by her people's religion, or by the actions of those around her (1:16-17).

6. It costs to love, but love has its rewards. Ruth gave up her parents, her country, her culture, and her language because of her love for Naomi. But her love was rewarded.

7. Proof of love is seen in service and in action, not just in words. Ruth proved her love for Naomi by going back with her to her country and working hard to care for her.

8. Those faced with forced adaptation are usually vulnerable and unprotected. When Ruth went to the field to gather grain, she was at risk of being raped (2:22). She was unable to protect herself, and she was grateful when Boaz offered her protection (2:9-14).

9. The person in need should take the initiative and do his part to work through his problems. Ruth went to the fields to pick up leftover grain (2:2-3), and she stayed at the task (2:7).

10. The unprotected person needs help from others in order to secure his rights; however, the act of seeking help puts him at risk of being exploited. Ruth was unprotected because she had no husband. She asked permission in order to gather grain left by the harvesters (2:2-3, 6-7). Since she was unprotected, she needed help from someone else in order to obtain her rights (2:19, 3:11-13, 4:1-8).

11. The poor, the needy and the unprotected are entitled to rights according to the Law of God. However, obtaining their rights depends upon the good will of people who have power and

wealth. The Law of God demanded that any grain that was dropped should be left for widows and the poor people to pick up. Gleaning was the term used to describe this activity (Lev 19:9; 23:22; Deut 24:19). But the poor depended upon the good will of the property owners to exercise their rights. Frequently, the harvest workers were cruel to the poor who gathered the grain that was left behind (Ru 2:9, 15).

12. Individuals have a responsibility to obtain social justice for others. Ruth was responsible for helping Naomi. Boaz was responsible for helping Ruth and permitting her the privilege of gleaning behind his harvesters as the Law demanded (Ru 2:20; 3:9). Boaz, being a near relative, had the duty of: being a kinsman-redeemer and preventing Naomi and Ruth from losing lands that was part of their family inheritance (Lev 25:23-25), of marrying Ruth, the deceased relative's widow, and of giving her children to preserve the deceased man's name (Lev 25:48-52).

13. The reason one person should help another in need should be the love of God. Reward for helping another comes from God (2:12).

14. Those who help people in need should treat them with respect. Boaz didn't provide Ruth with food. He helped her get food (2:9, 15-16); he encouraged her (2:11-12); he offered her protection (2:9, 16, 22) and he admired her as a person (2:11, 3:11).

15. No one is disqualified to be a part of the family of God because of race, sex, or national background. Ruth was a poor foreigner who belonged to a race that was despised by Israel. Boaz was a rich Jew. Ruth was blessed because of her faithfulness. She and Boaz were the great-grandparents of King David and direct ancestors of Jesus (4:17-22). Today, people of different races, nations and social levels can be part of the family of God, through faith in Jesus.

16. God can even bring blessings through sorrow and calamity. God brought blessings out of Naomi's tragedy. Ruth, her daughter-in-law, was better to her than seven sons would have been (4:15).

17. A person can not be aware of God's purpose for his life until he is able to look back through the perspective of eternity. The events recorded in Ruth were part of God's preparation for the births of David and Jesus. Ruth was unaware of this larger purpose in her life.

QUESTIONS

1. Why did Elimelech, Naomi and their two sons leave Bethlehem to live in Moab?
2. What tragedies did Naomi face?
3. How did Ruth help Naomi, her mother-in-law?
4. How did Naomi, Orpah and Ruth face their tragedies in different manners?
5. How did Boaz help Ruth?
6. What does Boaz's attitudes teach us about how to help a person in need?
7. What can you learn from Naomi and Ruth about how to face tragedies?
8. What does the story of Ruth teach us about the importance of family?
9. The book of Ruth emphasizes the fact that Ruth, a foreigner from Moab, was an ancestor of King David, who in turn was an ancestor of Jesus. Why is that important?
10. What did you learn from the story of Ruth, that will help you face a tragedy or a forced adaptation?

SAMUEL			
I Samuel 1:1 - 25:1			
PREPARATION FOR MINISTRY	MINISTRY UNKNOWN	PUBLIC MINISTRY	MINISTRY TO INDIVIDUALS
1:1 3:18	3:19 7:2	7:3 7:17	8:1 25:1
Serving the Priest	Serving God	God's Spokesman to the People	God's Spokesman to Individuals
▪Birth; answer to prayer (1:1-20); ▪Dedicated to the Lord (1:21-28); ▪Servant of Eli in the Tabernacle - (2:18-21); ▪God speaks to Samuel (3:1-18).	▪People realize that Samuel is a prophet (3:19-21); ▪For 20 years, the Israelites pray for the Lord to help them (7:2).	▪Samuel challenges Israel to return to the Lord (7:3-6); ▪He leads Israel to have victory over the Philistines (7:7-14); ▪He is the leader and judge of the people (7:15).	▪Samuel's sons were corrupt (8:1-5); ▪He resisted Israel's request for a king (8:6-22); ▪Samuel anointed Saul and crowned him king (9:15-10:27); ▪Samuel's farewell address (12:1-25); ▪Samuel announced God's judgment to Saul (13:6-14; 15:10-31); ▪Samuel anointed David as king (16:1-13); ▪Samuel's death (25:1).
1:1 3:18	3:19 7:2	7:3 7:17	8:1 25:1

SAMUEL: HEARD AND SPOKE THE WORD OF GOD
1 Samuel 1 - 8

STRUCTURE

Context:
Under Joshua's leadership, Israel conquered Canaan. Israel served the Lord during the lifetime of the leaders who had experienced the Lord helping them conquer Canaan. Another generation grew up that served the god Baal and goddess Ashtoreth. Then the Israelites experienced cycles of: The Lord raising up enemies who oppressed them; they cried for help; the Lord raised up a judge who delivered them; when the judge died, the people returned to their old ways and became worse than their fathers. During the time when judges ruled, Israel had no king; everyone did what he thought was right, and each generation became worse than the one of his parents.

Samuel was the last judge. The book of 1 Samuel records the transition from judges to kings.

Key-person: Samuel

Key-location: Israel: Shiloh and Ramah and Gibeah

Key-repetitions:
▪The Lord Almighty (1:3, 11; 44:15:2; 17:45).
▪Prayer (1:9-15; 2:1-10; 3:8-10; 7:8-9; 8:6; 12:12:17-18, 23).
▪The ark of the Lord (3:3; 4:3-22; 5:1-6:21; 7:1-2; 14:18).
▪Blessings result from faith in the Lord and obeying him; but afflictions result from unbelief and disobedience (2:30; 7:3; 12:13-15).
▪Family problems: Elkanah, Hannah and Peninnah (1:2-13); Eli and his sons (2:12, 22, 27-30; 3:11-14); Samuel and his sons (8:1-3) Saul and Jonathan (14:24-45).
▪The Lord's message: proclaimed by a holy man (2:27-36); proclaimed by Samuel to Eli (3:17), and to the people (7:3; 8:10-18).
▪The people want a king (8:4-5, 6, 19, 21).

Key-attitudes:
▪Rivalry between Hannah and Peninnah.
▪Hannah's agony because she had no children.
▪Hannah's joy when Samuel was born.
▪Eli's impotence with his sons.
▪The wickedness of Eli's sons.
▪The irreverent bossy attitude of Eli's sons.
▪The weakness of Eli even though he had good intentions.
▪Samuel was likeable and respected.
▪The Israelites feared the Philistines.
▪Samuel's displeasure when the people requested a king.
▪God's reluctance in giving the people a king.

Initial-problem:
Hannah, the wife of Elkanah, had no children.

Sequence of events:
Samuel's Birth and Childhood
▪Elkanah had two wives; Hannah and Peninnah. Hannah had no children. Every year when Elkanah

went to Shiloh to worship, Hannah would cry and refuse to eat (1:1-8).
- Hannah went to the tabernacle and prayed silently, asking for a son. Eli thought she was drunk. Hannah said that she was praying (1:9-18).
- Hannah gave birth to a son and named him Samuel (1:19-20).
- After weaning the boy, Hannah presented him to Eli, and dedicated him to God (1:21-28).
- Hannah sang a song praising the Lord (2:1-10).
- Samuel served the Lord under Eli (2:11).
- Eli's sons were wicked men; they disrespected meat sacrificed to the Lord (2:12-17).
- The boy Samuel served the Lord. Hannah had three more sons and two daughters (2:18-22).
- Eli talked to his sons about their evil actions (2:23-25).
- Samuel pleased the Lord and the people (2:26).
- A holy man pronounced judgment on Eli and his family (2:27-36).
- In those days it was rare for the Lord to speak directly to people (3:1).
- One night the Lord repeatedly called Samuel, and he thought it was Eli calling. The Lord informed Samuel about how he was going to punish Eli's family. Samuel told Eli everything the Lord said (3:1-18).
- The Lord continued to reveal himself to Samuel (3:19-21).

Israel Defeated; the Ark Captured
- In a battle, the Philistines killed 4,000 Israelite soldiers. The Israelites sent for the Ark of the Lord. Eli's sons, Hophni and Phinehas, accompanied the Ark. The Philistines defeated the Israelites, killing 30,000 Israelite soldiers. The Ark was captured, and Eli's two sons died. A Benjamite took the news to Shiloh. When Eli heard the news, he fell backward off his chair, broke his neck and died (4:1-18).
- The Philistines placed the Ark in Dagon's temple. Twice, the god Dagon fell to the ground before the Ark (5:1-5).
- The Lord punished the Philistines, and they sent the Ark back to Israel (5:6 - 6:21).

Samuel: Judge and Liberator of Israel
- About 20 years later, Samuel called for the Israelites to return to the Lord. So the Israelites put away their Baals and Ashtoreths, and served only the Lord. The Israelites assembled at Mizpah, fasted and confessed their sins (7:1-7).
- The Philistines went to Mizpah to attack the Israelites. Samuel offered a lamb as a whole-burnt-offering to the Lord, and he prayed for Israel. The Lord answered him. The Lord sent a huge thunderclap, the Philistines panicked and the Israelites slaughtered them. Samuel set up a stone and named it Ebenezer. The Philistines were defeated. Throughout Samuel's lifetime, the Lord fought against the Philistines (7:8-14).
- Samuel continued as judge. He went on a circuit from Bethel to Gilgal to Mizpah. But he always returned to his home at Ramah (7:15-17).

The Israelites Wanted a King
- When Samuel became an old man, he appointed his sons as judges. But they were dishonest in their judging (8:1-3).
- The leaders of Israel met Samuel at Ramah and requested a king. Samuel was displeased, and he prayed. The Lord replied that they were rejecting Samuel as they had always rejected him. Samuel was to give them a king after warning them about the way a king would treat them (8:4-9).
- Samuel told the people that a king would take their sons, daughters, fields, vineyards, olive groves, flocks and servants and that they would become his slaves. Then when they cried out to the Lord, he would not answer them (8:10-18).
- The people insisted that they wanted a king just like the other nations. The Lord told Samuel to give them a king. Then Samuel sent everyone home (8:19-21).

Final-situation:
The Israelites asked Samuel for a king. Samuel warned them about the way a king would treat them. But the people insisted they wanted a king just like the other nations.

BIBLE STORY

Samuel's Birth and Childhood

A man named Elkanah lived in Ramah with his two wives; one named Hannah and the other Peninnah. Peninnah had children, but Hannah had no children.

Every year Elkanah left his home in Ramah and went to Shiloh to worship and sacrifice to the Lord Almighty. Shiloh was where Eli and his two sons Hophni and Phinehas served as priests. When Elkanah sacrificed, he would give portions of the sacrificial meat to his wife Peninnah and to all her children. But to Hannah he gave a double portion because he loved her and because the Lord had made Hannah unable to have children. Peninnah kept provoking Hannah, never letting her forget that she had no children. This went on year after year. Every time Hannah went up to the house of the Lord, her rival provoked her until she cried and would not eat.

Her husband Elkanah would ask her: "Hannah, why are you crying? Why don't you eat? Why are you depressed? Don't I mean more to you than ten sons?" (1:1-8).

Once after they had eaten their meal in Shiloh, Hannah slipped away and entered the tabernacle. The Priest Eli was sitting on a chair by the entrance to the Lord's tabernacle. In bitterness of soul Hannah cried and cried. She prayed to the Lord and made a promise saying: "O Lord Almighty, if you will only look at my misery and remember me by giving me a son; I will give him back to you all the days of his life. No one will ever use a razor to cut his hair."

As she kept on praying to the Lord, Eli watched her mouth. Hannah was praying in her heart silently; her lips moved, but no words were heard. Eli thought she was drunk and said to her: "You're drunk! How long will you keep on getting drunk? Throw away your wine!"

Hannah replied; "Oh, no sir. I am a woman who is deeply troubled. I have not been drinking wine nor beer; I was pouring out my soul to the Lord. Do not think that I am a wicked woman; I have been praying because of my desperate torment and sorrow."

Eli answered: "Go in peace. And may the God of Israel give you what you have asked of him."

She said: "Please think well of me." Then she ate something, and her face was radiant (1:9-18).

Elkanah's family returned home to Ramah. Hannah became pregnant, gave birth to a son and named him Samuel, saying: "I asked the Lord for him" (1:19-20).

Hannah stayed at home and nursed her son until she had weaned him. Shortly after weaning Samuel, Elkanah and Hannah took him to the tabernacle of the Lord at Shiloh. Hannah presented the little child to Eli, and told him: "Sir, I am the woman who stood at this very spot, praying to the Lord. I prayed for this child, and the Lord gave me what I asked for. Now I give him back to the Lord. He is dedicated to God for all his life" (1:21-28).

Hannah sang a song praising the Lord (2:1-10).

Elkanah and Hannah went home to Ramah. The boy stayed and served the Lord under Eli the priest (2:11).

Eli's sons were wicked men; they had no regard for the Lord nor for the customs of the priests among the people. Ordinarily, whenever anyone offered a sacrifice, and while the meat was boiling, the priest would come with a three-pronged fork in his hand. He would plunge it into the cooking pot, and the priest would take for himself whatever the fork brought up. But this is how Eli's sons treated the Israelites who came to Shiloh to offer sacrifices to the Lord. Before they had even burned the fat to the Lord, the priest's servant would interrupt whoever was sacrificing and say: "Give the priest some meat to roast; he won't accept boiled meat from you, but only raw."

If the man replied: "Let the fat be burned up first, that's God's portion! Then take whatever you want," the servant would demand: "No, hand it over now; if you don't, I'll take it by force."

The young men's sin was horrible in the Lord's sight. They showed no respect for the offerings made to the Lord (2:12-17).

In the midst of all this, Samuel, a boy dressed in priestly robes, served the Lord. Each year his mother made him a little robe and took it to him when she went up with her husband for the annual sacrifice. Eli would bless Elkanah and his wife, saying: "May the Lord give you children to take the place of the one Hannah prayed for and gave back to the Lord." Then they would go home. The Lord was gracious to Hannah; she gave birth to three more sons and two daughters. Meanwhile, the boy Samuel grew up serving the Lord (2:18-22).

By this time, Eli was an old man. He kept hearing reports on how his sons were ripping off the people and how they slept with the women who served at the entrance to the tabernacle. He said to them: "Why do you do these evil things? I hear story after story about these wicked deeds of yours. If a man sins against another man, there is help; God's help. But if you sin against the Lord, no one can help you!" His sons, however, did not listen to their father (2:23-25).

The boy Samuel continued to grow up. He pleased the Lord and the people (2:26).

A holy man came to Eli and told him: "This is the Lord's message: I chose your ancestors out of all the tribes of Israel to be my priest. Why do you treat as mere loot these sacrificial offerings that I commanded for my worship? Why do you honor your sons more than me by letting them get fat on the best parts of the meat the Israelites bring to me? Therefore, the Lord God of Israel, declares: `I promised that your house and your father's house would be my priest indefinitely.' But now the Lord declares: `Those who honor me I will honor, but those who despise me will be despised. The time is coming when no one in your family will make it to old age! All your descendants will die in the prime of life. I will give you a sign: Both your sons, Hophni and Phinehas, will die on the same day. I will raise up for myself a true priest. He will do what I want him to do; he will be what I want him to be" (2:27-36).

The boy Samuel served the Lord under Eli's direction. In those days it was rare for the Lord to speak directly to people (3:1).

One night Eli was lying in bed. It was before dawn; the sanctuary lamp was still burning. Samuel was in bed in the tabernacle of the Lord, where the Ark of God stayed. Then the Lord called: "Samuel, Samuel!"

Samuel answered: "Yes, I'm here." Then he ran to Eli and said: "Here I am; you called me."

But Eli said: "I did not call; go back to bed." So Samuel went back to bed.

Again the Lord called: "Samuel, Samuel!"

Samuel got up, went to Eli and said: "Here I am; you called me."

Again Eli said: "Son, I did not call; go back and lie down."

Samuel did not yet know the Lord personally. The Lord had not yet spoken directly to him.

The Lord called a third time: "Samuel, Samuel! The boy got up and went to Eli and said: "Here I am; you called me."

Eli realized that the Lord was calling the boy and he told Samuel: "Go and lie down, and if he calls you, say: `Speak, Lord. I'm your servant, and I'm ready to listen.'" So Samuel returned to his bed.

The Lord called again: "Samuel! Samuel!"

Then Samuel said: "Speak Lord, I'm your servant, and I'm ready to listen."

And the Lord told Samuel: "I will do to Eli's family everything that I warned him of. I told Eli that I would punish his family forever because he knew that his sons were desecrating the Lord's name and the Lord's place, and he did nothing to stop them."

Samuel stayed in bed until morning. Then he opened the doors of the house of the Lord. He was afraid to tell Eli the vision, but Eli called him and said: "Samuel, my son."

Samuel answered: "Here I am."

Eli asked: "What was it he said to you? Do not hide it from me. I want it all, word for word as he said it to you." So Samuel told him everything. He held back nothing from him. Then Eli said: "He is the Lord; let him do whatever he thinks best" (3:1-18).

The Lord was with Samuel as he grew up. Samuel's prophetic words always came true. And all Israel recognized that Samuel was the real thing, a true prophet of the Lord. The Lord continued to reveal himself to Samuel through his word at Shiloh (3:19-21).

Whatever Samuel said was broadcast throughout Israel (4:1).

Israel Defeated; the Ark Captured

The Israelites went out to fight the Philistines. The Philistines won the battle, killing about four thousand Israelite soldiers. The Israelite soldiers returned to camp and their leaders asked: "Why did the Lord bring defeat upon us today with the Philistines? Let us bring the ark of the Lord's covenant from Shiloh; it will go with us and save us from the grip of our enemies."

Men went to Shiloh and brought back the Ark of the Covenant of the Lord Almighty. Eli's two sons, Hophni and Phinehas, accompanied the Ark of the Covenant of God.

When the ark of the Lord's covenant came into the camp, everyone cheered. The shout was like thunderclaps shaking the very ground. The Philistines asked: "What's all this shouting in the Hebrew camp?"

When they learned that the ark of the Lord had come into the camp, the Philistines panicked and said: "A god has come into the camp. We're in trouble! They are the gods who struck the Egyptians with all kinds of plagues in the desert. Be strong, Philistines! Be men, or you will be slaves to the Hebrews, as they have been to you. Be men, and fight!"

The Philistines fought and defeated the Israelites, killing thirty thousand Israelite foot soldiers. The Ark of God was captured, and Eli's two sons, Hophni and Phinehas, died.

A Benjamite ran from the battle line and went to Shiloh. He tore his clothes and put dust on his head. When he arrived, Eli was sitting on his chair by the side of the road; he was extremely worried about the Ark of God. When the messenger entered the town and told the bad news, the whole town cried loudly.

Eli heard the outcry and asked: "What is the meaning of this uproar?"

The messenger hurried over to Eli, who was ninety-eight years old. He told Eli: "I have just come from the battle line; barely escaping with my life."

Eli asked: "What happened, my son?"

The messenger replied: "Israel fled from the Philistines, and the army suffered heavy losses. Your two sons, Hophni and Phinehas, were killed, and the Ark of God was captured."

At the words: "Ark of God," Eli fell backward off his chair. When he fell, he broke his neck and died. He was an old man and fat. He had led Israel forty years (4:1-18).

After the Philistines captured the Ark of God, they took it to the town of Ashdod and placed it in Dagon's temple and set it beside the idol of Dagon. When the people of Ashdod rose early the next day, there was Dagon, flat on his face on the ground before the Ark of the Lord! They took Dagon and put him back in his place. But the following morning when they rose, there was Dagon, flat on his face on the ground before the Ark of the Lord! His head and hands had been broken off and were lying on the threshold; only his torso was in one piece. That is why the priests of Dagon and visitors to Dagon's shrine in Ashdod avoid stepping on the threshold (5:1-5).

The Lord punished the citizens of Ashdod and its vicinity by afflicting them with tumors. He let loose rats among them. Everyone was deathly afraid. The men of Ashdod said: "The Ark of the God of Israel must not stay here with us. We can't handle this, and neither can our god Dagon." So the Philistines sent the Ark back to Israel (5:6 - 6:21).

Samuel: Judge and Liberator of Israel

About twenty years later, Samuel addressed all the Israelites: "If you are returning to the Lord with all your hearts, clean house. Get rid of the foreign gods and the Ashtoreths. Commit yourselves to the Lord and serve him and him alone. He will deliver you from Philistine oppression." So the Israelites put away their Baals and Ashtoreths, and served only the Lord.

Next Samuel said: "Assemble all Israel at Mizpah, and I will pray to the Lord for you." They assembled at Mizpah and Samuel was their leader. They fasted all day and confessed: "We have sinned against the Lord" (7:1-7).

The Philistines heard that Israel had assembled at Mizpah and they came up to attack. The Israelites feared the Philistines. They said to Samuel: "Do not stop praying to the Lord our God for us. Ask the Lord to rescue us from the Philistines." Samuel took a suckling lamb and offered it as a whole-burnt-offering to the Lord. He cried out to the Lord, interceding for Israel. The Lord answered him.

While Samuel was sacrificing the burnt offering, the Philistines drew near to fight Israel. Just then, the Lord sent a huge thunderclap exploding among the Philistines. They panicked, mass confusion! They ran from Israel. The men of Israel rushed out of Mizpah and pursued the Philistines, killing them along the way to a point just beyond Beth Car.

Then Samuel took a stone and set it up. He named it Ebenezer, saying: "The Lord has helped us to this point." The Philistines were defeated and did not invade Israelite territory again. Throughout Samuel's lifetime, the Lord fought against the Philistines. The towns that the Philistines had captured from Israel were restored to her, and Israel delivered the neighboring territory from Philistine control. There was peace between Israel and the Amorites.

Samuel continued as judge over Israel his entire life. Every year he went on a circuit from Bethel to Gilgal to Mizpah, judging Israel in all those places. But he always returned to Ramah, where his home was. That is where he built an altar to the Lord (7:8-17).

The Israelites Wanted a King

When Samuel became an old man, he appointed his sons as judges for Israel. But his sons did not take after him. They sought dishonest gain, taking bribes and were dishonest in their judging.

So all the older leaders of Israel gathered together and met Samuel at Ramah. They said to him: "You are an old man, and your sons are not following in your ways; now appoint a king to lead us, just like all the other nations."

Samuel was displeased when they said: "Give us a king to lead us."

Samuel prayed to the Lord. And the Lord answered him: "Go ahead; give them what they want. It is not you they have rejected, but they have rejected me as their king. From the day I brought them up out of Egypt until this day, they have forsaken me and served other gods. Now they are doing the same to you. Let them have their way; but warn them about the way kings operate and let them know what they will get from a king."

Samuel told the people: "This is what your king will do: He will take your sons and make soldiers of them. He will put others to forced labor on his farms to plow his ground and reap his harvest. Others will make weapons of war and equipment for his chariots. The king will take your daughters. Some of your daughters will make perfume. Others will cook and bake for him. He will take your best fields and vineyards and olive groves and give them to his attendants. He will tax your grain, your vintage, your flocks and give riches to his officials. He will take for himself your menservants, your maidservants and your best cattle and donkeys. You yourselves will become his slaves. When that day comes, you will cry out in desperation because of the king you have chosen, but the Lord will not answer you."

But the people refused to listen to Samuel. They answered: "No!" "We want a king over us. Then we will be just like all the other nations. Our king will rule us, lead us and fight our battles."

The Lord told Samuel: "Do what they say. Give them a king."

Then Samuel dismissed the men of Israel: "Everyone go home to your town" (8:1-21).

LIFE-LESSONS DISCOVERED IN THE STORY

1. God answers prayers. He answered Hannah's prayers (1:9-20) and Samuel's prayers (3:8-10;7:8-9; 8:6-9;12:18, 23).

2. Parents need to recognize that their children come from God and they should consecrate their children to him. Hannah understood that baby Samuel was God's answer to her prayer, and she dedicated him to the Lord for all the days of his life (1:11, 28).

3. People are often mistaken when they judge others. Appearances can deceive. Eli was wrong when he judged Hannah to be intoxicated (1:14-18).

4. A person who receives a blessing from God in answer to prayer has reasons to celebrate. Hannah used poetic language to celebrate Samuel's birth. His birth was an answer to prayer (2:1-10).

5. Spiritual leaders should teach their children the way of the Lord, and they should discipline them when they disobey the Lord. When children of spiritual leaders are unfaithful to God, they hinder the future of divine work. Examples of this are revealed with Eli's sons (2:12-17, 29; 3:13) and Samuel's sons (8:1-5).

6. The spiritual leader who disobeys the Lord and despises the people of God is guilty of a great sin. Eli's sons were evil men who mistreated the people who came to worship the Lord, and they disrespected offerings made to the Lord (2:12-16). They were guilty of a great sin (2:17).

7. There are times in history when God avoids revealing himself to people. During the time when Eli was priest, it was rare for God to speak to people (3:1).

8. One may be guilty of sin by either doing wrong or by omitting to do right. Eli's sons were guilty of doing wrong (2:12-17, 22); Eli was guilty of omitting to discipline his sons (3:13).

9. God keeps his promises. God promised to destroy the family of Eli (2:27-34), and he did what he said (4:12-18).

10. A person can be faithful to God in an environment where others disobey him. Samuel was raised around Eli's sons who mistreated those who offered sacrifices to the Lord, who had no respect for offerings dedicated to the Lord (2:12-17) and who had sex with women that worked at the tabernacle's entrance (2:22). However, Samuel faithfully served the Lord (2:26).

11. Often, people do not understand when God is speaking to them. At first, the boy Samuel didn't understand that it was God who was calling him (3:5-6).

12. A person may need help to understand when God is speaking to him. The boy Samuel didn't understand that it was God who was calling him until Eli advised him (3:5-9).

13. God is a fair judge. Eli and his sons deserved the punishment they received from God (3:11-14; 4:12-18).

14. Believing God and obeying him brings blessings, while unbelief and disobedience results in misfortune. (See 1 Sm 2:30; 7:3; 12:13-15.)

15. The Lord God is the only true God. When the Ark of the Lord was put in the temple of Dagon, the idol of Dagon fell and was broken (5:1-5).

16. The desire to be similar to other people can lead the people of God to reject his leadership. All of Israel's neighboring nations had kings and the Israelites wanted to be like other nations. That desire led them to reject God as their King (8:5-9).

17. The people of God should be different from other people. The fact that the Lord chose them and they are dedicated to him should make them different. When the Lord's people want to be like everyone else, they reject God's leadership and lose their identity as the people of God. When Israel wanted to have a king like everyone else, she rejected the Lord God as her king (8:5-9).

18. People who are determined to get their way often refuse to consider potential problems that need to be dealt with. When the Israelites asked for a king, Samuel explained all the negative consequences of having a king, but they refused to listen (8:11-20).

QUESTIONS

1. What kind of family problems did Elkanah have?
2. How did Hannah become a mother?
3. What kind of upbringing did Samuel have?
4. What kind of family problems did Eli have?
5. What were some of the sins of Eli's sons?
6. What kind of experiences did the boy Samuel have with the Lord?
7. Did you learn anything from Elkanah's, Eli's or Samuel's family that can help your family?
8. What happened when the Ark of the Lord was put in Dagon's temple?
9. Why did the Israelites want a king?
10. What did you learn from this story that could help you?

THE KINGDOM OF ISRAEL					400 Years of Silence
United 1000 B.C.	**Divided** 931 B.C.	**Partial** 722 B.C.	**In Exile** 586 B.C.	**Remnant** 516 B.C.	
Saul David Solomon	**ISRAEL:** <u>North</u> Jeroboam *1st king* **JUDAH:** <u>South</u> Rehoboam *1st king*	Only JUDAH	In BABYLON	RESTORATION OF JUDAH	
112 years	209 years	136 years	70 years		400 years

SAUL		
1 Samuel 9 - 31		
CHOSEN KING BY GOD	**DISOBEDIENT; REJECTED BY GOD**	**REJECTED BY GOD**
HUMBLE (10:20-22)	**PRIDEFUL AND ARROGANT** (15:24-30)	**DESPERATE** (28:4-6)
Victorious in War	Courageous and Foolish, but Victorious in War	Destroyed in War
Holy Spirit with him (10:6, 10; 11:6)	Holy Spirit leaves him (16:14)	Tormented by an evil spirit (16:14-23; 19:9)
▪Was tall and handsome (9:1-2). ▪Anointed king by Samuel (9:3-10:1). ▪Became king (10:17-27). ▪Rescued city of Jabesh, defeats Ammonites (11:1-11). ▪Confirmed as king (11:12-15).	▪Became impatient at Gilgal; denounced by Samuel (13:5-15). ▪Took a foolish oath (14:24-46). ▪Victorious in war (14:1-35; 47-52; 15:1-8). ▪Disobeyed the Lord; rejected by God as king (15:10-35).	▪Felt jealous of David (18:6-16). ▪Tried to kill David (19-26). ▪Consulted a witch (28:3-25). ▪Wounded in battle and committed suicide (31).
9 11	13 16:14	16:14 31

SAUL: FROM GOD'S BEST TO A REJECT
United Kingdom
1 Samuel 9 - 15

STRUCTURE

Context:
Samuel was a judge who led the Israelites to have victory over their enemies. When Samuel became an old man, he appointed his sons as judges. But they were dishonest. Israel's leaders requested that Samuel give them a king. The Lord told Samuel to warn them about the way a king would treat them. Samuel told the people that a king would take their sons, daughters, fields, vineyards, olive groves, flocks and servants and they would become his slaves. Then when they cried out to the Lord, he would not answer them.

The people insisted that they wanted a king just like the other nations. The Lord told Samuel to give them a king.

Key-person: Samuel and Saul

Key-location: Ramah, Gibeah, Jabesh, Gilead and Gilgal

Key-repetitions:
- Saul becomes king: anointed in private by Samuel (10:1); at Mizpah before the people (10:17-26); kingship confirmed at Gilgal (11:14-15).
- Samuel pronounces God's message: to the people (10:17-19, 25; 12:1-25) and to Saul (9:20; 10:1-8; 13:13-14; 15:1-3, 14-29).
- God rejected: Saul's dynasty (13:13-14) Saul as king (15:23).
- Positive things about Saul at the beginning of his kingship: He was the best of the Israelites (9:2; 10:24); he was humble (9:21; 10:21-22); injustice made him angry (11:6); he did not seek revenge on those who had rejected him (11:12-13).
- Negative things about Saul after his kingship was established: He took credit for a battle won by Jonathan (13:3-4); he had no communication with Jonathan (14:1,17); he made a foolish curse (14:24); he ignored the well-being of his army (14:24, 29-31); he was willing to kill Jonathan who was responsible for a great victory (14:44); he partially obeyed God (15:3, 8-9); he built a monument in his own honor (15:13).

Key-attitudes:
- When Saul was first presented and at the beginning of his kingship, he pleased the Lord, Samuel and the people.
- After Saul's kingship was established, he troubled the people, and displeased God and Samuel.
- Positive attitude about Samuel.
- Saul's humility at the beginning of his kingship, but his arrogant foolishness after his kingship was established.
- Jonathan's goodness and courage.
- Samuel grieved for Saul after God rejected him.

Initial-problem:
Saul went searching for his father's lost donkeys.

Sequence of events:

Samuel and Saul
- Saul went searching for his father's lost donkeys. When he reached Samuel's home town, he sought his help (9:1-10).
- When Samuel saw Saul, the Lord revealed that he was the one who would govern his people. Samuel told Saul that Israel wants him and Saul asked why he would say such a thing. Saul dined with Samuel and spent the night at his house (9:11-27).
- Samuel anointed Saul king (10:1-2).
- Samuel summoned the Israelites to Mizpah and gave them the Lord's message condemning them for asking for a king. Samuel announced that Saul had been chosen king. Saul hid among the baggage. Samuel called Saul the best. The people shouted: "Long live the king!" (10:17-24).
- Samuel explained the rights and duties of the king (10:25).
- Samuel sent everyone to their homes. Some troublemakers despised Saul. But Saul kept silent (10:26-27).

Beginning of Saul's Kingship
- King Nahash of the Ammonites threatened to gouge everyone's right eye in Jabesh (11:1-3).
- When Saul heard the news, the Spirit of God came upon him, and he burned with anger. He called on Israel to follow him and Samuel. He gathered 330,000 men. They broke into the Ammonites' camp and killed them (11:4-11).
- Saul refused to execute those who had not wanted him to be their king. Then Samuel and the people reaffirmed the kingship (11:12-15).
- Samuel gave a farewell speech to Israel. He warned them to obey the Lord, or he would fight against them. The Lord sent thunder and rain to make them realize the wrong they did when they asked for a king (12:14-18).
- Samuel warned them not to turn away from the Lord after useless idols (12:19-22).
- Samuel would not sin by stopping to pray for them and he would teach them what is right. But if they persisted in sin, they and their king would be thrown out (12:23-25).
- Saul was 30 years old when he became king. He was king 42 years (13:1).
- Saul had 2,000 men with him. His son, Jonathan, had 1,000. Jonathan attacked the Philistine outpost at Geba. All Israel heard that Saul had attacked the Philistine outpost. Saul summoned the army to join him (13:2-4).
- The Philistines assembled to fight with 3,000 chariots, 6,000 men to ride in the chariots, and soldiers too many to count. The Israelites were afraid and hid (13:5-7).
- Saul waited seven days for Samuel. Soldiers began to scatter. Saul himself offered the whole-burnt-offering. Samuel arrived and told Saul that since he had disobeyed God, his kingdom would not endure (13:8-14).
- The Philistines did not allow anyone in Israel to be a blacksmith. So only Saul and Jonathan had a sword or spear (13:16-22).
- Jonathan with his armor-bearer crossed over to the Philistine outpost without telling Saul. They killed about 20 men. Panic struck the Philistine army. Then Saul and his men went to the battle. Hebrews who had previously defected to the Philistines joined the Israelites to fight with Saul and Jonathan. Israelites who had gone into hiding joined the battle. The Lord rescued Israel that day (14:1-23).
- Saul made his soldiers miserable by placing them under an oath not to eat until evening. There were honeycombs in the woods. Jonathan had not heard that his father put the army under oath so he ate some. Saul discovered that Jonathan had disobeyed the oath and was going to kill him. But the men rescued Jonathan, and he did not die (14:24-45).
- Saul fought against Israel's enemies and he always experienced victory. Whenever Saul saw a strong or brave man, he took him into his army (14:47-52).

Saul Rejected as King
- Samuel gave Saul the Lord's command to attack the Amalekites and destroy everything that belonged to them as an offering to the Lord (15:1-4).

- Saul defeated the Amalekites. He did not kill Agag king of the Amalekites nor the best of the sheep and cattle (15:5-9).
- The Lord told Samuel he was sorry he made Saul king. Samuel cried out to the Lord all night long (15:10-11).
- Samuel went to meet Saul and discovered that Saul had put up a victory monument in his own honor (15:12).
- Samuel caught up with Saul. Saul claimed he had obeyed the Lord's commands. Samuel asked why he was hearing sheep bleating and cattle mooing. Saul answered that the soldiers saved the best of the sheep and cattle to sacrifice to the Lord but had totally destroyed the rest (15:12-15).
- Samuel asked Saul why he had not obeyed the Lord. Saul defended himself, claiming he obeyed the Lord. He brought back only Agag their king, and the soldiers took the best sheep and cattle to sacrifice to the Lord (15:16-21).
- Samuel replied that to obey is better than sacrifice and that since Saul rejected the Lord's command, the Lord had rejected Saul as king (15:22-23).
- Saul confessed that he had sinned because he was afraid of the people so he gave in to them. He asked Samuel to forgive him and go with him to worship the Lord. Samuel refused and turned to leave. Saul grabbed his robe, and it tore. Samuel told Saul that the Lord had torn the kingdom of Israel from him. Saul insisted that Samuel honor him with his presence before the leaders and before Israel. So Samuel went back with Saul (15:24-31).
- Samuel killed King Agag of Amalek (15:32-33).
- Then Samuel left for Ramah. He never saw Saul again all the rest of his life. Samuel grieved for Saul. The Lord was sorry that he ever made Saul king over Israel (15:34-35).

Final-situation:

The Lord was sorry that he ever made Saul king over Israel (15:34-35).

BIBLE STORY

Samuel and Saul

Kish was an important man from the tribe of Benjamin. He had a son named Saul, a handsome young man who was a head taller than others.

Some of Kish's donkeys got lost. Kish said to his son Saul: "Take one of the servants and go find the donkeys." So Saul passed through the hill country of Ephraim and around Shalisha, but could not find them. They went on into the district of Shaalim, but no luck. Then he passed through the territory of Benjamin, but they did not find the donkeys.

When they reached Zuph, Saul said to his servant: "Let's go back, or my father will stop thinking about the donkeys and start worrying about us."

The servant replied: "A highly respected man of God is in this town; everything he says comes true. Maybe he can tell us where to go."

As they climbed the hill to enter the town, Samuel was coming toward them on his way up to the place of worship. The day before Saul arrived, the Lord had revealed this to Samuel: "About this time tomorrow I will send you a man from the land of Benjamin. Anoint him leader over my people Israel; he will deliver my people from the hand of the Philistines. Their cry for help has reached me."

The moment Samuel caught sight of Saul, the Lord told him: "This is the man I spoke to you about; he will govern my people."

Saul approached Samuel in the gateway and asked: "Would you please tell me where the seer's house is?" At that time in history, the prophet was called a seer.

Samuel replied: "I am the seer. Go up ahead of me to the place of worship. You are to eat with me. As for the donkeys you lost three days ago, do not worry about them; they have been found. At this moment, Israel wants you."

Saul answered: "But I am from the tribe of Benjamin, the smallest tribe of Israel. Why do you say such a thing to me?"

Samuel brought Saul and his servant into the hall and seated them at the head of the table. Saul dined with Samuel that day.

After they came down from the worship place to the town, Samuel talked with Saul on the roof of his house. They woke at daybreak. When Saul got ready, he and Samuel went outside together. As they reached the outskirts of town, Samuel told Saul: "Tell the servant to go on ahead of us; I have a message from God for you."

Then Samuel took a flask of olive oil, poured it on Saul's head and kissed him. Then he said: "The Lord has anointed you leader over his people. When you leave me today, you will meet two men who will tell you: 'The donkeys you set out to look for have been found. Your father has stopped thinking about them and is worried about you.'" Everything happened just as Samuel prophesied (9:1-10:2).

Samuel summoned the Israelites to Mizpah and gave them a message from the Lord: "I brought Israel up out of Egypt. I delivered you from the power of Egypt and all the kingdoms that oppressed you. Now you have rejected your God, who saves you out of all your calamities and distresses. And you have said: `No, we want a king over us.' Now present yourselves before the Lord by your tribes and clans."

Samuel got all the tribes of Israel lined up, and the tribe of Benjamin was chosen. Then he lined up the Benjamin tribe clan by clan. Finally Saul son of Kish was chosen. But when they looked for him, he was not to be found. Samuel inquired of the Lord: "Has Saul come here yet?"

The Lord answered: "Yes, he is hiding among the baggage."

They ran and brought him out. When Saul stood among the people, he was a head taller than anyone else. Samuel said to the people: "Do you see the man the Lord has chosen? He is the best. No one is like him in the whole country!"

The people shouted: "Long live the king!"

Samuel explained to the people the rights and duties of the king. He wrote them down on a scroll and placed it before the Lord. Then Samuel sent everyone to their homes.

Saul went to his home in Gibeah, accompanied by brave men whose hearts God had touched. But some troublemakers said: "How can this fellow save us?" They despised him and brought him no gifts. But Saul kept silent (10:17-27).

Beginning of Saul's Kingship

About a month later, Nahash, king of the Ammonites, went with his army and surrounded the city of Jabesh. The men of Jabesh said to him: "Make a treaty with us, and we will serve you."

Nahash replied: "I will make a treaty with you on one condition: that I gouge out the right eye of every one of you. I will bring disgrace on every last man and woman in Israel."

Jabesh's town leaders replied: "Give us seven days so we can send messengers throughout Israel; if no one comes to rescue us, we will accept your terms."

Messengers came to Saul's place in Gibeah and reported the news; then the people cried loudly. Saul returned from the fields with his oxen and heard the wailing. He asked: "What is wrong with the people? Why are they crying?" They repeated to Saul the message from Jabesh.

When Saul heard their words, the Spirit of God came upon him in power, and he burned with anger. He took a pair of oxen, cut them into pieces, and sent the pieces by messengers throughout Israel, proclaiming: "This is what will be done to the oxen of anyone who does not follow Saul and Samuel." The people became afraid of the Lord, and they came together as if they were one person. Saul gathered three hundred and thirty thousand soldiers.

The next day Saul separated his men into three divisions; before sunrise they broke into the Ammonites's camp and killed them until noon. Those who survived were scattered, so that no two of them were left together (11:1-11).

People then said to Samuel: "Who was it that did not want Saul as king? Bring them here and we will kill them."

But Saul said: "No one shall be executed today. On this day the Lord rescued Israel."

Then Samuel told the people: "Let us go to Gilgal and reaffirm the kingship." So all the people went to Gilgal and confirmed Saul as king. There they sacrificed fellowship offerings before the Lord. Saul and all the Israelites held a great celebration (11:12-15).

After Saul was reaffirmed as king, Samuel gave a farewell speech to Israel. In his speech he warned them: "If you fear the Lord, worship and obey him and keep his commands; if both you and the king who reigns over you follow the Lord your God, good! But if you do not obey the Lord, and if you rebel against his commands, the Lord will fight against you, as he did against your fathers. Pay attention! It is wheat harvest time, and the rainy season is over. But I am going to pray for the Lord to send thunder and rain. And you will realize the great wrong you did in the eyes of the Lord when you asked for a king."

Then Samuel prayed to the Lord, and that same day the Lord sent thunder and rain. All the people stood in awe of the Lord and of Samuel.

The people begged Samuel: "Pray to the Lord your God for your servants. Pray that we will not die, for we have added to all our other sins the evil of asking for a king."

Samuel replied: "You have committed great evil; but do not turn away from the Lord. Serve the Lord with all your heart. Do not turn away after useless idols. For the sake of his great name, the Lord will not reject his people. The Lord took delight in making you into his very own people. As for me, I will not sin against the Lord by stopping to pray for you. And I will teach you what is good and right. Be warned: If you persist in doing evil, both you and your king will be thrown out" (12:14-25).

Saul was thirty years old when he became king. He was king over Israel forty-two years (13:1).

Saul chose three thousand men from Israel; two thousand were with him in the hill country of Bethel, and a thousand were with his son Jonathan at Gibeah in Benjamin. He sent the rest of the men back to their homes.

Jonathan attacked the Philistine outpost at Geba. All Israel heard the news: "Saul attacked the Philistine outpost, and now the Philistines really hate us!." And the army was summoned to join Saul at Gilgal.

The Philistines assembled to fight Israel, with three thousand chariots, six thousand men to ride in the chariots, and soldiers as numerous as the sand on the seashore. The Israelites saw that they were outnumbered and in deep trouble. They hid in caves, in thickets, among the rocks, in pits and in cisterns.

Saul remained at Gilgal, and the soldiers still with him were shaking with fear. Saul waited seven days, the time set by Samuel; but Samuel failed to show up at Gilgal. The soldiers began to scatter. Saul said: "Bring me the whole-burnt-offering and the fellowship offerings." And Saul offered the whole-burnt-offering. Just as he finished, Samuel arrived. Saul greeted him.

Samuel asked: "What have you done?"

Saul replied: "I saw that my army was scattering, that you did not come at the set time, and that the Philistines were ready to fight, and I thought: 'The Philistines will come down against me at Gilgal, and I have not sought the Lord's help.' So I forced myself to offer the burnt offering."

Samuel told him: "You acted foolishly. You disobeyed the Lord's commands. If you had obeyed him, he would have established your kingdom over

Israel forever. But now your kingdom will not endure. The Lord has sought out a man after his own heart and appointed him leader of his people, all because you refused to follow the Lord's command" (13:2-14).

The Philistines prevented anyone in the land of Israel from being a blacksmith. This kept them from making swords and spears. All the Israelites went down to the Philistines to have their plowshares, mattocks, axes and sickles sharpened. So on the day of the battle not a soldier with Saul and Jonathan had a sword or spear in his hand; only Saul and his son Jonathan had them (13:16-22).

One day Saul's son Jonathan said to his armor bearer: "Come, let's go over to the Philistine outpost on the other side of the pass." But he did not tell his father. No one knew that Jonathan left.

There was a steep cliff on each side of the pass that Jonathan intended to cross to reach the Philistine outpost. Jonathan said to his young armor-bearer: "Come, let's go over to the outpost of those uncircumcised pagans. Maybe the Lord will act in our behalf. It doesn't matter if we have many people, or just a few. Nothing can hinder the Lord from giving us victory. We will cross over toward the men and let them see us. So both of them showed themselves to the Philistine outpost.

The Philistines said: "Look! The Hebrews are crawling out of the holes they were hiding in." The men of the outpost shouted to Jonathan and his armor-bearer: "Come up to us, and we'll teach you a lesson."

Jonathan told his armor-bearer: "Climb up after me; the Lord has given the Philistines to Israel!"

Jonathan climbed up on all fours with his armor-bearer right behind him. When the Philistines came running up to them, Jonathan knocked them flat. His armor bearer right behind finished them off, bashing their heads in with stones. In that first attack Jonathan and his armor-bearer killed about twenty men.

Panic struck the whole Philistine army; the ground shook. It was a panic sent by God.

Saul's sentries at Gibeah in Benjamin saw the army melting away in all directions. Saul discovered that Jonathan and his armor-bearer were not with them.

Then Saul and all his men assembled and went straight to the battle. They found the Philistines in total confusion, even striking each other with their swords. Hebrews who had previously defected to the Philistines joined the Israelites to fight with Saul and Jonathan. The Israelites who had hidden in the hill country heard that the Philistines were on the run. Then they joined the battle. The Lord rescued Israel that day (14:1-23).

Saul did something really foolish that day that made his soldiers miserable. Saul bound the army under an oath, saying: "Cursed be any man who eats food before evening comes, before I have avenged myself on my enemies!" So none of the troops ate food all day.

The entire army entered the woods, and there were many honeycombs there. When they went into the woods, they saw the honey oozing out, yet no one took any, because they feared the oath. But Jonathan had not heard that his father put the army under oath. So he reached out the tip of his staff and dipped it into the honeycomb. He raised his hand to his mouth, and his eyes lit up with renewed vigor. A soldier spoke up: "Your father bound the army under a strict oath, saying: `Cursed be any man who eats food today!' That is why the men are weak."

Jonathan said: "My father has made trouble for the country. See how quickly my energy returned when I tasted a little honey. How much better it would have been today if the men had eaten the food they took from their enemies. We could have killed many more Philistines!"

Saul discovered that Jonathan had disobeyed the oath by eating honey and was going to kill him. But the men challenged Saul: "Jonathan die? Never! He is responsible for saving Israel today! Never! As surely as the Lord lives, not a hair of his head will be harmed. He fought against the Philistines with God's help!" The men rescued Jonathan, and he did not die (14:24-45).

After Saul became king over Israel, he fought against their enemies on every side. He constantly experienced victory; he was invincible! He delivered Israel from the hands of those who had looted them. During all of Saul's life, there was bitter war with the Philistines. Whenever Saul saw a strong or brave man, he took him into his army (14:47-52).

Saul Rejected as King
Samuel told Saul: "The Lord sent me to anoint you king over his people Israel; now listen to the Lord's message. The Lord Almighty says: `I will punish the Amalekites for ambushing the Israelites who were coming up from Egypt. Now go, attack the Amalekites and totally destroy everything that belongs to them as an offering to the Lord. This is to be total destruction; put to death men and women, children and infants, cattle and sheep, camels and donkeys'" (15:1-4).

Saul called the army together; two hundred and ten thousand foot soldiers. Saul went to the city of Amalek and set an ambush in the canyon. Saul defeated the Amalekites. He took Agag king of the Amalekites alive. Everyone else was killed under the terms of the holy ban. But Saul and the army made an exception for Agag and the best of the sheep and cattle. They did not include them under the terms of the holy ban. But all the animals which were weak or useless, they destroyed as decreed by the holy ban (15:5-9).

Then the Lord spoke to Samuel: "I am sorry I made Saul king. He turned away from me and refuses to obey my commands." Samuel was upset, and he cried out to the Lord all night long (15:10-11).

Early the next morning Samuel got up and went to meet Saul. But the people told Samuel: "Saul went to Carmel where he put up a victory monument in his own honor; now he has gone to Gilgal."

When Samuel caught up with him, Saul said: "I carried out the Lord's commands."

Samuel replied: "Then why do I hear sheep bleating and cattle mooing?"

Saul answered: "The soldiers took them from the Amalekites. They saved the best of the sheep and cattle to sacrifice to the Lord your God, but we totally destroyed the rest as decreed by the holy ban" (15:12-15).

Samuel interrupted Saul: "Stop! Let me tell you what the Lord told me last night. When you started out, you were nothing, and you didn't think much of yourself. Then the Lord anointed you king over Israel. The Lord sent you on a mission, saying: `Go and completely destroy the wicked Amalekites under a holy ban; make war on them until all of them are dead.' Why did you not obey the Lord? Why did you pounce on the plunder and do what the Lord said was wrong?"

Saul defended himself: "But I did obey the Lord. I went on the mission the Lord assigned me. I completely destroyed the Amalekites under the terms of the holy ban. I only brought back Agag their king. The soldiers took the best sheep and cattle from the plunder to sacrifice to the Lord your God at Gilgal."

Samuel replied: "What pleases the Lord more: burnt offerings and sacrifices or obedience? To obey is better than sacrifice, and obedience is better than the fat of rams. Rebellion is as bad as the sin of divination. Arrogance is as bad as the evil of idolatry. Because you rejected the Word of the Lord, he has rejected you as king" (15:16-23).

Then Saul said to Samuel: "I have sinned. I violated the Lord's command and your commands. I was afraid of the people and so I gave in to them. Now I beg you, forgive my sin and come back with me, so that I may worship the Lord."

But Samuel said to him: "I will not go back with you. You rejected the command of the Lord, and the Lord has rejected you as king over Israel!"

As Samuel turned to leave, Saul grabbed his priestly robe, and it tore. Samuel said to him: "Just now, the Lord tore the kingdom of Israel from you and has given it to one of your neighbors, to one better than you. He who is the Glory of Israel does not lie or change his mind. He is not a man. He does not change his mind as men do."

Saul replied: "I have sinned. But don't abandon me! Honor me with your presence before the leaders of my people and before Israel. Come back with me, so that I may worship the Lord your God."

So Samuel went back with Saul, and Saul worshiped the Lord.

Then Samuel said: "Bring King Agag of Amalek to me."

Agag came to him confidently, thinking: "Surely the threat of death is past."

But Samuel said: "Your sword caused women to be without their children; now your mother will have no children."

And Samuel cut Agag to pieces before the Lord at Gilgal (15:24-33).

Then Samuel left for Ramah, but Saul went to his home in Gibeah. Samuel never saw Saul again all the rest of his life. Samuel grieved long and deeply for Saul. The Lord was sorry that he ever made Saul king over Israel (15:34-35).

LIFE-LESSONS DISCOVERED IN THE STORY

1. God may use common occurrences to lead a person to a life-changing experience; therefore one should consider each situation as a potential "divine appointment" designed to shape his life. Saul's search for stray donkeys took him to Samuel and an assignment to become king (9:3 - 10:1).

2. Those who govern must answer to divine authority. Samuel explained to the people the regulations of the kingship (10:25).

3. Criticism will always be directed toward those who lead because they are out in front. Some troublemakers despised Saul, the new king (10:26-27).

4. Anger directed at sin, mistreatment of others and injustice can be channeled by the Holy Spirit to bring about positive changes. Nahash, king of the Ammonites, threatened to gouge out the right eye of everyone in Jabesh. When Saul heard the news, the Spirit of God came upon him in power. He burned with anger, and he raised an army to defeat the Ammonites (11:6-8).

5. The spiritual leader should pray for those under his leadership and teach them to do right, even when they disappoint him. Samuel continued praying for the people and teaching them what was good and right, even though he condemned their decision to have a king (12:20, 23).

6. Those who govern have God-given responsibilities, and they must answer to him. Israel's kings were anointed by men of God (10:1; 16:13; 1 Kin 1:39; 2 Kin 9:6; 11:12). The anointing emphasized that as kings they were subject to the Lord God and that they had a responsibility to serve and obey him.

7. People need to be reminded of the great actions of Lord God in the past, in order to have faith to trust him for their future. In their farewells, Moses (Dt 31), Joshua (Jos 24) and Samuel (1 Sm 12) reminded the people of the Lord's past

actions, and they promised that the Lord would bless his people in the future, as long as they stayed faithful to him.

8. The leader only has the Lord's support when he is obeying the Word of God. The pre-condition for Saul to have divine support was for him to obey the Lord (12:14-15).

9. Arrogant pride controls the life of the person who takes credit for the accomplishments of others. Jonathan attacked and destroyed the Philistine outpost; however, Saul took credit for it (13:3-4). After Saul attacked and defeated the Amalekites, he set up a monument in his own honor (15:12). He did not give the Lord honor for the victory.

10. A person's character is revealed when he is under pressure, sees his resources slipping away, and thinks time is running out. Saul was under pressure from the approaching Philistines, his men scattering, and Samuel the priest delaying to come to offer sacrifices. Saul took matters into his own hands and disobeyed God by offering the sacrifices (13:8-14). This was against God's laws (Dt 12:5-14) and against Samuel's instructions (1 Sm 10:8).

11. If the person who was chosen and blessed by the Lord becomes unfaithful, the Lord may then reject and punish him. The Lord God chose Saul to save his people, and the Lord gave him great victories (11 - 14). However, after Saul began to disobey divine orders, the Lord rejected him as king and fought against him (13:13-14; 15:23-29).

12. God's best person may become disqualified to serve him. When the Lord chose Saul as king, he was the best man in Israel (9:2; 10:24). When Saul refused to obey God's commands, he became disqualified to serve him (13:13-14; 15:23-29).

13. God's servant should grieve when he is required to pronounce God's judgment. Samuel was faithful to pronounce God's judgment to Saul; however, he grieved for him (15:13, 35).

14. It is not enough to begin being faithful to God; one needs to remain faithful to the end. At the beginning of his kingship: Saul was the best of the Israelites (9:2; 10:24), he was humble (9:21; 10:21-22), injustice made him angry (11:6) and he did not seek revenge on those who rejected him as king (11:12-13). But after his kingship was established: He took credit for a battle won by Jonathan (13:3-4), he had no communication with Jonathan (14:1,17), he made a foolish curse (14:24), he ignored the well-being of his army (14:24, 29-31), he desired to kill his son Jonathan (14:44), he partially obeyed God (15:3, 8-9) and he built a monument in his own honor (15:13).

15. The leader, who has as his priority to please his followers, will displease the Lord. Saul's excuse for disobeying the Lord's command was: "I was afraid of the people and so I gave in to them" (15:24).

16. The impatient person who is unwilling to wait in order to follow God's plans will act foolishly. King Saul became impatient when the priest Samuel did not arrive at the appointed time. So, Saul officiated at a sacrifice that God's Law stated should be offered by a priest. Samuel accused Saul of acting foolishly (13:13).

17. The sinner usually makes excuses for his wrongdoing by shifting the blame to someone else. After Saul disobeyed God and offered a sacrifice himself instead of waiting for Samuel, he gave an excuse instead of admitting his wrongdoing (13:12-13). Saul shifted the blame to the soldiers for not obeying God's command to kill all the sheep and cattle (15:21). Beginning with Adam, the sinner seeks to make excuses and blame another for his sin. Adam shifted the blame to God and Eve (Gn 3:12). Eve shifted the blame to the snake (Gn 3:13). After Aaron made the golden calf, he shifted the blame to the people (Ex 32:21-24).

18. Decaying spiritual character destroys effective leadership. Saul had great victory when he was obedient to God. He rescued the city of Jabesh, (11:1-11) and he did not seek revenge on those who had formerly rejected him as king (11:12-13). But after his spiritual decay, he was a failure as a leader: He took credit for a battle won by Jonathan (13:3-4); he had no communication with Jonathan (14:1,17); he made a foolish curse (14:24); he ignored the well-being of his army (14:24, 29-31); he desired to kill Jonathan, the one who had enabled him to have great success (14:44); he partially obeyed God (15:3, 8-9) and he built a monument in his own honor (15:13).

19. Selective obedience is a form of disobedience. Saul was guilty because he and his men selected what they would destroy from the plunder, when God had commanded that everything be destroyed. Saul was guilty of disobeying God (15:3, 13-23).

20. The consequences of certain sins can not be undone. Saul refused to obey God's command, and this resulted in irreversible doom for his kingdom (15:16). The Lord rejected him as king (15:23) and the Lord is not one who will change his mind as men do (15:29). After eating the forbidden fruit, Adam and Eve were expelled from the garden and could not return (Gn 3:23-24).

21. Worship and sacrifice must be offered to the

Lord on his terms. Saul intended to sacrifice the best cattle to the Lord. He had good intentions; however, his delay in obeying the commanded destruction constituted flagrant violation of God's will (15:22). (See Ps 40:6-8; 51:16-17; Isa 1:11-15; Hos 6:6; Mk 12:32-33.)

22. Rejecting God's commands begets rejection by God. Saul refused to obey the Lord, and the Lord rejected him as king (15:23, 26, 28).

23. God demands obedience and not just participation in religious activities. God ordered Saul to destroy everything that belonged to the Amalekites. However, Saul spared the best sheep and cattle to sacrifice to the Lord. Samuel explained that it is better to obey God than to offer him sacrifices (15:22-23).

24. The person who disobeys God faces the risk that the Lord will begin to oppose him. Because Saul rejected the Word of the Lord, the Lord rejected him as king over Israel. The Lord began to oppose Saul while helping the one who would replace him as king (15:21-23, 28).

QUESTIONS

1. How did God arrange for Saul to encounter Samuel?
2. How did Samuel present Saul as king to the Israelites?
3. What did Saul do that resulted in the people's accepting and confirming him as king?
4. What were some of the positive things seen in Saul at the beginning of his kingship?
5. What warning did Samuel give in his farewell speech?
6. What were some of Saul's wrong actions after his kingdom was established?
7. What action on Saul's part led to God rejecting him as king?
8. How did Samuel react to Saul's disobedience?
9. What does this story teach us about God?
10. What can you learn from Samuel and Saul about leadership?

SAUL DESCENDS WHILE DAVID ASCENDS
United Kingdom
1 Samuel 16 - 31

STRUCTURE

Context:
Samuel was the last of the judges. He led the Israelites to have victory over their enemies. When Samuel became an old man, he appointed his sons as judges, but they were dishonest. Israel's leaders requested that Samuel give them a king.

Samuel anointed Saul king. Saul attacked the Philistines and defeated them. On one occasion, the Philistines assembled to fight with soldiers too many to count. Saul did not wait for Samuel to arrive to offer sacrifices to the Lord. Saul himself offered the whole-burnt-offering even though God's Law required that only priests offer burnt-offerings. Samuel arrived and told Saul that since he had disobeyed God, his kingdom would not endure. Saul fought against Israel's enemies and he always experienced victory.

Samuel gave Saul the Lord's command to attack the Amalekites and destroy everything that belonged to them as an offering to the Lord. Saul defeated the Amalekites. But, he did not kill the king of the Amalekites nor the best of the sheep and cattle.

Samuel informed Saul that since he had rejected the Lord's command, the Lord had rejected Saul as king. Samuel never saw Saul again all the rest of his life. Samuel grieved for Saul. The Lord was sorry that he made Saul king over Israel.

Key-persons: Saul, Jonathan and David

Key-locations: The house of Saul at Gibeah, Bethlehem, hideouts in back-country wilderness and deserts, land of the Philistines

Key-repetitions:
- Saul was afraid: of his soldiers (15:24); of David (18:12, 29); of the Philistines (13:7; 28:5); because of Samuel's words (28:20).
- David was loved: by Jonathan (18:1, 3; 20:17); by Judah (18:16); by Michal (18:20, 28).
- Saul's violent anger: when he tried to kill: David (18:11, 25; 19:1, 10, 12, 18), Jonathan (20:33); when he ordered the priest killed (22:18-19).
- The song: Saul has slain his thousands, and David his tens of thousands (18:6-9; 21:11; 29:5).
- David escaped from Saul (18:11; 19:10, 12, 18; 23:26-28).
- David and Jonathan made covenants (18:3; 20:16, 42; 23:18).
- David would not harm Saul, the Lord's anointed (1 Sm 24:6, 10; 26:9-11, 23; 2 Sm 1:14).
- Actions that resulted in Saul's self-destruction: impatience (13:12-13); disobedience (15:19-23); the Spirit of the Lord left him (16:14); dominated by jealousy (18:8-9); tried to kill David (18:10-11); killed priests (22:6-23); acted like a fool (26:21); sought counsel from a medium (28:6-20); suicide (31:4).
- Events that raised up David: Samuel anointed David (16:1-12); he was empowered by the Spirit of the Lord (16:13); he played the harp for Saul (16:14-23); killed Goliath (17:1-57); developed a friendship with Jonathan (18:1-5); women sang praises about David (18:6-16); he married Michal, Saul's daughter (18:17-29); the Lord was with David (18:28); he escaped when Saul tried to kill him (19:1-24); he spared Saul's life (24:3-22; 26:1-25); he and his men defeat the Amalekites (30:1-31).

Key-attitudes:
- The grief Samuel felt for Saul.
- Expressed by Saul: Arrogance, jealousy of David, fear/terror, violent temper, shame when David spared his life, and hatred.
- Saul's obsession with killing David.
- David felt confidence in God, courage, and commitment to do right.
- Love felt for David.
- Friendship between Jonathan and David.
- Conflict.

Initial-problem:
The Lord asked Samuel how long he would mourn for Saul. The Lord told Samuel that he had rejected Saul as king and had chosen one of Jesse's sons to be king.

Sequence of events:
David, a Servant of Saul
- The Lord told Samuel that he had rejected Saul as king and had chosen one of Jesse's son to be king (16:1-2).
- Samuel anointed David as king. The Spirit of the Lord entered David and empowered him (16:3-13).
- The Spirit of the Lord left Saul, and an evil spirit tormented him (16:14).
- David entered Saul's service to play his harp whenever the evil spirit came upon Saul (16:14-23).
- The Philistines prepared for war. Saul called up his troops (17:1-3).
- Goliath issued a dare for a man from the Israelite army to fight him. Saul and his troops were terrified of Goliath (17:4-11).
- Jesse's three oldest sons went with Saul to war. David went back and forth from helping Saul to tending his father's sheep (17:12-15).
- David took food to his brothers in Saul's camp. David went to the battle lines to greet his brothers. Goliath shouted his dare, and David heard it. The Israelites fell back in terror. David asked what would be done to reward the man who killed the

- Philistine (17:16-27).
- Eliab sneered at David (17:28-29).
- David's remarks were reported to Saul. David offered to fight the Philistine. Saul replied that David was only a boy. David answered that the Lord delivered him from the lion's teeth and the bear's claws, and he would also deliver him from the Philistine (17:30-37).
- David refused to wear Saul's armor. David took his shepherd's staff, five stones and his sling (17:38-40).
- Goliath ridiculed David (17:41-44).
- David answered that Goliath was coming against him with sword, spear and battle-ax. But David was coming against Goliath in the name of the Lord Almighty. David defeated Goliath with a sling and a stone (17:45-51).
- The Israelites defeated the Philistines (17:52-58).
- Saul kept David with him. Jonathan loved David, made a covenant with him and gave him gifts (18:1-4).
- Saul gave David a high rank in the army (18:5).
- Women sang: "Saul has killed thousands, and David has killed tens of thousands!" Saul became jealous of David (18:6-9).
- Saul threw a spear twice to nail David to the wall. Saul sent David away by giving him command over a thousand men. The Lord was with David. Saul was afraid of David, but all Israel loved him (18:10-16).
- Saul's daughter Michal was in love with David. Saul told David the price for the bride was 100 Philistine foreskins. David and his men killed 200 Philistines. Saul gave his daughter to David in marriage (18:17-27).
- Saul's fear of David increased. As long as Saul lived, he tried to kill David (18:28-30).

David, Fleeing from Saul
- Saul told Jonathan and his servants to kill David, but Jonathan warned David. Jonathan defended David to Saul, and Saul promised not to put David to death. Jonathan brought David back to Saul. But once again Saul tried to nail David to the wall with his spear (19:1-10).
- Saul sent men to David's house to kill him. But Michal helped David escape (19:11-17).
- David escaped to Samuel at Ramah (19:18).
- David sought Jonathan. Jonathan made a covenant with the house of David (20:1-17).
- Jonathan planned to warn David if Saul planned to harm him by shooting arrows in the direction of a boulder. At the New Moon festival, Saul exploded in anger at Jonathan, accusing him of siding with David. The next morning Jonathan went to the field and used his arrows to warn David to flee (20:18-43).
- David went to Nob, to see Ahimelech the priest, and he obtained bread and Goliath's sword. Saul's head shepherd, Doeg the Edomite, happened to be there that day (21:1-9).
- David went to Achish, king of Gath (21:10-15).

David, a Fugitive Living in Hideouts
- David escaped to the cave of Adullam. His father's household went to him, and about 400 men joined him (22:1-2).
- Saul criticized his officials: "None of you tells me that my son conspires with my servant David to ambush me!"
- Doeg the Edomite said that he saw David with the priest Ahimelech at Nob. Saul ordered Doeg to kill the priests. He killed 85 priests and carried the massacre into Nob (22:6-19).
- One son of Ahimelech, Abiathar escaped and fled to join David (22:20-23).
- David and his 600 men kept moving while Saul searched for them. God protected David. Jonathan visited David (23:7-18).
- In the wilderness of Maon, Saul was closing in on David when a messenger informed him that the Philistines had attacked the land (23:19-29).
- Saul with 3,000 men pursued David. David and his men were hiding in a cave when Saul entered. David cut off a corner of Saul's robe. After Saul left the cave, David called to him and used the cut robe as evidence that he would not harm Saul (24:1-22).
- Samuel died (25:1).
- In the Wilderness of Maon, Nabal insulted David, but Abigail, his wife, prevented David from avenging himself. Nabal fell into a coma and 10 days later died. David sent word to Abigail, asking her to become his wife (25:2-44).
- Saul searched for David in the Wilderness of Ziph. David entered the encampment by night and took Saul's spear and water jug, but spared his life (26:1-25).
- David went to Achish king of Gath in the land of the Philistines where Saul would not search for him. He took his two wives, and his 600 men took their families. David lived in Philistine territory a year and four months. Achish trusted David (27:1-12).

Saul's Defeat
- The Philistines gathered their forces to fight against Israel. Achish ordered David and his men to accompany him in the army (28:1-2).
- Samuel was dead. Saul had expelled mediums from the land. Saul saw the Philistine army and was terrified. He prayed to the Lord, but the Lord did not answer. Saul then consulted a medium, asking her to call up Samuel from the grave. Samuel told Saul that the Lord had become his enemy, he would hand over both Israel and Saul to the Philistines and that Saul and his sons would die. Saul had not eaten, and the medium prepared food for him (28:3-25).
- The Philistine commanders would not let David fight with them, so Achish sent David and his men away (29:1-11).
- The Amalekites had attacked Ziklag, the city where David and his men had been living. The Amalekites took captive all who were in the city. It took David's army three days to reach Ziklag. Then they pursued the raiding party. At Besor Ravine, 200 men were exhausted and stayed behind. David and 400 caught the raiding party and recovered everything the Amalekites had taken. David insisted that the 200 who stayed behind share in the plunder. David sent some of the plunder to the leaders of Judah (30:1-31).
- The Philistines made war on Israel and killed

three of Saul's sons. Archers wounded Saul. Saul took his own sword and fell on it (31:1-7).
- Saul died because he disobeyed the Lord. He consulted a medium to seek guidance (1 Chron 10:13-14).
- The next day the Philistines cut off Saul's head, put Saul's armor in the temple of the Ashtoreths, and hung his corpse to the wall of Beth Shan. Men from Jabesh went to Beth Shan, retrieved the bodies of Saul and his sons, brought them back to Jabesh, and gave them a dignified burial. They fasted in mourning for seven days (1 Sm 31:8-13).

Final-situation:
The Philistines made war on Israel and archers wounded Saul. Saul took his own sword and fell on it. Saul died because he disobeyed the Lord.

BIBLE STORY

David, a Servant of Saul

The Lord told Samuel: "How long will you mourn for Saul? I have rejected him as king of Israel. Fill your flask with oil and go. I am sending you to Jesse of Bethlehem. I have chosen one of his sons to be king."

Samuel went to Bethlehem and told the town leaders that he had come to sacrifice to the Lord. Then he invited Jesse and his sons to the sacrifice.

When Jesse's sons arrived, Samuel saw Eliab and thought: "This is the one, the Lord's anointed!"

But the Lord told Samuel: "Do not be impressed with his looks nor his height, for I have rejected him. The Lord judges people in a different way than humans do. Man looks at the outward appearance; the Lord looks at the heart."

Jesse had seven of his sons pass before Samuel, but Samuel told him: "The Lord has not chosen any of these. Are there no more sons?"

Jesse answered: "The youngest is out tending the sheep."

Samuel requested: "Send for him; we will not sit down until he arrives."

Jesse sent for the youngest, who was named David. He was the picture of health, tanned and good looking.

Then the Lord said: "Get up and anoint him; he is the one."

Samuel took the flask of oil and anointed David with his brothers watching. The Spirit of the Lord entered David and empowered him for the rest of his life. Samuel returned to Ramah (16:1-13).

Now the Spirit of the Lord left Saul, and an evil spirit from the Lord tormented him (16:14).

Saul's advisors sought someone to play the harp for Saul when the evil spirit tormented him. One servant mentioned that Jesse of Bethlehem had a son who played the harp. Saul sent messengers to Jesse and said: "Send me your son David."

David went to Saul and entered his service. Saul liked David and sent word to Jesse: "Allow David to remain in my service; I am pleased with him."

Whenever the evil spirit from the Lord came upon Saul, David got out his harp and played. Saul would feel better, and the evil spirit would leave him (16:14-23).

The Philistines prepared for war. Saul called up his troops to oppose them. The Philistines were on one hill and the Israelites on the opposing hill, with the valley between them (17:1-3).

The hero of the Philistine camp was Goliath, a giant who was over nine feet tall. He had a bronze helmet on his head and was dressed in bronze armor. He wore bronze shin guards and carried a bronze sword. His spear was like a fence rail; the spear tip weighed over fifteen pounds. Goliath shouted a challenge to the army of Israel: "No need for the whole army to fight. Choose one man and have him fight me. If he kills me, the Philistines will become your slaves; but if I kill him, you will become our slaves. I dare the army of Israel: Send one of your men to fight me!" When Saul and his troops heard Goliath's dare, they were terrified (17:4-11).

Jesse's three oldest sons, Eliab, Abinadab, and Shammah went with Saul to war. David, the youngest, went back and forth from helping Saul to tending his father's sheep at Bethlehem (17:12-15).

Each morning and evening for forty days the Philistine came forward and made his speech.

Jesse told his son David: "Take food to your brothers in Saul's camp. Check on them and bring me back some news."

Early the next morning David loaded up and set out. He arrived at the camp just as the army was moving into battle formation. Israel and the Philistines were forming their lines facing each other. David left the food with the keeper of supplies. Then he ran to the battle line and greeted his brothers. While they were talking, Goliath stepped forward and shouted his usual dare, and David heard it. When the Israelites saw the man, they fell back in terror.

The Israelite troops talked among themselves: "This man keeps coming out to challenge Israel. The king will give great wealth to the man who kills him. He will also give him his daughter as a bride and will exempt his father's family from paying taxes."

David asked the men standing near him: "What will be done to reward the man who kills this Philistine and removes this disgrace from Israel? Who does this uncircumcised Philistine think he is, defying the armies of the living God?"

Eliab, David's oldest brother, heard David talking. Eliab lost his temper and sneered at David: "What are you doing here? Who did you leave with those few sheep in the desert? You conceited kid, you came here hoping to see a bloody battle!"

David replied: "Now what have I done wrong? Can't I even talk?" He then turned away and ignored his brother. David's remarks were overheard and reported to Saul. Saul sent for him.

David told Saul: "I, your servant, will go and fight this Philistine."

Saul replied: "You can not fight this Philistine; you are only a boy. Goliath has been a warrior since his youth."

David answered Saul: "I have been tending sheep for my father. Whenever a lion or a bear took a sheep from the flock, I chased it, attacked it and rescued the sheep. I have killed both a lion and a bear. I will do the same to this uncircumcised Philistine who is challenging the armies of the living God. The Lord delivered me from the lion's teeth and the bear's claws. He will also deliver me from this Philistine."

Saul told David: "Go, and the Lord be with you." Saul outfitted David in his own armor.

David told Saul: "I cannot move with all this stuff; I am not used to it." So he took it off. Then David took his shepherd's staff, selected five smooth stones from the creek, put them in his shepherd's pouch and with his sling in his hand, approached the Philistine.

Meanwhile, Goliath kept coming closer to David. He saw that David was only a boy, and he sneered. He ridiculed David: "Do you think I am a dog, that you come after me with a stick?" Goliath cursed David and said: "Come here, and I'll give your flesh to the buzzards and the beasts of the field!"

David answered: "You come against me with sword, spear and battle-ax. I come against you in the name of the Lord Almighty, the God of the armies of Israel, whom you curse. Today the Lord will give you over to me. I'll kill you and I'll cut off your head. Then all the world will know that there is a God in Israel. It is not by sword or spear that the Lord saves; the battle belongs to the Lord."

Goliath moved closer to attack; David ran toward the Philistine, took a stone from his pouch, slung it and hit Goliath in the forehead. The stone sank into his forehead, and he fell face-down on the ground. David defeated Goliath with a sling and a stone. David ran to the Philistine, took Goliath's sword from its sheath and cut off his head (17:1-51).

The Philistines saw their hero dead! They ran for their lives. The men of Israel rushed forward, chased the Philistines and left many dead scattered along the roads (17:52-58).

From that day Saul kept David with him and did not let him return to his father's house. Jonathan, Saul's son, loved David as much as he loved himself. He made a covenant with David and gave him gifts: his royal robe and weapons including his armor, sword, bow and belt (18:1-4).

Saul sent David to fight in different battles. David was so successful that Saul gave him a high rank in the army. This pleased all the people, and Saul's officers as well (18:5).

As the men returned home after David had killed Goliath, women from all the villages of Israel greeted King Saul with singing and dancing. As they danced, they sang: "Saul has killed thousands, and David has killed tens of thousands!"

Saul became very angry; he thought: "They credit David with tens of thousands, but me with only thousands. What more can he get but the kingdom?" From then on Saul kept a jealous eye on David (18:6-9).

The next day an evil spirit from the Lord afflicted Saul while he was in his house. David was playing his harp. Saul had a spear in his hand, and he threw it to nail David to the wall. But David eluded him twice.

Saul was afraid of David. It was clear that the Lord was with David, but had left Saul. Saul sent David away by giving him command over a thousand men. David always had great success, because the Lord was with him. Saul was afraid of David, but all the Israelites in Saul's kingdom loved him (18:10-16).

Saul's daughter Michal was in love with David, and this pleased Saul. Saul planned to get the Philistines to kill David. Saul sent a message to David: "The king is pleased with you; now become his son-in-law. The king wants no other price for the bride than a hundred Philistine foreskins."

David and his men went out, killed two hundred Philistines, brought back their foreskins and counted them before the king. Saul then gave his daughter Michal to David in marriage (18:17-27).

Saul realized that the Lord was with David and that his daughter Michal loved David. Saul's fear of David increased. As long as Saul lived, he tried to kill David. Whenever the Philistine warlords came out to battle, David had more success than the rest of Saul's officers (18:28-30).

David, Fleeing from Saul

Saul told his son Jonathan and all his servants to kill David. But Jonathan warned David that Saul was looking for a chance to kill him.

Jonathan bragged on David to Saul his father: "Don't attack David. He has not wronged you. Look at all the good he has done!. He put his life on the line when he killed Goliath the Philistine. Why would you do wrong by killing an innocent man like David?"

Saul listened to Jonathan and promised: "As surely as the Lord lives, David will not be put to death."

Jonathan sent for David and told him the whole conversation. He brought David back to Saul, and David was with Saul as before.

But once again an evil spirit from the Lord came upon Saul. While David was playing the harp, Saul tried to nail him to the wall with his spear, but David dodged and escaped (19:1-10).

Saul sent men to David's house to watch it and to kill him in the morning. But Michal, David's wife let David down through a window, and he escaped (19:11-17).

David escaped to Samuel at Ramah and told him all that Saul had done to him (19:18).

David sought Jonathan and asked: "What have I done? How have I wronged your father, so that he is trying to kill me?"

Jonathan replied: "You have done nothing wrong and you are not going to die. I will get it out of my father how he feels about you. Then I will let you know what I learn. If my father still intends to kill you, I will let you know and send you away. If I continue to live, continue to be my covenant friend. If I die, keep the covenant friendship with my family. When God finally rids the earth of David's enemies, stay loyal to Jonathan!" So Jonathan made a covenant with the house of David. And Jonathan had David reaffirm his pledge of love and friendship for him, because he loved him as he loved himself (20:1-17).

Then Jonathan told David his plan: "Tomorrow is the New Moon festival. You will be missed when you don't show up for dinner. Three days from now, toward evening, go to the boulder where you hid when this trouble began. I will shoot three arrows in the direction of the boulder, as though I were shooting at a target. Then I will tell a boy: `Go, find the arrows.' If I yell to him: `Look, the arrows are on this side of you; retrieve them,' then you are safe; there is no danger. But if I yell to the boy: `Look, the arrows are farther out,' then you must run away."

So David hid in the field. When the New Moon festival came, the king sat down to eat, but David's place was empty. Saul said nothing that day. But the second day of the festival, David's place was empty again. Then Saul asked his son Jonathan: "Why hasn't the son of Jesse come to the meal, either yesterday or today?"

Jonathan answered: "David asked me for special permission to go to Bethlehem to attend a family reunion. That is why he has not come to the king's table."

Saul exploded in anger at Jonathan and screamed: "You son of a slut! I know that you have sided with the son of Jesse. You bring disgrace both on yourself and your mother! As long as Jesse's son lives on this earth, you will never be king nor have a kingdom. Bring David here; he must die!"

Jonathan stood up to his father: "Why should he be put to death? What has he done?"

Saul threw his spear at Jonathan, trying to kill him. Jonathan stormed from the table in fierce anger and was too upset to eat. He was grieved at his father's shameful treatment of David.

The next morning Jonathan went to the field for his appointment with David. A young boy was with him, and he told the boy: "Run and find the arrows I shoot." As the boy ran, he shot an arrow beyond him. The boy came to the place where Jonathan's arrow had fallen, and Jonathan yelled out: "The arrow is farther out! Hurry! Don't stop!" The boy picked up the arrow and returned to his master. Then Jonathan gave his bow and arrows to the boy and sent him back to town.

After the boy left, David left his hiding place beside the boulder and bowed down before Jonathan three times. They kissed each other and wept together, but David wept the most.

Jonathan told David: "Go in peace. We have vowed friendship with each other in the name of the Lord. The Lord is witness between you and me, and between our descendants forever." David left, and Jonathan went back to the town (20:18-43).

David went to Nob, to see Ahimelech the priest and told him: "The king charged me with urgent top-secret business. Now, give me five loaves of bread, or anything you can find."

The priest gave him holy bread, since there was no bread there except the bread of the Presence that had been removed from before the Lord and replaced by fresh bread at the same time.

Saul's head shepherd, Doeg the Edomite, happened to be there that day.

David asked Ahimelech: "Don't you have a spear or a sword here? I did not have a chance to grab my weapons, because the king's business was urgent."

The priest replied: "There is only the sword of Goliath the Philistine, whom you killed. If you want it, take it" (21:1-9).

David left there, fleeing from Saul and running for his life. David went to Achish, king of Gath (21:10-15).

David, a Fugitive Living in Hideouts

David left Gath and escaped to the cave of Adullam. His brothers and his father's household heard about it, and they went there to him. Also, misfits who were distressed, or in debt, or discontented gathered around him, and he became their leader. About four hundred men joined him (22:1-2).

Saul criticized his officials: "You have all conspired against me! No one tells me that my son makes a covenant with this outlaw son of Jesse. None of you tells me that my son conspires with my servant David to ambush me!"

But Doeg the Edomite, who was standing with Saul's officials, said: "I saw the son of Jesse come to the priest Ahimelech at Nob. Ahimelech prayed with him for the Lord's guidance, gave him food and armed him with the sword of Goliath the Philistine."

Saul sent for the priest Ahimelech along with the whole family of priests who were at Nob.

Then Saul ordered the guards at his side: "Kill the priests of the Lord, because they too have sided with David. They knew he was fleeing, yet they did not tell me."

But the king's men refused to raise a hand to strike the priests of the Lord.

The king then ordered Doeg: "You do it. Massacre the priests." So Doeg the Edomite killed them. That day he killed eighty-five priests. He also carried the massacre into Nob, the town of the priests; killing men and women, children and infants, cattle, donkeys and sheep (22:6-19).

Only one son of Ahimelech escaped; Abiathar. He

fled to join David. He told David that Saul had murdered the priests of the Lord. David told Abiathar: "That day, Doeg the Edomite was there, and I knew he would tell Saul. I am to blame for the death of your father's whole family. Stay with me. The man who is seeking your life is seeking mine also. You will be safe with me" (22:20-23).

David had about 600 men. They kept moving from place to place. David stayed in desert hideouts and in the back-country wilderness hills of the Desert of Ziph. Day after day Saul searched for him, but God protected David. Jonathan, Saul's son, visited David and helped David have stronger faith in God. The two of them made a covenant before the Lord. Then Jonathan went home.

David went to the wilderness of Maon, and Saul chased in pursuit. Saul was on one side of the mountain, and David and his men were on the other side, running to get away from Saul. Saul and his forces were closing in on David. But a messenger came to Saul, saying: "The Philistines just attacked the land." Then Saul broke off his pursuit of David and went to fight the Philistines (23:1-29).

After Saul chased off the Philistines, he took three thousand men and set out in pursuit of David and his men. Saul came to a cave and went in to relieve himself. David and his men were hiding far back in the same cave. Then David crept near Saul and cut off a corner of Saul's robe.

Immediately, David felt guilty. He told his men: "The Lord forbid that I should lift my hand against him; for he is the anointed of the Lord." David prevented his men from attacking Saul. And Saul left the cave and went on his way.

Then David went to the mouth of the cave and called to Saul: "My lord the king!" When Saul looked back, David bowed down and prostrated himself with his face to the ground. He called out: "Why do you listen when men say: `David is out to harm you'? Today, the Lord delivered you into my hands in the cave. But I spared you; I said: `I will not lift my hand against my master, because he is the Lord's anointed.' Look at this piece of your robe that I cut off! I cut off the corner of your robe but did not kill you. This is evidence: I'm no rebel. May the Lord punish you for the wrong you have done to me! But my hand will not harm you!"

Saul asked: "Is that your voice, David my son?" He wept in loud sobs and said: "You are right; I am wrong. You have done good to me; I have done bad to you. I know that you will be king and that the kingdom of Israel will be established in your hands. Now swear to me by the Lord that you will not kill off my descendants or wipe out my name from my father's family."

So David gave his promise to Saul. Saul returned home, but David and his men went up to the hideout (24:1-22).

Samuel died, and all Israel assembled and mourned for him. He was buried at his home in Ramah (25:1).

David moved again to the Wilderness of Maon. Nabal was a wealthy man who had property there; he had a thousand goats and three thousand sheep. Nabal's wife, Abigail, was intelligent and beautiful. But Nabal was cruel and mean.

David heard that Nabal was shearing sheep. He gave ten of his young men the order: "Greet Nabal in my name. Say to him: 'When your shepherds were with us, we did not mistreat them, and the whole time they were near us nothing of theirs was missing. Therefore, I am asking you to be generous with my young men. Please give your servants and your son David whatever you can find for them.'"

When David's men arrived, they gave Nabal this message in David's name.

Nabal insulted David's servants: "Who is this David? Many slaves are breaking away from their masters these days. Why should I take my bread and water, and the meat I have slaughtered for my shearers, and give it to men I've never laid eyes on?"

David's men turned around, went back and reported every word to David. David told his men to put on their swords. About four hundred men went up with David, while two hundred stayed with the supplies.

A servant told Nabal's wife Abigail: "David sent messengers to give our master his greetings, but Nabal hurled insults at them. Yet these men were very good to us. The whole time we were out in the fields near them, nothing was missing. See what you can do, because disaster is coming to our master and his household. He is such a wicked man that no one can talk to him."

Abigail hurried. She took two hundred loaves of bread, two leather bags of wine, five dressed sheep, a bushel of roasted grain, a hundred raisin cakes and two hundred fig cakes; and she loaded them on donkeys. She started toward David, but she did not tell her husband Nabal.

As she was riding her donkey into a mountain ravine, she met David and his men coming toward her. When Abigail saw David, she quickly got off her donkey and bowed down and said: "My lord, please let your servant speak to you. May my lord pay no attention to what that fool Nabal did. The Lord has kept you from bloodshed and from avenging yourself with your own hands. Let this gift be given to the men who follow you. Please forgive my presumption! But the Lord will certainly make a lasting dynasty for my master. Someone is chasing you to kill you, but the Lord your God will keep you alive. The Lord will throw away your enemies' lives as he would fling a stone from a sling. When the Lord has appointed you leader over Israel, you will not feel the guilt of needless bloodshed or of having avenged yourself."

David replied to Abigail: "Praise be to the Lord, the God of Israel, who sent you today to meet me. Bless you for your wisdom. Bless you for keeping me from murder and from avenging myself with my own hands. If you had not come to meet me, no one belonging to Nabal would be alive at daybreak."

Then David accepted what she had brought him.

When Abigail went home to Nabal, he was very drunk. So she told him nothing until the next morning. At daybreak, when Nabal was sober, his wife told him what she had done. His heart failed him, he fell into a coma and became like a stone. About ten days later, he died.

When David heard that Nabal was dead, he sent word to Abigail, asking her to become his wife. Abigail quickly got on a donkey and went with David's messengers and became his wife. David had also married Ahinoam of Jezreel, and they both were his wives. But Saul had given his daughter Michal, David's wife, to another man (25:2-44).

Saul went down to the Wilderness of Ziph, with three thousand soldiers, to search for David. David went to the place where Saul had set up camp. He saw where Saul and Abner, the commander of the army, were sleeping. David entered the encampment by night, took the spear and water jug near Saul's head, and left. No one woke up to see him.

Then David crossed over to the other side and stood on top of the hill some distance away. He shouted out to Abner: "Aren't you going to answer me, Abner?"

Abner replied: "Who are you who calls to the king?"

David said: "Why didn't you guard your lord the king? You and your men deserve to die because you did not guard your master, the Lord's anointed. Look around you. Where are the king's spear and water jug that were near his head?"

Saul recognized David's voice and said: "Is that you, David my son?"

David replied: "Yes it is, my lord the king. Why is my lord pursuing his servant? What have I done, and what crime am I guilty of?"

Saul responded: "I have sinned. Come back, David, my son. Because you considered my life precious today, I will not try to harm you again. Surely I have acted like a fool."

David answered: "Here is the king's spear. The Lord delivered you into my hands today, but I would not lay a hand on the Lord's anointed. Just as I valued your life today, so may the Lord value my life and rescue me from all trouble."

Saul replied to David: "Bless you, my son David. You will do great things and surely triumph."

Then David went on his way, and Saul returned home (26:1-25).

David decided to leave Israel and go the land of the Philistines where Saul would not search for him. So David and his six hundred men left and went over to Achish king of Gath. Each man had his family with him, and David had his two wives: Ahinoam of Jezreel and Abigail of Carmel, the widow of Nabal. When Saul was told that David had fled to Gath, he no longer searched for him.

David lived in Philistine territory a year and four months.

Achish trusted David (27:1-12).

Saul's Defeat
The Philistines gathered their forces to fight against Israel. Achish said to David: "You and your men will accompany me in the army."

David said: "Then you will see for yourself what I can do."

Achish replied: "Great, I will make you my bodyguard for life" (28:1-2).

Now Samuel was dead and buried. Saul had expelled mediums, who held seances with the dead, and fortune-tellers from the land.

The Philistines set up camp at Shunem. Saul set up camp at Gilboa. When Saul saw the Philistine army, terror filled his heart. He prayed to the Lord, but the Lord did not answer; neither by dream, nor by sign, nor by prophet. Saul ordered his attendants: "Find me a woman medium who calls up spirits, so I may go and inquire of her."

Saul disguised himself by putting on different clothes. Under the cover of night, Saul and two of his men went to the medium. Saul told her: "Consult a spirit for me. Call up the person I name."

But the woman told him: "Surely you know what Saul has done. He has forced the mediums from the land. Why have you set a trap to get me killed?"

Saul swore to her: "As surely as the Lord lives, you will not be punished for this."

The woman asked: "Who do you want me to bring up for you?"

Saul replied: "Bring up Samuel."

When the woman saw Samuel, she shouted: "Why did you lie to me? You are Saul!"

Saul assured her: "Don't be afraid. What do you see?"

The woman said: "I see a spirit ascending from the underground."

Saul asked: "What does he look like?"

The medium replied: "An old man wearing a priest robe is coming up."

Saul knew it was Samuel, and he bowed face down to the ground.

Samuel asked Saul: "Why have you disturbed me by calling me up?"

Saul replied: "I am in great trouble. The Philistines are making war against me and God has deserted me. He no longer answers me, so I called on you to tell me what to do."

Samuel said: "Why ask me, since the Lord left you and became your enemy? The Lord has done what he told you through me. The Lord ripped the kingdom out of your hands and gave it to David. You did not obey the Lord or carry out his fierce wrath against the Amalekites; therefore, the Lord has done this to you today. The Lord will hand over both Israel and you to the Philistines. Tomorrow you and your sons will be with me."

Immediately Saul dropped to the ground, terrified by Samuel's words. He was also very weak because he had eaten nothing all that day and night.

The medium told Saul: "Your maidservant obeyed you. I risked my life by doing what you told me to do. Now, it is your time to listen to your servant. Let me give you some food. Eat it, then you will have strength to go on your way."

Saul refused and said: "I will not eat."

Saul's men joined the woman in urging him to

eat, and he listened to them. He got up from the ground and sat on the couch. The woman butchered a fat calf and baked bread without yeast. Then she put the food before Saul and his men, and they ate. Then, they got up and left (28:3-25).

The Philistines gathered all their forces at Aphek, and Israel camped by the spring in Jezreel. David and his men were with the Philistine ruler Achish. The warlords of the Philistines asked: "What business do these Hebrews have being here?"

Achish replied: "This is David, ex-officer to Saul king of Israel. He has been with me for over a year, and from the day he defected from Saul until now, I have found no fault in him."

But the Philistine commanders were angry and ordered: "Send David back. He must not go with us into battle. He will switch sides in the middle of the fight. Isn't this the David they sang about in their dances: `Saul has killed thousands, and David has killed tens of thousands'?"

So Achish called David and told him: "You have been reliable, and I would be pleased to have you serve with me in the army, but the warlords don't approve of you."

So David and his men left at daybreak to go back to Philistine country, and the Philistines went on to Jezreel (29:1-11).

It took David and his men three days to reach Ziklag. When they arrived, they found that the Amalekites had attacked Ziklag. The city had been destroyed by fire and their families taken prisoner. David and his men wept aloud. The men threatened to stone David. They were bitter because of their sons and daughters. But David found strength in the Lord his God.

David and his six hundred men pursued the raiding party. When they came to the Besor Ravine, two hundred men were too exhausted to cross the ravine, and they stayed behind. But David and four hundred men continued the chase. When David caught up with the raiding party, they were lying around on the ground, eating, drinking and gorging themselves on the loot they had taken. David fought them and recovered everything the Amalekites had taken, including his two wives. Nothing was missing.

David came to the two hundred men who had stayed behind because they had been too weak to follow him. As David and his men approached, mean-spirited men among David's followers said: "They did not help with the rescue; we will not share with them any of the plunder we recovered. However, each man may take his wife and children and go."

David replied: "No, my brothers! The Lord kept us safe and handed over the raiders who attacked us. The share of the man who stayed with the supplies is to be the same as of the man who fought. All will share alike." David made this a statute and ordinance for Israel.

When David arrived in Ziklag, he sent some of the plunder to the leaders of Judah, who were his friends, saying: "Here is a present for you from the plunder of the Lord's enemies" (30:1-31).

The Philistines made war on Israel. The Philistines killed three of Saul's sons: Jonathan, Abinadab and Malki-Shua. The archers shot at Saul and wounded him critically.

Saul pleaded with his armor-bearer: "Draw your sword and put me out of my misery, lest these uncircumcised fellows come and make a game out of killing me."

But his armor-bearer was terrified and would not kill him; so Saul took his own sword and fell on it. When the armor-bearer saw that Saul was dead, he fell on his sword and died with him. So Saul, his three sons, his armor-bearer; the men closest to him, all died together that day (31:1-7).

Saul died because he disobeyed the Lord. He refused to obey the Word of the Lord. Instead of praying, he consulted a medium to seek guidance. So the Lord took his life (1 Chron 10:13-14).

The next day the Philistines came to strip the dead; they found Saul and his three sons dead. They cut off Saul's head and stripped off his armor. They put Saul's armor in the temple of the Ashtoreths and hung his corpse on the wall of Beth Shan.

The people of Jabesh Gilead heard what the Philistines had done to Saul. Their fighting men traveled all night to Beth Shan, retrieved the bodies of Saul and his sons, brought them back to Jabesh and gave them a dignified burial. They fasted in mourning for seven days (1 Sm 31:8-13).

LIFE-LESSONS DISCOVERED IN THE STORY

1. The person who has been walking with God, but refuses to obey divine instruction, will move away from God. When God and a person are walking together, it is as though they are following two parallel lines. The person who disobeys God, leaves his side of the parallel line and moves in another direction while God continues in the same direction. Therefore, the person is no longer accompanying God. A person is free to accompany the Lord or to go in another direction. God is unmovable and does not change his direction when a person makes a wrong turn. Saul was chosen by God to be king, and he walked with God until he began disobeying the Lord's orders.

2. It is difficult to explain the "evil spirit from the Lord" that tormented Saul (16:14). It may mean that when the Spirit of the Lord departed from Saul, God allowed an evil spirit, a demon, to torment him as judgment for his disobedience. This would show God's power over the spirit world. (See 1 Kings 22:19-23.)

3. The person who once served the Lord and was empowered by the Spirit of the Lord, but begins to disobey the Lord, faces the risk that he may be giving evil spirits freedom to torment him. At one time Saul was empowered by the Spirit of the Lord (11:6). But he disobeyed the Lord (15:23), and later an evil spirit tormented him (16:14).

4. The person who understands but disobeys the Word of God, risks being responsible for his self-destruction. That happened with Saul (15:17-19; 31:4). It also happened with Judas (Ac 1:17-18) and Ananias and Sapphira (Ac 5:1-10).

5. God doesn't judge as the people judge. People can judge wrongly when they look at outward appearances, but God sees the heart (16:7).

6. God's servant, who is empowered by the Spirit of God, has the capacity to do anything that God desires. David was empowered by the Spirit and could do everything that God wanted him to do (16:13).

7. Viewing difficult situations from God's point of view helps a person put giant problems in perspective. When Goliath challenged the Israelites, the soldiers saw a giant, while David saw a mortal man defying almighty God (17:26).

8. Criticism should not prevent a person from taking on a difficult task for God. Criticism didn't stop David (17:28-32).

9. A few resources, in the hands of the person committed to God, produce great results. To fight Goliath, David had in his hands a slingshot and some stones; however, with his head he believed in God, with his mouth he confessed confidence in the Lord Almighty, and with his hands he used the slingshot and a stone to kill Goliath (17:45-52). A child with only two fish and five pieces of bread provoked a miracle (Jn 6:5-13).

10. True friendship is invaluable! The friendship between Jonathan and David became a pattern of true friendship. It was born spontaneous and voluntarily (18:1-3). David and Jonathan based their friendship on commitment to God as well as to one another (18:1-4); family problems did not destroy their friendship (19:1-3), it lasted through severe testing (20:30-34, 41; 23:15-18); it was not destroyed by the death of one of the friends (2 Sm 9:7, 13).

11. The person who disobeys God may consider another person who faithfully serves God as his enemy. This happened to Saul when he became an enemy to David (18:29) and killed the priests (22:14-19).

12. There are occasions when a person needs to fight and other occasions when a person should flee from a fight. David faced and fought Goliath (17:32-51). However, David fled to escape from Saul. When Saul was pursuing David, twice David had the opportunity to kill Saul but spared him (24:3-7; 26:2-12).

13. It is necessary for God's servant to have patience to live with God's timing. David was a boy when he was anointed king (16:13). But he lived as a fugitive, fleeing from Saul for many years, before he in fact became king.

14. The person who is faithful to God may have enemies who hate him and even followers who turn against him. Saul was David's enemy (18:29). David's followers on one occasion talked of stoning him (30:6). Paul promised Timothy that everyone who wants to live a godly life in Christ will be persecuted (2 Tm 12).

15. A child should disobey a parent's order that would require him to sin and disobey God. Saul told his son Jonathan to kill David, but Jonathan disobeyed that order (19:1-2). Children should be respectful and obedient to their parents, but they are not to follow commands or advice that violate God's laws (Eph 6:1-3).

16. The person who faithfully serves God doesn't seek to avenge his enemies. He leaves the revenge up to God (Rm 12:19). Twice David had the opportunity to kill his enemy Saul; however, each time he spared Saul's life (24:1-11; 26:3-16). Abigal prevented David from avenging Nabal's insults (25:32-34).

17. Slander usually attacks the person of integrity. David begged Saul not to pay attention to slanderers (24:9). Slanderers won't inhabit the house of God (Ps 15:1-3). David was slandered; Job was slandered (Job 1:11; 2:4-5); Jesus was slandered (Mt 12:24); believers are slandered (Rm 3:8; 1 Pe 3:16); Satan is the accuser of the brothers (Rev 12:10).

18. A dysfunctional home cannot prevent a family member from doing right and serving God. Saul's anger and foolish actions didn't keep Jonathan from being faithful to God and to David (20:42).

19. The person who lies can bring harm to others. David lied when he told Ahimelech the priest that he was on a secret mission for the king. Ahimelech did not realize this when he helped David. Therefore, Ahimelech gave the appearance that he was against King Saul (21:1-7). The tragic consequence of David's lie was the death of Ahimelech and all the priests at Nob (22:13-19). Lying is wrong (Lev 19:11). The father of every lie is the devil (Jn 8:44).

20. The righteous will suffer in the nation that allows an evil system to flourish. This happened when Saul became an enemy of David (18:29) and killed the priests (22:14-19).

21. A person can become so evil that he interprets opportunities to do evil as signs of God's approval. Not every opportunity is sent from God. When Saul heard that David was trapped in a walled city, he thought God was putting David at his mercy (23:7).

22. A person should not compromise his moral standards by giving in to group pressure. David refused when his men pressured him to kill Saul (24:4, 10; 26:8).

23. Knowing what is right and denouncing what is wrong does not take the place of doing what is right. Saul had banned all mediums from Israel, When he was desperate, he turned to one for counsel. He had removed the sin of witchcraft from the land without removing it from his heart (28:3-8).

24. A person who disobeyed God's past instructions should not be surprised when God does not give further guidance. God did not answer Saul's supplications because Saul had disobeyed God's previous instructions (28:6, 15)

25. The person who doesn't hear and obey God's Word will seek guidance from the evil one. That happened with Saul, when he sought instruction from a medium (28:6-20; I Chr 10:13-14). (See Isaiah 8:19-20.)

26. It is a serious sin to consult the dead (Lev 20:27; Dt 18:9-14; Is 8:19-20; Gl 5:19-21; Rev 21:8). Saul committed a grave sin when he consulted a medium who held seances with the dead (1 Sm 28:6-20; I Chr 10:13-14).

27. Since the Bible gives strict instructions against contact with the kingdom of the dead, it is difficult to explain what happened when Saul consulted a medium. A possibility is that an evil spirit imitated Samuel, and the spirit was a pseudo-Samuel. Another possibility is that the woman expected to have contact with a demon representing Samuel; however, God allowed Samuel to appear with a message condemning Saul. The text declares that the spirit was Samuel (28:15-16, 20). The text doesn't say that the woman "brought up Samuel from the dead." The event doesn't give support to the witchcraft's false doctrine that they speak to the dead. The mediums don't have access to the dead; however, they communicate with evil spirits who imitate people who are dead. In 1 Kings 22:22, these spirits are called lying spirits.

28. When facing a crisis, do not look for someone to blame. Instead, search for a solution. When David's men faced the tragedy of losing their families, they looked for someone to blame and talked about killing David. David found strength in God and looked for a solution instead of a scapegoat (30:3-8).

29. Those who provide support services need to be respected equally with those who are on the front lines. David made a law that those who remained with the supplies were to be treated equally with those who fought the battle (30:24-25).

30. A person often responds to death the same way he responded to life. Saul confronted his death the same way he confronted life. He took things into his own hands without seeking God's guidance (31:4).

QUESTIONS

1. Why did God reject Saul?
2. What happened when Samuel went to anoint one of Jesse's sons as king of Israel?
3. How did God teach Samuel that the Lord judges people differently from the way people do?
4. What did the Holy Spirit do to Saul and to David?
5. How did David defeat Goliath?
6. What can you learn from Jonathan and David about true friendship?
7. What were the results of David's lying to Ahimelech the priest?
8. How did David react when he had an opportunity to kill Saul?
9. What happened when Saul consulted a medium?
10. With whom do you most identify:
    - With Saul on the road to self-destruction?
    - With Samuel who mourned because he felt betrayed by Saul, yet hoped for better days with David?
    - With Goliath, strong enough to challenge men and defy God?
    - With Abigail, doing damage control because of others' evil actions?
    - With David and Jonathan who experienced true friendship?
    - With David who was empowered by the Spirit of God to face great difficulties?

DAVID							
PROGRESS				SIN	PROBLEMS: the results of sin		
OBEDIENT				DISOBEDIENT	PUNISHMENT		
Ascending		Succeeding			Defeated	Frustrated	
YOUTH ■Shepherd ■Anointed ■Goliath ■Jonathan	FUGITIVE ■Fleeing from Saul, in hideouts in back-country wilderness and deserts	Spiritual	Political	In war	By the sin of adultery and murder	The consequences of sin:	
						for the family / for the nation / for himself: unstable		
SAUL IS KING	DAVID KING of Judah in Hebron for 7 ½ years	DAVID KING ■of all of Judah and Israel ■in Jerusalem for 33 years			Fleeing from Absalom	DAVID: Kingdom restored	
1 SAMUEL			2 SAMUEL				
16	21	31	1	6	8	11	12	15	19

KING DAVID
United Kingdom
2 Samuel 1 - 24; 1 Kings 1:1 - 2:12; 1 Chronicles 28 - 29

STRUCTURE

Context:
Samuel was the last of the judges. Israel's leaders requested that Samuel give them a king. The Lord led Samuel to anoint Saul as king.

On two occasions, Saul disobeyed the Lord. 1) Saul himself offered the whole-burnt-offering even though God's Law required that only priests offer burnt-offerings. 2) Samuel gave Saul the Lord's command to attack the Amalekites and destroy everything that belonged to them as an offering to the Lord. Saul did not kill their king nor the best of the sheep and cattle.

Since Saul rejected the Lord's command, the Lord rejected Saul as king. The Lord sent Samuel to anoint David as king. The Spirit of the Lord entered David and empowered him.

Saul became jealous of David and tried to kill him. David lived as a fugitive in wilderness hideouts with Saul pursuing him.

The Philistines made war on Israel and archers wounded Saul. Saul took his own sword and fell on it. Saul died because he disobeyed the Lord.

Key-persons: David, Joab, Bathsheba, Nathan, Absalom

Key-locations: Hebron, Jerusalem

Key-repetitions:
■Triumphs, one after the other in David's life, until he committed adultery.
■Frustrations, one after the other following David's sin, both in the family and in the nation.
■David sinned (2 Sm 11:1-15; 24:); confessed his sin (12:13; 24:) and was punished (12:10-14; 24:1-17).
■Crafted stories used to communicate ideas (2 Sm 12:1-4; 14:1-18).
■Beautiful people: Bathsheba (2 Sm 11:2); Tamar (2 Sm 13:1); Absalom (14:25); Absalom's daughter, Tamar (14:27); Adonijah (1 Kin 1:6).
■David did not deal with his children's sin-problems: Amnon (2 Sm 13:21); Absalom (2 Sm 14:23, 28); Adonijah (1 Kin 1:
■David's sons entered into rebellion: Amnon (2 Sm 13:1-19); Absalom (2 Sm 13:23 -18:18); and Adonijah (1 Kgs 1:1-31).
■Joab killed innocent men for revenge: Abner (2 Sm 3:22-27); Amasa; (2 Sm 20:9); David charged Solomon to remember Joab's crimes (1 Kin 2:5-6).

Key-attitudes:
■Progress experienced by David, until his sin.
■After David's sin, frustrations within David's family and within the nation.
■Conflict: war with enemies; within David's family and within the nation.
■Joab felt pride, hatred and revenge.

- The loyalty of Uriah to his leaders and army.
- The wisdom and courage of Nathan.
- David's grief when he faced the death of people he respected and loved.
- Tamar's bitter resentment.
- Absalom's hatred for Amnon.
- The arrogant pride and cunningness of Absalom.
- The arrogant selfishness of David's sons: Amnon, Absalom, and Adonijah.

Initial-problem:
A young man announces to David that the army of Israel was defeated in battle and that Saul and his son Jonathan were dead.

Sequence of events:
David, King of Judah; Ish-Bosheth, King of Israel
- A young man came to David from Saul's army and told him that Saul and Jonathan were dead. Saul was wounded and ordered the young man to put him out of his misery. So he killed Saul and brought his crown and his bracelet to David. David and his men mourned the death of Saul and Jonathan, and David ordered the youth killed (1:17-27).
- David moved to Hebron and was anointed king over the house of Judah (2:1-4).
- David sent a blessing to the men of Jabesh Gilead who had given Saul a dignified burial (2:4-7).
- Abner, the commander of Saul's army, took Ish-Bosheth son of Saul and made him king over all Israel (2:8-11).
- At Gibeon, Joab and David's men defeated Abner and the men of Israel (2:12-17).
- Abner killed Joab's brother Asahel. Number of men killed: 20 of David's men, but 360 of Abner's men (2:18-32).
- David grew stronger while the supporters of Saul grew weaker (3:1).
- Six sons were born to David in Hebron (3:2-5).
- Abner became angry at Ish-Bosheth and told him he would help David be king over the whole country, both Israel and Judah (3:6-11).
- David agreed to meet with Abner if he brought with him Michal, daughter of Saul (3:12-16).
- Abner conferred with the leaders of Israel and then went to Hebron to meet with David. David sent Abner away in peace with his blessing (3:17-21).
- Joab, without telling David, killed Abner to avenge the death of his brother Asahel (3:22-27).
- David blamed Joab for Abner's death and mourned his death (3:28-39).
- Two of Ish-Bosheth's men killed him while he slept and took his head to David. David ordered the two men killed (4:1-12).

David's Successes as King of All of Israel
- All the tribes of Israel came to Hebron and anointed David king over Israel. David was 30 years old when he became king, and he ruled 40 years (5:1-5).
- David's men captured Jerusalem and he took up residence there. He became more powerful, because the Lord was with him (5:6-10).
- The king of Tyre sent messengers to David, along with building materials and workmen to build him a palace (5:11-12).
- David constantly defeated the Philistines in battle (5:17-25).
- David took the Ark of God to Jerusalem (6:1-19).
- Michal criticized David for dancing in the streets, and David answered her in anger (6:16, 20-23).
- David wanted to build a Temple for the Lord. The Lord gave Nathan a message to tell David that he would not build a house for the Lord, but his son would. The Lord promised to establish David's kingdom forever (7:1-17).
- King David went into the tent and prayed to the Lord (7:18-29).
- David defeated the Philistines and conquered: Edom, Moab, the Ammonites and Amalek. The king of Hamath sent gifts to David. David dedicated these gifts to the Lord, as he had done with the plunder taken from conquered nations. The Lord gave David victory wherever he went (8:1-14).
- David reigned over all Israel, doing what was just and right for all his people (8:15).
- David showed Mephibosheth kindness for the sake of his father Jonathan (9:1-13).
- David defeated the Ammonites (10:1-19).

David, Guilty of Adultery and Murder
- David dispatched his fighting men to destroy the Ammonites, but he stayed in Jerusalem. He committed adultery with Bathsheba and she became pregnant. David ordered Joab to let Uriah, Bathsheba's husband, be killed in battle. Then David took Bathsheba as his wife (11:1-27).
- The Lord sent Nathan to confront David. Nathan told David a story about a rich man who took the one and only lamb of a poor man. David exploded with anger and Nathan told David he was the man and that he would be punished (12:1-12).
- David confessed his sin. Nathan replied that the Lord forgave him, but the son born to David and Bathsheba would die (12:13-14).

Problems in David's Family
- The child became sick and died. Then when David slept with Bathsheba, she became pregnant with Solomon (12:15-24).
- Joab captured Rabbah, the royal city of the Ammonites (12:26-31).
- Amnon fell in love with his half-sister Tamar and devised a devious plan where he could be with her. Amnon raped Tamar. David was furious; but he didn't discipline Amnon. Absalom hated Amnon for violating his sister Tamar (13:1-22).
- Two years later, Absalom invited all the king's sons to a celebration, and he had Amnon murdered. Absalom fled to Geshur where he stayed for 3 years (13:23-39).
- Joab sent a wise woman to speak to David about Absalom. Then David told Joab to bring Absalom back to Jerusalem. But Absalom was not permitted to see the king (14:1-24).
- Absalom lived two years in Jerusalem without seeing the king (14:25-33).

Absalom Leads a Revolution

■Absalom began riding in a horse-drawn chariot with 50 men running ahead of him. He would get up early and stand near the city gate. There he stole the hearts of everyone in Israel (15:1-6).

■Four years after Absalom returned to Jerusalem, he went to Hebron and made himself king. Ahithophel, David's counselor, supported Absalom (15:7-12).

■David fled Jerusalem with his officials, but he left ten concubines to take care of the palace. The priest Zadok with Levites who were carrying the Ark of the Covenant of God followed David. David sent Zadok and the priest back to Jerusalem. David sent his counselor Hushai back to Jerusalem to try to frustrate Ahithophel's advice (15:13-37).

■ Shimei cursed David, threw stones at him and showered him with dirt (16:5-14).

■Ahithophel advised Absalom to have sex with David's concubines and told him to take 12,000 men and immediately go after David. However, Hushai advised Absalom to only go after David when he had gathered all the fighting men of Israel. Absalom took Hushai's advice instead of Ahithophel's. The Lord determined to discredit Ahithophel's advice in order to bring disaster on Absalom. Hushai sent a message to David through the priest Zadok. Ahithophel hanged himself (16:15 - 17:23).

■Before the battle, David ordered each commander to be gentle with Absalom. The army of Absalom was defeated by David's men; 20,000 men died. Absalom was riding his mule under the thick branches of an oak when Absalom's head got caught in the tree. Joab took three spears and stabbed Absalom in the heart (18:1-18).

■David cried for Absalom. Joab rebuked David because he humiliated his men and showed that his commanders and soldiers meant nothing to him. So David took his seat at the city gate and his soldiers presented themselves to the king (18:19 - 19:8).

David Restored as King

■The Israelites complained to their leaders because they did not bring David back as king. The men of Judah escorted David across the Jordan. Shimei, the Benjamite, went with the men of Judah and begged David to forgive him. David told Shimei he would not die (19:9-23).

■The men of Israel complained to the men of Judah for not including them in bringing David back (19:41-43).

■Sheba, a Benjamite, sounded the trumpet and shouted: "We have no share in David; let's get out of here. Israel, head for your tents!" So all the men of Israel deserted David to follow Sheba. But the men of Judah stayed by David (20:1).

■David made Amasa the commander in place of Joab. David ordered Amasa to defeat Sheba. But Joab murdered Amasa and led the battle to defeat Sheba (20:2-22).

■David ordered Joab and the army commanders to get a count of the fighting men. God's Law prohibited a census (Ex 30:12-15; Num 1:2-4, 47-49). The Lord sent a plague and 70,000 Israelites died. The angel of the Lord stopped spreading the plague when he reached the threshing floor of Araunah the Jebusite. David bought the threshing floor and oxen, built an altar to the Lord there and sacrificed burnt offerings and fellowship offerings. The Lord answered David's prayer and the plague ended (24:1-25).

David as an Old Man

■David made preparations for the building of the House of the Lord. Then David charged his son Solomon to build a house for the Lord. David ordered the leaders of Israel to help his son Solomon build the temple (1 Chr 22:1-16).

■When King David was very old, his servants had Abishag, a Shunammite, lie beside David to keep him warm (1 Kin 1:1-4).

■Now Adonijah was David's oldest living son. He made a power move to become king, and Adonijah held a coronation feast (1 Kin 1:5-10).

■Bathsheba told David that Adonijah had taken over as king. David immediately ordered Nathan the prophet to anoint Solomon king over Israel (1 Kin 1:11-53).

■When David's time to die drew near, he gave a charge to Solomon his son for him to be strong and obey everything the Lord commands. He told Solomon not to forget that Joab had murdered two commanders of Israel's armies in peacetime and for him to have to deal with Shimei who called down curses on him (1 Kin 2:1-9).

■David died and was buried in the City of David. He had reigned 40 years over Israel, 7 ½ years in Hebron and 33 in Jerusalem. So Solomon sat on the throne of his father David (1 Kin 2:10-12).

Final-situation:

David reigned as king forty years over Israel. Before his death, David chose his son Solomon to succeed him as king.

BIBLE STORY

David, King of Judah; Ish-Bosheth, King of Israel

David returned to Ziklag after defeating the Amalekites. Three days later a young man showed up unannounced from Saul's army camp. He bowed facedown on the ground before David. Then he told David: "I escaped from the Israelite camp. The men fled from the battle. Many fell and died. And Saul and his son Jonathan are dead."

Then David asked: "How do you know Saul and Jonathan are dead?"

The young man answered: "On Mount Gilboa, I came upon Saul, wounded and leaning on his spear. The enemy was closing in on him. He called out to me, and ordered me to put him out of his misery. So I killed him, because I knew that he could not survive. I removed the crown from his head and the bracelet from his arm and brought them here to my lord."

David and his men ripped their clothes to show their sorrow. They wept and fasted the rest of the day. They cried because of the death of Saul and Jonathan, and because the army of Israel had been defeated.

David asked the young man: "Were you not afraid to kill the Lord's anointed king? You sealed your death sentence when you said you killed the Lord's anointed king." Then David ordered a soldier to kill the young man (1:1-16).

David composed a funeral song mourning the deaths of Saul and his son Jonathan (1:17-27).

David moved to Hebron along with his two wives. David's men and their families also went to live in and around Hebron. Then the men of Judah came to Hebron and anointed David king over the house of Judah (2:1-4).

David heard that the men of Jabesh Gilead had given Saul a dignified burial and he sent messengers to the men of Jabesh Gilead: "The Lord bless you for honoring your master Saul by burying him" (2:4-7).

Meanwhile, Abner the commander of Saul's army, took Ish-Bosheth son of Saul and made him king over all Israel. Ish-Bosheth was forty years old when he became king over Israel, and he ruled two years. The house of Judah, however, followed David (2:8-11).

Abner with the soldiers of Ish-Bosheth went to Gibeon. Joab and David's men went out and met them at the pool of Gibeon. Abner's group was on one side, Joab's on the other. The battle that day was very fierce, and David's men defeated Abner and the men of Israel (2:12-17).

Joab's brother Asahel was as fast as a wild deer. He chased after Abner. Abner warned him: "Stop chasing me! Don't force me to kill you! How could I face your brother Joab?"

But Asahel refused to quit; so Abner thrust the butt of his spear into Asahel's stomach, and he fell dead on the spot.

Joab pursued Abner, and as the sun was setting, they came to a hill on the way to the wasteland of Gibeon. The men of Benjamin took their stand with Abner on top of a hill.

Abner called out to Joab: "Must the sword kill forever? Don't you realize that this will end in bitterness? How long before you order your men to stop chasing their brothers?"

Joab answered: "As surely as God lives, if you had not spoken, the men would have continued to chase their brothers until morning."

So Joab blew the trumpet, and all the army of Judah came to a halt and stopped fighting Israel.

Twenty of David's men were killed, but three hundred and sixty of Abner's men died (2:18-32).

The war between the house of Saul and the house of David continued with David growing stronger and stronger, while the supporters of Saul grew weaker and weaker (3:1).

Six sons were born to David in Hebron: Amnon, Kileab, Absalom, Adonijah, Shephatiah, and Ithream (3:2-5).

Abner became the main leader among the supporters of Saul' family. Now Saul had a concubine named Rizpah. Ish-Bosheth asked Abner: "Why did you sleep with my father's concubine?"

Abner became angry and answered Ish-Bosheth: "Is this the thanks I get for being loyal to the house of your father Saul. Yet now you make an issue out of my going to bed with a woman! Now, I will help David accomplish what the Lord promised him. I will help transfer the kingdom from the house of Saul; I will make David king over the whole country, both Israel and Judah."

Ish-Bosheth was too afraid to say another word to Abner (3:6-11).

Then Abner sent personal messengers to David: "Make a treaty with me, and I will help you become the king of the whole country of Israel."

David replied: "Good, I will make an agreement with you. But I demand one thing of you: Bring Michal daughter of Saul when you come to see me." Then David sent messengers to Ish-Bosheth son of Saul, demanding: "Give me my wife Michal, whom I won as my wife at the cost of a hundred Philistine foreskins."

So Ish-Bosheth gave orders and had her taken away from her husband Paltiel. Her husband, however, went with her, weeping until Abner told him: "Go back home!" So he went back (3:12-16).

Abner conferred with the leaders of Israel and said: "You have wanted to make David your king. Now do it! For the Lord promised David: `I will save my people Israel from Philistine's oppression and from all their enemies through my servant David.'"

Abner then went to Hebron to tell David everything that Israel wanted to do. David prepared a feast for him and his men. Then Abner said to David: "Let me go at once and assemble all Israel for my lord the king. They will make a treaty with you authorizing you to rule as you see fit." So David sent Abner away in peace with his blessing (3:17-21).

After Abner left David, Joab returned from a raid. Joab was told that Abner had come to the king and David sent him away in peace. Without telling David, Joab sent messengers after Abner. When Abner returned to Hebron, Joab took him aside at the gate for a private word with him. And there Joab stabbed Abner in the stomach, killing him to avenge the death of his brother Asahel (3:22-27).

When David heard about this, he said: "I and my kingdom are forever innocent before the Lord of the blood of Abner. Joab and his entire family will be under a curse for this bloodguilt!"

They buried Abner in Hebron, and the king wept aloud at Abner's tomb. The king sang a funeral song for Abner. David told his servants: "A great man has fallen in Israel this day! And today, though I am the anointed king, I am weak, Joab is too strong for me. May the Lord repay the evildoer according to his evil deeds!" (3:28-39).

When Ish-Bosheth son of Saul heard that Abner had died in Hebron, he lost courage, and all Israel became alarmed. While Ish-Bosheth was taking a noonday nap, two of his military men entered his bedroom, stabbed him, and cut off his head. They took the head of Ish-Bosheth to David at Hebron and said to the king: "Here is the head of Ish-Bosheth son of Saul, your enemy. This day the Lord has avenged my lord the king against Saul and his offspring."

David answered the two men: "You wicked men killed an innocent man in his own house and in his own bed; I find you guilty of murder!"

So David gave an order to kill the two who had murdered Ish-Bosheth (4:1-12).

David's Successes as King of All of Israel

All the tribes of Israel came to David at Hebron and said: "When Saul was king over us, you were the one who led Israel on their military campaigns. And the Lord told you: `You will shepherd my people Israel; you will become their ruler.'"

David made a treaty with the leaders of all the tribes of Israel at Hebron in the presence of the Lord. They anointed David king over Israel.

David was thirty years old when he became king, and he ruled forty years. He was king over Judah in Hebron for seven years and six months. He was king over all Israel and Judah in Jerusalem for thirty-three years (5:1-5).

David and his men captured the city of Jerusalem. David then took up residence in the fortress and called it the City of David. And he became more and more powerful, because the Lord God Almighty was with him (5:6-10).

Now the king of Tyre sent messengers to David, along with cedar logs and carpenters and stonemasons, and they built a palace for David. David knew that the Lord had established him as king over Israel and had made his kingdom prominent for the sake of his people Israel (5:11-12).

David constantly defeated the Philistines in battle (5:17-25).

A multitude went with David to bring the Ark of God to Jerusalem. David, wearing a priest's linen robe, danced before the Lord with all his might. They brought up the Ark of the Lord with shouts and the sound of trumpets. They set the Ark in its place inside the tent that David had pitched for it. David sacrificed whole-burnt-offerings and fellowship offerings before the Lord. After he had finished sacrificing the offerings, he blessed the people in the name of the Lord Almighty. Then the people returned to their homes (6:1-19).

As the Ark of the Lord was entering the City of David; Michal, daughter of Saul, watched from a window. She saw King David leaping and dancing before the Lord and her heart filled with scorn (6:16). When David returned home, Michal confronted him: "The king of Israel did not dignify himself today. You exposed yourself in front of the servant girls of your officers as any vulgar fellow would!"

David replied to Michal: "I danced to celebrate in the Lord's presence. He chose me rather than your father or anyone from his house when he appointed me ruler over the Lord's people Israel. I will dance to God's glory even if I become more undignified than this. But these slave girls you are worried about, they will hold me in honor."

And Michal daughter of Saul was barren the rest of her life (6:16, 20-23).

David settled in his palace and the Lord gave him peace from all his enemies around him. Then he told Nathan the prophet: "I am living in a palace of cedar, while the Ark of God remains in a tent."

Nathan replied to David: "Do what you have in mind. The Lord is with you."

That night the Lord spoke his word to Nathan saying: "Tell my servant David: 'The Lord says: You are not the person to build a house for me to live in. I have not dwelt in a house from the day I brought the Israelites up out of Egypt till now. I have been moving from place to place with a tent as my dwelling. I never commanded any of Israel's rulers to build me a house of cedar.'

"The Lord Almighty says to David: I took you from the pasture tagging along after sheep to be ruler over my people Israel. I have been with you and I have mowed your enemies down before you. Now I will make you as famous as any of the great men on the earth. I will provide a place for my people Israel. Wicked people will not oppress them anymore. I will also give you rest from all your enemies. The Lord himself will establish a house for you. When your days are over and you die, I will raise up your child to succeed you and I will establish his kingdom. He will build a house to honor me, and I will make his kingdom strong forever. I will be his father, and he will be my son. When he does wrong, I will use other people to punish him. But I will not stop loving him as I stopped loving Saul. Your house and your kingdom will endure forever before me; your throne will be established forever."

Nathan reported to David all the words of this entire revelation (7:1-17).

Then King David went into the tent and prayed to the Lord: "Who am I, O Sovereign Lord, that you have brought me this far? O Sovereign Lord, you have also spoken about the future of my family. You have done this, not because of who I am, but because of who you are, and you made it known to me. How great you are, O Sovereign Lord! There is no God but you. And no one is like your people Israel; a nation unique on earth! You performed wonders by driving out nations and their gods from before your people. You freed your people from slavery in Egypt. You established your people Israel as your very own forever. And you, O Lord, became their God.

"And now, Lord God, keep the promise you have made concerning me and my family. O Lord Almighty, God of Israel, you have revealed this to your servant, saying, `I will build a house for you.' That is why I found courage to offer you this prayer. O Sovereign Lord, you are God! Your words are true, and you have promised these good things to me, your servant. Now, I ask you to bless my family, that it may continue forever before you. O Sovereign Lord, you have spoken, and with your blessing the house of your servant will be blessed forever" (7:18-29).

In the course of time, David defeated the Philistines. David also conquered: Edom, Moab, the Ammonites, and Amalek. The king of Hamath sent his son to King David to greet him, congratulate him on his victory and to give him articles of silver, gold and bronze. David dedicated these gifts to the Lord, as he had done with the silver and gold taken from all the nations he had conquered. The Lord gave David victory wherever he went (8:1-14).

David reigned over all Israel, doing what was just and right for all his people (8:15).

David asked: "Is anyone left from Saul's family. I want to show kindness to this person for Jonathan's sake?"
David discovered that Mephibosheth, son of Jonathan, and grandson of Saul, was still alive (9:1-3). Mephibosheth was five years old when the report came that Saul and Jonathan had been killed. The boy's nurse picked him up and fled. In her hurry to get away, she fell and the boy was crippled in both feet (4:4).
David sent for Mephibosheth. David told Mephibosheth: "Don't be afraid, for I will show you kindness for your father Jonathan's sake. I will restore to you all the land that belonged to your grandfather Saul. From now on, you will always eat at my table."
Mephibosheth bowed down and said: "You are very kind to me, your servant. And I am no better than a dead dog!"
David summoned Ziba, Saul's servant, and told him: "I have returned to your master's grandson everything that belonged to Saul and his family. You, your sons and your servants are to farm the land for him and bring in the crops, so that your master's grandson will be provided for. But, Mephibosheth, will always eat at my table" (9:1-13).

David, Guilty of Adultery and Murder
In the spring, it was the custom for kings to go off to war. David dispatched Joab with the king's fighting men to destroy the Ammonites and attack the city of Rabbah. But David stayed in Jerusalem.
One evening David got up from his bed and walked around on the roof of the palace. From the vantage point of the roof he saw Bathsheba, a beautiful woman, bathing. David sent messengers to get her. She came to him, and he went to bed with her. Then she returned home. Later, she sent word to David, saying: "I am pregnant."
So David sent word for Joab to send Uriah the Hittite, Bathsheba's husband to David. When Uriah came to him, David requested information about the war. Then David told Uriah: "Go to your house and have a good night's sleep." Uriah left the palace, but slept at the entrance to the palace with David's servants. He did not go home.
The next morning, David asked Uriah why he didn't go home.
Uriah answered: "The Ark and Israel and Judah are staying in tents. My master Joab and my lord's men are camped in the open fields. How could I go home to eat, drink and sleep with my wife?"
David told him: "Stay here today, tomorrow I will send you back." So Uriah remained in Jerusalem the rest of the day. The next day, David invited him to eat and drink with him, and David got him drunk. But Uriah went out to sleep on his mat with David's servants; he did not go home.
In the morning David wrote a letter to Joab and sent it with Uriah. In the letter he wrote: "Put Uriah in the front line where the fighting is most fierce. Let him be killed in battle."
Uriah's wife heard that her husband was dead and she grieved for him. After the time of mourning was over, David sent for her, and she became his wife and gave birth to his son. But the Lord did not like what David had done (11:1-27).

The Lord sent Nathan to David. Nathan told David: "There were two men in the same town, one rich and the other poor. The rich man had many sheep and cattle, but the poor man had nothing except one little female lamb which he bought and raised. It grew up with him and his children. It shared his food, drank from his cup and even slept in his arms. It was like a daughter to him. Now a traveler stopped to visit the rich man, but the rich man was too stingy to take one of his own sheep or cattle to feed the traveler. Instead, he took the poor man's lamb and cooked it for his guest to eat."
David exploded with anger and told Nathan: "The man who did this deserves to die! He must pay for that lamb four times over, for his crime and his stinginess!"
Nathan told David: "You are the man! This is what the Lord, the God of Israel, says: `I made you king over Israel, and I saved you from Saul. I gave you your master's daughter and other wives. I gave you both Israel and Judah. Why did you ignore the Lord's command and do this great evil? You murdered Uriah the Hittite with the sword of the Ammonites and you took his wife as your wife. Now, the sword will never depart from your house, murder and killing will continually plague your family. Out of your own family I am going to bring calamity upon you. I will take your wives and give them to one who is close to you, and he will lie with your wives in broad daylight. You did it in secret, but I will do it in broad daylight with all of Israel watching.'"
David told Nathan: "I have sinned against the Lord."
Nathan replied: "The Lord forgives your sin. You are not going to die for it. But because your sin made the enemies of the Lord lose all respect for him, the son born to you will die" (12:1-14).

Problems in David's Family

After Nathan returned to his home, the Lord caused the son of David and Bathsheba, Uriah's widow, to become sick. David pleaded with God for the baby. He refused to eat and went into his house and spent the nights lying on the ground. On the seventh day the baby died. David's servants were afraid to tell him that the baby was dead, for they thought: "While the baby was alive, he would not listen to a word we said. Now that the baby is dead, he may do something desperate."

David noticed that his servants were whispering among themselves and he realized the baby was dead. He asked: "Is the baby dead?"

The servants replied: "Yes, he is dead."

Then David got up from the ground, took a bath, changed his clothes and went into the house of the Lord and worshiped. Then he went to his house and asked for something to eat.

His servants asked him: "Why are you acting this way? While the baby was alive, you fasted and wept, but now that the baby is dead, you get up and eat!"

David answered: "While the baby was still alive, I fasted and wept. I thought: 'The Lord may be gracious and let the baby live.' But now that he is dead, I cannot bring him back to life. I will go to him, but he will not return to me."

Then David comforted his wife Bathsheba. When he slept with her, she became pregnant again and she had another son. They named him Solomon. The Lord loved the child (12:15-24).

Joab captured Rabbah, the royal city of the Ammonites (12:26-31).

David had a son named Absalom and a son named Amnon. Absalom had a beautiful sister named Tamar. Amnon fell in love with his half-sister Tamar. Amnon devised a devious plan. Amnon lay down in bed and pretended to be sick. When David went to see him, Amnon requested: "Please let my sister Tamar come and prepare food where I can watch her. Then she can feed me."

David sent word to Tamar: "Go to your brother Amnon's house and prepare a meal for him." So Tamar went to the house of her brother Amnon. She prepared bread as he watched. Then Amnon told Tamar: "Bring the food into my bedroom so I may eat from your hand." Tamar took the bread she had prepared into Amnon's bedroom. He grabbed her and said: "Sister, come to bed with me!"

Tamar answered: "No, brother! Don't force me. This kind of wicked thing should not be done in Israel! I could never get rid of my shame! And you would become a shameful fool in Israel. Please speak to the king; he will let you marry me."

But Amnon refused to listen. He was stronger than she; he raped her. After that, Amnon hated Tamar with intense hatred. He hated her much more than he had loved her before. Amnon ordered her: "Get up and leave!"

Tamar answered: "No!" Sending me away is a worse evil than what you just did to me."

Amnon ordered his personal servant to put her out and bolted the door after her. Tamar put ashes on her head, tore her long-sleeve gown, held her head in her hands and went away sobbing.

Her brother Absalom asked Tamar: "Has Amnon, your brother, forced you to have sex?" Then he told her: "Don't take this thing to heart. Don't talk about it. He is your brother." After being raped, Tamar lived in her brother Absalom's house, bitter and desolate.

When King David heard the whole story, he was furious; but he didn't discipline Amnon. Absalom quit speaking to Amnon. He did not say a word, good or bad to Amnon. He hated him for violating his sister Tamar (13:1-22).

Two years later, when Absalom's sheep-shearers were at Baal Hazor, he invited all the king's sons to come there for a celebration. Absalom ordered his men: "When Amnon is drunk from drinking wine, kill him!" Absalom's men obeyed his orders and killed Amnon.

Absalom fled and went to Geshur, but King David mourned for his son every day. Absalom stayed in Geshur for three years. When King David got over Amnon's death, he longed to be with Absalom (13:23-39).

Joab knew that the king longed for Absalom. So Joab sent a wise woman to speak to David. The wise woman bowed facedown on the ground to show respect and she said: "Help me, O king!"

David asked her: "What is troubling you?"

She answered: "My husband is dead. I had two sons. They were out in the field fighting and one son killed his brother. Now the whole clan is demanding: `Hand over the one who killed his brother, so that we may kill him for murdering his brother.' They would destroy the only heir I have left. If they kill him, my husband's name will be gone from the earth. Let the king invoke the Lord his God to prevent the relative who has the duty of avenging blood from killing my son."

King David told the woman: "Go home, and I will issue an order in your behalf. As surely as the Lord lives, not one hair of your son's head will be lost."

Then the woman said: "Let your servant speak a word to my lord the king."

David replied: "Speak."

The woman said: "Why then have you not done this very thing for God's people? In his verdict, the king convicts himself by not bringing home his banished son."

Then King David ordered the woman: "Answer truthfully the question I am about to ask you. Did Joab tell you to say these things?"

The woman answered: "Yes, it was your servant Joab who instructed me to do this and who put all these words into my mouth."

The king told Joab: "Very well, go, bring back the young man Absalom."

Joab went to Geshur and brought Absalom back to Jerusalem. But the king said: "He may return to his own house, but he must not come to see me." Absalom went to his own house but was not permitted to see the king (14:1-24).

No man in all Israel was as handsome as Absalom. There was no blemish in him.

Absalom lived two years in Jerusalem without seeing the king. Twice Absalom sent for Joab in order to send him to the king, but Joab refused to come to him. Then Absalom ordered his servants to set fire to Joab's barley field.

Joab went to Absalom's house and asked him: "Why did your servants burn my field?"

Absalom answered Joab: "I sent word to you so I can send you to the king to ask: "Why have I come from Geshur? It would be better for me to stay there!" ` I want to see the king's face, and if I am guilty of anything, let him put me to death."

Joab went to the king and told him what happened. The king summoned Absalom. When Absalom went to the king, he bowed facedown on the ground before the king. And the king kissed Absalom (14:25-33).

Absalom Leads a Revolution

As time went on, Absalom began riding in a horse-drawn chariot with fifty men running ahead of him. He would get up early and stand near the city gate. Whenever anyone came with a case for the king to settle, Absalom would say to him: "Look, your claims are valid and proper, but the king has no one to listen to you. If only I were appointed judge in the land! Then everyone who has a case could come to me and I would see that he gets justice."

People would come near Absalom to bow down. Absalom would reach out his hand, take hold of the person and then give the person a kiss. Absalom did this toward all the Israelites who came to the king asking for justice. He stole the hearts of everyone in Israel (15:1-6).

Four years after Absalom returned to Jerusalem, he went to Hebron, claiming he was going there to worship the Lord. While in Hebron, Absalom sent secret messengers throughout the tribes of Israel to say: "As soon as you hear the sound of the trumpets, shout: `Absalom is king in Hebron!'" Two hundred men from Jerusalem had accompanied Absalom to Hebron. Absalom also sent for Ahithophel, David's counselor. (Ahithophel was also Bathsheba's grandfather.) More and more people began to support Absalom (15:7-12).

A messenger came and told David: "The hearts of the men of Israel are with Absalom."

David told all his officials who were with him in Jerusalem: "Come! We must flee, or none of us will escape from Absalom!"

The king set out, with his entire household following him; but he left ten concubines to take care of the palace. The whole countryside wept aloud as all the people passed by. The priest Zadok was there, with all the Levites who were carrying the Ark of the Covenant of God.

King David told Zadok: "Take the Ark of God back into the city. You and your brother Abiathar take your two sons with you. I will wait at the fords in the desert until word comes from you telling me what is happening." So Zadok and Abiathar took the Ark of God back to Jerusalem and stayed there.

But David continued up the Mount of Olives, crying as he went; his head was covered and he was barefoot. All the people with him covered their heads too and were weeping as they went up. Someone told David that Ahithophel was among the conspirators with Absalom. So David prayed: "O Lord, turn Ahithophel's counsel into foolishness."

When David arrived at the top of the mountain, Hushai the Arkite came to meet him. David told Hushai: "If you go with me, you will be one more person to take care of. But you can help me by frustrating Ahithophel's advice if you return to the city and say to Absalom: `O king; I was your father's servant in the past, but now I will be your servant.' The priests Zadok and Abiathar will be there with you. Tell them any information you pick up in the king's palace. They in turn will send their sons to me with the news you hear."

So David's friend Hushai arrived at Jerusalem as Absalom was entering the city (15:13-37).

As King David approached Bahurim, Shimei, who was from the same clan as Saul's family, came out and cursed David. Shimei said: "Get out, you murderer, you scoundrel! The Lord has repaid you for all the people you killed in Saul's family. You stole Saul's kingdom. Now the Lord has given the kingdom to your son Absalom. You have come to ruin because you are a man of blood!"

Then Abishai, Joab's brother, said to the king: "Why should this dead dog curse my lord the king? Let me go over and cut off his head."

David then told Abishai and all his officials: "My son, who is of my own flesh, is trying to kill me. Compared to that, this Benjamite's curses are insignificant!"

David and his men continued on down the road while Shimei walked on the hillside on the other side of the road. Shimei continued cursing David, throwing stones at him and showering him with dirt (16:5-14).

Meanwhile, Absalom, Ahithophel and all the men of Israel came to Jerusalem. David's friend, Hushai the Arkite, went to Absalom and greeted him: "Long live the king! Just as I served your father, so I will serve you."

Absalom asked Ahithophel: "Give us your advice. What should we do?"

Ahithophel answered: "Have sex with your father's concubines whom he left to take care of the palace." So they pitched a tent for Absalom on the flat roof, and he lay with his father's concubines in the sight of all Israel.

Now in those days people thought Ahithophel's advice was as reliable as the Lord's words. Both David and Absalom regarded Ahithophel's advice as reliable.

Ahithophel told Absalom: "Choose twelve thousand men and go after David tonight. Attack him while he is weary and weak. Only kill David." This plan seemed good to Absalom and to all the leaders of Israel.

But Absalom said: "Summon Hushai, so we can hear what he has to say." When Hushai came to him, Absalom said: "Ahithophel has given this advice. Give us your opinion."

Hushai replied to Absalom: "Ahithophel's advice is not good this time. Your father and his men are experienced fighters; they are as fierce as a wild bear robbed of her cubs. So I advise you: Gather all the men of Israel, as numerous as the sand on the seashore, and you yourself lead them into battle. Don't leave either him or any of his men alive."

Absalom and the men with him agreed that Hushai's advice was better than that of Ahithophel. The Lord had determined to discredit Ahithophel's advice in order to bring disaster on Absalom.

Hushai told the priest Zadok and Abiathar to send a message to David to advise him to cross the river into the desert that night.

Ahithophel realized that his advice was not followed. He left for his home, put his house in order and then hanged himself (16:15 - 17:23).

David organized his forces and told the troops: "I myself will march with you."

But the men said: "No! You must not go with us. The enemy won't care about us, they only want you. Stay in the city."

David answered: "I will do what you think is best."

So the king stood beside the gate while all the men marched out. The king ordered each commander: "Be gentle with the young man Absalom for my sake." The whole army heard the king's orders concerning Absalom.

David's army went out to fight Israel's army that was loyal to Absalom. The battle took place in the forest of Ephraim. The army of Absalom was defeated by David's men; there was a terrible slaughter, twenty thousand men died. The forest claimed more lives that day than the sword.

Now Absalom ran into David's men. He was riding his mule. As the mule went under the thick branches of a large oak, Absalom's long hair got caught in the tree. He was left dangling in midair, while the mule ran out from under him.

A soldier told Joab: "I just saw Absalom hanging from an oak tree."

Joab replied to the man: "What! You saw him? Why didn't you kill him?"

The soldier replied: "I would not lift my hand against the king's son. We all heard the king command you: `Protect the young man Absalom for my sake.' I would have risked my life, and you would not have come to my defense."

Joab took three spears and stabbed Absalom in the heart. Joab then blew the trumpet, and the troops stopped pursuing the army of Israel. They took Absalom, threw him into a pit in the forest and piled up a large heap of rocks over him.

While alive, Absalom had erected for himself a pillar as a monument to himself because he had no son to carry on his name (18:1-18).

David heard that Absalom was dead. He went up to the room over the city gate and cried out: "O my son Absalom! My son, my son Absalom! If only I had died instead of you; O Absalom, my son, my son!"

Joab was told: "The king is weeping and mourning for Absalom." The day's victory turned into a day of mourning. The men came into the city that day demoralized. The king covered his face and cried aloud: "O my son Absalom! O Absalom, my son, my son!"

Joab went to the king and rebuked him: "Today you have humiliated your men. They saved your life and the lives of your sons, daughters, wives and concubines. You love those who hate you and hate those who love you. Today, you made it clear that commanders and soldiers mean nothing to you. You would be pleased if Absalom were alive and all of us were dead. Now go out and encourage your men. If you don't go to them, they will desert you; not a soldier will be left with you by nightfall. This will be the worst calamity you have ever faced!"

So the king got up and took his seat at the city gate and his soldiers presented themselves to the king (18:19 - 19:8).

David Restored as King

Meanwhile, the Israelites had fled to their homes. Throughout the tribes of Israel, the people were complaining to their leaders: "The king delivered us from the hand of our enemies; he is the one who rescued us from the Philistines. But he fled the country because of Absalom. Absalom, whom you anointed to rule over us, died in battle. Why don't you bring the king back?"

Now the men of Judah went to Gilgal to meet David and escorted him across the Jordan. Shimei, the Benjamite, hurried down with the men of Judah to meet King David. Shimei crossed the Jordan, fell facedown before the king and said to him: "May my lord not hold me guilty. Do not remember the wrong things I did on the day my lord the king left Jerusalem. I know that I have sinned, but I am the first of the whole house of Joseph to come down and meet my lord the king."

The king said to Shimei: "You shall not die" (19:9-23).

Soon the men of Israel came to David and asked him: "Why did our brothers, the men of Judah, steal the king away and escort him and his household across the Jordan?"

The men of Judah replied to the men of Israel: "We did this because the king is closely related to us. Why are you angry about it?"

Then the men of Israel argued: "We have ten tribes in the kingdom; we have a greater claim on David than you have. Why do you treat us with contempt? It was our idea to bring him back."

But the men of Judah responded more harshly than the men of Israel (19:41-43).

Just then, a troublemaker named Sheba, a Benjamite, sounded the trumpet and shouted: "We have no share in David; let's get out of here. Israel, head for your tents!"

So all the men of Israel deserted David to follow Sheba. But the men of Judah stayed by their king all the way from the Jordan to Jerusalem (20:1).

The king made Amasa the commander instead of Joab. The king ordered Amasa to defeat Sheba. The army was at the great rock in Gibeon. Joab was wearing his military uniform with a sheathed dagger strapped on his waist. Joab removed the dagger from its sheath to greet Amasa. Joab took Amasa by the beard with his right hand to kiss him. Amasa was not on his guard against the dagger in Joab's left hand, and Joab plunged it into his belly, killing Amasa. After Amasa had been killed, all the men went on with Joab to pursue Sheba. Sheba was killed (20:2-22).

David ordered Joab and the army commanders: "Take a census of the tribes of Israel and get a count of the fighting men." (2 Sm 24: 1). Satan incited David to count the fighting men (1 Chr 21:1). God's Law prohibited a census (Ex 30:12-15; Num 1:2-4, 47-49).

Joab resisted, but the king insisted, so Joab and the army commanders left the king to take a census of Israel. They took nine months and twenty days. Joab reported the number of the fighting men to the king: In Israel there were eight hundred thousand able-bodied men who could handle a sword, and in Judah five hundred thousand.

David was conscience-stricken after he had counted the fighting men, because he was replacing trust in the Lord with statistics. David prayed to the Lord: "I have sinned greatly in what I have done. Now, O Lord, I beg you, forgive me. I have done a very foolish thing."

The Lord sent a message to David: "The Lord says: I am giving you three options. Choose one of them. Do you want three years of famine in the land; or three months of running from your enemies while they chase you; or three days of plague in your land?"

David answered: "I would rather be punished by the Lord whose mercy is great than fall into the hands of men."

So the Lord sent a plague on Israel and seventy thousand Israelites died. When the angel stretched out his hand to destroy Jerusalem, the Lord was grieved because of the calamity. God ordered the angel who was spreading death: "Enough! Withdraw your hand." The angel of the Lord had just reached the threshing floor of Araunah the Jebusite.

David prayed: "I am the one who sinned. Punish me and my family, not them!"

God ordered David to build an altar on the threshing floor of Araunah the Jebusite. David went to Araunah the Jebusite. When Araunah saw the king and his men coming toward him, he went out and bowed facedown before the king.

Araunah asked: "Why has my lord the king come to see me?"

David answered: "To buy your threshing floor, so I can build an altar to the Lord, so he will put an end to this plague."

Araunah told David: "Let my lord the king take whatever pleases him and offer it up. Here are oxen for the burnt offering, and here is the wood."

But the king replied to Araunah: "No, I insist on paying you for it. I will not sacrifice to the Lord my God burnt offerings that cost me nothing."

So David bought the threshing floor and the oxen. David built an altar to the Lord there and sacrificed burnt offerings and fellowship offerings. Then the Lord answered David's prayer for the country, and that was the end of the plague on Israel (24:1-25).

David as an Old Man

David made preparations for the building of the House of the Lord. David thought: "My son Solomon is young and inexperienced, and the house to be built for the Lord should be of great magnificence and the talk of all nations. Therefore, I will make preparations for it."

Then David charged his son Solomon to build a house for the Lord, the God of Israel. David told him: "Now, my son, the Lord be with you, and may you have success and build the house of the Lord your God. May the Lord give you discretion and understanding when he puts you in command over Israel, so that you will keep the law that the Lord your God gave Israel. That is what will make you successful. Be strong and courageous. I have taken great pains to provide for the temple of the Lord. Now begin the work, and the Lord be with you."

David ordered the leaders of Israel to help his son Solomon build the temple (1 Chr 22:1-16).

When King David was very old, he could not keep warm even with covers heaped over him. So his servants found a young virgin, Abishag a Shunammite, to lie beside him to keep him warm (1 Kin 1:1-4).

Now Adonijah was David's oldest living son. He made a power move and said: "I will be king." His father had spoiled him, never once reprimanding him. Adonijah held a coronation feast. (1 Kin 1:5-10).

Bathsheba told David that Adonijah had taken over as king. David ordered Nathan the prophet to anoint Solomon king over Israel (1 Kin 1:11-53).

When David's time to die drew near, he gave a charge to Solomon his son: "I am about to go the way of all the earth. Be strong, and obey everything the Lord commands. If you and your descendants obey the Lord, you will always have a successor on Israel's throne.

"Don't forget what Joab did to me. He murdered two commanders of Israel's armies, Abner and Amasa. He murdered in peacetime as if he were in war and has been stained with blood ever since. Do not let him go to the grave in peace. You also have to deal with Shimei, the Benjamite, who called down bitter curses on me (1 Kin 2:1-9).

Then David died and was buried with his ancestors in the City of David. He had reigned forty years over Israel; seven years in Hebron and thirty-three in Jerusalem. So Solomon sat on the throne of his father David, and his rule was firmly established (1 Kin 2:10-12).

LIFE-LESSONS DISCOVERED IN THE STORY

1. A person may be chosen by God for a specific responsibility and still must wait for God's timing to assume the responsibility. David was anointed king during the reign of Saul; however, for many years David was either a servant of Saul or he was fleeing from Saul. He only became king after Saul's death.

2. Godliness does not guarantee a comfortable and carefree life. David was the only person who God described as: "a man after my own heart" (1 Sm 13:14; Ac 13:22). Yet David spent years living in desert hideouts fleeing from Saul (1 Sm 20 - 31). David had family problems: one son raped his half-sister (2 Sm 13:1-22); another son killed his half-brother (2 Sm 13:28-29) and incited the nation to rebel against David (14:1 - 18:33); another son made a power move to become king (1 Kin 1:1-27).

3. It is painful when marriage ends in separation. After David became a fugitive, Saul forced his daughter Michal to divorce David and required her to marry Paltiel. They lived together for at least 10 years. After David became king of Judah, he demanded that Michal be restored to him. Paltiel followed his wife for miles, weeping when she was torn from their home.

4. Desire for revenge may become the avenger's downfall. Moved by the desire for revenge, Joab killed Abner (3:22-27) and Amasa (20:9). Joab's action cost him: the support and esteem of David (2 Sm 3:28, 39; 19:13); resulted in his own death (1 Kgs 2:5-6, 31); and it provoked a curse on his descendants (2 Sm 3:29; 1 Kin 2:33).

5. Unchecked bitterness and resentment will destroy a relationship. Michal's contempt for her husband David escalated into a confrontation, and she was childless for life (2 Sm 6:16, 20-23).

6. Sometimes when a person desires to do something for God, the Lord says no. God did not want David to build a house for him (2 Sm 7:5).

7. Jesus Christ is the descendant of David who will reign forever. God promised that a descendant of David would reign forever (2 Sm 7:11-13; 16). This was a prophecy about Jesus, who is the King of Kings. This was the first of the prophecies that the Messiah would be a descendant of David (Ps 132:11; Is 9:7; 11:1; Jer 23:5; Eze 37:24-25). Acts 2:30 applied 2 Sm 7:11-13 to Christ.

8. God pours out his favor on his servants because of who he is and not because of a person's merit. God informed David that his son who would follow him as king would build the Temple, and that David's descendants would be kings (2 Sm 7:5-16). David responded in prayer that the Lord had done this, not because of who David was, but because of who God was (2 Sm 7:20-22).

9. A person can trust God to do what he promised. David knew God would do what he said he would (2 Sm 7:25).

10. Even great people who try to follow God are susceptible to temptation and sin. David was the only person who God described as: "a man after my own heart" (1 Sm 13:14; Ac 13:22). David was tempted and committed sin: when he saw Bathsheba taking a bath (2 Sm 11:2-4); and when he decided to take a census (2 Sm 24:1-3).

11. A first sin can provoke a person to commit other sins. David kept falling deeper and deeper into sin (2: Sm 11:1-17): he erred in staying home when he should have gone to war (11:1); he gave attention to a forbidden desire (11:3); he deliberately committed adultery with Bathsheba (11:4); he tried to cover up his sin by misleading another (11:6-15); he continued the cover-up by committing murder (11:15, 17).

12. Repeatedly sinning will dull a person's sensitivity to God's laws and other people's rights. David was insensitive to the news of Uriah's death because he had become callous to his own sin (2 Sm 11:23-25).

13. God hates sin and punishes the sinner. David suffered the consequences of his sins (2 Sm 12:10-12).

14. A person is unable to hide his sin from God. The Lord saw when David committed adultery with Bathsheba and when he used the Ammonites to murder Uriah (2 Sm. 11:1-17; 12:9).

15. Adultery brings disastrous consequences. To hide his sin, David planned the murder of an innocent man. David's son Amnon saw his father take the wife of another man, and he raped his half-sister (2 Sm 13:1-23). Absalom knew that his father had an innocent man murdered, and he murdered his brother who was guilty of incest-rape (2 Sm 13:28-29). Absalom saw his father usurp the place of Uriah (2 Sm 11:3), and he decided to usurp his father's throne (2 Sm 15:1-13).

16. Sin: so easy the act, so painful the result. It was so easy for David to go to bed with Bathsheba (2

Sm 11:4); however, the results were painful long lasting (2 Sm 12:9-14). The consequences of David's sin were irreversible.

17. Actions which a person strongly condemns in another may indicate his own character flaws. David burned with anger when he heard the story of the rich man who took the poor man's lamb, not realizing that in condemning the rich man, he was condemning himself (2 Sm 11:6-6).

18. The sins of the parents may contribute to their children's rebellion; however, the children are responsible for their own sins. The sins of David contributed to his children's rebellion Amnon (2 Sm 13), Absalom (2 Sm 13:27-29; 15:7-18:15) and Adonijah (I Kgs 1). However, each child was responsible for his actions and suffered the consequences of his own decisions.

19. A woman with a beautiful body may exploit sex in order to achieve rewards. However, such a woman is a curse and not a blessing. Whoever enjoys sexual pleasure with her is harmed and sows seeds of moral rottenness. Bathsheba used her body to achieve rewards: she became queen and later queen mother. Those who loved her were harmed: her husband was betrayed and murdered; David was punished for committing adultery with her.

20. Nathan is an example of God's spokesperson. From Nathan, we can learn that God's spokesperson must be submissive to God in order to: receive God's message and to know who should receive it (2 Sm 7:5-7); give the message to the person who God targets to receive it (2 Sm 7:8-17); have courage to denounce sin (2 Sm 12:1-12); have mercy to proclaim divine pardon (2 Sm 12:13).

21. Confessed sin is forgiven; however, its consequences will endure. The person who sows his wild oats and, at the time of harvest, prays for a crop failure will have his prayer denied by God. David confessed his sin and was forgiven; however, he suffered the consequences of his sin (2 Sm 12:10-14). The child that was the result of adultery died (2 Sm 12:14, 18); violence was experienced in David's family (2 Sm 12:10) when his son Amnon raped his half-sister Tamar (2 Sm 13:10-17) and Absalom killed his half-brother Amnon (13:23-29). God used David's own household to bring calamity upon him (2 Sm 12:11) when David's son Absalom lead a revolution (2 Sm 15:1-14) and was killed (2 Sm 18:14-15), and years later when another son Adonijah set himself up as king (1 Kin 1:5-10) and was killed (1 Kin 2:25). David committed adultery in secret, but his son would have sex with his wives in daylight (2 Sm 12:11-12), this happened when a tent was pitched for Absalom on the flat roof, and he lay with his father's concubines in the sight of all Israel (2 Sm 16:22).

22. Repentance is evident when the guilty person takes the responsibility for his wrong actions. David confessed: "I have sinned against the Lord" (2 Sm 12:13; 24:10, 17).

23. Uncontrolled sexual desires cause harm to the guilty person and to others. David looked at Bathsheba, a married woman, taking a bath. He didn't control his sexual desires (11:1-4). This resulted in the death of Uriah, Bathsheba's husband (12:11-16) and frustrations in David's family and nation (12 - 20). Amnon's desire for his step-sister Tamar led him to rape her (2 Sm 13:1-19). This provoked the hatred of Absalom (2 Sm 13:22).

24. Accepting advice from the wrong person leads to wrong conduct. Amnon accepted advice from his friend and first cousin Jonadab and raped his half-sister (2 Sm 13:3-14).

25. Love is different from lust: love is patient, lust wants immediate gratification; love is kind, lust is cruel, love does not require its own way, lust does. Amnon claimed to love Tamar, but he lusted after her. After he raped his half-sister, his "love" turned to hate (2 Sm 13:1, 14-17).

26. Family problems that are not dealt with, still exist and are destructive for the family. It is dangerous to keep silent and hope that destructive behavior in the family will go away. After Amnon raped Tamar, her brother Absalom told her: "Don't take this thing to heart. Let's keep it quiet" (2 Sm 13:20). When David heard the whole story, he was furious; but he didn't discipline Amnon (2 Sm 13:21). After being raped, Tamar lived in her brother Absalom's house, bitter and desolate (13:20). The unsolved situation led to Absalom's murder of Amnon and his flight (13:23-39) Later, David permitted Absalom to return, but David would not see his son (2 Sm 14:21-24). The unsolved problem ultimately resulted in Absalom's rebellion against his father (15:1-12).

27. Alcoholic drink can result in disaster. Amnon was drunk and could not fight off his attackers (2 Sm 13:28). The effects of drunkenness in the Bible are fatal: Noah lost composure and exposed himself (Gn 9:20-22); Lot lost consciousness and committed incest (Gn 19:32-35); Elah, king of Israel, died victim of his drunkenness. While Israel was at war, Elah got drunk in the home of a friend and was murdered by one of his officials (1 Kin 16:8-10); King Belshazzar became drunk and showed disrespect for sacred items; he lost his kingdom and his life (Dan 5:1-30).

28. Parents who do not discipline their children will suffer the consequences. David did nothing to correct Amnon after he raped his half-sister Tamar (2 Sm 13:21). After Absalom killed

Amnon and fled, David mourned for Absalom (2 Sm 13:37-39) establishing a discrimination among his children. David had spoiled his son Adonijah, never once reprimanding him, and Adonijah made a power move to become king (1Kg 1:6).

29. A "half-pardon" that partly forgives a person for his wrongdoing but continues to punish him, provokes anger. David forgave Absalom for killing his half-brother Amnon and allowed him to return to Jerusalem. But David continued to punish Absalom by not allowing him to see the king (2 Sm 14:24). David's "half-pardon" provoked an internal revolt in Absalom, which later was manifested in an open rebellion (17:1-12). God's pardon is complete and is expressed in his words recorded by the prophet: "I have swept away your offenses like a cloud, your sins like the morning mist (Is 44:22).

30. Sometimes it is necessary to flee in order to obtain victory. David escaped from Jerusalem and gained time to organize his soldiers in order to obtain victory in war (2 Sm 15:13-15; 18:6-8). Lot fled from Sodom and gained the right to continue living (Gn19:1-22); Joseph fled from Potiphar's wife and continued to experience the presence of the Lord with him. Later the Lord put him in a position of power (Gn 39:12; 41:56-57); Moses fled from the comfort of Egypt and saved the Israelites from slavery (Ex 2:15; 12:41; Heb 11:23-29).

31. The Lord confuses those who fight against his servants. He used Hushai to frustrate the advice of Ahithophel that would have harmed David (2 Sm 17:14), just as God had frustrated the curses of Balaam against the people of Israel (Nm 24:10).

32. The parent whose sins contribute to his children's rebellion will suffer bitterly. When Absalom died, David knew that his own sins contributed to Absalom's rebellion, and he cried bitterly for his son (2 Sm 18:33).

33. Often the person who is mourning for the dead must put aside showing his heartache in order to tend to the needs of the living. David was crying because of Absalom's death. Joab rebuked David and told him that if he did not go out and encourage his men, they would desert him. So David got up and took his seat at the city gate and his soldiers presented themselves to the king (18:33 - 19:8).

34. Spiritual leaders cannot take for granted the spiritual well-being of their children. David was used by God to lead the nation, but his children had sin-problems: Amnon raped his half-sister Tamar (2 Sm 13:10-17); Absalom killed his half-brother Amnon (13:23-29); Absalom lead a revolution against his father (2 Sm 15:1-14); Adonijah set himself up as king (1 Kin 1:5-10). Samuel was a spiritual leader whose children were dishonest (1 Sm 8:1-3).

35. The subordinate who has the best interest of his superior will reprove him when he is wrong. Joab told David that there would be dire results if he continued mourning for Absalom (2 Sm 19:4-7).

36. God's mercy is not separated from his justice. David confessed his sins of adultery and murder. He was forgiven, but suffered the consequences of his sin (2 Sm 12:10-14). David confessed his sin, after the counting of the fighting men. However, God punished him by sending a plague on Israel (2 Sm 24:10-15).

37. Parents need to set limits for their children in order to prepare them to live within limits. David had never interfered by opposing his son Adonijah. As a result, Adonijah always wanted his way and did not know how to respect limits that would restrict his desires (1 Kin 1:6).

QUESTIONS

1. What does the life of David teach us about God?
2. What was David's reaction when he learned that Saul and Jonathan were dead?
3. How did David become king of all of Israel?
4. What were the results of Joab's desire for revenge?
5. What happened when David desired to build a house for the Lord?
6. What victories did David experience?
7. What sins did David commit and what were their consequences?
8. What were some of the problems faced by David's family?
9. What are some of the positive and negative aspects about David?
10. What is the most important lesson you learned from the life of David?

SOLOMON			
2 Samuel	1 Kings		
PRINCE	**BECOMES KING**	**PROGRESSING**	**DECAYING**
▪Son of David and Bathsheba (12:24) ▪Raised in a dysfunctional family	▪Becomes king (1) ▪Eliminates his enemies (2)	▪Requests wisdom (3:1-15) ▪Judges with wisdom (3:16-28) ▪His fame (4) ▪The Temple (5-8) ▪His palace (7)	▪God's promise (9:1-9) ▪Gives away 20 cities (9:10-14) ▪Requires forced labor (9:15-28) ▪Queen of Sheba (10:1-13) ▪Much wealth (10:14-29) ▪Many women (11:1-3) ▪Idolatry (11:4-8) ▪Enemies (11:14-40) ▪Death (11:41-43)
Loved by God (12:24)	Loves God	Building for God	Abandoning God
Acquiring wisdom	Requesting wisdom	Living by wisdom	Abandoning wisdom
	Wrote: Song of Solomon ▪Reflects the feeling of a lover and his beloved. ▪Expresses the joy and beauty of human love within marriage.	Wrote: Proverbs ▪Teaches what a person should do.	Wrote: Ecclesiastes ▪Teaches what a person should quit doing.
2 Samuel	1 Kings		
12 18	1 2	3 8	9 11

SOLOMON: A WISE MAN WHO ABANDONED WISDOM

United Kingdom
1 Kings 1 - 11; 2 Chronicles 1 - 9

STRUCTURE

Context:
David reigned as king forty years over Israel. Before his death, David chose his son Solomon to succeed him as king.

Key-person: Solomon

Key-location: Jerusalem

Key-repetitions:
▪Solomon eliminated his enemies: Adonijah; Abiathar, Joab; and Shimei.
▪Solomon's wisdom: he was wise (1 Kin 2:9; 4:30-31; 10:23); he asked for wisdom (1 Kin 3:9-12); God gave him wisdom (1 Kin 4:29; 5:12); people knew Solomon had wisdom from the Lord (1 Kin 3:28); kings heard about Solomon's wisdom (1 Kin 4:34; 5:7); the queen of Sheba testified to Solomon's wisdom (1 Kin 10:4-7); people wanted to hear his wisdom (1 Kin 10:24).
▪ Solomon's wealth: God promised him wealth (1 Kin 3:13); he was wealthy (1 Kin 4:20-25); the queen of Sheba testified to his wealth (1 Kin 10:7); God multiplied Solomon's wealth (1 Kin 10:14-29); he was the richest king (1 Kin 10:23).
▪Temple (1 Kin 3:1-2; 5:3-5, 17-18; 6:1-38; 7:12-51; 8:1-65; 9:1-25).
▪Temple honoring the Name of the Lord (1 Kin 3:2; 5:3; 8:16-20, 23, 43, 44, 48; 9:3, 7).
▪The Lord spoke to Solomon (1 Kin 3:4-15; 6:11-13; 9:1-9 and 2 Chr 7:11-14; 1 Kin 11:9-13).
▪Solomon built: Temple (3:2; 5:3, 51, 58; 6:1-38; 8:13-27; 8:43-48; 9:1-3, 15) palaces (3:1; 7:2-7; 9:24); ships (9:26); other building projects (9:17-19); shrines for other gods (11:7).
▪Solomon's wrongdoings: he gave 20 towns in Galilee to Hiram king of Tyre (1 Kin 9:10-14); he required forced labor (1 Kin 5:13-14; 9:15-28); he multiplied his wealth (1 Kin 10:14-29); he married foreign women and they seduced him to abandon God (1 Kin 11:1-3); he practiced idolatry (1 Kin 11:4-8).

- God's promises: promises to David about his descendants: (2 Sm 7:25, 28; 1 Kin 2:4, 24; 6:12; 8:15; 9:5); God kept his promises (1 Kin 2:24; 5:12; 8:15; 20, 24, 56); conditioned on obedience (1 Kin 2:24; 8:25).

Key-attitudes:
- The Lord was pleased with Solomon when he requested wisdom.
- The impressions of Solomon's wisdom and wealth.
- The joy and celebration when the Temple was dedicated.
- Solomon's wisdom at the beginning of his reign.
- Danger expressed in God's warnings of the results of turning away from following him.
- Solomon's imprudence and arrogance when he married foreign women.
- God's pleasure with Solomon at the beginning of his reign.
- God's displeasure with Solomon after he married foreign women.

Initial-problem:
David chose his son Solomon to succeed him as king, but another son, Adonijah, made a power play to become king.

Sequence of events:

David Chose Solomon as King
- When David was old, Abishag a Shunammite, would lie beside him to keep him warm (1 Kin 1:1-4).
- Adonijah, David's oldest living son made a power move to become king. He had the support of Joab and Abiathar the priest (1 Kin 1:5-10).
- David ordered Nathan the prophet to anoint Solomon king over Israel (1 Kin 1:11-53).
- When David's time to die drew near, he gave a charge to Solomon and told him not to forget Joab's wrongdoing and to deal with Shimei, who called down curses on David (1 Kin 2:1-9).
- David died. Solomon sat on the throne of his father David (1 Kin 2:10-12).

Solomon Established His Kingdom
- Adonijah requested to marry Abishag the Shunammite. King Solomon gave orders for Adonijah to be killed (1 Kin 2:13-25).
- King Solomon stripped Abiathar of the priesthood (1 Kin 2:26-27).
- Joab took refuge in the tent of the Lord, seizing the horns of the altar. Solomon ordered Joab killed (1 Kin 2:28-35).
- Solomon prohibited Shimei from leaving Jerusalem. Three years later Shimei left Jerusalem to fetch escaped slaves. Solomon ordered him killed (1 Kin 2:36-46).
- The kingdom was firmly established in Solomon's hands (1 Kin 2:46).

Solomon Ruled with Wisdom
- Solomon made an alliance with Pharaoh king of Egypt and married his daughter (1 Kin 3:1).
- Solomon worshiped at local shrines, offering sacrifices and burning incense (1Kg 3:2-3).
- Solomon went to Gibeon to offer sacrifices. The Lord asked him in a dream: "What do you want me to give you?" Solomon requested a discerning heart. The Lord was delighted and promised Solomon wisdom, and as a bonus: riches, honor and a long life (1 Kin 3:4-15; 1 Chr 1:2-12).
- Solomon solved a case between two prostitutes. Everyone in Israel realized Solomon had wisdom from God to administer justice (1 Kin 3:16-28).
- One day's food supply for Solomon's household: 185 bushels of fine flour; 375 bushels of meal; 10 grain-fed cattle; 20 pasture-fed cattle and 100 sheep and goats, as well as deer, gazelles, roebucks and choice fowl. Solomon had 4,000 stalls for chariot horses, and 12,000 horses (1 Kin 4:22-26).
- Solomon had 12 district governors. Each one had a designated month to supply provisions for Solomon (1 Kin 4:27-28).
- God gave Solomon wisdom and deep insight. He spoke 3,000 proverbs and composed 1,005 songs. People came to listen to Solomon's wisdom (1 Kin 4:29-34).

Solomon Achievements
- King Hiram of Tyre helped Solomon in building the Temple. Hiram kept Solomon supplied with cedar and pine logs, and Solomon provided Hiram with food and olive oil (1 Kin 5:1-12).
- King Solomon drafted 30,000 Israelite men as laborers. He sent them to Lebanon in shifts of 10,000 each month. He had 70,000 unskilled laborers and 80,000 stone-cutters, plus 3,300 foremen (1 Kin 5:13-18).
- Four hundred and eighty years after the Israelites left Egypt, in the fourth year of Solomon's reign, Solomon began building the Temple. The Temple was 90 feet long, 30 feet wide and 45 feet high. The porch across the width extended out 15 feet. Solomon built a three story structure for side rooms against the walls of the main hall. Only blocks dressed at the quarry were used (1 Kin 6:1-10; 2 Chr 3:3-14).
- The Lord promised Solomon that if he obeyed his commands, God would fulfill the promise he gave to David and would take up residence among the Israelites (1 Kin 6:11-13).
- Solomon finished building the Temple. The Temple was paneled with cedar. The inner sanctuary, the Holy of Holies, was gold-plated. The two cherubim in the Holy of Holies were gold-plated. Solomon spent seven years building the Temple (1 Kin 6:14-37).
- It took Solomon 13 years to build his palace. The Palace of the Forest of Lebanon was 150 feet long, 75 feet wide and 45 feet high. He built the Hall of Justice and paneled it with cedar. And he built his personal residence behind the Hall of Justice. Solomon made an identical palace for his wife, Pharaoh's daughter (7:1-12).
- Solomon made all the furnishings for the Lord's Temple. When Solomon completed the Temple, he brought the items consecrated by David and placed them in the Temple (7:13-51).
- King Solomon summoned the leaders of Israel to Jerusalem to bring up the Ark of the Lord. The

priests carried the Ark, the Tabernacle and all the sacred furnishings in it to the Temple. When the priests withdrew from the Holy Place, the cloud filled the Temple of the Lord (8:1-13).

■Solomon turned to face the people and blessed them. Then he praised the Lord for keeping his promise to David (8:1-20; 2 Chr 5:2 - 6:11).

■Solomon faced the altar and prayed. He praised the Lord and requested that the Lord hear prayers made in the Temple. Solomon requested that when the Israelites sin and God punishes them with a disaster, and then they repent and pray in or facing the Temple, for God to forgive their sin and remove the disaster (1 Kin 8:22-53).

■Solomon closes his prayer with the request that the priests be clothed with salvation and the saints rejoice in God's goodness (2 Chr 6:40-42).

■Solomon finished praying and shouted a blessing to the congregation of Israel (8:54-61).

■The king and all Israel offered sacrifices. They celebrated for 14 days (8:62-66).

■The Lord appeared to Solomon a second time to tell him that if God sent a disaster and then the people turned back to God, God would hear their prayers from the Temple. God warned that if Solomon turned away from the Lord, God would uproot Israel and reject the Temple (2 Chr 7:11-22; 1 Kin 9:1-9).

■After building the Temple and the palace, Solomon gave 20 towns to Hiram king of Tyre. Hiram was not pleased with them (9:10-14).

■Solomon conscripted forced labor for his building projects. Slave labor was imposed on those who were descendants of those who were in the land before Israel conquered it. But Solomon did not make slaves of any of the Israelites (9:15-23).

■Three times a year Solomon worshiped at the Altar of God. He was generous with everything that had to do with the Temple (9:25).

■Solomon built ships and Hiram's men served in the fleet with Solomon's men. They brought back to Solomon 16 tons of gold (9:26-28).

■The queen of Sheba came to test Solomon with hard questions. She was overwhelmed when she experienced Solomon's wisdom and saw different things in Solomon's kingdom (10:1-13).

■Every year Solomon received 25 tons of gold in tribute (1 Kin 10:14-15).

■Solomon made a throne of ivory overlaid with a veneer of gold. All Solomon's serving utensils were gold. The king had a fleet of trading ships at sea with Hiram's ships. Every three years the fleet returned carrying gold, silver, ivory, apes and baboons. Solomon was wiser and richer than all the other kings on earth. He had 1,400 chariots and 12,000 horses (10:16-29).

Solomon Distances Himself from God

■The Lord had warned the Israelites not to marry people of other nations. Solomon had 700 wives from foreign royal families and 300 concubines. His wives seduced him away from the Lord. He worshiped Ashtoreth and Molech. He built sacred shrines for the god of each of his foreign wives (11:1-8).

■The Lord was furious with Solomon. The Lord promised to rip the kingdom away from Solomon and give it to one of his officers. He would leave Solomon's son one tribe to rule (1 Kin 11:9-13).

■Ahijah the prophet told Jeroboam that the Lord would rip ten tribes from Solomon and give them to Jeroboam to rule. God promised Jeroboam that if he obeyed the Lord's commands, the Lord would build him a dynasty similar to the one he had built for David (11:23-40).

■Solomon ruled for 40 years. He died, and his son Rehoboam succeeded him as king (1 Kin 11:41-43).

Final-situation:

Ahijah the prophet told Jeroboam that after the death of Solomon, the Lord would rip ten of the tribes of Israel away from Solomon's son and give them to Jeroboam to rule. The Lord was doing this because Solomon stopped following him and started worshiping many other gods.

Solomon died, and his son Rehoboam succeeded him as king.

BIBLE STORY

David Chose Solomon as King

In his old age, King David was cold even with covers heaped over him. His servants found a young virgin, Abishag a Shunammite, to lie beside him to keep him warm. Abishag was beautiful. She cared for the king, but the king did not have sex with her (1 Kin 1:1-4).

Adonijah was David's oldest living son. He made a power move and said: "I will be king." His father had spoiled him, never once reprimanding him. He was good-looking and was the son born after Absalom. Adonijah conferred with Joab and with Abiathar the priest, and they gave him their support. But Zadok the priest, Nathan the prophet, and David's bodyguards did not join Adonijah.

Adonijah held a coronation feast. He invited all his brothers, and all the royal officials of Judah. But he did not invite Nathan the prophet nor the king's bodyguards nor his brother Solomon (1 Kin 1:5-10).

Bathsheba told David that Adonijah had taken over as king. David immediately ordered Nathan the prophet to anoint Solomon king over Israel. Trumpets were sounded and everyone shouted: "Long live King Solomon!" And all the people joined the celebration, playing flutes and rejoicing greatly, so that the ground shook with the sound.

Adonijah and all his guests heard the uproar. On hearing the trumpet sound, Joab asked: "What's the meaning of the noise in the city?"

A messenger arrived with the answer: "Our lord King David has made Solomon king. Moreover, Solomon has taken his seat on the royal throne."

At this, all of Adonijah's guests rose in alarm and

dispersed (1 Kin 1:11-53).

When David's time to die drew near, he gave a charge to Solomon his son: "Be strong, obey everything the Lord commands and walk in his ways. Then you will prosper in all you do. If you obey the Lord, he will keep his promise to me: `If your descendants watch how they live, and if they walk faithfully before me with all their heart and soul, you will always have a successor on Israel's throne.'

"Don't forget what Joab did to me. He murdered two commanders of Israel's armies, Abner and Amasa. He acted in peacetime as if he were in war. You also have to deal with Shimei, the Benjamite, who called down bitter curses on me (1 Kin 2:1-9).

Then David died and was buried in the City of David. So Solomon sat on the throne of his father David, and his rule was firmly established (1 Kin 2:10-12).

Solomon Established His Kingdom

Adonijah went to Bathsheba, Solomon's mother, and told her: "All Israel looked to me as their king. But things changed, and the kingdom went to my brother. That was the Lord's doing. Now I have one request to make of you. Please ask King Solomon, since he will not refuse you, to give me Abishag the Shunammite as my wife."

Bathsheba replied: "I will speak to the king for you."

Bathsheba went to King Solomon to present Adonijah's request. Bathsheba requested: "Allow Abishag the Shunammite to marry your brother Adonijah."

Solomon answered his mother: "You request Abishag the Shunammite for Adonijah! You might as well request the kingdom for him since he is my older brother. He has Abiathar the priest and Joab on his side! Adonijah will pay with his life for this request! The Lord kept his promise; he established me firmly on the throne of my father David. Adonijah shall be put to death today!" So King Solomon gave orders for Adonijah to be killed (1 Kin 2:13-25).

King Solomon then told Abiathar the priest: "Go back to your fields. Even though you deserve to die, I will not put you to death, because you carried the Ark of the Sovereign Lord before my father David and shared in all his hard times." Solomon stripped Abiathar of the priesthood, fulfilling the Lord's word spoken at Shiloh regarding the family of Eli (1 Kin 2:26-27).

The news reached Joab, who had conspired with Adonijah. Joab took refuge in the tent of the Lord, seizing the horns of the altar. Solomon ordered: "Kill him and bury him. Free me and my father's house of the guilt of the innocent blood that Joab shed. Behind my father's back, he brutally murdered Abner, commander of Israel's army, and Amasa, commander of Judah's army. Both of them were better men and more upright than he. Joab and his family will be guilty for their deaths. But for David and his descendants, the verdict is the Lord's peace forever" (1 Kin 2:28-35).

Solomon sent for Shimei and said to him: "Build yourself a house in Jerusalem and live there. The day you leave Jerusalem, you will die; you will have decreed your own death sentence."

Shimei stayed in Jerusalem. But three years later, two of Shimei's slaves ran off. Shimei saddled his donkey and went looking for his slaves. He returned, bringing back his slaves.

Solomon summoned Shimei and told him: "I warned you: On the day you leave this area, you will die. You know in your heart all the wrong you did to my father David. Now the Lord will repay you for your wrongdoing. But King Solomon will be blessed, and David's throne will remain secure before the Lord forever."

Then the king gave the order for Shimei to be killed (1 Kin 2:36-46).

The kingdom was now firmly established in Solomon's hands (1 Kin 2:46).

Solomon Ruled with Wisdom

Solomon made an alliance with Pharaoh king of Egypt and married his daughter. He brought her to Jerusalem. The Temple had not been built, so the people were still sacrificing at the high places. Solomon showed his love for the Lord by living according to the ways of his father David. But Solomon also worshiped at local shrines on high places, offering sacrifices and burning incense (1Kg 3:1-3).

Solomon went to Gibeon, the most famous local shrine, to offer sacrifices. While he was at Gibeon, the Lord came to him in a dream during the night. God said: "What do you want me to give you?"

Solomon answered: "You have shown great kindness to my father David, because he was faithful to you. You continued your kindness to him by giving him a son to sit on his throne. Now, O Lord my God, you have made me king in my father's place. I am only a little child and do not have the wisdom to do my job. Here is what I want: give me a discerning heart to rule your people and to discern between right and wrong. For without wisdom, it is impossible to govern this great people of yours."

The Lord was delighted with Solomon's request. God told him: "You did not ask for a long life, or riches, or the death of your enemies. Since you asked for wisdom in dispensing justice, I will answer your request. I will give you a wise and discerning heart. There has never been one like you before, nor will there ever be. As a bonus, I will give you both riches and honor that you did not request. In your lifetime, no other king will be equal to you. And if you walk in my ways and obey my commands as your father David did, I will also give you a long life." Then Solomon awoke, and he realized it had been a dream.

Solomon returned to Jerusalem (1 Kin 3:4-15; 1 Chr 1:2-12).

Two prostitutes sought King Solomon. One said: "This woman and I live in the same house. I had a baby and three days later, this woman also had a baby. One night, the infant son of this woman died because she rolled over on him in her sleep. She got up in the middle of the night and took my son from my bed while I was sound asleep. She put my son by her breast and put her dead son by my breast. The next morning, I got up to nurse my son, and there was this dead baby! But when I looked at him in the morning light, I saw that it wasn't my baby."

The other woman countered: "No! Mine is the living baby; yours is the dead baby!"

But the first one insisted: "Not so! Your son is dead; my son is alive!" They argued back and forth in front of the king.

King Solomon requested: "Bring me a sword and cut the living baby in two; give half to one and half to the other."

The real mother of the living baby was full of love for her son and said to the king: "Please, my lord, give her the living baby! Don't kill him!"

But the other one said: "If I can't have him, neither will you. Cut him in two!"

The king gave his ruling: "Give the living baby to the first woman. She is the real mother."

Everyone in Israel heard of the king's verdict. They held the king in awe; they realized he had wisdom from God to administer justice (1 Kin 3:16-28).

One day's food supply for Solomon's household was: 185 bushels of fine flour; 375 bushels of meal; 10 grain-fed cattle; 20 pasture-fed cattle and 100 sheep and goats, as well as deer, gazelles, roebucks and choice fowl. Solomon ruled over all the kingdoms west of the Euphrates River, from Tiphsah to Gaza. Solomon had peace on all sides of his kingdom. During Solomon's lifetime, every one in Judah and Israel lived in safety and had plenty to eat.

Solomon had four thousand stalls for chariot horses, and twelve thousand horses.

Solomon had twelve district governors. Each governor had a designated month in which he supplied provisions for King Solomon. All who ate at the king's table had plenty to eat. The governors also brought their quotas of barley and straw for the horses (1 Kin 4:1-28).

God gave Solomon wisdom and deep insight. Solomon was wiser than any other person. He was famous in all the surrounding nations. He spoke three thousand proverbs and he composed a thousand and five songs. He knew about plant life, from the cedar that grew in Lebanon to the hyssop that grew in the cracks of a wall. He also taught about animals and birds, reptiles and fish. People came from far and near to listen to Solomon's wisdom (1 Kin 4:29-34).

Solomon's Achievements
King Hiram of Tyre heard that Solomon had succeeded his father David, and he sent ambassadors to Solomon. Solomon responded with a message to Hiram: "I intend to build a Temple to honor the Lord my God. The Lord told my father David: `Your son whom I will put on the throne in your place will build the Temple to honor my Name.' So give orders that cedars of Lebanon be cut for me. My men will work with yours, and I will pay whatever wages you set. We both know that you Sidonians are more skilled than anyone else in cutting timber."

When Hiram heard Solomon's message, he was delighted, exclaiming: "Praise the Lord today, for he has given David a wise son to rule over this great nation."

Hiram sent word to Solomon: "I received your request and will do all you want in providing the cedar and pine logs. All I request from you is food for my royal household."

Hiram kept Solomon supplied with all the cedar and pine logs he wanted, and Solomon provided Hiram with food and olive oil. There were peaceful relations between Hiram and Solomon, and the two of them made a treaty (1 Kin 5:1-12).

King Solomon drafted 30,000 men as laborers from all Israel. He sent them to Lebanon in shifts of ten thousand each month. They worked a month in Lebanon and were home for two months. Solomon also had 70,000 unskilled laborers and 80,000 stonecutters in the hills, plus thirty-three hundred foremen managing the project and directing the workmen. The craftsmen cut and prepared the timber and stone for the building of the Temple (1 Kin 5:13-18).

The four hundred and eightieth year after the Israelites came out of Egypt, which was the fourth year of Solomon's reign over Israel, Solomon began building the Temple of the Lord.

The Temple that King Solomon built to the Lord was 90 feet long, 30 feet wide and 45 feet high. The Temple's 30 foot wide porch extended out 15 feet. Solomon built a three story structure for side rooms against the walls of the main hall. The rooms on the ground floor were seven and a half feet wide; the middle floor rooms were nine feet wide; the third floor rooms were ten and a half feet wide. The rooms were seven and a half feet tall.

In building the Temple, only blocks dressed at the quarry were used. No hammer, chisel or any other iron tool was heard at the Temple site while it was being built.

The entrance to the ground floor was at the south end of the Temple; a stairway led to the second level and then to the third. So he built the Temple and completed it, roofing it with beams and cedar planks (1 Kin 6:1-10; 2 Chr 3:3-14).

The Word of the Lord came to Solomon: "About this Temple you are building; what is important is that you obey my commands. Then I will fulfill through you the promise I gave to David your father. I will take up my residence among the Israelites and will not abandon my people Israel" (1 Kin 6:11-13).

So Solomon finished building the Temple. He paneled the interior walls with cedar planks. For flooring, he used pine planks. He partitioned off thirty feet at the rear of the Temple with cedar planks from floor to ceiling. This formed the Holy of Holies. The main sanctuary in front was sixty feet long. The Temple was cedar, with carvings of fruits and flowers. Everything was covered with cedar; no stone was exposed.

He prepared the inner sanctuary, the Holy of Holies, for the Ark of the Covenant of the Lord. The inner sanctuary was a cube, thirty feet each way, all plated with gold. The altar of cedar was gold-plated. He made two identical cherubim, angel-like figures, from olive wood for the Holy of Holies. The outstretched wings of each cherubim measured fifteen feet. Each was fifteen feet high. The combined wing spread of the two stretched the width of the room. The wing of one cherub touched one wall, while the wing of the other touched the other wall, and their wings touched each other in the middle of the room. The cherubim were gold-plated.

On the walls all around the Temple, in both the inner and outer rooms, he carved cherubim, palm trees and open flowers. He also covered the floors of both the inner and outer rooms of the Temple with gold.

Solomon spent seven years building the Temple (1 Kin 6:14-37).

It took Solomon thirteen years; however, to finish building his palace. He built the Palace of the Forest of Lebanon. It was a hundred and fifty feet long, seventy-five feet wide and forty-five high. There were four rows with fifteen cedar columns supporting forty five cedar beams.

He built the throne hall, the Hall of Justice, where he would decide judicial matters, and paneled it with cedar. He built his personal residence behind the Hall of Justice on a similar plan. He made another palace exactly the same for his wife, Pharaoh's daughter.

All these buildings were made of blocks of high-grade stone cut to size and trimmed with a saw on their inner and outer faces (1 Kin 7:1-12).

King Solomon sent to Tyre and brought a skilled craftsman named Huram to do all the bronze work.

Solomon also made all the furnishings for the Lord's Temple: the golden altar; the golden table on which was placed the bread of the Presence; the lamp-stands of pure gold (five on the right and five on the left, in front of the inner sanctuary); the gold floral work and lamps and tongs; the pure gold basins, wick trimmers, sprinkling bowls, dishes and censers; and the gold sockets for the doors of the innermost room, the Holy of Holies, and also for the doors of the main hall of the Temple.

When Solomon completed all the work for the Temple, he brought in the items consecrated by his father David and placed them in the treasuries of the Lord's Temple (1 Kin 7:13-51).

Then King Solomon summoned the leaders of Israel, all the heads of the tribes and the family patriarchs, to come to Jerusalem to bring up the Ark of the Lord's Covenant from the City of David.

When leaders of Israel arrived, the priests carried the Ark of the Lord, the Tabernacle and all the sacred furnishings in it to the Temple. The priests took the Ark of the Lord to its place in the inner sanctuary of the Temple, the Holy of Holies, and put it beneath the wings of the cherubim. There was nothing in the Ark except the two stone tablets that Moses had placed in it at Horeb, where the Lord made a covenant with the Israelites after they came out of Egypt.

When the priests withdrew from the Holy Place, the glory of the Lord filled the Temple as a cloud, preventing the priests from performing their service.

Then Solomon said: "The Lord has told us that he lives in a dark cloud. O Lord, I have indeed built a magnificent Temple for you, a place for you to dwell forever."

While the people of Israel were standing, the king turned to face them and blessed them. Then he prayed: "Praise be to the Lord, the God of Israel, who has kept the promise he made to my father David who wanted to build a Temple honoring the Name of the Lord, the God of Israel. But the Lord told my father David: `You will not build the Temple, but your son will build the Temple for my Name.' The Lord has kept his promise: I am king in place of my father David and I have built the Temple to honor the Name of the Lord, the God of Israel" (1 Kin 8:1-20; 2 Chr 5:2 - 6:11).

Then Solomon faced the Lord's altar, spread his hands toward heaven and prayed: "O Lord, God of Israel, there is no God like you in heaven above or on earth below. You keep your covenant of love with your servants who truly follow you. You kept your promise to David my father; the proof is before us today! Now Lord, God of Israel, keep the other promises you made to David my father when you said: `You shall never fail to have a man rule Israel, on the condition that your sons are careful to walk before me as you have done.'

"The heavens cannot contain you. Certainly the Temple I have built cannot contain you! Yet I ask you to listen to my prayer and the prayers of your people Israel when they pray toward this place. Hear from heaven, your dwelling place, and when you hear, forgive. Judge between your servants; condemn the guilty and establish the innocence of the not guilty.

"Your people Israel will sin against you. Because of this, their enemies will defeat them. But when they turn back to you, confess your name, and pray to you in this Temple, then listen from heaven and forgive the sin of your people Israel.

"When your people sin against you and you stop the rain from falling; but when they pray toward this place, confess your name and turn from their sin, listen from heaven and forgive the sin of your people Israel. Teach them to do right and send rain on this land you gave your people.

"When disaster strikes, but then a prayer is

made by anyone of your people who spreads out his hands toward this Temple, then listen from heaven. Forgive and act; judge each person and deal with each one according to what is right. Do this and they will respect you.

"Listen to the prayers of the foreigner when he comes and prays toward this Temple. Then all the peoples of the earth may know your name and respect you.

"When your people go to war against enemies, then they pray to the Lord toward the Temple, listen to their prayer and do what is right for them.

"Your people will sin against you; you will become angry at them and let their enemy defeat them and take them captive to the enemy's land. If in the land of their captivity, they repent, turn back to you and pray to you toward this Temple, listen to their prayer and do what is best for them. Forgive your people, and move their conquerors to treat them with compassion.

"Pay attention to my prayers and the prayers of your people Israel. Listen to them when they cry out to you. For you handpicked them out from all the peoples on earth to be your people as you promised through your servant Moses when you brought our ancestors out of Egypt" (1 Kin 8:22-53).

Solomon closes his prayer with the request: "Now, my God, may your eyes be open and your ears attentive to the prayers offered in this place. Now arise, O Lord God, and come to your resting place. May your priests, O Lord God, be clothed with salvation, may your saints rejoice in your goodness" (2 Chr 6:40-42).

When Solomon finished praying to the Lord, he stood up. He had been kneeling in front of the altar with his hands spread out toward heaven. Standing, he shouted a blessing to the whole congregation of Israel: "Praise the Lord! He has given peace to his people Israel just as he promised. He kept every promise he gave through his servant Moses. May the Lord our God be with us as he was with our ancestors; may he never forsake us. May he turn our hearts to him, to walk in all his ways and to keep the commands he laid down for our ancestors. And may the Lord our God always remember this prayer, which I have prayed. I pray that he will help me and his people Israel every day. Then all the peoples of the earth will know that the Lord is the only true God. But your hearts must be fully committed to the Lord our God. You must obey his laws and commands" (1 Kin 8:54-61).

Then King Solomon and all Israel with him dedicated the Temple and offered fellowship sacrifices before the Lord. Solomon killed twenty-two thousand cattle and a hundred and twenty thousand sheep and goats. They celebrated before the Lord God for a total of fourteen days. Afterwards Solomon sent the people away. They blessed the king and then went home, joyful for all the good things the Lord had done for his servant David and his people Israel (1 Kin 8:62-66).

After Solomon had finished building the Temple, the royal palace, and had achieved all he had desired to do, the Lord appeared to him a second time, as he had appeared to him at Gibeon.

The Lord told Solomon: "I accept your prayer and have chosen this place for myself as a Temple for sacrifices and a house of worship. If I shut up the heavens so that there is no rain, or order locusts to devour the land or send a plague among my people; if my people, who are called by my name respond by humbling themselves, praying, seeking my face and turning from their wicked ways, then I will listen from heaven and will forgive their sin and will heal their land. Now my eyes will be open and my ears attentive to the prayers offered in this place.

"As for you, if you walk before me as David your father did, and do all I command, I will establish your royal throne, as I covenanted with David your father. But if you betray me and forsake my commands and go off to serve other gods and worship them, then I will uproot Israel from my land, and will reject this Temple I have consecrated to honor my Name. I will make it a byword and an object of contempt among all peoples" (2 Chr 7:11-22; 1 Kin 9:1-9).

By the end of twenty years, Solomon had built the Temple of the Lord and the royal palace. King Solomon then gave twenty towns in Galilee to Hiram, king of Tyre. Hiram had supplied him with all the cedar and pine and gold he wanted. But when Hiram went to see the towns that Solomon had given him, he was not pleased with them (1 Kin 9:10-14).

Solomon built widely and extravagantly in Jerusalem, in Lebanon and wherever he desired. King Solomon conscripted forced labor to build the Lord's Temple, his own palace and other building projects. Slave labor was imposed on those who were descendants of people who were in the land before Israel conquered it. But Solomon did not make slaves of any of the Israelites. The Israelites were his fighting men, officers, government officials, and officials in charge of supervising Solomon's projects (1 Kin 9:15-23).

Three times a year Solomon worshiped at the Altar of God, sacrificing offerings and burning incense in the presence of the Lord. He was generous with everything that had to do with the Temple (1 Kin 9:25).

King Solomon also built ships on the shore of the Red Sea. Hiram sent his men who knew the sea to serve in the fleet with Solomon's men. They sailed to Ophir and brought back to Solomon sixteen tons of gold (1 Kin 9:26-28).

The queen of Sheba heard about Solomon's fame. She came to test him with hard questions. She arrived at Jerusalem with a very great caravan. Solomon answered all her questions. The queen of Sheba was overwhelmed when she experienced Solomon's wisdom and saw with her own eyes the palace he had built, the food on his table, the seating of his officials, the attending servants, his cupbearers, and the burnt offerings he made at the Temple.

She told the king: "The report I heard in my own country about your achievements and your wisdom is true. But I did not believe these things until I came and saw with my own eyes. Praise be to the Lord your God, who has delighted in you and placed you on the throne of Israel."

She gave the king four and a half tons of gold plus many sacks of spices, and precious stones. King Solomon also gave the queen of Sheba all she desired and asked for. Then she returned to her own country (1 Kin 10:1-13).

Solomon received twenty-five tons of gold in tribute every year. This was beyond the taxes and profit on trade with merchants and money paid from different kings and governors (1 Kin 10:14-15).

The king made a massive throne of ivory overlaid with a veneer of gold. All of King Solomon's drinking cups, dinnerware and serving utensils were gold in the Palace of the Forest of Lebanon. The king had a fleet of trading ships at sea with Hiram's ships. Every three years the fleet returned, carrying gold, silver ivory, apes and baboons.

King Solomon was wiser and richer than all the other kings on earth. People came from all over the world to hear the wisdom God had put into his heart.

Solomon accumulated chariots and horses; he had fourteen hundred chariots and twelve thousand horses. The king made silver as common in Jerusalem as stones, and cedar as plentiful as fig trees in the foothills. Solomon's horses were imported from Egypt (1 Kin 10:16-29).

Solomon Distances Himself from God

King Solomon; however, loved many women who were not from Israel. Pharaoh's daughter was only the first of many foreign women he loved. The Lord had warned the Israelites: "You must not marry people of other nations because they will seduce you to follow their gods." Nevertheless, Solomon fell in love with these women. He had seven hundred wives from royal families and three hundred concubines; a thousand women. His wives seduced him away from the Lord. As Solomon grew old, his wives caused him to follow after foreign gods. He did not stay true to the Lord his God, as David his father had been. Solomon worshiped Ashtoreth, the whore goddess of the Sidonians, and Molech, the horrible god of the Ammonites. Solomon openly defied God; he did not follow the Lord completely, as his father David had done.

On a hill east of Jerusalem, Solomon built sacred shrines for the god of each of his foreign wives, who burned incense and offered sacrifices to their gods (11:1-8).

God was furious with Solomon for abandoning the Lord, the God of Israel. The Lord had appeared to Solomon twice and clearly commanded him not to fool around with other gods; yet he disobeyed God's orders. So the Lord told Solomon: "Since you have not kept my covenant and obeyed my commands, I will rip the kingdom away from you and give it to one of your officers. However, for the sake of David your father, I will not do it while you are alive. I will rip it away from your son when he becomes king. I will not take it all, I will leave him one tribe to rule (1 Kin 11:9-13).

The Lord raised up adversaries against Solomon. The most harmful one was Jeroboam, who had been in charge of the whole labor force of the house of Joseph. One day Jeroboam was going out of Jerusalem. Ahijah the prophet met him on the road, wearing a new cloak. The two of them were alone on a remote stretch of road. Ahijah took hold of his new cloak and ripped it into twelve pieces. Then he told Jeroboam: "Take ten pieces for yourself. The Lord, the God of Israel, says: `I am ripping the kingdom out of Solomon's hand and giving you ten tribes. But for the sake of my servant David and out of respect for Jerusalem, he will keep one tribe. Here is the reason: he stopped following me and started worshiping many other gods. He has not obeyed me, nor done what is right in my eyes, nor kept my commands and laws as David, his father, did. I will give one tribe to his son so that David my servant may always have a lamp before me in Jerusalem.

"'However, as for you, I will make you king over Israel. If you obey my commands and do what is right in my eyes, as David my servant did, I will be with you. I will build you a dynasty as enduring as the one I built for David. Israel will be yours. I will punish David's descendants because of this, but not forever.'"

Solomon ordered the assassination of Jeroboam, but he fled to Egypt where he remained in exile until Solomon's death (1 Kin 11:23-40).

Solomon reigned in Jerusalem over all Israel for forty years. Then he died and was buried in the city of David his father. His son Rehoboam succeeded him as king (1 Kin 11:41-43).

LIFE-LESSONS DISCOVERED IN THE STORY

1. Actions that bring short time benefits may result in long term disaster. Solomon's marriage to foreign women resulted in political alliances (1 Kin 3:1); however, his wives seduced him to follow other gods (1 Kin 11:3-4). Forced labor (1 Kin 5:13:13-18) enabled Solomon to build the Temple, the palaces and other projects in a hurry, but Solomon's people rebelled against his harsh labor and heavy yoke (1 Kin 12:4). Solomon received 25 tons of gold in taxes every year (1Kg 10:14). This made him the richest king in the world (10:23), but the people considered the taxes a heavy yoke (1 Kin 12:4).

2. Nothing can divert the sovereign purpose of God for his servant. Adonijah, the oldest living son of David, knew that David had proclaimed that Solomon would succeed him as king (1 Chr22:1-19; 28:1-8). Adonijah conspired to take the throne for himself. The conspiracy failed. He could not divert the sovereign purpose of God for Solomon (1 Chr 22:9-10).

3. Including religious ceremony as a part of an activity does not make it God's will. Adonijah offered sacrifices as a part of his coronation, but he was not God's choice to succeed David (1 Kin 1:9).

4. A person who gets himself in a dangerous situation as a result of making wrong choices and then seeks divine protection, will discover that God will not protect him from the consequences of his sin. After Joab had murdered two men, he sought God's protection by clinging to the horns of the sacred altar of burnt offering in the tabernacle court. But he was killed for his crime right at the altar (1 Kin 2:28-34).

5. Anger, hatred and the desire for revenge can destroy a person. Joab was a man who won all battles, except the one against the desire for revenge. He was a victim of violent anger, and he murdered two men who were better than he (1 Kin 2:28-34). (See Pr 16:32; Eph 4:31; 2 Cor 7:1.)

6. It is not enough to begin life serving God; it is important to end life being faithful to God. Solomon began well; however, he finished badly.

7. One wrong decision may be the first step that begins the process toward a future downfall. Solomon's decision to marry the daughter of Pharaoh, king of Egypt (1 Kin 3:1), was the beginning of his downfall that finally happened toward the end of his life (1 Kin 11:9-10).

8. A person can enjoy intimacy with God through prayer. Solomon's prayers when he asked God for wisdom (1 Kin 3:3-15; 2 Chr1:2-13), and when he dedicated the Temple (1 Kin 8:22-60) were examples of intimate conversation with God.

9. God hears and answers the prayer of the person who loves the Lord and values things that the Lord values. Solomon expressed adoration to God for his power and greatness (1 Kin 3:6-7); he recognized human weakness (1 Kin 3:7-8); he was not selfish, because he asked according to the divine will (1 Kin 3:9, 11); and according to his own needs (1 Kin 3:9).

10. The person who desires characteristics that please God will experience bonus benefits. Solomon asked God for wisdom. He received wisdom, but he received other bonuses, such as wealth and honor (1 Kin 3:11-14). The person who seeks the Kingdom of God (Mt 6:33) will receive other bonus benefits from God. He will discover that God will give him other good things (Rm 8:32).

11. God is the source of wisdom. It was the Lord who gave wisdom to Solomon (1 Kin 3:28).

12. God communicates with people. He communicated with Solomon (1 Kin 3:5, 11-14; 6:11; 11:9-11).

13. The person who does things for God, yet does not obey the Lord will not be rewarded by the Lord. Solomon was advised that the Lord's blessings would not be the results of his building the Temple. He would only be blessed if he obeyed the Lord (1 Kin 6:11-13).

14. People who face trouble should use prayer to reorientate their thinking. In prayer, they look away from the thing that troubles them and look toward God. Solomon suggests again and again that God's people who are in trouble need to "pray toward" the Temple (8:29, 30, 33, 35, 38, 42, 44, 48).

15. Solomon's prayer for the people of Israel can serve as a model for spiritual leaders who pray for their followers (1 Kin 8:55-60). Solomon requested: for God to be present with his people (8:56); for the people to have their hearts turned toward God (8:58); for them to obey the Lord's commands (8:58); for God to help with their daily needs (8:59); that all people may know that the Lord is the only true God (8:60).

16. The precondition for God being present in a building dedicated to him, is that those who gather in the building to worship must obey the Lord (1 Kin 9:3-9).

17. A precondition for receiving blessings from God is being faithful to him. No descendant of God's servant, nor organization, nor church building

can expect God's blessings after abandoning the Lord or disobeying his commands. The Lord promised Solomon that if he obeyed all God commanded, his descendant would govern Israel. But if Solomon were to forsake God's commands and serve other gods, then the Lord would uproot Israel from the land, and would reject the Temple (2 Chr 7:11-22; 1 Kin 9:1-9).

18. The person who serves the Lord, yet marries somebody who is committed to serve another god will compromise his faithfulness to God. Solomon abandoned the Lord as a result of marrying women who worshiped other gods (1 Kin 11:3-6). God had prohibited his people from marrying foreigners who served other gods (Ex 34:16; Dt 7:3-4). Foreign wives seduced Solomon to practice idolatry (1 Kin 11:1-6).

19. The person who uses methods which go contrary to God's commands in order to reach worthy goals will suffer the consequences of sin. Solomon's marriages with foreigners advanced political objectives; the pagan shrines were designed to make his wives and foreign merchants happy. However, those actions put in danger the purity of the true worship of God. God punished Solomon for his religious infidelity, raising up enemies in the exterior (1 Kin 11:14-25) and in the interior (1 Kin 11:26-39).

20. While God communicates his will to individuals, each person must decide if he will obey or disobey the Lord's orders. God had ordered Solomon not to follow other gods, but he disobeyed the Lord's commands (1 Kin 11:10).

21. No one can struggle against God and win. Solomon struggled against God, refusing to obey divine commands. The Lord determined how he would punish Solomon (11:9-13).

22. The continuation of divine blessings upon a government and nation depends on the fidelity of the leaders. The fulfilment of every promise that God made, to David (2 Sm 7:10-13; 1 Chr 22:8-10; 28:6-7) and to Solomon (1 Kin 6:12-13; 9:4), with reference to blessing the royal family and the nation of Israel, depended upon the kings' fidelity to God's precepts.

23. The continuation of divine favors depends upon the fidelity of the recipient of the blessings. The fulfilment of every promise that God had made to David and to Solomon with reference to blessing their families, depended upon their fidelity to divine precepts (1 Kin 9:4). God promised Jeroboam that God would make him a great king if he observed the Lord's commands and walked in his ways (1 Kin 11:29-38).

24. Parents who disobey God can cause harm to their descendants. Solomon's disobedience resulted in his son losing most of the kingdom (1 Kin 11:11-13).

QUESTIONS

1. What does Solomon's life teach us about God?
2. How did Solomon become king of Israel?
3. How did Solomon establish his kingdom?
4. How did Solomon free himself from enemies who had also troubled his father?
5. How did Solomon gain wisdom?
6. What did the case brought by the two prostitutes reveal about Solomon's wisdom and also about motherhood?
7. What importance did Solomon give to the Temple?
8. What can you learn from Solomon about prayer?
9. What were some of Solomon's successes?
10. How did some of Solomon's actions bring immediate prosperity, yet contributed to future problems?
11. What were some of Solomon's wrongdoings?
12. What caused Solomon to abandon the Lord?
13. Today, what causes people to abandon the Lord?
14. What were some of the consequences of Solomon abandoning the Lord?
15. Today, what are some of the consequences of abandoning the Lord?

COMPARING THE TWO KINGDOMS

ISRAEL North *10 tribes*	JUDAH South *2 tribes (Judah and Benjamin)*
KINGS	
Nine dynasties: 9 family lines. 1st king: Jeroboam	One dynasty: the family line of David 1st king: Rehoboam
▪All were evil and idolatrous. ▪All imitated King Jeroboam, sinning against the Lord and causing the people of Israel to sin.	▪Most were evil, a few were good. ▪Most imitated King Jeroboam, the first king of Israel, and sinned against God. A few imitated King David and served the Lord.
Most of the kings only reigned for a few years.	Most of the kings reigned for many years.
19 kings during 209 years.	20 kings during 345 years.
CAPITALS	
Samaria	Jerusalem
FALL	
722 B.C. ▪Defeated by Shalmaneser, king of Assyria. ▪Destroyed the capital.	586 B.C. ▪Defeated by Nebuchadnezzar, king of Babylon. ▪Destroyed the capital and the Temple.
AFTER THEIR FALLS	
Deported the important and strong people to Assyria.	Deported the important and strong people to Babylon.
Replaced those who were deported with conquered people from other nations.	Those deported from Judah were not replaced.
Those in Samaria worshiped the Lord God, yet at the same time they also followed the customs and served gods of the nations from which the newcomers had been deported.	In Babylon, those deported from Judah abandoned idolatry and returned to worship the Lord God.
Intermarried with other nationalities who served other gods.	Rejected intermarriage with other nationalities who served other gods.
MUCH LATER	
The deported Israelites never returned to Israel.	Seventy years after the fall of Judah, a remnant of the descendants of those deported to Babylon returned to Jerusalem.
Lost their identity as Israelites, the people of the Lord God. The mixed race became known as the Samaritans.	Held onto their identity as Israelites, the people of the Lord God.
Worshiped both the Lord God and idols of other gods.	Worshiped the Lord God and him alone.

THE KINGDOM IS DIVIDED
Divided Kingdom
1 Kings 12 -16; 2 Chronicles 10 - 16

STRUCTURE

Context:
Solomon was wiser and richer than all the other kings. High taxes and forced labor enabled him to obtain wealth and succeed with his building projects.

The Lord had warned the Israelites not to marry people of other nations. However, Solomon had 700 wives from foreign, royal families and 300 concubines. His wives seduced him away from the Lord.

The Lord was furious with Solomon. Ahijah the prophet told Jeroboam that after the death of Solomon, the Lord would rip ten of Israel's tribes away from Solomon's son and give them to Jeroboam to rule.

Solomon died and his son Rehoboam succeeded him as king.

Key-persons: Rehoboam, Jeroboam, and Asa

Key-locations: Tirzah, Samaria and Jerusalem

Key-repetitions:
- Sinned: Rehoboam, king of Judah (2 Chr 12:1, 14); the people of Judah (1 Kin 14:22-24); Abijah, king of Judah (15:3); Israel (12:30; 13:34); kings of Israel who sinned against the Lord and caused the people to sin: Jeroboam (1 Kin 14:16); Nadab (15:26); Baasha (16:2); Baasha and his son Elah (16:13); Zimri (16:19); Omri (16:25-26).
- Idolatry, idols or altar to other gods (1 Kin 12:25-33; 13:1-5, 32; 14:9, 21-31: 15:9-24; 16:13, 26).
- God of Israel (14:7, 13; 15:30; 16:13, 26).
- God spoke through prophets: **Shemaiah (1 Kin 12:21-24; 2 Chr 12:5-8)**; a man of God (1 Kin 13:1-10); Ahijah (1 Kin 14:1-16); Azariah (2 Chr 15:1-7); Hanani (2 Chr 16:7-9); Jehu (1 Kin 16:1-7).
- Written in the book of the annals/history of: Israel (1 Kin 14:19; 15:31; 16:5, 14, 20, 27); Judah (1 Kin 14:29; 15:7, 23).
- Followed the example of: Jeroboam (1 Kin 15:26, 34; 16:13, 26, 19, 26); Rehoboam (1 Kin 15:3); David (1 Kin 15:11).
- Seek the Lord (2 Chr 11:16; 12:14; 15:2, 15).

Key-attitudes:
- Rebellion against God.
- The selfish arrogant pride of Rehoboam.
- The Israelites had hope in Rehoboam when they first met with him, but after his harsh words they begrudged him.
- Jeroboam's insecurity and haughtiness.
- The persistence with idolatry of the kings of Israel.
- Asa was esteemed until he was reprimanded, then he was resented.
- The conspiracy and antagonism of Baasha.
- The courage of the prophets.

Initial-problem:
Jeroboam and the whole assembly of Israel told the newly anointed King Rehoboam: "Your father put a heavy yoke on us and made us work hard, but now lighten the harsh labor and the heavy yoke he put on us, and we will serve you."

Sequence of events:
Division of the Kingdom
- At Shechem, Jeroboam and the whole assembly of Israel asked Rehoboam to lighten the heavy yoke his father Solomon had put on them (1 Kin 12:1-4).
- Rehoboam told the people to return in three days. Older leaders advised Rehoboam to respond with compassion (1 Kin 12:5-7).
- Young men who were Rehoboam's peers advised him to answer with harsh words (1 Kin 12:8-11).
- Three days later, Rehoboam followed the advice of the young men and answered the people with cruel words (1 Kin 12:12-15).
- Ten tribes of Israel abandoned Rehoboam and went home. Rehoboam continued to rule the Israelites who lived in the towns of Judah (1 Kin 12:16-17).
- The Israelites stoned Adoniram, who was in charge of forced labor. King Rehoboam escaped to Jerusalem (1 Kin 12:18-19).
- The Israelites made Jeroboam king over all Israel (1 Kin 12:20).
- Rehoboam called up the men of the tribes of Judah and Benjamin to make war against the kingdom of Israel. But the word of God came to Shemaiah that they were not to go to war against the Israelites (1 Kin 12:21-24).

Israel: Jeroboam Creates New Worship
- Jeroboam made two golden calves. He built shrines on high places and recruited priests from all sorts of people. He created a new festival for the Israelites and went up to the altar at Bethel to make offerings (1 Kin 12:25-33).

Judah: Many from Israel Flee to Judah
- Priests, Levites and everyone from all the tribes of Israel who set their hearts on seeking the Lord migrated to Jerusalem and supported Rehoboam for three years (2 Chr 11:13-17).

Israel: Prophecy against Jeroboam
- A man of God, from Judah, cried out against Jeroboam's altar in Bethel. Jeroboam arm became paralyzed when he yelled for the man to be seized. The man of God prayed, and Jeroboam's arm was healed. Jeroboam invited the man of God to eat with him. The man replied that he was under God's orders not to eat nor drink in Israel (1 Kin 13:1-10).
- An old prophet lied to the man of God, telling him

that an angel ordered the prophet to take the man to his house to eat and drink water. While sitting at the table, the old prophet prophesied that because the man of God had disobeyed divine orders, he would not be buried in his family's grave (1 Kin 13:11-22).
- A lion killed the man of God. The old prophet buried him in his own grave (1 Kin 13:23-32).
- Jeroboam kept right on doing evil (1 Kin 13:33-34).
- Jeroboam's son, Abijah, became sick. Jeroboam's wife disguised herself and went to Shiloh to see Ahijah the prophet. Ahijah condemned Jeroboam for his sin of making gods of metal. He prophesied: the boy would die and be buried; all other members of Jeroboam's family would be killed; and the Lord would give Israel up because Jeroboam sinned and caused the people of Israel to sin (1 Kin 14:1-16).
- Jeroboam's wife returned home, and the boy died (1 Kin 14:17-18).
- Jeroboam reigned for 22 years. His son Nadab succeeded him as king (1 Kin 14:19-20).

Judah: Rehoboam
- Rehoboam was 41 years old when he became king. He ruled for 17 years (1 Kin 14:21).
- Rehoboam built up towns for defense in Judah (2 Chr 11:5-12).
- Rehoboam had 18 wives and 60 concubines, 28 sons and 60 daughters. He appointed his son Abijah to be the chief prince (2 Chr 11:18-23).
- After Rehoboam secured his kingdom, he did evil (2 Chr 12:1, 14). The people of Judah set up high places, sacred stones and Asherah poles (sex-and-religion idols). There were even male religious prostitutes (1 Kin 14:22-24).
- Shishak, king of Egypt, attacked Jerusalem in the 5th year that Rehoboam was king. The prophet Shemaiah told Rehoboam and the leaders of Judah that the Lord had abandoned them, because they had abandoned the Lord. The king and the leaders said: "The Lord is right." The Lord decided not to destroy them since they humbled themselves, but they would become Shishak's subjects (2 Chr 12:2-8).
- Shishak attacked Jerusalem and plundered the treasures of the Temple and the royal palace. He took the gold shields, but Rehoboam replaced them with bronze shields (1 Kin 14:25-28).
- Because Rehoboam repented and humbled himself, he was not totally destroyed (2 Chr 12:12).
- Rehoboam died. Abijah succeeded him as king (1 Kin 14:29-31).

Judah: Abijah; Asa
- Abijah reigned 3 years and sinned, just like his father before him. Abijah died, and Asa his son succeeded him as king (1 Kin 15:1-8).
- Asa reigned 41 years. His grandmother's name was Maacah (1 Kin 15:9-10).
- Asa did right, as his ancestor David had done. He expelled the male shrine prostitutes and got rid of all the idols. He removed his grandmother Maacah from her position as queen mother, because she had made a memorial to Asherah. Although he did not remove the sex-and-religion shrines, Asa's heart was committed to the Lord (1 Kin 15:11-15). He commanded Judah to seek the Lord (2 Chr 14:4).
- King Zerah from Cush marched to fight Judah. Asa called to the Lord his God. The Lord defeated the Cushites (2 Chr 14:9-15).
- Azariah told Asa that the Lord would be with him when he was with the Lord, but if he forsook the Lord, the Lord would forsake him. The prophecy of Azariah gave Asa courage to remove the idols from Judah and to repair the altar of the Lord. In the 15th year of his reign, he assembled all who had settled in Judah to make sacrifices to the Lord, and to enter into a covenant to seek the Lord with all their heart and soul (2 Chr 15:1-19).
- In Israel, King Jeroboam died and his son Nadab became king. Nadab was assassinated by Baasha.
- Baasha attacked Judah by building a fort at Ramah. Asa sent silver and gold to Ben-Hadad, king of Aram, for him to fight against the towns of Israel. Then Baasha stopped building Ramah (1 Kin 15:16-22; 2 Chr 16:1-6).
- Hanani the prophet condemned Asa because he relied on the king of Aram and not on the Lord. Asa put Hanani in prison and started being cruel to some of the people (2 Chr 16:7-10).
- In the 39th year of his reign, Asa was afflicted with a severe disease in his feet. He did not seek help from the Lord. Asa died in the 41th year of his reign and Jehoshaphat his son succeeded him (2 Chr 16:11-14; 1 Kin 15:23-24).

Israel: Nadab; Baasha
- Nadab became king of Israel in the 2nd year Asa was king of Judah. Nadab was king for two years. He sinned and caused Israel to sin (1 Kin 15:25-26).
- Baasha killed Nadab and succeeded him as king. Baasha was king of Israel for 24 years. Baasha killed Jeroboam's whole family (1 Kin 15:27-32).
- Baasha imitated Jeroboam, who both sinned and caused Israel to sin (1 Kin 15:33-34).
- The prophet Jehu condemned Baasha and prophesied that he would suffer the identical fate of Jeroboam. All members of his family would be killed (1 Kin 16:1-4).
- Baasha died, and Elah his son succeeded him as king (1 Kin 16:5-7).

Israel: Elah; Zimri; Omri
- Elah reigned two years. One day when Elah was drunk, Zimri killed him and became king. Zimri killed all of Baasha's family (1 Kin 16:8-14).
- Zimri was king for seven days. The Israelite army proclaimed their commander, Omri, king over Israel. Zimri set the palace on fire around himself (1 Kin 16:15-20).
- Omri built the city of Samaria. Omri sinned more than the kings who were before him. He imitated Jeroboam. Omri died, and Ahab his son succeeded him as king (1 Kin 16:21-28).

Final-situation:
Jeroboam, the first king of Israel, sinned by making idols. He sinned and caused the people to sin. All the kings of Israel followed the example of Jeroboam. Omri sinned more than the kings who

were before him.

The first two kings of Judah, Rehoboam and Abijah, also worshiped idols. But Asa did what was right, as David had done for 36 of his 41 years as king.

BIBLE STORY

Division of the Kingdom

Rehoboam went to Shechem, where all the Israelites had gone to make him king. To escape King Solomon's wrath, Jeroboam had taken asylum in Egypt. When Rehoboam became king, Jeroboam returned from Egypt. Jeroboam and the whole assembly of Israel went to Rehoboam and told him: "Your father put a heavy yoke on us and made us work hard. Loosen up the harsh labor and the heavy yoke he put on us, and we will serve you" (1 Kin 12:1-4).

Rehoboam replied: "Return in three days, and I will answer you." So the people left.

King Rehoboam consulted the elders, the older leaders, who had served his father Solomon when he was alive: "How do you advise me to answer these people?"

The elders replied: "If you will be a servant to these people and respond with compassion, they will always be your servants" (1 Kin 12:5-7).

But Rehoboam rejected the advice of the elders and asked the young men who had grown up with him: "What is your advice? How should we answer these people who are saying: `Lighten the yoke your father put on us'?"

The young men replied: "Tell these people: `My little finger is thicker than my father's waist. My father laid on you a heavy yoke; I will make it even heavier. My father beat you with whips; I will beat you with chains!'" (1 Kin 12:8-11).

Three days later Jeroboam and all the people returned to Rehoboam. The king followed the advice of the young men and answered the people with cruel words: "My father made your yoke heavy; I will make it even heavier. My father beat you with whips; I will beat you with chains!" The king refused to listen to the people. God caused this to happen in order to fulfill the prophecy spoken to Jeroboam through Ahijah (1 Kin 12:12-15).

When all Israel saw that the king refused to listen to them, they answered the king: "What do we have to do with David? To your tents, O Israel! Look after your own house, O David!"

So the Israelites went home. But Rehoboam continued to rule the Israelites who lived in the towns of Judah (1 Kin 12:16-17).

King Rehoboam sent out Adoniram, who was in charge of forced labor. The Israelites stoned him to death. King Rehoboam ran to his chariot and escaped to Jerusalem. Ten tribes of Israel remained in rebellion against the family of David (1 Kin 12:18-19).

The Israelites made Jeroboam king over all Israel (1 Kin 12:20).

When Rehoboam arrived in Jerusalem, he called up the men of the tribes of Judah and Benjamin, 180,000 fighting men, to make war against the house of Israel and to take back the kingdom for himself.

But the word of God came to Shemaiah to tell Rehoboam, along with everyone in Judah and Benjamin: "The Lord commands you not go up to war against your brothers, the Israelites. Go home, for this is my doing." They obeyed the Lord and returned to their homes (1 Kin 12:21-24).

Ten tribes rebelled against Rehoboam and followed Jeroboam. They called their new nation Israel or the Northern Kingdom. Its capital was Samaria.

Two tribes remained loyal to Rehoboam. Their kingdom was called Judah, or the Southern Kingdom. Its capital was Jerusalem. All the kings of Judah were descendants of David, while the kings of Israel were not.

Israel: Jeroboam Creates New Worship

Jeroboam thought: "The kingdom will probably go back to David's family. When these people go up to worship at the Temple of the Lord in Jerusalem, they will want to be ruled by Rehoboam king of Judah. They will kill me and go back to King Rehoboam."

After seeking advice, the king made two golden calves. He told the people: "It is too hard for you to go up to Jerusalem to worship. Here are your gods who brought you up out of Egypt." Jeroboam put one calf in Bethel, and the other in Dan. This was blatant sin.

Jeroboam built forbidden shrines on high places and recruited priests from all sorts of people. He created a new festival on the fifteenth day of the eighth month when he offered sacrifices on the altar he had built at Bethel. The Israelites went up to the altar to make offerings (1 Kin 12:25-33).

Judah: Many from Israel Flee to Judah

Priests and Levites throughout Israel sided with Rehoboam. The Levites abandoned their pastures and property, and moved to Judah and Jerusalem. Jeroboam had dismissed the Levites as priests of the Lord and appointed his own priests for worship centers where he installed goat and calf idols.

Everyone from all the tribes of Israel who set their hearts on seeking the Lord, the God of Israel, migrated with the Levites to Jerusalem. They strengthened the Kingdom of Judah. They supported Rehoboam for three years, during the time he was loyal to the ways of David and Solomon (2 Chr 11:13-17).

Israel: Prophecy against Jeroboam

Jeroboam was standing by the altar in Bethel to make an offering. A man of God, who had come from

Judah, cried out against the altar, pronouncing the Lord's words: "O altar, altar! The Lord says: `David's family will have a son named Josiah. Josiah will kill the priests of the high places who now make offerings here on you. Human bones will be burned on you. God gives this sign that these things will come to pass: the altar will be split apart and the ashes on it will fall onto the dirt.'"

King Jeroboam heard the man of God prophecy against the altar at Bethel. The king stretched out his arm, yelling: "Seize him!" But his arm became paralyzed and hung useless. At the same time, the altar broke apart and its ashes spilled into the dirt; the sign that the man of God had just given.

Then the king pleaded with the man of God: "Intercede for me! Pray to the Lord your God that my arm may be healed." The man of God prayed, and the king's arm was healed.

The king invited the man of God: "Come home and join me for a meal. I will give you a gift."

But the man of God answered the king: "Even if you were to give me half your kingdom, I will not go with you. I am here under the Lord's orders and he commanded: 'Do not eat bread. Do not drink water. Do not return by the way you came.'" The man of God took a different road than the one on which he had come to Bethel (1 Kin 13:1-10).

Now there was an old prophet living in Bethel. His sons told him the story of what the man of God had done in Bethel and what he had said to the king. Their father asked: "Which way did he go?" And his sons showed him which road the man of God had taken. The old prophet mounted a donkey and rode after the man of God. He found him sitting under an oak tree and asked: "Are you the man of God who came from Judah?"

The man replied: "I am."

The old prophet invited: "Come home with me and eat a meal."

The man of God replied: "I cannot go with you, nor can I eat bread or drink water with you. I was told by the Lord: `While you are in Israel, do not eat bread; do not drink water; do not return by the way you came.'"

The old prophet lied to the man of God: "I am a prophet, just like you. An angel came to me with a message from the Lord. He told me to bring you to my home so that you may eat bread and drink water. So the man of God returned with the old prophet and ate and drank in his house.

While they were sitting at the table, the Word of the Lord came to the old prophet. He cried out to the man of God from Judah: "You disobeyed the command the Lord your God gave you. You came back and ate bread and drank water in the place where God told you not to eat or drink. Therefore your body will not be buried in your family's grave" (1 Kin 13:11-22).

When the man of God finished eating, the old prophet saddled his donkey for him. The man of God went on his way, but a lion met him on the road and killed him. His body lay on the road, with both the donkey and the lion standing beside it. Some passers-by saw the body with the lion standing beside it. They reported the news in the city where the old prophet lived.

The old prophet heard what had happened and said: "It is the man of God who disobeyed the Lords' strict orders. The Lord sent a lion, which killed him, just as the Lord warned him."

The old prophet went and found the body on the road, with the donkey and the lion standing beside it. The lion had neither eaten the body nor hurt the donkey. So the prophet put the body of the man of God on the donkey, and brought it back to his own city to give him a decent burial. He placed the body in his own tomb, and they mourned over him.

After burying him, the old prophet told his sons: "When I die, bury me in the grave where the man of God is buried. For the message he declared by the Word of the Lord against the altar in Bethel and against all the sex-and-religion shrines in the towns of Samaria will come true" (1 Kin 13:23-32).

After this happened, Jeroboam kept right on doing evil, recruiting priests indiscriminately for the forbidden shrines. Anyone who wanted to become a priest, he consecrated for the local shrines. This was the root sin of Jeroboam's government. This was the sin that ruined him (1 Kin 13:33-34).

Jeroboam's son, Abijah, became sick. Jeroboam told his wife: "Disguise yourself, so you won't be recognized and go to Shiloh. Ahijah, the prophet who told me I would be king over this people, lives there. He will tell you what will happen to the boy." Jeroboam's wife went to Ahijah's house in Shiloh.

Now Ahijah was blind in his old age. The Lord advised Ahijah that Jeroboam's wife had disguised herself and was coming to ask about her sick son. When Ahijah heard the sound of her footsteps at the door, he said: "Come in, wife of Jeroboam. Why are you pretending to be someone else? Go, tell Jeroboam that the Lord, the God of Israel, says: `I raised you up from obscurity and made you a leader over my people Israel. I ripped the kingdom away from David's descendants and gave it to you. But you are not like my servant David, who kept my commands and followed me with all his heart. You have done more evil than anyone who ruled before you. You made other gods, idols of metal; you provoked me to anger and thrust me behind your back. Because of this, I am going to bring disaster on the family of Jeroboam. I will kill all the men in Jeroboam's family. The ones who die in the city will be eaten by stray dogs; the ones who die in the country will be eaten by birds!

"Go back home. When you set foot in your city, the boy will die. He is the only one of Jeroboam's family who will get a decent burial, because he is the only one in Jeroboam's family who pleases the Lord. The Lord will raise up a king over Israel who will wipe out Jeroboam's family. And the Lord will punish Israel. He will uproot Israel from this good land that he gave to their ancestors and scatter them to the four winds, because they provoked the Lord to anger by making Asherah sex-and-religion idols. He will give Israel up because Jeroboam sinned and caused the people of Israel to sin" (1 Kin 14:1-16).

Jeroboam's wife returned home. When she stepped through the door, the boy died. They buried him, and all Israel mourned for him, just as the Lord had said (1 Kin 14:17-18).

The other events of Jeroboam's reign, his wars, and how he ruled are written in the book of the history of the kings of Israel. He reigned for twenty-two years and then died. Nadab his son succeeded him as king (1 Kin 14:19-20).

Judah: Rehoboam

Rehoboam, son of Solomon, was 41 years old when he became king in Judah. He ruled for seventeen years in Jerusalem (1 Kin 14:21).

Rehoboam lived in Jerusalem and built up towns for defense in Judah. He strengthened their defenses and put commanders in them, with supplies of food, olive oil and wine. He put shields and spears in all the cities, and made them strong (2 Chr 11:5-12).

Rehoboam had 18 wives and 60 concubines, 28 sons and 60 daughters. Rehoboam appointed his son Abijah to be the chief prince among his brothers, in order to make him king. Rehoboam was shrewd in deploying his sons in all the fortress cities that made up his defense system in Judah and Benjamin (2 Chr 11:18-23).

By the time Rehoboam had secured his kingdom and was strong again, he and all Judah with him abandoned the law of the Lord. He did evil because he had not set his heart on seeking the Lord (2 Chr 12:1, 14). The people of Judah did what the Lord said was wrong. Their sins provoked the Lord's jealous anger more than their ancestors had done. They set up for themselves high places, sacred stones and Asherah poles (sex-and-religion idols) on high hills and under spreading trees. There were even male religious prostitutes in the places built to worship their gods. The people engaged in all the detestable practices of the nations the Lord had driven out before the Israelites (1 Kin 14:22-24).

Shishak was king of Egypt. He attacked Jerusalem in the fifth year that Rehoboam was king of Judah. He captured the fortified cities of Judah and came as far as Jerusalem.

Then the prophet Shemaiah came to Rehoboam and the leaders of Judah who had retreated to Jerusalem for fear of Shishak. The prophet told them: "The Lord says: `You abandoned me; therefore, I now abandon you to face Shishak alone.'"

The king and the leaders of Judah humbled themselves; they were sorry for what they had done and said: "The Lord is right."

The Lord saw that they were humbly repentant and the Word of the Lord came to Shemaiah: "Since they humbled themselves, I will not destroy them. My wrath will not be poured out on Jerusalem through Shishak. But, I will make them Shishak's subjects; they will learn the difference between serving me and serving kings of other nations" (2 Chr 12:2-8).

Shishak attacked Jerusalem and plundered the treasures of the Temple and the royal palace. He took the gold shields Solomon had made. King Rehoboam made bronze shields to replace the gold ones. Whenever the king went to the Lord's Temple, the guards carried the bronze shields (1 Kin 14:25-28).

Because Rehoboam was repentant and humbled himself, the Lord's anger turned from him, and he was not totally destroyed. There was some good in Judah (2 Chr 12:12).

Everything else King Rehoboam did is written in the book of the history of the kings of Judah. Rehoboam died and Abijah his son succeeded him as king (1 Kin 14:29-31).

Judah: Abijah; Asa

In the eighteenth year of the reign of Jeroboam in Israel, Abijah became king of Judah, and he reigned in Jerusalem three years.

Abijah continued to sin just like his father before him. His was not devoted to the Lord his God, as his ancestor David had been. However, for David's sake the Lord gave him a lamp in Jerusalem by raising up a son to succeed him and by making Jerusalem strong. For David had done what was right in the eyes of the Lord and had obeyed all the Lord's commands all the days of his life, except in the case of Uriah the Hittite.

There was war between Abijah and Jeroboam during Abijah's lifetime. The other events of Abijah's reign are written in the book of the history of the kings of Judah. And Abijah died and was buried in the City of David. Asa his son succeeded him as king (1 Kin 15:1-8).

In the twentieth year that Jeroboam was king of Israel, Asa became king of Judah. Asa reigned in Jerusalem forty-one years. His grandmother's name was Maacah (1 Kin 15:9-10).

Asa did what was right in the eyes of the Lord, as his ancestor David had done. He expelled the male shrine prostitutes from the land and got rid of all the idols made by his predecessors. He removed his grandmother Maacah from her position as queen mother, because she made a memorial to the whore goddess Asherah. Asa cut the idol pole down and burned it. Although he did not remove the sex-and-religion shrines, Asa's heart was committed to the Lord (1 Kin 15:11-15). He commanded Judah to seek the Lord, the God of their ancestors and to obey his commands (2 Chr 14:4).

King Zerah from Cush marched to fight Judah with a large army and 3,000 chariots. Asa went out to fight him, and they took up battle positions. Asa called to the Lord his God: "Lord, only you can help weak people against the mighty. Help us, O Lord our God; we fight this large army in your name, because we trust in you. O Lord, you are our God; do not let anyone defeat you."

The Lord defeated the Cushites before Asa and Judah. The Cushites fled, and Asa and his army pursued them (2 Chr 14:9-15).

The Spirit of God entered Azariah. He went to meet Asa and told him: "The Lord is with you when you are with him. If you seek him, he will be found by you; but if you forsake him, he will forsake you. Be strong and do not give up, for your good work will be rewarded."

When Asa heard the prophecy of Azariah, he took courage. He removed the detestable idols from the whole land of Judah and Benjamin and from the towns he had captured. He repaired the altar of the Lord that was in front of the Temple porch. Then he assembled all Judah and Benjamin and the people from other tribes of Israel who had settled among them. Many from Israel had left their homes and joined Asa when they saw that the Lord God was with him.

They assembled at Jerusalem in the fifteenth year of Asa's reign. They sacrificed to the Lord 700 cattle and 7,000 sheep and goats from the plunder they had brought back. They entered into a covenant to seek the Lord, the God of their ancestors, with all their heart and soul. All Judah rejoiced about the oath. They sought God eagerly, and he was found by them. The Lord gave them rest from war. There was no more war until the thirty-fifth year of Asa's reign (2 Chr 15:1-19).

Meanwhile in Israel, King Jeroboam died and his son Nadab became king. But Nadab was assassinated by Baasha, who became king of Israel.

There was war between Asa and Baasha king of Israel. Baasha attacked Judah by building a fort at Ramah and closing the border between Israel and Judah, so no one could enter or leave Judah.

Asa then took all the silver and gold that was left in the treasuries of the Lord's temple and of his own palace, and sent them to Ben-Hadad, the king of Aram, who was ruling in Damascus. He sent a message to King Ben-Hadad: "Let there be a treaty between me and you. I am sending you a gift of silver and gold. Now break your treaty with Baasha king of Israel so he will quit fighting against me."

Ben-Hadad agreed with King Asa and sent his troops to fight against the towns of Israel. Then Baasha stopped building Ramah and withdrew to Tirzah. Then King Asa issued an order to everyone in Judah, and they carried away from Ramah the stones and timber Baasha had been using there. With the stones and timber, King Asa fortified cities in Judah (1 Kin 15:16-22; 2 Chr 16:1-6).

Hanani the prophet went to Asa king of Judah and told him: "Because you relied on the king of Aram and not on the Lord your God, you have lost a victory over the army of the king of Aram. The Cushites and Libyans were a mighty army. Yet when you relied on the Lord, he delivered them into your hand. God is constantly on the lookout for people who are fully committed to him. He gives them victory. You have done a foolish thing; from now on you will be at war."

Asa lost his temper with the prophet Hanani and put him in prison. At the same time, Asa started being cruel to some of the people (2 Chr 16:7-10).

Asa was afflicted with a severe disease in his feet in the thirty-ninth year of his reign. He did not seek help from the Lord; he only sought help from the doctors. In the forty-first year of his reign, Asa died and was buried in the tomb that he had cut out for himself in the City of David. Jehoshaphat his son succeeded him as king (2 Chr 16:11-14; 1 Kin 15:23-24).

Israel: Nadab; Baasha
Nadab son of Jeroboam became king of Israel in the second year of Asa king of Judah. Nadab was king over Israel for two years. He did evil in the eyes of the Lord, following in the footsteps of his father, who both sinned and caused Israel to sin (1 Kin 15:25-26).

Baasha killed Nadab, king of Israel, and succeeded him as king. Baasha was king of Israel for twenty-four years. Baasha killed Jeroboam's whole family, just as the Lord's servant Ahijah had prophesied. This happened as punishment for Jeroboam, who sinned and caused Israel to sin. His sins provoked the Lord, the God of Israel, to anger (1 Kin 15:27-32).

Baasha did evil in the eyes of the Lord, walking in the footsteps of Jeroboam, who both sinned and caused Israel to sin (1 Kin 15:33-34).

Then the Word of the Lord came to Jehu for Baasha:"I lifted you up from being a nobody and made you leader of my people Israel, but you followed the footsteps of Jeroboam and caused my people Israel to sin. You provoke me to anger by their sins. So I am about to give you the identical fate of Jeroboam. All members of the family of Baasha will be killed. Stray dogs will eat those belonging to Baasha who die in the city, and birds will feed on those who die in the country" (1 Kin 16:1-4).

The other events of Baasha's reign are written in the book of the history of the kings of Israel. Baasha died and was buried in Tirzah. Elah his son succeeded him as king (1 Kin 16:5-7).

Israel: Elah; Zimri; Omri
Elah son of Baasha became king of Israel, and he reigned in Tirzah two years. One day when Elah was getting drunk, one of his officials named Zimri killed him and became king of Israel.

Zimri killed all of Baasha's family, just as the Lord said would happen through the prophet Jehu. Baasha and his son Elah sinned and caused Israel to sin. They provoked the Lord God of Israel to anger. because they made worthless idols.

The other events of Elah's reign, and all he did are written in the book of the history of the kings of

Israel (1 Kin 16:8-14).

Zimri was king for seven days. The Israelites' army proclaimed Omri, the commander of the army, king over Israel. Zimri then went into the citadel of the royal palace and set the palace on fire. He died because of the sins he had committed following in the footsteps of Jeroboam (1 Kin 16:15-20).

Omri became king of Israel in the thirty-first year that Asa was king of Judah. Omri was king for twelve years, six of them in Tirzah. He built a city on a hill, calling it Samaria.

But Omri did evil in the eyes of the Lord and sinned more than the kings who were before him. He followed the footsteps of Jeroboam who sinned and caused Israel to sin, provoking the Lord God to anger by worshiping worthless idols.

The other events of Omri's reign are written in the book of the history of the kings of Israel. Omri died and was buried in Samaria. Ahab his son succeeded him as king (1 Kin 16:21-28).

LIFE-LESSONS DISCOVERED IN THE STORY

1. Following bad advice may result in disaster. Rehoboam followed the advice of his peers and his kingdom was divided (1 Kin 12:8-17). Jeroboam sought the counsel of men who advised him to make golden calves. This sin resulted in the destruction of his family and nation (1 Kin 12:28; 14:9-11).

2. It is a narrow-minded person who only follows the advice of his peers. A peer group usually thinks alike. It is important to seek advice from those outside of one's peer group, who have more knowledge and experience. Rehoboam rejected the advice of Solomon's older counselors, preferring the advice of his peers (1 Kin 12:8-17).

3. The selfish person who constantly wants more, may wind up with little or nothing. Rehoboam had inherited the richest kingdom in the world, but, motivated by greed, he pressed for more and lost most of his kingdom (1 Kin 12:8-17).

4. False religions have their origin in human beings. The false religion of Jeroboam originated with his own thoughts (1 Kin 12:26) and was motivated by his selfish desires (1 Kin 12:27).

5. False religions provoke their followers to rebel against the Lord God. Jeroboam presented his invented religion as being advantageous for the people (1 Kin 12:28). However, his religion was a sin against the Lord (1 Kin 12:30; Ex 20:4) and people with low standards became spiritual leaders in his religion (1 Kin 12:31; 13:33).

6. Those who violate the Lord's commands are able to give positive rationalization for their actions; however, the results are negative and destructive. Jeroboam's intentions were political when he built the local shrines. He did not intend to substitute the Lord God for other gods (1 Kin 12:25-33). Jeroboam replaced the Ark of God, that symbolized the presence of God with a golden calf. However, the golden calf was used by others as an idol for the god Baal. The golden calf opened the door for compromising the worship of the Lord God with worship to Baal. (See Hos 13:1-2.) In making the golden calves, Jeroboam sinned and caused Israel to sin.

7. Using idols in worship results in worshiping false gods. The golden calves that Jeroboam made to use in the worship of God (1 Kin 12:25-33) could not represent God and became false gods that provoked the Lord to anger (1 Kin 14:9).

8. In order to seek the Lord, a person may need to suffer financial loss. Priests and Levites throughout Israel abandoned their property and migrated to Jerusalem to offer sacrifices to the Lord God (2 Chr 11:13-17).

9. Many of the faithful messengers of the Lord are never well-known; the important thing is to proclaim the Lord's message and be faithful to him. The Bible does not give the name of the man of God who prophesied against the altar of Jeroboam (1 Kin 13:1-10).

10. Those who serve the Lord may be caught unaware when temptation comes from someone who is respected within the family of God. The man of God immediately resisted temptation when it came from Jeroboam. However, the old prophet easily led him to disobey the Lord (1 Kin 13:7-22).

11. A person who is trusted needs to be cautious lest he use his influence to lead others to do wrong. The man of God trusted the old prophet who led him to disobey the Lord (1 Kin 13:7-22).

12. Disregard the person who claims to have a message from God that contradicts God's Word. The man of God died because he disobeyed the Lord by listening to an old prophet who claimed to have a message from God (1Kg 13:15-24).

13. When those who know the Lord and serve him become selfish, they may tempt others to do wrong. The old prophet of God selfishly wanted fellowship with the man of God, and his lies tempted the man of God (1 Kin 13:14-22).

14. Often, punishment in this life comes as the result of the guilty person being turned over to the evil forces that exist in this world. Ahijah

prophesied the destruction of Jeroboam's family (1 Kin 14:1-16). Baasha destroyed Jeroboam's family for political reasons, unaware that he was fulfilling the Lord's prophecy (1 Kin 15:25-31).

15. Punishment for rejecting God's revelation comes when a person believes false teachings; punishment for believing false teachings comes when a person practices immoral behavior accepted by the false religion. Passions for immorality stimulate a mental disposition to reject virtue and accept sin. The result is living in darkness, both in the present world and in eternity. (See Romans 1:18-32.)

16. The worst sinners are those who lead others to do wrong. Jeroboam sinned and caused Israel to sin (1 Kin 14:9, 16; 15:30). Jesus said it would be better for those who teach others to sin to have a millstone tied around their neck and be thrown into the sea (Mk 9:42).

17. Often it is more difficult to serve God in good times than in bad. During the first three years on the throne, Rehoboam was recovering from losing his kingdom and tried to serve the Lord. But when he became strong, he abandoned God (2 Chr 12:1-2). When Shishak of Egypt attacked Jerusalem, Rehoboam humbled himself and admitted his guilt (2 Chr 12:2-8).

18. It is a superficial person who settles for a cheap imitation in exchange for the real thing. Shishak attacked Jerusalem and took the gold shields. Rehoboam replaced the pure gold shields with bronze ones (1 Kin 14:25-28).

19. Anyone is qualified to represent a god that is worthless. To represent the Lord God Almighty; however, a person must live by God's standards, not man's. Jeroboam built forbidden shrines and recruited priests from all sorts of people (1 Kin 12:25-33). Jeroboam kept on indiscriminately recruiting priests for the forbidden shrines. Anyone who wanted to become a priest, Jeroboam consecrated for the local shrines (1 Kin 13:33-34).

20. The person who refuses to hear God's message, risks having his heart hardened against the Lord. Jeroboam followed the example of Pharaoh of Egypt (1 Kin 13:1-6; 33). The more signs the Lord gave, the less each repented and the more he hardened his heart against God (Ex 7:22; 8:15; 1 Kin 13:33).

21. The person who persists in the practice of evil will suffer God's judgment and punishment, and risks harming his own family. That is what happened to Jeroboam and his family. Jeroboam persisted in idolatry and in evil. This resulted in God's judgment against him and his family (1 Kin 13:34).

22. The worst sins are manifested in false religions. The false religion of Judah made idols and sheltered sex-and-religion prostitute-worship. Prostitution and homosexuality were practiced as part of those pagan cults (1 Kin 14:23-24).

23. A leader's sins makes it socially accepted for the people to sin. The idolatry of Jeroboam and of Rehoboam gave occasion for their people to practice idolatry.

24. Children whose parents are rebellious against God can faithfully serve the Lord. Asa is an example. The heart of Asa was totally committed to the Lord (1 Kin 15:14). Asa's reign was a time of powerful religious reform (1 Kin 15:12-15). However, Asa's father Abijah committed serious sins, following in the footsteps of Asa's grandfather Rehoboam (1 Kin 15:3). Asa's grandmother worshiped the whore-goddess Asherah (1 Kin 15:13).

25. God commands us to honor our parents; however, maintaining loyalty to God is an even higher priority. Asa removed his grandmother from the position of queen-mother because of her idol worship (1 Kin 15:13).

26. The person who is faithful to God may be required to break off fellowship with family members who reject the Lord. King Asa did what was right in the eyes of the Lord. He even removed his grandmother from her position as queen mother, because she made an idol to the god Asherah. He cut down and burned his grandmother's idol (1 Kin 15:9-15).

27. Serving the Lord requires both addition and subtraction. A person must do what is right and also remove what is offensive to God. King Asa did what was right in the eyes of the Lord and he removed idol worship from Judah. He commanded Judah to seek the Lord and he removed sex-and-religion places from the land (1 Kin 15:11-15; 2 Chr 14:2-6; 15:1-19).

28. The person who does not learn from other people's wrongdoings will repeat their mistakes. God destroyed Jeroboam's descendants for their sins; yet, Baasha repeated the same sins (1 Kin 16:1-7).

29. God's power works best through those who recognize their limitations. The secret for victory is: admit your inability to win and then trust God as you go into battle. Asa went out to fight King Zerah who had superior forces. Asa confessed that only the Lord could help weak people fight against the mighty, and that he was fighting the large army in God's name. The Lord defeated the Cushites before Asa and Judah (2 Chr 14:9-15). (See 2 Cor 12:9.)

30. God is seeking people who are committed to him. The prophet Azariah told Asa that if he sought the Lord, the Lord would be found (2 Chr 15:2). The people of Judah sought God and he was found by them (2 Chr 15:15). Hanani the prophet told Asa that the Lord seeks those who are committed to him (2 Chr 16:9).

31. A person cannot fight against God and win. Jeroboam thought he could fight against the Lord; however, he and his family were punished by God (1 Kin 15:25-31). All of the kings of Israel fought against the Lord and were punished by him.

32. Plans that produce the desired results may be disapproved by God. Asa came up with a brilliant plan to win a conflict with his enemy Baasha. He bribed King Ben-Hadad to break his alliance with Baasha. The plan worked; however, the Lord sent his prophet Hanani to condemn Asa's wrongdoing (2 Chr 16:1-9).

33. God always has a message for those who are leaders. The kings of Israel disobeyed the Lord's commands; however, God always sent messengers with a divine word for them. He also sent messengers to the kings of Judah.

34. Years of faithfulness to God will come to an end if a person rejects what God says in a specific situation. Asa faithfully served the Lord for 36 years. In the 36th year of his reign, Asa relied on the king of Aram and not on the Lord God during a war. The prophet Hanani brought Asa the Lord's Word reprimanding him. Asa put Hanani in prison and started being cruel to some of the people (2 Chr 16:7-10). When Asa was afflicted with a severe disease in the 39th year of his reign, he did not seek help from the Lord; he only sought help from doctors (2 Chr 16:11-14; 1 Kin 15:23-24).

35. God is sovereign. Even when evil men are in power, God knows what is happening and he stays in control.

36. It is a false assumption that all religions are good and that all religions take their faithful followers to God. It is not enough to have a religion; it is not enough to be sincere in one's religion. It is necessary to have the correct religion, the religion of the One True God who reveals himself to people. The story of this One True God is found in the Bible.

37. Combining religion with politics takes both down to decadence. When religion and politics walked hand in hand in Israel and Judah, the priests accepted an idolatrous religion (false gods), immorality (homosexual-priests and prostitute-priestesses) and sacrilegious actions (with mercenary and unmerciful leaders who even made human sacrifices).

38. The prophet is unfaithful to God if he only prophesies the good or only the evil. The prophet's message is the message from God and it is in agreement with the need of those who receive it.

QUESTIONS

1. The twelve tribes of Israel had been united in one kingdom. What happened to divide the kingdom?
2. How was King Rehoboam harmed by listening to unwise advice?
3. When you have to make an important decision, to whom do you turn for advice?
4. How were the two kingdoms similar? How were they different?
5. Who was the first king of Judah and who was the first king of Israel?
6. Which of the kingdoms had only kings who sinned and who caused their people to sin?
7. How did the old prophet lead the man of God to disobey the Lord?
8. What happened to the man of God who listened to the lies of the old prophet?
9. The kings of Israel caused the people of Israel to sin. The old prophet caused the man of God to disobey the Lord. Who has the ability to influence you to do wrong?
10. Why did Jeroboam introduce idiolatry into Israel?
11. How was Asa different from the kings of Judah who preceded him?
12. What were some of the consequences of worshiping false gods and of practicing idolatry?
13. What were some of the messages the prophets gave the kings?
14. What can the kings of both Judah and Israel teach us about the danger of having evil political leaders?

AHAB, A KING WHO FOUGHT THE LORD
ELIJAH, A PROPHET WHO FOUGHT FOR THE LORD
Divided Kingdom
1 Kings 16:29 - 22:40; 2 Kings 9:30 - 10:17

STRUCTURE

Context:
The book of 1 Kings covers about 120 years of history, beginning with Solomon's reign over the United Kingdom in 971 B.C., until 852 B.C. At that time, the Kingdom was divided, and Jehoshaphat was king of Judah, and Ahaziah was king of Israel. The book registers the history of the rebellion of the ten tribes of Israel against King Rehoboam, David's grandson, and how all the kings of Israel rejected the covenant with God.

1 Kings also registers how some of the kings of Judah imitated David and served the Lord, but most rejected the covenant with God.

1 Kings makes it clear that rejecting God's covenant is a sinful and rebellious action that results in divine judgment. While the kings rejected the covenant with God, the Lord constantly sent prophets who were his spokesmen.

Key-persons: Elijah, Ahab and Jezebel

Key-locations: Samaria, Jezreel and Jerusalem

Key-repetitions:
■Ahab's sins: He married Jezebel, served Baal and built a temple for Baal (1 Kin 16:29-34); let Ben-Hadad live when God had determined he should die (1 Kin 20:1-43); permitted the murder of Naboth (1 Kin 21:1-16).
■Miracles related to Elijah: predicted a prolonged drought (1 Kin 17:1); fed by ravens (1 Kin 17:3-6); a handful of flour and a little olive oil continued to feed Elijah, a widow and her son (17:8-16); brought a boy back to life (17:17-24); fire came from God on Mount Carmel (1 Kin 18:20-40); it rained in answer to his prayer (1 Kin 18:41-46); an angel fed him and he traveled 40 days and nights without eating (1 Kin 19:5-9); fire from heaven killed soldiers (2 Kin 1:9-14) he is taken to heaven (2 Kin 2:1-18).
■Ahab considered Elijah a troublemaker and his enemy (1 Kin 18:17-18; 21:17-29).
■Prophets spoke the Lord's words: Elijah (1 Kin 17:1; 18:1-40; 21:17-24); a prophet (1 Kin 20:35-43); Micaiah (1 Kin 22:1-23); Jehu (2 Chr 19:1-3); Jahaziel (2 Chr 20:14-17); Eliezer (2 Chr 20:37).
■The Word of the Lord (1Kg 17:1, 8, 16; 18:1, 31; 19:9; 20:35; 21:17, 28; 22:19, 38; 2 Kin 1:17; 9:26, 36).

Key-attitudes:
■The evilness of Ahab and Jezebel.
■Ahab sulking, upset and angry.
■The courage, solitude and depression of Elijah.
■Conflict between: Ahab and Elijah; Elijah and the prophets of Baal; Ahab and Ben-Hadad.
■Jehoshaphat's dedication to the Lord.

Initial-problem:
Ahab did more evil than any of the kings before him.

Sequence of events:
Israel: Elijah During the Drought
■Ahab did more to provoke the Lord God to anger than the previous kings of Israel (1 Kin 16:29-33).
■Elijah prophesied total drought. He hid at the Kerith Ravine where ravens fed him and he drank water from the brook (1 Kin 17:1-6).
■When the brook dried up, the Lord sent him to Zarephath in Sidon where a widow with only a handful of flour and a little oil was able to feed Elijah, her son and herself (1 Kin 17:7-16).
■The widow's son died. Elijah prayed, and the Lord brought the boy back to life (1 Kin 17:17-24).

Israel: Elijah on Mount Carmel
■The Lord sent Elijah to find Ahab. Elijah met Obadiah, who brought Ahab to Elijah. Ahab called Elijah the "troublemaker of Israel." Elijah accused Ahab of being the troublemaker and told him to assemble the Israelites at Mount Carmel and to bring the 450 prophets of Baal and the 400 prophets of Asherah (1 Kin 18:1-19).
■At Mount Carmel, Elijah challenged the people: "How long will you try to serve both Baal and the Lord?" Nobody said a word (1 Kin 18:20-21).
■Elijah challenged the 450 prophets of Baal to prepare an altar and a bull, and he would do the same. Each would pray to his god, and the god who answered by fire, he would be God. The people agreed (1 Kin 18:22-24).
■Baal's prophets prepared a bull and called on Baal, but nothing happened. Elijah taunted them. They continued until time for the evening sacrifice, but nothing happened (1 Kin 18:25-29).
■With 12 stones Elijah built an altar in honor of the Lord and dug a ditch around it. He put wood on the altar and laid the butchered bull on top. Then three times he ordered for the offering and the wood to be drenched with water. Elijah went near the altar and prayed. Immediately fire from the Lord fell (1 Kin 18:30-38).
■The people exclaimed: "The Lord, he is God!" (1 Kin 18:39).
■Elijah killed the prophets of Baal (1 Kin 18:40).
■Elijah told Ahab rain was coming. Elijah repeatedly prayed; told his servant to look toward

the sea; but the servant didn't see anything. The 7th time the servant saw a cloud no bigger than a man's hand. Elijah ordered Ahab to get down from the mountain before rain stopped him. Elijah ran in front of Ahab's chariot until they reached Jezreel (1 Kin 18:41-46).

Israel: Elijah on Mount Horeb
■Jezebel sent a messenger threatening to kill Elijah (1 Kin 19:1-2).
■Elijah was terrified and fled into the wilderness. He collapsed and prayed to die. Exhausted, he fell asleep. Twice, an angel brought him food. The food enabled him to walk for 40 days and nights until he reached Horeb. Elijah entered a cave and slept (1 Kin 19:1-9).
■The Lord asked Elijah why he was there. Elijah answered that he alone had been zealous for the Lord and they were trying to kill him. First came a wind, then an earthquake, then a fire, but the Lord was not in them. Then came a gentle whisper. The Lord ordered Elijah to go back through the Wilderness of Damascus and to anoint Hazael king over Aram, Jehu king over Israel, and Elisha to succeed him as prophet. The Lord told Elijah that he had 7,000 in Israel who had never bowed to Baal nor kissed his image (1 Kin 19:10-18).
■Elijah found Elisha plowing with oxen and threw his cloak around him. Elisha told his parents goodbye, slaughtered his oxen, burned the plowing equipment; then he followed Elijah (1 Kin 19:19-21).

Judah: Jehoshaphat
(when Ahab was king of Israel)
■Jehoshaphat became king of Judah and imitated the life of his father Asa. He did what was right. He was at peace with the king of Israel (1Kg 22:41-50).

Israel: War Between Ahab and Ben-hadad
■Ben-Hadad king of Aram allied himself with 32 kings and surrounded Samaria. A prophet promised Ahab that the Lord would defeat the vast army and Ahab would know that he was the Lord. Ahab defeated the Aramean army (1 Kin 20:1-21).
■The prophet warned Ahab that Ben-Hadad would attack again the following spring. Ben-Hadad's advisors told him that the gods of Israel were mountain gods. Ben-Hadad went to fight against Israel on the plains. A man of God told Ahab that the Lord would deliver the vast army into his hands, and he would know that he was the Lord. The Israelites killed 100,000 Aramean soldiers in one day. The rest of the army escaped to the city where the city wall collapsed on 27,000 of them. Ben-Hadad fled to the city and hid in a closet. Ahab made a peace treaty with Ben-Hadad and let him go free (1 Kin 20:23-34).
■A prophet told Ahab that since he had freed a man, the Lord had sentenced to die. It would be Ahab's life for Ben-Hadad's life. Ahab returned to his palace angry (1 Kin 20:35-43).

Israel: Naboth's Vineyard
■Ahab asked Naboth to sell him his vineyard that bordered Ahab's palace. Naboth refused. Ahab sulked and refused to eat (1 Kin 21:1-4).
■Jezebel promised Ahab she would get the vineyard for him. She wrote letters to the leaders who lived in Naboth's city with orders to stone him. Ahab went to take possession of Naboth's vineyard (1 Kin 21:5-16).
■Elijah found Ahab in Naboth's vineyard and told him that on the spot where the dogs lapped up Naboth's blood, dogs would lap up his blood; that the Lord would kill every male in Ahab's family; that dogs would devour Jezebel's flesh; and that dogs would eat the descendants of Ahab who died in the city, and buzzards would eat those who died in the country (1 Kin 21:1-26).
■Ahab humbled himself. The Lord told Elijah that because Ahab humbled himself, the disaster would not come during his lifetime, but on his son (1 Kin 21:27-28).

Israel: Ahab Killed
■Jehoshaphat visited Ahab. Ahab asked him to join in fighting the king of Aram to take back Ramoth Gilead. Jehoshaphat agreed but wanted guidance from the Lord. Ahab's 400 prophets predicted victory. Jehoshaphat asked if there were not a prophet of the Lord. Ahab sent for Micaiah. Zedekiah made iron horns and prophesied that Ahab would use those horns to gore the Arameans (1 Kin 22:1-13).
■Micaiah said that a lying spirit was speaking through Ahab's prophets to trick him so he would fight the king of Aram and be killed. Zedekiah punched Micaiah in the face. Ahab ordered for Micaiah to be put into prison (1Kg 22:14-28).
■Ahab disguised himself and went into battle. A soldier shot an arrow without aiming and hit Ahab. Ahab's blood pooled on the chariot floor. That evening he died. The king was buried in Samaria. They washed the chariot, and the dogs lapped up his blood. Things happened just as the Lord had promised (1 Kin 22:29-40).
■Ahaziah succeeded his father Ahab as king. Ahaziah ruled for two years, copying the evil example of his father (1 Kin 22:51-53). Ahaziah fell off the rooftop and died from his injuries. Ahaziah's brother, Joram, became the next king of Israel (2 Kin 1:1-18).

Judah: Jehoshaphat
(after the death of Ahab, king of Israel)
■Jehoshaphat returned safely to Jerusalem. Jehu the prophet criticized him because of his friendship with Ahab (2 Chr 19:1-3).
■Jehoshaphat appointed judges and told them that they were judging for the Lord (2 Chr 19:5-10).
■A vast army joined forces to make war against Jehoshaphat. Jehoshaphat called the people to seek the Lord. Jehoshaphat prayed, committing the situation to the Lord and acknowledging that only God could save the nation (2 Chr 20:1-13).
■The Lord spoke through Jahaziel saying that it was the Lord's battle, not theirs. They were to watch the Lord deliver them (2 Chr 20:14-17).
■Jehoshaphat and the people of Judah worshiped. The next morning, men marched in front of the army

singing praises to the Lord. The Lord set ambushes against the men who were invading Judah, and they mistakenly attacked their allies and destroyed one another. The men of Judah arrived and saw only dead bodies. Jehoshaphat and his men took three days to carry off their plunder. On the fourth day they assembled and praised the Lord. They returned rejoicing to Jerusalem and went to the Temple of the Lord (2 Chr 20:18-30).

- Later, Jehoshaphat made an alliance with Ahaziah to build ocean-going ships. But the Lord destroyed what they had built (Chr 20:35-37).
- Jehoshaphat was 35 years old when he became king of Judah, and he reigned 25 years. He did what was right (2 Chr 20:31-33). Jehoshaphat died, and his son Jehoram succeeded him as king (2 Chr 21:1).

Israel: Ahab's Family Punished

- Years later, the prophet Elisha had replaced Elijah. Elisha ordered a prophet to go to Ramoth Gilead and anoint Jehu king of Israel. The prophet anointed Jehu, told him that he was to destroy the house of Ahab and predicted that dogs would eat Jezebel (2 Kin 9:1-10).
- Jehu told his fellow officers what the prophet had said. The officers blew the trumpet and shouted: "Jehu is king!" (2 Kin 9:11-13).
- Jehu rode to Jezreel where Joram was recovering from injuries. King Ahaziah of Judah was visiting him. Joram and Ahaziah rode out, each in his own chariot. They met Jehu at the plot of ground that had belonged to Naboth. Jehu shot an arrow into Joram and ordered for his body to be thrown on the land that had been Naboth's. He also killed Ahaziah (2 Kin 9:14-29).
- Jehu went to Jezreel where Jezebel was posed at a window. Eunuchs threw her down, and horses ran over her body. Jehu went inside and ate. Then he ordered his men to bury Jezebel, but the men found nothing except her skull, feet and hands. Jehu said that things happened as the Lord promised through Elijah (2 Kin 9:30-37).
- Ahab's family had 70 sons living in Samaria. The leaders of the city killed all 70 of them, put their heads in baskets and sent them to Jehu. Jehu killed everyone who had any connection with Ahab. It happened just as the Lord had promised through Elijah (2 Kin 10:1-17).

Final-situation:

Ahab, his wife Jezebel, and all their male decedants were killed, just as the Lord had promised through his prophet Elijah.

BIBLE STORY

Israel: Elijah During the Drought

Ahab son of Omri became king of Israel during Asa's 38th year as king of Judah. Ahab reigned in Samaria for 22 years. Ahab did more evil than any of the kings before him. He copied the sins of Jeroboam. But he did worse things. He married Jezebel, daughter of the king of Sidon. He served Baal and built a temple for worshiping Baal in Samaria. Ahab made an idol to the sacred prostitute Asherah. He did more to provoke the Lord God to anger than did all the previous kings of Israel (1 Kin 16:29-33).

Elijah the Tishbite confronted Ahab: "As surely as the Lord lives, the God of Israel whom I serve, there will be total drought; no dew nor rain for the next few years until I say otherwise."

Then the Word of the Lord came to Elijah: "Get out of here, and hide in the Kerith Ravine, east of the Jordan River. You will drink from the brook. I have commanded ravens to feed you there."

Elijah obeyed the Lord and went and stayed at the Kerith Ravine. Ravens brought him bread and meat for both breakfast and supper. He drank water from the brook (1 Kin 17:1-6).

Eventually, the brook dried up because of the drought. Then the Word of the Lord came to Elijah: "Go to Zarephath in Sidon and live there. I have instructed a widow there to feed you." Elijah arrived at the town gate at Zarephath and saw a widow gathering sticks. Elijah asked her: "Bring me water to drink and please bring me a piece of bread."

The widow replied: "As surely as the Lord your God lives, I have no bread. I have a handful of flour in a jar and a little oil in a jug. I am gathering a few sticks to take home and cook a last meal for myself and my son. After we eat it, we will die."

Elijah told her: "Cook a small loaf of bread and bring it to me, and then make something for yourself and your son. For the Lord, the God of Israel, says: `The jar of flour will not become empty nor will the jug of oil run dry until the day the Lord sends rain and ends this drought.'"

The widow obeyed Elijah. There was food every day for Elijah, the woman and her family. The jar of flour and the jug of oil never ran out (1 Kin 17:7-16).

Time passed and the widow's son became sick. He grew worse and finally stopped breathing. The widow asked Elijah: "Man of God, what have you done to me? Did you come to expose my sin and kill my son?"

Elijah replied: "Give me your son." He took the boy from her arms, carried him to the loft where he was staying, and laid him on his bed. Then he prayed: "O Lord my God, this widow opened her home to me. Why have you brought tragedy upon her by causing her son to die?" Then three times he stretched himself full-length on the boy and cried to the Lord: "O Lord my God, let this boy's life return to him!"

The Lord answered Elijah's prayer, and the boy began breathing again. Elijah took the child to his mother and said: "Look! Your son is alive!"

The widow replied: "I know you are a man of God

and that when you speak, the Lord truly speaks through you" (1 Kin 17:17-24).

Israel: Elijah on Mount Carmel

Three years after Elijah had prophesied the drought, the Word of the Lord came to Elijah: "Go present yourself to Ahab, and I will send rain on the land." Elijah went to find Ahab.

The drought was severe in Samaria. Ahab summoned Obadiah, who was in charge of his palace. Obadiah was a true servant of the Lord. When Jezebel tried to kill all the Lord's prophets, Obadiah hid a hundred prophets in two caves and supplied them with food and water. Ahab ordered Obadiah: "Go through the land and locate all the springs and streams. Maybe we can find enough grass to keep the horses and mules alive." Ahab went one direction and Obadiah the other.

Elijah met Obadiah and told him: "Go tell your master: `Elijah is here.'"

Obadiah brought Ahab to Elijah. Ahab saw Elijah and said: "So it is you, you troublemaker of Israel?"

Elijah replied: "I have not caused trouble for Israel. But you and your father's family have. You abandoned the Lord's commands and now follow the Baals. Now assemble everyone in Israel at Mount Carmel. And bring the prophets who eat at Jezebel's table, the 450 prophets of Baal and the 400 prophets of the prostitute goddess Asherah" (1 Kin 18:1-19).

Ahab summoned everyone in Israel, especially the prophets, to Mount Carmel. Elijah challenged the people: "How long will you try to serve both Baal and the Lord? If the Lord is God, follow him; but if Baal is God, follow him."

Nobody said a word.

Elijah spoke: "I am the only prophet of the Lord's prophets left in Israel; but Baal has 450 prophets. Get two bulls for us. Let the Baal prophets butcher one bull and lay it on the wood, but not set fire to it. I will prepare the other bull and put it on the wood, but not set fire to it. Then you pray to your god, and I will pray to the Lord. The god who answers by fire, he is God."

The people agreed: "You have a good plan, do it!"

Baal's prophets took one of the bulls and prepared it. They called on Baal from morning till noon: "O Baal, answer us!" But nothing happened. Desperately, they danced around the altar they had made.

At noon Elijah began to taunt them: "Shout louder! He is a god! Perhaps he is off meditating, or busy, or traveling. Maybe he is sleeping and needs be awakened." Baal's prophets shouted louder and slashed themselves with swords and spears until their blood flowed. They tried every religious trick they knew until the time for the evening sacrifice. But nothing happened.

Then Elijah called the people to approach him. Elijah rebuilt the altar of the Lord, which was in ruins. Elijah took twelve stones, one stone for each of the tribes descended from Jacob. With the stones he built an altar in honor of the Lord, and he dug a ditch around it. He arranged the wood, butchered the bull and laid it on the wood. Then he ordered: "Fill four large jars with water and drench both the offering and the wood."

Elijah ordered: "Do it again," and they did it a second time. Then he ordered: "Do it a third time," and they did it a third time. The water ran down around the altar and filled the ditch.

At the time for the evening sacrifice, Elijah went near the altar and prayed: "O Lord, God of Abraham, Isaac and Israel, show these people that you are God in Israel, that I am your servant and have done all these things at your command. Answer me, O Lord, answer me, and reveal to these people that you, O Lord, are God, and that you are giving these people another chance at repentance."

Immediately fire from the Lord fell and burned up the sacrifice, the wood, the stones the soil, and even the water in the ditch.

The people saw it happen, they fell on their faces exclaiming: "The Lord, he is God! The Lord, he is God!"

Elijah commanded: "Seize the prophets of Baal. Don't let anyone get away!" The people seized them, and Elijah killed them (1 Kin 18:20-40).

Elijah told Ahab: "Celebrate! Eat and drink, for I hear the sound of a heavy rain." Ahab went off to eat and drink. Elijah climbed to the top of Carmel, bowed in prayer, with his face between his knees.

Elijah told his servant: "Look toward the sea."

The servant looked and said: "I see nothing there."

Seven times Elijah said: "Go back."

The seventh time the servant reported: "A small cloud no bigger than a man's hand is rising from the sea."

Elijah ordered his servant to tell Ahab: "Hitch up your chariot and get down from the mountain before the rain stops you."

The sky grew black with clouds, a heavy rain began to fall and Ahab rode off to Jezreel. The power of the Lord strengthened Elijah and, tucking his robe into his belt, he ran in front of Ahab's chariot until they reached Jezreel (1 Kin 18:41-46).

Israel: Elijah on Mount Horeb

Ahab told Jezebel everything Elijah had done. He told her how Elijah had massacred all the prophets. Jezebel sent a messenger to Elijah: "May the gods punish me, if by this time tomorrow I do not make you as dead as those prophets" (1 Kin 19:1-2).

Elijah was terrified and ran for his life. He left his servant and went by himself a day's journey into the wilderness. He came to a broom bush, collapsed in its shade and prayed to die: "Enough of this, Lord. Take my life!" Exhausted, he fell asleep under the lone broom bush.

An angel touched Elijah and said: "Get up and eat." By Elijah's head was a loaf of bread baked over hot coals, and a jug of water. He ate and drank and went back to sleep.

Later the angel of the Lord came back a second

time, awoke him and said: "Get up and eat, for you have a long journey ahead of you." So he got up and ate and drank. The food made him strong enough to walk for forty days and nights until he reached Horeb, the mountain of God. There Elijah crawled into a cave and slept through the night (1 Kin 19:1-9).

The Word of the Lord came to him: "Elijah, why are you here?"

Elijah replied: "I have been zealous for the Lord God Almighty. The Israelites have abandoned your covenant, destroyed your altars, and murdered your prophets. I am the only one left, and now they are trying to kill me."

The Lord said: "Go stand on the mountain in front of the Lord. The Lord will pass by."

A hurricane force wind ripped the mountains and shattered the rocks, but the Lord was not in the wind. Then came an earthquake, but the Lord was not in the earthquake. Then came a fire, but the Lord was not in the fire. Then came a gentle whisper. When Elijah heard it, he pulled his robe over his face and went out and stood at the mouth of the cave.

A quiet voice asked him: "Elijah, why are you here?"

Elijah replied: "I have been very zealous for the Lord God Almighty. The Israelites have abandoned your covenant, destroyed your altars, and murdered your prophets. I am the only one left, and now they are trying to kill me."

The Lord said: "Go back the way you came through the Wilderness of Damascus. When you get there, anoint Hazael king over Aram. Then anoint Jehu king over Israel, and anoint Elisha to succeed you as prophet. I have left 7,000 living in Israel. Those 7,000 have knees that never bowed down to Baal, and their mouths have not kissed his image" (1 Kin 19:10-18).

Elijah found Elisha who was in a field where there were twelve teams of yoked oxen at work plowing. Elisha was plowing with the twelfth team. Elijah went up to him and threw his cloak around him. Elisha then left his oxen and ran after Elijah and said: "Let me kiss my father and mother goodbye, and then I will follow you."

Elisha took his pair of oxen and slaughtered them. He burned the plowing equipment to cook the meat and gave it to the people, and they ate. Then he set out to follow Elijah (1 Kin 19:19-21).

Judah: Jehoshaphat (when Ahab was king of Israel)

Jehoshaphat son of Asa became king of Judah in the fourth year of Ahab king of Israel. Jehoshaphat was 35 years old when he became king, and he reigned in Jerusalem 25 years. Jehoshaphat imitated the life of his father Asa. He did what was right and pleased the Lord. But he failed to get rid of the high places with neighborhood sex-and-religion shrines. People continued to offer sacrifices and worship at those idolatrous shrines. He did get rid of the sacred prositutes left over from the days of his father Asa.

Jehoshaphat was at peace with the king of Israel (1Kg 22:41-50).

Israel: War Between Ahab and Ben-Hadad

About this time, Ben-Hadad king of Aram mustered his entire army. In addition, he recruited 32 kings with their horses and chariots. He surrounded Samaria ready to make war.

A prophet approached king Ahab and proclaimed the Lord's message: "Look at this big army! I will help you defeat it today. Then you will know that I am the Lord."

Ahab and his army set out at noon while Ben-Hadad and the 32 kings allied with him were in their tents getting drunk. Ahab's young officers marched out of the city with the army behind them, and each one struck down his opponent in hand-to-hand combat. The Arameans fled, with the Israelites in pursuit. But Ben-Hadad escaped on a horse with some of his cavalry. King Ahab defeated the Aramean army (1 Kin 20:1-21).

Afterward, the prophet came to King Ahab and warned him that the king of Aram would attack again the following spring.

Ben-Hadad's advisors told him that the gods of Israel were mountain gods and that the Arameans would have the advantage if they fought Israel on the flat land. The next spring Ben-Hadad mustered the Arameans and went to fight against Israel on the plains. The Israelites camped opposite them looking like two small flocks of goats, while the Arameans covered the countryside.

A man of God approached Ahab, king of Israel, saying: "The Lord says: `Because the Arameans say the Lord is a god of the mountains and not a god of the valleys, I will deliver this vast army into your hands, and you will know that I am the Lord.'"

The Israelites killed 100,000 Aramean foot soldiers in one day. The rest of the army escaped to the city of Aphek, where the city wall collapsed on 27,000 of the survivors. Ben-Hadad fled to the city and hid in a closet.

Ben-Hadad's officials went to King Ahab of Israel wearing sackcloth around their waists and ropes around their heads, and said: "Your servant Ben-Hadad requests: `Please let me live.'"

King Ahab answered: "Is he still alive? He is my brother."

Then Ben-Hadad's officials quickly picked up his word and replied: "Yes, Ben-Hadad is your brother!"

Ahab told them: "Go and get him." When Ben-Hadad came out, Ahab had him come up into his chariot. Ahab said: "On the basis of a peace treaty I will set you free." So the two kings made a peace treaty and Ahab let Ben-Hadad go free (1 Kin 20:23-34).

One of the prophets ordered a soldier to strike him. The soldier hit and wounded the prophet. Then the prophet disguised himself with a bandage over his eyes and stood by the road waiting for the king.

As the king passed by, the prophet called out: "Your servant was in the thick of the battle, when one of our men came to me with a prisoner saying: `Guard this man. If he is missing, it will be your life for his life.' I was busy doing other things, and the prisoner escaped."

King Ahab replied: "You have pronounced your own verdict."

The prophet removed the bandage from his eyes, and Ahab knew he was one of the prophets. He told the king: "The Lord says: `You freed a man I sentenced to die. So it is your life for his life, your people for his people.'" Ahab returned to his palace in Samaria upset and angry (1 Kin 20:35-43).

Israel: Naboth's Vineyard

Naboth owned a vineyard that bordered Ahab's palace. Ahab asked Naboth: "Let me have your vineyard to use for a vegetable garden, since it is next to my palace. In exchange I will give you a better vineyard or I will pay you money for it."

Naboth replied: "The Lord forbid that I should sell you the land that belongs to my family."

Ahab went home, sulking and angry. He lay on his bed sulking and refused to eat.

Jezebel his wife came to him and asked: "Why are you sulking? Why won't you eat?"

Ahab answered: "Because I asked Naboth to sell me his vineyard and he refused."

Jezebel said: "Is this any way for the king of Israel to act? Get up! Eat! Cheer up! I'll get you Naboth's vineyard!"

Jezebel wrote letters over Ahab's signature, placed his official seal on them, and sent them to the leaders who lived in Naboth's city. Jezebel wrote: "Proclaim a day of fasting and seat Naboth at the head table. But seat two scoundrels opposite him and have them testify that he cursed both God and the king. Then take him out and stone him to death."

The leaders in Naboth's city followed Jezebel's instructions. They proclaimed a fast and seated Naboth at the head table. Two scoundrels sat opposite him and brought charges against Naboth before the people, saying: "Naboth cursed both God and the king." So they took him outside the city and stoned him to death. Then they sent word to Jezebel: "Naboth has been stoned to death."

Jezebel told Ahab: "Get up and take possession of the vineyard that Naboth refused to sell you. He is dead." When Ahab heard that Naboth was dead, he got up and went down to take possession of Naboth's vineyard.

The Word of the Lord came to Elijah the Tishbite: "Go to King Ahab who is now in Naboth's vineyard, claiming it as his own. Tell him: `The Lord says: You murdered Naboth and seized his property! The very spot where the dogs lapped up Naboth's blood, dogs will lap up your blood!'"

Ahab told Elijah: "So you found me, my enemy!"

Elijah answered: "I found you, because you sold yourself to do evil, defying the Lord. The Lord says: `I am going to destroy you. I will kill you and every male in your family. Your family will be like that of Jeroboam and that of Baasha, because you provoked me to anger and caused Israel to sin. Now concerning Jezebel: Dogs will devour Jezebel's flesh by the wall of Jezreel. Dogs will eat the descendants of Ahab who die in the city, and buzzards will feed on the corpses of those who die in the country.'"

There was never a man like Ahab, who openly did evil before the Lord, urged on by Jezebel his wife. He indulged in outrageous obscenities by going after idols, copying the Amorites whom the Lord had earlier driven out of Israelite territory.

When Ahab heard these words, he ripped his clothes, put on sackcloth, fasted and went around meekly.

The Word of the Lord came to Elijah the Tishbite: "Because Ahab has humbled himself, I will not bring this disaster during his lifetime; I will bring the disaster on his son" (1 Kin 21:1-28).

Israel: Ahab Killed

For three years there was no war between Aram and Israel. During the third year Jehoshaphat king of Judah went down to visit Ahab the king of Israel. Ahab asked Jehoshaphat: "Will you go with me to fight against the king of Aram and take back Ramoth Gilead?"

Jehoshaphat answered Ahab: "I am as you are, my people as your people, my horses as your horses. But, first seek guidance from the Lord."

Ahab brought together about 400 prophets and asked them: "Should I attack Ramoth Gilead, or should I wait?"

The prophets answered: "Attack, for the Lord will give victory to the king."

But Jehoshaphat asked: "Is there not a prophet of the Lord here whom we can consult?"

Ahab answered: "Micaiah is the only other prophet. We could ask the Lord through him. I hate him. He never prophesies anything good about me, but always bad."

Ahab ordered one of his officials: "Bring Micaiah at once."

King Ahab and King Jehoshaptat were dressed in their royal robes and sitting on their thrones. All the prophets staged a prophecy-performance for them. Zedekiah made iron horns and prophesied: "The Lord declares that you will use these horns to gore the Arameans until they are destroyed."

All the other prophets prophesied: "Attack Ramoth Gilead! God will give you victory!"

The messenger who summoned Micaiah told him: "Look, all the other prophets are predicting success for the king. Agree with them and speak favorably."

Micaiah replied: "As surely as the Lord lives, I can tell him only what the Lord tells me."

Micaiah told King Ahab: "I saw the army of Israel scattered on the hills like sheep without a shepherd. I saw the Lord sitting on his throne with all the angels standing at attention around him on his right and on his left. And the Lord asked: `Who will trick Ahab into attacking Ramoth Gilead and going to his death?'

"One suggested one thing, and another something else. Finally, an angel stepped forward, and said: 'I will trick him. I will be a lying spirit in the mouths of all his prophets.'

"The Lord said: 'You will succeed in tricking him. Go and do it.'

"So now the Lord has filled the mouths of your puppet prophets with lies. The Lord has ordained disaster for you."

Just then Zedekiah went up and punched Micaiah in the face saying: "Since when did the Spirit of the Lord leave me to speak to you?"

Micaiah replied: "You will find out on the day you frantically look for a place to hide."

Ahab ordered: "Put Micaiah in prison and keep him on bread and water until I return safely."

Micaiah declared: "If you return safely, the Lord has not spoken through me" (1Kg 22:1-28).

Ahab, king of Israel and Jehoshaphat king of Judah attacked Ramoth Gilead. Ahab told Jehoshaphat: "I will enter the battle in disguise, but you wear your royal robes." King Ahab of Israel disguised himself and went into battle.

The king of Aram had ordered his 32 commanders: "Do not fight with anyone except the king of Israel." The chariot commanders saw Jehoshaphat, and they thought: "There he is, the king of Israel!" So they took after him, but when Jehoshaphat cried out, the chariot commanders saw that he wasn't the king of Israel, and they let him go.

A soldier shot an arrow without aiming at anyone. But he hit Ahab between the sections of his armor. Ahab told his chariot driver: "Turn around and get me out of the fighting. I'm wounded." King Ahab was propped up in his chariot and watched the battle from the sidelines. Blood from his wound pooled on the chariot floor, and that evening he died. The king's body was brought to Samaria and buried. They washed the chariot at a pool in Samaria where the prostitutes bathed, and the dogs lapped up his blood. These things happened just as the Lord had promised (1 Kin 22:29-40).

Ahab died and his son Ahaziah succeeded him as king. Ahaziah ruled for two years, copying the evil example of his father (1 Kin 22:51-53). Ahaziah fell off the rooftop and died from his injuries. Because Ahaziah had no son, his brother Joram became the next king of Israel (2 Kin 1:1-18).

Judah: Jehoshaphat (after the death of Ahab, king of Israel)

Jehoshaphat king of Judah returned safely to Jerusalem. Jehu the prophet told him: "Should you help the wicked and love those who hate the Lord? Because of this, the Lord is angry with you. However, good is in you, for you have rid the land of the Asherah sex-and-religion poles and have set your heart on seeking God" (2 Chr 19:1-3).

Jehoshaphat appointed judges in the land and told them: "Consider carefully what you do, because you are not judging for man but for the Lord, who is with you whenever you give a verdict. Now let the fear of the Lord be upon you. Judge carefully, for with the Lord there is no injustice or partiality or bribery. In every case that comes before you, warn the people not to sin against the Lord; otherwise his wrath will come on you and your brothers" (2 Chr 19:5-10).

A vast army of the Moabites, Ammonites and the Meunites joined forces to make war against Jehoshaphat. Alarmed, Jehoshaphat resolved to pray, and he proclaimed a fast for all Judah. The people of Judah came together to seek help from the Lord.

Jehoshaphat stood up in front of the courtyard of the Temple and prayed: "O Lord, God of our ancestors, you rule over all the kingdoms of the nations. Power and might are in your hand, and no one can withstand you. O God, did you not drive out the inhabitants of this land before your people Israel and give it forever to the descendants of Abraham? They have lived in it and have built in it a house of worship to honor you. If calamity comes upon us, whether the sword of judgment, or plague or famine, we will stand in your presence before this Temple that bears your Name and will cry out to you in our distress, and you will hear us and save us.

"But now men from Ammon, Moab and Mount Seir are coming to drive us out of the possession you gave us as an inheritance. O our God, will you not judge them? We have no power to face this vast army that is attacking us. We do not know what to do; we are looking to you."

Then the Spirit of the Lord came upon Jahaziel a Levite and he said: "This is what the Lord says to you: `Do not be afraid of this vast army. This is God's battle; it is not yours. Tomorrow march against them. They will be climbing up by the Pass of Ziz, and you will find them at the end of the ravine in the wilderness of Jeruel. You will not have to fight this battle. Take up your positions and watch the Lord deliver you. Do not be afraid. Boldly face them tomorrow, and the Lord will be with you.'"

Jehoshaphat knelt with his face to the ground, and all the people of Judah fell down in worship before the Lord. Then some Levites loudly praised the Lord.

Early in the morning they left for the wilderness of Tekoa. Jehoshaphat appointed men to sing to the Lord. They marched at the front of the army, singing: "Give thanks to the Lord, for his love endures forever."

As soon as they began to sing and praise, the Lord set ambushes against the men who were invading Judah. The men of Ammon and Moab mistakenly attacked their allies from Mount Seir and killed them all. After they finished slaughtering the men from Seir, they started fighting each other and destroyed one another.

When the men of Judah came to a high place that overlooks the wilderness, they saw only dead bodies lying on the ground; no one had escaped. So Jehoshaphat and his men went to carry off their plunder. There was so much plunder that it took three days to collect it. On the fourth day they assembled and praised the Lord.

Then, Jehoshaphat and all the men of Judah returned rejoicing to Jerusalem. They went to the Temple of the Lord with stringed instruments and trumpets (2 Chr 20:1-30).

Later, Jehoshaphat king of Judah made an alliance with Ahaziah, the wicked king of Israel. He became a partner with him to build ocean-going ships. Eliezer prophesied against Jehoshaphat, saying: "Because you made an alliance with Ahaziah, the Lord will destroy what you have built." The ships wrecked, and nothing came of the partnership (Chr 20:35-37).

Jehoshaphat was thirty-five years old when he became king of Judah, and he reigned in Jerusalem twenty-five years. He did what was right in the eyes of the Lord (2 Chr 20:31-33). Jehoshaphat died and his son Jehoram succeeded him as king of Judah (2 Chr 21:1).

Israel: Ahab's Family Punished

Years later, the prophet Elisha had replaced Elijah. One day Elisha summoned a young prophet and ordered him: "Take this flask of oil and go to Ramoth Gilead and find Jehu. Get him away from his companions. Take the flask and pour the oil on his head and declare: `The Lord says: I anoint you king over Israel.' Then open the door and run away fast!"

The young prophet, went to Ramoth Gilead where he found the army officers sitting together, and he told Jehu: "I have a message for you, commander."

Jehu got up and went into the house. The prophet poured the oil on Jehu's head and declared: "The Lord, the God of Israel, says: `I anoint you king over the Lord's people Israel. Your assignment is to destroy the house of Ahab your master. I will avenge the massacre of my servants the prophets and the blood of all the Lord's servants shed by Jezebel. Everyone in Ahab's family will die. I will cut off from Ahab every last male in Israel. I will make the family of Ahab like the family of Jeroboam and like the family of Baasha. As for Jezebel, dogs will eat her carcass in the open fields of Jezreel. No one will bury her.'" Then the prophet opened the door and ran (2 Kin 9:1-10).

When Jehu went out to his fellow officers, one of them asked him: "Is everything all right? Why did this madman come to you?"

Jehu replied: "You know the man and the sort of things he says."

They said: "That's not true! Tell us."

Jehu said: "He told me: `The Lord says: I anoint you king over Israel.'"

The officers hurried and took their robes and spread them under Jehu on the bare steps. Then they blew the trumpet and shouted: "Jehu is king!" (2 Kin 9:11-13).

Jehu got into his chariot and rode to Jezreel where Joram was recovering from injuries. King Ahaziah of Judah was visiting him.

When the lookout standing on the tower in Jezreel saw Jehu's troops approaching, he called out: "I see troops coming. The driving is like that of Jehu, he drives like a madman."

Joram king of Israel and Ahaziah king of Judah rode out, each in his own chariot, to meet Jehu. They met him at the plot of ground that had belonged to Naboth. Joram saw Jehu and asked: "Have you come in peace, Jehu?"

Jehu replied: "How can there be peace, as long as all the idolatry, witchcraft, and promiscuous whoring of your mother Jezebel pollutes the country?"

Joram wheeled his chariot around and fled, calling out to Ahaziah: "Treachery, Ahaziah!"

Then Jehu drew his bow and shot an arrow between the shoulders of Joram. The arrow pierced his heart, and he slumped down in his chariot. Jehu ordered a chariot officer: "Pick him up and throw him on the field that belonged to Naboth. Remember how you and I were riding together in chariots behind Ahab his father when the Lord made this prophecy about him: `Yesterday I saw the blood of Naboth and the blood of his sons. I will make you pay for it on this exact plot of ground.' Now pick him up and throw him on that plot. Carry out the Lord's words."

Ahaziah king of Judah fled. Jehu chased him, shouting: "Kill him too!" They wounded him and he died (2 Kin 9:14-29).

Then Jehu went to Jezreel. Jezebel heard about Jehu's arrival; she painted her eyes, arranged her hair and posed at the window. As Jehu entered the gate, she asked: "Have you come in peace, Zimri, you who murdered your master?"

Jehu looked up at the window and called out: "Who is on my side?" Two or three eunuchs looked down at him. Jehu ordered: "Throw her down!" So they threw her down, and horses ran over her body. Her blood spattered the wall and the horses as they trampled her underfoot.

Jehu went inside and ate his lunch. Then he ordered: "Bury that cursed woman for she was a king's daughter." When they went out to bury her, they found nothing except her skull, her feet and her hands. They came back and told Jehu. He said: "This is the Word of the Lord that he spoke through his servant Elijah the Tishbite: On the plot of ground at Jezreel, dogs will devour Jezebel's flesh. Jezebel's body will become dog manure on the ground in Jezreel, so no one will be able to say: `This is Jezebel'" (2 Kin 9:30-37).

Ahab's family had 70 sons living in Samaria. Jehu wrote letters to the leaders in Samaria: "If you are willing to follow me, decapitate your master's sons and bring their heads to me in Jezreel tomorrow."

The leaders of the city received the letter. They took the royal princes and slaughtered all 70 of them. They put their heads in baskets and sent them to Jehu in Jezreel.

The next morning Jehu went out. He stood

before all the people and said: "You should know that not a word the Lord has spoken against the house of Ahab will fail. The Lord has done what he promised through his servant Elijah."

Jehu proceeded to kill everyone in Jezreel who had any connection with Ahab's family. It happened just as the Lord had promised through Elijah (2 Kin 10:1-17).

LIFE-LESSONS DISCOVERED IN THE STORY

1. God communicates with people. God sent his messengers to the kings who rebelled against him. The prophets often received the Word of the Lord.

2. The Holy Spirit was and is still active in the world. When God chose the prophets, the Holy Spirit came on them, in order to give them understanding and the Word of the Lord. The prophets communicated the Lord's words to the kings and the people.

3. God often uses nature to punish people who rebel against him. When the Israelites served and worshiped the false god Baal, God decreed a drought against Israel (1 Kin 17:1).

4. The Lord listens to and answers his servants' prayers. God answered the prayers of Elijah (1 Kin 17:19-22; 18:42-45; Ja 5:16-18) and Jehoshaphat (2 Chr 20:5-17).

5. The person who rejects the Lord will consider the Lord's messenger a troublemaker and may even consider him an enemy. That was Ahab's reaction to Elijah (1 Kin 18:17-18; 21:17-29).

6. The sinner does not recognize that he is responsible for damaging himself, his health and society. He places the blame on others. Ahab accused Elijah of being a troublemaker and did not assume responsibility for the consequences of his own sins (1 Kin 18:17-18).

7. Faith in God enables a person to face difficulties with a calm confidence. Elijah was calm when he faced conflict with Baal's prophets on Mount Carmel (1 Kin 18:34-35). Jehoshaphat marched into battle against superior forces singing praises to God (2 Chr 20:20-21).

8. The Lord God is the only true God with power to act. The competition between Baal's prophets and Elijah on Mount Carmel wasn't to decide which of them, the Lord or Baal, was the most powerful. It was to determine which was the only true God. Elijah's word (1 Kin 18:22-25), his prayer (1 Kin 18:37), and the acclamation of the people (18:39) show that it was a battle to determine who was the only true God. Monotheist faith was determined.

9. Spiritual leaders who are not servants of the Lord God are false prophets. The competition between Baal's prophets and Elijah on Mount Carmel revealed who was a servant of the true God and who were false prophets of false gods (1 Kin 18:22-39). The false prophets of Ahab were inspired by a lying spirit (1 Kin 22:23).

10. The main reason God acts is to convert people to become his servants. The reason for the Mount Carmel miracle was to prove to the Israelites that the Lord is the only God, that they should convert in order to worship and serve only him (1 Kin 18:37).

11. Miracles from God don't break down barriers of unbelief. God's miraculous demonstration on Mount Carmel didn't tear down Jezebel's barrier of unbelief (1 Kin 19:2).

12. After a great spiritual victory, a person may become discouraged. That happened to Elijah. After the victory on Mount Carmel, Elijah fell into despair, self-pity and desired to die (1 Kin 19:3-4).

13. Those who serve the Lord are imperfect. Elijah was a hero of the faith; however, he became afraid of Jezebel, he became discouraged, acted like a person without faith (1 Kin 19:3-4) and became full of self-pity (1 Kin 19:10). God's servants are still mud vessels (2 Cor 4:7; Ja 5:17).

14. The depressed person should both take care of his body and act to assume responsibility. When Elijah was depressed, God let him sleep (1 Kin 19:5), provided him with food (19:6) and gave him the responsibility to anoint two kings and a prophet (19:15-16).

15. Unity exist between the Law of Moses, the ministry of Elijah the prophet, and the salvation work of Jesus. God revealed himself to Moses on Mount Sinai (Ex 3:1-6). It was on Sinai that God established his covenant with Israel (Ex 19 and 20; 24:12-14; 34:1-3). Another name for Mount Sinai was Mount Horeb. When Elijah went to Mount Horeb, (1 Kin 19:8-13), he went to the place where Moses met God and later where the Lord gave him the Law. Centuries later, Moses, Elijah, and Jesus would meet together on a mountain top when Jesus experienced his transfiguration (Mt 17:1-8; Lk 9:28-36).

16. An assignment from God may demand a renunciation of one's profession and current lifestyle. Elijah threw his robe on Elisha. Then

Elisha said good-bye to his parents, sacrificed his oxen and burned his plow (1 Kin 19:19-21). When Elisha sacrificed his oxen and destroyed his plow, he abandoned his previous lifestyle and renounced his profession as a farmer. Gideon also sacrificed the bull he used in his work (Jdg 6:25-26). The fishermen Peter, Andrew, James and John left their nets and boats to follow Jesus (Mt 4:18-22).

17. Every disobedience to God is punished, even when the disobedience is for motives that human culture considers praiseworthy. When King Ahab battled against Ben-Hadad, a prophet advised Ahab on how to defeat Ben-Hadad. It was God's intention for Ben-Hadad to be killed. Ahab defeated Ben-Hadad, but made a peace treaty and let him go free (1 Kin 20:1-34). God sent a prophet with a message condemning Ahab (1 Kin 20:35-43). King Saul was also punished for letting a king live whom the Lord had determined should die (1 Sm15:22-28).

18. Evil people believe that they have the right to practice injustice in order to reach their objectives. Ahab and Jezebel considered that they had the right to eliminate Naboth in order to obtain his vineyard (1 Kin 21:7-16).

19. People willing to do anything to obtain material possessions sells themselves out to evil. Ahab sold himself out to evil in order to gain Naboth's vineyard. He was judged and punished by God (1 Kin 21:17-26). (See 1 Tm 6:9-10.) The person who gains the whole world, yet forfeits his soul makes a bad business deal (Mk 8:36).

20. Spiritual leaders who serve an institution may benefit from it, even though the institution turns them into false prophets. The 400 prophets of Ahab (1 Kin 22:6) prospered because they were in the king's service, while the prophets who were committed to the Lord were persecuted by Jezebel (1 Kin 18:4, 13; 19:1).

21. False prophets please their listeners with lying promises of prosperity. The false prophets of Ahab prophesied success in the battle against Syria (1 Kin 22:5-6). (See Jer 28:8-9.)

22. False prophets are guided by lying spirits. The false prophets of Ahab were guided by a lying spirit (1 Kin 22:19-23). (See 2 Tm 4:1-4.)

23. Accomplishments that are achieved by means that violate God's plans and principles do not have durable value. Ahab completed many construction projects (1 Kin 22:39), but his kingdom terminated when Ahab's royal blood was mixed with sewage water and lapped up by dogs (1 Kin 22:38). (See Ps 127:1; 1 Cor 3:10-15.)

24. The person who refuses to believe the truth will believe a lie. Ahab rejected the Lord's truth, and an evil spirit deceived him with a lie (1 Kin 22:23; 2 Chr 18:20-21). (See 2 Th 2:11-12.)

25. God is honest and fulfills his promises. He fulfilled his promises of punishing Ahab, Jezebel and their descendants (1 Kin 21:20-24). Ahab died and the dogs lapped his blood (1 Kin 22:38). Dogs devoured the body of Jezebel (2 Kin 9:30-37) and the male descendants of Ahab were murdered by Jehu (2 Kin 10:1-17).

26. The godly person courts disaster when he enters into a partnership with people who reject God's leadership. The one who serves the Lord must compromise divine values in order to have a partnership with the ungodly. Jehoshaphat, the godly king of Judah, suffered because he made alliances with the wicked kings of Israel: Ahab (2 Chr 19:1-2) and Ahaziah (2 Chr 20:35-37). (See 2 Cor 6:14-15.)

27. Fear is profitable when it helps a person who faces danger to seek the Lord in prayer. When an enormous army came to attack Jehoshaphat, he became afraid and prayed (2 Chr 20:2-3).

28. The godly person who is caught up in an undesirable conflict can learn from the way Jehoshaphat dealt with the attack by Edom (2 Chr 20:6-27). 1) He prayed, committing the problem to God; 2) he acknowledged that only God had power to resolve the problem; 3) he professed his dependence on God to deliver him from the conflict (20:6-13); 4) he took comfort in God's promises, praising God even before he went into battle (2 Chr 20:18-21); 5) he praised God after the victory (2 Chr 20:26-27).

29. Even a godly leader will make wrong choices. Jehoshaphat made a mistake in making alliances with the wicked kings of Israel: Ahab (2 Chr 19:1-2) and Ahaziah (2 Chr 20:35-37).

QUESTIONS

1. Why did God send his prophets to people who did not want to hear his message?
2. Why is Ahab considered more evil than all the other kings of Israel?
3. What were some of the evil things that Ahab and Jezebel did?
4. What do Ahab and Jezebel illustrate about government leaders who reject God's laws?
5. How did God provide for Elijah during the prolonged drought?
6. Compare the prophets of Baal to Elijah, the prophet of the Lord.
7. What does Elijah's life teach about a spiritual leader who is faithful to the Lord?
8. What does the conflict on Mount Carmel teach about the conflict between false religion and true religion?
9. What does the conflict between Ahab and Jezebel against Elijah teach about the conflict between good and evil?
10. What does the suffering in Israel when Ahab was king, teach about reasons why good people suffer?
11. How can a person who suffers with depression be helped by Elijah's experience with self-pity and depression?
12. What does the life of Ahab and Jezebel teach about the consequences of doing evil?
13. How did God punish Ahab and Jezebel?
14. Today, where is the conflict between good and evil most prevalent?

JONAH				
1	2		3	4
1st COMMISSION			2nd COMMISSION	
Disobedience > Results			Reluctant Obedience > Results	
KEY-SUBJECTS Jonah The Great Sea			**KEY-SUBJECTS** Nineveh The Great City	
Jonah running	Jonah praying		Jonah preaching	Jonah complaining
God sending	God hearing		God changing his plans	God instructing
THE POWER OF GOD God's mercy with Jonah			**THE MERCY OF GOD** God's mercy with Nineveh	
1	2		3	4

THE PROBLEM	ACTIONS RELATED TO THE CITY OF NINEVEH	CONSEQUENCES
NINEVEH Wicked (1:2) and violent (3:8).	God sent Jonah to preach to the city.	The people of Nineveh turned from their sins and God spared the city.
JONAH God wanted to save Nineveh while Jonah wanted it destroyed.	Jonah did not want to go to Nineveh.	Jonah was angry with God.
	Jonah preached about God's judgment, but neglected to mention his mercy.	God instructed Jonah.

JONAH: THE RELUCTANT PROPHET
Jonah 1 - 4

STRUCTURE

Context:
From 2 Kings 14:25, we learn that Jonah was a prophet in the Kingdom of Israel when Jeroboam II was king. After King Solomon's death, there was civil war among the Israelites. Ten tribes rejected Rehoboam, Solomon's son, as king. They chose Jeroboam as their king and formed a new kingdom, called Israel. Jeroboam led Israel to idol worship.

Jeroboam II was the thirteenth (13th) king of Israel. His kingship was a time of prosperity and strong feelings of nationalism.

Assyria, Israel's great enemy, was famous for their cruelty toward conquered nations. The capital city of Assyria was Nineveh.

Jonah was the only Old Testament prophet sent to a heathen nation and the only one who tried to get out of delivering his message.

Key-person: Jonah

Key-location: Nineveh

Key-repetitions:
- People turned to God: the sailors (1:14-16); Jonah inside the fish (2:2-7) the people of Nineveh (3:5); the king of Nineveh (3:6).
- Things/people that obeyed God: the storm (1:4); the sailors (1:11-16); the fish (1:17; 2:10); the residents of Nineveh (3:5-9); the plant (4:6); the worm (4:7); the east wind (4:8).
- Jonah speaking with God (2:1-9; 4:1-4, 8-9).
- God speaking/sending (1:1, 4, 17; 2:10; 3:1; 4:4, 6, 7, 8, 9, 10).
- Fear: the sailors (1:5-10); Jonah (2:2-7); the people of Nineveh (3:5-9).

Key-attitudes:
- Jonah's reluctance to go to Nineveh.
- The sailors' fear of the storm.

- The helplessness of Jonah when he was thrown overboard.
- Jonah's prejudice and hatred of Nineveh.
- Jonah's anger with God.
- The people of Nineveh were afraid of God's punishment.
- The awe of God felt by the sailors and the Ninevites.
- God's mercy and compassion for both Jonah and Nineveh.

Initial-problem:
The Lord told Jonah to go to the great city of Nineveh and preach against it.

Sequence of events:
Jonah: the Disobedient Servant of God
- The Lord told Jonah to go to the wicked city of Nineveh and preach against it (1:1-2).
- In Joppa, Jonah boarded a ship bound for Tarshish to get away from the Lord (1:3).
- The Lord sent a storm. The terrified sailors cried out to their gods and threw the cargo overboard. The captain finds Jonah asleep (1:4-5).
- The sailors drew straws; Jonah got the short straw. They interrogated Jonah. He confessed his responsibility for the storm. Jonah told them to throw him overboard. When they threw him overboard, the sea grew calm (1:6-16).
- The Lord provided a large fish to swallow Jonah. Jonah was inside the fish for 3 days and nights (1:17).
- Jonah prayed to the Lord God (2:1-9).
- The Lord spoke to the fish and it vomited Jonah onto dry land (2:10).

Jonah: the Reluctant Servant of God
- Again the Lord told Jonah to go to Nineveh and proclaim his message (3:1-2).
- In Nineveh, Jonah proclaimed: "Forty more days and Nineveh will be destroyed!" The Ninevites believed God, declared a fast and put on sackcloth (3:3-5).
- The king dressed himself with sackcloth, decreed a fast and called on the people to turn from their wicked ways (3:6-9).
- God saw what the people did and change his mind about destroying Nineveh (3:10).
- Jonah was furious and yelled at God. He told God why he ran off to Tarshish. He asked God to kill him. God questioned his right to be angry (4:1-4).
- Jonah built a shelter to the east of the city. The Lord provided a vine to give Jonah shade. Then he sent a worm to kill the vine. Jonah wished he were dead (4:5-8).
- God questioned Jonah's right to be angry and Jonah said he had reason to be angry (4:9).
- The Lord compared Jonah's concern for the vine to his own concern for Nineveh (4:10-11).

Final-situation:
God expressed his concern for Nineveh to Jonah.

BIBLE STORY

Jonah: the Disobedient Servant of God

The Lord spoke to Jonah: "Go to the great city of Nineveh and preach against it. It's wickedness has caught my attention" (1:1-2).

But Jonah headed for Tarshish, running away from the Lord. He went down to the port of Joppa, where he found a ship bound for Tarshish. He paid his fare, went aboard and sailed for Tarshish. He wanted to get as far away from the Lord as possible (1:3).

However, the Lord sent a great wind that created a violent storm with gigantic waves. The ship was in danger of breaking apart. The sailors were terrified. In desperation, each sailor cried out to his own god. And they threw the cargo overboard to lighten the ship.

Meanwhile, Jonah had gone below deck into the hold of the ship to lie down. He fell into a deep sleep. The captain came to him and said: "How can you sleep? Get up and pray to your god! Maybe your god will notice our desperate situation and rescue us."

Then the sailors said to one another: "Let us draw straws to find out who is the culprit on the ship responsible for this calamity." They drew straws and Jonah got the short straw.

So they interrogated him: "Confess! Why are you responsible for our disaster? What do you do? Where do you come from? What is your country? Who are your people?"

Jonah confessed that he was running away from the Lord and told them: "I am a Hebrew. I worship the Lord, the God of heaven, who made sea and land."

Jonah's confession increased their terror! The raging storm became more turbulent. The sailors demanded: "What have you done? What should we do to you to get rid of this storm?"

Jonah replied: "Throw me overboard into the sea, then it will become calm. I know that I am the cause of the storm. Get rid of me and you will get rid of the storm."

Instead, the men tried to row back to land. But they made no headway. The storm grew worse; the sea grew even wilder than before. The sailors cried to the Lord: "O Lord, please do not let us die because of this man's life. Do not blame us for killing an innocent man. You caused all this to happen." Then they took Jonah and threw him overboard. Immediately the raging sea grew calm. At this the men were no longer terrified by the sea, but they were in awe of the Lord. They offered a sacrifice to the Lord and made vows to him (1:4-16).

Old Testament Bible Stories © Jackson Day

Meanwhile, back to Jonah. The Lord provided a large fish to swallow him, and Jonah was inside the stomach of the fish for three days and three nights (1:17).

Jonah was in the stomach of the fish. He prayed to the Lord his God: "In my distress I called to the Lord, and he answered me. From the mouth of the grave I cried: 'Help!' You heard my cry. You cast me into the ocean's depths. I went down into the heart of the sea. Currents swirled about me; ocean waves crashed over me. I said: `I have been cast out from your sight; I will never again see your holy temple.' Sea waters closed over me. Undercurrents pulled me to the depths of the ocean; seaweed wrapped itself around my head. I sank down to the valley between sea mountains; I hit bottom! The gates of death were closing in on me. But you pulled me up alive from the grave, O Lord my God. When my life was slipping away, I remembered you Lord. Lord, I prayed to you and you heard me in your holy temple. People who worship worthless idols forfeit the grace that could be theirs. But I will worship you with a song of thanksgiving; I will sacrifice to you. I will do what I promised to do. Salvation comes from the Lord!" (2:1-9).

The Lord spoke to the fish and it vomited Jonah out of its stomach onto dry land (2:10).

Jonah: the Reluctant Servant of God

Then the Lord spoke to Jonah a second time: "Go to the great city of Nineveh and proclaim to them the message I give you" (3:1-2).

This time, Jonah obeyed the Lord and went to Nineveh. Now Nineveh, the capital of Assyria was a very large city; it took a person three days to walk across it. The first day that Jonah entered into the city, he proclaimed: "Forty more days and Nineveh will be destroyed!"

The Ninevites believed God. They declared a citywide fast; and everyone of them, from the greatest to the least, from the richest to the poorest, from the most famous to the most obscure, put on sackcloth (3:3-5).

When the message reached the king of Nineveh, he got up from his throne, took off his royal robes, dressed himself with sackcloth and sat down in the dirt. Then he issued a public proclamation throughout Nineveh: "By the decree of the king and his nobles: Do not drink one drop of water. Do not eat one bite of food. This is an order for all men, women and animals. Every person and every animal must be clothed with sackcloth. Let everyone cry out to God. Everyone must turn around, stop doing evil and stop doing violence. Maybe God will change his mind and show compassion. Maybe he will stop being angry and let us live" (3:6-9).

God saw what the people did. He saw that they turned from their evil ways. So God changed his mind about destroying them. He showed compassion by not bringing upon them the threatened destruction (3:10).

But Jonah was furious, he lost his temper. He yelled at God: "O Lord, this is what I said would happen when I was back home! That is why I ran off to Tarshish. I knew that you are a kind God who shows mercy. You are not easily angered. You are rich in love. You would rather change your plans for calamity into a program of forgiveness! Lord, if you won't kill them, kill me! I'm better off dead!"

But the Lord replied: "Do you have the right to be angry?" (4:1-4).

Jonah went east, out of the city, and sat down on a hill. There he made himself a shelter of leafy branches and sat in its shade waiting to see what would happen to the city. Then the Lord God provided a broad-leaf vine and made it grow up over Jonah to give shade for his head. This made a cool place for him to sit. Jonah was very happy with the vine and enjoyed its shade. Then the Lord sent a worm. By dawn of the next day the worm had chewed the vine and it withered. The sun rose and the Lord sent a scorching east wind. The sun beat down on Jonah's head so that he grew light-headed. He wished he were dead. He prayed to die: "It would be better for me to die than to live!"

But God asked: "Jonah, do you have a right to be angry about the vine?"

Jonah replied: "I do. It is right for me to be angry enough to die."

But the Lord said: "You showed concern for this vine. You did nothing for the vine, you neither planted it nor cultivated it. It sprang up one night and died the next night. But Nineveh has more than a hundred and twenty thousand childlike people who cannot tell their right hand from their left. There are also many animals in the city. Should I not be concerned about this great city?" (4:5-11).

LIFE-LESSONS DISCOVERED IN THE STORY

1. God speaks to people. The book of Jonah begins and finishes with the Lord speaking to Jonah. God used Jonah to communicate his Word to Nineveh.

2. God has a plan for people's lives. God spoke to Jonah and he told him to go to Nineveh and proclaim his Word to that wicked city (1:1-2).

3. A people group that is characterized by evil is predestined to destruction. The city of Nineveh was characterized by wickedness. The city was full of evil (1:2; 3:8) and violence (3:8). The prophet Nahum called Nineveh a city full of bloodshed, full of lies, full of plunder and full of victims. The kings of Nineveh were constantly at war. They bragged that their enemy's blood ran

like a river. It was also a city of sorcery and witchcraft (Nah 3:1-4).

4. The judgment of God predestines the destruction of a people characterized for their wickedness (1:2). God judges and punishes people individually. However, when a people who form a society join together in their wickedness, together as a society they will suffer divine punishment.

5. God is omniscient and he sees the wickedness of a people group. God knew about the wickedness in Nineveh (1:2).

6. A people group, who deserves divine punishment, has hope when God acts in their favor. God wanted to save the wicked city of Nineveh. He acted to liberate Nineveh from destruction:
   ■ He saw the city (1:2; 3:10);
   ■ He sent his prophet to the city (1:2);
   ■ He ave his prophet a message to proclaim to the city (3:2);
   ■ He disciplined the indisposed prophet in order to get him to Nineveh (1:4-2:10);
   ■ When the people turned from their evil ways, God saved the city from destruction (3:10).

7. God's salvation plans include everyone. Everyone in Nineveh, from the greatest to the least put on sackcloth (3:3-5). The king of Nineveh called for everyone in the city to cry out to God, to turn around, to stop doing evil and stop doing violence (3:6-9).

8. People who serve God are often reluctant to help God save the city. Just as Jonah resisted going to Nineveh (1:3), many evangelicals are reluctant to take God's message to the city.

9. The person who seeks to escape from God-given responsibility leaves others in danger, and he becomes a curse to those who are around him. Jonah tried to escape from God's plan for him (1:3). Jonah became a curse for the sailors who were with him (1:4-14) and, if it were not the intervention of God, Nineveh would have been destroyed because of his omission (3:1-10).

10. People who run from God don't realize when they are responsible for the suffering of others. When Jonah was running from God, he was responsible for the storm that afflicted the sailors; yet he was asleep (1:5).

11. The person who seeks to flee from the Lord's presence will pay a high price. It cost Jonah when he fled from the Lord. He suffered in the storm. He faced the burden of knowing he was responsible for the sailors' suffering. He had to listen to their accusations. He had a near death experience and was inside the stomach of a fish for three days and three nights. He also suffered depression and self-pity (1:4-17; 4:1-9).

12. God seeks the person who is fleeing from him. The Lord sought Jonah when he was running away from his presence (1:17; 3:1).

13. God is omnipresent and omniscient. Jonah could not escape from God. The Lord was in the ocean (1:4; 1:17) and heard him from the stomach of a fish (2:7). God is everywhere. (Read Ps 139:1-18.)

14. God's messenger is responsible for proclaiming God's Word; he is not responsible for the listener's response. Jonah was responsible for proclaiming God's Word (1:2; 3:2). He was not responsible for what the people of Nineveh would do with it.

15. God's messenger should proclaim all of God's Word. Jonah only proclaimed judgment (3:4). He knew about the mercy of God (4:1), but failed to preach about it.

16. People who are hated by God's servants are loved by God and he desires to save them. Assyria was the principal enemy of Jonah's country. So Nineveh was the capital city of Jonah's enemies. But God wanted to save Jonah's enemies, and he wanted Jonah to help him(1:1-2; 3:2; 4:10-11). The heart of God that was willing to forgive the wicked and violent, is seen in contrast to Jonah's attitude that was narrow, full of prejudices and indisposed to forgive.

17. God is able to work through and with inept people. The story of Jonah portrays God working with and around Jonah's ineptness to accomplish his purpose through him.

18. God is omnipotent and is in charge of the whole world: the sky, the sea, the earth, animals, plants and human beings. He ordered the storm, he calmed the sea (1:15), he prepared a large fish to swallow Jonah (1:17), he made a vine grow (4:6), he sent a worm to attack the plant (4:7) and he sent a scorching east wind (4:8).

19. Sinful man needs God to save him from deserved punishment. Man is unable to save himself. The desperate condition of Jonah in the stomach of the fish (1:17 - 2:9) is similar to that of sinful man. Jonah could not remove himself from the stomach of the fish; neither can the sinner liberate himself from the power of sin. Only God can save the sinner.

20. God offers salvation from destruction to everyone; however, only those who hear the offer, believe in God and repent from their sins are liberated from divine punishment. Nineveh's residents heard God's message (3:4); they believed in God (3:5); they repented of their wicked behavior (3:5) and they turned away from

an evil life and violence (3:8).

21. The person who is reluctant to obey God needs to value what God values most: people. Jonah didn't value the residents of Nineveh because they were enemies of Israel. He valued the plant that gave him shade, while God valued the people of Nineveh (4:9-11).

22. God wants his servants to willingly obey him. When God gave Jonah an order Jonah, he expected obedience (1:1-4; 3:1-2).

23. The person who reluctantly obeys God does not have joy in serving the Lord. Jonah reluctantly obeyed God and went to Nineveh. Jonah's preaching resulted in a great victory. Everyone in the city repented and turned from his wicked ways; however, Jonah experienced anger, depression and self-pity (4:1-4, 8-9).

24. The Lord is a God of love who is always ready to forgive and save people; both citizens who belong to a nation that professes to worship the Lord and citizens from a nation that considers the people of God their enemies. God was willing to forgive the prophet Jonah, who was indisposed to obey him, as well as the violent residents of Nineveh who considered themselves enemies of Israel, the people of God.

25. A person can be honest with God, even when he is angry at the Lord. God allowed Jonah the freedom to express his anger. The Lord questioned Jonah's right to be angry, but did not condemn him for expressing his anger (4:3-4).

26. God's messenger has the duty to proclaim that God is aware of man's evilness and cruelty. The task given to Jonah is still given to those who have the job of proclaiming God's Word (1:2; 3:2).

27. The one who proclaims God's message should expect the lives of his listeners to be transformed. When Jonah announced God's Word, lives were changed: people believed in God and turned away from evil and violence (3:1-9).

28. The death and resurrection of Jesus Christ was illustrated by the three days and three nights that Jonah spent in the stomach of the fish (Mt 12:39-41; 16:4; Lk 11:29-30).

QUESTIONS

1. Why did God send Jonah to Nineveh, the capital city of his enemies?
2. What were Jonah's reactions when he received orders to go to Nineveh?
3. What did the Lord do when Jonah fled from him?
4. How were other people hurt because Jonah fled from God?
5. Who would be hurt if you fled from the Lord?
6. What happened to Jonah when he was thrown overboard?
7. What happened in Nineveh when Jonah proclaimed the Lord's message?
8. Why did God change his mind about destroying Nineveh?
9. How did God use the plant to teach Jonah about divine mercy?
10. What does the story of Jonah teach us about God and his desire to save wicked people?

PROPHETS TO REBELLIOUS PEOPLE
Divided Kingdom
2 Kings 1 - 17

STRUCTURE

Context:
When Saul, David and Solomon were kings, all 12 tribes of Israel were together in one kingdom. After the death of Solomon, the Kingdom was divided. Ten tribes rebelled against the king who was David's descendant and became the Kingdom of Israel. Two tribes remained loyal to the king who was David's grandson and became the Kingdom of Judah.

All of the kings of Israel rejected the covenant with God and served sex-and-religion idols. Israel's worst king was Ahab, who was influenced by his wicked wife, Jezebel.

Some of the kings of Judah imitated David and served the Lord, but most rejected the covenant with God and imitated the kings of Israel.

God constantly sent prophets to the two kingdoms.

Key-persons: Elisha and the kings of both Israel and Judah

Key-location: Samaria and Jerusalem

Key-repetitions:
- Miracles by Elisha: divided the river and crossed it (2 Kin 2:13-15); healing of the water (2 Kin 2:19-22); told the kings of Israel, Judah and Edom how to defeat the Moabites (2 Kin 3:11-24); multiplied the widow's oil (2 Kin 4:1-7); boy restored to life (2 Kin 4:8-37); poison removed from stew (2 Kin 4:38-41) twenty loaves of bread fed 100 men (2 Kin 4:42-44); Naaman healed of leprosy (2 Kin 5:1-19); an axhead floated (2 Kin 6:1-7); told the king of Israel the military plans of the king of Aram (2 Kin 6:8-12); Arameans blinded and trapped (2 Kin 6:13-19); foretold events that would happen on the following day (2 Kin 7:1-2, 17-20).
- Elisha helped the kings of Israel during war: (3:1-3; 6:8 - 7:20).
- All the kings of Israel did evil, imitating the sins of Jeroboam who caused Israel to sin: Ahaziah (1 Kin 22:51-52); Joram (2 Kin 3:1-6); Jehu (2 Kin 10:29); Jehoazah (2 Kin 13:2); Jehoash (2 Kin 13:11); Jeroboam II (2Kg 14:24); Zechariah (2 Kin 15:9); Menahem (2 Kin 15:18); Pekah (2 Kin 15:28); Hoshea (2 Kin 17:2).
- Some of the kings of Judah did evil by imitating the kings of Israel: Jehoram (2 Kin 8:18); Ahaziah (2 Kin 8:27); Queen Athaliah (2 Kin 11:1); Ahaz (2 Kin 16:2-3).
- Some of the kings of Judah did right and imitated David: Joash (2 Kin 12:2); Amaziah (2 Kin 14:2) Uzziah/Azariah (2 Kin 15:3); Jotham (2 Kin 15:34).
- Kings of Judah who did right as long as they were instructed by a man of God; afterwards they did evil: Joash as long as Jehoiada lived (2 Kin 12:2); Uzziah (Azariah) during the days of Zechariah (2 Chr 26:4-5).

Key-attitudes:
- The solitude of Elijah who was often alone.
- Elijah's authority.
- The sociability of Elisha who was often with others.
- The hope of Naaman when he went to Israel.
- The greed of Gehazi.
- The stubborn insubordination of the kings and people of Israel.
- The calamity of the fall of Samaria.
- The instability of the Israelites that made them vulnerable to the influences of their leaders.
- The inconsistency of the kings of Judah.
- The dependance of Joash and Uzziah (Azariah) on the influence of godly teachers. When they lost their teachers, they turned away from God.
- The stability and fidelity of Elisha.

Initial-problem:
Ahaziah, king of Israel, fell off the rooftop. He sent messengers to consult Baal-Zebub to find out if he would recover.

Sequence of events:

Israel: Ahaziah and Elijah
- Ahaziah ruled for two years imitating the evil example of his father, Ahab (1 Kin 22:51-53).
- Ahaziah fell off the rooftop. He sent messengers to consult Baal-Zebub to find out if he would recover (2 Kin 1:1-2).
- Elijah intercepted Ahaziah's men and gave them God's Word that the king would die (2 Kin 1:3-4).
- Ahaziah sent a captain with 50 men to Elijah. Fire from heaven cremated the men. This happened a second time. The third captain fell on his knees before Elijah. Elijah then went and told the King he would die. Ahaziah's brother, Joram, succeeded him as king (2 Kin 1:5-19).

Israel: Elijah Taken up to Heaven
- At Gilgal, Bethel, and Jericho; Elijah asked Elisha to stay. Each time Elisha refused to leave Elijah. Elijah hit the river with his robe, the water divided and Elijah and Elisha crossed over (2 Kin 2:1-8).
- Elisha requested to inherit a double share of Elijah's spirit. A chariot of fire and horses of fire separated Elijah from Elisha, and Elijah went up to heaven in a whirlwind (2 Kin 2:9-12).
- Elisha picked up Elijah's fallen robe, hit the river with it, the water divided and Elisha crossed over (2 Kin 2:13-18).

Israel: Some of Elisha's Miracles
- In Jericho, Elisha used a new bowl and salt to heal the water (2 Kin 2:19-22).

■Forty-two youth who jeered Elisha were mauled by two bears (2 Kin 2:23-25).

■Elisha told King Joram of Israel, King Jehoshaphat of Judah and the king of Edom to defeat Moab by digging ditches all over the valley. The Lord filled the ditches with water which looked like blood when the sun rose. This deceived the Moabite army (2 Kin 3:1-27).

■A widow, whose only possession was a little jar of oil, asks Elisha for help in paying her husband's debts. The oil was multiplied (2 Kin 4:1-7).

■A woman and her husband in Shunem prepared a room and furnished it for Elisha. Elisha promised her a son. When the boy died, Elisha prayed, and God restored his life (2 Kin 4:8-36).

■Naaman, commander of the army of Aram, had leprosy. A slave Israelite girl told Naaman's wife that a prophet in Samaria would cure Naaman. The king of Aram sent Naaman with a letter for the king of Israel. The king of Israel read the letter and ripped his robes in distress. Elisha sent word to the king to send Naaman to him (2 Kin 5:1-8).

■So Naaman went to Elisha's house. Elisha sent a message for Naaman to immerse himself 7 times in the Jordan River. Naaman went away angry. Naaman's servants talked him into obeying Elisha. Naaman immersed himself in the Jordan 7 times and was healed. Naaman returned to Elisha with gifts. Elisha refused the gifts. Naaman promised to worship only the Lord (2 Kin 5:9-19).

■Gehazi ran after Naaman to obtain the gifts for himself. He also received Naaman's leprosy (2 Kin 5:20-27).

Israel: Elisha's Knowledge During War

■Elisha warned the king of Israel the locations where Ben-Hadad, king of Aram, had set up ambushes. Ben-Hadad dispatched an army to Dothan to capture Elisha. Elisha's servant was terrified. Elisha prayed and the Lord opened the servant's eyes so that he saw the hills full of horses and chariots of fire (2 Kin 6:8-18).

■Elisha prayed, and the Lord made the soldiers blind. Elisha took them to Samaria and told the king to feed them and send them home (2 Kin 6:8-23).

■Ben-Hadad laid siege to Samaria. This brought on a famine and prices went up (2 Kin 6: 24-25).

■A woman cried to the king for help. The king ripped his robes and swore that Elisha would die (2 Kin 6:26-31).

■Elisha told the king that by the next day, 7 quarts of flour would sell for 2/5 of an ounce of silver. And 13 quarts of barley would sell for 2/5 of an ounce of silver at the gate of Samaria. The king's officer said that it could not happen. Elisha told the officer that he would see it but would not eat any of the food (2 Kin 6:32-7:2).

■Four lepers went to the Aramean camp, but nobody was there. The lepers ate and carried away silver, gold and clothes. Then they realized that they were doing wrong, so they reported the news to the gatekeepers. The people went out and looted the Aramean camp. So food was the price that Elisha had predicted. The officer who had said it could not happen was trampled to death at the city gate. Things happened just as Elisha had foretold (2 Kin 7:3-19).

Judah: Jehoram and Ahaziah

■Jehoram was 32 years old when he began his 8 year reign in Jerusalem. He married a daughter of Ahab and did evil. Jehoram killed all his brothers. Jehoram died and Ahaziah his son succeeded him as king (2 Kin 8:16-24; 2 Chr 21:2-4).

■Ahaziah was 33 years old when he began his one-year reign. His mother, Athaliah, was a daughter of Ahab. He copied the ways of Ahab's family. Ahaziah allied himself with king Joram of Israel. Ahaziah went to Jezreel to visit Joram, his wounded ally (2 Kin 8:25-29).

Israel: Jehu

■Elisha ordered a young prophet to go to Ramoth Gilead to anoint Jehu king of Israel. Jehu rode to Jezreel where Joram was recovering from injuries. King Ahaziah was also there. Jehu killed both king Joram of Israel and King Ahaziah of Judah (2 Kin 9:1-29).

■Jehu went to Jezreel where Jezebel was killed. Things happened as the Lord promised through Elijah (2 Kin 9:30-37).

■Jehu proceeded to kill everyone who had any connection with Ahab. It happened just as the Lord had promised through Elijah (2 Kin 10:1-17).

■Jehu summoned all the prophets of Baal to a sacrifice. They crowded into the temple of Baal. Jehu's officers killed everyone in the temple. Then the temple of Baal was demolished (2 Kin 10:18-29).

■The Lord promised Jehu that his descendants would be kings of Israel for four generations. Jehu did not turn away from the sins of Jeroboam. Jehu reigned over Israel in Samaria for 28 years. Jehu died, and Jehoahaz his son succeeded him as king (2 Kin 10:18-35).

Judah: Athaliah and Joash

■After Ahaziah was killed, his mother Athaliah massacred the whole royal family. Ahaziah's sister hid Ahaziah's son, Joash. Joash was hidden at the temple for six years (2 Kin 11:1-3).

■In the seventh year, Jehoiada, the priest, brought out Joash and crowned him king (2 Kin 11:4-12; 2 Chr 23:1-11).

■Queen Athaliah was killed (2 Kin 11:13-16).

■Jehoiada then made a covenant between the Lord, the king, and the people. The people tore Baal's temple down and killed Baal's priest (2 Kin 11:17-21).

■Joash was 7 years old when he became king, and he reigned in Jerusalem 40 years. Joash did right for as long as Jehoiada the priest instructed him. However, the sacred fertility shrines were not removed (2 Kin 12:1-3).

■Jehoiada chose two wives for Joash (2 Chr 24:3).

■Joash ordered the priests to repair the temple (2 Kin 12:4-16).

■The priest Jehoiada died when he was 130 years old. Then the king listened to the officials of Judah,

abandoned the Lord's temple and worshiped idols of the sex goddess Asherah. Zechariah, son of Jehoiada the priest, condemned Joash. Joash gave the order for Zechariah to be killed (2 Chr 24:15-22).
- Two of Joash's officials assassinated him. His son Amaziah succeeded him (2 Kin 12:19-21).

Judah: Amaziah, Uzziah, Jotham and Ahaz
- Amaziah reigned in Judah for 29 years and did what was right (2 Kin 14:1-22). However, after Amaziah had victory over the Edomites, he brought back their gods and worshiped them (2 Chr 25:14-16).
- Amaziah died, and his son Uzziah (Azariah) succeeded him as king. Uzziah was 16 years old when he became king, and he reigned for 52 years (2 Kin 15:1-7).
- Uzziah (Azariah) did what was right during the days of Zechariah. As long as Uzziah sought the Lord, God gave him success (2 Chr 26:4-5).
- After Uzziah became powerful, his pride led to his downfall. He burned incense on the altar of incense. Azariah with 80 other priests confronted him. Uzziah was raging at the priests when leprosy broke out on his forehead. Then Uzziah's son, Jotham, governed the nation. Uzziah died, and Jotham his son succeeded him as king (2 Chr 26:16-22).
- Jotham was 25 years old when he became king of Judah, and he reigned 16 years. He did what was right (2 Kin 15:32-38).
- When Jotham died, his son Ahaz succeeded him as king. Ahaz was 20 years old when he became king. He reigned in Judah for 16 years. He imitated the kings of Israel and even sacrificed his son in the fire (2 Kin 16:1-20).

Israel: Kings who Succeeded Jehu
- All the kings of Israel who succeeded Jehu did evil by following the sins of Jeroboam, who had caused Israel to sin. So the Lord's anger burned against Israel (2 Kin 13:1 - 15:31).
- Hoshea was the last king of israel. He did evil in the eyes of the Lord (2 Kin 17:1-4).

Israel: Israel Exiled
- Shalmaneser, king of Assyria, captured Samaria and relocated the Israelites in other countries (2 Kin 17:5-6).
- The exile came about because the Israelites had sinned against the Lord their God. The Lord warned Israel and Judah through all his prophets. But they would not listen. They followed worthless idols, and they themselves became worthless. So the Lord became so angry with Israel that he removed them from his presence. Only the tribe of Judah was left, but Judah followed the practices Israel had introduced (2 Kin 17:7-23).
- The Israelites were exiled to Assyria. The king of Assyria relocated people from other nations in the towns of Samaria. The newcomers did not worship the Lord; so he sent lions who mauled and killed the people. Then one of the exiled priests from Samaria, returned to Bethel and taught them how to worship the Lord. These people both worshiped the Lord and served their idols. This was the beginning of the Samaritan people (2 Kin 17:24-41).

Final-situation:
The people of Israel followed worthless idols, and they themselves became worthless. The Lord became so angry with Israel that he removed them from his presence. The king of Assyria captured Samaria and relocated the Israelites in other countries. He also relocated people from other nations in the towns of Samaria. The newcomers tried to worship the Lord and their own idols at the same time.

Only the tribe of Judah was left, but Judah followed the practices Israel had introduced.

BIBLE STORY

Israel: Ahaziah and Elijah

Ahaziah succeeded his father Ahab as king. Ahaziah ruled for two years imitating the evil example of his father (1 Kin 22:51-53).

Ahaziah fell off the rooftop of his palace and was injured. Ahaziah sent messengers to consult Baal-Zebub, the god of Ekron, to find out if he would recover from his injury.

Elijah met Ahaziah's men and told them to return to the king with God's Word: "Is it because there is no God in Israel that you are running off to consult Baal-Zebub, the god of Ekron?' This is what the Lord says: `You will not leave the bed you are in. You will die!'"

Ahaziah received Elijah's message. Then he sent a captain with 50 men to Elijah. Elijah was sitting on the top of a hill. The captain ordered him: "Man of God, the king orders: `Come down!'"

Elijah answered: "If I am a man of God, may fire come down from heaven and cremate you and your 50 men!" Fire fell from heaven and cremated the captain and his men.

King Ahaziah sent to Elijah another captain with his 50 men. The captain said to him: "Man of God, the king orders you to come down at once!"

Elijah replied: "If I am a man of God, may fire come down from heaven and cremate you and your 50 men!" Then fire fell from heaven and cremated the captain and his 50 men.

King Ahaziah sent a third captain with his fifty men. This third captain went up and fell on his knees before Elijah and begged: "Man of God, please have respect for my life and the lives of these 50 men, your servants!"

Elijah got up and went down with him to see the king. Elijah told King Ahaziah: "The Lord says: Because you sent messengers to consult Baal-Zebub, the god of Ekron, as if there were no God in Israel to whom you could pray, you will never leave your bed alive. You will die!"

King Ahaziah died. Since Ahaziah had no son,

his brother Joram succeeded him as king (2 Kin 1:1-19).

Israel: Elijah Taken up to Heaven

Just before God took Elijah to heaven in a whirlwind, Elijah and Elisha were walking out of Gilgal. Elijah said to Elisha: "Stay here; the Lord has sent me to Bethel."

Elisha answered: "As surely as the Lord lives and as you live, I will not leave you." So they both went down to Bethel.

The company of the prophets at Bethel met Elisha and asked: "Do you know that the Lord is going to take your master away from you today?"

Elisha replied: "Yes, I know, but do not talk about it."

At Bethel Elijah told him: "Stay here, Elisha; the Lord has sent me to Jericho."

Elisha replied: "As surely as the Lord lives and as you live, I will not leave you." So they both went to Jericho.

The company of the prophets at Jericho went to Elisha and asked him: "Do you know that the Lord is going to take your master away from you today?"

Elisha replied: "Yes, I know, but do not talk about it."

Then Elijah said to him: "Stay here; the Lord has sent me to the Jordan." But Elisha stayed with Elijah.

Fifty men of the company of the prophets gathered some distance away while Elijah and Elisha stopped at the Jordan. Elijah took his robe rolled it up and struck the water with it. The water divided, and the two men crossed over on dry ground (2 Kin 2:1-8).

When they reached the other side, Elijah asked Elisha: "What can I do for you before I am taken from you?"

Elisha replied: "Let me inherit a double share of your spirit."

Elijah said: "You have asked a hard thing. But if you see me when I am taken from you, it will be yours. If you do not, it will not happen."

They were walking along and talking together. Suddenly a chariot of fire and horses of fire separated Elijah from Elisha. Then Elijah went up to heaven in a whirlwind. Elisha saw it and shouted: "My father! My father! The chariots and horsemen of Israel!" Elisha saw him no more. Then he grabbed his own clothes and ripped them apart (2 Kin 2:9-12).

Elisha picked up the robe that had fallen from Elijah. He returned to the bank of the Jordan. Then he took Elijah's robe and hit the river with it and asked: "Where now is the Lord, the God of Elijah?" When he hit the river, the water divided and Elisha crossed over.

The company of the prophets from Jericho were watching. They said: "Elisha now has the spirit Elijah had" (2 Kin 2:13-18).

Israel: Some of Elisha's Miracles

Elisha went to Jericho. The men of the city told Elisha: "Look, this town is well situated, but the water is bad and the land is unproductive."

Elisha said: "Bring me a new bowl, and put salt in it." So they brought it to him.

Then Elisha went out to the spring and threw the salt into it, saying: "The Lord says: `I have healed this water. Never again will it cause death or make the land unproductive.'" And the water became wholesome, just as Elisha said (2 Kin 2:19-22).

As Elisha was walking to Bethel, some youths came out of the town and jeered him: "Go up, you baldhead! Out of our way, skinhead!" He turned, looked at them and called down a curse on them in the name of the Lord. Two bears came out of the woods and mauled 42 of the youths (2 Kin 2:23-25).

King Joram of Israel, King Jehoshaphat of Judah and the king of Edom became allies to fight against Moab. The prophet Elisha advised the kings to dig ditches all over the valley. The Lord filled the ditches with water.

When the Moabite army got up early in the morning, the sun was shining on the water. To the Moabites, the water reflecting the sun looked red, like blood. They said: "That's blood! Those kings must have fought and massacred each other. Now to the plunder, Moab!"

But when the Moabites entered the camp of Israel, the Israelites rose up and slaughtered the Moabites (2 Kin 3:1-27).

The wife of a man from the company of the prophets called out to Elisha: "Your servant my husband is dead. You know that he was devoted to the Lord. But now his creditor is coming to take my two boys as his slaves."

Elisha replied to her: "How can I help you? Tell me, what do you have in your house?"

The widow answered: "Nothing at all, except a little jar of oil."

Elisha said: "Go around and ask all your neighbors for empty jars. Don't ask for just a few. Then go inside and close the door behind you and your sons. Pour oil into all the jars. When each is filled, set it aside."

She did what he said. She shut the door. Only she and her sons were in the house. As they brought the jars to her, she poured the oil. When all the jars were full, she said to her son: "Bring me another jar."

Her son replied: "No jar is left." Then the oil stopped flowing.

The widow went to Elisha and told him what happened. Elisha said: "Go, sell the oil and pay your debts. You and your sons can live on what is left" (2 Kin 4:1-7).

A wealthy woman in Shunem suggested to her husband that they make a room for Elisha to stay with them when he was in their town. They added a small room to the roof of their house and put in it a bed, a table, a chair and a lamp for Elisha.

The woman's husband was old and they had no son. Elisha promised the woman: "About this time next year, you will hold a son in your arms."

The woman became pregnant. The next year she gave birth to a son, just as Elisha had promised.

The child grew. One day he went to his father, who was with the men harvesting grain. The boy screamed: "My head! My head!"

His father ordered a servant: "Carry him to his mother." The servant took the boy to his mother and he sat on her lap until noon. Then he died. The mother took the boy and laid him on Elisha's bed, then she shut the door and left to find Elisha.

When she reached the man of God, she grabbed his feet. Elisha's servant Gehazi came over to push her away, but Elisha said: "Leave her alone! She is in bitter distress."

Elisha went to the house and found the boy lying dead on his bed. He went in the room and shut the door. Only he and the boy were there. Elisha prayed. Then he got on the bed and lay on the boy, mouth to mouth, eyes to eyes, hands to hands. As he stretched out over him, the boy's body grew warm. Elisha got up and paced back and forth in the room. Then he got on the bed and stretched out upon the boy again. The boy sneezed seven times and opened his eyes.

Elisha summoned the boy's mother and said: "Take your son." She came in, fell at his feet and bowed to the ground. Then she took her son and went out (2 Kin 4:8-36).

Naaman was commander of the army of the king of Aram. The king highly regarded Naaman. Naaman was a valiant soldier, but he had leprosy.

The Arameans had taken captive an Israelite girl who became a maid to Naaman's wife. She told her mistress: "If my master could see the prophet in Samaria, he would cure him of his leprosy."

Naaman went to his king and reported what the Israelite girl had said. The king told him to go to Israel. Naaman took about 750 pounds of silver, 150 pounds of gold and ten sets of clothes. The king of Aram prepared a letter for the king of Israel which read: "With this letter I am sending my servant Naaman to you so that you may cure him of his leprosy."

When the king of Israel read the letter, he ripped his robes and said: "Am I God? Can I kill and bring back to life? Why does this fellow send someone to me to be cured of his leprosy? He is trying to pick a fight with me!"

Elisha sent word to the king: "Why have you ripped your robes? Have the man come to me and he will learn that there is a prophet in Israel" (2 Kin 5:1-8).

So Naaman went with his horses and chariots and stopped at the door of Elisha's house. Elisha sent a servant who told Naaman: "Go, immerse yourself seven times in the Jordan River, and your skin will be healed and you will be cleansed."

Naaman went away angry and said: "I thought that he would personally come out and stand before me and call on the name of the Lord his God. I thought he would wave his hand over the diseased spot and cure me of my leprosy. Are not the rivers of Damascus cleaner than any of the rivers of Israel? Couldn't I wash in them? Then I would be clean." So he turned and went off in a rage.

Naaman's servants told him: "My father, if the prophet had asked you to do something hard and heroic, would you not have done it? So why not this simple: `Wash and be cleansed'!" So Naaman went down and immersed himself in the Jordan seven times. His skin was healed and became clean like that of a young boy.

Then Naaman and all his attendants went back to the man of God. He stood before Elisha and said: "Now I know that there is no God anywhere in the world except the God in Israel. Please accept a gift from me."

Elisha answered: "As surely as the Lord lives, whom I serve, I will accept nothing from you." Naaman insisted, but Elisha refused.

Naaman requested: "Please give me as much dirt as a pair of mules can carry, because I will never again make burnt offerings and sacrifices to any other god but the Lord. But there is one thing for which I need God to forgive me: My master goes to the temple of Rimmon to worship. When he goes, he will lean on my arm. When he bows down, I must bow in that temple. May the Lord forgive me for this."

Elisha said: "Go in peace" (2 Kin 5:9-19).

Gehazi, the servant of Elisha, said to himself: "My master was too easy on Naaman by not accepting gifts from him. I will run after him and get something from him."

So Gehazi hurried after Naaman. When Naaman saw him running toward him, he got down from the chariot and asked: "Is something wrong?"

Gehazi answered: "Everything is all right, but something came up. My master sent me to say: `Two young men from the company of the prophets have just showed up from the hill country of Ephraim. Please give them 75 pounds of silver and two sets of clothing.'"

Naaman said: "By all means, take 150 pounds of silver. He tied up the silver in two bags, with two sets of clothing. He sent two servants to carry the gifts. Gehazi took the things from Naaman and stored them away in his own house. Then he returned and stood before his master Elisha.

Elisha asked: "Where have you been, Gehazi?"

Gehazi answered: "Your servant didn't go anywhere."

Elisha replied: "This is not the time to take money, or to accept clothes, olive groves, vineyards, flocks, herds, or menservants and maidservants! Naaman's leprosy will cling to you and to your descendants forever." Then Gehazi walked away from Elisha's presence, and his skin was leprous, as white as snow (2 Kin 5:20-26).

Israel: Elisha's Knowledge During War

Ben-Hadad king of Aram was at war with Israel. Time and again Elisha warned the king of Israel the location where Ben-Hadad had set up an ambush.

Ben-Hadad was enraged. He summoned his officers and demanded: "Tell me who is leaking information to the king of Israel!"

One of the king's officers replied: "None of us, my lord the king. Elisha, the prophet who is in Israel, tells the king of Israel the very words you whisper in your bedroom."

Elisha was in Dothan. The king dispatched an army with horses and chariots to capture Elisha. They surrounded the city during the night. Elisha's servant got up early the next morning and saw the army all around the city. The servant cried out: "Oh, my master, what shall we do?"

Elisha answered: "Don't be afraid. There are more on our side than on their side." Elisha prayed: "O Lord, open his eyes and let him see." The Lord opened the servant's eyes, and he saw the hills full of horses and chariots of fire surrounding Elisha.

As the enemy attacked, Elisha prayed: "Lord, strike these people blind!" God made them blind.

Elisha told them: "This is not the road. This is not the city. Follow me, and I will lead you to the man you are looking for." And he led them to Samaria.

After they entered the city, Elisha said: "Lord, open the eyes of these men so they can see." Then the Lord opened their eyes and the Aramean army saw that they were trapped inside Samaria.

When the king of Israel saw them, he asked Elisha: "Shall I kill them? Shall I kill them?"

Elisha answered: "Do not kill them. Set a feast before them so that they may eat and drink and then go back to their master." After they had finished eating and drinking, they returned to their master. The soldiers from Aram stopped raiding Israel's territory (2 Kin 6:8-23).

Some time later, Ben-Hadad king of Aram mobilized his entire army and laid siege to Samaria. This brought on a terrible famine in the city; the siege lasted so long that a donkey's head sold for two pounds of sliver, and a bowl of field greens for two ounces of silver (2 Kin 6: 24-25).

The king of Israel was passing by on the wall and a woman cried to him: "Help me, my lord the king!"

The king replied: "If the Lord does not help you, how can I get help for you? What's the matter?"

She answered: "This woman said to me: `Give up your son so we may eat him today, and tomorrow we'll eat my son.' So we cooked my son and ate him. The next day I said to her: `Give up your son so we may eat him,' but she had hidden him."

When the king heard the woman's words, he ripped his robes. Underneath his robe, he was wearing sackcloth. He said: "May God punish me, if the head of Elisha remains on his shoulders today!" (2 Kin 6:26-31).

Elisha was sitting in his house, and the elders were sitting with him. Elisha said to the elders: "This murderer is sending someone to cut off my head? His master is behind him."

While Elisha was still talking to them, the executor arrived. Then the king arrived and said: "This disaster is from the Lord. I am fed up with the Lord!"

Elisha said: "Hear the Word of the Lord. About this time tomorrow, seven quarts of flour will sell for 2/5 of an ounce of silver. And 13 quarts of barley will be sold for 2/5 of an ounce of silver at the gate of Samaria."

The officer who was close to the king answered Elisha: "Look, even if the Lord should open trapdoors from heaven, that could not happen!"

Elisha answered: "You will see it with your own eyes, but you will not eat any of it!" (2 Kin 6:32-7:2).

There were four lepers sitting outside the city gate. They said to one another: "Why stay here until we die? If we enter the famine-struck city, we will die. If we stay here, we will die. Let's go over to the Aramean camp. If they receive us, we live; if they kill us, then we die."

At nightfall they went to the Aramean camp. They reached the edge of the camp, not a man was in camp! The Lord had caused the Arameans to hear the sound of chariots and horses and a mighty army marching. They said to one another: "The king of Israel has hired the Hittite and Egyptian kings to attack us!" They panicked and fled in the darkness, abandoning tents, horses and donkeys. They left the camp standing and ran for their lives.

The four lepers entered the camp and entered one of the tents. They ate and drank, and carried away silver, gold and clothes, and hid them. They returned and entered another tent and looted it and hid their plunder.

Then they said to each other: "We're doing wrong. Today we have good news and we are keeping it to ourselves. If we wait until daylight, we will be punished. Let's report this news to the king's palace."

So they went and called out to the city gatekeepers and told them what had happened: "We went into the Aramean camp and the place was deserted, only tethered horses and donkeys." The gatekeepers shouted the news, and it was reported within the palace.

The king sent out two chariots with horses after the Aramean army. The men found the road strewn with clothing and equipment the Arameans had thrown away in their panic. The messengers returned and reported to the king. Then the people went out and looted the Aramean camp. So seven quarts of flour sold for 2/5 of an ounce of silver. And 13 quarts of barley sold for 2/5 of an ounce of silver, as the Lord had said.

The king had put the officer who was close to him to guard the gate. But the people turned into a mob and trampled him to death at the city gate. Things happened just as Elisha had foretold the king: "About this time tomorrow, seven quarts of flour will sell for 2/5 of an ounce of silver. And 13 quarts of barley will be sold for 2/5 of an ounce of silver." Things happened as Elisha foretold the officer: "You will see it with your own eyes, but you will not eat any of it!" That is exactly what happened to him, for the people trampled him to death at the city gate (2 Kin 7:3-19).

Judah: Jehoram and Ahaziah

In the fifth year of Joram king of Israel, Jehoram son of Jehoshaphat began his reign as king of Judah. He was 32 years old when he became king, and he reigned in Jerusalem eight years. He imitated the ways of the kings of Israel, as the family of Ahab had done, for he married a daughter of Ahab. He did evil in the eyes of the Lord. Nevertheless, for the sake of his servant David, the Lord was not willing to destroy Judah. He had promised to maintain a lamp for David and his descendants forever. When Jehoram established himself firmly over his father's kingdom, he killed all his brothers.

Jehoram died, and Ahaziah his son succeeded him as king (2 Kin 8:16-24; 2 Chr 21:2-4).

Ahaziah was twenty-two years old when he became king, and he reigned in Jerusalem one year. His mother Athaliah was a daughter of Ahab. He copied the ways of the family of Ahab and did evil in the eyes of the Lord.

Ahaziah allied himself with King Joram of Israel to war against Hazael king of Aram at Ramoth Gilead. The Arameans wounded Joram of Israel, and he returned to Jezreel to recover. King Ahaziah went to Jezreel to visit his wounded ally, King Joram of Israel (2 Kin 8:25-29).

Israel: Jehu

Elisha ordered a young prophet to go to Ramoth Gilead, get Jehu away from his companions and anoint him king of Israel. The prophet anointed Jehu, told him that he was to destroy the house of Ahab and predicted that dogs would eat Jezebel. Jehu rode to Jezreel where Joram was recovering from injuries. King Ahaziah of Judah was visiting him. Joram and Ahaziah rode out, each in his own chariot, to meet Jehu. They met him at the plot of ground that had belonged to Naboth. Jehu shot an arrow into Joram and ordered that Joram's body be thrown on the land that had been Naboth's, thereby carrying out the Lord's Words. Jehu also killed Ahaziah (2 Kin 9:1-29).

Jehu went to Jezreel where Jezebel was posed at a window. Eunuchs threw her down, and horses ran over her body. Jehu went inside and ate. Then he ordered his men to bury Jezebel, but the men found nothing except her skull, feet and hands. Jehu said that things happened as the Lord promised through Elijah (2 Kin 9:30-37).

Ahab's family had 70 sons living in Samaria. The leaders of the city slaughtered all 70 of them, put their heads in baskets and sent them to Jehu in Jezreel. Jehu proceeded to kill everyone who had any connection with Ahab. It happened just as the Lord had promised through Elijah (2 Kin 10:1-17).

Then Jehu brought all the people together and said to them: "Ahab served Baal small-time; Jehu will serve him big-time! Summon all the prophets of Baal, because I am going to hold a great sacrifice for Baal." But Jehu was lying. He planned to destroy the prophets of Baal.

All the worshipers of Baal came and crowded into the temple of Baal. Jehu went into the temple of Baal and said: "Make sure there are no worshipers of the Lord here with you, only worshipers of Baal." Now Jehu had posted eighty men outside. As soon as Jehu had finished making the burnt offering, he ordered the guards and officers: "Enter and kill them; let no one escape." So they killed them with the sword. The guards and officers threw the corpses out and then entered the inner shrine of the temple of Baal. They demolished the sacred stone of Baal and tore down the temple of Baal, and people used it for a latrine (2 Kin 10:18-29).

Jehu destroyed Baal worship in Israel. The Lord said to Jehu: "Because you have done well in accomplishing what is right in my eyes and have destroyed the house of Ahab, your descendants will sit on the throne of Israel to the fourth generation." Yet Jehu was not careful to keep the law of the Lord, the God of Israel, with all his heart. He did not turn away from the sins of Jeroboam, the worship of the golden calves at Bethel and Dan, which caused Israel to sin. Jehu reigned over Israel in Samaria for 28 years. Jehu died, and Jehoahaz his son succeeded him as king (2 Kin 10:18-35).

Judah: Athaliah and Joash

Athaliah, the mother of Ahaziah, saw that her son was dead and she massacred all her grandsons except Joash, who was hidden by his Aunt Jehosheba. Joash remained hidden with Jehosheba at the temple of the Lord for six years while Athaliah ruled the land (2 Kin 11:1-3).

In the seventh year, Jehoiada the priest sent for the military commanders, the Levites and the heads of Israelite families from all the towns. They came to Jerusalem and made a covenant with the boy Joash at the temple of the Lord. Jehoiada armed the men and stationed them around the temple and around the young king.

Jehoiada brought out Joash and put the crown on him; he presented him with a copy of the Lord's covenant and proclaimed him king. They anointed him, and the people clapped and shouted: "Long live the king!" (2 Kin 11:4-12; 2 Chr 23:1-11).

Athaliah heard the shouting and she went to the temple of the Lord. Astonished, she saw the king flanked by the officers and the trumpeters. All the people were rejoicing and blowing trumpets. Then Athaliah ripped her robes and called out: "Treason! Treason!"

Jehoiada the priest ordered the troops: "Drag her outside and kill anyone who tries to follow her!" They dragged her out to the palace's horse corral; there they killed her (2 Kin 11:13-16).

Jehoiada then made a covenant between the Lord and the king, and the Lord and the people: they were the Lord's people. The people went to the temple of Baal and tore it down. They smashed the altars and idols to pieces and killed Baal's priest in front of the altars.

Then King Joash took his place on the royal throne, and all the people of the land rejoiced. And the city was quiet, because Athaliah had been slain (2 Kin 11:17-21).

Joash was seven years old when he became king and he reigned in Jerusalem forty years. Joash did what was right in the eyes of the Lord for as long as Jehoiada the priest instructed him. However, the sacred fertility shrines were not removed; the people continued to offer sacrifices and burn incense there (2 Kin 12:1-3).

Jehoiada chose two wives for Joash, and he had sons and daughters (2 Chr 24:3).

Joash ordered the priests to collect all the money that was brought into the temple for holy offerings and use it to repair whatever damage was found in the temple. Jehoiada the priest took a chest and bored a hole in its lid. He placed it beside the altar. The royal secretary and the high priest gave the money to the men appointed to supervise the work on the temple (2 Kin 12:4-16).

The priest Jehoiada died when he was 130 years old. After the death of Jehoiada, the king listened to the officials of Judah. The king and the officials abandoned the Lord's temple and worshiped idols of the sex goddess Asherah. Because of their guilt, God's anger came upon Judah and Jerusalem. The Lord sent prophets to bring the people back to him; however, they refused to listen.

Then the Spirit of God moved Zechariah, son of Jehoiada the priest, to speak up. He stood before the people and said: "God says: 'Why do you disobey the Lord's commands? You will not prosper. Because you have forsaken the Lord, he has forsaken you.'"

King Joash gave the order for Zechariah to be killed in the courtyard of the Lord's temple. King Joash did not remember the kindness Zechariah's father had shown him. He murdered Jehoiada's son. Zechariah's last words were: "May the Lord see this and punish you" (2 Chr 24:15-22).

Two of Joash's officials assassinated him. His son Amaziah succeeded him as king (2 Kin 12:19-21).

Judah: Amaziah, Uzziah, Jotham and Ahaz
Amaziah reigned in Judah for 29 years and he did what was right in the eyes of the Lord (2 Kin 14:1-22). However, after Amaziah had victory over the Edomites, he brought back their gods and worshiped them (2 Chr 25:14-16). Amaziah died, and his son Uzziah (Azariah) succeeded him as king. Uzziah was sixteen years old when he became king, and he reigned for 52 years (2 Kin 15:1-7).

Uzziah (Azariah) did what was right in the eyes of the Lord. He sought God during the days of Zechariah, who instructed him in the fear of God. As long as he sought the Lord, God gave him success (2 Chr 26:4-5).

After Uzziah became powerful, his pride led to his downfall. One day, he entered the temple of the Lord to burn incense on the altar of incense. Azariah with 80 other priests confronted him and said: "It is not right for you, Uzziah, to burn incense to the Lord. Only the priests, descendants of Aaron, who have been consecrated for the work are permitted to burn incense. Leave the sanctuary! You are unfaithful; you will not be honored by the Lord God."

Uzziah, censer in hand, was already burning incense. He became angry. While he was raging at the priests, leprosy broke out on his forehead. The Lord had afflicted him. King Uzziah had leprosy until the day he died. He lived in a separate house. Jotham his son governed the people of the land. Uzziah died, and Jotham his son succeeded him as king (2 Chr 26:16-22).

Jotham was 25 years when he became king of Judah, and he reigned 16 years. He did what was right in the eyes of the Lord (2 Kin 15:32-38). When Jotham died, his son Ahaz succeeded him as king.

Ahaz was 20 years old when he became king. He reigned in Judah for 16 years. Unlike David his ancestor, he did not do what was right in the eyes of the Lord. He imitated the kings of Israel and even sacrificed his son in the fire (2 Kin 16:1-20).

Israel: Kings who Succeeded Jehu
All the kings of Israel who succeeded Jehu did evil in the eyes of the Lord by following the sins of Jeroboam, who had caused Israel to sin, and they did not turn away from them. So the Lord's anger burned against Israel (2 Kin 13:1 - 15:31).

Elisha died and was buried (2 Kin 13:20).

During this period of history, many prophets, such as Hosea, Amos, Jonah, Micah and Isaiah, began collecting and writing their prophecies.

Hoshea was the last king of israel. He did evil in the eyes of the Lord (2 Kin 17:1-4).

Israel: Israel Exiled
Shalmaneser, king of Assyria invaded all the land of Israel. He laid siege to Samaria for three years. He captured Samaria and deported the Israelites to Assyria. He relocated them in other countries which he had captured (2 Kin 17:5-6).

The exile came about because the Israelites had sinned against the Lord their God, who had delivered them from Egypt and the brutal oppression of Pharaoh king of Egypt. They worshiped other gods. They followed the practices of the nations the Lord had driven out before them. They also followed the evil practices that the kings of Israel introduced. The Israelites secretly did things that were offensive to the Lord their God. They openly built sex-and-religion shrines in all their towns. They set up sacred stones and Asherah poles on every high hill and under every spreading tree. The Lord warned

Israel and Judah through all his prophets: "Turn from your evil ways. Observe my commands and decrees, in accordance with the Law that I commanded your fathers to obey and which my prophets keep reminding you to obey."

But they were more stiff-necked than their stubborn ancestors and would not listen. They followed worthless idols, and they themselves became worthless. They forsook all the commands of the Lord their God. They made for themselves two idols cast in the shape of calves, and an idol to the prostitute goddess Asherah. They bowed down to all the starry hosts, and they frequented the sex-and-religion shrines of Baal. They sacrificed their sons and daughters in the fire. They practiced divination and sorcery and prostituted themselves to do every kind of evil in the eyes of the Lord, provoking him to anger.

So the Lord became so angry with Israel that he removed them from his presence. Only the tribe of Judah was left, and even Judah did not keep the commands of the Lord their God. Judah followed the practices Israel had introduced (2 Kin 17:7-23).

The people of Israel were taken from their homeland into exile in Assyria. The king of Assyria brought people from other nations he had conquered and relocated them in the towns of Samaria, replacing the exiled Israelites. They took over Samaria and lived in its towns. When they first moved in, they did not worship the Lord; so he sent lions among them, and people were mauled and killed.

Then the king of Assyria gave this order: "Have a priest you took captive from Samaria go back to live there and teach the people what the god of the land requires." One of the priests who had been exiled from Samaria returned to live in Bethel and taught them how to worship the Lord.

Nevertheless, each national group made its own gods in the towns where they settled, and set them up in the sex-and-religion shrines the citizens of Samaria had left behind. They worshiped the Lord, but they also served their own gods in accordance with the customs of the nations from which they had been exiled. These people tried to worship both the Lord and serve their idols. Their descendants continued to do as their fathers did. This was the beginning of the Samaritan people (2 Kin 17:24-41).

LIFE-LESSONS DISCOVERED IN THE STORY

1. God communicates with people. Even though all the kings of Israel rebelled against the Lord, he continued to send his prophets who proclaimed God's message.

2. The skeptic does not nullify God's existence; neither does he limit God's power. Ahaziah did not believe in the Lord God, and ordered his messengers to consult the god Baal-Zebub. God ordered Elijah to tell the king's messengers that the king would die. The king ordered soldiers to arrest Elijah; however, fire from heaven cremated them. The Lord determined the death of the king who did not believe in him (2 Kin 1:1-17).

3. The wise person observes the consequences of other people's mistakes, and avoids repeating them. Twice, King Ahaziah ordered an official with 50 soldiers to arrest Elijah. Each time the official ordered Elijah to come down and each time fire from heaven cremated the official and his men. The third official didn't repeat the mistake of the first two. He humbled himself and asked for mercy (2 Kin 1:9-15).

4. People who serve God have different personalities, and their ministry and methods will be different. The same Spirit that was on Elijah was also on Elisha (2 Kin 2:15). The Spirit and the authority were the same for both Elijah and Elisha. But, their personalities were different, and their ministries were different. Elijah lived in solitude and hit high points in his fight against false gods and sin; however, he also fell into the valley of despair. Elisha was constantly with the people. He gave advice to solve their problems and brought healing. Elijah was a lonely prophet, while Elisha was constantly with other people, especially with those who were in the school of prophets.

5. Divine power has two sides. It helps some and punishes others. Elisha possessed divine power. The city of Jericho sought Elisha's help, and he healed their water. Youth jeered Elisha and two bears mauled them (2 Kin 2:19-25).

6. To ridicule one of God's servants is to show contempt against the God he serves. The youth who jeered Elisha were killed by two bears (2 Kin 2:23-25).

7. The spiritual leader who takes a stand for God becomes vulnerable to verbal abuse. Elisha was jeered by the youth (2 Kin 2:23-25).

8. The person who desires to benefit from God's miracle-working power needs to obey the Lord's orders. God multiplied the olive oil for the widow. However, the widow followed Elisha's instructions when she borrowed empty jugs, poured the olive oil into the jugs and sold the oil (2 Kin 4:1-7). God cured Naaman; however, he had obeyed God, immersing himself seven times in the Jordan River (2 Kin 5:1-14).

9. The head of the home needs to avoid debts that could bring hardships on his family. The widow sought help from Elisha, because her dead

husband left a debt she could not pay, and a creditor was going to take their two children as his slaves (2 Kin 4:1-7).

10. A person who is in a humble position can still spread God's Word. Naaman's slave girl was an Israelite, kidnapped from her country. Yet, she told Naaman's wife about the prophet in Israel (2 Kin 5:3-4).

11. A person who desires for God to act in his favor, must humble himself. Naaman the hero was a proud man, and he expected the prophet of God to give him special treatment (2 Kin 5:11-13). All people are equal before God. The Lord does not show partiality; therefore, each person must humble himself in the presence of the Lord.

12. God's requirement for people often seems too simple. Naaman had trouble accepting God's cure: wash in a dirty river and be clean (2 Kin 5:11-14).

13. God's favor can not be purchased. Elisha refused Naaman's gifts to show that God's favor cannot be purchased (2 Kin 5:16).

14. God's servant becomes a mercenary if he gives into temptation to seek personal gain ahead of serving God. Gehazi had been a faithful servant to Elisha. But when he took the opportunity to get rich by asking for the reward Elisha had refused, he became a mercenary (2 Kin 5:20-27). One cannot serve both God and money (Mt 6:24).

15. The mercenary religious leader wants to use his God-given position for his own financial gain; however, he will be punished by the Lord God. Gehazi wanted to profit from Naaman's cure (2 Kin 5:19-27) Gehazi, Elisha's disciple, can be compared to Judas, Jesus' disciple. Both had lingering and intimate contact with God's messengers. However, each sought to use his privileged religious position for his own financial gain. Some examples of mercenary religious leaders are: Balaam (Nm 22-24, 31:16); Gehazi (2 Kin 5:19-27); Judas (Jn 12:4-6); Simon, the magician (Ac 8:18-20).

16. The person who prays and has faith may experience God's power using simple objects of little value to accomplish great things. Each time that Elisha helped people with their difficulties, he used a simple object that was easily available to accomplish a problem solving miracle: salt (2 Kin 2:21); olive oil (2 Kin 4:2-7); breath (2 Kin 4:34); flour (2 Kin 4:41); bread (2 Kin 4:42-44) and a piece of wood (2 Kin 6:6). These objects didn't have any power; God's power operated in Elisha, a person who prayed and had faith.

17. God's servant is freed from fear when he has a spiritual perception of life's problems. Elisha's assistant was terrified when he saw troops surrounding their city. Elisha prayed and the servant received the ability to see divine protection (2 Kin 6:14-17). (See Ps 34:7; 119:18.)

18. God is always doing more for his people than they can realize through their sight and understanding. God opened the eyes of Elisha's servant so he could see God's mighty heavenly army (2 Kin 6:16-17).

19. Skepticism is a sin against God and deprives individuals of blessings that God is ready to grant. The king's official who disbelieved Elisha's prediction that cheap food would be available the next day, was unable to participate in the blessing (2 Kin 7:1-2, 16-20). Skepticism on the part of individuals, can have national consequences. Nu 13:25-14:38 tells how the Israelites had to wander in the wilderness for forty years because of unbelief. (See Hb 3:16-19 and Mt 13:58.)

20. The person who is blessed by God should share the news with others so they too can receive the same blessing. The lepers, who found the Arameans camp vacated, discovered wealth beyond their wildest dreams. It was a time of good-news. It would be wrong to hide the news (2 Kin 7:3-9).

21. The person who has a godly heritage should not marry someone who doesn't have faith in God. King Jehoshaphat, king of Judah, sought the Lord and followed his commands (2 Chr 17:3-4). However, his son Jehoram married Athaliah, a daughter of Ahab. Jehoram followed the evil example of Ahab's family (2 Kin 8:18; 2 Chr 21:6-13). Jehoram's marriage was politically advantageous, but spiritually it was deadly.

22. A person can be active in doing things for God, yet not give God his heartfelt obedience. Jehu obeyed many of the Lord's commands, but he did not obey the Lord with all his heart (2 Kin 10:30-31).

23. The leader whose counselors are wise, godly men will do what is right. King Joash did what was right all the years when Jehoiada the priest was his counselor (2 Chr 24:2.) King Uzziah sought God during the days of Zechariah, who instructed him in the fear of God (2 Chr 26:5). The opposite is also true; the leader whose counselors are ungodly men will do evil. Joash did evil after Jehoiada the priest died and he started listening to the ungodly officials of Judah (2 Chr 24:17-18).

24. While it is important to learn from teachers, a person needs to be able to make the right choices independently of others. King Joash did what was right all the years when Jehoiada the priest was alive (2 Chr 24:2.) But Joash did evil after Jehoiada the priest died (2 Chr 24:17-18). King

Uzziah sought God during the days of Zechariah (2 Chr 26:5).

25. The person who desires God's help needs to be faithful to him. As long as Uzziah sought the Lord, God gave him success (2 Chr 26:4-5). After Uzziah became powerful, his pride led to his downfall and to his having leprosy (2 Chr 26:16-22).

26. The traitor will be betrayed. King Joash killed Zechariah whose father, Jehoiada, had been his counselor (2 Chr 24:17-21). Later Joash was killed by his officials (2 Chr 25:25).

27. Religious syncretism that mixes worship of the Lord God with worship of other gods, is both rejected and punished by God. The author of First and Second Kings shows that religious schism was the great sin of the Israelites (1 Kin 12:25-33), the main sin remembered against each king of Israel, and it was the original sin of Israel (2 Kin 17:7, 21-23).

28. People who know the Word of God and who have experienced his acting in their behalf, yet sin against him, will be punished. The destruction of Israel happened because the Israelites sinned against God and worshiped other gods (2 Kin 17:7).

29. Secret sins are known by God, and secret insubordination is as evil as open rebellion. Israel was punished for both their public sins and their secret sins. They committed idolatry in public, but they committed even worse sins in private (2 Kin 17:9).

30. The worldliness that surrounds God's people attracts them to spiritual impurity and immorality. The paganism that surrounded Israel attracted them to idolatry and immorality. The Israelites thought that the key to prosperity and wisdom was found in the pagan worship and in the customs of the people who surrounded them. When they deviated from worshiping the true God, they brought God's punishment upon themselves.

31. People can know God as either their Savior or their destroyer. God delivered his people from slavery in Egypt, and he desired to always be their Savior, liberator and protector. After the Israelites abandoned God to follow the sex-and-religion gods of the people around them, God became their punisher; he destroyed Israel (2 Kin 17:7-18).

QUESTIONS

1. How did Elijah depart from this world?
2. How were Elijah and Elisha similar?
3. How were Elijah and Elisha different?
4. How was Naaman cured from his leprosy?
5. What does Naaman's cure teach us about the way God treats important people?
6. What do Elisha's miracles teach us about God?
7. What was Gehazi's sin?
8. How was Gehazi punished?
9. What was the lepers' reaction when they found wealth in the Arameans' abandoned camp?
10. What happened to the king's official who was skeptical when Elisha predicted that food would be cheap the next day?
11. What influence did the Priest Jehoiada have over King Joash?
12. What teacher has most influenced you to serve the Lord?
13. Why did God keep sending prophets to kings and people who constantly rebelled against him?
14. Why did God use the king of Assyria to punish and to destroy Israel?
15. What was the main sin that caused God to destroy Israel?
16. What should the people of God today learn from Israel's sins and God's punishment?

NEBUCHADNEZZAR'S INVASIONS OF JERUSALEM

INVASION	KING OF JUDAH	YEAR	TEXT	EVENTS
1st	Jehoiakim	605 B.C.	2 Kin 24:1; Jer 46:2-13; Dan 1:1-7	Nebuchadnezzar invaded Judah, and Jehoiakim submitted to him without resistence. The Babylonians took some objects of value from the Temple and some intelligent youths to Babylon. Daniel and his friends were taken in this group (Dan 1:2-7; 2 Kin 24:1). After three years, Jehoiakim rebelled against Nebuchadnezzar (2 Kin 24:1-7).
2nd	Jehoiachin	597 B.C.	2 Kin 24:8 - 17	Nebuchadnezzar advanced on Jerusalem. Jehoiachin surrendered to him. Nebuchadnezzar took captive the important people of the city and treasures from the Temple and the palace.
3rd	Zedekiah	587 B.C.	2 Kin 24:20 - 25:30	Nebuchadnezzar captured Jerusalem. He destroyed the city, the temple and the city walls. He carried the populace of Judah into exile (2 Kin 25:1-21).

INSTABILITY IN THE PARTIAL KINGDOM
Partial Kingdom
2 Kings 18 - 25; 2 Chronicles 29 - 36

STRUCTURE

Context:
When Saul, David and Solomon were kings, all 12 tribes of Israel were together in one kingdom. After the death of King Solomon, the Kingdom was divided. Ten tribes rebelled against the king who was David's descendant and became the Kingdom of Israel. Two tribes remained loyal to the king who was David's grandson and became the Kingdom of Judah.

All of the kings of Israel rejected the covenant with God and served sex-and-religion idols.

Some of the kings of Judah imitated David and served the Lord, but most rejected the covenant with God and imitated the kings of Israel.

The people of Israel followed worthless idols. So the Lord became so angry with Israel that he removed them from his presence. The king of Assyria captured Samaria and relocated the Israelites in other countries.

Only the tribe of Judah was left, but Judah followed the practices Israel had introduced.

Key-persons: Kings of Judah: Hezekiah, Manasseh, Josiah; King Shalmaneser of Assyria; King Nebuchadnezzar of Babylon. Prophets: Isaiah, Jeremiah

Key-location: Jerusalem

Key-repetitions:
- Provoked the Lord to anger: (2 Kin 21:6, 15; 22:13, 17; 23:19, 26; 24:20).
- Kings who did right in the eyes of the Lord and imitated David: Hezekiah (2 Kin 18:3); Josiah (2 Kin 22:2).
- Kings who did evil in the eyes of the Lord and caused the people to sin. They imitated the kings of Israel, or their ancestors: Manasseh (2 Kin 21:2); Amon (2 Kin 21:20); Jehoahaz (2 Kin 23:32); Johoiakim (2 Kin 23:37); Jehoiachin (2 Kin 24:9); Zedekiah (2 Kin 24:19).
- Prophets received the Word of the Lord and spoke the Word of the Lord: Isaiah; Huldah; Jeremiah; Ezekiel; Habakkuk; and prophets whose names are not mentioned.
- Fathers and sons who had an opposite kind of relationship with God: Jotham did right (2 Kin 15:34), but his son Ahaz did evil (2 Kin 16:2-3). Hezekiah did right (2 Kin 18:3), but his son was an evil man (2 Kin 21:2-9); Amon did evil and was an idolater (2 Kin 21:19-22), but his son Josiah constantly did what was right, he served the Lord with all his heart (2 Kin 22;2; 23:24-25), but his son Jehoahaz did evil (2 Kin 23:32) and his son Jehoiakim (2 Kin 23:37) did evil.
- Judah was attacked by enemy kings: Sennacherib, king of Assyria (2 Kin 18:13 - 19:37); Nebuchadnezzar; king of Babylon attacked three times.

Key-attitudes:
- The righteousness of kings Hezekiah and Josiah; but, the wickedness of the other kings of Judah.
- The arrogance of the Assyrians when they attacked Jerusalem.
- The anguish of Jeremiah.
- The calamity of the nation of Judah.
- The arrogance and cruelty of the Babylonians.
- The Lord felt both anger and love for Judah.
- The sovereignty of the Lord God.

Initial-problem:
When the Assyrians conquered Israel because the Israelites had sinned against the Lord, Hezekiah was king of Judah.

Sequence of events:

King Hezekiah and the Prophet Isaiah

- Hezekiah was 25 years old when he became king of Judah. He ruled 29 years. He did right. He destroyed the worship of false gods. The Lord was with him (2 Kin 18:1-8).
- In King Hezekiah's fourth year, Shalmaneser, king of Assyria, captured Samaria (2 Kin 18:9-12).
- The king of Assyria sent his military chiefs to ask King Hezekiah if he were depending on the Lord (2 Kin 18:17-25).
- Hezekiah's officials asked the field commander to speak in Aramaic instead of Hebrew. The commander shouted in Hebrew for those sitting on the wall to hear. He shouted for them not to let Hezekiah fool them into trusting in the Lord (2 Kin 18:26-35; Is 36:1-20).
- The people were silent (2 Kin 18:36-37).
- King Hezekiah sent officials to the prophet Isaiah. Isaiah sent word to Hezekiah that the king of Assyria would retreat to his own country where he would be killed (2 Kin 19:1-7; Is 37:1-7).
- Sennacherib received a report that the king of Egypt was marching out to fight against him. Sennacherib sent a letter to Hezekiah telling him that the Lord would not prevent Jerusalem from falling to the king of Assyria (2 Kin 19:9-13; Is 37:8-13).
- Hezekiah took the letter to the Temple, spread it out before the Lord and prayed (2 Kin 19:14-19; Is 37:14-20).
- Isaiah sent Hezekiah a message that the Lord had heard his prayer and that the king of Assyria would not enter Jerusalem (2 Kin 19:20-34; Is 37:21-35).
- That night the Lord massacred 185,000 Assyrian soldiers. Sennacherib headed home for Nineveh. There, two of his sons killed him (2 Kin 19:35-37; Is 37:36-38).
- Hezekiah became deathly sick. Isaiah told him to prepare to die. Hezekiah prayed, and the Lord let him live 15 more years (2 Kin 20:1-11; Is 38:1-22).
- Hezekiah became arrogant. This provoked God to anger. Then Hezekiah repented, and the Lord withdrew his anger (2 Chr 32:24-26).
- The son of the king of Babylon sent Hezekiah a gift. Hezekiah gave the Babylonian messengers a tour of all his prized possessions. Isaiah told Hezekiah that everything in his palace would be taken away to Babylon. Some of his sons would become eunuchs in Babylon (2 Kin 20:12-19; Is 39:1-8).

King Manasseh

- Hezekiah died and Manasseh his son succeeded him as king. Manasseh was 12 years old when he became king, and he ruled 55 years. He did evil. He reintroduced the practices of the nations the Lord had driven out before the Israelites. He rebuilt the sex-and-religion shrines his father Hezekiah had destroyed. He erected images to the sex god Baal and the sex goddess Asherah. He put the idol of the sex goddess Asherah in the temple. He shed innocent blood (2 Kin 21:1-9).
- The Lord spoke through his prophets condemning Manasseh and predicting the destruction of Judah (2 Kin 21:10-15).
- Manasseh and his people ignored the Lord's Word. The king of Assyria took Manasseh prisoner. In his distress he sought the Lord, and God brought him back to Jerusalem. Then Manasseh knew that the Lord is God (2 Chr 33:10-17).
- Manasseh died, and Amon his son succeeded him. Amon became king when he was 22. He did evil, and his officials assassinated him. Josiah his son became the next king (2 Kin 21:19-26).

King Josiah

- Josiah was 8 years old when he became king, and he ruled 31 years. He did what was right and copied his ancestor David (2 Kin 22:1-2).
- Zephaniah, Nahum and Habakkuk were prophets during the time when Josiah was king.
- In the eighteenth year of his reign, Josiah ordered that the Temple be repaired. Hilkiah the high priest found the Book of the Law. When King Josiah heard the words of the Book of the Law, he ripped his robes. He ordered his officials to inquire of the Lord. The prophetess Huldah told them that the Lord would bring catastrophe on Judah. Everything written in the book would happen. But Josiah would not live to see the disaster (2 Kin 22:3-20; 2 Chr 34:1-28).
- King Josiah assembled all the leaders of Judah and renewed the covenant to follow the Lord and keep his commands (2 Kin 23:1-3).
- Josiah ordered the high priest Hilkiah to remove from the Temple everything made for Baal, Asherah and all the stars of heaven. He did away with the pagan priests. He took the Asherah pole from the Temple. He tore down the living-quarters for the male shrine prostitutes and made impure the local religious shrines. He hauled off the horse statues dedicated to the sun god. He made impure the sex-and-religion shrines that Solomon had built (2 Kin 23:4-14).
- Josiah demolished and made impure the altar at Bethel made by Jeroboam, who had caused Israel to sin. This happened as the Lord had said it would to Jeroboam years before. Josiah removed and made impure all the sex-and-religion shrines in Samaria and slaughtered all the priests of those shrines. Then he returned to Jerusalem (2 Kin 23:15-20).
- The king ordered the people to celebrate the Passover (2 Kin 23:21-23).
- Josiah obeyed the Lord. Nevertheless, the Lord's fierce anger continued to burn against Judah because of all that Manasseh had done (2 Kin 23:24-27).
- Josiah was killed in a battle with Pharaoh Neco from Egypt. Josiah's son Jehoahaz became king (2 Kin 23:28-30).

Prophet Jeremiah

- Jeremiah served as a prophet for more the 40 years. The Word of the Lord came to Jeremiah. Jeremiah replied that he was only a boy. The Lord answered that he was to go wherever the Lord sent him and say whatever he commanded (Jer 1:1-8).
- The Word of the Lord ordered Jeremiah to stand at the gate to the Lord's Temple and proclaim God's message calling on the people to reform their ways and actions (Jer 7:1-11).
- The Word of the Lord told Jeremiah not to marry and have children (Jer 16:1-4).
- God gave Jeremiah a visual lesson at the potter's house: the moist marred clay jar can be remade (Jer 18:1-40; however, the dry marred clay pot can only be broken (Jer 19:10-11).
- God's Words were like a fire in Jeremiah's heart and he could not keep silent (Jer 20:7-9).
- Jeremiah announced God's Words against the leaders who were like shepherds who butchered and scattered sheep (Jer 23:1-3).
- The Lord gave Jeremiah words for the evil prophets and priests, who: committed adultery, lived a lie and encouraged people to keep on doing evil (Jer 23:9-17).

First Two Invasions of Judah

- Two years after Josiah's death, Babylon became a major power. Jeremiah asserted that Judah should submit to Babylon. Judah's leaders considered him a traitor (Jer 25 - 28).
- The prophet Habakkuk was perplexed because of the wickedness in Judah. Habakkuk asked God why the wicked in Judah were not being punished for their sin (Hab 1:2-4). God answered that he would use Babylon to punish Judah (Hab 1:5-11). Habakkuk then asked how God could use wicked Babylon (Hab 1:12-2:1). God answers that the wicked will always be punished; however, the righteous will live by faith (Hab 2:2-20). Habakkuk ended with an affirmation of commitment (Hab 3:16-19).
- Jehoahaz was king for three months. Then his brother Jehoiakim became king. Jehoiakim was 25 years old when he became king, and he reigned 11 years. He did evil (2 Kin 23:31-37).
- The prophet Jeremiah dictated the Lord's words to Baruch, who wrote on a scroll. Jehoiakim cut the scroll into pieces, and threw them into a fire (Jer 36:1-27).
- Nebuchadnezzar began his reign in Babylon and destroyed the Egyptian armies (Jer 46:2).
- Nebuchadnezzar invaded Judah. Jehoiakim submitted to him. The Babylonians took some objects of value and some intelligent youths to Babylon. Daniel and his friends were taken in this group (Dan 1:2-7; 2 Kin 24:1). *(This was Babylon's 1st invasion into Judah. It took place during the first year Nebuchadnezzar was king of Babylon in 605 B. C.)*
- Jeremiah prophesied that the exile in Babylon would be 70 years (Jer 25:8-14).
- After three years, Jehoiakim rebelled against Nebuchadnezzar. Jehoiakim died and Jehoiachin his son succeeded him as king (2 Kin 24:1-7).
- Jehoiachin was 18 years old when he became king. His rule lasted three months. He did evil. Nebuchadnezzar advanced on Jerusalem, took Jehoiachin prisoner, emptied the treasures of both the Temple of the Lord and the palace, and carried the capable people of Jerusalem into exile (2 Kin 24:8-17). *(This was Babylon's 2nd invasion into Judah. It took place during the eighth year Nebuchadnezzar was king in 597 B.C.)*
- Ezekiel was one of the captives taken to Babylon.
- Nebuchadnezzar chose 21-year-old Zedekiah to be his puppet king in Judah. He reigned 11 years and did evil (2 Kin 24:18-19; Jer 52:1-3).
- The Lord ordered Jeremiah to make a yoke and put it on his neck. Jeremiah told king Zedekiah to harness himself to the yoke of the king of Babylon and not to listen to lying false prophets (Jer 27:1-15).
- The prophet Hananiah confronted Jeremiah in the Temple. He predicted that the Lord would break the yoke of the king of Babylon within two years (Jer 28:1-9).
- Hananiah grabbed Jeremiah's yoke and smashed it. Then he told the people that the Lord would break the yoke of Nebuchadnezzar off the neck of all the nations within two years. Jeremiah told Hananiah that he would die within the year because he had made the people of Judah trust in lies. In the seventh month of that year, Hananiah died (Jer 28:1-17).

Third Invasion and Destruction of Jerusalem

- Zedekiah rebelled against Babylon. Nebuchadnezzar marched against Jerusalem and kept the city under siege for two years (2 Kin 25:1-2).
- Jeremiah was confined to jail because he had prophesied that Judah would be handed over to the king of Babylon (Jer 32:1-44).
- God made promises to Jeremiah about the future of Jerusalem (Jer 33:6-13).
- Nebuchadnezzar kept Jerusalem under siege for two years. There was no food to eat. An opening in the city wall was made. The king and the army escaped at night. But the Babylonians captured the king. The Babylonians executed Zedekiah's sons as he watched, then they put out his eyes (2 Kin 25:1-7).
- Then the Babylonians set fire to all of Jerusalem and they broke down the walls around the city. They carried into exile all the people, except they left behind some of the poorest. They took from the Temple all the articles made of bronze, gold or silver (2 Kin 25:8-21). *(This was Babylon's 3rd invasion into Judah, when the city of Jerusalem was destroyed. It took place during the eighteenth year Nebuchadnezzar was king in 587 B.C.)*

Final-situation:

The Babylonians conquered Jerusalem, destroyed the city and carried into exile its citizens.

BIBLE STORY

King Hezekiah and the Prophet Isaiah

Hezekiah was 25 years old when he became king of Judah, and he ruled 29 years in Jerusalem. He did what was right in the eyes of the Lord; he kept to the standards of his ancestor David. He removed the local fertility shrines, smashed the sacred stones and cut down the sex-and-religion Asherah poles. He broke into pieces the bronze snake Moses had made, for the Israelites had been burning incense to it. Hezekiah trusted in the Lord, the God of Israel. There was no one like him among all the kings of Judah, either before or after. He held fast to the Lord. He obeyed the commands the Lord had given Moses. The Lord was with him; he had success in everything he did (2 Kin 18:1-8).

In King Hezekiah's fourth year, Shalmaneser, king of Assyria, attacked Samaria, laid siege to it, and after three years captured it. So Samaria was captured in Hezekiah's sixth year. This happened because the Israelites had not obeyed the Lord their God (2 Kin 18:9-12).

The king of Assyria sent his top three military chiefs to King Hezekiah in Jerusalem. They stood outside the city walls. Two of Hezekiah's men, Shebna the secretary, and Joah the recorder went out to meet them.

The Assyrian field commander was the spokesman for the king of Assyria. He gave a message for King Hezekiah: "The great king of Assyria, says: On what are you basing your confidence? On whom are you depending? You can not say to me: 'We are depending on the Lord our God;' because Hezekiah eliminated the people's access to God by getting rid of the local god-shrines" (2 Kin 18:17-25).

Then Hezekiah's officials told the field commander: "Please speak to us in Aramaic. Don't speak to us in Hebrew with everyone crowded on the city wall listening."

The commander replied: "This is not a private message for your king; this is a public message. The men sitting on the wall will have to eat their own dung and drink their own urine, like you."

The commander shouted in Hebrew: "Hear the word of the great king of Assyria! Do not let Hezekiah fool you. Do not let Hezekiah persuade you to trust in the Lord. The king of Assyria says: Make peace with me. Then I will take you to a land of grain and new wine, a land of bread and vineyards, a land of olive trees and honey. Choose life and not death! Do not listen to Hezekiah's lies when he says: 'The Lord will deliver us.' Has the god of any nation ever delivered anyone from the king of Assyria? The Lord cannot deliver Jerusalem from me!" (2 Kin 18:26-35; Is 36:1-20).

But the people were silent, because the king had commanded: "Do not answer him."

Hezekiah's men reported to him what the field commander had said (2 Kin 18:36-37).

King Hezekiah ripped his clothes, put on sackcloth and went into the Temple of the Lord. He sent officials, all wearing sackcloth, to the prophet Isaiah. They told Isaiah what Hezekiah had said: "This is a day of distress and disgrace, just like when it is time for a baby to be born, but the mother has no strength to deliver it. Maybe the Lord your God will hear what the commander said. Maybe the Lord will punish him for ridiculing the living God. Therefore, pray for the remnant that still survives."

Isaiah sent word to King Hezekiah: "The Lord says: Do not be afraid of what you have heard from the king of Assyria's errand boys. They have blasphemed me. The king will hear a report, he will retreat to his own country, and there I will cause him to die by the sword" (2 Kin 19:1-7; Is 37:1-7).

Sennacherib received a report that the Cushite, king of Egypt, was marching out to fight against him. He sent a letter to Hezekiah: "Do not let the god you depend on deceive you when he says: 'Jerusalem will not fall to the king of Assyria.' The kings of Assyria have destroyed country after country. The gods of those people did not deliver them?" (2 Kin 19:9-13; Is 37:8-13).

Hezekiah read the letter. Then he went up to the Temple of the Lord and spread it out before the Lord. Hezekiah prayed: "O Lord, God of Israel, you are the one and only God, sovereign over all the kingdoms of the earth. You made heaven and earth. O Lord, listen to the words Sennacherib has sent to insult the living God. It is true, Lord, the Assyrian kings have laid waste these nations and their lands. The Assyrian kings threw their gods into the fire and destroyed them. But they were only wood and rock statues that men made. Now, O Lord our God, deliver us so that all kingdoms on earth may know that you are the one and only God" (2 Kin 19:14-19; Is 37:14-20).

Isaiah sent Hezekiah a message: "The Lord, the God of Israel, says: I have heard your prayer concerning Sennacherib king of Assyria. He has insulted and blasphemed the Holy One of Israel! But I know where he stays, when he comes and goes, and how he rages against me. The king of Assyria will not enter this city, nor shoot a single arrow here. I will defend this city and save it, for my sake and for David's sake" (2 Kin 19:20-34; Is 37:21-35).

That very night an angel of the Lord massacred 185,000 Assyrian soldiers. The next morning, there were all those corpses! Sennacherib king of Assyria broke camp and headed home for Nineveh. One day, while he was worshiping in the temple of his god Nisroch, two of his sons killed him (2 Kin 19:35-37; Is 37:36-38).

Some time later, Hezekiah became deathly sick. The prophet Isaiah visited him and said: "The Lord says: Put your affairs in order because you are about to die."

Hezekiah turned his face to the wall and prayed: "Remember O Lord, how I have always obeyed you. I have lived to please you." And Hezekiah wept bitterly.

Isaiah was halfway across the courtyard when the Word of the Lord came to him: "Go back and tell Hezekiah: 'The Lord, the God of your ancestor David, says: I heard your prayer and saw your tears; I will heal you. I will add fifteen years to your life. And I will save you and this city from the king of Assyria. I will defend this city for my sake and for my servant David's sake'" (2 Kin 20:1-11; Is 38:1-22).

During Hezekiah's near-death experience, the Lord answered his prayer and gave him a miraculous sign. Instead of being grateful, Hezekiah became arrogant. This provoked God to anger. The Lord's wrath was on Hezekiah, on Judah and on Jerusalem. Then Hezekiah repented of his arrogance, and the Lord withdrew his anger while Hezekiah lived (2 Chr 32:24-26).

The son of the king of Babylon heard about Hezekiah's illness and sent him letters and a gift. Hezekiah received the messengers and gave them a guided tour of all his prized possessions. He showed them everything of value.

Isaiah the prophet went to King Hezekiah and told him what the Lord said: "The time will come when everything in your palace, and everything your ancestors have passed down to you, will be taken away to Babylon. Some of your sons will end up as eunuchs in the palace of the king of Babylon."

Hezekiah replied: "The Word of the Lord you have spoken is good." He was thinking: "It won't happen during my lifetime. There will be peace and security in my lifetime" (2 Kin 20:12-19; Is 39:1-8).

King Manasseh

Hezekiah died, and Manasseh his son succeeded him as king. Manasseh was 12 years old when he became king, and he ruled 55 years in Jerusalem. He did evil in the eyes of the Lord. He reintroduced the detestable practices of the nations the Lord had driven out before the Israelites. He rebuilt the sex-and-religion shrines his father Hezekiah had destroyed. He erected images to the sex god Baal and the sex goddess Asherah as Ahab king of Israel had done. He built altars in the Temple of the Lord to all the stars and worshiped them. He consulted astrologists. He sacrificed his own son in the fire. He practiced black-magic and fortune-telling. He held seances and consulted spirits from the underworld. He provoked the Lord to anger. He took the carved pole to the sex goddess Asherah and put it in the Lord's temple. Manasseh led the people astray, so that they did more evil than the nations the Lord had destroyed ahead of the Israelites. Manasseh killed so many innocent people that he filled Jerusalem with blood from end to end (2 Kin 21:1-9, 16).

The Lord spoke through his servants the prophets: "Manasseh king of Judah has committed these detestable sins. He has led Judah to sin with his idols. I am going to bring catastrophe on Jerusalem and Judah. I will stretch out over Jerusalem the measuring line used against Samaria and the plumb line used against the house of Ahab. I will wipe out Jerusalem as one wipes a dish, wiping it and turning it upside down. They have done evil in my eyes and have provoked me to anger from the day their ancestors left Egypt until this day" (2 Kin 21:10-15).

Manasseh and his people ignored the Lord's Word. So the Lord directed the army commanders of the king of Assyria. They took Manasseh prisoner, put a hook in his nose, bound him with shackles and took him to Babylon. In his distress he sought the Lord his God and humbled himself before the God of his ancestors. Manasseh prayed, and the Lord listened to his plea. God brought him back to Jerusalem and to his kingdom. Then Manasseh knew that the Lord is God (2 Chr 33:10-17).

Manasseh died. Amon his son succeeded him. Amon became king when he was twenty-two years old, and he reigned two years. He did evil just like his father Manasseh. Amon's officials assassinated him, and Josiah his son became the next king (2 Kin 21:19-26).

King Josiah

Josiah was eight years old when he became king, and he ruled 31 years in Jerusalem. He did what was right in the eyes of the Lord and copied the ways of his ancestor David (2 Kin 22:1-2).

Zephaniah, Nahum and Habakkuk were prophets during the time when Josiah was king.

In the eighteenth year of his reign, King Josiah sent his secretary, Shaphan to Hilkiah the high priest with orders to repair the Temple.

Hilkiah the high priest told Shaphan the secretary that he had found the Book of the Law in the Temple of the Lord. He gave it to Shaphan, who read it. Shaphan went to the king and reported: "Hilkiah the priest gave me a book." And Shaphan read it to the king.

When King Josiah heard the words of the Book of the Law, he ripped his robes. He ordered his officials: "Inquire of the Lord about what is written in this book. Great is the Lord's anger that burns against us because our ancestors have not obeyed the words of this book."

The king's officials went to speak to the prophetess Huldah. She told them: "The Lord says: I will bring catastrophe on this place and its people. Everything written in the book read by the king will happen. Because they forsook me and burned incense to other gods and provoked me to anger by all the idols they have made, my anger will burn against this place. Tell King Josiah: Because your heart was responsive and you humbled yourself before the Lord and wept, I heard you. Therefore, you will be buried in peace. You will not see the disaster I will bring on this place" (2 Kin 22:3-20; 2 Chr 34:1-28).

King Josiah assembled all the leaders of Judah and Jerusalem to the Temple of the Lord. He read to them all the words of the Book of the Covenant. The king renewed the covenant to follow the Lord and keep his commands with all his heart and all his soul. Then all the people pledged themselves to the covenant (2 Kin 23:1-3).

Josiah ordered the high priest Hilkiah and his associates to remove from the Temple of the Lord everything made for Baal, Asherah and all the stars of heaven. He burned them outside Jerusalem in the fields of the Kidron Valley and disposed of the ashes at Bethel. He did away with the pagan priests appointed by the kings of Judah to burn incense at the local sex-and-religion shrines. He took the Asherah pole from the Temple of the Lord to the Kidron Valley outside Jerusalem and burned it. He tore down the living quarters of the male shrine prostitutes, who were in the Temple of the Lord. This was where women did weaving for the sex goddess Asherah.

Josiah brought all the priests from the towns of Judah and made impure the local religious shrines where the priests had burned incense. He made impure Topheth, the iron furnace griddle set up in the Valley of Ben Hinnom for sacrificing children in the fire to Molech. He hauled off the horse statues dedicated to the sun god that the kings of Judah had set up near the Temple entrance. The king also made impure the sex-and-religion shrines that King Solomon had built. Josiah smashed the sacred stones and cut down the Asherah poles and covered the sites with human bones (2 Kin 23:4-14).

Josiah demolished the altar at Bethel, the religious shrine made by Jeroboam, who had caused Israel to sin. He burned the shrine and ground it to powder, and burned the Asherah pole. Then Josiah had bones removed from tombs that were nearby and had them cremated on the altar to make it impure. These things happened as the Lord had said it would through the man of God to Jeroboam years before.

Josiah removed and made impure all the sex-and-religion shrines that the kings of Israel had built in the towns of Samaria that had provoked the Lord to anger. Josiah slaughtered all the priests of those shrines and burned human bones on the shrines. Then he went back to Jerusalem (2 Kin 23:15-20).

The king ordered all the people: "Celebrate the Passover to the Lord your God as it is written in this Book of the Covenant." The Passover had not been celebrated since the days when the judges judged Israel (2 Kin 23:21-23).

There was no king like Josiah before or after him. He obeyed the Lord with all his heart, soul and strength. Nevertheless, the Lord's fierce anger continued to burn against Judah because of all that Manasseh had done to provoke him to anger. The Lord said: "I will remove Judah from my presence as I removed Israel" (2 Kin 23:24-27).

King Josiah was killed in a battle with Pharaoh Neco, king of Egypt. Josiah's son Jehoahaz became king in place of his father (2 Kin 23:28-30).

Prophet Jeremiah

Jeremiah began his ministry when Josiah was king. The Word of the Lord came to Jeremiah in the thirteenth year of Josiah's reign over Judah, and through the reign of Jehoiakim, down to the eleventh year of Zedekiah, when the people of Jerusalem went into exile. That was a period of over 40 years.

The Word of the Lord came to Jeremiah saying: "Before I shaped you in the womb, I knew you; before you were born, I made plans for you; I appointed you as a prophet to the nations."

Jeremiah replied: "Sovereign Lord, I do not know how to speak; I am only a boy."

The Lord answered: "Do not say: `I am only a boy.' Go wherever I send you and say whatever I command you. Do not be afraid of them, for I am with you and will rescue you" (Jer 1:1-8).

The Word of the Lord ordered Jeremiah to stand at the gate to the Lord's Temple and proclaim this message: "Hear the Word of the Lord, people of Judah who come through these gates to worship the Lord. The Lord Almighty, the God of Israel, says: Reform your ways and your actions, and I will let you live in this place. Change your ways and deal with each other justly. Stop oppressing the foreigners, the fatherless or the widow. Stop shedding innocent blood. Stop following other gods. If you do these things, then I will let you live in this place. This is the land I gave your ancestors to keep for ever and ever. Will you steal and murder? Will you commit adultery and perjury. Will you burn incense to Baal and follow other gods? Will you do these things and then come to this house, set apart to worship me? Can you say you are safe to do all these detestable things? Has this Temple, built to worship me become a den of robbers to you? I have been watching you declares the Lord!" (Jer 7:1-11).

The Word of the Lord came to Jeremiah: "Do not marry and do not have children in this place. Children born in this land will die. Their mothers and their fathers will die of deadly diseases. They will not be mourned or buried. They will become decomposing corpses lying on the ground and stinking like dung. Their corpses will become food for buzzards and wild beasts" (Jer 16:1-4).

God gave Jeremiah a visual lesson at the potter's house. The jar that is marred can be remade when the clay is moist (Jer 18:1-40). However, the marred clay pot that is dried, can only be broken and thrown away (Jer 19:10-11).

Jeremiah felt no pleasure in prophesying

disaster for Judah. He felt an obligation to pronounce God's Words. God's Words were like a fire in his heart, and he could not keep silent (Jer 20:7-9).

Jeremiah announced God's Words against the leaders: "The Lord declares: 'Woe to the shepherds who butcher and scatter my sheep! You scattered my sheep, you drove them away, you did not take care of them; therefore, I will punish you for the evil you have done. I myself will gather the remnant of my sheep out of all the countries where I have driven them. I will bring them back to their pasture, where they will recover and flourish. I will place shepherds over them who will take care of them. They will no longer be afraid or terrified. There will be no lost sheep'" (Jer 23:1-3).

The Lord gave Jeremiah words for the prophets and priests: "Both prophet and priest are evil; even in my Temple I find their wickedness. The prophets of Jerusalem commit adultery and live a lie. They encourage evil people to keep on doing evil, so that no one turns from his wickedness. The Lord Almighty says: "Do not listen to the prophets! They fool you with false hopes. They speak visions from their own minds. They did not get their visions from the mouth of the Lord" (Jer 23:9-17).

First Two Invasions of Judah
Two years after Josiah's death, Babylon became a major power. Jeremiah asserted that Judah should submit to Babylon. Judah's leaders did not listen to him. They considered him a traitor; he was rejected, persecuted and imprisoned (Jer 25 - 28).

The prophet Habakkuk was perplexed because of the wickedness in Judah. Habakkuk asked God why the wicked in Judah were not being punished for their sin (Hab 1:2-4). God answered that he would use world-conquering Babylon to punish Judah (Hab 1:5-11). Habakkuk then asked how God could use Babylon. Judah was wicked, but it was more righteous than Babylon (Hab 1:12-2:1). God answers that the wicked will always be punished; however, the righteous will live by faith (Hab 2:2-20).

Habakkuk ends with an affirmation: "I will wait patiently for the day of calamity to descend upon the nation invading us. Though the fig tree does not blossom, though there are no grapes on the vines, though the olive crop fails, though the wheat fields produce no food, though there are no sheep in the pen and no cattle in the stalls, yet I will rejoice in the Lord, I will rejoice in God my Savior. The Sovereign Lord is my strength" (Hab 3:16-19).

Jehoahaz was king for three months. Then his brother Jehoiakim became king. Jehoiakim was twenty-five years old when he became king. He reigned in Jerusalem eleven years. Jehoiakim did evil in the eyes of the Lord, just as his ancestors had done (2 Kin 23:31-37).

The prophet Jeremiah dictated to Baruch, who wrote down on a scroll, the words the Lord gave Jeremiah. When the scroll was read to King Jehoiakim, he cut the scroll into pieces and threw them into a fire (Jer 36:1-27).

During the reign of Jehoiakim, Nebuchadnezzar began his reign in Babylon. Nebuchanezzar's first official act was to destroy the Egyptian armies (Jer 46:2).

Nebuchadnezzar invaded Judah. Jehoiakim submitted to him without resistence. The Babylonians took some objects of value from the Temple and some intelligent youths to Babylon. Daniel and his friends were taken in this group (Dan 1:2-7; 2 Kin 24:1). *(This was Babylon's 1st invasion into Judah. It happened the first year Nebuchadnezzar was king of Babylon in 605 B.C.)*

Jeremiah prophesied that the exile in Babylon would be 70 years (Jer 25:8-14).

Jehoiakim was subject to Babylon for three years; then he changed his mind and rebelled against Nebuchadnezzar. Jehoiakim died, and Jehoiachin his son succeeded him as king (2 Kin 24:1-7).

Jehoiachin was eighteen years old when he became king. His rule in Jerusalem only lasted three months. He did evil in the eyes of the Lord. He was just like his father.

The army of Nebuchadnezzar, king of Babylon, advanced on Jerusalem. Jehoiachin surrendered to him. In Nebuchadnezzar's eighth year as king, he took Jehoiachin prisoner. Nebuchadnezzar emptied the treasures of both the Temple of the Lord and the royal palace. He took away all the gold furnishings that King Solomon had made for the Temple of the Lord. He carried into exile from Jerusalem: all the leading men, the officers and fighting men, and all the craftsmen and artisans. Only the poorest people of the land remained (2 Kin 24:8-17). *(This was Babylon's 2nd invasion into Judah. It took place during the eighth year Nebuchadnezzar was king in 597 B.C.)*

Ezekiel was one of the captives taken to Babylon. He began his ministry after Nebuchadnezzar's second invasion into Judah. Ezekiel announced God's Word to both the captives in Babylon and to those remaining in Jerusalem.

Nebuchadnezzar chose Zedekiah to be his puppet king in Judah. Zedekiah was twenty-one years old when he became king, and he reigned eleven years. He did evil in the eyes of the Lord (2 Kin 24:18-19; Jer 52:1-3).

Shortly after Zedekiah became king of Judah, the Lord ordered Jeremiah: "Make a yoke out of straps and crossbars and put it on your neck."

Jeremiah told Zedekiah king of Judah: "Harness yourself to the yoke of the king of Babylon; serve him and his people, and you will live. Do not listen to the lying false prophets who tell you: `You will not serve the king of Babylon" (Jer 27:1-15).

Later, that same year, prophet Hananiah confronted Jeremiah in the Temple in front of the priests and the people: "The Lord Almighty, the God of Israel, says: 'I will break the yoke of the king of Babylon. Within two years I will bring back to this place all the articles from the Lord's house that Nebuchadnezzar king of Babylon hauled to Babylon. I will also bring back all the exiles who were taken to Babylon. I will break the yoke of the king of Babylon."

Prophet Jeremiah replied to prophet Hananiah before the priests and the people: "The old prophets, the ones before our time, prophesied war, disaster and plague against many countries and kingdoms. But the prophet who prophesies peace will be recognized as one truly sent by the Lord only if his prediction comes true" (Jer 28:1-9).

Then the prophet Hananiah grabbed the yoke off Jeremiah's neck and smashed it. Then he told the people: "The Lord says: 'In the same way will I break the yoke of Nebuchadnezzar king of Babylon off the neck of all the nations within two years.'"

Jeremiah told the prophet Hananiah: "This is what the Lord says: You have broken a wooden yoke, but in its place you will get an iron yoke. I will put an iron yoke on the necks of all these nations to make them serve Nebuchadnezzar king of Babylon.' Listen, Hananiah! The Lord has not sent you, yet you have made the people of Judah trust in lies. Therefore, the Lord says: 'I am about to remove you from the earth. You will die this year because you taught the people to turn against the Lord.'"

In the seventh month of that same year, Hananiah the prophet died (Jer 28:1-17).

Third Invasion and Destruction of Jerusalem

Zedekiah rebelled against the king of Babylon. So Nebuchadnezzar marched against Jerusalem with his whole army. The city was kept under siege for two years. The famine in the city became so severe that there was no food to eat (2 Kin 25:1-2).

When Nebuchadnezzar was besieging Jerusalem, Jeremiah the prophet was confined to jail in the royal palace of Judah. Zedekiah, king of Judah, imprisoned him because Jeremiah prophesied: "The Lord says: I am about to hand this city over to the king of Babylon. Zedekiah king of Judah will be handed over to the king of Babylon. He will take Zedekiah to Babylon. The Babylonians will come and burn this city down. The people of Israel and Judah have provoked me by all the evil they have done" (Jer 32:1-44).

God made promises to Jeremiah about the future of Jerusalem: "Nevertheless, I will bring health and healing to this city. I will heal my people and will let them enjoy peace and security. I will bring Judah and Israel back from captivity and will rebuild them. They will be as strong as in the past. They sinned against me, but I will cleanse them from their sin. Then this city will make me famous. All nations on earth that hear of all the good things I do for it; and they will be shocked at the prosperity and peace I provide for it" (Jer 33:6-13).

Nebuchadnezzar kept Jerusalem under siege for two years. Hunger in the city became severe. There was no food to eat. An opening in the city wall was made. The king and the army escaped at night. But the Babylonians chased and captured the king. Zedekiah was taken to the king of Babylon. The Babylonians executed Zedekiah's sons as he watched. The execution of his sons was the last thing he saw, because then they put out his eyes, bound him with chains and took him to Babylon (2 Kin 25:1-7).

Then the Babylonians set fire to the Temple of the Lord, the royal palace, all the houses of Jerusalem and every important building. The Babylonian army broke down the walls around Jerusalem. They carried into exile the people who were in the city, along with the rest of the populace of Judah. But they left behind some of the poorest people of the land to work the vineyards and fields.

The Babylonians destroyed the Temple. They broke up and took from the Temple all the articles made of bronze, gold or silver.

So Judah went into captivity, away from her land (2 Kin 25:8-21). *(This was Babylon's 3rd invasion into Judah, when the city of Jerusalem was destroyed. It took place during the eighteenth year Nebuchadnezzar was king in 587 B.C.)*

LIFE-LESSONS DISCOVERED IN THE STORY

1. Religious revival should begin with the spiritual leader and then precede to the people. King Hezekiah ordered the Levites to sanctify themselves (2 Chr 29:5-9).

2. The person who faithfully serves the Lord may find himself in a difficult situation where, from a human viewpoint, he has no hope; however, he still has hope for God's intervention. When the Assyrians attacked, King Hezekiah didn't see any hope from the human viewpoint; however, he had hope that the Lord would rescue him (2 Kin 18 - 19).

3. The person who is arrogant and blasphemes God will bring upon himself divine punishment. The arrogance and the blasphemy of the Assyrians (2 Kin 18:22, 33-35) resulted in God's punishing them (2 Kin 19:19, 35-37).

4. The person who is sincere and honest when he prays to God will have his prayer answered. When Hezekiah received the letter from the Assyrian king with its threats, he took the problem before God in prayer (2 Kin 19:14-19), and God used his sovereign power to send the

Assyrians back to their country (2 Kin 19:35-36).

5. Many argue that faith in God is the result of human weakness and ignorance; however, those who criticize God do not obstruct his divine power. King Sennacherib of Assyria made fun of the hope that Hezekiah put in God. But it was God who defeated Sennacherib (2 Chr 32:10-21).

6. Spiritual lessons can be learned in a time of disease or suffering. A terrible disease taught King Hezekiah to depend only on the Lord (2 Kin 20:1-11; Is 38:1-8). In his suffering Manasseh prayed with fervor to the Lord, and he repented of his sins (2 Chr 33:10-17).

7. Prayer should be the first response to a crisis. When Hezekiah received the letter from the Assyrian king with its threats, he took the problem before God in prayer (2 Kin 19:14-19). When Hezekiah was close to death, he prayed, and God allowed him to live 15 more years (2 Kin 20:1-6).

8. The person who receives a great blessing from the Lord often faces the temptation to degenerate into vanity and self-congratulations. After God delivered Hezekiah from his illness, he became proud (2 Chr 32:24-26).

9. Prayer should seek above everything else the glory of God. Hezekiah's prayer (2 Kin 19:14-19; Is 37:15-16) is a worthy model of a prayer. He did not just ask for the deliverance from the Assyrians, he implored for God's name to be glorified (2 Kin 19:19).

10. Parents don't determine their children's relationship with God; each one decides for himself what his relationship with God will be. King Jotham did what was right before God (2 Kin 15:34); however, his son Ahaz was unjust and perverse (2 Kin 16:2-3). Hezekiah did what pleased God (2 Kg18:3); however, his son Manasseh sinned against Him (21:2-9). Amon did evil and worshiped idols (2 Kin 21:19-22); however, his son Josiah restored the worship of the Lord to the Temple (2 Kin 22:2-7) and served the Lord with all his heart and strength (2 Kin 23:24-25). Josiah's son Jehoahaz did evil (2 Kin 23:32). His other son Jehoiakim also did evil (2 Kin 23:37).

11. The person with doubts should take them to God. The prophet Habakkuk was perplexed because of the wickedness in Judah. He took his questions to God. Habakkuk asked God why the wicked in Judah were not being punished for their sin (Hab 1:2-4). Habakkuk asked how God could use Babylon. Judah was wicked, but it was more righteous than Babylon (Hab 1:12-2:1).

12. God should be worshiped because of who he is, not because of what God can do for the worshiper. Habakkuk affirmed that he would rejoice in the Lord, even when everything was going wrong. "Though the fig tree does not blossom, though there are no grapes on the vines, though the olive crop fails, though the wheat fields produce no food, though there are no sheep in the pen and no cattle in the stalls, yet I will rejoice in the Lord, I will rejoice in God my Savior. The Sovereign Lord is my strength" (Hab 3:16-19).

13. Sin moves the person away from the Bible, or the Bible moves the person away from sin. During the reign of the idolatrous and wicked Manasseh, the Law of Moses was lost. During the reign of Josiah who served the Lord, the Law was found (2 Kin 22:8-10). The reading of the Law resulted in repentance, and the king and people worshiped the Lord again (2 Kin 23:1-3; 2 Chr 34: 29-33).

14. Sin provokes God to anger. Manasseh did much evil, provoking the Lord to anger (2 Kin 21:6).

15. No one is too young to take God seriously and obey him. Josiah was eight years old when he became king. He always did what was right in the eyes of the Lord (2 Kin 22:1-2). The Word of the Lord came to Jeremiah. Jeremiah replied that he was only a boy. The Lord answered that he was to go wherever the Lord sent him and say whatever he commanded (Jer 1:1-8).

16. God often uses women to speak for him. The prophetess Huldah was consulted by priest Hilkiah on behalf of King Josiah, and she pronounced the Word of the Lord (2 Kin 22:14-20). There were other women that had the talent of prophecy, for instance: Miriam, the sister of Moses (Ex 15:20); Deborah (Jdg. 4:4) and Philip's daughters (Ac 21:8-9).

17. The Lord honors the person who serves him with everything he has. The Bible honors Josiah by saying that there had never been another king like him. Josiah turned to the Lord with all his heart, with all his soul and with all his strength (2 Kin 23:25). (See Luke 10:27.)

18. Religious reforms that correct activities and ceremonies only have durable effects if the lives of the worshipers are transformed. Josiah brought reforms that purified the religious ceremonies of Judah; however, the hearts of the people were not changed, and the reforms died with Josiah.

19. God chooses people to speak for him. Isaiah (Is 6:1-8) and Jeremiah (Jer 1:5-9) were chosen to pronounce the Word of God.

20. God is faithful to keep his promises. He kept his promises and punished Israel and Judah when they abandoned him to serve other gods.

21. Opportunity for repentance will pass and it will become too late for a person to regret his wrongdoing, change his actions, be transformed by God and receive forgiveness from God. by God. The visual lesson of the potter's vase reveals that a vase with flaws can be remade when it is still wet (Jer 18:1-4); however, after it becomes dry and hard, a vase with flaws can only be broken and thrown into the garbage (Jer 19:10-11).

22. The spiritual leader should be faithful to God both, when people hear and respect him and when he is hated and persecuted. King Hezekiah respected Isaiah and looked to him for advice. Jeremiah supported King Josiah's reforms; however, the kings after Josiah hated and persecuted Jeremiah. Yet, he still pronounced the Word of the Lord.

23. The Word of God cannot be destroyed. The missing Book of the Law was discovered during the reign of Josiah (2 Kin 22:8-10). When King Jehoiakim cut the scroll of the Word of God into pieces and burned them in the fire, God ordered Jeremiah to write again everything that the king had burned (Jer 36:1-6, 23, 27-28, 32).

24. People who rebel against the Lord do not want to hear his Word, nor do they respect those who pronounce God's message. King Jehoiakim cut the scroll with the Words of the Lord and burned them in the fire (Jer 36:1-6, 23). King Zedekiah confined the prophet Jeremiah to jail because Jeremiah prophesied the Lord's words (Jer 32:1-44). Zedekiah did not humble himself before the prophet Jeremiah when he spoke the Word of the Lord (2 Chr 36:12).

25. The person who loves God with all his heart will: obey him, reject contaminated worship and reject idiolatry. The religious reform of Josiah led the people to adore God and also to fight against practices and habits common in worship of other gods that had contaminated the worship of the Lord God (2 Kin 23:4-20).

26. God's enemies can arrest, persecute and limit the activities of those who serve the Lord; however, they cannot limit God's actions. Jeremiah was arrested and imprisoned; however, God communicated with him about what he was doing in the present and what he would do in the future (Jer 32:1-44; 33:6-13).

27. God is sovereign in relation to history. He used Nebuchadnezzar as his instrument to crush Judah politically, economically, and religiously (2 Kin 24:20 - 25:7).

QUESTIONS

1. Describe the reign of Hezekiah, king of Judah.
2. What was the relationship between Hezekiah and Isaiah?
3. What were some of the evil things done by Manasseh, king of Judah?
4. What were some of the reforms done by Josiah, king of Judah?
5. What was King Josiah's reaction to the Book of the Law that was found in the Temple?
6. Why didn't the reforms of Josiah continue after his death?
7. What do you learn from the life of the prophet Jeremiah?
8. What lesson can be learned from the fact that the potter's jar with flaws can be remade while it is still wet (Jer 18:1-4); however, after already hard, if it has flaws, it can only be broken and thrown into the trash (Jer 19:10-11)?
9. How did King Jehoiakim react when he received the scroll with the words the Lord had given to the prophet Jeremiah?
10. Why was Jerusalem conquered and destroyed by Nebuchadnezzar?
11. When Jerusalem was conquered, what happened to its residents?
12. What does the destruction of Jerusalem teach us about God?

BABYLONIAN EXILE
2 Kings 24:8-14; 25:18-21; Daniel 1 - 6; Jeremiah 29:1-23

STRUCTURE

Context:

Judah, the Southern Kingdom, had twenty kings during 390 years. During this time, Judah experienced a spiritual decay that was interrupted by the reforms of Kings Asa, Jehoshaphat, Joash, Hezekiah, Uzziah, Jothan, Hezekiah and Josiah. During this spiritual decay the kings, religious leaders and the people sinned more and more, following the wicked examples of pagan neighbors and the evil kings of Israel. They worshiped worthless gods and they became worthless, like the gods they worshiped. The Lord sent his prophets to the kings and the people, but they rejected their messages and ridiculed them. Finally, God became so angry with Judah that he made Nebuchadnezzar, king of Babylon, conquer and destroy Judah.

Babylon's first invasion into Judah took place during the first year Nebuchadnezzar was king in 605 B. C.. Daniel and his friends were taken captive at this time. Babylon's second invasion into Judah took place during the eighth year that Nebuchadnezzar was king in 597 B.C.. The Babylonians emptied the treasures of both the Temple and the palace, and carried the capable people of Jerusalem into exile. Babylon's third invasion into Judah took place during the eighteenth year that Nebuchadnezzar was king, in 587 B.C. The Babylonians set fire to Jerusalem, broke down the city walls and carried into exile most of the people.

Key-persons: The Jews Daniel, Shadrach, Meshach, and Abednego; and the Kings Nebuchadnezzar, Belshazzar and Darius

Key-location: Babylon

Key-repetitions:
- Nebuchadnezzar lived like an animal: his dream and its interpretation (Dan 4:1-27); he became like an animal (4:28-37); Daniel reminds Belshazzar (5:18-24).
- Conspiracy/hostility against the Jews (Dan 3:8-12; 6:3-16).
- Temptation resisted: to be defiled with the king's food (Dan 1:8-16); to worship the gold statue (3:1-18); to pray to the king (6:1-10).
- God rescued his servants: from impure food (Dan 1:8-16); from the furnace (3:21-27); from the lions' den (6:16-23).
- Dreams/mystery: Nebuchadnezzar's dreams (Dan 2:1-49; 4:4-27); Belshazzar, writing on the wall (Dan 5:1-7); Daniel's dreams (Dan 7:1-14; 8:1-27; 10:1 - 12:13).
- Daniel and his friends faced dangers: to be impure (Dan 1:8); to be killed (Dan 2:12); the furnace (Dan 3:19-30); the lions' den (Dan 6:1-22).
- Daniel's successes (Dan 1:9, 20; 2:48-49; 6:2-3).
- Daniel was loved by God (Dan 9:23; 10:11, 19).
- Daniel prayed (Dan 2:17-8; 6:10; 9:4, 20-23).
- The destiny of people/nations is determined by God (Dan 2:20-21, 41; 4:17, 25, 30-37; 7:25-27; 9:20-27).
- Arrogant pride resulted in divine punishment Nebuchadnezzar (Dan 4:30-37); Belshazzar (Dan 5:22-30).

Key-attitudes:
- The arrogant pride of Nebuchadnezzar.
- The curiosity to understand dreams and divine mysteries.
- The commitment of Daniel and his Jewish friends to be loyal to the Lord.
- Conflict and hostility.
- The courage of Daniel and his Jewish friends.
- The antagonism of the wicked against those who served the Lord.
- The pride and irreverence of Belshazzar.

Initial-problem:

Nebuchadnezzar, king of Babylon, invaded Judah and took some Jews into exile. Among the exiles were four Jewish youth: Daniel, Hananiah, Mishael and Azariah.

Sequence of events:

The Captives; Jeremiah's Letter
- Nebuchadnezzar invaded Judah and took Daniel and his friends to exile in Babylon (Dan 1:1-2; 2 Kin 24:1).
- Jeremiah sent a letter to Jewish leaders exiled to Babylon. It advised them to seek the prosperity of the city and to pray for Babylon's well-being. He established 70 years as the time for the exile (Jer 29:1-32).

Young Israelites' Training in Babylon
- King Nebuchadnezzar told Ashpenaz to choose some Israelite youth for three years of training. They were to eat from the same menu served at the king's table (Dan 1:3-5).
- Four young men from Judah were selected. They were Daniel, Hananiah, Mishael and Azariah. Their names were changed to Belteshazzar, Shadrach, Meshach and Abednego (Dan 1:6-7).
- Daniel determined not to defile himself with the royal food and wine. He obtained permission to eat vegetables and to drink water (Dan 1:8-16).
- God gave the four Jewish youth wisdom and the ability to learn. Daniel also understood visions and dreams. After three years of training, they entered the king's service (Dan 1:17-21).

Daniel Interprets Nebuchadnezzar's Dream
- Nebuchadnezzar started having dreams that

disturbed him. He asked his wise men to tell him the dream, then interpret it. They could not, so he ordered the execution of all the Babylonian wise men. The order included Daniel and his companions (Dan 2:1-13).

■Daniel went in to the king and asked for time. Daniel asked his friends Hananiah, Mishael and Azariah to pray for mercy. That night the secret was revealed to Daniel. Daniel praised the Lord. Daniel went to Arioch and said he would interpret the king's dream (Dan 2:14-24).

■Daniel told the king that no man could explain the king's secret. But God reveals mysteries, and the secret had been revealed to Daniel so that the king would know the future. In his dream, the king saw a statue. The head was gold, its chest and arms were silver, its belly and thighs were bronze, its legs were iron, its feet were an iron-clay mixture. A rock cut out of a mountain by an invisible hand struck the statue, smashing its iron-clay feet. The pieces became like chaff, and the wind blew them away. The rock became a huge mountain (Dan 2:25-35).

■Daniel interpreted the dream. The king was the head of gold on the statue. After him, an inferior kingdom would rise. Next, a third kingdom, one of bronze. Finally, there would be a fourth kingdom, iron-like in strength that would crush and break the previous kingdoms. Just as the feet and toes were partly clay and partly iron, so this would be a divided kingdom that would not bind together. Throughout those kingdoms, God would be building an eternal kingdom that would crush all those kingdoms (Dan 2:25-45).

■Nebuchadnezzar honored Daniel and recognized that his God is the God of gods, the Lord of kings and a revealer of secrets. The king made Daniel ruler over the province of Babylon and put him in charge of its wise men. He appointed Daniel's friends to administrative posts (Dan 2:46-49).

The Gold Statue and the Furnace

■Nebuchadnezzar had a gold statue made. He summoned leaders to the dedication of the statue. When the band played, they were to fall to their knees and worship the statue. Anyone who disobeyed would be thrown into a furnace (Dan 3:1-7).

■Astrologers accused the Jews Shadrach, Meshach and Abednego of ignoring the king's order. Nebuchadnezzar gave them a second chance. The Jews replied that God was able to save them from the furnace, but even if he did not, they would not worship the statue. The king ordered the furnace heated 7 times hotter than usual. Soldiers bound the Jews and threw them into the furnace (Dan 3:8-23).

■King Nebuchadnezzar saw four men walking in the fire. The Jews exited the furnace unharmed. Nebuchadnezzar praised God and prohibited anyone from criticizing him. Then he promoted the Jews (Dan 3:24-30).

Nebuchadnezzar Humbled by God

■King Nebuchadnezzar described in a letter an experience he had with the Lord. He had a nightmare that his wise men could not interpret. The king described to Daniel his dream. Nebuchadnezzar saw a towering tree. A holy watchman gave orders to cut down the tree, but to leave the stump and its roots in the ground. Let this go on for seven seasons. This would happen so that everyone living may know that the Most High is sovereign (Dan 4:1-18).

■Daniel was upset. He told the king he wished the dream were about the king's enemies. He said that the king was the tree. He would be forced away from people and would live with wild animals. Seven seasons would pass before he recognized that the Most High rules. Then his kingdom would be restored to him. Daniel advised the king to renounce his sins and start doing right (Dan 4:19-27).

■Twelve months later, Nebuchadnezzar was forced away from people and lived like a wild animal. At the end of 7 years, he looked up to heaven and praised the Most High. His sanity was restored, and he was returned to his throne. The king praised the King of Heaven who is able to humble the proud (Dan 4:28-37).

The Writing on the Wall

■Belshazzar gave a banquet and ordered to bring in the gold and silver cups taken from the Lord's Temple. They drank wine from the gold cups and praised man-made gods. A human hand appeared and wrote on the palace wall. The king was terrified. His wise men could not read the writing nor interpret it. The king's mother told the king about Daniel (Dan 5:1-12).

■Daniel reminded the king that when Nebuchadnezzar became arrogant, his throne was taken away, and he lived with wild donkeys and ate grass like cattle. Belshazzar knew all this, but he had the drinking cups from the Lord's Temple brought to him. He and his guests drank wine from them and praised man-made gods. Daniel read the writing and interpreted it: "*Mene*: God has numbered the days of your reign and they do not add up; *Tekel*: You have been weighed on the scales and found wanting; *Peres*: Your kingdom is divided and given over to the Medes and Persians" (Dan 5:13-28).

■Daniel was proclaimed third in command in the kingdom. That night Belshazzar was slain, and Darius the Mede took over the kingdom (Dan 5:29-31).

Daniel During King Darius' Reign

■Daniel was reading the Scriptures. He understood from the prophet Jeremiah that Jerusalem would lie in ruins for seventy years. Daniel prayed to the Lord God. He confessed the sins of his people and that they were covered with shame because they had sinned against the Lord. He remembered how the Lord had delivered his people from Egypt. He then asked God to have mercy because his city and his people were named after him (Dan 9:1-19).

■Darius appointed 120 governors and chose three supervisors over the governors; one of whom was Daniel. The supervisors and governors tried to find some scandal that they could use against Daniel. They concluded that they could find nothing against

him, unless it had something to do with the religion of his God (Dan 6:1-5).
- The supervisors and governors recommended that the king issue a decree that anyone who prayed to any god or man, except to the king, be thrown into the lions' den (Dan 6:6-9).
- Daniel continued to pray three times a day. The conspirators reminded the king about his royal decree and accused Daniel of defying it. The king tried to save Daniel, but the conspirators reminded the king that according to the law of the Medes and Persians the king's decree can never be canceled (Dan 6:10-14).
- The king ordered Daniel thrown into the lions' den. At daybreak he approached the den, called out and Daniel answered. The king gave orders to take Daniel out of the den. Then he commanded that those who conspired against Daniel be thrown into the lions' den, along with their families (Dan 6:15-24).
- Darius published a decree to all the people in his land to fear and worship the God of Daniel who is the living God who rescues and saves (Dan 6:25-27).
- Daniel prospered during the reign of Darius (Dan 6:28).
- Daniel was greatly loved by God (Dan 9:23; 10:11, 19).

Final-situation:
The Lord rescued Daniel from the lions' den and made him prosper. Daniel was greatly loved by God.

BIBLE STORY

The Captives; Jeremiah's Letter
In the first year that Nebuchadnezzar was king of Babylon, he invaded Judah. The Babylonians took some intelligent Jewish youth into exile in Babylon. Daniel and his friends were taken in this group (Dan 1:1-2; 2 Kin 24:1).

The prophet Jeremiah sent a letter from Jerusalem to the Jewish leaders whom Nebuchadnezzar had taken from Jerusalem to Babylon. It said: "The Lord Almighty, the God of Israel, says to all those I have taken into exile from Jerusalem to Babylon: Build houses and settle in the land; plant gardens and eat the food you grow. Get married and have children; find wives for your sons and give your daughters in marriage, so that they too will have children. Have many children and increase in number there; do not decrease. Seek the peace and prosperity of the city to which I have taken you into exile. Pray for Babylon's well-being, because if it prospers, you too will prosper."
The Lord says: "When seventy years are up for Babylon, I will come to you and bring you back to Jerusalem. I know the plans I have for you. I have good plans for you. I do not plan to harm you. I plan to give you the future you hope for. Then you will call on me and come and pray to me, and I will listen. You will seek me with all your heart and you will find me. I will bring you back to the place from which I sent you into exile" (Jer 29:1-32).

Young Israelites' Training in Babylon
King Nebuchadnezzar told Ashpenaz, chief official of his palace, to choose some Israelite youth from the royal family and the nobility who were healthy with no handicaps, handsome, intelligent, well-educated, quick to understand, and qualified for leadership positions in the king's palace. Ashpenaz was to teach them the language and literature of the Babylonians. The king ordered that they be served from the same menu served at the king's table: the best food, the finest wine. After three years' training, they were to enter the king's service (Dan 1:3-5).

Four young men from Judah were among those selected. They were: Daniel, Hananiah, Mishael and Azariah. The chief official gave them Babylonian names: Daniel was named Belteshazzar; Hananiah was named Shadrach; Mishael was named Meshach; and Azariah was named Abednego (Dan 1:6-7).

Daniel determined not to defile himself with the royal food and wine. He asked the chief official to exempt him from the royal diet. God caused Ashpenaz to be kind and to show sympathy to Daniel, but he told Daniel: "I am afraid of my master the king, who has determined your diet. If the king sees that you look worse than the other young men your age, he will cut off my head."
Daniel asked the guard responsible for them: "Please test your servants for ten days on a simple diet of nothing but vegetables to eat and water to drink. Then compare us with the young men who eat the royal food. Decide on our diet on the basis of what you see."
The guard agreed and tested them with vegetables and water for ten days. At the end of the ten days they looked healthier than the young men who ate the royal food. So the guard exempted them from the royal menu of food and wine and gave them vegetables instead (Dan 1:8-16).

God gave these four young men wisdom and the ability to learn. Daniel could also understand all kinds of visions and dreams.
At the end of the three years set by the king for their training, the chief official presented them to Nebuchadnezzar. The king found Daniel, Hananiah, Mishael and Azariah superior to all the other young men; so they entered the king's service (Dan 1:17-21).

Daniel Interprets Nebuchadnezzar's Dream
In the second year of his reign, Nebuchadnezzar started having dreams that disturbed him, and he could not sleep. The king summoned the Babylonian magicians, wizards, sorcerers, astrologers and fortune-tellers to interpret his dream. The king told

them: "I had a dream that disturbs me and I want to know what it means."

The wise men answered the king: "O king, live forever! Tell us your dream, and we will interpret it."

The king told the wise men: "You must tell me the dream; then you must interpret it. If you do not tell me the dream and interpret it, I will have you cut into pieces. If you tell me the dream and explain it, you will receive gifts and honor. Now, tell me the dream and interpret it."

Once more they replied: "Let your majesty tell us the dream, and we will interpret it."

The king answered: "If you do not tell me the dream, there is just one penalty for you. Now, tell me the dream, and I will know that you can interpret it for me."

The wise men answered the king: "Nobody anywhere can do what the king asks! No king has ever asked anything like this from any magician or wizard or fortune-teller. What the king asks is impossible. No one can reveal it to the king except the gods."

This made the king so angry that he ordered the execution of all the Babylonian wise men. Daniel and his companions were included in this death warrant (Dan 2:1-13).

When Arioch, the commander of the king's guard, was making arrangements for the execution, Daniel spoke to him with wisdom and tact. He asked the king's officer: "Why did the king issue such a harsh decree?" Arioch explained everything to Daniel. Daniel went to the king and asked for time, so that he might interpret the dream.

Daniel returned to his house and explained the story to his friends Hananiah, Mishael and Azariah (Shadrach, Meshach, and Abednego). Daniel urged them to pray for mercy from the God of heaven, so that the four of them might not be executed. That night the secret was revealed to Daniel in a vision. Daniel praised the God of heaven and said: "Praise be to the Name of God forever and ever; wisdom and power are his. I thank and praise you, O God of my ancestors. You gave me wisdom and power; you showed me what we asked of you; you made known to me the king's dream."

So Daniel went to Arioch, the man in charge of the execution and told him: "Do not execute the wise men of Babylon. Take me to the king, and I will interpret his dream" (Dan 2:14-24).

Arioch took Daniel to the king and said: "I found a man from the exiles of Judah who can interpret the king's dream."

The king asked Daniel: "Are you able to tell me my dream and interpret it?"

Daniel replied: "No wise man, wizard, magician or diviner can explain the king's secret. But there is a God in heaven who reveals mysteries. He has shown King Nebuchadnezzar what will happen in days to come. As you lay on your bed, your mind turned to things to come, and the revealer of secrets showed you what is going to happen. This secret has been revealed to me, not because I have greater wisdom than other men, but so that you, O king, will understand what you dreamed.

"O king, in your dream, you saw a huge statue in front of you. The head of the statue was pure gold, its chest and arms were silver, its belly and thighs were bronze, its legs were iron, its feet were an iron-clay mixture. While you were watching this statue, a rock cut out of a mountain by an invisible hand struck the statue, smashing its iron-clay feet. Then the whole thing fell to pieces. Iron, clay, bronze, silver and gold were broken to pieces and became like chaff on a threshing floor in the summer. The wind swept them away without leaving a trace. But the rock that struck the statue became a huge mountain and filled the whole earth.

"Now we will interpret the dream for the king. You are the most powerful king on earth. The God of heaven has given you power, strength and glory. You are the head ruler all over the world. You are the head of gold on that statue.

"After you, another kingdom will rise, inferior to yours. Next, a third kingdom, one of bronze, will rule over the whole earth. Finally, there will be a fourth kingdom, iron-like in strength. Just as iron breaks things to pieces, so it will crush and break all the previous kingdoms. Just as you saw that the feet and toes were partly baked clay and partly iron, so this will be a divided kingdom; yet it will have some of the strength of iron in it. As the toes were partly iron and partly clay, so this kingdom will be partly strong and partly breakable. That kingdom will not bind together any more than iron and clay bind together.

"Throughout the time of those kings, the God of heaven will be building a kingdom that will never be destroyed. It will crush all those kingdoms and bring them to an end, but it will endure forever. This is the meaning of the vision of the rock cut out of a mountain by invisible hands, a rock that broke to pieces the iron, the bronze, the clay, the silver and the gold.

"The great God has shown the king what will take place in the future. The dream is true and the interpretation is accurate" (Dan 2:25-45).

King Nebuchadnezzar fell facedown to the ground before Daniel and ordered that an offering and incense be presented in Daniel's honor. The king told Daniel: "Your God is the God of gods and the Lord of kings and a revealer of secrets. I know because you were able to reveal this secret."

Then the king showered Daniel with gifts and made him ruler over the province of Babylon and in charge of all its wise men. At Daniel's request, the king appointed Shadrach, Meshach and Abednego to administrative posts (Dan 2:46-49).

The Gold Statue and the Furnace

King Nebuchadnezzar had a gold statue made. It was 90 feet high and nine feet thick. He set it up in the province of Babylon. He summoned all the important leaders in the province to come to the dedication of the statue. They came and stood before the statue.

The master of ceremonies loudly proclaimed:

"Attention, everyone! As soon as you hear the musical instruments of the band, fall to your knees and worship the gold statue that King Nebuchadnezzar has set up. Whoever does not fall to his knees and worship will immediately be thrown into a blazing furnace."

As soon as they heard the band's musical instruments, all the people groups of every language fell to their knees and worshiped the gold statue that King Nebuchadnezzar had set up (Dan 3:1-7).

Some astrologers accused the Jews to King Nebuchadnezzar: "O king, live forever! There are some Jews whom you have set over the affairs of the province of Babylon, Shadrach, Meshach and Abednego, who ignore you. They neither serve your gods nor worship the gold statue you set up."

Enraged, Nebuchadnezzar summoned Shadrach, Meshach and Abednego. Nebuchadnezzar asked: "Is it true, Shadrach, Meshach and Abednego, that you do not serve my gods or worship the gold statue I have set up? I am giving you a second chance. When you hear the band music, fall to your knees and worship the statue I made. But if you do not worship it, you will be thrown immediately into a blazing furnace. Then no god will be able to rescue you from my power!"

Shadrach, Meshach and Abednego replied: "O Nebuchadnezzar, if we are thrown into the blazing furnace, the God we serve is able to save us from it. But even if he does not, we will not serve your gods or worship the gold statue you have set up."

Nebuchadnezzar was furious with Shadrach, Meshach and Abednego. He ordered the furnace heated seven times hotter than usual. He commanded some of the strongest soldiers in his army to tie them up and throw them into the blazing furnace. Shadrach, Meshach and Abednego were fully dressed when they were tied up and thrown into the blazing furnace. The king was in such a hurry and the fire so hot that the flames killed the soldiers who threw them into the blazing furnace (Dan 3:8-23).

Then King Nebuchadnezzar leaped to his feet in surprise and shouted: "Weren't there three men that we tied up and threw into the fire? Look! I see four men walking around in the fire. They are not tied up. They are unharmed. The fourth man looks like a son of the gods."

Nebuchadnezzar approached the door of the blazing furnace and shouted: "Shadrach, Meshach and Abednego, servants of the Most High God, come here!"

So Shadrach, Meshach and Abednego walked out of the fire. The government leaders crowded around them. They saw that the fire had not harmed the three men; not a hair singed, not a scorch mark on their clothes, and there was no smell of smoke on them.

Then Nebuchadnezzar said: "Praise be the God of Shadrach, Meshach and Abednego, who sent his angel and rescued his servants who trusted in him! They defied the king's command. They laid their lives on the line rather than serve or worship any god except their own God. Therefore, I decree that anyone of any nation or language who says anything against the God of Shadrach, Meshach and Abednego be cut into pieces. No other god can save in this way."

Then the king promoted Shadrach, Meshach and Abednego in the province of Babylon (Dan 3:24-30).

Nebuchadnezzar Humbled by God

King Nebuchadnezzar described in a letter an experience he had with the Lord. Nebuchadnezzar was at home in his palace, happy and successful. He had a nightmare that terrified him. So he commanded that all the wise men of Babylon be brought to him, but they could not interpret his dream. Finally, Daniel came into the king's presence.

Nebuchadnezzar said: "Daniel, chief of the magicians, I know that the spirit of the holy gods is in you. No mystery is too difficult for you. Listen to my dream and interpret it for me. I saw a big towering tree at the center of the world. The tree grew large and strong. Its top reached the sky; it was visible from all over the earth. Its leaves were beautiful, its fruit abundant; it had enough food for everyone. Wild animals were sheltered under it, and birds lived in its branches. Everything living was fed and sheltered by it. A holy watchman descended from heaven and called out in a loud voice: `Cut down the tree, trim off its branches; strip its leaves and scatter its fruit. Chase the animals from under it and chase the birds from its branches. But leave the stump and its roots in the ground in the grassy meadow. Let the man be soaked with dew, and let him eat with animals that graze plants. Let his mind be changed from that of a man into the mind of an animal. Let this go on for seven seasons. This will happen so that everyone living may know that the Most High is sovereign over human kingdoms and gives kingdoms to anyone he wishes'" (Dan 4:1-18).

Then Daniel was upset and terrified. So the king said: "Daniel, do not let the dream or its meaning scare you."

Daniel answered: "My lord, I wish the dream were about your enemies and its meaning for your adversaries! You, O king, are that tree! Your greatness has grown until it reaches the sky, and your rule extends all over the earth. You saw a holy angel descending from heaven and saying: `Cut down the tree, but leave the stump and its roots in the ground in the grassy meadow. Let him be soaked with dew, and let him eat with animals that graze plants.' This applies to you. You will be forced away from people and will live with wild animals. You will graze on grass like cattle and be soaked with the dew. Seven seasons will pass by until you recognize that the Most High rules over human kingdoms and gives them to anyone he wishes. The command to leave the stump of the tree with its roots means that your kingdom will be restored to you when you recognize that Heaven rules your kingdom. Therefore, take my advice: Renounce your sins and start doing what is right. Quit your wickedness, and start being kind to poor people" (Dan 4:19-27).

Twelve months later, as King Nebuchadnezzar was walking on the roof of the royal palace in Babylon, he said: "Look at this, Babylon the great! I built a royal palace to show how great I am!"

The words were still in his mouth when a voice from heaven spoke: "This is the verdict for you, King Nebuchadnezzar: Your royal authority has been taken from you. You will be forced away from people and will live with wild animals; you will eat grass like cattle. Seven seasons will pass by until you recognize that the Most High rules over human kingdoms and gives them to anyone he wishes."

Immediately, Nebuchadnezzar was forced away from people and ate grass like cattle. His body was soaked with the dew. His hair grew like the feathers of an eagle and his nails like the claws of a bird.

Seven years later, Nebuchadnezzar looked up toward heaven. His sanity was restored. Then he praised the Most High. He honored and glorified the Lord who lives forever. At the same time that his sanity was restored, he was restored to his throne and became even greater than before. Nebuchadnezzar praised and glorified the King of Heaven, because everything the Lord does is right, and he is able to humble the proud person (Dan 4:28-37).

The Writing on the Wall
When Nebuchadnezzar died, his son Belshazzar became king. King Belshazzar gave a big banquet for a thousand nobles. Belshazzar was drinking wine when he ordered his servants to bring in the gold and silver cups that his father Nebuchadnezzar had taken from the Lord's Temple in Jerusalem. The king, his nobles, his wives and his concubines drank wine from the gold cups taken from the Lord's Temple. Drunkenly they praised the gods made of gold, silver, bronze, iron, wood and stone.

Suddenly a human hand appeared, and its fingers wrote on the palace wall. The king watched the hand as it wrote. His face turned pale; he was so scared that his knees knocked together and he was too weak to stand up.

The king yelled for the wise men of Babylon and told them: "Whoever reads this writing and interprets it will be famous and rich. He will be third in command in the kingdom."

All the king's wise men came in, but they could not read the writing nor interpret it. King Belshazzar became even more terrified.

The king's mother heard the hysteria and came into the banquet hall. "O king, live forever! A man in your kingdom has the spirit of the holy gods in him. Daniel is his name. During your father Nebuchadnezzar's reign, he was famous for his insight, intelligence and spiritual wisdom. Call for Daniel, and he will tell you what the writing means" (Dan 5:1-12).

So Daniel was called in. The king asked him: "Are you Daniel, one of the Jewish exiles my father brought from Judah? I heard that you are incredibly wise. If you can read this writing and interpret it, you will be famous and rich. You will be third in command in the kingdom."

Daniel answered the king: "You may keep your gifts or give them to someone else. Nevertheless, I will read and interpret the writing for the king. The Most High God gave your father Nebuchadnezzar a great kingdom. When he became arrogant and stubborn, his royal throne and his glory were taken away. He was forced away from people, given the mind of an animal, and he lived with the wild donkeys and ate grass like cattle. His body was soaked with dew until he recognized that the Most High God rules over the kingdoms of men, and he puts in charge anyone he wishes.

"You are his son. You knew all this. Yet you are arrogant and set yourself up against the Lord of heaven. You had the drinking cups from the Lord's Temple brought to you. You, your nobles, your wives and your concubines drank wine from them. You praised the gods of silver, gold, bronze, iron, wood and stone. They are not really gods; they cannot see or hear or understand. You treat with contempt the living God who has power over your life. God sent the hand that wrote on the wall. These are the words that were written: MENE, MENE, TEKEL, PARSIN. These words mean:
- *Mene*: God has numbered the days of your reign and they do not add up.
- *Tekel*: You have been weighed on the scales and found wanting.
- *Peres*: Your kingdom is divided and given over to the Medes and Persians" (Dan 5:13-28).

Belshazzar did what he promised. Daniel was clothed in purple, a gold chain was placed around his neck, and he was proclaimed third in command.

That very night Belshazzar, king of the Babylonians, was slain, and Darius the Mede took over the kingdom (Dan 5:29-31).

Daniel During King Darius' Reign
During the first year that Darius ruled over the Babylonian kingdom, Daniel was reading the Scriptures. He understood from the words the Lord gave to the prophet Jeremiah, that Jerusalem would lie in ruins for seventy years.

Daniel prayed to the Lord God. He fasted and put on sackcloth and ashes. He prayed and confessed: "O Lord, you are great and awesome. You keep your covenant of love with all who love you and obey your commands. But we have sinned and done wrong. We have been wicked; we rebelled; we turned away from your commands. We turned a deaf ear to your servants, the prophets, who spoke in your name to our kings and leaders, and to all the people of the land. Lord, we and our kings, our leaders and our ancestors are covered with shame because we have sinned against you. The Lord our God is merciful and forgiving, even though we have rebelled against him. The curses and judgments written in the Law of Moses have been poured out on us, because we sinned against you. All this catastrophe has come upon us, yet we persist in ignoring you.

"O Lord our God, you delivered your people from Egypt with a mighty hand. We have sinned, we have done wrong. O Lord, in keeping with all your righteous acts, please stop being angry with Jerusalem, your city. Now, Lord, listen to the prayers of your servant. For your sake, O Lord, have mercy on your ruined sanctuary. We do not make requests of you because we are righteous, but because of your great mercy. O Lord, listen to us! O Lord, forgive us! O Lord, hear and act! For your sake, O my God, do not delay, because your city and your people are named after you" (Dan 9:1-19).

Darius appointed 120 governors to administer all parts of the kingdom. He chose three men as supervisors over the governors; one of whom was Daniel. Daniel did so much better that the other supervisors and governors, that the king planned to put him in charge of the whole kingdom. The supervisors and governors tried to find some scandal that they could use against Daniel, but were unable to find anything. He was trustworthy and neither corrupt nor negligent. Finally these men said: "We will never find any evidence of negligence or misconduct against Daniel; unless, it has something to do with the religion of his God" (Dan 6:1-5).

So the supervisors and governors conspired together and went as a group to the king. They said: "King Darius, live forever! We convened your supervisors, governors and all your leading officials. We all agreed that the king should issue the following decree: 'Anyone who prays to any god or man during the next thirty days, except to you, O king, shall be thrown into the lions' den.' Now, O king, issue the decree and put it in writing so that it cannot be altered; in accordance with the laws of the Medes and Persians." So King Darius put the decree in writing (Dan 6:6-9).

Daniel learned that the decree had been published. He went home to his upstairs room where the windows opened toward Jerusalem. Three times a day he got down on his knees and prayed, giving thanks to his God, just as he had done before. The conspirators went as a group and found Daniel praying and asking God for help. So they went to the king and reminded him about his royal decree: "Did you not publish a decree that during the next thirty days anyone who prays to any god or man except to you, O king, would be thrown into the lions' den?"
The king answered: "The decree stands. In accordance with the laws of the Medes and Persians, it cannot be canceled."
Then they told the king: "Daniel, one of the Jewish exiles, ignores you and defies your degree. He still prays three times a day." The king heard this and was greatly distressed. He was determined to rescue Daniel and made every effort until sundown to save him.
Then the conspirators returned to the king and said: "Remember, O king, that according to the law of the Medes and Persians the king's decree can never be canceled" (Dan 6:10-14).

So the king gave the order to bring Daniel and throw him into the lions' den. The king said to Daniel: "May your God, whom you loyally serve, rescue you!"
A stone slab was placed over the lions' den. The king returned to his palace and spent the night fasting. He could not sleep. At daybreak, the king got up and hurried to the lions' den. As he approached the den, he called out anxiously: "Daniel, servant of the living God, has your God, whom you serve so loyally, saved you from the lions?"
Daniel answered: "O king, live forever! My God sent his angel, who shut the lions' mouths so they would not hurt me. I was found innocent in God's sight. And I have never done you any wrong."
The king was overjoyed and gave orders to take Daniel out of the den. When Daniel was lifted from the den, no scratch was found on him. He had trusted his God.
Then the king commanded that those who conspired against Daniel be thrown into the lions' den, along with their wives and children. Before they hit the floor of the den, the lions had them in their jaws, tearing them to pieces (Dan 6:15-24).

Then King Darius published a decree to all the people in his land: "I decree that people must fear and worship the God of Daniel in all parts of my kingdom. He is the living God; he endures forever; his kingdom is eternal; he rescues and saves; he performs miracles. He rescued Daniel from the power of the lions" (Dan 6:25-27).

From then on, Daniel prospered during the reign of Darius and also in the following reign of Cyrus the Persian (Dan 6:28).

Daniel was greatly loved by God (Dan 9:23; 10:11, 19).

LIFE-LESSONS DISCOVERED IN THE STORY

1. God wants his people to be a useful and necessary part of the community where they live. God advised the Jews, who were captive in Babylon, to seek the good of the city (Jer 29:5-7).

2. The person who faithfully announces God's message will proclaim both good news and also the bad news that the people don't want to hear. However, false preachers/teachers will proclaim lies, promising good things that their listeners want to hear. Jeremiah gave the bad news that the time of the captivity would be 70 years, while false prophets were deceiving the people and promising a brief exile (Jer 29:1, 8-10, 15, 31-32).

3. God reveals himself to people who are ready to give to the Lord everything they have and are. God promised that those who seek him with all their heart would find him (Jer 29:13).

4. The pagan world seeks to integrate youth who serve God into the pagan religion and culture. The change of the Jewish youths' names was an attempt to change their religion from Judah's God to Babylonia's gods. In Hebrew, Daniel means: "God is my Judge. His name was changed to Belteshazzar meaning: "Bel, protect his life." Hananiah means: "The Lord shows grace," his new name Shadrach means "under the command of Aku" (the moon god). Azariah means "The Lord helps," his new name, Abednego means "Servant of Nego" (Dan 1:7).

5. The youth who lives just like everyone else in his social setting will become impure and will be contaminated spiritually. Daniel and his friends decided not to be contaminated. They made a choice to maintain a lifestyle different from the other youth in training (Dan 1:8).

6. The one who serves God is often able to resolve trouble with those in authority; however, he will not obey an authority who requires him to disobey God. Daniel resolved not to defile himself with the royal diet. He made a request, not a demand, and he offered a practical suggestion that resolved the official's problem as well as his own (Dan 1:8-14). In another situation, Daniel's friends refused to obey the king and kneel down to a statue (Dan 3:12-18). Also, Daniel refused to obey the royal decree which required him to abstain from praying to God (Dan 6:10).

7. When culture does not violate God's commands, it can help the person who serves God to accomplish his purpose. Daniel and his companions studied the Babylonian literature (Dan 1:4, 17).

8. Sometimes God's servants who are loyal to him experience success in the world. Daniel is an example of one who was loyal to God and prospered in a pagan kingdom (Dan 1:9, 20; 2:48-49; 6:2-3). Joseph in Egypt is another example (Gen 41:41-49).

9. The person who serves God often faces crises. Daniel and his friends were taken captive from their home and exiled to another country (Dan 1:1-2); were under the death penalty (Dan 2:12); three were thrown into the furnace (Dan 3:19-30); and Daniel was thrown into the lions' den (Dan 6:1-22).

10. When facing a crisis, God's servant should go to God in prayer, ask for mercy, place the problem under God's control and be committed to do God's will. The person who does this will have reasons to praise the Lord. When threatened with death, Daniel and his companions prayed, God answered their prayers, and Daniel praised the Lord (Dan 2:17-23).

11. Prayer opens the door to talk with the Living God. It was through his prayers that Daniel had constant access to God (Dan 2:17-18; 6:10; 9:4, 20-23).

12. God often demonstrates achieving the impossible through those who serve him. The astrologers told the king that no one could know the dreams of another person (Dan 2:10-11). But God revealed the dream and its interpretation to Daniel (Dan 2:19).

13. God often reveals his secrets to his servants who are loyal and obedient. Daniel is an example of one to whom God revealed his secrets (Dan 2:19, 22, 47). (See Job 14:21.)

14. The person who takes a prayer request to God, should express gratitude to God when his prayer is answered. Daniel asked God to reveal Nebuchadnezzar's dream to him. When God answered his prayer, he praised the Lord (Dan 2:19-23).

15. Jesus Christ is sovereign and determines the destiny of governments. He is the stone that breaks the kingdoms of this world (Dan 2:34-35, 44). (See Mt 22:42-44.)

16. A person should not take credit for himself for what God does through him. Before Daniel interpreted the king's dream, he stated that God had revealed the dream and interpretation to him (Dan 2:27-30).

17. People who faithfully serve the Lord will be considered enemies by those who are responsible for government-sponsored religion. Daniel's three companions refused to worship the statue that King Nebuchadnezzar set up; they were

condemned to die (Dan 3:6-20).

18. The person who faithfully serves God does not have as his priority: sensual favors, or physical protection, or health, or benefits or wealth. His priority is a commitment to serve God, no matter what it costs. Shadrach, Meshach and Abednego would not worship the king's statue. They did not know if God would save them from the blazing furnace, though they knew that he could save them (Dan 3:16-18). The greatest surprise is not that they were unharmed by the fire, but that they entered the furnace without knowing if God would protect them.

19. Those who faithfully walk with God will experience intimate communion with him when they suffer tribulation and persecution. When Shadrach, Meshach and Abednego were in the furnace, they walked with an angel, or possibly they experienced a visit from Jesus before his birth (Dan 3:24-25).

20. Pride is self-destructive, because pride denies God's right to govern; it is also self-adoration. The consequence of Nebuchadnezzar's pride was that God punished him with insanity (Dan 4:30-37); the consequence of Belshazzar's pride was that he lost his kingdom and his life (Dan 5:22-30).

21. No one is so powerful that God can not reach him with divine punishment. The most powerful kings suffered divine punishment. Here are the examples of King Nebuchadnezzar (Dan 4:30-37) and of King Belshazzar (Dan 5:22-30). Pharaoh of Egypt, King David, King Solomon and all of the kings of Judah and Israel also could not escape God's punishment.

22. The person who serves God may have esteem for and friendship with another person who rejects God. Daniel had true esteem for Nebuchadnezzar, the king whom he served. This friendship brought sadness when he understood that God would punish Nebuchadnezzar (Dan 4:19).

23. Suffering can become a road that takes a person to God. Those who do not come to God because he loves them, may come to him when they are in pain. King Nebuchadnezzar spent seven years insane, living like a wild animal, until he recognized God and praised him. His suffering became a road that led him to recognize God (Dan 4:28-35).

24. A person may convert to God, regardless of past actions. Any sinner that recognizes his sins, humbles himself and searches for God will be transformed. The proud Nebuchadnezzar was transformed when he humbled himself, praised God, and recognized that God Almighty has control over nations and individuals (Dan 4:28-37).

25. God is sovereign, and the destiny of people and nations is controlled by him (Dan 2:20-21, 41; 4:17, 25, 30-37; 7:25-27; 9:20-27).

26. Truth should be told, regardless of the pressure one faces. Daniel told Belshazzar the truth, even though kings often killed the bearer of bad news (Dan 5:22).

27. A person should not use for selfish purposes that which has been dedicated to God. Belshazzar used cups from the Temple for his party, and God condemned him (Dan 5:24).

28. Alcoholic drink can provoke a person to mock and profane that which is sacred. King Belshazzar became cheerful after drinking wine; he began to mock and profane religious things, using the cups taken from the Lord's Temple to drink wine (Dan 5:2-4).

29. The effects of the alcoholic drink may prove fatal. The effects of alcoholic drink in the Bible often proved fatal: Noah lost his composure and exposed himself (Gn. 9:20-22); Lot lost his awareness and committed incest (Gn. 19:32-35); Amnon died victim of his drunkenness; drunk, he could not resist when attacked (2 Sm 13:28); Elah, king of Israel, died victim of his addiction; in a time when Israel was at war, he was at home in an alcoholic stupor and was murdered by his official (1 Kin 16:8-10); Belshazzar lost his sobriety, his kingdom and his life (Dan 5:1-30).

30. The person who is faithful to God will suffer threats and persecutions when his virtue enters into conflict with the culture of those who surround him. Then his own virtue becomes a reason to condimn him. Daniel had enemies who used his fidelity to God as a reason for killing him (Dan 6:5, 12-16).

31. The cynical person, who is harmed by the virtues of one who serves God, will surrender to Satan's ambitions. The men who were jealous of Daniel surrendered to Satan's ambition to accuse and condemn him (Dan 6:5). Satan is the accuser of the brethren (Rev 12:10), and he is a murderer from the beginning (Jn 8:44).

32. The person who serves God should have a disciplined prayer life. Daniel continued to pray three times a day as he always had (Dan 6:10).

33. God loves the person who is faithful to him. Daniel is one of the few people written about in the Bible with no mention of his doing anything wrong. Daniel was greatly loved by God (Dan 9:23; 10:11, 19).

QUESTIONS

1. What can you learn from the letter that Jeremiah sent to the captives in Babylon (Jer 29)?
2. How did the Jewish youth, Daniel and his companions, become servants of the king of Babylon?
3. What kind of problems did Daniel and his friends face?
4. Which of these problems are faced by people who serve God today?
5. What happened when Daniel refused to defile himself by eating the food and drinking the wine that was on the royal diet?
6. What happened when the three Jewish youth refused to worship King Nebuchadnezzar's statue?
7. What can you learn from the story of Daniel about how to deal with problems with authority?
8. What was the result of King Nebuchadnezzar's pride?
9. When Daniel's enemies were seeking a scandal to accuse him, what evidence were they able to use against him?
10. What happened to Daniel in the lions' den?
11. What does the story of Daniel and his friends teach us about God?
12. What does the story of Daniel and his friends teach us about privileges enjoyed by those who serve the Lord?
13. What does the story of Daniel and his friends teach us about problems faced by those who faithfully serve the Lord?

CHRONOLOGICAL ORDER OF THE HISTORICAL BOOKS OF THE RECONSTRUCTION
Ezra, Nehemiah and Esther

BOOK	Ezra 1-6	Esther	Ezra 7-10	Nehemiah
KEY-PERSON	Zerubbabel	Esther and Mordecai	Ezra	Nehemiah
RETURN TRIP	1st Return trip		2nd Return trip	3rd Return trip
KEY-ACTIVITY	Rebuilding the Temple	Problems of the scattered Jews who did not return to Jerusalem	Reforms, undoing mixed marriages	Rebuilding the walls of Jerusalem
PROPHETS	Haggai, Zechariah			Malachi
YEAR, B.C.	538 516	483 473	457	444 425

RESTORATION OF JUDAH
Ezra and Nehemiah

STRUCTURE

Context:
The Babylonians conquered Jerusalem, destroyed the city and carried its citizens into exile. After the destruction of Jerusalem, the Jews lived as exiles in Babylon. They had been in Babylon for 70 years when Cyrus, king of Persia conquered Babylon.

Key-persons: Ezra, Nehemiah

Key-location: Jerusalem

Key-repetitions:
- Prayers: of Ezra (Ezr 8:21-23; 9:1-10:2; Neh 8:5-6); of Nehemiah (Neh 1:4-11; 2:4; 5:19; 6:9, 14; 9:6-37; 13:22, 29, 31).
- Reconstructions: Temple, houses, wall.
- Mixed marriages condemned (Ezr 9:1-4; 10:2,10-18, 44; Neh 13:23-28).
- Opposition to work done for God: to reconstructing the Temple: enemies wanting to participate (Ezr 4:1-2); false accusations (Ezr 4:6); political interference (Ezr 5:3-17). To rebuilding the city walls: ridicule (Neh 4:1-3); physical aggression (Neh 4:8); weariness (Neh 4:10); rumors (Neh 6:5-8); false prophets (Neh 6:10-14); fear (Neh 6:1-14) undermining because of family relations (Neh 6:17-19).
- Celebration after completing a task: foundation of Temple (Ezr 3:10-13), Temple (Ezr 6:16); city walls (Neh 12:27-43).

Key-attitudes:
- The holiness and determination of Ezra.
- Opposition against those who helped the Jews.
- The inconsistency of the Jews in Jerusalem.
- Mixed anger and grief of Ezra and Nehemiah when they saw the sins of the Jews.
- Celebrations of achievements.
- The determination and persistence of Nehemiah.

Initial-problem:
The Jews had lived as exiles in Babylon for 70 years when Cyrus, king of Persia, conquered Babylon and issued a proclamation permitting the Jews to return to Jerusalem.

Sequence of events:
First Return: Temple Rebuilt
- Cyrus, king of Persia conquered Babylon and permitted the exiled Jews to return to Jerusalem and rebuild the Temple. Everyone who wanted to go set out, taking gifts from their neighbors and articles belonging to the Temple (Ezr 1:1-11). The first return was in 538 B.C.
- The returning group numbered 42,360 (Ezr 2:64-70).
- When they arrived in Jerusalem, the priests built the altar and sacrificed burnt offerings (Ezr 3:1-6).
- They began the reconstruction of the Temple. When the foundation was laid, many of the older people wept aloud, while others shouted for joy (Ezr 3:7-13).
- The Samaritans offered to help the Jews build the Temple. The Jewish leaders refused their offer (Ezr 4:1-3).
- The surrounding peoples set out to harass the people of Judah and make them afraid to go on building. When Artaxerxes became king, they wrote him a letter. King Artaxerxes issued an order for the Jews to stop work on the Temple (Ezr 4:4-24).
- The prophets Haggai and Zechariah prophesied to the Jews in Judah (Ezr 5:1).
- Haggai told the Jews that life was hard because

Old Testament Bible Stories © Jackson Day

God's Temple remained a wreck, while each of them was busy with his own house (Hag 1:1-11).
- The people began to work on the Temple (Hag 1:12-13; Ezr 5:2). They finished building it and celebrated its dedication with joy (Ezr 6:13-18).
- They celebrated the Passover (Ezr 6:19-22).

Second Return: Ezra

- Almost 80 years had passed since the first group of exiles returned from Babylon to Jerusalem, when Ezra led a second group of exiles to return to Jerusalem. God's hand was on Ezra, and King Artaxerxes granted him everything he requested. Ezra had devoted himself to the study and observance of the Law of the Lord and to teaching it to the Israelites (Ezr 7:1-10).
- King Artaxerxes ordered his treasurers to provide whatever Ezra asked (Ezr 7:21-22).
- Ezra praised the Lord. He gathered leading men from Israel to go to Jerusalem with him (Ezr 7:27-28).
- Ezra sought out Levites to return to Jerusalem with him (Ezr 8:15-20).
- Before leaving on the trip, Ezra proclaimed a fast. He was ashamed to ask the king for soldiers and horsemen to protect them from bandits on the road. They fasted and petitioned God, and he answered their prayer (Ezr 8:21-23).
- In Jerusalem, Ezra discovered that the Israelites had adopted the customs of the surrounding people, and the men had married foreign women (Ezr 9:1-2).
- Ezra ripped his clothes, pulled his hair and slumped to the ground. Others surrounded him. Ezra fell on his knees with his hands spread out and prayed confessing both the sins of their ancestors and the sins of the present day Jews (Ezr 9:3-15).
- Many gathered around Ezra weeping. The people made a covenant with God to send away the foreign women and their children (Ezr 10:1-17).

Third Return: Nehemiah

- Fourteen years passed after Ezra went to Jerusalem, in the year 444 B.C. Visitors from Jerusalem who were in Susa, told Nehemiah that the wall of Jerusalem was broken and its gates were burned (Neh 1:1-3).
- Nehemiah mourned, fasted and prayed. He confessed the sins of the Israelites and reminded God of his promise to Moses (Neh 1:4-11).
- Nehemiah, the cupbearer, took wine to King Artaxerxes. The king asked him why he was sad. Nehemiah replied that the city of his ancestors was in ruins. He asked the king to send him to Judah so he could rebuild it. The king sent him (Neh 2:1-9).
- Nehemiah arrived in Jerusalem. Three days later, under cover of night, he examined the broken walls and its gates. Nehemiah challenged the Jewish leaders to rebuild the wall of Jerusalem. They agreed (Neh 2:11-18).
- The surrounding non-Jews were angry that someone had come to promote the welfare of the Israelites (Neh 2:10). Sanballat, Tobiah, and Geshem ridiculed them. Nehemiah answered that God would give them success (Neh 2:19-20).
- The builders of the walls were organized. Each group was assigned a section to rebuild (Neh 3:1-32).
- Sanballat exploded in anger. He ridiculed the Jews. Tobiah joked that even a fox would knock the walls down. Nehemiah prayed because of the insults (Neh 4:1-5).
- The Jews rebuilt the wall till it was halfway to its intended height. Sanballat, Tobiah and others plotted to fight against Jerusalem. Nehemiah prayed to God and posted guards. Half the men did the work, while the other half were equipped with weapons. The laborers worked with one hand and held a weapon in the other. The man who sounded the trumpet stayed with Nehemiah (Neh 4:6-23).
- Men and their wives complained against their fellow Jews who were exploiting them with high interest. Nehemiah became angry; he accused the nobles and officials of wrongdoing, prohibited them from charging interest, and demanded that they return property and money (Neh 5:1-13).
- Nehemiah was appointed governor in Judah, but did not use the privileges allotted to him as governor (Neh 5:14-19).
- Sanballat, Tobiah, and Geshem heard that Nehemiah had rebuilt the wall, even though he had not yet installed the gates. They requested that he meet with them in one of the villages. Nehemiah replied that he was doing a great work and could not go down. This happened four times. The fifth time, Sanballat accused Nehemiah of conspiring to become king of the Jews. Nehemiah denied the accusation and prayed for strength (Neh 6:1-9).
- Shemaiah warned Nehemiah to flee to the Temple for protection. Nehemiah asked if a man like him should run away. Tobiah and Sanballat had hired Shemaiah to prophesy against Nehemiah. Nehemiah prayed that God would remember the prophets who tried to intimidate him (Neh 6:10-14).
- The wall was completed in fifty-two days. The enemies of the Jews knew that the work had been done with the help of God (Neh 6:15-16).
- All during this time letters were constantly going back and forth between the nobles of Judah and Tobiah (Neh 6:17-19).
- The city was large and spacious, but few people lived in it (Neh 7:4).

Other Reforms

- The Israelites in Judah assembled in Jerusalem. Ezra read from the Book of the Law from daybreak till noon with the people listening. Ezra stood on a high platform. As he opened the book, the people stood up. The Levites explained the meaning so that the people could understand what was being read (Neh 8:1-8).
- Nehemiah, Ezra and the Levites told the people not to mourn or weep, because the joy of the Lord was their strength. Then the people ate, drank and celebrated because they understood the reading of God's Word (Neh 8:9-12).
- On another occasion, the Israelites gathered together, fasting and wearing sackcloth with dust on their heads. They had separated themselves from all foreigners. They stood and confessed their sins and

the wickedness of their ancestors. Then they praised the Lord God (Neh 9:1 - 10:39).
- The leaders of the people settled in Jerusalem. The people cast lots to bring one out of every ten to live in Jerusalem (Neh 11:1).
- The wall of Jerusalem was dedicated to God with great joy (Neh 12:27-47). The Book of Moses was read aloud (Neh 13:1).
- Nehemiah left Jerusalem. When he returned he discovered many wrongdoings and initiated reform: priests had provided Tobiah a room in the Temple. Nehemiah threw out Tobiah's household goods (Neh 13:4-9); Nehemiah called the Levites and singers back to Jerusalem and put them back on their jobs (Neh 13:10-14) Nehemiah stopped the profaning of the Sabbath day (Neh 13:15-22); Nehemiah made the Jews take an oath not to marry their children to the children of other people (Neh 13:23-30).

- With the reforms by Nehemiah and prophets, the remnant that returned to Judah became a nation consecrated to God. With the passing of time, their religion became more of a formality rather than a commitment to the Lord God. After the prophet Malachi, a time period of 400 years passed without God sending a prophet or giving anyone a special revelation.

Final-situation:

With the reforms by Nehemiah and the other prophets, the remnant that returned to Judah became a nation consecrated to God. They rejected idiolatry and mixed marriages. They observed the Sabbath. But with the passing of time, their religion became more of a formality rather than a commitment to the Lord God.

BIBLE STORY

First Return: Temple Rebuilt

After the destruction of Jerusalem, the Jews lived as exiles in Babylon. The Jews had been in Babylon for almost 70 years when Persia became a new power. Finally, Cyrus, king of Persia conquered Babylon.

In the first year that Cyrus was king of Persia, the Lord caused the king to make a proclamation throughout his kingdom permitting exiled Jews to return to Jerusalem and rebuild the Temple for the Lord. This proclamation fulfilled the Word of the Lord spoken by Jeremiah.

During the 70 years of exile in Babylon, a new generation grew up. Many preferred the security of Babylon over the challenge of reconstructing a nation. Everyone whose heart God made to want to go, set out to build the Temple of the Lord in Jerusalem. All their neighbors helped them with articles of silver and gold, with goods and livestock, and valuable gifts. Moreover, King Cyrus turned over to them the articles belonging to the Temple of the Lord, which Nebuchadnezzar had hauled from Jerusalem. King Cyrus provided a full inventory listing all those items and turned them over to Sheshbazzar, the prince of Judah, who was responsible for them, when the exiles left Babylon to return to Jerusalem (Ezr 1:1-11). The first return was in 538 B.C.

The first group of Jews to return from exile to Jerusalem numbered 42,360. They took with them offerings for the reconstruction of the Temple (Ezr 2:64-70).

When they arrived in Jerusalem, the priests began to build the altar of the God of Israel to sacrifice burnt offerings on it. Before laying the foundation of the Temple, they built the altar and sacrificed burnt offerings on it to the Lord (Ezr 3:1-6).

They began the reconstruction of the Temple. When the foundation of the Temple was laid, the priests stood up with trumpets, and the Levites with cymbals, to praise the Lord. The people gave a shout of praise to the Lord. Many of the older people, who had seen the former Temple, wept aloud while the others shouted for joy. No one could distinguish the sound of the shouts of joy from the sound of weeping, because the people made so much noise. The sound was heard far away (Ezr 3:7-13).

The Jews were surrounded by people of the land: the Samaritans and some old enemies who had invaded the land left unoccupied when the Jews were taken captive to Babylon. Those who surrounded the Jews considered that the land and political rights now belonged to them. The Samaritans mixed the worship of the Lord God with the worship of other gods. The Samaritans heard that the returned exiles were building a Temple for the Lord, the God of Israel. They came to the Jewish leader Zerubbabel and the other leaders and said: "Let us help you build the Temple because, like you, we seek your God and have been sacrificing to him."

The Jewish leaders knew that if the surrounding people helped build the Temple, they would also use it for their worship. They would contaminate the worship of the Lord by including worship to other gods. The Jewish leaders replied: "You have no part with us in building a Temple to our God. We alone will build it for the Lord, the God of Israel" (Ezr 4:1-3).

Then the surrounding peoples set out to harass the people of Judah and make them afraid to go on building. They hired consultants to work against them and frustrate their plans during the entire reign of Cyrus king of Persia. When Xerxes became king, they lodged a written accusation against the people of Judah. Later Artaxerxes became king and they wrote him a letter. After receiving their letter, King Artaxerxes issued an order for the Jews to stop work on the Temple. Thus the work on the Temple of

God in Jerusalem came to a standstill (Ezr 4:4-24).

Life was hard for the returned exiles. The prophets Haggai and Zechariah prophesied to the Jews in Judah and Jerusalem in the name of the God of Israel (Ezr 5:1).

The Word of the Lord came through the prophet Haggai to the governor Zerubbabel and the other leaders: "Is it a time for you yourselves to be living in your paneled houses, while God's Temple remains a ruin? Give careful thought to your ways. You planted much, but harvested little. You eat, but are always hungry. You drink, but are always thirsty. You put on clothes, but cannot get warm. You earn wages, but put them in a purse with holes in it. Why? Because of my house, which remains a wreck, while each of you is busy with his own house."

Then the governor Zerubbabel and all the people obeyed the voice of the Lord their God spoken through the prophet Haggai (Hag 1:1-11).

The people began to work on the Temple of the Lord Almighty. And the prophets of God were with them, helping them (Hag 1:12-13; Ezr 5:2). They continued to build, and the work prospered under the preaching of the prophets Haggai and Zechariah. They finished building the Temple according to the command of God. Then the people of Israel celebrated the dedication of the Temple of God with joy. And they installed the priests and the Levites in their groups to serve God in the Temple at Jerusalem (Ezr 6:13-18).

Then the returned exiles celebrated the Passover (Ezr 6:19-22).

Second Return: Ezra

Almost eighty years had passed since the first group of exiles returned from Babylon to Jerusalem, when in 458 B.C., Ezra led a second group of exiles to return to Jerusalem.

During the reign of Artaxerxes king of Persia, Ezra came to Jerusalem from Babylon. He was a teacher well versed in the Law of Moses. Because God's hand was on Ezra, the king had granted him everything he requested.

Ezra had devoted himself to the study and observance of the Law of the Lord, and to teaching its decrees and laws to the Israelites (Ezr 7:1-10).

King Artaxerxes ordered his treasurers to provide whatever Ezra the priest asked of them within established limits (Ezr 7:21-22).

Ezra praised the Lord who caused the king to want to honor the Temple of the Lord in Jerusalem, and that the Lord showed him his love. Because the hand of the Lord God was on Ezra, he took courage and gathered leading men from Israel to go to Jerusalem with him (Ezr 7:27-28).

Ezra was disappointed because there were no Levites with him. So he sought out Levites to return to Jerusalem with him (Ezr 8:15-20).

Before leaving on the trip, Ezra proclaimed a fast, so that the returning exiles might humble themselves before God and ask him for a safe journey. Ezra was ashamed to ask the king for soldiers and horsemen to protect them from bandits on the road, because he had told the king: "The gracious hand of our God is on everyone who seeks him, but his anger is against all who forsake him." They fasted and petitioned God, asking for safety, and he answered their prayer (Ezr 8:21-23).

After they arrived in Jerusalem, Ezra faced the problem of the Israelites who had adopted the customs of the surrounding people, and of men who had married women who worshiped other gods. The leaders and officials had been the first in this unfaithfulness (Ezr 9:1-2).

Ezra describes in his own words his actions when he learned of the Jews' unfaithfulness: "I ripped my robe and coat, pulled hair from my head and beard and slumped to the ground appalled. Then everyone who trembled at the Words of the Lord gathered around me because of this betrayal by the exiles. And I sat there appalled until the evening sacrifice. Then, at the evening sacrifice, I rose from my self-abasement, with my ripped clothes, and fell on my knees with my hands spread out to the Lord my God and prayed."

In his prayer, Ezra confessed both the sins of his ancestors and the sins of the present day Jews (Ezr 9:3-15).

While Ezra was praying and confessing, weeping and throwing himself down before the Temple of God, a large crowd gathered around him. They too wept bitterly. Then Shecaniah, one of the leaders, acting as spokesman, said to Ezra: "We have been unfaithful to our God by marrying women from the peoples around us. But in spite of this, there is still hope for Israel. Now let us make a covenant with our God to send away all these women and their children, just as you and all those who honor God's commandments are counseling. Let it be done according to the Law."

A notice was then issued throughout Judah and Jerusalem for all the exiles to assemble in Jerusalem. The assembly confessed their sins, and they all agreed that everyone who had married a foreign woman would put her away (Ezr 10:1-17).

Third Return: Nehemiah

About fourteen years passed after Ezra went to Jerusalem. In the year 444 B.C., Nehemiah was a cupbearer to King Artarxerxes at Susa. Hanani, one of Nehemiah's brothers, along with some fellow Jews, traveled from Judah to Susa. Nehemiah asked them about the Jewish remnant who survived the exile, and about Jerusalem.

They told him: "Those exiled survivors who are back in Judah are in great trouble and disgrace. The wall of Jerusalem is still broken down, and its gates are still burned with fire" (Neh 1:1-3).

When Nehemiah heard the report, he sat down and wept. For several days he mourned and fasted and prayed before the God of heaven. In his prayers, he confessed the sins of the Israelites. Then he reminded God of his promise to Moses: "If you are unfaithful, I will scatter you among the nations, but if you return to me and obey my commands, I will gather these scattered peoples and bring them to the place I have chosen to mark with my Name" (Neh 1:4-11).

Nehemiah was cupbearer to the king. Since many kings had been poisoned, the cupbearer was a trusted person. Nehemiah took wine to King Artaxerxes. The king asked him: "Why does your face look so sad? This can be nothing but sadness of heart."

Even though he was afraid: Nehemiah replied: "May the king live forever! My face is sad because the city where my ancestors are buried lies in ruins, and its gates have been destroyed by fire."

The king asked Nehemiah: "What is it you want?"

Nehemiah silently prayed to God, and then answered the king: "Send me to the city in Judah where my ancestors are buried so that I can rebuild it."

It pleased the king to send Nehemiah (Neh 2:1-9).

Nehemiah arrived in Jerusalem. After staying there three days he set out during the night with a few men. He had not told anyone what God had put in his heart to do for Jerusalem. Under cover of night he examined the broken walls of Jerusalem, and its gates, which had been destroyed by fire. The officials did not know where he had gone or what he was doing.

Then Nehemiah told the Jewish leaders: "You see the trouble we are in: Jerusalem lies in ruins, and its gates have been burned with fire. Come, let us rebuild the wall of Jerusalem, and we will no longer be in disgrace."

They replied: "Let us start rebuilding." So they began the good work (Neh 2:11-18).

The non-Jews who lived close to Jerusalem were very angry that someone had come to promote the welfare of the Israelites (Neh 2:10). When Sanballat the Horonite, Tobiah the Ammonite official and Geshem the Arab heard about the rebuilding of the walls, they mocked and ridiculed the Jews: "What is this you are doing?"

Nehemiah answered them: "The God of Heaven will give us success. We his servants will start rebuilding, but as for you, you have no share in Jerusalem or any historic right to it" (Neh 2:19-20).

The builders of the walls were organized, and each group was assigned to a section to rebuild (Neh 3:1-32).

When Sanballat heard that they were rebuilding the wall, he exploded in anger. He ridiculed the Jews, and in the company of his friends and the Samaritan army, he said: "What are those feeble Jews doing? Will they restore their wall? Can they bring the stones back to life from those heaps of trash and ashes?"

Tobiah the Ammonite was with him and said: "If even a fox climbed up that wall, it would fall to pieces under his weight!"

Nehemiah prayed: "Hear us, O our God, for we are despised. Boomerang their insults back on their own heads. Do not cover up their guilt or blot out their sins from your sight, for they have insulted the builders (Neh 4:1-5).

The Jews rebuilt the wall until it was halfway up to its intended height; the people worked with all their heart.

But when Sanballat, Tobiah, the Arabs, the Ammonites and the Ashdodites heard that the repairs to Jerusalem's walls had gone ahead and that the gaps in the wall were being closed, they were furious. They plotted together and decided to fight against Jerusalem. Nehemiah prayed to God and posted guards day and night to meet this threat. From that day on, half the men did the work, while the other half were equipped with spears, shields, bows and armor. Military officers posted themselves behind all the people of Judah who were building the wall. The laborers on the wall did their work with one hand and held a weapon in the other. Each of the builders wore his sword at his side as he worked. But the man who sounded the trumpet stayed with Nehemiah. Nehemiah told the people: "The work is extensive and spread out, and we are widely separated from each other along the wall. Wherever you hear the sound of the trumpet, join us there. Our God will fight for us!"

So they continued the work, with half the men holding spears (Neh 4:6-23).

The men and their wives complained loudly against their fellow Jews: "We are mortgaging our fields, our vineyards and our homes to get grain during the famine."

Others complained: "We had to borrow money to pay the king's tax on our fields and vineyards. We are of the same flesh and blood as our countrymen and our children are just as good as theirs. Yet we have to sell our children off as slaves. Some of our daughters have already been enslaved, but we are powerless, because our fields and our vineyards belong to others."

Nehemiah became very angry. He accused the nobles and officials: "You are exacting high interest from your own countrymen! You are selling your brothers into debt slavery!" They kept quiet, because they could find nothing to say.

Nehemiah continued: "What you are doing is not right. Shouldn't you fear our God and avoid the reproach of our Gentile enemies? I, my brothers, and the men who work for me are also lending the people money and grain. But let the exacting of interest stop! Give back to them immediately their fields, vineyards, olive groves and houses, and also the interest you are charging them."

The nobles and officials replied: "We will give it back, and we will not demand anything more from them. We will do as you say." And the leaders did as they had promised (Neh 5:1-13).

Nehemiah was appointed governor in Judah, but did not use the privileges allotted to him as governor. The governors preceding him had placed a heavy burden on the people, and their assistants lorded it over the people. Nehemiah did not act like that. Instead, he devoted himself to the work on the wall. He did not acquire any land. Every day, a hundred and fifty Jews and officials ate at his table, but he never demanded the food allotted to the governor, because the demands would be hard for the people. Nehemiah prayed that God would remember everything he did for the people (Neh 5:14-19).

Word reached Sanballat, Tobiah, Geshem the Arab, and the rest of the Jews' enemies that Nehemiah had rebuilt the wall, even though he had not yet installed the gates. Sanballat and Geshem sent Nehemiah this message: "Come, let us meet together in one of the villages on the plain of Ono."

But they were scheming to harm him; so he sent messengers to them with this reply: "I am doing a great work and cannot go down. Why should the work stop while I leave it and go down to you?" Four times they sent him the same message, and each time he gave them the same answer.

Then, the fifth time, Sanballat sent his aide with the same message, but he also sent an unsealed letter in which he accused Nehemiah of conspiring to become king of the Jews.

Nehemiah replied: "Nothing you are saying is true; you are making it up in your head."

They were all trying to frighten the Jews so they would stop rebuilding the walls. But Nehemiah prayed: "Now give me strength" (Neh 6:1-9).

One day Nehemiah visited the home of Shemaiah who warned Nehemiah: "Let us meet inside the Temple of God. Let us lock the Temple doors because men are coming by night to kill you."

Nehemiah replied: "Should a man like me run away? Should one like me go into the Temple to save his life? I will not go!" Shemaiah had prophesied against Nehemiah because Tobiah and Sanballat had hired him. They wanted to intimidate Nehemiah so that he would commit a sin by going into hiding. Then they would discredit him.

Nehemiah prayed that God would remember the prophetess and the prophets who tried to intimidate him (Neh 6:10-14).

The wall was completed in fifty-two days. When the enemies of the Jews heard the news, all the surrounding nations were afraid and lost their self-confidence. They knew that the work had been done with the help of God (Neh 6:15-16).

All during this time, letters were constantly going back and forth between the nobles of Judah and Tobiah. Many nobles were obligated to him; some were related to him through marriage. The nobles kept telling Nehemiah about the good deeds of Tobiah, and kept Tobiah informed about everything Nehemiah said (Neh 6:17-19).

Now the city was large and spacious, but few people lived in it. The houses had not yet been rebuilt (Neh 7:4).

Other Reforms

All the Israelites in Judah assembled in Jerusalem. They told Ezra the scribe to bring out the Book of the Law of Moses.

Ezra the priest brought the Book of the Law to the assembly made up of men and women and all who were able to understand. He read it aloud from daybreak till noon as he faced the square in the hearing of all who could understand. And all the people listened attentively to the Book of the Law.

Ezra the scribe stood on a high wooden platform built for the event. Ezra opened the book. All the people could see him because he was standing above them. As he opened it, the people all stood up. The Levites taught the people the Law while the people stood. They read from the Book of the Law of God, and explained the meaning so that the people could understand what was being read.

Then Nehemiah the governor, Ezra the priest and scholar, and the Levites who were instructing the people said to them all: "This day is sacred to the Lord your God. Do not mourn or weep." For all the people had been weeping as they listened to the words of the Law.

Nehemiah said: "Go and enjoy choice food and sweet drinks. This day is sacred to our Lord. Do not grieve, for the joy of the Lord is your strength."

Then all the people went away to eat and drink, and to celebrate with great joy, because they understood the reading of God's Word that had been given to them (Neh 8:1-12).

On another occasion the Israelites gathered together, fasting and wearing sackcloth and having dust on their heads as signs of repentance. The Israelites had separated themselves from all foreigners. They stood up and confessed their sins and the wickedness of their ancestors. Then they praised the Lord God: "Blessed be your glorious name. You alone are the Lord. You made the heavens. You give life to everything. You are the Lord God, who chose Abram and changed his name to Abraham. You made a covenant with him to give his descendants the land of the Canaanites. You freed our ancestors from Egypt. You came down on Mount Sinai; you spoke to them from Heaven. You gave them regulations and laws that are just and right. But they, our ancestors, became arrogant and did not obey your commands. But you are a forgiving God, compassionate, slow to anger and abounding in love. Therefore, you did not desert them, even when they cast for themselves an image of a calf. By day, the pillar of cloud guided their path; by night, the pillar of fire led them. You gave them manna; you gave them water. For forty years you sustained them in the desert; their clothes did not wear out nor did their feet become swollen. You brought them into the land that you promised their ancestors. You subdued before them the Canaanites, who lived in the land. But they were disobedient and rebelled against you.

They killed your prophets; they committed awful blasphemies. You warned them through your prophets to return to your Law, but they became arrogant and disobeyed your commands. For many years you were patient with them. Yet they paid no attention, so you abandoned them to the neighboring peoples.

"We are slaves today, slaves in the land you gave our forefathers. Because of our sins, its abundant harvest goes to the kings you have placed over us. They rule over our bodies and our cattle. We are in great distress. Because of this, we are making a binding agreement and putting it in writing. We bind ourselves with a curse and an oath to follow the Law of God. We promise not to marry our children to the peoples around us. We will not buy merchandise from the neighboring people on the Sabbath or on any holy day. We also assume responsibility for bringing to the house of the Lord each year the first-fruits of our cattle, crops and trees. We will not neglect the house of our God" (Neh 9:1 - 10:39).

The leaders of the people settled in Jerusalem. The rest of the people cast lots to bring one out of every ten to live in Jerusalem, while the remaining nine were to remain in their own towns (Neh 11:1).

The wall of Jerusalem was offered as a gift to God. At the dedication of the wall of Jerusalem, the Levites celebrated joyfully with songs of thanksgiving and with music. The singers were there. Nehemiah and the leaders of Judah went up on top of the wall. He assigned two large choirs to give thanks. One was to proceed on top of the wall to the right. The second choir proceeded to the left. God gave them great joy. The men, women and children rejoiced. The sound of rejoicing could be heard far away (Neh 12:27-47). On that day the Book of Moses was read aloud in the hearing of the people (Neh 13:1).

Nehemiah left Jerusalem to be with Artaxerxes, king of Persia. Some time later he received permission to return to Jerusalem. At his return, he discovered many wrongdoings and initiated reform.

Nehemiah learned that priests had provided Tobiah a room in the courts of the Temple of God. He threw all Tobiah's household goods out of the room, gave orders to purify the rooms, and then put back into them the equipment of the Temple of God (Neh 13:4-9).

Nehemiah learned that the food allotments assigned to the Levites had not been given to them, so the Levites and singers responsible for the Temple service had gone back to their own farms. Nehemiah rebuked the officials and asked them: "Why is the Temple of God neglected?" Then he called the Levites and singers back and put them back on their jobs.

Nehemiah prayed: "Remember me with favor, O my God" (Neh 13:10-14).

Nehemiah saw men in Judah bringing in grain, wine, grapes, figs and all other kinds of loads into Jerusalem on the Sabbath. Nehemiah rebuked the nobles of Judah and said to them: "You are profaning the Sabbath day."

When evening shadows fell on the gates of Jerusalem before the Sabbath, Nehemiah ordered the gates to be shut and not opened until the Sabbath was over. He stationed some men at the gates so that no merchandise could be brought in on the Sabbath day. Once or twice the merchants and traders spent the night camped outside Jerusalem. But Nehemiah warned them: "If you do this again, I will lay hands on you." From that time on they no longer came on the Sabbath.

Nehemiah prayed: "Remember me with favor, O my God" (Neh 13:15-22).

Nehemiah saw men of Judah who had married foreign women. Half of their children spoke the language of some other people and did not know how to speak the language of Judah. Nehemiah made them take an oath in God's name not to marry their children to the children of other people.

Nehemiah prayed: "Remember me with favor, O my God" (Neh 13:23-30).

With the reforms by Nehemiah and the prophets, the remnant that returned to Judah became a nation consecrated to God. They rejected idolatry and mixed marriages. They observed the Sabbath. With the passing of time, their religion became more of a formality rather than a commitment to the Lord God. A few short years later, the prophet Malachi wrote, reprimanding the formality of their religion that was accompanied by corrupt priests and people who sinned against the family. They were also stingy in their offerings to God. With the passing of centuries, their religion became a strict following of rules and regulations without manifestation of love for God or for their fellow man. After Malachi, a time period of 400 years passed without God sending a prophet or giving anyone a special revelation through a dream.

LIFE-LESSONS DISCOVERED IN THE STORY

1. God does what he promises. He kept his promise registered in Jeremiah 29:14 and brought the exiles back to Jerusalem.

2. God's people can become content with the lifestyle of the pagan world, or they can trust God's promises and have the courage to face difficult challenges. Many Jews preferred the comfort of civilized Babylon to the challenge of rebuilding an impoverished Judah.

3. The providence of God can cause people who serve other gods to become his instruments in accomplishing his work. God caused King Cyrus of Persia to sponsor the first return of captives from Babylon to Jerusalem (Ezr 1:1-11). God

caused King Artaxerxes of Persia to sponsor Ezra on the second return (Ezr 7:1, 12-28) and to send Nehemiah on the third return (Neh 2:1-9). Several times God caused people who did not serve him to become his instrument; for instance: in the exodus (Ex 11:3; 12:36), in the return from captivity (Ezr 1:4; 7:1-28; Neh 2:7-8) and in the beginning of the proclamation of the Gospel (Ac 2:47).

4. The nation that wishes to prosper should begin by putting the Kingdom of God and his justice in first place. When the Israelites first returned to Jerusalem, their first action was to build an altar to God. The altar was a place to offer sacrifices and prayer to God (Ezr 3:1-6). (See Mt 6:33.)

5. When faced with opposition, the people of God have a choice: they can become afraid and stop working for God, or they can obey God and proceed forward. Those who returned to Jerusalem allowed their enemies to stop them from constructing the Temple (Ezr 4:1-24).

6. A person's zeal to serve God can become weakened by the influence of the world; therefore, the people of God must continually remember their commitment to give God first place in their lives. The first group to return from Babylon to Jerusalem immediately built an altar as a symbol that their priority was serving and obeying God (Ezr 3:1-13). The years passed and they forgot God's laws and gave themselves to mixed marriages with pagan women (Ezr 9:1-2; Neh 13:23-27) and they stopped observing the Sabbath (Neh 13:15-22). The history of Israel proves that religious devotion is weakened by pagan influence.

7. Disobedience to God results in God holding back his blessings. When the Jews stopped building the Temple for the Lord, God held back blessings; this resulted in their experiencing hard times (Ezr 5:1; Hag 1:6).

8. A person should become a student of the Bible before he becomes a Bible teacher. Ezra had devoted himself to the study and observance of the Law of the Lord, and to teaching its decrees and laws to the Israelites (Ezr 7:10).

9. The hypocrite speaks about trusting God; however, when trouble comes, he depends upon a human force for protection. After speaking about his trust in God, Ezra refused to ask the king for an army to protect them from bandits. He committed his trip to the Lord (Ezr 8:22). (See Ps 20:7; 2 Chr 14:11.)

10. Prayer produces results. God answered Ezra's prayer for protection on the trip to Jerusalem (Ezr 8:23). When Ezra prayed for the Israelites who abandoned God's laws, they recognized their sins (Ezr 10:1). Nehemiah prayed before asking the king's permission to return to Jerusalem, and the king granted his request (Neh 1:11; 2:4-6).

11. The person who weeps and prays when confronted with the sins of others is the one who will most likely lead the sinner to repent. Ezra wept and prayed when he learned of the detestable practices of the Israelites (Ezr 9:3-5; 10:1). Jesus wept over the city of Jerusalem (Lk 19:41). Paul feared that when he visited the church at Corinth he would be grieved over many who were sinning (2 Cor 12:23).

12. Prayer should be based upon the Word of God. Ezra's prayer, in Ezr 10:11-15, is based upon Deuteronomy and the prophets.

13. Those who yield to temptation need to repent. Those who had entered mixed marriages recognized and admitted their sin (Ezr 9:1-10:2).

14. The person who prays about a need may become the instrument God uses to resolve it. Nehemiah prayed about the walls of Jerusalem that were in ruin (Neh 1:4-11), and he became the human instrument God used to rebuild the walls. Jesus told the disciples to pray for the Lord to send out workers into his harvest field (Mt 9:38). Then he called and sent out the twelve disciples (Mt 10:1, 5).

15. The one who serves God should make prayer an important part of his life. The scripture records many occasions when Ezra and Nehemiah prayed. Prayers of Ezra (Ezr 8:21-23; 9:1-10:2; Neh 8:5-6); prayers of Nehemiah (Neh 1:4-11; 2:4; 5:19; 6:9, 14; 9:6-37; 13:22, 29, 31).

16. Prayer and action go together hand in hand. The story of Nehemiah constantly emphasizes both his prayers and his actions.

17. A person needs to be both spiritual and practical. Nehemiah faced the threats of aggression with prayer and guards (Neh 4:9, 17).

18. Threats to the work of God come from both outside and within. Barriers for the construction of the walls came from enemies outside who attacked the workers (Neh 4) and from rich Jews within who exploited their fellow citizens (Neh 5:1-12).

19. The enemies of the work of God are persistent and use many methods of attack. Some of the methods used to stop the construction of the walls were: ridicule (Neh 4:1-3); physical aggression (4:8); exhaustion from fatigue (4:10); rumors (6:5-8); false prophets (6:10-14); terror (6:1-14) and subversion through family ties (6:17-19).

20. The person who is inspired by God will never counsel another person to be weak in faith. A

prophet warned Nehemiah to hide in the Temple because enemies were coming to kill him. Nehemiah recognized that such counsel was not from God (Neh 6:10-12).

21. The enemies of the faith create opportunities for God's people to grow in communion with God and to become stronger. Nehemiah's enemies frequently provoked him to go to God with spontaneous prayers. This developed his communion with God and as a result, Nehemiah became stronger after each attack.

22. The Bible prohibits God's servants from marrying someone who serves another god. Marriage with foreigners was prohibited by the Law to combat idolatry that pagan spouses could introduce into their homes (Dt 7:1-4). When Ezra arrived in Jerusalem, he faced the problem of the Israelites involved in mixed marriages (Ezr 9:1-2). Mixed marriages were condemned by Nehemiah (Neh 13:23-28). (See 2 Cor 6:14-15.)

23. In public worship, the Word of God should be read and explained. Ezra read the Law and the Levites explained the meaning so the people could understand it (Neh 8:1-8).

24. Understanding God's Word is a reason to rejoice. The people rejoiced because they understood the words that had been read to them (Neh 8:12).

25. The person who completes a task for God should celebrate. The Israelites celebrated when they completed the foundations of the Temple (Ezr 3:10-13), the construction of the Temple (Ezr 6:16) and the walls of the city (Neh 12:27-43).

26. People, who are committed to obeying God, risk returning to old habits with the passing of time. Those who first returned to Jerusalem separated themselves from the people who surrounded them (Ezr 4:2). When Ezra returned 60 years later he found mixed marriages (Ezr 9:1). Nehemiah left Jerusalem to return to the king of Persia (Neh 13:6). Later, when Nehemiah returned to Jerusalem he discovered serious wrongdoings and initiated reforms (Neh 13:7-31).

QUESTIONS

1. Describe the major event of each of the three groups that returned from Babylon to Jerusalem.
2. When the first group returned, what was their first action?
3. What problems did the Israelites face in rebuilding the Temple?
4. Why did the Israelites refuse the Samaritans' offer to help rebuild the Temple?
5. When Ezra led the second group that returned to Jerusalem, what was the spiritual situation of the city?
6. How did Ezra react when he discovered the detestable behavior of the Jews in Jerusalem?
7. What can you learn from both Ezra and Nehemiah on prayer?
8. What can you learn from both Ezra and Nehemiah on leadership?
9. What were some barriers that Nehemiah had to overcome to rebuild the walls of Jerusalem?
10. How did he face each barrier?
11. What can you learn from Ezra and Nehemiah that will help you face your crisis in life?
12. What were some of the occasions that the Israelites celebrated in the times of Ezra and Nehemiah?
13. After Nehemiah built the city walls, he left Jerusalem. When he returned, what were some evidences he found of spiritual decadence, and what reforms did he initiate?
14. What do the Israelites in the time of Ezra and Nehemiah teach us about the tendency of the people of God to grow weak in their commitments to him?
15. In what areas do you have a tendency to be weak in your commitment to God?

www.ingramcontent.com/pod-product-compliance
Lightning Source LLC
Chambersburg PA
CBHW081219170426
43198CB00017B/2662